# Lecture Notes in Computer Scien

T0237998

Commenced Publication in 1973
Founding and Former Series Editors:
Gerhard Goos, Juris Hartmanis, and Jan van Leeuwen

Muhammad Ali Babar   Ian Gorton (Eds.)

# Software Architecture

4th European Conference, ECSA 2010
Copenhagen, Denmark, August 23-26, 2010
Proceedings

 Springer

Volume Editors

Muhammad Ali Babar
IT University of Copenhagen
Software Development Group
Rued Langgaards, Vej 7
2300, Copenhagen, S., Denmark
E-mail: malibaba@itu.dk

Ian Gorton
Pacific Northwest National Laboratory
Computational and Information Sciences
PO Box 999, MS: K7-90
Richland, WA, 99352, USA
E-mail: ian.gorton@pnl.gov

Library of Congress Control Number: 2010931870

CR Subject Classification (1998): D.2, D.3, F.3, H.4, C.2, K.6

LNCS Sublibrary: SL 2 – Programming and Software Engineering

ISSN      0302-9743
ISBN-10   3-642-15113-2 Springer Berlin Heidelberg New York
ISBN-13   978-3-642-15113-2 Springer Berlin Heidelberg New York

springer.com

© Springer-Verlag Berlin Heidelberg 2010

Typesetting: Camera-ready by author, data conversion by Scientific Publishing Services, Chennai, India
Printed on acid-free paper      06/3180

# Preface

Welcome to the European Conference on Software Architecture (ECSA), which is the premier European software engineering conference. ECSA provides researchers and practitioners with a platform to present and discuss the most recent, innovative, and significant findings and experiences in the field of software architecture research and practice. The fourth edition of ECSA was built upon a history of a successful series of European workshops on software architecture held from 2004 through 2006 and a series of European software architecture conferences from 2007 through 2009. The last ECSA was merged with the 8th Working IEEE/IFIP Conference on Software Architecture (WICSA).

Apart from the traditional technical program consisting of keynote talks, a main research track, and a poster session, the scope of the ECSA 2010 was broadened to incorporate other tracks such as an industry track, doctoral symposium track, and a tool demonstration track. In addition, we also offered several workshops and tutorials on diverse topics related to software architecture.

We received more than 100 submissions in the three main categories: full research and experience papers, emerging research papers, and research challenges papers. The conference attracted papers (co-)authored by researchers, practitioners, and academics from 30 countries (Algeria, Australia, Austria, Belgium, Brazil, Canada, Chile, China, Colombia, Czech Republic, Denmark, Finland, France, Germany, Hong Kong, Iceland, India, Ireland, Israel, Italy, The Netherlands, Poland, Portugal, Romania, Spain, Sweden, Switzerland, Tunisia, United Kingdom, United States).

Based on the recommendations of the Program Committee, we accepted only 19 full papers out of 75 full papers submitted. The acceptance rate for the full papers was 25.33% for ECSA 2010. In the "Emerging Research" category, we accepted only 2 out of 21 papers submitted. Based on the reviews and quality of the submissions, 18 full papers were invited to be converted into "Emerging Research" papers. For the "Research Challenges" (Poster) category, 5 out of 10 submissions were accepted. Two full research papers and three "Emerging Research" papers were invited to be presented as poster papers. Hence, there were 11 papers in this category. The Tool Demonstration Chairs accepted three out of six submitted papers.

It was a great pleasure to have three eminent keynote speakers at ECSA 2010. The opening day keynote was delivered by Jan Bosch from Intuit, USA. He spoke on "Architecture in the Age of Compositionality"; The second keynote was presented by Philippe Kruchten from the University of British Columbia, Canada, on "Where Did all This Good Architectural Knowledge Go?" The third and final keynote was delivered by Jim Webber from Thoughtsworks UK. Jim spoke about "REST Style Architectures in Practice for Building Very Large Scale Enterprise Systems."

We are grateful to the members of the Program Committee for helping us to seek submissions and provide valuable and timely reviews. Their efforts enabled us to put together a high-quality technical program for ECSA 2010. We are also indebted to members of the Organizing Committee of ECSA 2010 for playing an enormously important role in successfully organizing the event with several new tracks and collocated events. We also thank the workshop organizers and tutorials presenters, who also made significant contributions to the success of an extended version of ECSA. A very special thanks is due to Vibeke Ervø for her enormous help in putting these proceedings together. The ECSA 2010 submission and review process was extensively supported by the EasyChair Conference Management System. We acknowledge the prompt and professional support from Springer, who published these proceedings in printed and electronic volumes as part of the *Lecture Notes in Computer Science* series. Finally, we are grateful to the management team of the IT University of Copenhagen, Denmark, for providing its facilities and professionally trained staff for the organization of ECSA 2010.

June 2010

Muhammad Ali Babar
Ian Gorton

# Organization

ECSA 2010 was hosted by the IT University of Copenhagen, Denmark.

## Organizing Committee

| | |
|---|---|
| General Chair: | Ian Gorton (Pacific Northwest Laboratory, USA) |
| Program Chair: | Muhammad Ali Babar (IT University of Copenhagen, Denmark) |
| Industry Chairs: | Ronny Kolb (Honeywell, Switzerland) |
| | Martin Naedele (ABB Corporate Research, Switzerland) |
| Workshop Chairs: | Rafael Capilla (Rey Juan Carlos University, Spain) |
| | Danny Weyns (Katholieke Universiteit Leuven, Belgium) |
| Tutorial Chairs: | Kasper Østerbye (IT University of Copenhagen, Denmark) |
| | Juha Savolainen (Nokia, Finland) |
| Tool Demo Chairs: | Andrzej Wasowski (IT University of Copenhagen, Denmark) |
| | Michel Wermelinger (The Open University, UK) |
| Doctoral Symposium Chairs: | Eila Ovaska (VTT Technical Research Centre, Finland) |
| | Claudia Raibulet (University of Milano-Bicocca Italy) |
| Publicity Chair: | Jennifer Perez Benedi (Technical University of Madrid (UPM), Spain) |
| Local Organizing Chairs: | Pia Dyrhagen (IT University of Copenhagen, Denmark) |
| | Yvonne Dittrich (IT University of Copenhagen, Denmark) |
| Digital Media Chair: | Hataichanok Unphon (IT University of Copenhagen, Denmark) |

## Program Committee

| | |
|---|---|
| Eduardo Santana de Almeida | Federal University of Bahia, Brazil |
| Yamine Ait Ameur | ENSMA, France |
| Paris Avgeriou | University of Groningen, The Netherlands |
| Jesper Andersson | V%ₒjö University, Sweden |
| Dharini Balasubramaniam | University of St. Andrews, UK |
| Thais Batista | University of Rio Grande do Norte - UFRN, Brazil |

| | |
|---|---|
| Marco Bernardo | University of Urbino, Italy |
| Antoine Beugnard | ENST Bretagne, France |
| Jan Bosch | Intuit, USA |
| Alan W. Brown | IBM Rational, USA |
| Sorana Cîmpan | University of Savoie, France |
| Ivica Crnkovic | Mälardalen University, Sweden |
| Carlos Cuesta | Rey Juan Carlos University, Spain |
| Paulo Roberto F. Cunha | Federal University of Pernambuco, Brazil |
| Rogerio De Lemos | University of Kent, UK |
| Khalil Drira | LAAS-CNRS, University of Toulouse, France |
| Laurence Duchien | INRIA and University of Lille, France |
| Katrina Falkner | University of Adelaide, Australia |
| John Favaro | Intecs, Italy |
| Régis Fleurquin | University of South Brittany - VALORIA/INRIA Rennes - Bretagne Atlantique, France |
| Cristina Gacek | City University, London, UK |
| David Garlan | Carnegie Mellon University, USA |
| Holger Giese | University of Potsdam, Germany |
| Paul Grefen | Eindhoven University of Technology, The Netherlands |
| Volker Gruhn | University Duisburg-Essen, Germany |
| Wilhelm Hasselbring | University of Oldenburg, Germany |
| Klaus Marius Hansen | University of Iceland, Iceland |
| Juan Hernández | University of Extremadura, Spain |
| Paola Inverardi | University of L'Aquila, Italy |
| Rick Kazman | University of Hawaii, USA |
| Kai Koskimies | Tampere University, Finland |
| Gerald Kotonya | Lancaster University, UK |
| René Krikhaar | VU University Amsterdam, The Netherlands |
| Patricia Lago | VU University Amsterdam, The Netherlands |
| Frédéric Lang | INRIA Rhône-Alpes, France |
| Nicole Levy | University of Versailles St-Quentin en Yvelines - PRiSM, France |
| Anna Liu | University of New South Wales, Australia |
| Antonia Lopes | University of Lisbon, Portugal |
| Leszek Maciaszek | Macquarie University, Australia |
| Sam Malek | George Mason University, USA |
| Esperanza Marcos | Rey Juan Carlos University, Spain |
| Tomi Männistö | Aalto University, Finland |
| Robert L. Nord | Software Engineering Institute, USA |
| Flavio Oquendo | University of South Brittany - VALORIA, France |
| Mourad Oussalah | University of Nantes - LINA, France |
| Claus Pahl | Dublin City University, Ireland |
| George A. Papadopoulos | University of Cyprus, Cyprus |
| Dewayne Perry | University of Texas at Austin, USA |
| Paulo de Figueiredo Pires | University of Rio Grande do Norte - UFRN, Brazil |
| Frantisek Plasil | Charles University, Czech Republic |
| Amar Ramdame-Cherif | LISV - University of Versailles , France |

Isidro Ramos                    Polytechnic University of Valencia, Spain
Ralf Reussner                   University of Karlsruhe, Germany
Raghu Sangwan                   Penn State University, USA
Clemens Schäfer                 IT factum GmbH, Germany
Bradley Schmerl                 Carnegie Mellon University, USA
Judith Stafford                 Tufts University, USA
Clemens Szyperski               Microsoft Research, USA
Miguel Toro                     University of Sevilla, Spain
Brian Warboys                   University of Manchester, UK
Claudia Maria Lima Werner       Federal University of Rio de Janeiro, Brazil
Eoin Woods                      BlackRock, UK
Uwe Zdun                        Technical University of Vienna, Austria

## ECSA Steering Committee

Flavio Oquendo  (Chair)         University of South Brittany - VALORIA, France
Carlos E. Cuesta                Rey Juan Carlos University, Spain
Esperanza Marcos                Rey Juan Carlos University, Spain
John Favaro                     INTECS, Italy
Volker Gruhn                    University Duisburg-Essen, Germany
Ron Morrison                    University of St. Andrews, UK
Mourad Oussalah                 University of Nantes - LINA, France
George A. Papadopoulos          University of Cyprus, Cyprus
Brian Warboys                   University of Manchester, UK

## Subreviewers

Achilleas Achilleos             Zoya Durdik
Abdelkrim Amirat                Rik Eshuis
Samuil Angelov                  Sören Frey
Fadila Aoussat                  Gregor Gabrysiak
Marco Autili                    Jean-Marie Gilliot
Vlastimil Babka                 Qing Gu
Paul Bannerman                  Stephan Hildebrandt
Matthias Book                   Anthony Hock-koon
Ismael Bouassida Rodriguez      Thomas Hubbard
Tobias Brückmann                Pavel Jezek
Erik Burger                     Lucia Kapova
Trosky B. Callo Arias           Ali Khalili
Fernando Castor                 Klaus Krogmann
Pericles Cheng                  Olivier Le Goaer
Jose Maria Conejero             Marcos Lopez-Sanz
Rafael Corchuelo                Francisca Losavio
Flavia Delicato                 Andréa Magdaleno
Davide Di Ruscio                Julien Mallet

Michal Malohlava
Tiago Massoni
Radu Mateescu
Silvia Mazzini
Christos Mettouris
Mohamed Nadhmi Miladi
Amparo Navasa
Stefan Neumann
Alex Norta
José Antonio Parejo Maestre
Patrizio Pelliccione
Tomas Poch
Stefano Puri
Sakkaravarthi Ramanathan
Chris Rathfelder
Maryam Razavian

Antonia M. Reina-Quintero
Gwen Salaun
German Sancho
André L. Santos
Rodrigo Santos
Ricardo Seguel
Ondrej Sery
Mark Staples
Dan Tofan
Uwe van Heesch
Andre van Hoorn
Sylvain Vauttier
Thomas Vogel
Hiroshi Wada
Jan Waller
Bechir Zalila

# Table of Contents

## Emerging Research Papers

## Research Challenges Papers

## Tool Demo Papers

# Architecture in the Age of Compositionality

Jan Bosch

Intuit, Mountain View, CA
Jan@JanBosch.com

**Abstract.** The nature of software engineering is changing. Whereas building systems was the predominant activity, more recently the focus has shifted toward composing systems from open-source, commercial and proprietary components and to only build the functionality that truly is competitively differentiating. In addition, the way software is developed has changed as well, especially focusing on short development cycles and frequent, or even continuous, deployment. Because of these requirements, often teams are organized around features, rather than components, and can change all components in the system, including their interfaces. A third trend is the increasing adoption of software ecosystems, where significant development of functionality relevant for customers occurs outside the platform organization. Obviously, however, the quality attributes that are necessary for system success remain important as well as the ability to easily incorporate new requirements in the system in a cost effective fashion. Because of the above, the role of software architecture and in particular the software architects is more important in this new world, but there is significant evolution in the implementation of the role. The paper starts by characterizing the new approach to software engineering and the role of compositionality. It then explores the implications for software architecture and the role of the software architect, Finally, it defines a number of research challenges for the ECSA community to explore.

**Keywords:** Software architecture, compositionality.

## 1 Setting the Context

Software engineering continues to evolve at an enormous rate, both in terms of the size of systems built as well as the speed at which these systems are deployed and evolve. This requires software engineering practitioners, including architects, to continuously develop new approaches to manage the consequent implications for the complexity of software.

For large classes of systems, this now means that most software development is more concerned with composition of existing open-source, commercial and internally developed components in creative configurations than with the creation of significant amounts of new software. The new software development is constrained to the truly differentiating functionality that definesthe competitive advantageforthe system. The consequence of this is obviously that easy composition of software assets increases in importance.

M. Ali Babar and I. Gorton (Eds.): ECSA 2010, LNCS 6285, pp. 1–4, 2010.

A second major transition in the software engineering industry is the adoption of lean and agile development approaches. The principal elements of these approaches include small teams, short development iterations and frequent or continuous deployment. As these approaches increasingly are deployed in the context of medium to large-sized systems, the consequence is that multiple teams are working in parallel on the same system. These teams often have responsibility for components of the system and that again increases the need for compositionalityas for these teams to be successful, they need to be as decoupled in their work as possible.In response to the latter, increasingly teams are organized around features instead of components, can make changes to all code in the system and integrate their branches during the integration stage.

The third trend is concerned with the increased adoption of a software ecosystem approach by companies that have successful software systems or software product lines. As companies increasingly aim to reposition as networked organization and reduce their own headcount, outside partners perform significant parts of development. In addition, companies are introducing app-store styled approaches to increase the richness of functionality provided to their customers. However, it is difficult, if not impossible, to enforce process on external companies, and consequently the partners and third party developers need to be able to deploy independently. This requires increased compositionality of the system and the architecture of the system presents a, if not the, key enabler for achieving compositionality.

## 2  Role of Architecture and the Architect

With the evolution of software engineering, there are implications to the role of software architecture as well as the software architect. Research attention has mostly been directed to the early stages of designing for a green-field system and stressed the importance of designing architectures carefully as the cost of re-architecting was considered to be prohibitively high. In practice, most software architects spend all their time in existing systems and focus on re-architecting and the addition of new functionality against the lowest investment. The adoption of lean and agile approaches even further deemphasizes the initial design stage.

The role of the architect in this modern world can be viewed as focused on three main responsibilities:

- **Define and enforce end-to-end quality requirements:** As multiple, largely independent, teams work in the context of the evolving system, there is a need for a central authority to define and enforce end-to-end quality requirements. Especially operational quality requirements such as response times, performance and reliability do not have a logical owner in a highly distributed and composition-oriented world. The architect or architects have a responsibility to evaluate the impact of ongoing development efforts on the quality attributes.
- **Evolve the architecture and fight design erosion:** Component teams, but especially feature teams, are strongly focused on adding new functionality to the system. This requires additions and changes to the interfaces between components and, as a consequence, over time the design of the system starts to erode. The architect has a role to work with teams to steer interface evolution in the right direction to

minimize erosion. In addition, the formulation and execution of refactoring efforts also needs to be initiated and, potentially, executed by the architect team.

- **Decoupling:** Lean, agile development demands that teams can perform their work with minimal dependency on other teams. Only in this way, the main inefficiency, dependencies between components and between teams and the consequent coordination cost can be avoided.Consequently, the architect has to strife for simplicity and backward compatibility of subsequent versions of components. In many systems, architectural simplicity is not sufficiently prioritized, causing inefficiency as teams need to understand too much about the context in which their software will operate.

## 3  Research Challenges

The evolution of the approach to software development as described earlier in the paper, as well as the implications for software architecture and the architect, results in a number of research challenges. These challenges mirror the changes in the role of architecture and the architect discussed in the previous section.

- **Define and architect end-to-end qualities into the system:** The architect needs to formulate end-to-end qualities for the system, often in collaboration with product management. However, it is not trivial how to identify, define, architect and enforce the qualities.
- **Design erosion:** Especially with multiple, independent teams, the architecture will erode over time, requiring effort to assess, prioritize and address design erosion. Some teams use very pragmatic approaches, such as a list in a document or on a whiteboard, to identify when shortcuts are taken and priority of fixing the erosion. However, ways to quantify design erosion as well as its life time cost and the ROI of refactoring efforts still have not been broadly adopted in industry.
- **Managing architecture in an ecosystem context:** In the case of a software ecosystem, the normal approaches employing software process as a mechanism to control and coordination no longer work as the external partners and third party developers cannot be subjected to these processes. Consequently, the architecture of the system needs to shoulder this responsibility and help independent and mostly decoupled teams evolve their part of the system without causing major issues as well.

Finally, I would like take this opportunity to call on the research community to refocus efforts on the industrial application of research results. Of course we need the development of new techniques and approaches, but these should be developed in response to problems that companies actually experience and then validated in the context of those companies to determine whether the proposed approach actually delivers a benefit.

Reflecting on the progress of the software architecture community, that I have been a part of for more than 15 years, I worry about the increasing dichotomy between industrial practice and academic research. Academics may feel that the techniques and approaches that industry would benefit from have already been developed over the last decade and all that is needed is the adoption of these techniques. Industry, however, will not adopt a technology until it is clear that it provides a real and clear benefit to the organization and, unfortunately, not all technologies proposed by academia provide that benefit.

The second reason that I feel it is so important for academia and industry to strengthen their interactions is that in many ways practice leads research. Many new research areas start from new problems identified by companies and solved in an ad-hoc fashion that addresses the immediate needs of the organization. When multiple companies run into the same issue, the next step is the identification of the generic problem area and research becomes involved. However, as researchers, we have the responsibility to go full circle and make sure that our solutions really do improve on the original problem in its specific industrial context.

Finally, I want to stress that software architecture research falls under software engineering and not computer science. Whereas science can drive activities that have no apparent benefit or relevance, engineering research should not only prove feasibility but also relevance. Relevance can be achieved by several means, but typically requires that the research results improve the current practice through, for example, productivity improvement, reduction in time-to-market or improved customer satisfaction. Consequently, software architecture research has an obligation to provide satisfactory qualitative or quantitative evidence of the benefit.

Concluding, I would like to encourage all members of the software architecture research community to continuously work to decrease the dichotomy between research and industrial practice and to seek validation of research results in industrial contexts.

# Where Did All This Good Architectural Knowledge Go?

Philippe Kruchten

Electrical and Computer Engineering
University of British Columbia
2332 Main mall, Vancouver BC V6T1Z4 Canada
pbk@ece.ubc.ca

**Abstract.** Software architecture represents a significant intellectual asset. But much of the architectural knowledge in organizations is still tacit knowledge. Different parties involved in software development have different needs in terms of architecture at different point in time, not limited to the architects themselves. How can we deliver the right information at the right time to the right person, as schedules are compressed? And where would the information be coming from? And how good is it? Various strategies have been tried, from central, bureaucratic accumulation of data--codification strategies, to simply giving access to the right person--personalization strategies, and a few hybrid strategies in between. This goes beyond mere software documentation, we need to effectively support the reasoning of the architects and developers.

**Keywords:** software architecture, knowledge management.

## 1   Beyond Mere Architecture Documentation...

Organizations developing large software-intensive software have slowly realized that software architecture represents a significant intellectual asset [1]. But as Rus & Lindvall stated, "the major problem with intellectual capital is that it has legs and walks home every day" [2]. Indeed, much of the architectural knowledge we have still resides mostly in peoples' head. The different parties involved in software develop-ment have different needs in terms of architecture information at different points in time, and this is not limited to the architects themselves.

How can we deliver the right information at the right time to the right person, as schedules are compressed? And where would the information be coming from? And how good is it?

Various strategies have been tried, from central, bureaucratic accumulation of data—codification strategies, to simply giving access to the right person—personalization strategies, and a few hybrid strategies in between. The problem is getting more complicated as we move to software product lines and software "eco-systems" [3], involving many more parties, across multiple organizational boundaries. But there is more than just architectural documentation [4].

M. Ali Babar and I. Gorton (Eds.): ECSA 2010, LNCS 6285, pp. 5–6, 2010.
© Springer-Verlag Berlin Heidelberg 2010

## 2    Tools and Processes for Architectural Reasoning

Beyond the mere documentation of the architecture of a given system, or reusable recipes, tactics, methods on how to develop an architecture for a software-reliant system, we need ways to support (and reuse) reasoning about the evolving architecture of such systems: guidance that would increase the efficiency of the software architects while designing an architecture.

The focus of our community has shifted over the last few years from software architecture as a variant or subset of software design to software architecture as a decision-making process. By making architectural decisions first-class citizens, we have also raised up the bar, as well as the expectations, in process, methods, tools, and techniques to support and exploit reasoning. Guiding people in decisions making is not easy, and trying to do this with tools maybe even harder than educating people in software architecture.

We are still far from a solution to these issues; the tools and processes that have been proposed so far [4] are difficult to scale up, and to effectively transfer to practitioners. The point solutions to various problems cited above are hard to integrate.

We've done tremendous progress in the last 20 years in understanding software architecture. But we are hardly keeping up with the challenges ahead of us. How can we put all this good architectural knowledge effectively to work?

## References

1. Ali Babar, M., Dingsøyr, T., Lago, P., van Vliet, H. (eds.): Software Architecture Knowledge Management: Theory and Practice. Springer, Berlin (2009)
2. Rus, I., Lindvall, M.: Knowledge Management in Software Engineering. IEEE Software 19, 26–38 (2002)
3. Bosch, J.: From Software Product Lines to Software Ecosystems. In: Muthig, D., McGregor, J.D. (eds.) 13th International Software Product Line Conference (SPLC 2009) San Francisco, CA, pp. 111–119. ACM, New York (2009)
4. Clements, P., Bachmann, F., Bass, L., Garlan, D., Ivers, J., Little, R., Nord, R., Stafford, J.: Documenting Software Architectures: Views and Beyond. Addison-Wesley, Boston (2002)
5. Tang, A., Avgeriou, P., Jansen, A., Capilla, R., Ali Babar, M.: A comparative study of architecture knowledge management tools. Journal of Software and Systems 83, 352–370 (2010)

# REST in Practice

Jim Webber

ThoughtWorks, 168-173 High Holborn, London, United Kingdom, WC1V 7AA
Jim.Webber@ThoughtWorks.com

**Abstract.** The Web has emerged as a viable platform for building distributed systems beyond its traditional scope as a scalable means of sharing and disseminating information. In this paper I present observations from recent industrial development projects where commodity Web infrastructure and common patterns have been used to create large, scalable, and dependable computer systems.

**Keywords:** Dependability, ESB, REST, Scalability, SOA.

## 1 Introduction

Over the years we've seen many systems architecture approaches come and go as we've worked hard in IT to keep up with the pace of business change. While agile delivery methods have helped enormously on a project-by-project basis, enterprise system portfolios remain notoriously resistant to change.

Although we've seen significant progress in the way we analyze and govern enterprise systems through business-aligned SOA, the technology choices we make all too often undermine those efforts. But for almost two decades the enterprise architecture most of us have dreamed of has been sitting in plain sight. The Web has become the world's foremost example of a scalable, resilient, and loosely coupled system of systems, which are precisely the characteristics we want in enterprise solutions.

In contrast the Web succeeds by avoiding inappropriate technology choices, which bow to vendor pressure over business imperatives, while delivering all of the "ilities" that we demand from enterprise-grade systems. Not only is the Web more than a match for traditional middleware from a technology perspective, but from a cost perspective too. The keynote talk affiliated with this paper addresses financial and risk in software architecture using case studies from recent projects.

**Acknowledgments.** The author would like to thank Ali Babar and Ian Gorton for the opportunity to deliver these observations to ECSA and to the delivery teams at ThoughtWorks for sharing their delivery experiences.

# An ADL-Approach to Specifying and Analyzing Centralized-Mode Architectural Connection

Guoxin Su[1], Mingsheng Ying[1,2], and Chengqi Zhang[1]

[1] Centre for Quantum Computation and Intelligent Systems, Faculty of Engineering and Information Technology, University of Technology, Sydney, NSW 2007, Australia
[2] State Key Laboratory of Intelligent Technology and Systems, Department of Computer Science and Technology, Tsinghua University, Beijing 100084, China
{guoxin,mying,chengqi}@it.uts.edu.au

**Abstract.** A rigorous paradigm coordinating components is important in the design stage of large-scale software engineering. In this paper we propose a new Architecture Description Language, called ACDL, to represent the centralized-mode architectural connection in which all components are linked by a single connector. Following one usual approach to architectural description, in which component types and components are distinguished, and connectors integrate behaviors of components by specifying their coordination protocols, ACDL describes connectors in such a way that connectors are insensitive to the numbers of attached same-type components. Based on ACDL, we develop analytic techniques to facilitate the system checking of temporal properties of an architecture. In particular, our method shows to what extent one can add, delete and replace components without making the whole system lose desired temporal properties, and improves the system checking in several ways, for example enhancing the use of previous checking results to deal with new checking problems.

## 1 Introduction

As the complexity of software designs increases, apart from algorithmic and data-structure-related problems, attention is focused on how to compose subsystems into an overall system [1]. A rigorous paradigm coordinating components is important in the design stage of large-scale software engineering.

Many approaches exist in the literature, from application-oriented to theory-emphasized, to deal with issues related to component-based engineering [2]. Architecture Description Languages (ADLs) emerged as a promising way to formally describe some essential features of an architecture. Although the software architecture community agrees, more or less, that a description of an architecture should consist of three parts, i.e. components, connectors, and architectural configuration [3], each ADL has its own modeling focus, fleshing out features of an architecture from its own viewpoint. We consider components as interfaces performing running-time behaviors, i.e. sequences of input, output and internal actions, and connectors as a special kind of components whose functionality is to integrate components, and whose interfaces can be seen as protocols coordinating behaviors of components. Similar understanding of components and connectors can be found in ADLs such as Wright [4] and $\pi$-ADL [5].

M. Ali Babar and I. Gorton (Eds.): ECSA 2010, LNCS 6285, pp. 8–23, 2010.

In this paper we propose a new ADL, called ACDL (an acronym for Architectural Connection Description Language), in which component types and components are distinguished, and connectors are described to be insensitive to the numbers of attached same-type components. ACDL provides a suitable formal specification for both the structural and the behavioral features of centralized-model architectural connection in which components are linked by a single connector. Centralized-mode architectural connection emphasizes the central status of connectors in star-topology architectures. Advantages of such architectural topology have been recognized in the literature, such as [6] in which it was called coordinator-based architecture style.

Based on ACDL, we develop analytic techniques to facilitate the system checking of temporal properties of an architecture. The compositional analyses use a partition to divide the whole set of components in an architecture into parts, and allow to check each part against the central connector to obtain the correctness of the architecture. The type-based analyses allow to do the checking on the architecture-type level instead of the individual-architecture level, and show to what extent one can add, delete and replace components without making the whole system lose desired temporal properties. Together, these techniques can improve the system checking in four ways:

- Our method enhances the use of previous checking results to deal with new checking problems;
- It helps identify the part of an architecture leading to an undesired property;
- It reduces the complexity of checking by safely skipping over some components;
- It facilitates the reusability of ACDL-specifications by showing to what extent the system checking can be carried out in the type level.

## 1.1 Novelty

This paper is novel in the way that ACDL describes architectures, in particular, connectors. The idea that connectors integrate components by specifying the coordination protocols for their behaviors is not new, but connectors described in ACDL are structurally flexible in the sense that protocols implemented in them have no restriction on the numbers of attached same-type components. This structural flexibility of connectors is achieved by allowing some components to send information to inform the connector what components are involved in the interactions. Therefore ACDL need not distinguish connector types and instances as Wright does. The formal descriptions of connectors in ACDL provides the centralized-mode architectural connection a generic representation, which is important both in theory and in practice (see Sect. 2).

Another innovation is the analytic techniques of temporal properties of an architecture, which are developed based on ACDL. By employing $\pi$-calculus [7] to be its formal semantics, ACDL allows reasoning about temporal properties of the system. We show how it deals with deadlock-freedom and an important liveness property called interaction-liveness. Interaction-liveness formulates the property of a system that, at each stage during the running-time of the system, each component is able to get involved into the interaction with the rest of the architecture at some future time, or alternatively, the system will never proceed to a situation in which some of its components can no longer interact with the environment. The idea of using Process Algebras reasoning about properties of an architecture is not new and has been carried out in the previous literature, such as [4] and [8]. But the main novelty of our method is that, firstly, more general than the acyclic/cyclic sharp division in [8], it uses a partition on the whole set of components in architecture to achieve the finest-grain of the compositional analyses, and secondly, it allows to do the checking on the architecture-type level and shows to what extent one can add, delete and replace components in an architecture without making the system lose the desired properties. On the other hand, although some ADL-relevant works like [9] and [10] did indicate that their methods apply to the analysis of liveness properties, ours, which seriously deals with interaction-liveness, is still enlightening.

## 1.2   Other Related Works

The architectural topology that we consider, i.e. centralized-mode architectural connection, is close to the coordinator-based architecture style investigated in [6], in which the authors were motivated by the following problem: how to assemble a set of off-the-shelf software components into an overall system which enjoys desired properties. They achieved this goal by delegating the interactions of components to a single coordinator which restricts the interaction-patterns of components.

Related ADLs includes Darwin [11], which also employs $\pi$-calculus as its semantics. But Darwin considers components as interfaces for providing and requesting (references of) services, and does not explicitly model a connector as a first-class entity in an architecture. $\pi$-ADL [5] is a powerful formal specification language based on the high-order typed $\pi$-calculus, and is equipped with the analysis language $\pi$-AAL [12] which is able to express safety and other temporal properties. However, despite of their expressive and analytic power, $\pi$-ADL and $\pi$-AAL do not aim to facilitate the system checking and the reusability of specifications by providing a suitable representation of centralized-mode architectural connection, which is the primary goal of our approach.

The remainder of this paper is organized as follows: In Sect. 2 we use client-server systems as examples to motivate our modeling approach. In Sect. 3 we recall relevant definitions of $\pi$-calculus. In Sect. 4 we present the structure of our description language ACDL and a complete textual notation of a client-server system which is treated as the working example in the sequel. In Sect. 5 we describe the translation of expressions in ACDL into processes in $\pi$-calculus. In Sect. 6 we present several theorems dealing with analyses of architectural properties based on the description of ACDL and illustrate their significance by the working example. Finally, in Sect. 7 we conclude our paper and report the future work. The proofs of the theorems are provided in the Appendix.

## 2   Motivating Examples

We motivate our modeling approach by considering the simple client-server system shown in Fig. 1(a), which consists of two clients and one server linked by a black-box middleware embodying the functionality of procedure-callings from the clients to the server. One modeling viewpoint considers this system as a composition of two subsystems as shown in Fig. 1(b). In other words, two clients are linked to the server via two

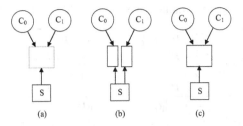

**Fig. 1.** Client-Server Systems

independent procedure-call connectors. We call this kind of connection the dispersed-mode connection. An obvious advantage of dispersed-mode connection is that, because each links one client and one server only, two connectors can be formally described as instances of the same connector type in ADLs such as Wright and PADL [8]. The dispersed-mode connection also applies to multi-client-server cases. However, this model disperses the connected middleware, and hence, is unable to implement within the connectors some global strategies of coordination of clients and servers, for example, a fairness strategy for access of clients to a server. The implementation of such coordination strategies in a connector is particularly desirable if we consider a connector as a first-class entity in an architecture, whose advantages have been increasingly recognized [13].

Given the above considerations, it is reasonable therefore to adopt another modeling viewpoint, i.e. the centralized-mode connection (as contrary to dispersed-mode connection), in which (take our client-server system for example) both clients are linked to the server via a single procedure-call connector, as shown in Fig. 1(c). However, one obvious difficulty for the centralized-mode connection is how to find a generic representation of connectors that are able to be attached to different numbers of clients (and servers). The significance of such a representation is two-fold. It is theoretically interesting. For example, the three connectors in Figure 1(b) and (c) can be seen as three instances of such a representation. On the other hand it favors the implementing practices. For example, the applicability of this representation in other client-server systems with different numbers of clients and servers advocates the reusability principle in software architecture [14] [15]. In this paper we offer a solution to this problem by developing ACDL to formally describe connectors in a manner where they are insensitive to the number of attached same-type components.

## 3  $\pi$-Calculus

In this section we summarize relevant definitions of a version of $\pi$-calculus, which is treated as the semantics of ACDL. For a reference to $\pi$-calculus we refer to [16].

We assume an infinite set of names, ranged over by $a, b, c, x, y$ and $z$. The $\pi$-calculus syntax is given by the following grammar:

$$P ::= \pi.P \mid \mathbf{0} \mid P + Q \mid P\|Q \mid P\backslash N \mid I$$

**Table 1.** SOS of $\pi$-calculus

| | |
|---|---|
| $a(x).P \xrightarrow{a\langle y\rangle} P\{y/x\}$ | $\alpha.P \xrightarrow{\alpha} P$ if $\alpha \neq a(x)$ |
| $\dfrac{P \xrightarrow{\alpha} P'}{P+Q \xrightarrow{\alpha} P'}$ | $\dfrac{P \xrightarrow{\alpha} P'}{Q+P \xrightarrow{\alpha} P'}$ |
| $\dfrac{P \xrightarrow{\alpha} P'}{P\|Q \xrightarrow{\alpha} P'\|Q}$ | $\dfrac{P \xrightarrow{\alpha} P'}{Q\|P \xrightarrow{\alpha} Q\|P'}$ |
| $\dfrac{P \xrightarrow{\overline{a}\langle x\rangle} P' \quad Q \xrightarrow{a\langle x\rangle} Q'}{P\|Q \xrightarrow{\tau} P'\|Q'}$ | $\dfrac{P \xrightarrow{\overline{a}\_c} P' \quad Q \xrightarrow{a\_c} Q'}{P\|Q \xrightarrow{\tau} P'\|Q'}$ |
| $\dfrac{P \xrightarrow{\alpha} P', \quad ch(\alpha) \neq N}{P\backslash N \xrightarrow{\alpha} P'\backslash N}$ | $\dfrac{P \xrightarrow{\alpha} P', \quad I \stackrel{\text{def}}{=} P}{I \xrightarrow{\alpha} P'}$ |

where $P$ is called a *process*, $\pi$ is called a *prefix* and ranges over $\overline{a}\langle x\rangle, a(y), \overline{a}\_c, a\_c$ and $\tau$ (the silent action), $N$ is called a *channel* and ranges over $a$ and $a\_c$, and $I$ ranges over *process identifiers*.

An *action* $\alpha$ ranges over $\pi$ and $a\langle x\rangle$. The *structural operational semantics* (SOS) of $\pi$-calculus is a set of derivative rules defining a relation called *transition* $\mathcal{O} \subseteq$ Process $\times$ Action $\times$ Process. We write $P \xrightarrow{\alpha} Q$ if $(P, \alpha, Q) \in \mathcal{O}$. The SOS of our $\pi$-calculus is given in Table 1.

The SOS compiles a $\pi$-calculus process $P$ into a *Labeled Transition System* (LTS) called the LTS *of* $P$. A *transition path* $\varphi$ (of the LTS) of $P$ is a *maximum* concatenation of transitions, i.e., either an infinite concatenation of transitions or a finite concatenation of transitions such that the last process has no more transitions. $Q$ is *reachable* from $P$ if there is a finite concatenation of transitions from $P$ to $Q$. Furthermore, $ch(\alpha)$ refers to the channel of $\alpha$. $\text{Ch}(P)$ denotes the set of channels of actions labeled in the transition paths of the LTS of $P$. $P \xrightarrow{\alpha}$ means $P \xrightarrow{\alpha} P'$ for some $P'$. Given a specific occurrence of $P$ in $Q$, $P \xrightarrow{\alpha}$ *in* $Q$ means that, $P \xrightarrow{\alpha} P'$ for some $P'$ and, in addition, this transition is a primitive of the derivation of $Q \xrightarrow{\beta} Q'$ for some $Q', \beta$ according to the SOS in Table 1.[1] For example, $\overline{a}\langle b\rangle.P \xrightarrow{\overline{a}\langle b\rangle}$ in $(\overline{a}\langle b\rangle.P\|a(x).Q)\backslash a$. Let $\mathcal{I} = \{N_0, \ldots, N_n\}$, $P\backslash\mathcal{I}$ abbreviates $P\backslash N_0 \cdots \backslash N_n$; $(\pi + \pi').P$ abbreviates $\pi.P + \pi'.P$.

**Definition 1.** *$P$ is* deadlock-free, *if there is no finite transition path of $P$.*

**Definition 2.** *$P$ is* strongly deadlock-free, *if $P$ is deadlock-free and all its transition paths contain infinite non-silent actions, i.e. $\alpha$'s such that $\alpha \neq \tau$.*

Strong deadlock-freedom means processes interact with the environment infinitely often.

**Definition 3.** *$P_1, \ldots, P_n$ are* mutually interaction-live against (the restriction of) $\mathcal{I}$, *if for each $Q = (Q_1\| \cdots \|Q_n)\backslash\mathcal{I}$ reachable from $P = (P_1\| \cdots \|P_n)\backslash\mathcal{I}$ and each $i \in [1, n]$, there is $R = (R_1\| \cdots \|R_n)\backslash\mathcal{I}$ reachable from $Q$ such that $R_i \xrightarrow{\alpha}$ in $R$ for some $\alpha \neq \tau$ where $ch(\alpha) \in \mathcal{I}$.*

---

[1] Throughout this paper when $P \xrightarrow{\alpha}$ *in* $Q$ is written, the specific occurrence of $P$ in $Q$ is clear in the context.

When $P_1, \ldots, P_n$ represent all components (including the connector) of a system, and $\mathcal{I}$ is the set of communication channels of the system, interaction-liveness formulates the property that, this system will not proceed to a situation in which some of its components can no longer interact with the rest of the system.[2]

## 4   Specifying Architectural Connection

In this section we present the architecture description language ACDL and a working example throughout the remainder of this paper. A textual notation in ACDL consists of two parts: an architecture type and an architecture. The former specifies the component types and the connector; the latter specifies the components of corresponding types. The structure of ACDL is given in the following template:

```
ArchitectureType {"name"}
  ComponentType {"name"}
    Input {...}
    Output {...}
    Control {...}
    Behavior {...} %in Process-Algebra form%
  Connector {"name"}
    Protocol {...} %in Process-Algebra form%
  Architecture {"name"}
    Configuration {"Component : ComponentType"}
```

A *ComponentType* is defined as a function of *Input, Output, Control* and *Behavior*. Elements in *Input* and *Output* are indexed by their component-type name, and elements in *Control* convey component-type names (their own and others). *Behavior* of a *ComponentType* is specified in the Process-Algebra form and its prefixes are the elements in *Input, Output* and *Control*. A *Connector* is defined as a function of *Protocol*, which is also specified in Process-Algebra form and whose prefixes are derived from elements in *Input, Output* and *Control* of every *ComponentType* in this way: if *act_name* is in *Input* or *Output* of some *ComponentType*, then *act_x* is a *possible* prefix of *Protocol*; if *act⟨name⟩* is in *Control* of some *ComponentType*, then *act(y)* is a *possible* prefix of *Protocol*. Note that *act(y)* binds variable *y*. We further require that no free occurrence of variables appears in *Protocol*.

Our working example is the complete textual notation of a simple client-server system named *SimpleCS*, in which three clients, $Client_0$, $Client_1$ and $Client_2$, and two servers, $Server_0$ and $Server_1$, are linked by a procedure-call connector *ProCall*:

```
Architecture Type {Client-Server}
  ComponentType {C} %for Client%
    Input {result_C}
    Output {request_C}
    Control {log<C>, target<S>}
```

---

[2] Note that the interaction-liveness is strictly weaker than that each component will interact with other components in the system infinitely often. In our working example, the latter property is not desirable.

```
    Behavior {Client = internalCompute.log<C>.
        target<S>.request_C.result_C.Client}
  ComponentType {S} %for Server%
    Input {involve_S}
    Output {return_S}
    Behavior {Server = involve_S.internalCompute.
        return_S.Server}
  Connector {ProCall}
    Protocol {ProCall = log(x).target(y).request_x.
        involve_y.return_y.result_x.ProCall}
Architecture {SimpleCS}
  Configuration {C0,C1,C2:C; S0,S1:S}
```

There are three important points to be observed. First, behaviors of components are derived from *Behavior* of their types, so we need not specify them in the textual notation. Secondly, the connector *ProCall* obtains its knowledge of involved components from the information conveyed in *log* and *target*, and consequently, the specification of architecture type *Client-Server* need not have any restriction on the number of components, i.e. instances of *Client* and *Server*. In this way, a component-number-insensitive connector *ProCall* is formally described. This is the main feature of ACDL. Finally, the architecture type/instance separation in ACDL implies that the specification of *Client-Server* may be reused when describing other architectures of the same type.

## 5 Formal Semantics

In this section, we bridge ACDL and $\pi$-calculus. For the convenience of discussion, we set down some notations in Table 2.

**Table 2.** Notation Convention

| STRUCTURES | NOTATIONS | SEMANTICS |
|---|---|---|
| architecture type | $\mathbb{A}$ | - |
| architecture | $\mathcal{A}$ | $[\mathcal{A}]$ |
| component type | $\mathbb{E}$ | - |
| component | $\mathcal{E}$ | $[\mathcal{E}]$ |
| connector | $\mathcal{G}$ | $[\mathcal{G}]$ |

The semantics $[\mathcal{E}]$ of component $\mathcal{E}$ is the *process identifier* whose recursive definition is naturally obtained from the behavior of $\mathcal{E}$ (not its component type) according to the input-, output- and silent-nature of the prefixes (elements in *Control* are output-nature). Similar treatment applies to the semantics $[\mathcal{G}]$ of a connector $\mathcal{G}$. But prefixes in $[\mathcal{G}]$ are dual to prefixes in some $[\mathcal{E}]$ provided that $\mathcal{E}, \mathcal{G}$ are in one architecture. As an example, Table 3 gives the semantics of the components $Client_0$, $Server_0$ and the connector *ProCall* in the *SimpleCS* system.

In the sequel, we assume that $\mathcal{E}_1, \ldots, \mathcal{E}_n$ list all components in $\mathcal{A}$, and $\mathcal{G}$ is the connector in $\mathcal{A}$. Let $\mathcal{I}_{\mathcal{E}_i}$, called *the set of channels of* $\mathcal{E}_i$, be the set of channels in *Input*,

**Table 3.** Semantics Samples

$[Cliento] = \tau. \overline{log}\langle C_0 \rangle. (\overline{target}\langle S_0 \rangle + \overline{target}\langle S_1 \rangle). \overline{request\_C_0}. result\_C_0. [Cliento]$

$[Server_0] = involve\_S_0. \tau. \overline{return\_S_0}. [Server_0]$

$[ProCall] = log(x). target(y). request\_x. \overline{involve\_y}. return\_y. \overline{result\_x}. [ProCall]$

*Output* and *Control* of $\mathcal{E}_i$. For example, $\mathcal{I}_{C_0} = \{log, target, request\_C_0, result\_C_0\}$. The semantics of $\mathcal{A}$ is defined by

$$[\mathcal{A}] = ([\mathcal{E}_1]\| \cdots \|[\mathcal{E}_n]\|[\mathcal{G}])\backslash\mathcal{I}_\mathcal{A} \ ,$$

where $\mathcal{I}_\mathcal{A} = \bigcup_{i=1}^n \mathcal{I}_{\mathcal{E}_i}$. Note that the positions of $[\mathcal{E}_1], \ldots, [\mathcal{E}_n]$ and $[\mathcal{G}]$ do not affect the analyses of temporal properties of $\mathcal{A}$. The following propositions formulate some neccessary properties of ACDL to formulate or prove the theorems later. Let $i, j, k \in [1, n]$.

**Proposition 1.** *If $\mathcal{E}_i, \mathcal{E}_j$ and $\mathcal{E}_k$ are of the same type, then (i) $\mathcal{I}_{\mathcal{E}_i} \cap \mathcal{I}_{\mathcal{E}_j} = \mathcal{I}_{\mathcal{E}_i} \cap \mathcal{I}_{\mathcal{E}_k}$, and, (ii) $\mathcal{I}_{\mathcal{E}_j} = \{N\{b/a\} : N \in \mathcal{I}_{\mathcal{E}_i}\}$ and $[\mathcal{E}_i] = [\mathcal{E}_j]\{b/a\}$, where $a, b$ are the names of $\mathcal{E}_i, \mathcal{E}_j$, respectively.*

Proposition 1 formalizes that same-type components share the same *Control* and that their *Input* and *Output* are parameterized on their names.

**Proposition 2.** *(1)* $\text{Ch}([\mathcal{E}_i]) \subseteq \mathcal{I}_{\mathcal{E}_i}$ *for each $\mathcal{E}_i$ . (2) For each $P = (P_1\| \cdots \|P_n\|P_{n+1})$* $\backslash\mathcal{I}_\mathcal{A}$ *reachable from* $([\mathcal{E}_1]\| \cdots \|[\mathcal{E}_n] \|[\mathcal{G}])\backslash\mathcal{I}_\mathcal{A}$, *if $P_{n+1} \xrightarrow{\alpha}$ in $P$, then either $\alpha = \tau$ or* $ch(\alpha) \in \mathcal{I}_\mathcal{A}$.

The first clause of Proposition 2 justifies the name of $\mathcal{I}_{\mathcal{E}_i}$, i.e. the set of channels of $\mathcal{E}_i$. The second clause justifies the definition of $[\mathcal{A}]$ above by showing all channels of $\mathcal{G}$ are in $\mathcal{I}_\mathcal{A}$, and implies that $\mathcal{G}$ indeed functions to coordinate behaviors of components in $\mathcal{A}$ only.

## 6   Analyzing Architectural Properties

In this section we develop formal techniques to analyze deadlock-freedom and interaction-liveness based on the framework of ACDL. To improve the readability we put all the proofs of theorems in the Appendix. The utilities of the theorems are illustrated by the working example – the *SimpleCS* system.

We say $\mathcal{A}$, $\mathcal{E}$ or $\mathcal{G}$, respectively, is *deadlock-free*, if $[\mathcal{A}]$, $[\mathcal{E}]$ or $[\mathcal{G}]$, respectively, is deadlock-free; $\mathcal{E}'_1, \ldots, \mathcal{E}'_m$ (selected from $\mathcal{E}_1, \ldots, \mathcal{E}_n$) and $\mathcal{G}$ are *mutually interaction-live against (the restriction of) $\mathcal{I}$*, if $[\mathcal{E}'_1], \ldots, [\mathcal{E}'_m]$ and $[\mathcal{G}]$ are mutually deadlock-free against $\mathcal{I}$; $\mathcal{A}$ is *interaction-live* if $\mathcal{E}_1, \ldots, \mathcal{E}_n$ and $\mathcal{G}$ are mutually interaction-live against $\mathcal{I}_\mathcal{A}$.

We still need to formulate one property expressing that the connector fits the components: $\mathcal{G}$ is *compatible with* $\{\mathcal{E}'_1, \ldots, \mathcal{E}'_m\}$ *against $\mathcal{I}$*, if each transition path of $([\mathcal{E}'_1]\| \cdots \| [\mathcal{E}'_m]\|[\mathcal{G}])\backslash\mathcal{I}$ contains infinitely many processes $P = (P_1\| \cdots \| P_m\|P_{m+1})\backslash\mathcal{I}$ such that: if $P_{m+1} \xrightarrow{\alpha}$ and $ch(\alpha) \in \mathcal{I}$, then $P_{m+1} \xrightarrow{\alpha}$ in $P$.

## 6.1 Compositional Analyses

For convenience, we use the collection of the elements in the architecture $\mathcal{A}$ to denote $\mathcal{A}$ itself, i.e. $\mathcal{A} = \{\mathcal{E}_1, \ldots, \mathcal{E}_n, \mathcal{G}\}$. To carry out the compositional analyses, we need an auxiliary definition. Let $\mathcal{P}$ be the *finest* partition on $\mathcal{A} - \{\mathcal{G}\}$ such that $\mathcal{E}_j \in \mathcal{P}(\mathcal{E}_i)$ whenever $\mathcal{I}_{\mathcal{E}_j} \cap \mathcal{I}_{\mathcal{E}_i} \neq \emptyset$. We let

$$\mathcal{A} - \{\mathcal{G}\} = \{\mathcal{E}_1^1, \ldots, \mathcal{E}_1^{k_1}, \ldots, \mathcal{E}_m^1, \ldots, \mathcal{E}_m^{k_m}\} \ ,$$

where $\sum_{i=1}^{m} k_i = n$ and $\mathcal{P}(\mathcal{E}_i^1) = \{\mathcal{E}_i^1, \ldots, \mathcal{E}_i^{m_i}\}$, and let $\mathcal{I}_{\mathcal{P}(\mathcal{E}_i)} = \bigcup_{\mathcal{E}_j \in \mathcal{P}(\mathcal{E}_i)} \mathcal{I}_{\mathcal{E}_j}$. Note that by Proposition 1 either $\mathcal{P}(\mathcal{E}_i^1) = \{\mathcal{E}_i^1\}$ or $\mathcal{P}(\mathcal{E}_i^1)$ is the super set of the set of same-type components including $\mathcal{E}_i$. This partition sets the stage for the compositional analyses: analyses of the architecture are decomposed into analyses of parts according to the partition, while "finest" refers to the possibly finest-grained decomposition. This renders our compositional analytic method (for deadlock-freedom, i.e. Theorem 1) more general than that in [8] where components in an acyclic-topology architecture share no channels due to the definition of PADL.

**Theorem 1.** *If $\mathcal{G}$ is deadlock-free and compatible with $\mathcal{P}(\mathcal{E}_i^1)$ against $\mathcal{I}_{\mathcal{P}(\mathcal{E}_i^1)}$ for each $i \in [1, m]$, then $\mathcal{A}$ is deadlock-free.*

The proofs of Theorem 1 and other theorem below are given in the Appendix. Theorem 1 allows us to reduce the checking of the deadlock-freedom of $\mathcal{A}$ to the checking of the deadlock-freedom of $\mathcal{G}$ and compatibility of $\mathcal{G}$ with parts of $\mathcal{A}$, i.e. $\{\mathcal{E}_i^1, \ldots, \mathcal{E}_i^{m_i}\}$ where $i \in [1, m]$. For the *SimpleCS* system, to check the deadlock-freedom of the whole system, it suffices to check: (1) the deadlock-freedom of *ProCall*, and, (2) the compatibility of *ProCall* with $\{Client_0, Client_1, Client_2\}$ against $\mathcal{I}_{c0} \cup \mathcal{I}_{c1} \cup \mathcal{I}_{c2}$, with $\{Server_0\}$ against $\mathcal{I}_{s0}$, and with $\{Server_1\}$ against $\mathcal{I}_{s1}$, respectively. By decomposing the analyses, we may be able to use previous checking results to check other similar architectures, and detect which part of an architecture is responsible for deadlocks (if any) and hence, make diagnoses.

**Theorem 2.** *If $\mathcal{A}$ satisfies the conditions in Theorem 1, all components in $\mathcal{A}$ are strongly deadlock-free, and $\mathcal{G}$ is mutually interaction-live against $\mathcal{I}_{\mathcal{P}(\mathcal{E}_i^1)}$ for each $i \in [1, m]$, then $\mathcal{A}$ is interaction-live.*

If $\mathcal{A}$ satisfies the conditions in Theorem 1, Theorem 2 licenses us to reduce the checking of the interaction-liveness of $\mathcal{A}$ to the checking of the following two: the strong deadlock-freedom of each component in $\mathcal{A}$, and the mutual interaction-liveness of $\mathcal{E}_i^1, \ldots, \mathcal{E}_i^{k_i}, \mathcal{G}$ against $\mathcal{I}_{\mathcal{P}(\mathcal{E}_i^1)}$ for each $i \in [1, m]$. For the *SimpleCS* system, to check the mutual interaction-liveness of $\mathcal{A}$, it suffices to check: (1) the strong deadlock-freedom of all clients and servers, and, (2) the mutual interaction-liveness of $Client_0$, $Client_1$, $Client_2$ and *ProCall* against $\mathcal{I}_{c0} \cup \mathcal{I}_{c1} \cup \mathcal{I}_{c2}$, of $Server_0$ and *ProCall* against $\mathcal{I}_{s0}$, and of $Server_1$ and *ProCall* against $\mathcal{I}_{s1}$, respectively. The significance of Theorem 2 is similar to Theorem 1, as described above. Theorem 2 also shows that the checking of interaction-liveness can be based on the checking of deadlock-freedom according to Theorem 1.

**Theorem 3.** *If $\mathcal{E}_i$ and $\mathcal{E}_j$ are of the same type and $\mathcal{I}_{\mathcal{E}_i} \cap \mathcal{I}_{\mathcal{E}_j} = \emptyset$, then (1) $\mathcal{G}$ is compatible with $\{\mathcal{E}_i\}$ against $\mathcal{I}_{\mathcal{E}_i}$ if and only if $\mathcal{G}$ is compatible with $\{\mathcal{E}_j\}$ against $\mathcal{I}_{\mathcal{E}_j}$, (2) $\mathcal{E}_i$ is strongly deadlock-free if and only if $\mathcal{E}_j$ is strongly deadlock-free, and, (3) $\mathcal{E}_i$ and $\mathcal{G}$ are mutually interaction-live against $\mathcal{I}_{\mathcal{E}_i}$ if and only if $\mathcal{E}_j$ and $\mathcal{G}$ are mutually interaction-live against $\mathcal{I}_{\mathcal{E}_j}$.*

In the *SimpleCS* system, according to Theorem 3 we have that, for example, *Procall* is compatible with $\{Server_0\}$ against $\mathcal{I}_{s0}$ if and only if *Procall* is compatible with $\{Server_1\}$ against $\mathcal{I}_{s1}$, and $Server_0$ is strongly deadlock-free if and only if $Server_1$ is strongly deadlock-free. With this theorem we can safely skip over the checking of some parts of an architecture.

## 6.2  Type-Based Analyses

The compositional analyses are carried out in the level of architecture instance. We now develop analytic techniques in the level of architecture type.

Similar to an architecture, we treat an architecture type $\mathbb{A}$ as a collection of component types, together with a connector. In this section we assume $\mathbb{E} \in \mathbb{A}$. Note that $\mathbb{E}$ is disjointed if and only if $\mathcal{P}(\mathcal{E}^{\mathbb{E}}) = \{\mathcal{E}^{\mathbb{E}}\}$ for some $\mathcal{P}$. Let $\mathcal{E}^{\mathbb{E}}$ refer to a component of type $\mathbb{E}$ and $\mathcal{A}^{\mathbb{A}}$ an architecture of type $\mathbb{A}$. We say $\mathbb{A}$ is *open for deadlock-freedom* on $\mathbb{E}$, if $\mathcal{A}^{\mathbb{A}} \cup \{\mathcal{E}^{\mathbb{E}}\}$ and $\mathcal{A}^{\mathbb{A}} - \{\mathcal{E}^{\mathbb{E}}\}$ are deadlock-free whenever $\mathcal{A}^{\mathbb{A}}$ is deadlock-free;[3] $\mathbb{A}$ is *open for interaction-liveness* on $\mathbb{E}$, if the proposition of the same form holds for interaction-liveness. Informally, if $\mathbb{A}$ is open for deadlock-freedom on $\mathbb{E}$, then every new architecture obtained from a deadlock-free architecture of type $\mathbb{A}$ via adding, deleting and replacing instances of $\mathbb{E}$ is also deadlock-free, and if $\mathbb{A}$ is open for interaction-liveness on $\mathbb{E}$, then every new architecture obtained from an interaction-live architecture of type $\mathbb{A}$ via adding, deleting and replacing instances of $\mathbb{E}$ is also interaction-live. We are going to set down some reasonable conditions on component types to ensure these two properties hold.

We say $\mathbb{E}$ is *disjointed*, if $\mathcal{I}_{\mathcal{E}_1^{\mathbb{E}}} \cap \mathcal{I}_{\mathcal{E}_2^{\mathbb{E}}} = \emptyset$ for any components $\mathcal{E}_1^{\mathbb{E}}, \mathcal{E}_2^{\mathbb{E}}$; $\mathbb{E}$ is *excluded*, if for any component $\mathcal{E}_1^{\mathbb{E}}, \mathcal{E}_2^{\mathbb{E}}$ the following holds: for each $P = (P_1 \| P_2 \| P_3) \backslash \mathcal{I}_{\mathcal{E}_1^{\mathbb{E}}} \cup \mathcal{I}_{\mathcal{E}_2^{\mathbb{E}}}$ reachable from $([\mathcal{E}_1^{\mathbb{E}}] \| [\mathcal{E}_2^{\mathbb{E}}] \| [\mathcal{G}]) \backslash \mathcal{I}_{\mathcal{E}_1^{\mathbb{E}}} \cup \mathcal{I}_{\mathcal{E}_2^{\mathbb{E}}}$, there is $\alpha \neq \tau$ such that $P_i \xrightarrow{\alpha}$ in $P$ for each $i \in \{1, 2\}$, only if $P_j$ where $j = 3 - i$ is reachable from $[\mathcal{E}_j^{\mathbb{E}}]$ via a finite concatenation of transitions labeled by $\tau$ only. Informally, a component type is disjointed if and only if its *Control* is empty. The definition of "excludedness" implies the following lemma which says, informally, that each component of that type must not start its interaction if any other component of the same type is in the middle of interaction, and whose proof follows immediately from the definition of excludedness.

**Lemma 1.** *Suppose $\mathcal{E}_1', \ldots, \mathcal{E}_m'$ ($m \geq 2$) are all instances of $\mathbb{E}$ in $\mathcal{A}^{\mathbb{A}}$, and $\mathbb{E}$ is excluded, then: For each $P = (P_1 \| \cdots \| P_m \| P_{m+1}) \backslash \bigcup_{i=1}^{m} \mathcal{I}_{\mathcal{P}(\mathcal{E}_i')}$ reachable from $([\mathcal{E}_1'] \| \cdots \| [\mathcal{E}_m'] \| [\mathcal{G}]) \backslash \bigcup_{i=1}^{m} \mathcal{I}_{\mathcal{P}(\mathcal{E}_i')}$, $P_i \xrightarrow{\alpha}$ in $P$ where $\alpha \neq \tau$ for each $i \in [1, m]$, only if $P_j$ where $j \in [1, m] - \{i\}$ is reachable from $[\mathcal{E}_j']$ via a finite concatenation of transitions labeled by $\tau$ only.*

---

[3] For $\mathcal{A}^{\mathbb{A}} - \{\mathcal{E}^{\mathbb{E}}\}$ we have to suppose $\mathcal{A}^{\mathbb{A}}$ has more than one instances of type $\mathbb{E}$, for there must be at least one instance for each component type in an architecture.

We now demonstrate the relationship between disjointedness, excludedness, deadlock-freedom and interaction-liveness.

**Theorem 4.** *If $\mathbb{E}$ is disjointed, then $\mathbb{A}$ is open both for deadlock-freedom and for interaction-liveness on $\mathbb{E}$.*

Theorem 4 allows us to add and delete components of disjointed types without making the architecture lose deadlock-freedom and interaction-liveness, if the architecture enjoyed these two properties originally. We illustrate the application of Theorem 4 by our working example – the *SimpleCS* system. Since the the component type *Server* does not have any *Control* actions, it is not hard to prove that *Server* is disjointed. If we have already obtained the result that *SimpleCS* is deadlock-free (resp. interaction-live), then we can build new systems based on *SimpleCS* that are also deadlock-free (resp. interaction-live), such as:

$$MultiServerCS = SimpleCS \cup \{Server_2, \ldots, Server_n\} - \{Server_0, Server_1\} \ .$$

If we do not know the deadlock-freedom and interaction-liveness of *SimpleCS*, we check the following simpler system with one server only:

$$SingleServerCS = SimpleCS - \{Server_1\} \ .$$

**Theorem 5.** *If $\mathbb{E}$ is excluded, then $\mathbb{A}$ is open both for deadlock-freedom and for interaction-liveness on $\mathbb{E}$.*

The significance of Theorem 5 is just like Theorem 4 in that it allows us to add and delete components of excluded types without making the architecture lose deadlock-freedom and interaction-liveness, if the architecture enjoyed these two properties originally. In the *SimpleCS* system, since the $\overline{log}$ actions in each *Client* instance has to synchronize with the *log* actions in the connector *ProCall*, it is not hard to verify that component type *Client* is excluded. As above, if we already have the result that *SimpleCS* is deadlock-free (resp. interaction-live), then we can build new systems based on *SimpleCS* that are also deadlock-free (resp. interaction-live) (combining Theorem 4), such as:

$$MultiCS = MultiSeverCS \cup \{Client_3, \ldots, Client_m\} - \{Client_0, Client_1, Client_2\} \ .$$

If we do not know the deadlock-freedom or interaction-liveness of *SimpleCS*, we check the following elementary system with one client and one server only (combining Theorem 4):

$$SingleCS = SingleServerCS - \{Client_1, Client_2\} = \{Client_0, Server_0, ProCall\} \ .$$

In total, what Theorem 4 and Theorem 5 tell us is when and to what extent the checking of deadlock-freedom and interaction-liveness of an architecture can be carried out in the type level. A final point worthy to be noticed is that, combining with the compositional analytic techniques (Theorem 1 and 2), the checking of *SingleCS* can be splitted into the checking of the following two subsystems:

$$SingleCS_C = \{Client_0, ProCall\}, \quad SingleCS_S = \{Server_0, ProCall\} \ .$$

### 6.3 Discussions

We have shown how our analytic techniques, i.e. the compositional analyses and the type-based analyses, deal with the deadlock-freedom and the interaction-liveness of an architecture. We now summarize how these techniques improve the system checking in the following four ways and explain them by examples.

- First, our method enhances the use of previous checking results to deal with new checking problems. For example, if we already know that *ProCall* is compatible with $Server_0$ against $\mathcal{I}_{s_0}$, then we can deduce that *ProCall* is compatible with $Server_1$ against $\mathcal{I}_{s_1}$.
- Secondly, our method helps make diagnoses of those architectures failing to satisfy a desired property. This is due to the compositional nature of our first analyses. Suppose a client-server architecture *BadCS* contains a deadlock and we detect that the *ProCall* is not compatible with the client type, say, *BadClient*. By fixing *BadClient* we may obtain a deadlock-free architecture.
- Thirdly, our method reduces the complexity of system checking. For example, we can reduce the checking of deadlock-freedom and interaction-liveness of the system *SimpleCS* to the checking of those properties of the system *SingleCS*.
- Finally, while the architecture-type/instance distinction in ACDL makes the reusability of architecture-type specifications to describe new architectures possible, our type-based analyses facilitate this reusability by showing when and to what extent the system checking of some properties can be undertaken in the type level.

## 7 Conclusions and Future Work

In this paper we consider components in software-intensive systems as interfaces performing behaviors of input, output, and internal actions, and connectors as a special kind of components that glue components by specifying coordination protocols for their behaviors. Our focus is the centralized-mode architectural connection in which all components are linked by a single connector. We have proposed a new ADL called ACDL, the key feature of which is that it describes connectors in such a way that they are insensitive to the numbers of attached same-type components. We develop two kinds of analytic techniques customizing ACDL, i.e. compositional analyses and type-based analyses, to improve the system checking of temporal properties, such as deadlock-freedom and interaction-liveness, of an architecture. The latter property is a liveness property formulating that, during the running-time of the system, each component will never be trapped in a situation where no future interactions with the rest of the system is possible.

Our future work will follow two directions. First, the interaction-liveness is only one kind of liveness properties, but we foresee that our method applies to other liveness properties. Therefore one challenging problem is to find out what range of liveness properties can be dealt with by our method, and to give them a formal definition.

The other important direction is the tool support for ACDL. A tool-set accompanying an ADL is, strictly speaking, not part of the language itself, but the purpose of developing formal languages for architectural description is because their formality implies their suitability to be manipulated by software tools [3]. However, until now we have not offered (in this paper or elsewhere) any tool support for ACDL, such as a parser which analyzes the syntactic correctness of a piece of written ACDL textual notation, and this renders ACDL rather conceptual. A "shortcut" to overcome this shortcoming is mapping a conceptual language like ACDL to a standard language equipped with a well-developed toolkit such as UML (currently UML2.0 [17]), so an ACDL user can leverage the tools customizing UML like a code-generator and be favor of the theoretic merits of ACDL in practice. Nonetheless, the applicability of the mapping depends on whether and to what extent UML supports modeling the abstractions formally described by ACDL, especially given the fact that UML is a semi-formal language. Optimistically, UML has an extension mechanism permitting one use Object Constraint Language (OCL) [18], which is based on set theory and predicate logic, to provide a precise description of the information unable to be expressed in standard UML diagrams. The general applicability of using UML to model software architectures as several representatives of ADLs do has been evaluated in the literature [19]. In our case, however, a thorough examination is needed.

## Acknowledgements

The authors would like to thank the anonymous referees for their helpful comments to improve the draft of this paper.

## References

1. Garlan, D., Shaw, M.: An introduction to software architecture. Technical report, Pittsburgh, PA, USA (1994)
2. Sifakis, J.: A framework for component-based construction. In: Proceedings of the 3rd IEEE International Conference on Software Engineering and Formal Methods (2005)
3. Medvidovic, N., Taylor, R.: A classification and comparison framework for software architecture description languages. IEEE Transactions on Software Engineering 26(1), 70–93 (2000)
4. Allen, R., Garlan, D.: A formal basis for architectural connection. ACM Transactions on Software Engineering and Methodology 6(3), 213–249 (1997)
5. Oquendo, F.: $\pi$-ADL: an architecture description language based on the higher-order typed $\pi$-calculus for specifying dynamic and mobile software architectures. ACM SIGSOFT Software Engineering Notes 29(3), 1–14 (2004)
6. Tivoli, M., Inverardi, P.: Failure-free coordinators synthesis for component-based architectures. Science of Compututer Programming 71(3), 181–212 (2008)
7. Milner, R., Parrow, J., Walker, D.: A calculus of mobile processes. Information and Computation 100(1), 1–77 (1992)
8. Bernardo, M., Ciancarini, P., Donatiello, L.: Architecting families of software systems with process algebras. ACM Transactions on Software Engineering and Methodology 11(4), 386–426 (2002)
9. Inverardi, P., Wolf, A.L., Yankelevich, D.: Static checking of system behaviors using derived component assumptions. ACM Transactions on Software Engineering and Methodology 9(3), 239–272 (2000)

10. Aldini, A., Bernardo, M.: On the usability of process algebra: An architectural view. Theoretical Computer Science 335(2-3), 281–329 (2005)
11. Magee, J., Dulay, N., Eisenbach, S., Kramer, J.: Specifying distributed software architectures. In: Proceedings of the 5th European Software Engineering Conference, pp. 137–153 (1995)
12. Mateescu, R., Oquendo, F.: π-AAL: an architecture analysis language for formally specifying and verifying structural and behavioural properties of software architectures. ACM SIGSOFT Software Engineering Notes 31(2), 1–19 (2006)
13. Shaw, M., Garlan, D.: Software Architecture: Perspectives on an Emerging Discipline. Prentice-Hall, NJ (1996)
14. Spitznagel, B., Garlan, D.: A compositional formalization of connector wrappers. In: Proceedings of the 25th International Conference on Software Engineering (2003)
15. Giesecke, S.: Taxonomy of architectural style usage. In: Proceedings of the 2006 Conference on Pattern Languages of Programs (2006)
16. Sangiorgi, D., Walker, D.: π-calculus: A Theory of Mobile Processes. Cambridge University Press, NY (2001)
17. Booch, G., Rumbaugh, J., Jacobson, I.: Unified Modeling Language User Guide, 2nd edn. Addison-Wesley Professional, Reading (2005)
18. Warmer, J., Kleppe, A.: The Object Constraint Language: Getting Your Models Ready for MDA. Addison-Wesley, Boston (2003)
19. Medvidovic, N., Rosenblum, D.S., Redmiles, D.F., Robbins, J.E.: Modeling software architectures in the unified modeling language. ACM Transaction on Software Engineering Methodology 11(1), 2–57 (2002)

# Appendix

*Proof of Theorem 1.* To improve readability we use $\{[\mathcal{E}_i^1]\}$ refering to $[\mathcal{E}_i^1]\| \cdots \|[\mathcal{E}_i^{k_i}]$, for each $i \in [1, m]$. Hence $[\mathcal{A}] = (\{[\mathcal{E}_1^1]\}\| \cdots \|\{[\mathcal{E}_m^1]\}\|[\mathcal{G}])\backslash \mathcal{I}_\mathcal{A}$. We decompose the proof of Theorem 1 into the following three lemmas.

**Lemma 2.** *If $P = (P_1\| \cdots \|P_m\|P_{m+1})\backslash \mathcal{I}_\mathcal{A}$ is reachable from $[\mathcal{A}] = (\{[\mathcal{E}_1^1]\}\| \cdots \| \{[\mathcal{E}_m^1]\}\|[\mathcal{G}])\backslash \mathcal{I}_\mathcal{A}$, then $(P_i\|P_{m+1})\backslash \mathcal{I}_{\mathcal{P}(\mathcal{E}_i^1)}$ is reachable from $(\{[\mathcal{E}_i^1]\}\|[\mathcal{G}])\backslash \mathcal{I}_{\mathcal{P}(\mathcal{E}_i^1)}$ for each $i \in [1, m]$.*

*Proof.* The proof is by induction on the number of transitions from $[\mathcal{A}]$ to $P$. Suppose $Q = (Q_1\| \cdots \|Q_m\|Q_{m+1})\backslash \mathcal{I}_\mathcal{A}$, $Q \xrightarrow{\alpha} P$, and $Q$ is reachable from $[\mathcal{A}]$. W.r.t. Proposition 2 and the partition $\mathcal{P}$, there are only two cases on the derivation of $Q \xrightarrow{\alpha} P$. (1) Suppose $Q \xrightarrow{\alpha} P$ is derived from $Q_i \xrightarrow{\tau} P_i$ for some $i \in [1, m + 1]$. Then clearly $(Q_j\|Q_{m+1})\backslash \mathcal{I}_{\mathcal{P}(\mathcal{E}_j^1)}$ for each $j \in [1, m]$. By induction hypothesis we are done. (2) Suppose $Q \xrightarrow{\alpha} P$ is derived from $Q_j \xrightarrow{\beta} P_j$ for some $j \in [1, m]$ and $Q_{m+1} \xrightarrow{\beta'} P_{m+1}$ where $\beta'$ is dual to $\beta$. Then $(Q_j\|Q_{m+1})\backslash \mathcal{I}_{\mathcal{P}(\mathcal{E}_j^1)} \xrightarrow{\beta} (P_j\|P_{m+1})\backslash \mathcal{I}_{\mathcal{P}(\mathcal{E}_j^1)}$, $(Q_k\|Q_{m+1})\backslash \mathcal{I}_{\mathcal{P}(\mathcal{E}_k^1)} \xrightarrow{\beta} (Q_k\|P_{m+1})\backslash \mathcal{I}_{\mathcal{P}(\mathcal{E}_k^1)}$, and $Q_k = P_k$ where $k \in [1, m] - \{j\}$. By induction hypothesis, we have the result.

**Lemma 3.** *If $\mathcal{G}$ is compatible with $\mathcal{P}(\mathcal{E}_i^1)$ for each $i \in [1, m]$, then $\mathcal{G}$ is compatible with $\mathcal{A} - \{\mathcal{G}\}$ against $\mathcal{I}_\mathcal{A}$.*

*Proof.* Suppose $P = (P_1\|\cdots\|P_m\|P_{m+1})\backslash\mathcal{I}_\mathcal{A}$ is reachable from $[\mathcal{A}]$, and $P_{m+1} \xrightarrow{\alpha}$ for some $\alpha$. By Proposition 2, $ch(\alpha) \in \mathcal{I}_{\mathcal{P}(\mathcal{E}_i^1)}$ for some $i \in [1,m]$. By Lemma 2, $(P_i\|P_{m+1})\backslash\mathcal{I}_{\mathcal{P}(\mathcal{E}_i^1)}$ is reachable from $([\mathcal{E}_i]\|[\mathcal{G}])\backslash\mathcal{I}_{\mathcal{P}(\mathcal{E}_i^1)}$. Since $\mathcal{G}$ is compatible with $\mathcal{P}(\mathcal{E}_i^1)$, $P_{m+1} \xrightarrow{\alpha}$ in $(\{[\mathcal{E}_i^1]\}\|[\mathcal{G}])\backslash\mathcal{I}_{\mathcal{P}(\mathcal{E}_i^1)}$. Therefore $P_{m+1} \xrightarrow{\alpha}$ in $[\mathcal{A}]$.

**Lemma 4.** *If $\mathcal{G}$ is deadlock-free and compatible with $\mathcal{A} - \{\mathcal{G}\}$ against $\mathcal{I}_\mathcal{A}$, $\mathcal{A}$ is deadlock-free.*

*Proof.* The result is obvious by the definitions.

*Proof of Theorem 2.* We first show a small lemma:

**Lemma 5.** *$\mathcal{E}_i$ and $\mathcal{E}_j$ are strongly deadlock-free, the $[\mathcal{E}_i]\|[\mathcal{E}_j]$ is strongly deadlock-free; and this can be generalized to any number of components.*

*Proof.* This lemma can be proved by show that if $[\mathcal{E}_i]\|[\mathcal{E}_j]$ has a finite transition path or a infinite path failing the satisfying the non-silent-label requirement, then one of $\mathcal{E}_i$ and $\mathcal{E}_j$ must be failed; this can be easily generalized to any finite number of components.

Then we prove Theorem 2:

*Proof.* Suppose $\mathcal{A}$ satisfies the conditions in Theorem 1, and $\{[\mathcal{E}_j]\}$ is strongly deadlock-free for each $j \in [0,m]$, we show that if for some $i \in [1,m]$ there is an infinite transition path $\varphi$ of $[\mathcal{A}]$ containing only finitely many $P$ such that there is $Q$ reachable from $P$ and $Q_i \xrightarrow{\alpha}$ in $Q$ for some $\alpha \neq \tau$, then there is an infinite transition path $\psi$ of $(\{[\mathcal{E}_i^1]\}\|\mathcal{G})\backslash\mathcal{I}_{\mathcal{P}(\mathcal{E}_i^1)}$ containing only finitely many $P'$ such that there is $Q'$ reachable from $P'$ and $Q_i' \xrightarrow{\alpha}$ in $Q'$ for some $\alpha \neq \tau$, and hence prove the theorem. More specifically, $\psi$ is constructed in the following procedure: Suppose $P$ is reachable from $[\mathcal{A}]$ via $n$ transitions in $\varphi$ and also $P \xrightarrow{\alpha} Q$ is in $\varphi$, and let $\widehat{\psi}_n$ be a finite concatenation of transitions starting at $(\{[\mathcal{E}_i^1]\}\|\mathcal{G})\backslash\mathcal{I}_{\mathcal{P}(\mathcal{E}_i^1)}$ and ending at $(P_i\|P_{m+1})\backslash\mathcal{I}_{\mathcal{P}(\mathcal{E}_i^1)}$,

1. $\widehat{\psi}_0 = (\{[\mathcal{E}_i^1]\}\|\mathcal{G})\backslash\mathcal{I}_{\mathcal{P}(\mathcal{E}_i^1)}$ ;
2. If $P \xrightarrow{\alpha} Q$ is derived from $P_i \xrightarrow{\tau} Q_i$ (thus $\alpha = \tau$), then $\widehat{\psi}_{n+1} = \widehat{\psi}_n \xrightarrow{\tau} (Q_i\|Q_{m+1})\backslash\mathcal{I}_{\mathcal{P}(\mathcal{E}_i^1)}$ where $Q_{m+1} = P_{m+1}$;
3. If $P \xrightarrow{\alpha} Q$ is derived from $P_i \xrightarrow{\beta} Q_i$ and $P_{m+1} \xrightarrow{\beta'} Q_{m+1}$ where $\beta'$ are dual to $\beta$ (thus $\alpha = \tau$), then $\widehat{\psi}_{n+1} = \widehat{\psi}_n \xrightarrow{\tau} (Q_i\|Q_{m+1})\backslash\mathcal{I}_{\mathcal{P}(\mathcal{E}_i^1)}$ ;
4. If $P \xrightarrow{\alpha} Q$ is derived from $P_j \xrightarrow{\beta} Q_j$ where $j \neq i \in [1,m]$ and $P_{m+1} \xrightarrow{\beta'} Q_{m+1}$ where $\beta'$ are dual to $\beta$, then $\widehat{\psi}_{n+1} = \widehat{\psi}_n \xrightarrow{\beta'} (Q_i\|Q_{m+1})\backslash\mathcal{I}_{\mathcal{P}(\mathcal{E}_i^1)}$ where $Q_i = P_i$;
5. If $P \xrightarrow{\alpha} Q$ is derived from $P_j \xrightarrow{\tau} Q_j$ where $j \neq i \in [1,m]$ (thus $\alpha = \tau$), then $\widehat{\psi}_{n+1} = \widehat{\psi}_n$ .

The strong deadlock-freedom of each $\{[\mathcal{E}_j]\}$ guarantees that there are only finitely many $k_1$'s and $k_2$'s such that $k_1 \neq k_2$ and $\widehat{\psi}_{k_1} = \widehat{\psi}_{k_2}$ . Therefore it not hard to verify that $\lim_{n\to\infty} \widehat{\psi}_n$ is the $\psi$ we want.

*Proof of Theorem 3.* Clause (1) and (3) in Theorem 3 immediately follow from Theorem 4 (see below) and Clause (2) is obvious.

*Proof of Theorem 4.* We decompose the proof of Theorem 4 into the following three lemmas.

**Lemma 6.** *Provided $\mathbb{E}$ is disjointed, $P = (P_1 \| P_2) \backslash \mathcal{I}_{\mathcal{E}_1^{\mathbb{E}}}$ is reachable from $R = ([\mathcal{E}_1^{\mathbb{E}}] \| [\mathcal{G}]) \backslash \mathcal{I}_{\mathcal{E}_1^{\mathbb{E}}}$ if and only if $P' = (P_1 \sigma \| P_2 \sigma) \backslash \mathcal{I}_{\mathcal{E}_2^{\mathbb{E}}}$ is reachable from $R' = ([\mathcal{E}_2^{\mathbb{E}}] \| [\mathcal{G}]) \backslash \mathcal{I}_{\mathcal{E}_2^{\mathbb{E}}}$, where $\sigma = \{p, q/q, p\}$ and $p, q$ are the IDs of $\mathcal{E}_1, \mathcal{E}_2$, respectively.*

*Proof.* Note that by Proposition 1, we have that $P' = P\sigma$ and $R' = R\sigma$, and that $\alpha \in \mathcal{I}_{\mathcal{E}_1^{\mathbb{E}}}$ iff $\alpha\sigma \in \mathcal{I}_{\mathcal{E}_2^{\mathbb{E}}}$. We firstly consider the direction from left to right. The proof is by induction on the number of transitions from $R$ to $P$. Suppose $Q = (Q_1 \| Q_2) \backslash \mathcal{I}_{\mathcal{E}_1^{\mathbb{E}}}$ is reachable from $R$ and $Q \xrightarrow{\alpha} P$. By induction hypothesis $Q' = Q\sigma = (Q_1 \sigma \| Q_2 \sigma) \backslash \mathcal{I}_{\mathcal{E}_2^{\mathbb{E}}}$ is reachable from $R'$. Similar to the proof of Lemma 2, we proceed by two cases on the derivation of $Q \xrightarrow{\alpha} P$. (1) Suppose $Q \xrightarrow{\alpha} P$ is derived from $Q_2 \xrightarrow{\alpha} P_2$ and $\alpha \notin \mathcal{I}_{\mathcal{E}_1^{\mathbb{E}}}$, then $Q\sigma \xrightarrow{\alpha\sigma} P\sigma$ is derived from $Q_2\sigma \xrightarrow{\alpha\sigma} P_2\sigma$ for $\alpha\sigma \notin \mathcal{I}_{\mathcal{E}_2^{\mathbb{E}}}$. (2) Suppose $Q \xrightarrow{\alpha} P$ is derived from $Q_1 \xrightarrow{\tau} P_1$ (thus $\alpha = \tau$), then $Q\sigma \xrightarrow{\tau} P\sigma$ is derived from $Q_1\sigma \xrightarrow{\tau} P_1\sigma$. (3) Suppose $Q \xrightarrow{\alpha} P$ is derived from $Q_1 \xrightarrow{\beta} P_1$ and $Q_2 \xrightarrow{\beta'} P_2$ where $\beta'$ is dual to $\beta$ (thus $\alpha = \tau$), similarly we have the same result. Hence $P' = P\sigma$ is reachable from $R'$. By symmetric of substitution we complete the proof.

**Lemma 7.** *Provided $\mathbb{E}$ is disjointed, $\mathcal{G}$ is compatible with $\{\mathcal{E}_1^{\mathbb{E}}\}$ against $\mathcal{I}_{\mathcal{E}_1^{\mathbb{E}}}$ if and only if $\mathcal{G}$ is compatible with $\{\mathcal{E}_2^{\mathbb{E}}\}$ against $\mathcal{I}_{\mathcal{E}_2^{\mathbb{E}}}$.*

*Proof.* Lemma 7 is based on Lemma 6 in the same vein that Lemma 3 is based on Lemma 2.

**Lemma 8.** *Provided $\mathbb{E}$ is disjointed, $\mathcal{E}_1^{\mathbb{E}}$ and $\mathcal{G}$ are mutually interaction-live against $\mathcal{I}_{\mathcal{E}_1^{\mathbb{E}}}$ if and only if $\mathcal{E}_2^{\mathbb{E}}$ and $\mathcal{G}$ are mutually interaction-live against $\mathcal{I}_{\mathcal{E}_2^{\mathbb{E}}}$.*

*Proof.* Let $\sigma = \{p, q/q, p\}$ where $p, q$ are the IDs of $\mathcal{E}_1, \mathcal{E}_2$, respectively. We show that if $P = (P_1 \| P_2) \backslash \mathcal{I}_{\mathcal{E}_1^{\mathbb{E}}}$ is reachable from $([\mathcal{E}_1]^{\mathbb{E}} \| [\mathcal{G}]) \backslash \mathcal{I}_{\mathcal{E}_1^{\mathbb{E}}}$ and $P_i \xrightarrow{\alpha}$ in $P$ $(i = 1, 2)$, then $P\sigma = (P_1\sigma \| P_2\sigma) \backslash \mathcal{I}_{\mathcal{E}_2^{\mathbb{E}}}$ is reachable from $([\mathcal{E}_2]^{\mathbb{E}} \| [\mathcal{G}]) \backslash \mathcal{I}_{\mathcal{E}_2^{\mathbb{E}}}$ and $P_i\sigma \xrightarrow{\alpha\sigma}$ in $P\sigma$. The proof is similar to the proof of Lemma 6.

*Proof of Theorem 5.* The proof of Theorem 5 is decomposed into three lemmas below whose proofs are similar to those of previous lemmas.

**Lemma 9.** *Provided $\mathbb{E}$ is excluded, if $\mathcal{G}$ is compatible with $\{\mathcal{E}_i^{\mathbb{E}}\}$ against $\mathcal{I}_{\mathcal{E}_i^{\mathbb{E}}}$ for some $i \in [1, m]$, then $\mathcal{G}$ is compatible with $\{\mathcal{E}_1^{\mathbb{E}}, \ldots, \mathcal{E}_m^{\mathbb{E}}\}$ against $\bigcup_{i=1}^{m} \mathcal{I}_{\mathcal{E}_i^{\mathbb{E}}}$.*

**Lemma 10.** *If $[\mathcal{E}_1^{\mathbb{E}}]$ is strongly deadlock-free, then $[\mathcal{E}_1^{\mathbb{E}}] \| \cdots \| [\mathcal{E}_m^{\mathbb{E}}]$ is strongly deadlock-free.*

**Lemma 11.** *Provided $\mathbb{E}$ is excluded, if $\mathcal{E}_i^{\mathbb{E}}$ and $\mathcal{G}$ are mutually interaction-live against $\mathcal{I}_{\mathcal{E}_i^{\mathbb{E}}}$ for some $i \in [1, m]$, then $\mathcal{E}_1^{\mathbb{E}}, \ldots, \mathcal{E}_m^{\mathbb{E}}$ and $\mathcal{G}$ are mutually interaction-live against $\bigcup_{i=1}^{m} \mathcal{I}_{\mathcal{E}_i^{\mathbb{E}}}$.*

# Naive Architecting - Understanding the Reasoning Process of Students

## A Descriptive Survey

Uwe van Heesch[1,2] and Paris Avgeriou[1]

[1] University of Groningen, The Netherlands
[2] Fontys University of Applied Sciences Venlo, The Netherlands
uwe@vanheesch.net, paris@cs.rug.nl

**Abstract.** Software architecting entails making architecture decisions, which requires a lot of experience and expertise. Current literature contains several methods and processes to support architects with architecture design, documentation and evaluation but not with the design reasoning involved in decision-making. In order to derive a systematic reasoning process we need to understand the current state of practice and propose ways to improve it. In this paper we present the results of a survey that was conducted with undergraduate software engineering students, aiming to find out the innate reasoning process during architecting. The results of the survey are compared to the existing architecture literature in order to identify promising directions towards systematic reasoning processes.

## 1 Motivation

One of the responsibilities of software architects is to make decisions, which are usually called architectural decisions [4,12,29] and determine the overall structure and behavior of the system. Making architectural decisions involves understanding and addressing relevant requirements, business goals and issues, identifying and choosing among alternative solutions while adhering to constraints and mitigating risks. Architectural decisions form the basis for all other detailed decisions and are crucial for the success or failure of the whole project. This decision-making process is one of the major challenges during architecting since it requires a lot of experience and expertise by the architect.

Various methods exist to support software architects in their work. Hofmeister et al. derived a common model for architecture design from five industrial approaches [10], including the Rational Unified Process [21] and Attribute-Driven Design [3]. Other approaches deal with documenting the architecture in terms of multiple architectural views or with the help of architecture frameworks [2,7,16]. Furthermore, different methods exist to support the systematic evaluation of architectures [14,18,19]. More recently some approaches propose the documentation of the actual decisions as first-class entities by defining their attributes and relations [4,27]. However, all of these approaches deal with the core part of

M. Ali Babar and I. Gorton (Eds.): ECSA 2010, LNCS 6285, pp. 24–37, 2010.

architecting: prioritizing architecturally significant requirements, selecting architecture patterns, styles and tactics, partitioning the system into components and connectors, assessing the design and documenting the result with architectural views, frameworks and architecture description languages. In contrast, there has been very little research on the reasoning part of the decision-making process; one can only find fragments about sound reasoning in the literature.

Recent work emphasizes the importance of design reasoning and design rationale [4,23]. Ideally a systematic reasoning process can shorten the gap between experienced and inexperienced architects: design reasoning can support designers step-by-step in making sound decisions and subsequently documenting the rationale behind them as first class entities. However, so far, architects are not trained on how to reason: making architectural decisions is often described as an ad-hoc creative process [5,32,33] that relies heavily on the personal experience and expertise of the architect. Research is required to explore the current state of practice in design reasoning and subsequently to find ways to enhance it.

Our work is towards this direction: investigating how the reasoning process takes place and identifying potential areas for improvement. This can be done either by studying beginners (bottom-up) or experienced architects (top-down). In the former case one can establish the baseline reasoning process that is based on common sense instead of experience. In the latter case one can discover best practices in successful architecting examples and synthesize them into an ideal reasoning process. Eventually one can propose an approach to close the gap between the baseline and the ideal process and package it appropriately to train current or future architects.

This paper deals with the former case; we leave the latter case as future work. In particular we have studied the most inexperienced subjects: students of software engineering. We asked 22 students to design an architecture for a large web application and carefully observed their reasoning during this process. After that, the students were interviewed about the way they thought and acted to come up with a software architecture. As a result, we identified the basic reasoning process of inexperienced designers, which we compared to established architecting processes in the literature in order to come up with promising directions for improvement.

The rest of this paper is organized as follows. Section 2 presents related Work. In Sect. 3, the design of the study is introduced. The next section presents an analysis of the results, which are interpreted in Sect. 5. The paper ends with conclusions and directions for further work.

## 2    Related Work

The survey presented in this paper is related to the software architecture research field, namely architecting processes, architecting practice in the industry and design reasoning.

Hofmeister et al. derive a general model of architecture design from five industrial approaches [10]. They identify the following common activities:

*Architectural analysis* is concerned with identifying architecturally significant requirements from architectural concerns and system contexts; *Architectural synthesis* is the activity of finding candidate solutions for architecturally significant requirements; Architectural evaluation makes sure that the candidate solutions are the right ones.

Jansen et al. specialize this generic model from the perspective of architectural decisions [13]. They describe the architecting process as a cycle of activities that are followed iteratively until the architecture is complete. In accordance with Hofmeister et al.'s categorization, in architectural analysis, the problem space is scoped down to problems that can be solved by single architectural decisions. Candidate decisions are proposed during architectural synthesis, while decisions are chosen during architectural evaluations, which also entails modifying and describing the architecture in multiple architectural views. In addition to Hofmeister et al.'s approach, which focuses mainly on architecting activities and artifacts, Jansen et al. indicate reasoning processes within the activities.

Various studies have attempted to define the role of software architects in the industry [8,9,17,31]. Clerc et al. have conducted survey-based research [8] to gain insights in the daily working processes of architecture practitioners. They found out that architecture use cases [28] concerning risk assessment and requirements trade-off analysis are not regarded as particularly important by the architects. In contrast, use cases concerned with requirements, architecture design and implementation, and the traceability among these were rated as important. The authors reckon that the architects' workflow follows a linear (i.e. non-iterative) approach to designing architecture that satisfies the requirements subsequently. In a different survey, Farenhorst et al. [9] describe that more experienced architects (in terms of working years) are more often involved in auditing activities and quality assurance. Kruchten defines the typical roles and responsibilities that architects should take in software projects [17]. Besides making architectural decisions, other central activities of architects include maintaining the architectural integrity, risk assessment and risk mitigation. Finally, Clements et al. compare duties, skills, and knowledge of software architects from the perspectives of literature, education and practice [31]. They found that architecture evaluation and analysis are regarded as less important in architecture practice, whereas knowledge of technologies and platforms, as well as technology-related duties are regarded more important in architecture practice than in the literature and education. We will revisit these results on architecting practice and relate them to our findings in Sect. 6.

The significance of design reasoning in software architecture has been recently emphasized. Tang and Lago describe design reasoning tactics [24] to support architects in structuring architectural problems and extracting design issues. In his previous work [23,25], Tang declares the importance of design reasoning and design rationale in the area of software architecture. It supports architects in making well-founded decisions and provides guidance to explore and manage the solution space. They state that the use of a reasoning approach significantly improves the quality of architectural design, especially for inexperienced architects [23].

# 3  Design of the Study

## 3.1  Goal

The goal of the study is to get insight into the innate reasoning that students follow while they are architecting. To make this goal more concrete we need to consider the fundamental reasoning activities that take place during the architecting process. As a reference architecting process, we use the one defined in our previous work [13], which explicitly takes into account the reasoning aspects and maps onto the process of Hofmeister et al. (see Sect. 2). We thus refine our research goal into the following three research questions:

**RQ1:** How do students scope and prioritize the problem space during architectural analysis?
**RQ2:** How do students propose solutions during architectural synthesis?
**RQ3:** How do students choose among solutions during architectural evaluation?

RQ1 is concerned with finding out how students scope and prioritize requirements and issues to define concrete problems that are small enough to be addressed by one architectural decision. RQ2 applies to finding candidate solutions based on the problems identified in the previous step. Finally, the aim of RQ3 is to discover how students make choices between the candidate solutions and how they evaluate their choices with respect to previously made decisions. It is noted that the requirements engineering activity, though closely related, is performed before the architecting process and is therefore out of the scope of this study (an initial set of requirements was made available to the students). Furthermore the activity of modifying and describing the architecture (see [13]) was omitted, because of time constraints in conducting the study.

## 3.2  Study Design and Execution

To find answers to the research questions, a descriptive survey [30] was conducted with students from the seventh semester, in a four-year software engineering programme of study at the Fontys University of Applied Science in Venlo, The Netherlands. At that time, the students had at least 3 years of OO-programming experience from small software development projects withing the study programme. Some of them had additional experience from side jobs. They had followed two lectures (three hours in total) specifically on software architecture. The following topics were covered in this course: the 4+1 architectural views [16], the recommended Practice for Architectural Description of Software-Intensive Systems [2], the concept of architectural decisions mainly using the template by Tyree and Akerman [27] and software architectural patterns [6]. In total, 22 students took part, who were divided into 11 pairs.

To produce an architecting experience, we asked the students to create a new software architecture of a non-trivial software system (later referred to as *phase one*). Right after that, the students were asked to fill in a questionnaire, in order to report about their individual architecting experiences (*phase two*). The questionnaire was designed and evaluated according to [20].

The architecting case used in phase one was a document describing architecturally relevant functional and non-functional requirements for an online selling platform comparable to Amazon.com [1]. The case study included requirements for user management, selling books, multimedia and other products, searching for products, notification of sellers and buyers. The non-functional requirements included interoperability, availability, performance and security. In total, nine functional and nine non-functional requirements were given. The students were explicitly allowed to supplement or modify the given requirements, for example because of specific trade-offs, if they could justify why.

The architecting activity (phase one) in the experiment took 60 minutes. The students were asked to make all necessary architectural decisions and to document the process of decision making in a mind map. The purpose of the mind map (created on flip charts) was to conserve as much reasoning and as many thoughts of the participants during the decision making process as possible. No architecting method was imposed on them, nor did they have knowledge about any existing systematic approach. The students were also asked to document design options and design decisions using a minimal template. Laptops with an internet connection were allowed to search for arbitrary information, e.g. to find design options like software patterns or technologies. To gather data in phase

**Table 1.** Question Mapping

| Code | Question | RQ1 | RQ2 | RQ3 |
|------|----------|-----|-----|-----|
| Q1 | Have you understood and considered the given requirements? | X | | |
| Q2 | Have you reasoned about the most challenging requirements? | X | | |
| Q3 | Have the quality attribute requirements played a prominent role during the design? | X | | |
| Q5 | Have you considered alternatives for the decisions you made? | | X | |
| Q6 | Have you relaxed requirements to have more design options? | X | X | |
| Q7 | Have you thought about the pros and cons of each alternative that you have considered? | | | X |
| Q9 | Have you preferred well-known solutions rather than searching for better alternatives? | | X | |
| Q10 | Have you sometimes made multiple decisions at the same time? | | X | X |
| Q11 | Have you rejected decisions? | | | X |
| Q12 | Have you made trade-offs, while making decisions, between multiple requirements? | X | | X |
| Q13 | Have you come across dependencies between decisions? | | X | X |
| Q14 | How long did it take since you had a first architectural vision in mind? | | | X |
| Q15 | Does the final architecture significantly differ from your initial vision? | | | X |
| Q16 | How have you come from one decision to the next decision? | X | X | X |
| Q17 | What has gone on in your head when you have thought about the architecture? | X | X | X |

two of the experiment, a group-administered questionnaire (see [26]) was handed out to the students right after they finished phase one. The students used their documented decisions and the mind map as help to reflect on the process while answering the questions. The questionnaire contained a mix of structured and un-structured questions. The structured questions had a five-point interval-level response format, also referred to as Likert-scale [26]. To mitigate the risk of ambiguous or poorly understood questions that comes along with questionnaires [20], an instructor explained the questions to the participants one by one. That way the students could clarify questions before answering. Table 1 shows a mapping of the questionnaire questions to the research questions formulated in Sect. 3.1. Some questions have a relation to more than one research question; in these cases, the bold-faced 'X' denotes the most relevant research question (except for Q16 and Q17 where all three research questions are relevant). Additionally, two more questions were asked, which do not directly map to the research questions: "Do you have the skills to design and program the given system?" (Q4) and "Are you confident that your decisions and the resulting design are sound?" (Q8).

The participation in the study was mandatory. The students received grades for the architecture documentation on the flip charts. It was clearly communicated to the students that the answers in the questionnaire in phase two were not taken into consideration for the grading. This issue will be further discussed in Sect. 5.1.

# 4  Analysis

We use descriptive statistics to visualize the collected data in the analysis. This section contains one subsection for every research question. Subsection 4.4 presents results concerning all three research questions. There are eleven valid datapoints for each question, one for each student pair.

## 4.1  RQ1 - Architectural Analysis

Questions Q1,Q2 and Q3 from the questionnaire are primarily related to the treatment of architecturally relevant requirements during architectural synthesis. Figure 1 shows a stacked bar chart presenting cumulative percentaged frequencies of answers to the respective questions. The vast majority of the participants ($> 90\%$) affirmed that they understood and considered the given requirements (Q1). The median answer was 'affirmation'. The answers to question two, concerning the reasoning about the most challenging requirements, do not show a clear trend (Q2, median 'neutral'). More than 80% affirmed that quality attribute requirements played a prominent role during the design (Q3, median 'strong affirmation').

## 4.2  RQ2 - Architectural Synthesis

Figure 2 shows the frequencies of answers to questions Q5,Q6 and Q9, related to finding candidate solutions during architectural synthesis (RQ2). More than 70%

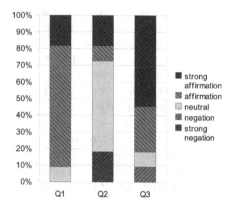

**Fig. 1.** Cumulative frequencies of answers to questions related to RQ1

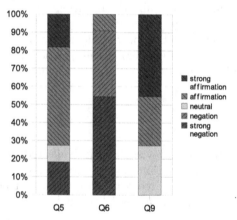

**Fig. 2.** Cumulative frequencies of answers to questions related to RQ2

of the participants affirmed that they considered alternatives for the decisions they made (Q5, median 'affirmation'). The majority of participants did not relax requirements to have more design options (Q6, > 90%, median 'strong negation') and, without any negations, more than 70% of the participants affirmed that they preferred well-known solutions rather than searching for better alternatives (Q9, median 'affirmation').

## 4.3   RQ3 - Architectural Evaluation

Questions Q7, Q10-Q15 refer to the making of choices between candidate solutions and the evaluation of the choices with previously made decisions. Figure 3 shows the frequencies of answers. The answers to Q7, referring to the consideration of pros and cons of alternative solutions, show a clear tendency towards affirmation (median 'affirmation'). Q10, related to the making of multiple decisions at the same time, does not receive a clear result. Although the most

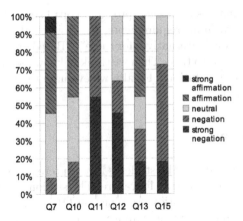

**Fig. 3.** Cumulative frequencies of answers to questions related to RQ3

frequent answer was 'affirmation', the median answer was 'neutral'. 100% of the participants negated the question about rejecting decisions (Q11, median 'strong negation'). The students also did not consciously make trade-offs between requirements (Q12, > 60%, median 'negation'). The answers to question 13 concerning dependencies between decisions do not show a clear tendency (median 'neutral'). Question 14 did not have predefined answers. The participants were asked how long it took in minutes since they had a first architectural vision in mind (Q15 refers to this vision). On average, the participants took 13,36 minutes for a first vision. The standard deviation is 9,067 (min: 5min, max: 30min). Finally, without a single affirmative answer, more than 70% negated that the final architecture significantly differed from the initial architectural vision (Q15, median 'negation').

## 4.4  Open Questions Concerning the Whole Architecting Process

Besides structured questions, we asked the participants to answer two open questions (Q16 and Q17) that concern all three research questions.

In question 16, we asked the students to describe how they got from one decision to the next decision. Four of the pairs stated that they made decisions along the requirements (e.g. "Reading requirements one by one"). Two groups mentioned that they used common combinations of technologies as orientation in the decision making process (e.g. Spring as web framework, then Hibernate as object-relational mapper), one group explicitly stated that they first created a list of things to be decided and then made the decisions one by one.

In question 17, the students were asked to freely describe what went on in their heads when they thought about the architecture. The following workflow of decision making can be derived from the given answers: Analyze requirements, find candidate solutions based on own experience, search for alternative solutions, evaluate pros and cons of all candidate solutions, make decision. Exemplary verbatim answers are: "We started with own knowledge and experience, then we thought about alternatives and made pros and cons lists.", "We thought about what was necessary to fulfill requirements, we thought about known technologies, we tried to find some alternatives for these", "Based on the requirements we think about the decisions to take. Then we think of known solutions/technologies and research on further solutions. Finally we evaluate the different possibilities and make the decisions".

## 5   Interpretation

In this section, the behavior of the students is interpreted and compared to existing approaches in the architecture literature. The section is organized according to the three architecting activities. Findings on Q16 and Q17 that concern all three activities are mentioned where appropriate.

**Architectural Analysis.** Architectural analysis involves articulating [10] and scoping down [13] architecturally significant requirements (ASR). The quality attribute requirements play a prominent role in this activity [3,11]. Usually the ASRs are further prioritized [13] to identify key issues or problematic requirements [11,21] that require special attention, because they are critical for the architecture. They sometimes become risks [21].

The analysis of the students' results showed that most of them intuitively followed these activities. They tried to understand and consider the ASRs and put emphasis on the quality attribute requirements. The only discrepancy is that many students did not identify the most challenging requirements, nor did they prioritize them. It is noticeable that the students do not seem to be aware of risks and consequently do nothing to mitigate them. However, two student pairs strongly affirmed that they did think about the most challenging requirements. A correlation analysis (Kendall's tau [22]) showed that students who affirmed the statement also had strong confidence in the soundness of their resulting designs (Q8) (corr.-coefficient 0,618, sig. 0,023), which allows the conclusion that risk assessment leads to higher confidence in the quality of the architecture.

**Architectural Synthesis.** Architectural synthesis is the process of finding candidate architectural solutions that (partially) address the distilled ASRs [10,13]. This activity requires the architect to identify and distill relevant knowledge from own experience and external knowledge repositories [10,24], needed to create design solutions. To have more design options, it is sometimes advisable to relax requirements that put too many constraints on possible solutions [24].

In the study, the students affirmed that the identification of design options was driven by the requirements. However, they did not relax requirements to have more design options and they also declared that they preferred well known solutions in favor of unknown alternatives. Also, they do not seem to be aware of limitations and constraints that solutions impose on other decisions. Their answers to the open questions reflect that the requirements were used as a kind of checklist to ensure that all of them are covered by at least one solution without taking into account the relationships and dependencies between decisions. A similar behavior was also observed for practising architects by Clerc et al., who state that the architects' workflow follows a linear approach that satisfies the requirements sequentially [8].

**Architectural Evaluation.** During architectural evaluation the candidate solutions are weighed against the ASRs [10] to make a design decision. Therefore, the pros and cons of each design option have to be considered [13,24]. Choosing solutions can entail making trade-offs [10,13] between requirements. This activity also involves identifying and documenting constraints that decisions impose on future decisions [3]. Evaluation further ensures that a decision does not violate previously made decisions. Therefore the architecture is regularly evaluated as a whole after a few iterations [11]. Some approaches emphasize the need of risk assessment during architectural evaluation [21,24] to ensure that no hidden assumptions or constraints behind decisions exist and to assess if additional risks are introduced by a decision.

The study shows strong deviation of the students' behavior from these activities. Although they weighted pros and cons for the design options, they did not consciously make trade-offs between requirements and also neglected to validate the decisions against each other. This explains why the students did not reject decisions. They do not seem to be aware of dependencies and relationships between architectural decisions. Only few students stated that they came across dependencies. In line with these observations, the students quickly came up with a first architectural vision ( 13$mins$) and did not significantly deviate from this vision any more. This is another indicator that students do not critically evaluate their decisions. This is not very surprising. As mentioned in Sect. 2, Clerc et al. [8] found out that even practising architects do not regard risk assessment and requirements trade-off analysis as particularly important.

Additionally, it was observed that no clear statement was made about the question if they made multiple decisions at the same time. Some students described that they used a kind of reference architecture they knew from comparable projects as a basis, others started from scratch and made decisions strictly sequentially. A correlation analysis (Kendall's tau [22]) showed that students who made multiple decisions at the same time also relaxed requirements to have more design options (corr.-coefficient 0,584, sig. 0,045).

## 5.1 Threats to Validity

In this section, possible limitations of the study are presented by discussing internal validity, construct validity and external validity [15,22].

With respect to internal validity, the questionnaire design and the fact that an instructor verbally explained the questions before they were answered ensured that the questions were unambiguous and focused on the research questions. Furthermore, the fact that the study was done as a classroom assignment introduces a potential risk. The students received grades for the performance in phase one of the study. Although the questionnaires were not taken into consideration for the grading, some students might have tried to impress the lecturer by giving specific answers. This risk, however, is considered rather low: no evidence in favor of it could be found in the results; and it was not possible to determine which answer would be rated positively or negatively.

Concerning construct-validity, the fact that only one specific architecting experience was used as a basis for the study introduces the risk that the cause construct was under-represented. The architecting process could be different for other architecting case studies. In this study, the students already had experience building simple web applications. In totally unknown domains, they would have been forced to uncover design options they did not know before. However, the risk is regarded as rather low as working in unknown domains is unrealistic especially for inexperienced designers. It can further be assumed that the architecting process for the used system is representative for those of large and medium-size software projects. We also used multiple variables to cross-check the results concerning the research questions. The risk of researchers bias was mitigated for the most part, as the structured questions with pre-defined answers do not leave space for interpretation. However, some open questions do exist that were interpreted by the researchers.

With respect to external validity, the subject population in the study might not be representative for the larger population of inexperienced software architects. The participants of the study were undergraduate students in the last year of a software engineering study programme. Their state of knowledge is comparable to the lowest level of architecture knowledge that software architects in practise have. Thus, it can be assumed that this risk is mitigated.

The instrumentation used in phase one of the study might have been unrealistic or old-fashioned. This risk was mitigated by creating a working environment that corresponds to those of practicing architects. The students were allowed to use laptops with internet connections without any restrictions and they could discuss all issues with their partners. In real software projects however, additional constraints (e.g. time, cost, corporate culture, politics) exist that can hardly be simulated in a classroom environment.

## 6   Conclusions and Future Work

To gain insights into the innate reasoning processes of students during architectural design, we conducted a descriptive survey with software engineering students. The architecting process the students followed was compared to existing architecture practices in the literature.

The comparison showed that the students' activities during architectural analysis closely match with the activities advocated in existing architecture approaches. However, during architectural synthesis and architectural evaluation large discrepancies were observed. As pointed out, some of these were also observed in studies with professional architects, which leads to the conclusion that the problems do not only result from the low level of experience. To move towards a systematic reasoning process, we list the areas that need to be improved and invite the research community to work on providing the necessary methodological and tooling support:

- Prioritize requirements [13] and identify risks in terms of the most challenging requirements [11,21] that are hard to fulfill.
- Relax requirements to have more design options, where required [24].
- Search for alternatives, even if known solutions exists that seem to solve the design issue.
- Document why one option was chosen over another one [24] to ensure that design options were not only chosen because of personal bias towards known solutions.
- Reason about possible limitations and constraints that solutions impose on future decisions [3].
- Actively consider relationships and dependencies between decisions [11,12].
- Identify situations, in which decisions cannot satisfy two requirements at the same time. Try to find optimal trade-offs between the requirements [10,13,14].
- Determine constraints that decisions impose on future solutions [3].
- Assess and actively mitigate risks throughout the architecting cycle [17].

We hypothesize that systematic support in these areas can verifiably improve the reasoning process and we plan to conduct controlled experiment to test these hypotheses. As mentioned in the introduction, we also plan to study the reasoning practices of successful architects, in order to derive an ideal reasoning process and compare it with the aforementioned areas. However one major issue remains: finding and identifying suitable design options during architectural synthesis is a task that requires the combination of experience and personal design knowledge with new knowledge and unknown design solutions. This task is highly creative and dependent on personal skills and experience and we doubt whether it can be fully supported by systematic architecting approaches.

## Acknowledgements

We would like to thank the students from the JEE course 2009 at the Fontys University of Applied Sciences Venlo for taking part in the study.

## References

1. Amazon.com. http://www.amazon.com, 2010.
2. IEEE-Std-1471-2000. Recommended Practice for Architectural Description of Software-Intensive Systems. Technical report, IEEE, 2000.
3. L. Bass, P. Clements, and R. Kazman. *Software architecture in practice*. Pearson Education, 2003.
4. J. Bosch. Software architecture: The next step. *Lecture notes in computer science*, Springer, pages 194–199, 2004.

5. J. Bosch and P. Molin. Software architecture design: evaluation and transformation. In *IEEE Conference and Workshop on Engineering of Computer-Based Systems, 1999. Proceedings. ECBS'99*, pages 4–10, 1999.

6. F. Buschmann, R. Meunier, H. Rohnert, P. Sommerlad, and M. Stal. *Pattern-Oriented Software Architecture, Volume 1: A System of Patterns*. John Wiley & Sons, Inc. New York, NY, USA, 1996.

7. P. Clements, D. Garlan, L. Bass, J. Stafford, R. Nord, J. Ivers, and R. Little. *Documenting software architectures: views and beyond*. Pearson Education, 2002.

8. V. Clerc, P. Lago, and H. Van Vliet. The Architect's Mindset. In *Software Architectures, Components, and Applications*, Springer, pages 231–249, 2007.

9. R. Farenhorst, J. F. Hoorn, P. Lago, and H. V. Vliet. The Lonesome Architect. In *Joint Working IEEE/IFIP Conference on Software Architecture & European Conference on Software Architecture (WICSA/ECSA 2009)*, Cambridge, UK, September 14-17, 2009.

10. C. Hofmeister, P. Kruchten, R. Nord, H. Obbink, A. Ran, and P. America. Generalizing a Model of Software Architecture Design from Five Industrial Approaches. In *Proceedings of the 5th Working IEEE/IFIP Conference on Software Architecture*, IEEE Computer Society, 2005.

11. C. Hofmeister, R. Nord, and D. Soni. *Applied Software Architecture*. Addison-Wesley Professional, 2009.

12. A. Jansen and J. Bosch. Software architecture as a set of architectural design decisions. In *Proceedings of the 5th Working IEEE/IFIP Conference on Software Architecture*, pages 109–120., 2005.

13. A. Jansen, J. Bosch, and P. Avgeriou. Documenting after the fact: Recovering architectural design decisions. *The Journal of Systems & Software*, Elsevier, 81(4):536–557, 2008.

14. Kazman, R., Klein, M., Barbacci, M., Longstaff, T., Lipson, H., Carriere, J.: The architecture tradeoff analysis method. In: ICECCS, Published by the IEEE Computer Society (1998)

15. B. Kitchenham, S. Pfleeger, L. Pickard, P. Jones, D. Hoaglin, K. El Emam, and J. Rosenberg. Preliminary guidelines for empirical research in software engineering. *IEEE Transactions on Software Engineering*, 28:721–734, August 2002.

16. P. Kruchten. The 4+ 1 view of architecture. *IEEE software*, 12(6):45–50, 1995.

17. P. Kruchten. What do software architects really do? *Journal of Systems and Software*, 81:2413–2416, 2008.

18. Kazman, R., Bass, L., Webb, M., Abowd, G.: SAAM: A method for analyzing the properties of software architectures. In: Proceedings of the 16th international conference on Software engineering, IEEE Computer Society Press (1994) 81–90

19. Williams, L., Smith, C.: PASA SM: a method for the performance assessment of software architectures. In: Proceedings of the 3rd International Workshop on Software and Performance, ACM (2002) 189

20. T. Lethbridge, S. Sim, and J. Singer. Studying software engineers: Data collection techniques for software field studies. *Empirical Software Engineering*, 10(3):311–341, 2005.

21. P. Kruchten. The Rational Unified Process An Introduction. *Addsion-Wesley Publishing Company*, 2000.

22. F. Shull, J. Singer, and D. Sjøberg. *Guide to Advanced Empirical Software Engineering*. Springer-Verlag New York, Inc. Secaucus, NJ, USA, 2007.

23. A. Tang, M. Babar, I. Gorton, and J. Han. A survey of architecture design rationale. *Journal of systems and software*, Elsevier, 79(12):1792–1804, 2006.

24. A. Tang and P. Lago. Notes on design reasoning tactics. Technical report, Swinburne University of Technology, 2009.
25. A. Tang, M. Tran, J. Han, and H. Vliet. Design reasoning improves software design quality. *QoSA 2008, LNCS*, 5281:28–42, 2008.
26. W. Trochim. *The Research Methods Knowledge Base*. Atomic Dog Publishing, 2001.
27. J. Tyree and a. Akerman. Architecture Decisions: Demystifying Architecture. *IEEE Software*, 22:19–27, 2005.
28. J. Van Der Ven, A. Jansen, P. Avgeriou, and D. Hammer. Using architectural decisions. *2nd International Conference on the Quality of Software Architectures (QoSA 2006)*, Västerås, Sweden, 2006
29. J. Van Der Ven, A. Jansen, J. Nijhuis, and J. Bosch. Design Decisions: The Bridge between Rationale and Architecture. *Rationale management in software engineering*, Springer, pages 329–348, 2006.
30. C. Wohlin, M. Host, and K. Henningsson. Empirical research methods in software engineering. *Empirical Methods and Studies in Software Engineering*, Springer, pages 145–165, 2003.
31. P. Clements, R. Kazman, M. Klein, D. Devesh, E. Reddy, P. Verma. The Duties, Skills, and Knowledge of Software Architects. *in Proceedings of the Sixth Working IEEE/IFIP Conference on Software Architecture*, 2007.
32. U. Zdun. Systematic pattern selection using pattern language grammars and design space analysis. *Software Practice and Experience*, John Wiley & Sons, Inc., 37(9):1016, 2007.
33. O. Zimmermann, U. Zdun, T. Gschwind, and F. Leymann. Combining Pattern Languages and Reusable Architectural Decision Models into a Comprehensive and Comprehensible Design Method. *Seventh Working IEEE/IFIP Conference on Software Architecture (WICSA 2008)*, pages 157–166, 2008.

# Towards Architecture-Centric Software Generation

Chung-Horng Lung[1], Balasangar Balasubramaniam[2], Kamalachelva Selvarajah[1],
Poopalasinkam Elankeswaran[2], and Umatharan Gopalasundaram[2]

[1] Department of Systems and Computer Engineering
Carleton University, Ottawa, Ontario, Canada
[2] Nortel Networks, Ottawa, Ontario, Canada
chlung@sce.carleton.ca

**Abstract.** Architecture-centric software generation has the potential to support flexible design and large-scale reuse. This paper describes the development of an architecture-centric framework that consists of multiple architecture alternatives, from which the architect can select and generate a working prototype in a top-down manner through a user interface rather than building it from scratch. The framework is primarily built with well-understood design patterns in distributed and concurrent computing. The development process involves extensive domain analysis, variability management, and bottom-up component engineering effort. The framework enables the architect or designer to effectively conduct upfront software architecture analysis and/or rapid architectural prototyping.

**Keywords:** domain analysis, variability management, architecture-centric development, generative technique, patterns, concurrency.

## 1 Introduction

In today's highly competitive age, the success or failure of a product could be determined by the time taken to develop the software. Architecture-centric software generation has the potential to support rapid development and/or evaluation of target systems. In addition, software architecture captures the design decisions at an early stage, which is difficult to change and has far-reaching effects on downstream development. Unfortunately, software development time often runs over schedule in practice. Another challenging issue often faced at the architecture level is estimating software qualities, such as software performance. Software Performance Engineering (SPE) [21, 26] has been recognized as a vital approach for addressing this issue. It is generally accepted that SPE should be conducted early in the life cycle. Unfortunately, conducting SPE, especially at the early stages of the development, is difficult and requires a high skill level. To perform SPE effectively, the architect has to have extensive knowledge and experience in the application domain, software design, and performance engineering, which is often scarce.

The performance or even general quality-of-service (QoS) issue becomes even more challenging for systems with high complexity, such as distributed systems and increasing hardware complication due to threading and parallelism. Many design

M. Ali Babar and I. Gorton (Eds.): ECSA 2010, LNCS 6285, pp. 38–52, 2010.
© Springer-Verlag Berlin Heidelberg 2010

patterns in distributed and concurrent systems have been captured and documented [20]. However, those patterns in distributed and concurrent areas are specialized and may not be easy to understand or implement. In addition, designers may want to focus primarily on the application level rather than the lower-level base system.

As an example, consider a real industrial case of which one of the authors was a team member. The project was a study of an advanced network routing technique to support network traffic engineering. Some features of the traffic engineering included, among others, network protocols, load balancing, QoS, resource utilization, and path protection and restoration. When the project started, there were no suitable simulation tools available and the customers requested a working prototype for concept demonstration. A lot of efforts were spent on software solutions involving three and a half designers to facilitate the traffic engineering applications which along took three designers.

We also learned from the re-architecting experience that it can be a time-consuming task [15]. In another case study, a system needed to be restructured to support additional QoS requirements. The existing system was limited due to its original architecture: messages received from the network were processed non-preemptively. The Half-Sync/Half-Async (HS/HA) architectural pattern [20] was a natural fit for the restructuring. However, due to complicated concurrency controls and interactions among various parts and with the application level, the restructuring itself took much longer than expected, even though the new design was well-understood and documented in the pattern literature. Further, the re-architected system requires tremendous efforts for verificatin and it may not perform better than the original one.

The research presented in this paper was originally motivated by asking the following question. "How can we help the architect or designer rapidly or incrementally develop, and subsequently evaluate the software architecture effectively?" The question can also be stated in another way: "How can we provide the architect robust alternatives, so that she/he can choose and experiment with those alternatives for rapid development or effective evaluation?"

The approach adopted in this research is to study the feasibility of an architecture-centric generative framework. A framework in this paper is meant to provide an infrastructure to build an executable architectural prototype. To support this goal, our approach is to incorporate multiple architectural alternatives into the framework through a variability management process. Those alternatives are built with robust software components based on recognized patterns and existing solutions. The framework can then be used to instantiate specific types of software architecture, as selected by the user. The architect or designer can then conduct experiments to gather specific quality information for the selected alternative or the application.

Such a framework facilitates reuse of previous domain analysis and domain engineering effort to support rapid prototype development at the architecture level for more effective architecture evaluation or alternatives comparison early in the life cycle. Rapid software prototyping in general can also support requirements validation and communication between stakeholders, because it can generate quantitative and concrete operational information, or collect more accurate or realistic data such as workloads, throughput, processing delay, and packet losses.

The structure of the rest of the paper is as follows: Section 2 discusses the development process of the generative framework. Section 3 demonstrates the components and structure of the framework. Section 4 shows how the framework can be used to support of new application development. Section 5 is an evaluation of the framework. Section 6 describes the related work. Finally, Section 7 contains the summary.

## 2 Development of the Architecture-Centric Generative Framework

The framework was not developed totally from scratch. Before the framework was developed, we had re-engineered existing working systems with well-known patterns in networked systems. Specifically, we restructured the systems from the single thread (ST) approach in C++ to HS/HA and Leader-Followers (LFs), separately [1, 14, 15]. The size of the original system was about 30 KLOCs, not including the user interface, third party software or underlying lower level protocols. The main part that was reengineered had about 10 KLOCs. Furthermore, other relevant patterns at lower levels, e.g., *Monitor Object, Scoped Locking idiom, Reactor, Connector,* and *Acceptor* [20], were selected and implemented.

The first re-engineered software system was a peer-to-peer (P2P) network routing system. The other two working systems were mainly used to study the server side software of the client-server model. These two client-server systems were implemented based on an industrial pre-paid phone system by different groups for a course project. Extensive studies and evaluations of these systems and relevant well-recognized patterns in this field [Schmidt00] were conducted. These systems were re-engineered [1, 14, 15] using various architectural and design patterns, including HS/HA and LFs.

A framework was then developed based on those previous studies and working systems. Two core technical areas are variability management of architectural alternatives and construction of components and the subsequent framework. These two key areas are discussed in the following.

### 2.1 Variability Management

Each architectural variation has a set of features which in turn may consist of variation points at lower level and their associated variations. On the other hand, some features or components may be common or only slightly different among architecturally different alternatives or variations. Those features or components have been captured and built in a way that is reusable across variations. The variability modeling process consists of the following steps.

- Identify variations at the architecture level
- Identify variation points at lower layers and potential variations for each variation point
- Identify components and their relationships for each architectural variation
- Identify component composition rules for each architectural variation
- Identify commonalities and differences of components that are shared by different architectural variations

Note that the process is iterative and incremental in nature; some steps may even been conducted in parallel. Each step is illustrated in more detail as follows:

The first step is to identify architectural variations, since the variation point is raised to the architecture level for our study. For our target domain, for instance, three basic architectural alternatives are selected from the concurrency management perspective. They are the traditional single thread (ST) approach using the Reactor pattern, HS/HA, and Leader/Followers (LFs) [20]. ST was selected, primarily due to its simplicity and, further, because it was the style originally used in the existing software under study. The other two alternatives were included mainly due to their acceptance in this field [20]. Dynamic creation/termination of threads based on requests is another variation; however, it was not included in the study due to its high overhead. The variability is open [6]; in other words, other possible architectural variations can be analyzed and added to the framework if appropriate.

Figure 1 displays these three alternatives: ST, HS/HA, and LFs, at the *Architecture Patterns* layer. (See Section 2.2 for detailed description of the figure.) Selection of ST often leads to scalability concerns. This can be improved using either HS/HA or LFs pattern as the overall architecture. In LFs, multiple threads function similarly to that in the ST example and synchronization of those threads is provided. However, only one thread at a time—the leader—waits for an event to occur. Other threads—the followers—can queue up, waiting for their turn to become the leader. Once the leader detects an event, it promotes one of the followers to be the leader. The previous leader then becomes a service-processing thread. HS/HA, on the other hand, divides the system into three layers: asynchronous layer, queuing layer, and synchronous layer. The asynchronous layer reads messages and stores them in the queuing layer. Multiple worker threads will read messages from the queue in a synchronous fashion and handle those messages subsequently. Readers are referred to Schmidt et al. [20] for detailed descriptions of those patterns and their benefits and limitations.

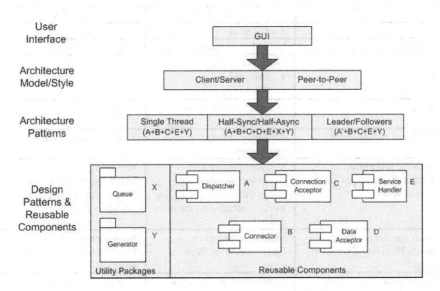

**Fig. 1.** Structure and Reusable Components of the Generative Framework [17]

The second step is to identify possible variation points and their variations at lower levels. This step involves identification of features and their relationships or interactions. The selection of one variation or feature may enable or disable the selection of other features or variations. For instance, selecting HS/HA means that a queuing layer is required. Furthermore, the selected feature may consist of more variations. The queuing layer, for example, could consist of a single queue or multiple queues, each for one priority type for various QoS requirements. TABLES 1 and 2 demonstrate the main features that were identified from various systems. Detailed design of each component can be found in [1].

The third step is to model the components and their connections for each architectural variation, including its associated lower layer variations. This step is an extension of traditional architecture analysis and design. It also shares concepts with product line architecture modeling, see section 4 for more descriptions on related work. For our target domain, the basic components and their relationships have been well documented in the patterns community. Hence, a similar description is not repeated here. In addition, each architectural variation also serves as a base architecture which consists of variation points and their associated variations at various levels of abstraction.

Considering the HS/HA pattern as an illustration, one of the variation points is the queuing layer as described in the previous step. Different queuing disciplines have different components and connections; additional components may also be needed for some variations. Fair share queuing, for instance, needs a component to dynamically monitor the resource (system and/or bandwidth) usage for different message types or service level agreements (SLAs). Another simple variation point for HS/HA is the number of threads in the synchronous layer. A more detailed example is that a

**Table 1.** Abstracted Features from the Client/Server Systems – Server Side

| ST | HS/HA | LFs |
|---|---|---|
| Socket setup | Socket setup | Socket setup |
| Initial buffer setup | Initial buffer setup | Initial buffer setup |
| Thread creation<br>• *Main thread* | Thread creation<br>• *Main thread*<br>• *Worker threads* | Thread creation<br>• *Leader/Followers threads* |
| No queue | Queuing layer (one or multiple queues) | No queue |
| No thread management | No Join/Promote thread management | Thread management for Join/Promote |
| Message processing: Exchange messages and process data | Message processing: Exchange messages and process data (Synchronizing worker threads and the main thread) | Message processing: Exchange messages and process data (processing threads or Followers) |
| Main functionalities: Insert/ Retrieve/ Remove msgs | Main functionalities: Insert/ Retrieve/ Remove msgs | Main functionalities: Insert/ Retrieve/ Remove msgs |
| Application: transaction-oriented computations | Application: transaction-oriented computations | Application: transaction-oriented computations |

**Table 2.** Abstracted Features from the P2P Systems

| ST | HS/HA | LFs |
|---|---|---|
| Socket setup | Socket setup | Socket setup |
| Thread creation<br>• *Destination threads*<br>• *Statistics thread* | Thread creation<br>•*Destination threads*<br>•*Statistics thread*<br>•*Worker Threads* | Thread creation<br>• *Destination threads*<br>• *Statistics thread*<br>• *LFs threads* |
| No queue | Multiple queues for QoS | No queue |
| No thread management | No thread management for Join/Promote | Thread management for Join/Promote |
| Main functionalities:<br>Perform network emulation tasks | Main functionalities:<br>Perform network emulation tasks and synchronize worker threads and the main thread | Main functionalities:<br>Perform network emulation tasks (Processing Threads) |
| Other functionalities:<br>Supporting functionalities | Other functionalities:<br>Supporting functionalities | Other functionalities:<br>Supporting functionalities |
| Application: traffic engineering | Application: traffic engineering | Application: traffic engineering |

variation related to the thread scheduling at the synchronous layer could consist of a dedicated thread for a particular queue in a multi-queue system for quality-of-service (QoS) requirements.

The fourth step is to determine composition rules that bind components and variants at lower levels of abstraction to realize variation points at higher levels. Similar to feature selection, selection of one component may enable or disable the selection of other components. This step is repeated from the base components and up until it reaches the architecture level. The concept is similar to that of parameterization and GenVoca [3]. To continue the previous example, a particular queuing approach in HS/HA may consist of a set of components and the queuing layer also interacts with components in two other layers. Subsequently, lower level components are first grouped together to form the queuing layer which is then associated with components in synchronous and asynchronous layers. If there is a dedicated thread for the queuing layer for a critical queue or a particular message type or customer due to high QoS requirements, the association rules of relevant components also need to be specified.

Currently, component composition for our framework primarily relies on manual efforts at the feature analysis and design stages. There are a few reasons: First, the number of architectural variations usually is small and the variations are mostly stable. Next, it is easier to identify high-level domain constraints or design rules that govern the compatibility of features or legal composition of components. In other words, the architecture has already captured the main components and their relationships. For instance, if HS/HA is selected, a queuing layer is automatically included based on the nature of the architecture. Similarly, if LFs system is the choice, a feature to manage the Leader and Followers threads is a must. Third, this framework is mainly for proof-of-concept and feasibility study. This phase could be improved if the number of variations becomes large or the components mostly are at the implementation-level. Thaker, et al [23] advocate algebraic equations to specify legal combinations of implementation-level features or components. Research is still needed to investigate propagating feature selections in a feature model into other development artifacts, including requirements, architecture, and code modules [23].

The last step of the modeling process is to identify commonalities and differences in various architectural variations. Some lower level components may be common or only slightly different even though the high-level architectural variations are diverse. The components that are common could be directly reused across multiple architectural variations. On the other hand, techniques such as parameterization or inheritance could be used for components that only vary a little. For example, some parts, e.g., the *Reactor* pattern [20], are common to all three architectural alternatives.

However, slight differences may exist among some elements for those alternatives. A specific example is the difference of dispatching feature (*Dispatcher* pattern [20]) between ST and LFs. Using the ST approach, a message is read in from the lower level and processed by the same thread sequentially. With LFs, however, after a message is read, the leader will elect a follower to be the leader before it processes the message. For HS/HA, the message received is stored in the queue first and will be processed by another worker thread. The components that realize the dispatching feature for these three patterns share similarities and differences. Identification of commonalities and differences can support the development of reusable components and the framework. Further, maintenance effort could be reduced if components that are common could be captured and designed. Otherwise, same or similar modifications to multiple architectural alternatives need to be made if there are any changes. Section 3 illustrates this point in more detail.

## 2.2  Construction of Reusable Components and the Framework

The main extension of our work is integrating different software architectural patterns into one framework. In other words, in our approach the variation point or variability modeling starts at the architecture level. Variation points can occur at different levels, e.g., architecture, design, and code, and represent the binding time when a system is configured. There are tradeoffs between those levels. Variation points at the finer-grain component level or later in the binding time could result in larger footprints or more alternatives. On the other hand, variant selection at the architecture level occurs at design time, which can support a more flexible design and could be more effective for specific requirements. In addition, a framework that provides high-level alternatives does not preclude it from supporting lower level variations, as advocated in step 2 of the modeling process.

The next major phase is to build the framework from reusable components that are developed based on patterns (both architectural and design patterns) and variability analysis, if appropriate. Different types of patterns were adopted, as described earlier. The reusable components are mainly developed based on features at lower layers, which are shared among different architectural variations. In addition, the association or composition rules discovered in the variability modeling phase provide guidelines to select components at lower levels of abstraction.

Figure 2 demonstrates the overall concept and structure of the framework. The framework itself is organized as layers. The focus of this research is feasibility study and the development of the framework to support architectural prototyping. But applications for validation purposes had been added through the *Service Handler* (component E shown in Figure 2). The component basically is an interface to the application level. Other applications can also be integrated using the *Service Handler*.

The GUI on top of Figure 1 is an optional interface through which the user can select an architectural style and an architectural pattern. Distributed applications could be either client-server or P2P style. Each style can be built using any of the three architectural patterns: ST, HS/HA, or LFs.

The architectural style and pattern selection is made through the GUI. However, the association of an architectural pattern and lower-level design patterns is performed at design time as a result of the variability modeling and framework development process. During the modeling process, component composition rules have been identified, which are used to glue components together to realize an architectural alternatives or variations. The architectural patterns layer shown in Figure 1 includes the component composition policy. For this framework, all three architectural variations are derived from patterns, which may not be true in other cases as new alternatives could be developed and incorporated into the framework.

Each architectural alternative is made up of generic, reusable components (represented by the letters A, B, C, and D in Figure 1) plus, if necessary, a specific component X for HS/HA. The '+' signs shown in Figure 1 represent composition of components. For instance, the ST architectural variation is made up of components A, B, C, E, and Y, e.g., A+B+C+E+Y. Figure 1 also illustrates that the LFs architectural pattern is created using generic components A' (a slight variation of A), B, and C, and other components specific to an application (E and Y), as described below.

Considering the LFs, as an example, once it has been selected, the GUI will invoke a method in the LFs package to start the LFs application. The *start* method for LFs in turn will establish connection(s) with other node(s) (generic to all three different alternatives) and create a thread pool (specific to LFs). The thread pool will also manage the promotion of a follower to be the leader in cooperation with the *Dispatcher* component.

There could be more variations at the architecture level, e.g., dynamic thread creation upon a request. Additional variations could be added to the framework. The framework is built in a way that it is expandable to include those variations as well. However, in practice, not all variations may be practically useful if there are no evident advantages or special requirements. A framework that is very generic, to support many varieties, may have a negative impact on the usage. That is, the user may be confused, or it may be tedious for the user to go through all the steps. Further, there may be extra execution overhead.

## 3  Usage of the Framework

Using the framework with the GUI is straightforward. The user simply goes through the interface, chooses the desired architecture model and pattern, and inputs network data (machine names or IP addresses, for example) to set up the connection. After those steps, an operational prototype is built instantaneous.

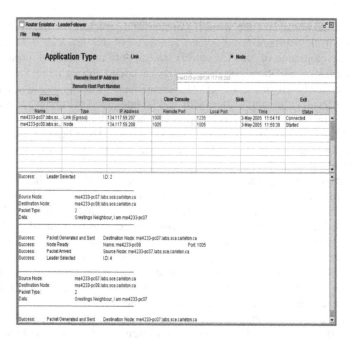

**Fig. 2.** Network Router Emulation Application Using the P2P Model and the Leader/Followers Pattern for the "Server" Side

Figure 2 shows a screen shot of the network router emulation application using the P2P model and the Leader/Followers pattern (shown at the top). The highlighted *Node* option under *Application Type* indicates that this particular node serves as a "server." The *Link* option under the *Application Type* is selected for the corresponding client counterpart. A network of routers can be set up using different architecture alternatives, which can facilitate the comparison of those alternatives.

Once an architectural style (client-server or P2P) and an architectural pattern have been chosen, and the configuration of a network is completed, a working network system can be generated immediately. Figure 2 demonstrates that data packets have been generated (Source Node) and forwarded (Destination Node) to the routers. The figure also shows which thread (I.D.: 4) is selected as the Leader during the execution. Note that this figure is only for the network connections rather than the output of the application level.

A text-based domain-specific configuration support is also available for network generation. The main usage of the text-based approach is to eliminate repetitive creations of the same network topology or to support large network topologies for evaluation purpose.

The designers can validate application requirements using the framework by adding features or modifying existing ones in the top application-level *Service Handler* (component E), shown in Figure 1. The *Service Handler* can be used to validate functional and/or evaluate non-functional requirements. Validation of functional requirements can be enhanced using the tool to generate an executable prototype for proof-of-concept or to facilitate communications among stakeholders.

Evaluation of non-functional aspect could also be improved by collecting realistic performance data. Examples of performance data that were monitored in the systems under study include throughput, packet delay and jitter, packet loss, resource utilization, failure detection and switchover time. Other performance data could be easily collected by adding appropriate instrumentation in the code. The data can be used together with or without a modeling tool for further scalability analysis or planning.

This paper focuses on the development of the framework instead of the actual performance of a specific application based on the framework. Detailed performance evaluation of a routing application on different architectural patterns was conducted earlier in [1, 12].

The performance overhead of the framework compared to the baseline systems mainly lies in the initial user selection stage in order to associate current components. After a final architectural variation is selected, a program will be synthesized by combining appropriate executable components only once, from which point on architectural variations do not play any role or have any impact on performance. In other words, composition of components is primarily decided in the analysis and design stages. Hence, performance overhead of the framework is negligible.

The main emphasis is to advocate the idea of raising the level of abstraction and the development of a framework using proven software patterns. The framework can be used to instantiate specific architectural alternatives. Moreover, more realistic or precise data and a working system can provide more insights for supporting quantitative software architecture evaluation. The point is essential for some qualities such as performance for scalability analysis or availability for reliability evaluation. A framework that can be used to generate multiple architectural prototypes also provides key insights for supporting learning and finding a better architectural fit.

**Table 3.** Average Response Time of Three Architectural Alternatives: an Illustration

| # of Clients | ST | HS/HA, 5 worker threads | LFs, 5 threads |
|---|---|---|---|
| 2 | 1024,484 | 1019,226 | 1036,773 |
| 3 | 1043,425 | 1020,871 | 1046,862 |
| 4 | 1068,592 | 1022,428 | 1054,467 |
| 5 | 1078,578 | 1025,483 | 1084,914 |

TABLE 3 depicts a performance comparison (in ms) of three architectural alternatives instantiated from the framework with a simple client/server messaging application. In this application, clients send messages to the server. Upon receiving a message, the server does a table lookup and sends a reply message back to the sender. The example demonstrates how quantitative evaluation of architectural alternatives using a generative approach can be efficiently realized. For a new application, only the *Service Handler* has to be tailored once. Then, a quantitative evaluation of different alternatives can be collected. The results in TABLE 3 are average response times of each client sending 10,000 messages to the server using systems with Intel Core2 2.0GHZ Duo processor and 1022MB memory in a lab environment. The inter-arrival time between two consecutive messages is 0.1 second. In this particular case, the results reveal that the performance of HS/HA is steadier with respect to the number of clients than the other two options; hence, it is more likely to scale well. Performance of LFs is the worst, which is contrary to what is generally believed [20]. Though the difference is not significant for a small number of clients, the results could show higher discrepancy for large number of clients or high arrival rates. It is not our intention to claim that a system based on the LFs pattern always has the worst performance just from this simple case study. However, the experiment outcome does demonstrate the potential challenge of SPE that we have described earlier.

## 4   Related Work

This paper is an extension of our earlier workshop paper [17] which focused on design recovery and re-engineering of existing systems. Additions in this paper include detailed discussions on variability management which serves as a more general model, component composition, actual performance measurements, and broader discussions on related work. This following describes related work in domain engineering, generative programming, software architecture prototyping and evaluation, and software architecture and performance modeling.

### 4.1   Domain Engineering and Generative Programming

Since the 1980s, the concept of the generative approach has been discussed extensively in the areas of domain analysis and engineering and has been adopted in many application domains. The generative approach will potentially become more popular [4, 7] and practical in the future as more applications are becoming mature for automation.

Model Integrated Computing (MIC) [22] has had success in system synthesis in embedded applications. Application developers use this approach to facilitate analysis of the models and to automatically synthesize applications from the models. However, MIC has less success in areas of classical software applications [4].

GenVoca [Batory97] is a composition model used for program generation. The main commonality of our approach and GenVoca is the idea of component composition. However, GenVoca is based on the concept of feature modularity to support programming-by-difference. In our case, the differences or variations have been identified and built into the framework. Those variations become options for the user. Another difference is that the level of abstraction discussed in GenVoca generally is lower than the architecture, as advocated in our approach. AHEAD [4] extends GenVoca to express diverse representations, such as code, rule, and makefile. AHEAD offers an infrastructure to modularize problem domains by features and a mechanism to generate applications by composing features.

The concept of product line architecture [5, 6, 19] is another area that shares similarities with our approach. Typically, a product line approach starts with some kind of base product architecture which is used to establish the base for the commonality and variability analysis. The variabilities for product line architecture are often captured at a lower level than architecture, e.g., component, class, method, and even variables.

In addition, Batory [5] argues that several technologies are emerging, including generative techniques, product line architecture, and metaprogramming. Metaprogramming is proposed to raise the level of abstraction in software development with large pieces or components [24]. Trujilo et al [25] introduce the concept of generative metaprogramming which is an approach to metaprogram generation that will synthesize a target program of a product line. The main idea is to accelerate the development of metaprograms by generating them rather than implementing them from abstract specifications.

## 4.2  Software Components, Architecture Prototyping and Evaluation

Overall, the approach proposed in this paper is distinguished from most other generative approaches in that their aim is primarily to generate a system or develop a program—in some cases, the "final" system. Our framework is primarily used to support rapid or incremental architecture development by providing executable systems (infrastructure rather than the final system), using different architecture alternatives from which the architect can build specific applications. The approach can support the comparison of architectural alternatives and evaluation against quality attributes by instantiating working systems using different architectures. Architecture tradeoff or sensitivity analysis [11, 13] has been discussed extensively. One challenge in this area is that more concrete information is often needed to provide more precise evidence for various quality attributes. Our approach can have a complementary role by providing quantitative or more concrete information to support architecture tradeoff or sensitivity analysis, especially in performance, scalability, and availability.

Based on our experience, it is often necessary to actually build a low-cost executable system that reflects the critical architectural elements and qualities of the target system [16], which is also the main theme of architectural prototyping advocated by Bardram et al. [2] and Martensson et al. [18]. Architectural prototyping allows the architect to explore different alternatives and receive concrete feedback, which could provide valuable information for balancing qualities and evaluating architecture.

Component-based software engineering (CBSE) [9] is also related to our approach. One main difference between CBSE or even a catalog of well-documented patterns and the proposed approach is that our approach emphasizes the problem on the architecture perspective. CBSE does not address software architecture explicitly. There may be many ways to glue the components. Without architecture or high-level design rules, composition of components may not be trivial.

From the performance modeling perspective, the framework can play a complementary role. Performance modeling, e.g., Layered Queuing Networks [8] or Stochastic Process Algebras [10], can be adapted more easily to a variety of applications and is useful for scalability analysis. On the other hand, each performance modeling technique has limitations, such as modeling of lost messages or packets, failure scenarios, or state explosion. Secondly, performance modeling often depends on realistic estimations, such as execution time or probabilities for diverse decision points for different execution paths, and it may be difficult or time-consuming to obtain these for complicated system interactions within an application or between the application and the computing resources. By quickly generating a working system, the data from various working prototypes can be measured much more efficiently and precisely. The data could be stored in a performance knowledge base [27] and fed into performance models for further sensitivity or scalability analysis. Woodside et al. [27] also advocate describing the system with different values of factors, including variations in design.

## 5 Conclusion and Future Work

Software architecture has been recognized as a crucial factor in successful software development. Practicing architects, unfortunately, have few tools available to them for conducting front-end analysis. Evaluations of architectures are often performed on high-level descriptions. This paper advocated an architecture-centric generative approach to support software architects in requirements gathering, evaluating architecture qualities, and developing a system stepwise. A trend of software development is to raise the level of abstraction; as the level increases, so does the degree of software automation and generation [5].

The paper also reported our empirical experience in the development of such a generative framework in distributed and concurrent applications. The framework was primarily built using well-understood design patterns and through reengineering existing robust systems. As a result, the framework consists of robust reusable components and practically useful architecture or design alternatives.

The framework can be further expanded to support other new design alternatives or adapted to other problem domains. For instance, multi-core systems have become popular. New design techniques may be developed to make better use of parallelism. Hence, new patterns may be discovered in the future, which could be added to the framework. New patterns can be inserted into the framework as a totally separate entity. But similarities may be present between the new pattern and existing pattern(s). With variability management (as discussed in Section 2.1), common components can be identified to reduce maintenance efforts. For a new application domain, similar concept or process, e.g., variability management (Section 2.1) and construction of reusable components and the framework (Section 2.2) could be applied.

Another point is that the proposed framework needs to be modeled only once and then it can be used repeatedly. In other words, more effort needs to be spent on the front-end analysis by incorporating multiple alternatives into a framework and identifying commonalities and variabilities of components. The concept is similar to domain analysis or development for reuse. The proposed approach is better suited for environments where systems in an area are repeatedly needed to be built (e.g., the communication framework that will be repeatedly used for different service applications) or for third party evaluators who provide services to other companies or organizations.

A GUI-based interface was used in the experiment for network topology creation and alternative selection. GUI is easy to use, but is not effective if the network becomes large. A text-based domain-specific configuration support can be used to eliminate repetitive creations of the same network topology or to support large network topologies for evaluation purposes. A text-based domain-specific support is also useful for automation.

# Acknowledgements

We would like to thank Nortel Networks for providing us with a network routing software system for research and education. The project is partially funded by NSERC (National Sciences and Engineering Research Council) of Canada.

# References

1. Alhussaini, A., Balasubramaniam, B., Chandrabose, P., Kasinathan, A.: Software Restructuring and Performance Evaluation, Project Report, Department of Systems & Computer Eng., Carleton University (2004)
2. Bardram, J.E., Christensen, H.B., Hansen, K.M.: Architectural Prototyping: An Approach for Grounding Architectural Design and Learning. In: Proc. of the 4th Working IEEE/IFIP Conf. on Software Architecture, pp. 15–24 (2004)
3. Batory, D., Chen, G., Robertson, E., Wang, T.: Design Wizards and Visual Programming Environments for GenVoca Generators. IEEE Trans. on Soft. Eng. 26(5), 441–452 (2000)
4. Batory, D., Sarvela, J.D., Rauschmayer, A.: Scaling Step-Wise Refinement. IEEE Trans. Soft. Eng. 30(6), 355–371 (2004)
5. Batory, D.: Multi-Level Models in Model Driven Development, Product-Lines, and Metaprogramming. IBM Systems Journal 45(3), 1–13 (2006)
6. Bosch, J.: Design and Use of Software Architectures: Adopting and Evolving a Product-Line Approach. Addison-Wesley, Reading (2000)
7. Czarnecki, K., Eisenecker, U.W.: Generative Programming Methods, Tools, and Applications. Addison Wesley, Reading (2000)
8. Franks, G., Al-Omari, T., Woodside, M., Das, O., Derisavi, S.: Enhanced Modeling and Solution of Layered Queueing Networks. IEEE Transactions on Software Engineering 35(2), 148–161 (2009)
9. Heineman, G.T., Councill, W.T.: Component Based Software Engineering: Putting the Pieces Together. Addison-Wesley, Reading (2001)
10. Hillston, J.: A Compositional Approach to Performance Modelling. Cambridge University Press, Cambridge (1996)
11. Kazman, R., Klein, M., Barbacci, M., Longstaff, T., Lipson, H., Carriere, J.: The Architecture Tradeoff Analysis Method. In: Proc. of the 4th Int'l. Conf. on Eng. of Complex Comp. Sys., pp. 68–78 (1998)
12. Lee, J.-C., Zhang, X.: Performance Investigation of a Network System on Different Linux Kernels. Project Report 2004, Dept. of Systems & Comp. Eng., Carleton University (2004)
13. Lung, C.-H., Kalaichelvan, K.: A Quantitative Approach to Software Architecture Sensitivity Analysis. Int'l. Journal of Software Eng. and Knowledge Eng. 10(1), 97–114 (2000)
14. Lung, C.-H., Zhao, Q., Xu, H., Mar, H., Kanagaratnam, P.: Experience of Communications Software Evolution and Performance Improvement with Patterns. In: Proc. of IASTED Software Engineering, Feburary 2004, pp. 321–326 (2004)
15. Lung, C.-H., Zhao, Q.: Pattern-Oriented Reengineering of a Network System. Journal of Systemics, Cybernetics and Informatics 2(5) (2004)
16. Lung, C.-H., Zaman, M., Goel, N.: Reflection on Software Architecture Practices – What Works, What Remains to Be Seen, and What Are the Gaps. In: Proc. of the 5th Working Conf. on Software Architecture (2005)
17. Lung, C.-H., Balasubramaniam, B., Selvarajah, K., Elankeswaran, P., Gopalasundaram, U.: Architecture-Centric Software Generation: An Experimental Study on Distributed

Systems. In: Proc. of Generative Programming and Component Engineering for QoS Provisioning in Distributed Systems (October 2006)

18. Martensson, F., Grahn, H., Mattsson, M.: Prototype-based Software Architecture Evaluation – Component Quality Attribute Evaluation. In: Proc. of the $4^{th}$ Conf. on Software Engineering Research and Practice, Sweden, pp. 11–17 (2004)

19. Northrop, L.M., Clements, P.C.: A Framework for Software Product Line Practice, Version 5.0. Software Engineering Institute, Carnegie Mellon University (2005)

20. Schmidt, D., Stal, M., Rohnert, H., Buschmann, F.: Pattern-Oriented Software Architecture: Patterns for Concurrent and Networked Objects. Wiley, Chichester (2000)

21. Smith, C.U., Williams, L.G.: Performance Solutions A Practical Guide to Creating Responsive and Scalable Software. Addison-Wesley, Reading (2001)

22. Sztipanovits, J., Karsai, G.: Generative Programming for Embedded Systems. In: Proc. of the 1st Conf. on Generative Programming and Component Eng., pp. 32–49 (2002)

23. Thaker, S., Batory, D., Kitchin, D., Cook, W.: Safe Composition of Product Lines. In: Proc. of the 6th Int'l. Conf. on Generative Programming and Component Eng., pp. 95–104 (2007)

24. Trujillo, S., Batory, D., Diaz, O.: Feature Oriented Model Driven Development: A Case Study for Portlets. In: Proc. of the 29th Int'l. Conf. on Software Eng., pp. 44–53 (2007)

25. Trujillo, S., Azanza, M., Diaz, O.: Generative Metaprogramming. In: Proc of the $6^{th}$ Int'l Conf. on Generative Programming and Component Engineering, October 2007, pp. 105–114 (2007)

26. Williams, L.G., Smith, C.U.: PASA: An Architectural Approach to Fixing Software Performance Problems. In: Proceedings of CMG (2002)

27. Woodside, C.M., Franks, G., Petriu, D.C.: The Future of Software Performance Engineering. In: Proc. of the 29th International Conference on Software Engineering, pp. 171–187 (2007)

# An Architectural Blueprint for Model Driven Development and Maintenance of Business Logic for Information Systems

Tobias Brückmann[1] and Volker Gruhn[2]

[1] University of Leipzig, Klostergasse 3, 04107 Leipzig, Germany
brueckmann@ebus.informatik.uni-leipzig.de
[2] University of Duisburg-Essen, Schützenbahn 70, 45127 Essen, Germany
volker.gruhn@uni-due.de

**Abstract.** Despite of ongoing development of model-driven development approaches in industry and academia, we believe that in particular for business logic aspects of information systems there is a lack of integrated support considering all phases of a model driven software process, from analysis until code generation. In our work we developed a framework consisting of meta-models, model transformations and tools that address a consistent support of development and maintenance tasks. As contribution of this article, we present an architecture for generated business logic code as part our infrastructure blueprint. We aim at the generation of robust business logic layers and consider particularly maintenance and integration issues of complex information systems with external dependencies. For this purpose, our infrastructure supports the specification of global domain states and local conditions in visual software models and generates corresponding code artifacts which assure these conditions automatically.

## 1 Introduction

Model driven software engineering is a software engineering approach that considers software models as "first class citizens"[6]: They are the premiere artifacts in a software process and used to provide a tool for structured descriptions of systems [18] or aspects of a reality [15]. Through the application of automated model processing tasks, model driven approaches aim at the automated execution of former manual actions, such as translating a model into another modeling language or producing program code. We believe that for utilizing the potential strengths of model driven software engineering a consistent support of all phases of a software process is needed from early analysis and design until implementation and maintenance. For this purpose, the following aspects have to be considered by a project infrastructure that supports a consistent model driven software process:

– Visual software models have to support different levels of detail considering all phases from analysis models until detailed design models as well as all

M. Ali Babar and I. Gorton (Eds.): ECSA 2010, LNCS 6285, pp. 53–69, 2010.

required modeling paradigms, such as structural, state, scenario, or process modeling;

- Quality assurance tasks for complex visual software models have to support modelers in preventing a faulty and inconsistent set of requirements;
- A clear interface between visual software models and code generators is needed, in particular if several visual modeling languages and several code generators are deployed;
- With regard to the integration of generated code artifacts and handcrafted code, the architecture of the generated program code has to support developers in manual integration tasks; and
- With regard to maintenance and modification tasks, modelers and developers have to be supported in impact analysis and program understanding tasks.

As a consequence, a proper technical infrastructure is needed that provides meta models, modeling tools, model verification, and model processing rules under consideration of project specific requirements. As part of our work, we developed an architectural blueprint that supports a consistent model driven development process of business logic for information systems. This blueprint is structured in several architectural layers. Each layer supports specific tasks, such as visual modeling, impact analysis, model verification, and code generation. These tasks are performed on different levels of abstraction: starting with a general purpose software model, followed by a domain specific model, and a formal representation and finally resulting in generated code artifacts.

In our work, we focus on business logic aspects of web-based information systems. In contrast to reactive systems, which are used to control time-critical or live-critical physical machines, information systems support industrial business processes. In the following, we use the term business logic to address parts of an information system that connect user interfaces (presentation layer) with storage systems (persistency layer). The business logic layer (application layer) provides the implementation of business processes and contains processing instructions for business data. We consider page flow and navigation logic as part of the presentation layer and not as part of the business logic layer. Based on the following two assumptions, we explicitly address not only the initial development process of systems but rather reoccurring modification and maintenance tasks: First, we assume that the business logic of industrial information systems often depends on external functions or systems such as internal and external web services, public APIs, or further systems of an enterprise application landscape. As a consequence, possibly unsafe program code that was not generated automatically has to be connected manually to critical parts of a system. Second, a complex system (or a landscape of systems) supporting complex and probable critical business processes has to be developed and maintained over several years and with changing project teams. Parts of the original system are reworked, added, or removed due to changed domain requirements and documentation artifacts often lack and are not up to date so that code maintenance becomes a complex and risky task. It can easily happen that during work on a minor change request important domain constraints become accidentally violated. In such a case the consequences are not easily predictable and may lead to inconsistencies in the data base or unexpected behavior in business critical systems. Both assumptions, need for integration as well as long-term operation, led us to the conclusion that a project infrastructure for the development and maintenance of business logic must particularly consider specific requirements:

- The generated code artifacts that implement defined business processes contain business critical control structures;
- External systems as well as persistency layer and presentation layer have to be connected to the generated critical business logic code; and
- Despite of dependencies and interconnections to further subsystems, the business logic has to assure that business processes are supported as specified. Any inconsistency in the domain data set, which probably has to be shared with other applications, has to be avoided.

The contribution of this article is to introduce robustness features that are in particular relevant for generated business logic artifacts and to provide an architecture for generated business logic layers of information system that considers the above outlined assumptions. Moreover, we show how specific robustness features are supported in each layer of our proposed architectural blueprint.

The remainder of this article is structured as follows: After the discussion of related work in Sect. 2, we provide a brief introduction of our architectural blueprint in Sect. 3. Afterwards an example model for business logic is presented in Sect. 4, before we introduce concrete robustness criteria in Sect. 5. Sect. 6 discusses architectural details of a generated business logic layer for industrial information systems, followed by concrete implementation examples in Sect. 7, before we conclude in Sect. 8.

## 2   Related Work

For the study of related work, we started with a focus on architectures and tool chains that address modeling, model verification, and code generation of information systems. Compared to the presentation and persistency layer, existing approaches for automation of business logic layer development usually do not support a comparable level of automation considering all phases of a software process from analysis until maintenance. Hence, we also examined approaches from the embedded systems domain. Concluding the analysis of the related work, we found no approach covering all aspects that have to be addressed for a consistent support of the development and maintenance of business logic. They either

- Do not support process modeling concepts as required for large business logic models (Mohan et al. [11], Schattkowsky et al. [17], Fleurey et at. [5], Konrad et al. [10], Engels et al. [4], Meier et al.[19]); and/or
- Do not consider model quality analysis tasks (Köhler et al. [9], Schattkowsky et al. [17], Fleurey et at. [5]); and/or

- Support code generation only for proprietary platforms (Mohan et al. [11], Köhler et al. [9], Schattkowsky et al. [17]) or do not support code generation (Engels et al. [4], Jurack et al. [7]); and/or
- Focus only on the reactive (embedded) systems domain and not on information systems (Engels et al. [4], Konrad et al. [10], Meier et al. [19]).

Mohan et al. present in [11] "a state machine based work flow system (FlexFlow) which formally describes internet applications using statecharts" and implement an engine that uses these descriptions to control the execution of web applications. Mohan et al. address the application logic of information systems considering the logical connection to the user interface layer. They use state charts as visual modeling paradigm under consideration of the whole live cycle from design until maintenance. As a difference to Mohen et al., our visual model is used to cover all required concepts as needed to generate business logic artifacts (including user and systems functions) and not only abstract navigation paths through user interface artifacts. A further difference is that Mohen et al. only support a proprietary execution engine.

Koehler et al. introduces their Business-Driven Development (BDD) approach in [9]. It is focused on business processes and applies visual business process models that are transformed into executable business process languages as part of a consistent service-oriented environment. Compared to our work, the Business-Driven Development approach considers all phases of the development process of an information system, from analysis and design until code generation. The visual model as used by Koehler et al. is provided by the IBM Websphere Business Modeler tool and the target platform for generated code artifacts is BPEL/WDSL. Further visual modeling languages and target platforms, such as J2EE, are not supported.

Schattkowsky and Müller presented in [17] a model-driven development and maintenance process for embedded systems that addresses design and execution of UML models for embedded systems. They developed a virtual machine for UML (UVM) that executes UML models directly. Compared to our work Schattkowsky and Müller support structural and behavioral modeling concepts. However, they support only sequence and state diagrams as behavioral diagrams, which are the common supported types of diagrams in the context of embedded systems. Moreover, Schattkowsky and Müller aim at the direct execution of the model and do not consider code generation and integration tasks.

Bordbar et al. address in [1] robust system maintenance for data-centric applications considering maintenance issues. They provide a project infrastructure consisting of a visual software model and its automated processing. However, Bordbar et al. focus only on the persistency layer without any consideration of business logic or integration purposes of the persistency layer and business logic. Fleurey et al. developed in [5] a model-driven approach for the modernization and migration of information systems. They support the whole process from processing the old code base into an abstract model until code generation of the target platform. Fleurey et al. strongly focused on code migration projects, where running systems have to be migrated into another platform, for example, from CORBA into J2EE. Our proposed infrastructure blueprint also comprises different models and model processing tasks. Instead of code migration, we focus on changed domain requirements related to the business logic.

Model driven development platforms, such as openMDX (www.openmdx.org) or AndroMDA (www.andromda.org), provide code generation environments that can be used as technical frameworks supporting the code generation step. However, they do not consider visual modeling tasks and do not provide native support for robustness features of business logic layers as proposed by our approach.

## 3   Architectural Blueprint of an Amabulo Infrastructure

For the development and maintenance of business logic for information systems, we developed an architectural blueprint consisting of meta models, tools, and a method support for model driven development and maintenance of business logic (from analysis to code generation). This blueprint, which we call "Amabulo infrastructure", provides concepts and tools to set up and apply concrete infrastructures for model driven development projects. Modeling languages can be applied as needed. In this paper, we focus on business logic layers of J2EE application. However, concrete code generation rules can be easily adapted for different target platforms.

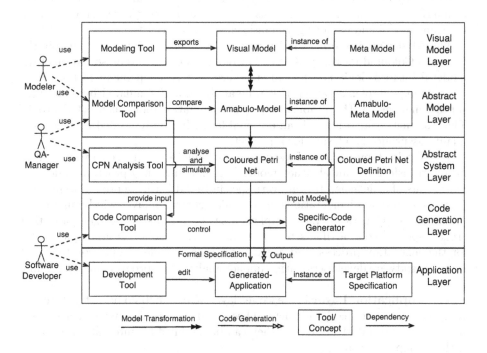

**Fig. 1.** Overview of Amabulo Infrastructure Blueprint

An Amabulo infrastructure consists of five different layers (see Fig. 1): The **Visual Model Layer** is responsible for all visual modeling tasks of a development process. For this purpose, the visual modeling language and the modeling tool of this layer are used by human modelers to specify domain and technical requirements. Depending on actual requirements, yet existing modeling languages (such as UML [12], BPMN [13], or EPC [8]) and tools can be reused. If needed, multiple Visual Model Layers can be part of one concrete project setup and modelers can switch between them. To illustrate this point, at the very beginning of a project, when talking to domain experts, a business process modeling language (such as EPC) can be the best choice for visual modeling. Afterwards, when the domain requirements are complete and a technical modeling language is needed, the visual model layer can be switched to the Unified Modeling Language (UML).

The **Abstract Model Layer** provides an abstract (non-visual) view onto the business logic model in the form of a domain specific modeling model (Amabulo model), as introduced in [2]. It is reduced to pure logical information concerning business logic aspects and focused on information that is relevant for code generation. For this purpose, an Amabulo model integrates concepts for process modeling, state modeling, and structural modeling. It is used as a common interface between visual modeling languages and code generators. Moreover, it helps to reduce the complexity of the interface between models and code generators. Compared to UML with its more than 250 defined elements, an Amabulo model consists only of 13 precisely defined elements. This layer also provides a model comparison tool that is used to assist users in comparing different versions of the same model and exploring semantic changes between them.

The **Abstract System Layer** provides a formal view onto the system in the form of a Coloured Petri Net (CPN). A Coloured Petri Net representation of the modeled business logic is a formal structure that is independent of the actual business logic implementation. It can be analyzed and simulated by quality assurance managers with suitable analysis and simulation tools, such as CPNTools. The Abstract System Layer is an optional layer. It is only needed if automated quality assurance is relevant for a project.

The **Code Generation Layer** is responsible for code generation, which means transforming an abstract model automatically into program code. Requirements of code generators are very specific and differ from project to project. Hence, concrete implementations of the code generation layer will be unique. A concrete Code Generation Layer implements two concepts: A code generator that creates specific code artifacts based on an abstract model as input parameter for the generation process, and a generator specific code comparison tool that supports software developers during impact analysis and program understanding tasks.

The **Application Layer** is the target layer of an Amabulo infrastructure and comprises generated code artifacts. These artifacts are instances of a specific target platform specification, and they can be modified for integration purposes with development tools.

# 4    Example Model

The UML model in Fig. 2 provides an example for a business logic model as created with a concrete Visual Model Layer that defines an UML profile for business logic as described in [2]. This model specifies a detailed part of an industrial four eyes decision process. It comprises three different diagrams: A process view, a structural view, and a state view. In general, we use the state modeling paradigm to refine structural entities at property scope as described in [3]: The attribute "decision" of the business object "Offer" is refined by the state view. The state view defines four different states and transitions between them. Using only the structural view together with the state view, a modeler gets an overview of the relevant steps of the live cycle of an "Offer". The process view provides a complementary view. As modeled in the activity diagram, two "UserActions" have to be supported: During the "first decision" action a first manual decision has to be made. This action requires and modifies an instance of "Offer" and a precondition forces the incoming offer to be in the state "undecided". Additionally, a postcondition requires the outgoing offer to be either in the state "declined" or in the state "firstDeciderAccepted". Afterwards, if the offer was declined, the action "send declinature message" is called. This action is executed automatically (it is stereotyped "SystemAction") and requires an offer to be started (modeled as InputPin). In contrast to "first decision" action the "send declinature message" action does not modify an offer ("Offer" is modeled only as InputPin). During the execution of this system action, an internal implemented function or an external integrated function is called and no user input is necessary. If the first decider accepts the user action "second decision" is called. After finishing the "second decision", a further control flow decision has to be made depending on the current state of the offer. If the offer was declined, the above mentioned "send declinature message" is called. Otherwise, the "send acceptance message" action is executed automatically.

# 5    What Robustness Means

As described above, the robustness of complex business information systems that are part of application landscapes is an important concern in particular for business logic implementations, because critical code artifacts have to provide interfaces to external functions and subsystems. For supporting developers in development and maintenance tasks, our architectural blueprint considers three main aspects of robust, generated business logic code:

## 5.1    Assurance of Local Conditions

Whenever a system reuses implemented functionality of other systems it has to be assured that external data input does not violate internal domain constraints. This class of errors (improper input validation) is listed as "one killer of healthy software" in the SANS List of Top 25 Most Dangerous Programming Errors

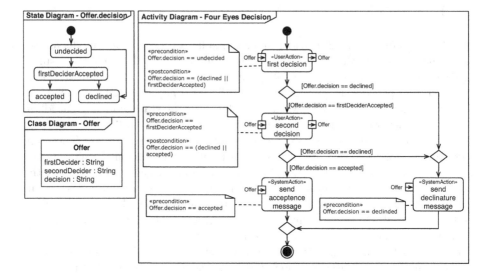

**Fig. 2.** Four Eyes Decision Process, UML Model

[14]. For example: A function X is called by function Y and expects either the value A or B as results of function X. Now, if function X returns a value C, an exception handling routine has to be started in Y. This seems to be a trivial use case, but considering that systems run several years and complex result types of integrated external functions may change due to maintenance tasks after running several months, it is important to guarantee that reused external functions never cause internal errors. Therefore, the specification of local conditions for each function is a modeling concept to prevent faulty behavior at a local scope of single processes or functions. By the use of preconditions and postconditions, the modeler can specify domain conditions, which have to be asserted automatically by the generated system. Considering the detailed model example as introduced in Fig. 2, each function comes with a specified precondition and two functions have also defined postconditions. If a condition is not satisfied, an exception handling routine has to be executed, and the control flow has to be stopped. Moreover, it has to be prevented that probable inconsistent data sets are stored in the persistency layer.

## 5.2   Assurance of Global Domain States

Beside local conditions, which are modeled as preconditions and postconditions, domain states of business objects can often be identified. Such domain states are interpreted as domain constraints and must not be violated by the supporting system. Domain states are modeled as the refinement of attributes of business objects. If an attribute is related to a state chart, the business logic layer abode by the following rules:

- The values of the attribute are restricted to elements of the set of defined states.
- If a new instance of a business object is created, the value of all state chart refined attributes is restricted to one of the possible initial states.
- If an object is going to be modified it has to be assured that the values of all attributes that are refined by a state chart follow the modeled transitions of the corresponding state chart. Attributes may remain unchanged. However, if an attribute value is changed, it has to be assured that the new value is a valid successor of the previous value of the attribute.

If any of this rules is violated by business logic implementations, the control flow has to be stopped. These rules overrule even modeled local conditions. (An inconsistent specification of local conditions and global domain states can lead to unexpected system behavior. We are currently working on the automated detection of such inconsistencies through an automated transformation of visual models into CPN and a tool-supported automated analysis as part of the Abstract System Layer of our infrastructure, which is not considered in this paper.) When during a maintenance task a developer implements a function or a process that executes a domain state transition that is not specified, this violation is detected and handled automatically. Providing an example with regard to the example model in Fig. 2: if the user function "first decision" tries to change the value of the attribute "decision" to "accepted", which is not allowed when following the state chart, a domain state violation handling routing has to be invoked and the process has to be stopped.

## 5.3   Clear Separation of Concerns

As motivated above, generated business logic artifacts usually have to be integrated with further code artifacts, such as handcrafted code, otherwise generated code, or legacy code. On the one hand, a reliable and robust implementation of modeled domain requirements has to be guaranteed: Manual additions to generated parts of an application are not allowed everywhere. Critical code fragments, such as the assurance of modeled conditions or domain constraints, must not be modified after generation. On the other hand, there should be no artificial hurdles for developers performing manual integration tasks. As a consequence, the generated business logic code consists of parts that are critical and that have to be protected. Furthermore, it contains parts that have to be modified manually by developers. For integration as well as for tracking and versioning purposes it is essential to separate both types of code fragments at file level. As described in Sect. 6: we recommend to generate a single file for each part of the system that has to be edited by developers and to integrate the handwritten code using object-oriented design concepts and patterns, such as delegation and interfaces. Using the results of the code comparison tool from the Code Generation Layer, the code generator produces only code that is needed to reflect actual model changes and not the entire business logic. It does not delete or overwrite manually modified files without an explicit confirmation by the developer. If the developer chooses not to overwrite existing sources and the scheduled changes affect structural aspects for the program code, such as the addition of attributes, compiler errors provide a help to identify and fix updates manually.

# 6    Architecture of Business Logic Layers of Generated J2EE-Applications

The architecture of business logic layers generated by an Amabulo infrastructure is discussed with regard to robustness supporting aspects as introduced in the previous section. If the design of generated business logic layers as introduced in this section is considered during the design and implementation of its code generator, the generator output will satisfy our robustness features and support later integration and maintenance tasks. Focusing on web-based information systems, we focus on business logic layers of J2EE applications, which also include simple code artifacts of the persistency layer and the presentation layer. The result of the generation process is a J2EE application that implements standards such as Java Beans, Enterprise Java Beans (EJB), and Java Server Faces (JSF). It reuses the Seam Framework [16] and can be deployed directly on a JBoss application server. Fig. 3 provides an architectural overview of a generated J2EE application: The business logic layer contains Session EJBs for processes that implement the modeled control flow including all decisions and constraints, and it contains Session EJBs for system functions that provide the actual implementation of a function. Business objects are accessible as JavaBeans, which also implement the domain state assurance logic. The presentation layer is implemented by JavaServerFaces and supports all modeled user functions. Entity EJBs are used for the persistency layer implementation. Additionally, the rows in Fig. 3 indicate whether a component is a critically generated code artifact that must not be modified manually or a component that is expected to be modified manually.

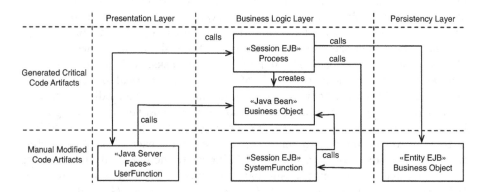

**Fig. 3.** Application Tier Overview

## 6.1  Business Objects

For each modeled business object a corresponding triple is generated: an unique interface, a Java Bean, and an Entity Enterprise Java Bean (see Fig. 4 at the top). The generated **interface** provides all required functions of a business object, such as getter and setter functions, as well as administrative attributes, such as identifiers. The interface is implemented by both, the Entity Bean and the Java Bean. The Java Bean is used as **data transfer object**. It is a critical code artifact and must not be modified manually. Implemented (system and user) actions access business objects only through transfer objects that are managed by process implementations. Moreover, the generated transfer objects are responsible for domain-state assertions (as introduced in Sect. 5.2): If attributes are modeled with a refining state chart, the transfer object assures that only defined state transitions are processed when the value of an attribute is changed. By the support of the domain-state assertion logic, no invalid state transition can be executed or passed to any persistent object in any function of the business logic. This prevents inconsistent application data, even if the business logic depends on several external systems that modify business objects. The **Entity Enterprise Java Bean (Entity EJB)** connects business logic with persistency layer and contains information about object-relational data mapping in form of standardized annotations. If needed, the Entity EJB can be completely rewritten, for example, to support bean-managed persistence. However, to keep the modified Entity EJB integrated with the generated code artifacts, it has to keep its name and has to provide a valid implementation of the generated interface.

## 6.2  Processes

For each modeled process a Session EJB and its Local Session EJB Interface is generated, see Fig. 4 at the bottom left. The implementation of the modeled process is generated as a **Session EJB**. It contains all the control flow logic of the process, which determines initial and final functions, sub-processes, and succession relations. The actual order of called functions or sub-processes

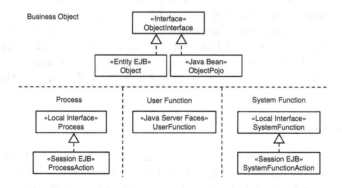

**Fig. 4.** Generated Business Object Triple, Generated Processes and Actions

is processed at runtime depending on modeled succession relations between the model elements and the current state of the data model. Moreover, the process implementation provides connections to the persistency layer: It loads all needed business objects that are needed during process execution from the persistency layer into transfer objects and stores the modified objects back in the persistency layer. Session EJBs generated for processes are the most critical and most complex generated artifacts: They must not be edited manually. Beside control flow decisions, they are responsible for condition evaluation (as introduced in Sect. 5.1): Each modeled precondition and postcondition has to be assured by the process implementation. If a condition is violated, a defined exception handling starts and interrupts the current executed process to prevent an inconsistent data model.

## 6.3   System Functions

For each system function, a Session EJB stub including its **local interface** is generated, see Fig. 4 bottom right. The generated code for a system function provides a connection to the handwritten program code and enables the integration of external functions, applications, and legacy systems. Therefore, the generated **Session Bean** consists of one method with an empty body and has to be extended manually for integration purposes. All required parameters are accessible through class attributes, which are provided by "bijection" mechanisms of the Seam Framework. Additionally, as part of its containing process, a **call-method** is generated for each system function. This call-method is part of the Session EJB that is generated for the parent processes containing the system function. A call-method prepares all required business objects (input parameters) and is responsible for the precondition assurance. Then, it calls the (manually modified) implementation of the system function and is responsible for postcondition assurance. Moreover, it also passes changed objects back to the persistency layer. Fig. 5 illustrates a scenario of a successful call and return of a System Function: If the process implementation `Process.findNext()` decides to invoke a system function, the system function implementation `SystemFunctionCall()` is called. This function prepares all required input parameters from the persistency connection `BusinessObjectEJB` and is responsible for the assurance of preconditions. Then, the actual system function implementation `SystemFunction.java` is processed. After the collected data were returned to the `SystemFunctionCall()` method, specified postconditions are assured and output parameters are stored in the persistency layer. Finally, the control flow is handed over to the process implementation.

## 6.4   User Functions

A modeled user function is generated as a simple **Java Server Faces (JSF) file**, see Fig. 4, bottom center. The internal state of all required business objects (input parameters) is rendered in a read-only view, so that all attributes and their current values can be seen by the user. Moreover, the internal state of all created

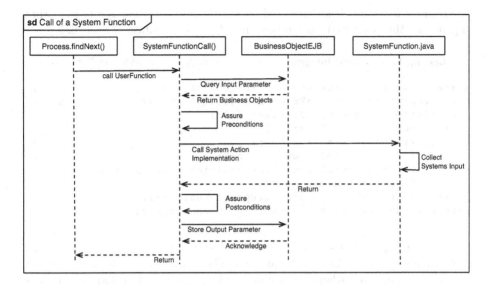

**Fig. 5.** UML Sequence Diagram: Call of a User Function

or modified business objects (output parameters) can be edited by the user in the user interface. After the user decides to finish the current action, the control flow is passed back to the business logic layer. Depending on project specific needs, the generated UI implementation can be modified or completely replaced, for example by otherwise generated or hand-written UIs, which is particularly relevant for industrial information systems. Comparable to system functions, specific methods that manage the connections to the persistency layer and assure all modeled conditions are generated for each user function.

## 7   Robustness at Code Level

For validation purposes we implemented a concrete Amabulo infrastructure with UML as visual modeling language, Coloured Petri Nets for quality assurance, and J2EE/JBoss-Seam as target platform. Subsequently, we applied it in an industrial scenario, which was derived from project experiences with our industrial partners. With regard to the contribution of this paper, this section focuses on robustness features at code level. The subsequently described listings contain excerpts from the generated business logic layer that was generated from the UML model of Fig. 2. This model is part of a complex offer negotiation process as supported by e-business systems of our partners from the insurance and reinsurance business. List. 1 shows a generated "call-method" **sendAcceptenceMessage()** related to the modeled system action "SendAcceptanceMesssage" of Fig. 2. This method is part of the generated control flow logic and must not be modified manually after generation. The actual implementation of the system function is provided by a session bean (referred as `sendAcceptanceMessage` object) that implements the generated session bean interface as described in Sect. 6.

**Listing 1.** Generated Integration Code of "SendAcceptanceMessage" Action

```
private String sendAcceptanceMessage () throws                    1
SystemFunctionExcecutionException , ViolatedConditionException {  2
   em.find(Offer.class , offer.getId ());                         3
   offer.merge(offerEJB , offer );                                4
   if (!(evaluateExpression("offer.decision=='accepted'"))) {     5
         throw new ViolatedConditionException ("                  6
      Violated precondition(offer.decision=='accepted')           7
      in function bindContract");}                                8
   sendAcceptanceMessage.sendAcceptanceMessage ();                9
return findNextFunction("sendAcceptanceMessage");           }    10
```

After preparing an `offer` object from the persistency layer (LOC 3+4), the modeled preconditions have to be assured. The `decision` attribute of contract has to be `accepted`. Otherwise, a constraint violation is detected an a proper exception has to be raised (LOC 5-8). Then an accepted offer will be handed over to the manual implementation or integrated functionality (the session bean `sendAcceptanceMessage`) in LOC 9. The data transfer object `offer` is accessible through the session context of the application. Postcondition assurance and storage functions are not needed in this function, because the offer was modeled readonly. Read-only means that only an InputPin was defined at Visual Model Layer indicating that an object must not be modified. Finally, the control flow is passed back to the process implementation (LOC 10). As mentioned above, the actual modification of the offer object is done in the data transfer object `offer`. Following the design of Sect. 6, this object implements the domain state assurance logic for its attribute state as specified in the state diagram (see Fig. 2) List. 2 shows the generated `setDecision(String state)` method of `Offer`: Depending on the current value of `state`, the new value of `state` is checked against the modeled transitions. For example, in the user action "Second Decision", the decision has to be switched from `firstDeciderAccepted` into `accepted` or `declined`. The domain state assurance for state `firstDeciderAccepted` starts in LOC 9. Only `accepted` or `declined` are accepted new states of `decision`. Any further state would lead to an `IllegalArgumentException`.

**Listing 2.** Generated Domain State Assurance Logic for Attribute "Offer.decision"

```
public void setDecision(String state) throws                     1
      IllegalArgumentException {
   boolean isValid = false;                                       2
   if (state.equals(this.state)) isValid = true;                 3
   else if (this.state.equals("")) {                             4
   if ("undecided".equals(state)) isValid = true;                5
   }                                                              6
   else if ("accepted".equals(this.state)) {                     7
```

```
}                                                               8
else if ("firstDeciderAccepted".equals(this.state)) {          9
   if ("accepted".equals(state)) isValid = true;              10
   if ("declined".equals(state)) isValid = true;              11
}                                                              12
else if ("declined".equals(this.state)) {                     13
}                                                              14
else if ("undecided".equals(this.state)) {                    15
   if ("declined".equals(state)) isValid = true;              16
   if ("firstDeciderAccepted".equals(state)) isValid = true;  17
}                                                              18
if (isValid) this.state = state;                              19
else throw new IllegalArgumentException("No valid value for   20
   Contract.state. Current state: "+this.state+",
   Proposed new state: "+state + ".");  }
```

## 8  Conclusion

As part of our work, we developed an architectural blueprint that supports a consistent model driven development process of business logic for information systems. Each layer of the blueprint supports specific tasks, such as visual modeling, model verification, and code generation. As contribution of this article we introduced an architecture for generated business logic code, which is part of the Code Generation Layer of our architectural blueprint. We assumed, that external functions have to be connected manually to generated critical parts of a system and that complex systems are developed and operated over several years and with changing project teams and reoccurring modification and maintenance tasks. For this purpose, we considered particularly maintenance and integration issues and focused on the generation of robust business logic layers. Therefore, our infrastructure supports the specification of global domain states and local conditions in visual software models and generates corresponding code artifacts, which assures these conditions automatically. Moreover, manual integration tasks are supported through a consistent separation of generated critical code artifacts and code that was modified manually at file level.

We demonstrated the robustness features with a sample implementation of an Amabulo infrastructure and their application in an industrial scenario. The experiences with our sample implementation show that a consistent support of a model driven development and maintenance process for the business logic of information systems requires huge initial efforts. Its application is only reasonable for long-term operated systems, where the initial setup as well as the maintenance of the project infrastructure demands less efforts than the n-times manually executed development process. Moreover, only if future changes of domain requirements can be classified and expressed by a software model and corresponding code generation rules can be implemented, a model driven approach provides an alternative to conventional software development without automated model processing.

# References

1. Bordbar, B., Draheim, D., Horn, M., Schulz, I., Weber, G.: Integrated model-based software development, data access, and data migration. In: Briand, L.C., Williams, C. (eds.) MoDELS 2005. LNCS, vol. 3713, pp. 382–396. Springer, Heidelberg (2005)
2. Brückmann, T., Gruhn, V.: Amabulo-a model architecture for business logic. In: ECBS 2008. 15th Annual IEEE International Conference and Workshop on the Engineering of Computer Based Systems (2008)
3. Brückmann, T., Gruhn, V.: Modellierung und Qualitätssicherung von UML-Modellen der Geschäftslogik von Informationssystemen (in German). Software Engineering 143 (2009)
4. Engels, G., Küster, J.M., Heckel, R., Groenewegen, L.: A methodology for specifying and analyzing consistency of object-oriented behavioral models. In: European Software Engineering Conference, ESEC/FSE (2001)
5. Fleurey, F., Breton, E., Baudry, B., Nicolas, A., Jézéquel, J.-M.: Model-driven engineering for software migration in a large industrial context. In: Engels, G., Opdyke, B., Schmidt, D.C., Weil, F. (eds.) MODELS 2007. LNCS, vol. 4735, pp. 482–497. Springer, Heidelberg (2007)
6. Frankel, D.: Model Driven Architecture: Applying MDA to Enterprise Computing. John Wiley and Sons, Inc., Chichester (2002)
7. Jurack, S., Lambers, L., Mehner, K., Taentzer, G.: Sufficient criteria for consistent behavior modeling with refined activity diagrams. In: Czarnecki, K., Ober, I., Bruel, J.-M., Uhl, A., Völter, M. (eds.) MODELS 2008. LNCS, vol. 5301, pp. 341–355. Springer, Heidelberg (2008)
8. Keller, G., Nüttgens, M., Scheer, A.-W.: Semantische Prozessmodellierung auf der Grundlage "Ereignisgesteuerter Prozessketten (EPK)". Veröffentlichungen des Institutes für Wirtschaftsinformatik, Universität des Saarlandes (1992)
9. Koehler, J., Hauser, R., Küster, J., Ryndina, K., Vanhatalo, J., Wahler, M.: The Role of Visual Modeling and Model Transformations in Business-driven Development. Graph Transformation and Visual Modeling Techniques, GT-VMT 2006 (2006)
10. Konrad, S., Goldsby, H.J., Cheng, B.H.C.: i2MAP: An Incremental and Iterative Modeling and Analysis Process. In: Engels, G., Opdyke, B., Schmidt, D.C., Weil, F. (eds.) MODELS 2007. LNCS, vol. 4735, pp. 451–466. Springer, Heidelberg (2007)
11. Mohan, R., Cohen, M., Schiefer, J.: A State Machine Based Approach for a Process Driven Development of Web-Applications. In: Pidduck, A.B., Mylopoulos, J., Woo, C.C., Ozsu, M.T. (eds.) CAiSE 2002. LNCS, vol. 2348, p. 52. Springer, Heidelberg (2002)
12. Unified Modeling Language (UML): Superstructure, Version 2.1.2. Object Management Group, OMG (2007)
13. Business Process Modeling Notation (BPMN) 1.2. Object Management Group (OMG) (January 2009)

14. Paller, A., Martin, B., Brown, M., Christey, S.: 2009 CWE/SANS Top 25 Most Dangerous Programming Errors. Technical report, SANS Institute (2009)
15. Pohl, K.: Requirements Engineering - Grundlagen, Prinzipien, Techniken. dpunkt.verlag (2007)
16. Red Hat, Inc. Seam framework (2009-02-11), http://www.seamframework.org
17. Schattkowsky, T., Müller, W.: Model-based design of embedded systems. In: 7th IEEE International Symposium on Object-Oriented Real-Time Distributed Computing (ISORC 2004), Vienna, Austria (2004)
18. Seidewitz, E.: What models mean. IEEE Software 20(5), 26–32 (2003)
19. Seybold, C., Meier, S., Glinz, M.: Scenario-driven modeling and validation of requirements models. In: 5th Intl.Wworkshop on Scenarios and State Machines, SCESM (2006)

# A Model for Dynamic Reconfiguration in Service-Oriented Architectures

José Luiz Fiadeiro[1] and Antónia Lopes[2]

[1] Department of Computer Science, University of Leicester
University Road, Leicester LE1 7RH, UK
jose@mcs.le.ac.uk
[2] Faculty of Sciences, University of Lisbon
Campo Grande, 1749–016 Lisboa, Portugal
mal@di.fc.ul.pt

**Abstract.** The importance of modelling the dynamic architectural characteristics of software systems has long been recognised. However, the nature of the dynamic architectural characteristics of service-oriented applications goes beyond what is currently addressed by existing architecture description languages (ADLs). At the heart of the service-oriented approach is the logical separation of *service need* from the need-fulfillment mechanism, i.e., the *service provider*: the binding between the two is deferred to runtime and established at the instance level, i.e. each time the need for the service emerges. In this paper we present an architecture-oriented model for dynamic reconfiguration that paves the way for the definition of ADLs that are able to address the specification of dynamic architectural characteristics of service-oriented applications.

## 1 Introduction

Several architectural aspects arise from service-oriented computing (SOC), loosely understood as a paradigm that supports the construction of complex software-intensive systems from entities, called services, that can be dynamically (i.e. at run time) discovered and bound to applications to fulfil given business goals. On the one hand, we have so-called service-oriented architecture (SOA), normally understood as a (partially) layered architecture in which business processes can be structured as choreographies of services and services are orchestrations of enterprise components. SOAs are supported by an integration middleware providing the communication protocols, brokers, identification/binding/composition mechanisms, and other architectural components that support a new architectural style. This style is characterised by an interaction model between service consumers and providers that is mediated by brokers that maintain registries of service descriptions and are capable of binding the requester who invoked the service to an implementation of the service description made available by a provider that is able to enter into a service-level agreement (SLA) with the consumer.

On the other hand, this new style and form of enterprise-scale IT architecture has a number of implications on the nature of the configurations (or run-time architectures) of the systems that adhere to that style (what we will call service-oriented systems). If we take one of the traditional concepts of architecture as being "concerned with

M. Ali Babar and I. Gorton (Eds.): ECSA 2010, LNCS 6285, pp. 70–85, 2010.

the selection of architectural elements, their interactions and the constraints on those elements and their interactions necessary to provide a framework in which to satisfy the requirements and serve as a basis for the design" [30], it is possible to see why service-oriented systems fall outside the realm of the languages and models that we have been using so far for architectural description: for service-oriented systems, the selection of their architectural elements (components and connectors) is not made at design time; as new services are bound, at run time, to the applications that, in the system, trigger their discovery, new architectural elements are added to the system that could not have been anticipated at design time. In other words, the new style is essentially 'dynamic' in the sense that it applies not only to the way configurations are organised but, primarily, to the way they evolve.

For example, a typical business system may rely on an external service to supply goods; in order to take advantage of the best deal available at the time the goods are needed, the system may resort to different suppliers at different times. Each of those suppliers may in turn rely on services that they will need to procure. For instance, some suppliers may have their own delivery system but others may prefer to outsource the delivery of the goods; some delivery companies may have their own transport system but prefer to use an external company to provide the drivers; and so on. In summary, the structure of a service-oriented system, understood as the components and connectors that determine its configuration, is intrinsically dynamic. Therefore, the role of architecture in the construction of a service-oriented system needs to go beyond that of identifying, at design time, components and connectors that developers will need to implement. Because these activities are now performed by the SOA middleware, what is required from software architects is that they identify and model the high-level business activities and the dependencies that they have on external services to fulfil their goals.

Run-time architectural change is itself an area of software engineering that has deserved a lot of attention from the research community [3,19,26,27,29,32], mainly as a response to the need for mechanisms for enhancing adaptability and evolvability of systems in the face of changing requirements or operating conditions. Although the dynamic nature of the architecture of service-oriented systems could be thought to fall within this general remit, there are a number of specificities that suggest that a more focused and fundamental study of dynamic reconfiguration in SOA is needed. Indeed, dynamic reconfiguration is clearly intrinsic to the computational model of SOC, i.e. it is not a process that, like adaptability or evolvability, is driven by factors that are external to the system. Naturally, self-adaptation is a key concern for many systems but, essentially, this means reacting to changes perceived in the environment in which the system operates. In the case of services, the driver for dynamic reconfiguration (through change of the source of provision each time a service is required) is not so much the need to adjust the behaviour in response to changes in the environment: it is part of the way systems should be designed to meet goals that are endogenous to the business activities that they perform. In both cases, the aim is to optimise the way quality-of-service requirements are met. However, while in architectural-based approaches to self-adaptation the optimisation process is programmed in terms of reconfiguration actions, in the case of services the optimisation process is determined by quality-of-service requirements that derive from business goals.

Our purpose in this paper is to put forward a mathematical model that can be used as a semantic domain for service-oriented architectural description languages. Our starting point is the graph-based approach that we and other authors have used for architectural reconfiguration [12,32]. Essentially, we introduce a mechanism of reflection (as used in other approaches to dynamic reconfiguration [14,21]) by which configurations are typed with models of business activities and service models define rules for dynamic reconfiguration. This mathematical model was used in the SENSORIA project to define the dynamic semantics of the language SRML [18]. A full definition of the model itself cannot be provided here; a more detailed account can be found in [17]. For illustrating our approach, we use the financial case study developed in SENSORIA.

The paper is organised as follows. In Section 3, we define a model for business-reflective configurations of systems. In Section 4, we put forward a model of services as rules for the dynamic reconfiguration of systems and we outline an operational semantics for the rules defined by services. We discuss related work in Section 5 and conclude in Section 6 by pointing to other aspects that are being investigated.

## 2    Motivation and Example

At a certain level of abstraction, configurations of service-oriented applications can be seen to be a particular case of component-connector architectural configurations: a graph of *components* (applications deployed over a given execution platform) linked through *wires* (interconnections between components over a given network)[1]. We denote by **COMP** and **WIRE** the universes of components and wires, respectively.

As it often happens in the presence of dynamic reconfiguration, it is necessary to consider the execution state of the configuration elements as well. Every component $c \in$ **COMP** and wire $w \in$ **WIRE** of a configuration may be in a number of states (e.g. valuations of local state variables), the set of which is denoted by **STATE**$_c$ and **STATE**$_w$, respectively. We denote by **STATE** the corresponding indexed family of sets of states.

### Definition 1 (Configuration and State Configuration)

- A configuration *is a simple graph* $\mathcal{G}$ *such that* $nodes(\mathcal{G}) \subseteq$ **COMP** *(i.e. nodes are components) and* $edges(\mathcal{G}) \subseteq$ **WIRE** *(i.e. edges are wires). Each edge e is associated with a (unordered) pair of nodes that we denote by* $e : n \leftrightarrow m$.
- A state configuration $\mathcal{F}$ *is a pair* $\langle \mathcal{G}, \mathcal{S} \rangle$, *where* $\mathcal{G}$ *is a configuration and* $\mathcal{S}$ *is a configuration state, i.e., a mapping that assigns an element of* **STATE**$_c$ *to each* $c \in nodes(\mathcal{G})$ *and an element of* **STATE**$_w$ *to each* $w \in edges(\mathcal{G})$.

Configurations of service-oriented applications change as a result of the creation of new business activities and the execution of existing ones: new components or wires may be added to a configuration because the execution of a business activity triggered the discovery of and binding to a service that is required. In order to illustrate our approach, we use a (simplified) scenario in which there is a financial services organisation that offers a mortgage-brokerage service MORTGAGEFINDER that, in addition to finding

---

[1] In SOC, message exchanges are essentially peer-to-peer and, hence, for simplicity, we take all connectors to be binary.

the best mortgage deal for a mortgage request, opens a bank account associated with a loan (if the lender does not provide one) and procures an insurance policy (if required by either the customer or the lender). The provision of this service depends on three other services — a *Lender*, a *Bank*, an *Insurance* — that are assumed to be provided by other organisations and procured at run time, each time they are needed, according to the profile of the customer and market availability.

In this context, let us consider a situation in which there is a business activity $A_{Bob}$ processing a mortgage request issued through a user interface *BobHouseUI* on behalf of a customer (Bob), and that this activity is being served by MORTGAGEFINDER. Suppose that the active computational ensemble of components that collectively pursue the business goal of this activity in the current state is as highlighted (through a dotted line) on the left-hand side of Figure 1 — the component *BobMortAg* is orchestrating the delivery of MORTGAGEFINDER, which requires it to interact with the component *BobEstAg* that is acting on behalf of Bob (who is using the interface *BobHouseUI*), and a database *MortRegistry* of trusted lenders. Other components may be present in the current configuration that account for other business activities running in parallel with $A_{Bob}$, say activities processing other mortgage requests that share the same database *MortRegistry* or, as depicted in Figure 1, updating that registry with new lenders. That is, $A_{Bob}$ is in fact a sub-configuration of a larger system.

Let us further imagine that the discovery of a provider of the service *Lender* is triggered by *BobMortAg*. As illustrated in the right-hand side of Figure 1, as a result of the execution of the discovery and binding process, a new component — *RockLoans* — is added to the current configuration and bound to the component *BobMortAg* that is orchestrating the delivery of MORTGAGEFINDER. This new component is responsible for the provision of the service by the selected provider of *Lender*.

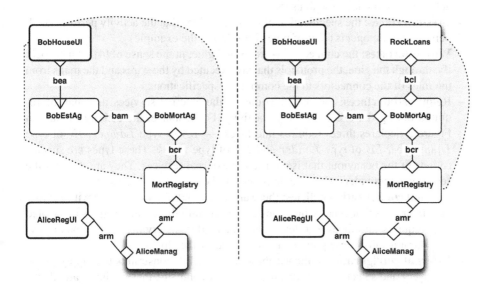

**Fig. 1.** Two configurations that shows the sub-configuration that corresponds to the business activity $A_{Bob}$ before and after the discovery of a provider of the service *Lender*, respectively

This example illustrates why, in order to capture the dynamic aspects of SOC, we need to look beyond the information available in a state — configurations account only for which components are active and how they are interconnected, not why they are active and interconnected in that way. Therefore, we need to have available information that accounts for the dependencies that the activity has on externally provided services, the situations in which they need to be discovered, and the criteria according to which they should be selected. The approach that we developed achieves this by making configurations *business reflective*, i.e. by labelling each sub-configuration that corresponds to a business activity with a model of the workflow that implements its business logic. The models that we propose for this effect are called *activity modules*, whose operational semantics defines the rules according to which service-oriented systems are dynamically reconfigured. We discuss this form of reflection in Section 3.

## 3    Business-Reflective Configurations

Activity modules are specification artefacts that we use for typing the sub-configurations that, in a given state, execute the business activities that are running. Figure 2 depicts the activity module that types the configuration of the activity $A_{Bob}$ on the left-hand side of Figure 1, i.e. before the discovery of a provider of the service *Lender*. The different elements of an activity module are:

- **Component-interfaces:** the specifications that type the components that, in the sub-configuration, execute the business activity. For example, $MA$ is a component-interface declared to be of type *MortgageAgent*.
- **Serves-interface:** the specification of the interface ($HUI$ in the example) that the activity uses to interact with users.
- **Uses-interfaces:** the specification of the interactions that the activity performs with persistent components ($MR$ of type *Registry* in the example).
- **Wire-interfaces:** the connectors — roles and glue, in the sense of [4] — that specify, through the glue, the protocols that are executed by the wires and the maps from the roles of the connectors to the component specifications.
- **Requires-interfaces:** the specifications of the external services that may be required during the execution of the activity. For instance, the activity module in Figure 2 declares three 'requires-interfaces' — $LA$ of type *Lawyer*, $IN$ of type *Insurance*, $LE$ of type *Lender* and $BA$ of type *Bank*. These types are specifications of the behaviour that is required of external services. They are used for the selection of providers when the discovery of the services is triggered.
- **Internal configuration policies:** these are state conditions associated with component interfaces that specify how they should be initialised, and triggers associated with requires-interfaces that determine when external services need to be discovered. Graphically, these policies are identified by the clocks.
- **External configuration policies:** these are the SLA constraints that apply to the discovery and selection of external services. Graphically, these policies are identified by the rulers.

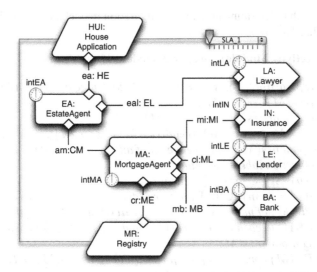

**Fig. 2.** The activity module that types the sub-configuration that corresponds to $A_{Bob}$ as shown on the left-hand side of Figure 1

The nature of the specifications used for defining the interfaces is not relevant for the purpose of this paper. In [18] we have used both a declarative language and an extension of UML statecharts for component-interfaces, and temporal logic for requires-interfaces, but other formalisms could be used. For generality, we assume that all specifications belong to a universe **SPEC**. We distinguish between the different kinds of interfaces because they have different roles in the dynamic re-configuration of the activity as explained further on. We also abstract from the nature of the connectors that are used in wire-interfaces and work over a generic universe **CNCT**. Details on the kind of connectors that we have found useful for service modelling can be found in [1].

The specific language used for specifying initialisation conditions and triggers is also of no particular importance for this paper, so we assume that we have available a set **STC** of conditions over **STATE**. Finally, we adopt so called 'soft constraints' for expressing SLA constraints. These generalise the notion of constraint: while a constraint is a predicate over a certain set of variables $X$ and, hence, divides the set of valuations of $X$ in two disjoint subsets (those that satisfy the constraint and those that do not), a soft constraint is a function mapping each valuation of $X$ into some domain $D$ (e.g., the interval of real numbers $[0, 1]$) that captures different degrees of satisfaction. Soft constraints are commonly used for describing problems where it is necessary to model fuzziness, preferences, costs, inter alia. In particular, they have shown to be useful for supporting the negotiation of service-level agreements [7]. Some well-known soft constraint formalisms are *Valued Constraint Satisfaction Problems* [16] and *Semiring-based Soft Constraints* [6]. The particular formalism that is adopted is not relevant for this paper; in SRML [18], we adopted [6].

In summary, an activity module includes all the information that defines the business aspect of the activity on a particular state. This includes the specifications of the components and connectors that execute the activity on that state but also the dependencies on external services that determine how that configuration may change. Activity modules are also formalised as graphs:

**Definition 2 (Activity Module).** *An* activity module $M$ *consists of*

- *A simple graph* $graph(M)$; *we use* $nodes(M)$ *to denote the set of its nodes.*
- *A set* $requires(M) \subseteq nodes(M)$.
- *A set* $uses(M) \subseteq nodes(M) \setminus requires(M)$.
- *A node* $serves(M) \in nodes(M) \setminus (requires(M) \cup uses(M))$.
  *We use* $components(M)$ *to denote the set of all remaining nodes.*
- *A labelling function* $label_M$ *such that*
    • $label_M(n) \in$ **SPEC** *for every node* $n$.
    • $label_M(e : n \leftrightarrow m) \in$ **CNCT** *for every edge* $e$.
- *A pair* $intPlc(M)$ *of mappings* $\langle trigger_M, init_M \rangle$ *such that* $trigger_M$ *assigns a condition in* **STC** *to each* $n \in requires(M)$ *and* $init_M$ *assigns a condition in* **STC** *to each* $n \in components(M)$.
- *A pair* $extPlc(M)$ *consisting of a soft constraint system* $cs(M)$ *and a set* $sla(M)$ *of soft constraints over* $cs(M)$.

*We denote by* $body(M)$ *the (full) sub-graph of* $graph(M)$ *that forgets the nodes in* $requires(M)$ *and the edges that connect them to the rest of the graph.*

We can now also formalise the typing of state configurations with activity modules motivated before, which makes configurations business-reflective. We consider a space $\mathcal{A}$ of business activities to be given, which can be seen to consist of reference numbers (or some other kind of identifier) such as the ones that organisations automatically assign when a service request arrives.

**Definition 3 (Business Configuration).** *A* business configuration *is a triple* $\langle \mathcal{F}, \mathcal{B}, \mathcal{C} \rangle$ *where*
- $\mathcal{F}$ *is a state configuration.*
- $\mathcal{B}$ *is a partial mapping that assigns an activity module* $\mathcal{B}(a)$ *to each activity* $a \in \mathcal{A}$ *— the workflow being executed by* $a$ *in* $\mathcal{F}$. *We say that the activities in the domain of this mapping are those that are active in that state.*
- $\mathcal{C}$ *is a mapping that assigns an homomorphism* $\mathcal{C}(a)$ *of graphs* $body(\mathcal{B}(a)) \rightarrow \mathcal{F}$ *to every activity* $a \in \mathcal{A}$ *that is active in* $\mathcal{F}$. *We denote by* $\mathcal{F}(a)$ *the image of* $\mathcal{C}(a)$ *— the sub-configuration of* $\mathcal{F}$ *that corresponds to the activity* $a$.

A homomorphism of graphs is just a mapping of nodes to nodes and edges to edges that preserves the end-points of the edges. Therefore, the homomorphism $\mathcal{C}$ of a business configuration types the nodes (components) of $\mathcal{F}(a)$ with specifications of the roles that they play in the activity — i.e. $\mathcal{C}(a)(n) : label_{\mathcal{B}(a)}(n)$ for every node $n$ — and the edges (wires) with connectors — i.e. $\mathcal{C}(a)(e) : label_{\mathcal{B}(a)}(e)$ for every edge $e$.

In Figure 3, we represent a business configuration for the state configuration depicted on the left-hand side of Figure 1. For simplicity, we only show the node mappings of the homomorphisms. In addition to the business activity $A_{Bob}$ that we have been discussing, Figure 3 reveals another business activity — $A_{Alice}$ — in which the registry of trusted lenders $MortRegistry$ is also involved. The activity module that types $A_{Alice}$

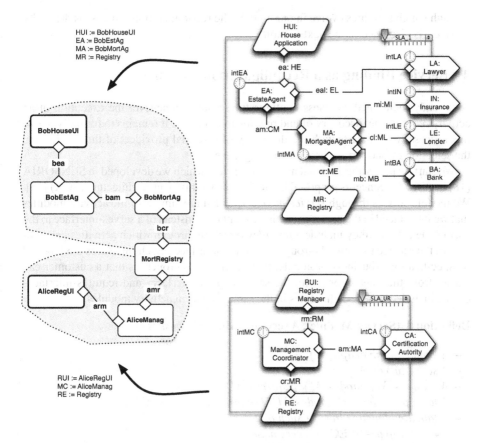

**Fig. 3.** A business conguration that shows the sub-congurations that correspond to the business activities $A_{Bob}$ (top part) and $A_{Alice}$ (bottom part) and the activity modules that type them

defines that the business goal of this activity is to update the registry with new lenders; in the particular state being depicted, this activity still requires an external service to be discovered that can certify the new lender.

The fact that the homomorphism is defined over the body of the activity module means that the requires-interfaces are not used for typing components of the state configuration. Indeed, as discussed above, the purpose of the requires-interfaces is for identifying dependencies that the activity has, in that state, on external services. In particular, this makes requires-interfaces different from uses-interfaces as the latter are indeed mapped, through the homomorphism, to a component of the state configuration.

In summary, the homomorphism makes state configurations reflective in the sense of [14] as it adds meta (business) information to the state configuration. This information is used for deciding how the configuration will evolve (namely, how it will react to events that trigger the discovery process). Indeed, reflection has been advocated as a means of making systems adaptable through reconfiguration, which is similar to the mechanisms through which activities evolve in our model. The reconfiguration process, as driven by services, is discussed in the next section.

## 4   Service Binding as a Reconfiguration Action

As already mentioned, business configurations change whenever the execution of an activity requires the discovery of and binding to a service. It remains to formally define this process, which starts with the discovery of potential providers of the service and the selection of one service provider among these.

We start by providing a formal notion of service, which we developed in SENSORIA [18] inspired by concepts proposed in the Service Component Architecture (SCA) [25]. We model services through *service modules*, which are similar to the activity modules that we introduced in the previous section except that, instead of a serves-interface to the user of the activity, they include a *provides-interface* through which activities can connect to the service (identified through a requires-interface). Such interfaces are labelled by specifications (business protocols) that describe the properties that a customer can expect from the interactions with the service. Uses-interfaces and requires-interfaces can be included in service modules in the same way as in activity modules.

**Definition 4  (Service Module).** *A service module $M$ consists of*

- *A simple graph $graph(M)$.*
- *A set $requires(M) \subseteq nodes(M)$.*
- *A set $uses(M) \subseteq nodes(M) \setminus requires(M)$.*
- *A node $provides(M) \in nodes(M) \setminus (requires(M) \cup uses(M))$.*
- *A labelling function $label_M$ such that*
  - *$label_M(n) \in \textbf{SPEC}$ for every node $n$.*
  - *$label_M(e : n \leftrightarrow m) \in \textbf{CNCT}$ for every edge $e$.*
- *An internal configuration policy $intPlc(M)$ as in definition 2.*
- *An external configuration policy $extPlc(M)$ as in definition 2.*

In Figure 4 we present the structure of the service module that models the mortgage-brokerage service MORTGAGEFINDER described before. A complete definition of this service using the modelling language SRML, including all the specifications involved, is presented in [18]. The module specifies that the service is provided through an interface $CR$ and wire $CC$ that can bind to any activity that requests an external service through a requires-interface that is matched by the specification $Customer$. The orchestration of the provision of the service is specified through the component-interface $MA$ of type $MortgageAgent$ which may require external services that match the requires-interfaces $LE$ of type $Lender$ (for securing a loan), $BA$ of type $Bank$ (for opening a bank account), and $IN$ of type $Insurance$ (for procuring an insurance). The orchestration also requires the binding to a persistent component $RE$ of type $Registry$ (that stores information about trusted lenders).

In order to formalise the processes of discovery and binding, let $r$ be a requires-interface of an activity $a$. The discovery of services to which $r$ can be bound involves finding services $M$ that (i) through their provides-interface $p$ are able to satisfy the

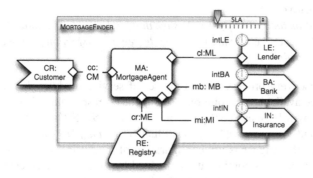

**Fig. 4.** The structure of a service module that models MORTGAGEFINDER

specification associated with $r$, and (ii) through their external configuration policies offer SLA constraints that are compatible with those of $a$ and, therefore, make it possible to reach a service-level agreement. For simplicity, we limit our attention to service modules where there is exactly one component-interface connected to the provides-interface and to activity modules where each requires-interface is connected to a single component-interface (the formulation of the general case can be found in [17]).

For the formulation of condition (i) above we assume that the universe **SPEC** of specifications is equipped with a notion of *refinement* such that $\rho : r \to p$ means that the behavioural properties offered by $p$ entail the properties required by $r$, up to a suitable translation between the languages of both. For example, if using temporal logic for specifying the business protocols associated with $r$ and $p$ as in [18] refinement corresponds to entailment (logical consequence).

The formulation of condition (ii) above relies on a composition operator $\oplus$ that is applicable to soft constraint systems that are compatible (see [6] for an example) and to sets of constraints over compatible constraints systems. Soft constraint systems also provide a notion of *best level of consistency* that assigns a non-negative numerical value $blevel(C)$ to each set of constraints $C$ — the degree of satisfaction that we can expect for $C$. A set of constraints is said to be *consistent* if and only if $blevel(C) > 0$. If $C$ is consistent, a valuation for the variables of $C$ is said to be a *solution* of $C$.

**Definition 5 (Service matching).** *Let $A$ be an activity module and $r{\in}requires(A)$. We denote by* $\mathbf{match}(\mathbf{A}, \mathbf{r})$ *the set of pairs $\langle M, \rho \rangle$ such that:*

- *$M$ is a service module such that the constraint systems $cs(M)$ and $cs(A)$ are compatible and $blevel(sla(M){\oplus}sla(A)) > 0$;*
- *$\rho$ is a refinement mapping from $label_A(r)$ to $label_M(provides(M))$.*

That is, the matching process for an activity module and one of its requires-interfaces returns all service modules whose provides-interface refines the requires-interface of the activity module and whose constraint systems are compatible and whose constraints are consistent.

**Definition 6 (Service Discovery).** *Let $A$ be an activity module and $r{\in}requires(A)$. We denote by* $\mathbf{discover}(\mathbf{A}, \mathbf{r})$ *the set of triples $\langle M, \rho, \Delta \rangle$ such that:*

- $\langle M, \rho \rangle \in \mathbf{match}(\mathbf{A}, \mathbf{r})$;
- $\Delta$ *is a solution for* $sla(M) \oplus sla(A)$ *such that* $bvalue(sla(M) \oplus sla(A))$ *is maximal for* $\mathbf{match}(\mathbf{A}, \mathbf{r})$, *i.e.* $\Delta$ *maximises the degree of satisfaction for the combined set of SLA constraints.*

That is, the discovery process returns the set of service modules that offer the best possible service available, the solution $\Delta$ being the corresponding SLA agreement.

Consider now a business configuration $\mathcal{L} = \langle \langle \mathcal{G}, \mathcal{S} \rangle, \mathcal{B}, \mathcal{C} \rangle$, $a$ an active business activity in $\mathcal{L}$ and $r \in requires(\mathcal{B}(a))$ such that $trigger_{\mathcal{B}(a)}(r)$ evaluates to *true* in $\mathcal{S}$. The reaction to this trigger is a reconfiguration of the business configuration, which results in a new business configuration obtained by binding an element $\langle M, \rho, \Delta \rangle$ of $\mathbf{discover}(\mathcal{B}(a), \mathbf{r})$ to $a$. We now define this binding process.

**Definition 7 (Service Binding).** *Let* $\mathcal{L} = \langle \langle \mathcal{G}, \mathcal{S} \rangle, \mathcal{B}, \mathcal{C} \rangle$ *be a business configuration, $a$ an active business activity in* $\mathcal{L}$, $r \in requires(\mathcal{B}(a))$, $M$ *a service module,* $\rho$ *a refinement mapping from $r$ to* $provides(M)$ *and* $\Delta$ *a constraint. Binding* $\langle M, \rho, \Delta \rangle$ *to $r$ induces a business configuration* $\langle \langle \mathcal{G}', \mathcal{S}' \rangle, \mathcal{B}', \mathcal{C}' \rangle$ *such that:*

- $\mathcal{B}'(x) = \mathcal{B}(x)$, *if* $x \neq a$.
- $\mathcal{B}'(a)$ *is an activity module* $M'$ *such that:*
    - $graph(M')$ *is obtained from the sum (disjoint union) of the graphs of* $\mathcal{B}(a)$ *and $M$ by identifying $r$ with the node of $M$ to which* $provides(M)$ *is connected and identifying the corresponding edges.*
    - $requires(M') = requires(M) \cup requires(\mathcal{B}(a)) \backslash \{r\}$, *i.e. we eliminate $r$ and add the requires-interfaces of $M$.*
    - $uses(M') = uses(M) \cup uses(\mathcal{B}(a))$, *i.e. we add to* $\mathcal{B}(a)$ *the uses-interfaces of $M$.*
    - $serves(M') = serves(M)$, *i.e. we keep the serves-interface.*
    - *the labels provided by* $label'_M$ *are those that are inherited from the graphs of* $\mathcal{B}(a)$ *and $M$. The edge that connected $r$ is now labelled with the label of the edge that connects* $provides(M)$ *in $M$.*
    - $intPlc(M')$ *has the triggers and initialisation conditions that are inherited from* $\mathcal{B}(a)$ *and $M$.*
    - $extPlc(M') = \langle cs(M) \oplus cs(\mathcal{B}(a)), sla(M) \oplus sla(\mathcal{B}(a)) \cup \{\Delta\} \rangle$.
- $\mathcal{G}'$ *is obtained from* $\mathcal{G}$ *by adding:*
    - *For each node $n$ of* $components(M)$, *a component $c_n$ in* **COMP** *that implements the specification* $label_M(n)$ *and, for each edge connecting $n$, a wire that implements the connector that labels the edge.*
    - *For every node $n$ of* $uses(M)$, *a component $c_n$ of $\mathcal{G}$ that implements the specification* $label_M(n)$ *is selected and, for every edge connecting $n$ in $M$, a wire that implements the connector that labels the edge is added to* $\mathcal{G}$.
    *That is to say, implementations of component-interfaces of $M$ are added to the graph and existing components are chosen for uses-interfaces. Wires are added that implement the connectors specified in $M$.*
- $\mathcal{S}'$ *coincides with* $\mathcal{S}$ *in the nodes of* $\mathcal{G}$ *and assigns, to every new node $c_n$ where* $n \in components(M)$, *a state that satisfies* $init_M(n)$.

– $C'$ is the homomorphism that results from updating $C$ with the mappings defined above, i.e. for each node $n$ of $body(M)$, $C'(n) = c_n$, and similarly for the edges.

In order to illustrate how binding works, consider the business configuration in Figure 5, which shows $A_{Bob}$ at an earlier stage of execution (i.e. earlier than the configuration depicted in the left-hand side of Figure 1). Assume that, in the current state, the trigger $intMG$ is true and that the service module shown in Figure 4 is returned by the discovery process described in Definition 6 for the requires-interface $MG$. A possible result of the binding is depicted in Figure 3.

Note that a new component — $BobMortAg$ — is added to the configuration of $A_{Bob}$ as an instance of $MortgageAgent$, but that the uses-interface $RE$ of MORTGAGEFINDER does not give rise to a new component: it is mapped to $MortRegistry$. This is the means through which effects of services can be made 'persistent', i.e. the execution of the service can interfere with other activities in the current configuration. For instance, if $A_{Alice}$ registers a new lender, $A_{Bob}$ will be able to consider that lender when discovering an external service that responds to the trigger $intLE$ of the requires-interface $LE$ of type $Lender$. On the other hand, the serves-interface of the activity

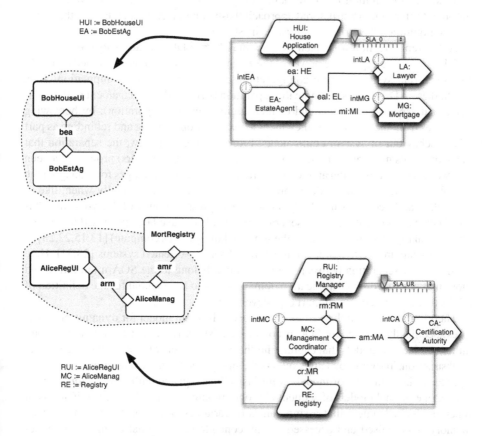

**Fig. 5.** A business conguration that precedes that of Figure 3

module remains invariant through the evolution of the business configuration. This captures the fact that the activity relies on the same interface to interact with its user. Also notice that the new activity module that types $A_{Bob}$ acquires the requires-interfaces of $MortgageAgent$, i.e. the business activity evolves both at the level of its configuration and its type.

## 5  Related Work

In the last decade, different approaches to architectural specification have been proposed that permit the representation of dynamic architectures [3,5,12,29,32,33]. The focus of these approaches is on the description of a control (reconfiguration) layer on top of a managed system. The dynamic architectural changes that have to be performed in the managed system are specified explicitly, for instance in terms of reconfiguration rules [5,12,32], configurator processes [3] or reconfiguration scripts [29,33]. Although different semantic domains have been used in those aforementioned works, their underlying mechanisms can be defined in terms of operations that rewrite state configurations in the sense of Definition 1. The work that we presented in this paper follows on this tradition but offers a more structured approach (based on reflection) that targets the forms of reconfiguration that arise, specifically, in SOC.

A different direction was taken by Darwin [24], $\pi$-ADL [27] and ARCHWARE [26], which explore the expressive power of the $\pi$-calculus — a calculus developed precisely for concurrent systems whose configurations may change during computation. As a result, these ADLs do not promote the separation between the management of the computational aspects of systems and of their architecture (configuration); by borrowing primitives from the $\pi$-calculus, they include instantiation, binding and rebinding as part of the behaviour of system components. From our point of view, the separation that the approaches mentioned in the previous paragraph (including ours) promote between the two levels (computation and reconfiguration) has clear advantages for managing the complexity that arises in modern software-intensive systems, especially when, like in SOC, their architecture is highly dynamic. The expressive power of the $\pi$-calculus has also been explored within SOC: several service calculi have been proposed to address operational foundations of SOC (in the sense of how services compute) [13,15,22,23] as well as to capture the dynamic architectures of service-oriented systems [28,31]. Here again, a clear separation between the aspects that belong to the SOA middleware and those that derive from the application domain seems to be essential for the definition of ADLs that can effectively support high-level design.

Therefore, the reason that led us to propose a different model for dynamic architectures specifically targeted for SOC is not the lack expressiveness of existing models but, rather, the lack of models that capture the 'business' aspects of SOC at the 'right' level of abstraction. To our knowledge, ours is the first proposal in this direction.

Indeed, the definition of models is intrinsically associated with *abstraction*. For example, operational models of sequential programming are typically defined in terms of functions (called states) that assign values to variables, which abstract from the way memory is organised and accessed in any concrete conventional computer architecture. Paradigms such as SOC superpose further layers of abstraction (creating a richer middleware) so that systems can be built and interconnected by relying on a software infrastructure that adds to the basic computation and communication platform a number of facilities that, in the case of SOAs, support service publication, discovery and binding. This means that designers or programmers working over a SOA do not need to implement these mechanisms: they can rely on the fact that they are available as part of the *abstract operating system* that is offered by the middleware. Just like any Java programmer does not need to program the dynamic allocation, referencing and de-referencing of names, a programmer of a complex service should not need to include the discovery, selection and binding processes among the tasks of the orchestrator.

This is why we perceive that the architectural aspects of SOC are best handled over graph-based representations that separate computation from reconfiguration such as the ones proposed in this paper. Drawing an analogy with the semantics of programming languages, we could say that we proposed a notion of (typed) state and state transition for such dynamic aspects of SOC: states are graphs of components and connectors that capture configurations that execute business activities, and transitions are reconfigurations that result from binding to selected services. Our model captures the nature of SOA-middleware approaches and generalises them, offering a more abstract level of modelling in which the business aspects that drive reconfiguration can be represented explicitly and separately from the orchestration of the interactions through which services are delivered.

## 6   Concluding Remarks

In this paper we presented a mathematical model that can be used as a semantic domain for service-oriented architectural description languages. The static aspects of our model were inspired by the concepts proposed in the Service Component Architecture (SCA) [25] towards a general assembly model and binding mechanisms for service components and clients that may have been programmed in possibly many different languages, e.g. Java, C++, BPEL, or PHP. We have transposed those concepts to a more abstract level of modelling and enriched them with primitives that address the dynamic aspects (run-time service discovery, selection and binding) of service-oriented systems. This model paves the way for the definition of ADLs that are able to address the specification of dynamic architectural characteristics of service-oriented applications and, moreover, contribute to overcome the lack of models that capture the 'business' aspects of SOC.

The advantages of this approach have been explored in the language SRML that we defined in SENSORIA [18] but our model is general enough that it can be used to support other ADLs. For example, at a methodological level, we have extended the traditional use-case method to define the structure of both activity and service modules from business requirements [9], which was validated in a number of case studies, including automotive [10] and telco systems [1] in addition to more classical business-oriented domains such as the one used in the paper. Another advantage of the separation of reconfiguration from computation is that different orchestration languages can be used for modelling the components and connectors through which services are provided without affecting the way activities or services are structured in modules: for example, transformations were defined from BPEL to SRML [11], UML state machines were used for supporting model-checking [2], and transformations to PEPA [20] were used for supporting quantitative analysis [8].

## Acknowledgments

We would like to thank our colleagues in the SENSORIA project for many useful discussions on the topics covered in this paper, in particular João Abreu and Laura Bocchi for their contribution to the definition of SRML.

## References

1. Abreu, J., Bocchi, L., Fiadeiro, J., Lopes, A.: Specifying and Composing Interaction Protocols for Service-Oriented System Modelling. In: Derrick, J., Vain, J. (eds.) FORTE 2007. LNCS, vol. 4574, pp. 358–373. Springer, Heidelberg (2007)
2. Abreu, J., Mazzanti, F., Fiadeiro, J., Gnesi, S.: A Model-Checking Approach for Service Component Architectures. In: Lee, D., Lopes, A., Poetzsch-Heffter, A. (eds.) FMOODS 2009. LNCS, vol. 5522, pp. 219–224. Springer, Heidelberg (2009)
3. Allen, R., Douence, R., Garlan, D.: Specifying and analyzing dynamic software architectures. In: Astesiano, E. (ed.) ETAPS 1998 and FASE 1998. LNCS, vol. 1382, pp. 21–37. Springer, Heidelberg (1998)
4. Allen, R., Garlan, D.: A formal basis for architectural connection. ACM Trans. Softw. Eng. Methodol. 6(3), 213–249 (1997)
5. Batista, T., Joolia, A., Coulson, G.: Managing dynamic reconfiguration in component-based systems. In: Morrison, R., Oquendo, F. (eds.) EWSA 2005. LNCS, vol. 3527, pp. 1–17. Springer, Heidelberg (2005)
6. Bistarelli, S., Montanari, U., Rossi, F.: Semiring-based constraint satisfaction and optimization. Journal ACM 44(2), 201–236 (1997)
7. Bistarelli, S., Santini, F.: A nonmonotonic soft concurrent constraint language for sla negotiation. ENTCS 236, 147–162 (2009)
8. Bocchi, L., Fiadeiro, J., Gilmore, S., Abreu, J., Solanki, M., Vankayala, V.: A formal approach to modelling time properties of service oriented systems (submitted, 2009)
9. Bocchi, L., Fiadeiro, J., Lopes, A.: A Use-Case Driven Approach to Formal Service-Oriented Modelling. In: Leveraging Applications of Formal Methods, Verification and Validation. CCIS, vol. 17, pp. 155–169. Springer, Heidelberg (2008)
10. Bocchi, L., Fiadeiro, J., Lopes, A.: Service-oriented modelling of automotive systems. In: The 32nd Annual IEEE International on Computer Software and Applications, COMPSAC 2008, pp. 1059–1064. IEEE, Los Alamitos (2008)
11. Bocchi, L., Hong, Y., Lopes, A., Fiadeiro, J.: From bpel to srml: a formal transformational approach. In: Dumas, M., Heckel, R. (eds.) WS-FM 2007. LNCS, vol. 4937, pp. 92–107. Springer, Heidelberg (2008)
12. Bruni, R., Bucchiarone, A., Gnesi, S., Hirsch, D., Lluch Lafuente, A.: Graph-based design and analysis of dynamic software architectures. In: Degano, P., De Nicola, R., Meseguer, J. (eds.) Concurrency, Graphs and Models. LNCS, vol. 5065, pp. 37–56. Springer, Heidelberg (2008)
13. Carbone, M., Honda, K., Yoshida, N.: A calculus of global interaction based on session types. ENTCS 171(3), 127–151 (2007)
14. Coulson, G., Blair, G., Grace, P., Taiani, F., Joolia, A., Lee, K., Ueyama, J., Sivaharan, T.: A generic component model for building systems software. ACM Trans. Comput. Syst. 26(1), 1–42 (2008)

15. Boreale, M., et al.: Scc: A service centered calculus. In: Bravetti, M., Núñez, M., Zavattaro, G. (eds.) WS-FM 2006. LNCS, vol. 4184, pp. 38–57. Springer, Heidelberg (2006)
16. Fargier, H., Lang, J., Martin-Clouaire, R., Schiex, T.: A constraint satisfaction framework for decision under uncertainty. In: Proc. of the 11th Int. Conf. on Uncertainty in Artificial Intelligence, pp. 175–180 (1996)
17. Fiadeiro, J., Lopes, A., Bocchi, L.: An abstract model of service discovery and binding, http://www.cs.le.ac.uk/people/jfiadeiro
18. Fiadeiro, J., Lopes, A., Bocchi, L., Abreu, J.: The Sensoria reference modelling language, http://www.cs.le.ac.uk/people/jfiadeiro
19. Garlan, D., Cheng, S.-W., Huang, A.-C., Schmerl, B., Steenkiste, P.: Rainbow: Architecture-based self-adaptation with reusable infrastructure. Computer 37(10), 46–54 (2004)
20. Gilmore, S., Hillston, J.: The PEPA Workbench: A Tool to Support a Process Algebra-based Approach to Performance Modelling. In: Haring, G., Kotsis, G. (eds.) TOOLS 1994. LNCS, vol. 794, pp. 353–368. Springer, Heidelberg (1994)
21. Kon, F., Costa, F., Blair, G., Campbell, R.H.: The case for reflective middleware. Communications ACM 45(6), 33–38 (2002)
22. Lapadula, A., Pugliese, R., Tiezzi, F.: A Calculus for Orchestration of Web Services. In: De Nicola, R. (ed.) ESOP 2007. LNCS, vol. 4421, pp. 33–47. Springer, Heidelberg (2007)
23. Lucchi, R., Mazzara, M.: A pi-calculus based semantics for ws-bpel. Journal of Logic and Algebraic Programming (2005)
24. Magee, J., Kramer, J.: Dynamic structure in software architectures. SIGSOFT Softw. Eng. Notes 21(6), 3–14 (1996)
25. Beisiegel, M., et al.: Service Component Architecture Specifications (2007)
26. Morrison, R., Kirby, G., Balasubramaniam, D., Mickan, K., Oquendo, F., Cmpan, S., Warboys, B., Snowdon, B., Greenwood, R.: Support for evolving software architectures in the ArchWare ADL. In: 4th Working IEEE/IFIP Conference on Software Architecture (2004)
27. Oquendo, F.: π-adl: an architecture description language based on the higher-order typed π-calculus for specifying dynamic and mobile software architectures. SIGSOFT Softw. Eng. Notes 29(3), 1–14 (2004)
28. Oquendo, F.: Formal approach for the development of business processes in terms of service-oriented architectures using pi-adl. In: SOSE, pp. 154–159 (2008)
29. Oreizy, P., Taylor, R.: On the role of software architectures in runtime system reconfiguration. IEEE Proceedings- Software Engineering 145(5), 137–145 (1998)
30. Perry, D., Wolf, L.: Foundations for the study of software architecture. SIGSOFT Softw. Eng. Notes 17(4), 40–52 (1992)
31. López-Sanz, M., Qayyum, Z., Cuesta, C.E., Marcos, E., Oquendo, F.: Representing service-oriented architectural models using pi-adl. In: Morrison, R., Balasubramaniam, D., Falkner, K. (eds.) ECSA 2008. LNCS, vol. 5292, pp. 273–280. Springer, Heidelberg (2008)
32. Wermelinger, M., Fiadeiro, J.: A graph transformation approach to software architecture reconfiguration. Sci. Comput. Program. 44(2), 133–155 (2002)
33. Wermelinger, M., Lopes, A., Fiadeiro, J.: A graph based architectural (re)configuration language. In: ESEC/FSE-9, pp. 21–32. ACM, New York (2001)

# Integrating Requirements and Design Decisions in Architecture Representation

Rainer Weinreich[1] and Georg Buchgeher[2]

[1] Johannes Kepler University Linz, Austria
`rainer.weinreich@jku.at`
[2] Software Competence Center Hagenberg, Austria
`georg.buchgeher@scch.at`

**Abstract.** It has been proposed to make architectural design decisions first-class entities in software architecture representation. The actual means of capturing, representing, and managing architectural design decisions is still an open issue of research. We present an approach for capturing requirements and design decisions during design and development. We integrate design decisions, requirements, scenarios, and their relationships along with other architectural elements directly in a single, consistent, and formally defined architecture model. Capturing, visualizing, and tracing of architectural knowledge are supported by an integrated set of tools working on this model. The approach supports comprehensive tracing between requirements, design decisions, other architectural elements, and implementation artifacts, impact analysis, and architecture analysis and evaluation.

**Keywords:** Software Architecture Models, Design Decisions, Software Architecture Tools, Software Architecture Knowledge Management.

## 1 Introduction

Design decisions are an important element in software architecture. An early definition of the term software architecture provided by Perry and Wolf [20] already includes rationale in addition to elements and form. According to Perry and Wolf rationale "captures the motivation for the choice of architectural style, the choice of elements, and the form".

Though rationale has already been identified early in the history of software architecture research, it has been neglected in software architecture representation. As Kruchten [16] points out, research in this area has concentrated on representing and documenting a system's architecture from different perspectives, called architectural views. While architectural views and corresponding view frameworks are an important means for documentation, they focus on the result of the design process and lack information about the actual decisions and their rationale [26]. If design decisions are not documented, they remain tacit knowledge [12], which is easily lost [5,26]. Bosch [5] identified the resulting knowledge vaporization as the key problem of design erosion [13] and was one of the

M. Ali Babar and I. Gorton (Eds.): ECSA 2010, LNCS 6285, pp. 86–101, 2010.
© Springer-Verlag Berlin Heidelberg 2010

first to point out the importance of design decisions in software architecture. He proposed to view software architecture as a composition of design decisions and demanded a first class-representation of design decisions [5].

While capturing design decisions and rationale provides a number of benefits [25], the means for capturing this information is still an open issue of research. Approaches for rationale management exist [11] but suffer from a number of problems. Van der Ven et al. [26] provide some examples like the overhead involved in capturing the required information, and the missing connection between design decisions and architectural elements. In addition, design decisions are closely related to requirements [4,18,21,26]. And requirements, as well as design decisions, are central to many architectural analysis methods [16].

We present an approach for capturing requirements and design decisions and for integrating them in a formally defined architecture representation. A consistent model for requirements, design decisions, and scenarios - called *architectural issues* in our approach - supports architecture knowledge activities like impact analysis and tracing from requirements to architecture elements and implementation artifacts. The same model can be used for architecture analysis and evaluation by connecting architectural issues with analysis state and analysis data. Capturing issues and their relationships is supported as an integrated activity in design and development. The main benefits of our approach are the deep integration of support for architectural issues in design and development, the usage of the same model for architecture knowledge management and architecture analysis, and the integration into a consistent architecture representation, which supports system evolution and enables tracing from requirements to architecture and implementation.

The remainder of this paper is structured as follows: In Section 2 we comment on previous work that has been used as the basis for the work presented in this paper. The section includes an overview of the LISA model, a meta-model for architecture description, and the LISA toolkit. The section also includes references to previous work where appropriate. In Section 3 we give a conceptual overview of our approach. This includes a conceptual model of requirements, design decisions, and scenarios, their relationships to each other, as well as relationships to other architectural elements. In Section 4 we describe tool support for three important aspects of our approach in more detail: capturing, visualizing, and analyzing requirements, design decisions, and scenarios. Section 5 describes the steps we have taken to validate our approach. In Section 6 we present related work. Section 7 summarizes the main aspects of our work.

## 2   Previous Work

The work presented in this paper is part of the *Software Architecture Engineering* project for supporting architecture-centric software development [7]. The project aims at supporting architecture-related activities like modeling, documenting, and analyzing software architectures in an integrated and incremental way. Integrated means that architecture-related activities are integrated seamlessly in all software development activities, from analysis to design, and implementation. Incremental means that we aim to provide support for both agile and non-agile project settings with potential interleaved analysis, design, and implementation activities.

The main results of the project are the LISA model, a meta-model for software architecture representation, and the LISA toolkit, which is a set of tools for working on LISA architecture models.

The LISA model has been designed for ease of integration and synchronization with a system's implementation to prevent architectural erosion and architectural drift. It provides not only components and connectors for describing dynamic system structures and configurations, but also lower-level abstractions for describing packages, classes, and modules. These parts of a LISA model can be extracted from and easily synchronized with a system implementation and enable us to support dependency analysis as provided by typical software architecture management tools (AMTs) like Lattix, SonarJ, and Structure101. In this sense LISA combines the concepts of lower-level AMTs, i.e., strong tool support and tight implementation integration, with the concepts of higher-level architecture representation and analysis as supported by architecture description languages (ADLs).

The LISA toolkit is integrated in the Eclipse IDE. Architecture modeling, analysis, and implementation can be performed incrementally and interleaved [27]. The toolkit supports multiple architectural views, which are derived from a single, consistent LISA-based architecture model. Using a single model avoids inconsistencies among views. Architecture/implementation synchronization is supported through continuous forward and reverse engineering [6]. Developers always have an up-to-date architecture description available, which acts as a blueprint for the implementation.

Technology independence is achieved through technology-specific binding models [6]. Currently we support bindings for languages like Java and C# and for component models and technologies like Spring, OSGi, EJB, and SCA.

Both the LISA model and the LISA toolkit are extensible. The LISA model is based on XML-Schema and can be extended with additional sub-models. In this sense it is similar to xADL [9]. The LISA toolkit can be extended with additional architectural views for documentation and visualization, with additional constraints for architecture analysis and validation, and with additional components for architecture/implementation synchronization.

The approach has been developed to support different analysis approaches in one single consistent environment. This includes automatic analysis approaches as offered by ADLs and architecture management tools, and manual analysis techniques like scenario-based evaluation methods.

## 3 Conceptual Overview

A LISA-based architecture description is organized in modules. Modules are the units of deployment and versioning. LISA-modules can be bound to and deployed with implementation modules in different implementation technologies. This way an architecture representation can be deployed with an implementation.

LISA modules contain architectural elements and relations between these elements. Examples for architectural elements are classes, components, ports, connections, layers, features, configurations, and systems. Architectural elements can have assigned attributes, which are a kind of high-level specification of semantics that is necessary for validation and verification of certain system properties. Architectural elements can be bound to implementation artifacts through technology-specific implementation bindings. The synchronization engine of the LISA toolkit uses these implementation bindings for keeping architecture description and implementation synchronized. Synchronization is performed incrementally, at each change to either the architecture description or the implementation.

Following the model described above, design decisions, requirements, and their relations are also architectural elements in our model and are part of LISA architecture modules. This means that requirements and design decisions are captured as first-class elements of the architecture representation.

Fig. 1 shows design decisions and requirements in the context of the LISA approach. The LISA toolkit provides different editors and views on a LISA architecture model. The model can be bound to an implementation. As shown in the figure, requirements and design decisions are captured as part of a LISA architecture model. We will describe later how requirements and design decisions are represented in the LISA model, and how requirements and design decisions can be captured and described. For now, we will focus our description on how requirements and design decisions can be related to other architectural elements of a LISA architecture description. As shown in Fig. 1, the starting point for architectural decisions are usually architecturally significant requirements (ASRs). Architecturally significant requirements are requirements upon a software system, which influence its architecture [19]. Like other requirements on a software system, ASRs are typically captured during requirements analysis. Nuseibeh [18] and Pohl/Sikora [21] point out that it may also make sense to capture requirements incrementally and interleaved with architecture design for certain kinds of systems, particularly for innovative systems. We support both scenarios. We support importing requirements from issue management systems for requirements that have been captured beforehand with other tools. For incremental analysis and design we support capturing requirements and design decisions during design and implementation.

As shown in Fig. 1 requirements may lead to design decisions, which may lead to subsequent design decisions. In fact, design decisions may act as requirements for subsequent decisions, which blurs the line between requirements and design decisions. De Boer and van Vliet [4] discuss the similarity between requirements and architectural design decisions and even state: "architecturally significant requirements are architectural design decisions and vice versa". In our model, requirements and design decisions are both modeled as special kinds of issues. The difference is mainly the kind of description and the source of the issue. Requirements are usually the result of analyzing the problem space, while design

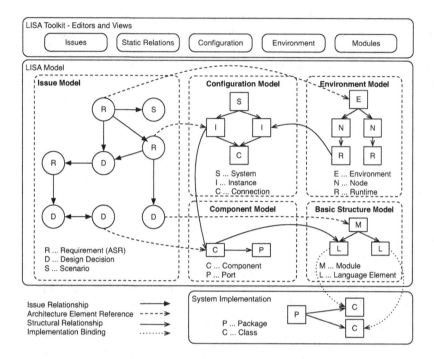

**Fig. 1.** Requirements and Design Decisions in LISA

decisions are the result of exploring the solution space. As can be seen from Fig. 1, design decisions may also uncover new requirements. For this reason, there may exist a directed relationship from design decisions to requirements in our model.

The defined relationships allow comprehensive tracing. As shown in Fig. 1 requirements and design decisions can be traced to other architectural elements, and through implementation bindings, even to potential implementation artifacts. This depth of integration of requirements and design decisons is also reflected in our toolkit, which supplies markers in an implementation indicating requirements and design decisions that would be affected by changing a particular implementation artifact (see Section 4). Implementation artifacts are not only code fragments but also configuration files [6].

Fig. 2 shows in more detail how requirements and design decisions are modelled in our approach. The central abstraction for representing both requirements and design decisions is an architectural issue. Requirements and design decisions are just special kinds of issues. This reflects the close relationship between requirements and design decisions mentioned before. As can be seen from the figure, issue kinds have not been modelled as subclasses but as attributes of the issue class. This has only technical reasons and facilitates changing an issue kind at run-time without compromising already existing dependencies.

Issues have a summary attribute providing a short description of the issue. The summary is essentially the issues logical name. More detailed descriptions and rationale can be provided as part of specific issue kinds. Issues can be architecturally

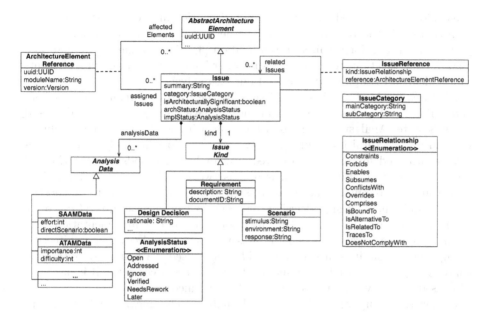

**Fig. 2.** Requirements Sub-Model

significant. We introduced this field because we also support capturing and describing requirements and design decisions that are not architecturally significant - though the focus of our work lies on ASRs and ADDs. Issues can be assigned to a category, which consists of a main category and a sub category. The category can be used for sorting issues and for automatically building a utility tree as provided by the Architecture Tradeoff Analysis Method (ATAM).

All issues support references to related issues and references to affected architectural elements. References to related requirements and design decisions have been identified as an important element of design decisions [25]. As shown in Fig. 2 we support different kinds of relationships, which are essentially modelled after a taxonomy for design decisions and requirements that has been proposed by Kruchten in [17]. Relations are also used for capturing potential alternative decisions. Capturing alternative design decisions is important for preserving architectural knowledge. Van der Ven et al. [26] even define design decisions as "A description of the choice and considered alternatives that (partially) realizes one or more requirements". Dingsøyr and van Vliet [10] also list alternatives as an important element of a design decision. The second kind of reference that is visible in the model are references to architectural elements that are affected by a change of a requirement or a decision. These references are used for tracing and impact analysis as described above.

A third kind of issue shown in Fig. 2 is *Scenario*. A scenario is a special kind of requirement that enforces a specific description. Kazman [15] defines a scenario as "a brief description of a single interaction of the stakeholder with a system". A scenario is similar to a use case but encompasses the interactions of multiple stakeholders as opposed to the user only. Scenarios may encompass many requirements [15] and requirements may be derived from scenarios. Scenarios are particularly useful for architecture evaluation [3]. Since scenarios are a special kind of issue, relations from scenarios to other issues and architectural elements can be defined to support tracing and impact analysis.

All three kinds of architectural issues can be used for architecture analysis and evaluation. For this reason, each issue can have associated analysis data and analysis state. Analysis data is used for associating analysis-specific attributes with an architectural issue, like priority and cost. Specific analysis data types can be provided for different architectural analysis methods like SAAM and ATAM as shown in Fig. 2. Each issue has two kinds of analysis state, since evaluating architectural issues is a two-step process. First, it has to be checked that a requirement, design decision, or scenario has been addressed correctly in the architecture. A second step is used for checking the implementation. The initial state of each issue is "open". If an issue has been addressed in architecture or implementation, its status is changed to "addressed". A manual or automatic analysis step ensures that the issue has been addressed correctly. If it has been addressed correctly, the status is changed to "verified".

Currently we support mainly manual analysis. This means that status updates have to be provided by hand. We are currently working on integrating automated analysis on the basis of configurable rules and predefined architectural knowledge. The aim is to provide a combined approach and to enhance and replace manual analysis through automated analysis where possible.

## 4   Tool Support

Capturing and visualizing architectural issues is supported by the LISA toolkit. The toolkit provides a set of plug-ins that integrates seamlessly with the Eclipse IDE. Editors for defining and visualizing architectural issues are presented in the same environment as other architecture and implementation editors as shown in Fig. 3. The central architecture dashboard shows the modular organization of a LISA-based architecture representation and is depicted in the lower left part of Fig. 3. The main area depicts a form-based editor for capturing information about a particular architectural issue. The lower right part of the figure shows a global or context-specific list of requirements and design decisions, along with issue life-cycle information.

### 4.1   Capturing Architectural Issues

We provide several options for capturing architectural issues. A central aim has been to support capturing as an integrated activity during design and implementation without the need for switching tools. In the following, we briefly describe the supported means for capturing requirements, design decisions, and their relationships.

*Importing Issues from Issue Management Systems.* Requirements that have been defined during requirements analysis and specification can be imported

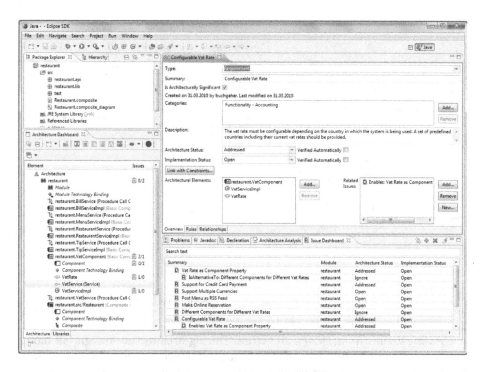

**Fig. 3.** Issue Views and Editors in the LISA toolkit

from issue management systems. We have implemented an import component for
Eclipse *Mylyn*, which acts as a front-end for multiple issue management systems
like JIRA and *Bugzilla*. Currently, only importing requirements is supported. A
synchronization component supporting two-way synchronization between issue
management systems and architecture description is a topic of future work.

*Creating Issues Manually.* Issues can be created and edited using the form-
based editor shown in Fig. 3. The editor is used for manually entering attributes
like summary, description/rationale, and category. It can also be used for explicitly defining relationships between issues and between issues and other architectural elements, like components and modules.

*Defining Relationships.* Relationships can easily be created by dropping related elements onto the corresponding fields in the issue editor. An issue can
also be created directly for an architectural element by selecting the element
and choosing the "create issue" entry from the provided context menu. This implicitly creates a relation between architectural element and issue and eliminates
the need for creating this relationship explicitly. Once an architecture element
has been assigned to an issue - be it a requirement, design decision, or scenario -
the toolkit also automatically proposes relations to other architecture elements
that might be affected by this issue. The proposed elements are determined by
analyzing existing relationships between architecture elements.

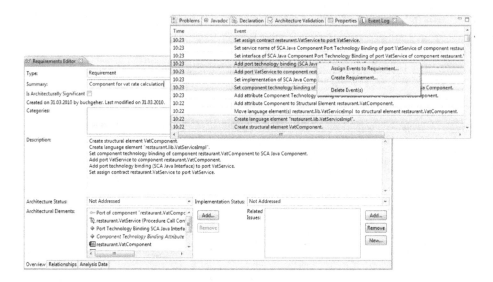

**Fig. 4.** Creating Issues from Design Activity Logs

*Creating Issues from Design Activities.* During architecture design, all modifications of the architecture representation are logged. Log entries contain a description of the modification and a list of the architecture elements that are affected by the modification. New requirements and design decisions can be created from the logged activities as shown in Fig. 4. Information about the logged activities is added as part of the description of the new issue and architectural elements that are part of the performed modifications are automatically associated with the new issue. Information from logged activities can also be added to existing issues.

## 4.2   Visualizing Architectural Issues

Kruchten [16] shows some options for visualizing a set of design decisions, including tables and graphs. Tables lack information about relationships among decisions and graphs may easily become very complex, even for a small set of decisions. For this reason, mechanisms for dealing with this complexity like eliding, filtering, focusing, and sequencing are necessary [16]. In our case, not only design decisions and their relationships are visualized but also requirements, scenarios, and relations to other architecture elements. However, the main challenges of reducing the inherent complexity remain the same. In the following, we provide a short overview of the means for visualizing and editing architectural issues and their relationships in our approach.

*Issue Dashboard.* The issue dashboard (see Fig. 3) shows all issues that have been defined in the architecture description. Issues can be sorted by name, type, containing module or category. It is also possible to search for specific issues (filtering). A global issue list shows for each issue the relationships to other

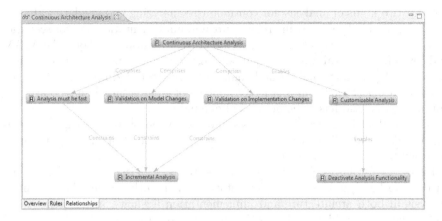

**Fig. 5.** Dependency Graph

issues. The dashboard can also be configured to show only issues for currently selected architecture elements (focusing). When a user selects an architecture element in one of the architecture diagrams, the dashboard shows all issues that have been assigned to this element. New issues can also be created for selected elements and are automatically assigned to the selected element. The dashboard can also be used for changing the analysis status of an issue without opening the editor for this issue.

*Dependency Graph.* The issue editor contains an extra page for visualizing the relationships between issues as a directed graph as shown in Fig. 5. This way it is possible to explore the relationships from the viewpoint of a particular issue (focusing) instead of viewing a global relationship graph.

*Issues as Part of Architecture Diagrams.* Architecture elements that have assigned issues are annotated with a note marker that informs the user that issues have been assigned to that element (see Architecture Dashboard in Fig. 3). The marker also shows the number of assigned issues. Information about the assigned issues is shown as a tool tip.

*Resource Markers.* Issues can be linked to architecture elements. In turn, architecture elements can be bound to implementation artifacts like source and configuration files through implementation bindings. This enables tracing issues to implementation artifacts. Issues that are related to an implementation artifact are shown as markers in implementation editors. For example, markers are shown in source code editors as icons with tool tips and inform developers about requirements and design decisions that apply to the currently edited implementation.

### 4.3   Analyzing Architectural Issues

Architectural issues are also the basis for certain kinds of architectural analysis. We mentioned in Section 2 that we integrate multiple approaches for architecture analysis in one consistent environment. Analysis of architectural issues is typically used for two kinds of analysis: for continuously analyzing and validating that issues are addressed correctly in architecture and implementation and for scenario-based architecture evaluation using architecture evaluation methods like ATAM and SAAM. In general, we aim at supporting incremental and continuous analysis. While dependency analysis and analysis of architecture/implementation conformance are performed automatically, analysis of architectural issues is currently not automated and has to be performed manually.

As described in Section 3, analysis and validation of architectural issues is supported through life-cycle attributes and through analysis data that can be attached to architectural issues.

Life-cycle attributes indicate the analysis status of an issue in the architecture on the one hand and in the implementation on the other hand. The status of analysis in both architecture and implementation is shown in the issue editor and in the issue dashboard. Issues that have not been addressed and issues that have not been addressed correctly are visualized as architecture problems in the architecture diagrams provided by the LISA toolkit.

Analysis data is used for supporting particular architecture evaluation methods. Analysis data can be captured in separate panes for each issue. Additional views can be added for method-specific visualizations. For example, for ATAM we support capturing importance and difficulty, which are used for prioritizing scenarios. The architecture utility tree can be generated automatically based on the defined scenarios and their categories. We also support partly automated analysis like the detection of possible sensitivity and tradeoff points by analyzing architecture elements that have multiple scenarios assigned.

We are currently working on support for automatic analysis of architectural issues on the basis of user-defined element attributes and constraints. The main idea is to support a user in defining issue-specific validation criteria using role-attributes that are assigned to architectural elements.

## 5   Validation

The benefit of connecting requirements, design decisions, solution structures, and implementation, has been argued widely and is also shown in several approaches and case studies (see section on related work). Main questions that remain are how the required information is captured efficiently and how the captured information can be made easily accessible. We view the main contribution of our approach in reducing the overhead of capturing architectural knowledge and the required relations through integration in one consistent model and environment and in ensuring the consistency of architectural knowledge, representation, and implementation. Therefore, the main aim of validation has been to check the usefulness and usability of the presented approach in practice.

In order to validate the approach we used LISA in a small industrial project for the development of a medical information system. The project was scheduled for one and a half person years, included three developers, and followed a SCRUM/XP process. At the beginning of the project we briefed the users (developers, project leader/architect) in using the toolkit. We gave an overview of the provided functionality and its intended use. We focused on the supported means for capturing and analyzing requirements and design decisions. We also supported the users during the development process by answering their questions. In order to collect relevant information we observed the usage of LISA with a dedicated monitoring plug-in that logged user interactions in terms of issues captured, including capturing time and owner. Additionally, we conducted interviews with the users to find out about their experiences and the perceived usefulness of our approach. Finally, we reviewed the created architecture description to determine the kind of information captured by users.

*Findings.* Initially developers had reservations regarding the usefulness of our approach. A particular concern was the additional effort involved in capturing requirements and design decisions. This applied especially for requirements that had already been specified in a separate requirements document. After using the tool for some time this attitude changed and parts of our approach were considered useful. The central benefit perceived was the linking of issues to architecture elements. Capturing requirements and design decisions gave additional meaning to architecture elements. It turned out that users often captured requirements after they had created corresponding architecture elements.

The users doubted the usefulness of defining relationships between issues. Even more, they did not see any benefit from specifying these relationships. They also did not understand the different relationship kinds. One user complained that there "are too many of them and one does not know which to choose". Analyzing the captured requirements and their relationships revealed that primarily functional requirements had been captured. Relationships were typically used for splitting coarse-grained requirements into multiple smaller requirements. In addition, users were unsure about the difference between requirements and design decisions.

*What was good?* The users particularly liked the seamless integration into the IDE, which facilitated the capturing of requirements and design decisions (as well as the creation and maintenance of the entire architecture description). The issue editor was perceived similar to existing issue management systems, which raised its acceptance among the project team. The general usability of the toolkit was perceived as good with some space for future improvements.

*What needs to be improved?* The users asked us to provide additional diagrams for visualizing and analyzing the relationships between issues and architecture elements. Particularly they asked for a diagram showing which architecture elements are affected by a set of issues. Currently we only support tracing from one issue to related elements. The users missed additional fields for defining references to other artifacts like existing requirement documents, project guidelines and issues/bugs-ids.

*Observations of the research team.* IDE integration and traceability from requirements to architectural artifacts have been viewed as the main benefit by the users in the conducted case study. Despite our efforts in reducing the overhead in capturing information, users neglected the knowledge management features. We attribute this mainly to the lack of immediately perceived value in capturing this information. We think that additional research in making these benefits more clearly might raise the acceptance for such an approach. The support for architecture analysis has not been examined in the described case study.

# 6 Related Work

Our work combines aspects of architecture description languages (ADLs), software architecture management tools (AMTs), and of tools for software architecture knowledge management (AKM).

ADLs and AMTs focus on automatic architecture analysis. Typical ADL-based approaches lack the level of implementation and IDE integration that is provided in our approach [6]. AMTs provide this integration, but they lack higher-level architectural abstractions and support for analyzing particular quality attributes as supported by ADLs. Representatives of both approaches usually provide no support for capturing and managing requirements and design decisions. The main topics presented in this paper, i.e., capturing and managing requirements and design decisions, support for tracing and impact analysis, and support for scenario-based architecture analysis and architecture evaluation are usually offered by architecture knowledge management tools. A variety of AKM tools exist. Most of them are research prototypes.

PAKME [1] is a web based architecture knowledge management tool, which supports capturing of design decisions and scenarios. It also supports scenario-based architecture analysis. Contrary to our approach, requirements and design decisions are managed independently from architecture representation. Also, PAKME provides no integration with other kinds of analysis and is not integrated in an IDE. The lack of integration leads to overhead for capturing and keeping captured information synchronized with architecture description and implementation. The additional workload through duplication of requirements has been identified as potential problem in using PAKME [2].

Archium [14] also integrates design decisions with architecture description and implementation. Aside from capturing design decisions as first-class entities to prevent knowledge vaporization, the approach also aims at keeping architecture and architectural knowledge consistent during system evolution. This is achieved by integrating a design decision model, an ADL-like architecture model, a composition model, and an implementation in one language (an extension to Java). Archium provides a textual representation, a compiler and a runtime system. This is already an important difference to our approach, which binds and synchronizes an architecture model with an implementation but is independent from particular implementation technologies and run-time systems. From a conceptual viewpoint Archium takes current definitions of software architecture literally; it requires designing software systems by composing design decisions and thus requires a new way of thinking during design. We integrate design decisions differently. Rather than composing a design from design decisions, we bind design decisions to design solutions. Support for architectural analysis and IDE integration as supported in our approach is not available in Archium.

SEURAT [8] is an approach for rationale management in software development, which also provides integration in the Eclipse IDE. Rationale is captured in a semi-formal representation (RATSpeak), which supports the description of decisions, alternatives, and relations to requirements and implementation. The approach supports traceability from requirements and decisions to code. Contrary to our approach, SEURAT provides no architecture representation but connects rationale directly with source code. The authors mention integration with UML as a topic of future work to support rationale management in other software development phases.

AREL [22,24] is an extension to UML. It adds stereotypes for representing architecture elements (AE) and architecture rationale (AR) to UML diagrams. This way rationale and relations to architectural elements are directly modeled in UML using a standard UML tool. Forward and backward traceability is supported through an additional tool, which is implemented in .NET. AREL lacks the deep integration of support for architectural knowledge management into development and design tools that is supported by our approach. This is mainly due to the use of a standard UML tool ([23] p. 201). Also, the combination of architectural knowledge with architectural analysis and validation is not provided.

## 7   Conclusion

Our approach integrates requirements and architecture design decisions with single consistent architecture representation, the LISA model. A LISA architecture model is continuously checked for consistency and supports continuous synchronization with a potential system implementation. Therefore, the approach supports consistency of the captured requirements and decisions with architectural structures and implementation. Support for consistency is important in wake of incremental development and system evolution. The approach also supports forward and backward tracing from requirements to architecture and implementation and vice versa. We aimed at reducing the overhead in capturing architectural knowledge through IDE integration, through support for defining issue relations by capturing information from design activities, and by suggesting additional relations on the basis of existing ones. Visualization of architectural issues is supported through specific views with support for focusing and filtering. Architectural issues are also presented in other views on architecture and implementation creating an ongoing awareness of related requirements and design decisions during design and development. We have also integrated support for analysis and validation of captured architectural issues and for scenario-based architecture evaluation in our model and toolset. Finally, we have conducted a case study for validating the approach in an industrial project. Integration of architectural issues with architecture representation and implementation and the support for tracing have been well received. Other knowledge management features, like capturing more complex relations between architectural issues, failed to show immediate value to users of the approach. Making the benefits of particular relations more explicit is a necessity for raising the acceptance of such an approach.

# References

1. Babar, M.A., Gorton, I.: A tool for managing software architecture knowledge. In: SHARK-ADI 2007: Proceedings of the Second Workshop on SHAring and Reusing Architectural Knowledge Architecture, Rationale, and Design Intent, p. 11+. IEEE Computer Society, Washington (2007)
2. Babar, M.A., Northway, A., Gorton, I., Heuer, P., Nguyen, T.: Introducing tool support for managing architectural knowledge: An experience report. In: IEEE International Conference on the Engineering of Computer-Based Systems, vol. 1, pp. 105–113. IEEE, Los Alamitos (2008)
3. Babar, M.A., Zhu, L., Jeffery, R.: A framework for classifying and comparing software architecture evaluation methods. In: ASWEC 2004: Proceedings of the 2004 Australian Software Engineering Conference, p. 309+. IEEE Computer Society, Washington (2004)
4. de Boer, R., van Vliet, H.: On the similarity between requirements and architecture. Journal of Systems and Software (November 2008)
5. Bosch, J.: Software architecture: The next step. In: Oquendo, F., Warboys, B.C., Morrison, R. (eds.) EWSA 2004. LNCS, vol. 3047, pp. 194–199. Springer, Heidelberg (2004)
6. Buchgeher, G., Weinreich, R.: Connecting architecture and implementation. In: Meersman, R., Herrero, P., Dillon, T. (eds.) OTM 2009 Workshops. LNCS, vol. 5872, pp. 316–326. Springer, Heidelberg (2009)
7. Buchgeher, G., Weinreich, R.: Software Architecture Engineering. In: Buchberger, et al. (eds.) Hagenberg Research, pp. 200–214. Springer, Heidelberg (2009)
8. Burge, J.E., Brown, D.C.: Seurat: integrated rationale management. In: ICSE 2008: Proceedings of the 30th international conference on Software engineering, pp. 835–838. ACM, New York (2008)
9. Dashofy, E.M., van der Hoek, A., Taylor, R.N.: A comprehensive approach for the development of modular software architecture description languages. ACM Trans. Softw. Eng. Methodol. 14(2), 199–245 (2005)
10. Dingsøyr, T., Vliet, H.: Introduction to software architecture and knowledge management. In: Ali Babar, M., Dingsøyr, T., Lago, P., Vliet, H. (eds.) Software Architecture Knowledge Management, ch. 1, pp. 1–17. Springer, Heidelberg (2009)
11. Dutoit, A.H., McCall, R., Mistrík, I., Paech, B. (eds.): Rationale Management in Software Engineering: Concepts and Techniques. Springer, Heidelberg (2006)
12. Farenhorst, R., Boer, R.C.: Knowledge management in software architecture: State of the art. In: Ali Babar, M., Dingsøyr, T., Lago, P., Vliet, H. (eds.) Software Architecture Knowledge Management, ch. 2, pp. 21–38. Springer, Heidelberg (2009)
13. van Gurp, J., Bosch, J.: Design erosion: problems and causes. Journal of Systems and Software 61(2), 105–119 (2002)
14. Jansen, A., Bosch, J.: Software architecture as a set of architectural design decisions. In: 5th Working IEEE/IFIP Conference on Software Architecture, WICSA 2005, pp. 109–120. IEEE Computer Society, Washington (2005)
15. Kazman, R., Carrière, S., Woods, S.: Toward a discipline of scenario based architectural engineering. Annals of Software Engineering 9(1), 5–33 (2000)
16. Kruchten, P.: Documentation of software architecture from a knowledge management perspective design representation. In: Ali Babar, M., Dingsøyr, T., Lago, P., Vliet, H. (eds.) Software Architecture Knowledge Management, ch. 3, pp. 39–57. Springer, Heidelberg (2009)

17. Krutchen, P.: An ontology of architectural design decisions in software intensive systems. In: 2nd Groningen Workshop Software Variability, October 2004, pp. 54–61 (2004)
18. Nuseibeh, B.: Weaving together requirements and architectures. Computer 34(3), 115–117 (2001)
19. Obbink, H., Kruchten, P., Kozaczynski, W., Hilliard, R., Ran, A., Postema, H., Lutz, D., Kazman, R., Tracz, W., Kahane, E.: Report on software architecture review and assessment, SARA (2002)
20. Perry, D.E., Wolf, A.L.: Foundations for the study of software architecture. SIG-SOFT Softw. Eng. Notes 17(4), 40–52 (1992)
21. Pohl, K., Sikora, E.: COSMOD-RE: Supporting the co-design of requirements and architectural artifacts. In: IEEE International Conference on Requirements Engineering, pp. 258–261 (2007)
22. Tang, A., Jin, Y., Han, J.: A rationale-based architecture model for design traceability and reasoning. Journal of Systems and Software 80(6), 918–934 (2007)
23. Tang, A.: A rationale-based model for architecture design reasoning. Ph.D. thesis (2007)
24. Tang, A., Han, J., Vasa, R.: Software architecture design reasoning: A case for improved methodology support. IEEE Software 26(2), 43–49 (2009)
25. Tyree, J., Akerman, A.: Architecture decisions: Demystifying architecture. IEEE Software 22(2), 19–27 (2005)
26. van der Ven, J., Jansen, A., Nijhuis, J., Bosch, J.: Design decisions: The bridge between rationale and architecture. In: Dutoit, A.H., McCall, R., Mistrík, I., Paech, B. (eds.) Rationale Management in Software Engineering, ch. 16, pp. 329–348. Springer, Heidelberg (2006)
27. Weinreich, R., Buchgeher, G.: Paving the road for formally defined architecture description in software development. In: 25th ACM Symposium on Applied Computing (SAC), Sierre, Switzerland, March 22-26. ACM, New York (2010)

# Flexible *Working Architectures*: Agile Architecting Using PPCs

Jennifer Pérez, Jessica Díaz, Juan Garbajosa, and Pedro P. Alarcón

Technical University of Madrid (UPM), E.U. Informática, Madrid, Spain
jenifer.perez@eui.upm.es, yesica.diaz@upm.es,
{jgs,pedrop.alarcon}@eui.upm.es

**Abstract.** Software systems need software architectures to improve their scalability and maintenance. However, many agile practitioners claim that the upfront design of software architectures is an investment that does not pay off, since customers can rarely appreciate the value delivered by architectures. Furthermore, conventional architectural practices may be considered unacceptable from the Agile values and principles perspective. In this paper, the development of *working architectures* in agile iterations is presented as an attempt to solve the problem of designing software architectures in Agile. This contribution is based on the new concept of Plastic Partial Component (PPC). PPCs are highly malleable components that can be partially described, what increases the flexibility of architecture design. PPCs based architectures let reinforce some of the agile values and principles. Our experience of putting this contribution into practice is illustrated through the agile development of a Testing Framework for Biogas Plants.

## 1 Introduction

It is a well accepted fact in Software Engineering that architectures make software systems simpler and more understandable. Software architectures describe the structure of a software system by hiding the low-level details and abstracting the high level important features [1]. Software architectures also accommodate non-functional requirements. The design, specification, and analysis of the structure of software-intensive systems have become critical issues in software development [2]. As a result, software architectures emerged as a solution for the design and development of large and complex software systems.

The Agile Manifesto [3] is the basis of agile methodologies. It establishes the following two principles: *"Working software is the primary measure of progress"* and *"Delivering working software frequently, from a couple of weeks to a couple of months, with a preference to the shorter timescale"*. These two agile principles imply that, the limited time that the development of a *working product* takes the developers, should be mostly invested in coding to satisfy the delivery deadline. Therefore, agile practitioners often consider that the upfront design and definition of software architectures is an investment in time and effort that is not paid off.

M. Ali Babar and I. Gorton (Eds.): ECSA 2010, LNCS 6285, pp. 102–117, 2010.

Literature is full of references that advocates against architecture in Agile, as customers rarely can appreciate the value that architecture delivers. A common belief is that *"If you are sufficiently agile, you don't need an architecture - you can always refactor it on the fly"*. However, it has been argued that an inaccurate architectural design leads to the failure of large software systems and large refactoring might create significant defects [4]. As it is illustrated by Dybå and Dingsøyr in [5], several authors advocate that the lack of focus on architecture is bound to engender suboptimal design-decisions. This lack is in contradiction with an Agile principle that establishes that *"Continuous attention to technical excellence and good design enhances agility"*. In addition, according to Babar and Abrahamsson [6] software architectures may be also essential to improve and scale up *Agile Software Development*[1] in large software-intensive systems. Cockburn [7] claims that the issue with architecture in Agile is not either *architecture yes* or *architecture no*: he thinks that the issue is how much effort should be invested in architecture, assuming that (architecture) practices can be valuable for the customer. Kruchten concludes in [8] that in software architectures there are cost and value, also for agile. Then, the key question is: *"Are we able to avoid the obstacles that hamper agile practitioners to design software architectures without renouncing their values and principles?"*. There are some works [7,8,9,10,11] that intend to harmonize Agile and architecture by outlining high level approaches or organizational guidelines, but do not provide specific techniques or practices to design architectures that favor agile values and principles. Our understanding is that having flexibility at the time of defining software architectures is essential, so that, practices can be aligned with Agile values and principles.

In this paper, we deal with the problem of designing software architectures in Agile. From the wide-scope of tasks that software architectures comprise: (i) to analyze and describe the properties of systems at a high level of abstraction; (ii) to validate software requirements; (iii) to estimate the cost of the development and maintenance processes; (iv) to reuse software; and (v) to establish the bases and guidelines for the design of large complex software systems [1]. Our contribution is focused on the structural viewpoint of software architectures, i.e. the description of software architectures.

We present our experience using *Plastic Partial Components* (PPCs) [12] to specify software architectures in an Agile context. A Plastic Partial Component (PPC) is a new concept to support internal variation of architectural components by hooking *crosscutting* and *non-crosscutting* concerns (*aspects* and *features*) that are unaware of the linking context. Despite the fact that PPCs were originally defined for Software Product Lines (SPLs) [13], we have taken advantage of their extension mechanisms for designing software architectures in Agile. Using PPCs, architectural components can be iteratively and incrementally developed in each iteration and, by extension, the software architecture that they make up. This architecture is incrementally and iteratively designed in each iteration by adding/removing: (i) aspects and/or features to/from its PPCs, and (ii) components and connections to/from the architecture. From this proposal, a new concept in

---

[1] In this article we will use the term Agile representing Agile Software Development.

software architectures emerges, called *working architecture*. A *working architecture* is the architecture that is obtained along with each *working product* in each agile iteration. We illustrate our proposal of using PPCs in Agile through our experience of developing a framework, in cooperation with industrial partners, for monitoring, testing and operating biogas power production plants.

It is necessary to emphasize that our contribution is focused on the structural viewpoint of software architecture, i.e. the description of software architectures. Software architectures address: (i) the description of systems properties at a high level of abstraction; (ii) validation of software requirements; (iii) estimation of the cost of the development and maintenance processes; (iv) software reusability; and (v) establish the bases and guidelines for the design of large complex software systems [1].

The structure of the paper is as follows: Section 2 introduces the main notions of agile and PPCs. In addition, it explains the agile methodology SCRUM. Section 3 discusses related works about software architecture practices in Agile. Section 4 explains why and how PPCs fit for use with Agile. It also explains our proposal about how to specify *working architectures*. Section 5 presents a case study that is used to illustrate our contribution, and exemplifies the use of PPCs in Agile. Finally, conclusions and further work are presented in section 6.

## 2    Background

### 2.1    Agile Software Development

Agility is just an umbrella term for a variety of methods structured into values, principles and practices, with a common reference in the Agile Manifesto [3]. Shore et al. [14] define *values* as ideals, *principles* as the application of these ideals to the industry, and *practices* as principles applied to a specific type of project. The relevance of values and principles is increasing as long as large organizations are requiring their application [15]. Some of these agile principles are: *customer satisfaction through early and continuous delivery of valuable software*; *continuous attention to technical excellence*; or *welcome changing requirements, even late in development*. Some common Agile methods are eXtreme Programming (XP) [16], Lean Development [17], and Scrum [18], the one used within this work.

Scrum implements an iterative and incremental life cycle (see Figure 1). Three roles, the *Product Owner*, *Team*, and *ScrumMaster* make up all together the *Scrum Team* [18]. The Product Owner represents the key stakeholder interests. The Team is in charge of developing the product functionality and the customer is often a membership of the team. The Scrum process is responsibility of the ScrumMaster. Requirements are captured as User Stories (USs) by the customer together with the rest of the Scrum Team members during the *pre-game phase*, at the beginning of the project. The list of USs is stored in the *product backlog*. Later on in the process, USs are prioritized and divided into short time-framed iterations called *sprints*. A sprint is a 2-4 weeks period of development time. The scope and *goals* of each sprint are agreed at its beginning by the Product Owner

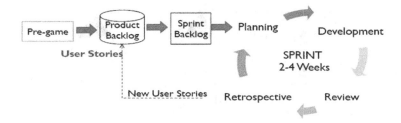

**Fig. 1.** Scrum Lifecycle

and the Team at the *sprint planning meeting*. The output from this meeting is stored in the *sprint backlog*. Each sprint should deliver a valuable increment of the final product functionality. During the execution of each sprint, the Team will *meet daily* in a 15-minute meeting to track work progress. At the end of each sprint, the *sprint review* and *retrospective* meetings will be held. In the sprint review meeting the Product Owner will communicate whether goals were met, and might introduce changes into the USs. In the retrospective meeting the Team and ScrumMaster discuss what went well, and what could be improved for the next sprint, and works as an estimation and tracking activity to put into practice continuous improvement.

### 2.2   An Overview of Plastic Partial Components (PPCs)

The notion of *Plastic Partial Component (PPC)*[2] was originally defined for Software Product Lines Engineering (SPLE) [13]. SPLE adoption requires explicitly to specify the commonalities and variabilities of SPLs at the architectural level. This implies not only to specify variants for modifying the configuration of software architectures, but also to define variations inside components. PPCs are a solution to support the internal variation of architectural components.

PPCs variability mechanisms are based on Invasive Software Composition Principles [19]. Invasive Software Composition defines components as fragment boxes that hook a set of reusable fragments of code. Specifically, these fragments of reusable code can be aspects making components easier to be maintained and by extension software architectures. The variability of a PPC is specified using *variability points*, which hook fragments of code to the PPC. These fragments of code are specific features of a software product, which can crosscut the software architecture or not. For this reason, we classified these features into: *crosscutting-features* and *non-crosscutting-features*. A *crosscutting-feature* is a common feature of the software architecture, which is encapsulated into a separate entity called *aspect*. Whereas, a *non-crosscutting-feature* is the specific functionality of a component, which is encapsulated into a separate entity called *feature*. Therefore, variability points can hook *aspects* or *features* to the PPC. A PPC is defined by specifying: (i) its variability points; (ii) the aspects and/or

---

[2] This section presents just an overview of PPCs. A broader description with additional references to literature sources can be found in [12].

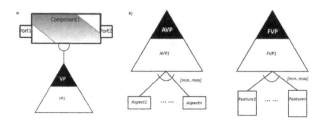

**Fig. 2.** a) Linking Plastic Partial Components and Variability Points. b) Variability Points and Variations (Aspects and Features).

features that are necessary to complete the definition of the component for any software product; and (iii) the hooks between the variability points and the aspects and/or features. As a result, the complete definition of a PPC for a specific product is done by means of the selection of aspects and/or features through the variability points.

A PPC is a specialization of a component and inherits all the properties and behavior of a component. A PPC is characterized by the definition of a set of variability points, i.e. the place where the different variants are hooked to the PPC (see Figure 2.a). A ***variability point*** of a PPC is characterized by three properties: (i) the kind of variation, (ii) the type of variability point depending on the variants that it offers to be selected (i.e. crosscutting or non-crosscutting features), and (iii) the weaving between variants and the component.

The *kind of variation* is based on the variability management of software architectures that Bachmann and Bass set out [20]. This property is provided to support variability, and it defines the number of variants of a product family that must be selected (*mandatory*) or can be selected (*optional*) for developing a specific product of the family. The kind of variation is specified as cardinality (0..1, 1..1, 0..n, 1..n, m..n).

There are two *types of variability points* (see Figure 2.b): (i) those that permit the selection of variants that are *crosscutting-features* (*aspects*); (ii) and those that permit the selection of variants that are *non-crosscutting features* (*features*). An *Aspect Variability Point (AVP)* can only offer aspects to be selected; and a *Feature Variability Point (FVP)* can only offer features to be selected. It is important to emphasize that both aspects and features can be linked to more than one variability point to facilitate reuse.

Variability points allow us to specify the *weaving* between the PPC and the variant. The weaving principles of Aspect-Oriented Programming (AOP)[21] provide the needed functionality to specify *where* and *when* extending the PPCs using variants. Therefore, AOP weaving primitives (*pointcuts, weavings* and *aspects*) are applied to weave a PPC with both, aspects and features. The *pointcut* definition consists of defining *where* to insert the code of the variant. An example of pointcut could be calling a service that the PPC provides. The definition of the *weaving operator* consists of establishing *when* to insert the code of the variant with regard to the pointcut: *before*, *after* or *instead of* (around). In our proposal, it will be before, after or insteadOf the call of the service of the PPC. Thereby, the PPC, the pointcut, the weaving operator and the variant are the elements that define a *weaving*.

However, there are some differences between our definition of aspects and weavings and those AOP provides. In our proposal, the pointcut and the weaving operator are specified outside the aspects and features, and inside variability points. As a result, unlike AOP, our aspects and features are unaware of the linking context, and they are completely reusable.

The description of working architectures using PPCs is supported by a graphical modeling tool called Flexible-PLA. Flexible-PLA has been developed following the MDD approach [22,23] to take advantage of its metamodel definition and its corresponding graphical metaphor [12]. It has been automatically generated from the metamodel and the graphical metaphor. It was possible because they were specified using the Eclipse Modeling Framework (EMF) and its Graphical Modeling Framework(GMF) [24]. As a result, Flexible-PLA is an open-source tool that is available for the research community.

## 3    Related Work

To make come true agile software architectures, it is necessary: (i) to provide mechanisms to flexibly describe them and (ii) to define how they should be designed throughout the Agile software life cycle, i.e, how to perform agile architecting. In any case, Agile values and principles should be respected.

On the one hand, with regard to software architecture description, Scott Ambler in [25] proposes a model based on views and concerns for designing software architectures in Agile. We take a step forward and define a specific formalism to systematically introduce crosscutting and non-crosscutting features in the Agile Software Development of architectures. This is due to the fact that we realized that it is necessary to be flexible enough for supporting not only *external changes* (modification of the architectural configuration by adding or removing components or connections), but also *internal changes* (modification inside components). It is important to keep in mind that these internal changes must preserve abstraction and encapsulation (black boxes) of software architectures and Agile flexibility requirements. So, internal changes are treated as crosscutting and non-crosscutting features that are easily added and removed to/from agile software architectures.

On the other hand, with regard to agile architecting, one of the main Agile issues is to improve the scalability of their products by designing their software architectures. Several proposals have been outlined to fix this issue [9,10,11]. Most of them agree with the idea that Agile should incorporate architectural information when it is applied to develop large-scale software-intensive systems. However, the proposed approaches are rather "high-level". Cockburn [7] proposes to start with a simple architecture that handles all the *big rocks*. Then, it can be evolved or refactored as other requirements appear; but it should not be an objective to get the architecture at the end of the project. Boehm and Turner [9] recognize that hybrid approaches to balance agile and plan-driven approaches are necessary; McMahon [10] recommends employing in agile architectures two levels. The first level develops a high-level agile architecture including the major system components, assumptions, and a brief description of each component. The second level focuses on the high-risk areas for each iteration (big rocks). M. Ali Babar et al. [11] analyze the role of the architecture in Agile through a case study by integrating software product lines and agile practices, and carry out a description of the organizational processes. All these works recognize and recommend the role of architectures in Agile but the practices they provide are rather general.

From our point of view, it is not necessary to create new mechanisms from scratch to design software architectures in Agile. We can adopt existing mechanisms that assists architects to flexibly develop software architectures. This flexibility can be obtained from mechanisms that allow us to specify variability. Agile methodologies can take advantage of variability mechanisms to flexibly adapt software architectures and to incrementally develop them together with the working product. In fact, our proposal uses PPCs [12] to incrementally design software architectures in Agile.

## 4   Flexible Working Architectures

Agile establishes an iterative and incremental software development, in which iterations are short time-framed and always deliver valuable software (*working product*). When Agile Methodologies are applied to develop large-software intensive systems, software architectures are required to scale their working and final products. Software architectures bridge the gap between requirements and implementation [1], and by extension between USs and the implementation. Therefore, mechanisms for designing flexible architectures along with the working product in each agile iteration are required to deal with the obstacles that hamper agile practitioner to design software architectures. These mechanisms must support for easily adding/removing components and connections (external variation) and adding/removing features and aspects inside components (internal variation), considering variation like incremental steps in software development. These assumptions and PPCs are the base of our proposal for developing software products in Agile by designing their software architectures and preserving the Agile values and principles. In this section, it is explained how PPCs can help us to flexibly build *working architectures* throughout the ASD life cycle.

### 4.1   Plastic Partial Components in Agile

PPCs variability mechanisms are successfully applied to SPLs to support internal variation of architectural components among the products of a SPL. However, in Agile, variability mechanisms are not used to define variations (aspects and features) among products. On the contrary, they are used to flexibly add, remove and modify aspects and/or features throughout the iterations of an Agile lifecycle. Variability mechanisms behave as extensibility mechanisms to flexibly compose pieces (aspects, features, components) of software as if we were building a puzzle. As a result, PPCs get closer and closer to customer needs by means of specifying the aspects and features only when they are strictly required by a working product. From the PPC definition it is possible to conclude that PPCs facilitate to meet the agile principle and values:

- **Partial:** PPCs are Partial because they can be incompletely specified. They can be *working components* delivered and refined each iteration as part of the working product. Therefore, PPCs allow us to incrementally develop architectural components by only taking into account the required functionality for each iteration, and to construct them in time to the working product.
- **Plastic:** PPCs are Plastic because they are highly malleable. This is thanks to their extensibility mechanisms, which allow us to flexibly adapt software components by easily adding or removing fragments of code. As a result, they are ready to be extended or modified at any moment.

PPCs are always composed of *mandatory* aspects or features and every variability point of a PPC is either *mandatory and unique* or *mandatory multiple and multiple*. In agile, aspects and features of PPCs are mandatory unless they will be removed over iterations. So, the kinds of variation are constrained to the following cardinalities:

- 1..1: *mandatory and unique:* it is mandatory to select the unique aspect or feature of the variability point.
- m..n: *mandatory and multiple:* variability point is not used in Agile as a point of decision, therefore it is mandatory to select the multiple features or aspects of the variability point. For this reason, the number of selections m is equals to the number of variants n, and the cardinality is n..n.

Therefore, when PPCs are applied in Agile, the two types of variability points are characterized by the kind of addition, update or deletion, not by the kind of selection that performs. An *Aspect Variability Point (AVP)* can only add, modify or remove aspects; and a *Feature Variability Point (FVP)* can only add, modify or remove features.

## 4.2 Agile Architecting

In this section, we present our experience of applying PPCs in Agile. In our proposal, all the components of the architecture are PPCs, that are incrementally developed in time to the working product. They constitute the new concept of *working architecture*. A working architecture is the architecture that is iteratively and incrementally designed together with the working product. This idea was also proposed in [26,27,28] as continuous architecting. Continuous architecting allow us to tackle architecture degradation and keep the system in sync with changing conditions. In addition, successful agile architecting requires to define the role of the architect in an Agile team. The *architecture team* is part of the Agile team and interacts with the rest of members at the making-decision process by tracking architectural concerns and balancing them with business priorities.

Thereby, architecture can also support one of the agile values, communication [29]. Next, from our experience we explain how to develop agile *working architectures* using PPCs. We make a distinction between the first performed iteration and the others.

### – First Iteration

Once the architecture team, the development team, and the customer have defined the USs of the software product, the customer selects the USs for being developed in the first iteration. This selection is performed taking into account the priorities of the customer and the advice and recommendations of the development and architecture teams. Next, the development and architecture teams can start the architecture design and implementation of the selected USs. Before implementing USs, it is important to analyze them to identify *candidate components* for a *working architecture* of the working product. Whereas traditional software development classifies requirements into functional and non-functional, Agile does not make this distinction in USs. In fact, most USs are related to functional requirements due to the fact that they are those requirements that the customer perceives as the result he/she requires. However, it often happens that non-functional requirements, such as distribution or security, have to be implicitly considered and implemented to meet the functional requirements, i.e. customer needs. As a result, the architecture team must keep in mind non-functional requirements to identify them in the USs. In consequence, we understand that the architecture team must analyze USs to identify:

1. *PPCs:* Units of basic functionality, also known as major software components [10]. They are *candidate components* of the software architecture of the working product. They make up the *working architecture*.
2. *Features:* Features represent *non-crosscutting features* (see section 2.2). They are usually functional requirements that are not relevant enough for being major software components. They constitute additional functionality of the final product, which is susceptible of being removed over time. Thus, they are part of the functionality that a PPC provides.
3. *Aspects:* Aspects represent *crosscutting features* (see section 2.2). They are usually non-functional requirements. They are part of the functionality that one or more PPCs provide.
4. *Architectural Connections*: Connections to coordinate PPCs and configure a working architecture.

From this iteration, a first version of the *working architecture* is obtained.

### – Subsequent Iterations

As in the first iteration, the customer, the architecture and development teams select the USs that are going to be developed during the current iteration. However, in this case the selection can be also guided and supported by the *working architecture* obtained from the previous iteration. This is due to the fact that software architectures not only can help us study the feasibility of the development of software systems, but also can help us determine which requirements are reasonable and viable [30], and by extension which USs could be selected. There are different criteria of selection that can be assisted by the architecture knowledge such as scalability, reusability or the impact of changes. Therefore, the knowledge of a *working architecture* is a value which may enrich the agile process.

Once the customer, architecture and development teams have selected the USs for the iteration, the architecture and development teams can start the architecture design and implementation of the selected USs as in the first iteration. Finally, after completing the last iteration, a *final software architecture* is obtained as part of the *final product*.

It is important to emphasize that the unique difference among the first iteration and the rest of them is the fact that the first iteration starts from scratch the software architecture. We do not define a ZFR (Zero Feature Release) where the customer does not participate as other approaches propose [16,10]. We consider that the investment of time and cost in this ZFR does not guarantee that the decisions taken will be definitive and the ZFR architecture will be preserved. So, our first iteration is just one more, where the customer participates. In each iteration, PPCs, Aspects, Features or Connections from the software architecture are updated, added and removed in a flexible way and without any restriction.

### 4.3 Analysis of PPCs and *Working Architectures* from the Agile Perspective

PPCs facilitate to meet the agile principles and values and to carry out some of the agile practices. PPCs and *working architectures* match with the four agile values: (i) *Individuals and interactions over processes and tools*: The architecture team is part of the Agile team and participates in its meetings; (ii) *Working software over comprehensive documentation*: PPCs are part of a working architecture, which is software that is delivered in each working product; (iii) *Customer collaboration over contract negotiation*: The architecture team interacts with the customer throughout the agile process; and (iv) *Responding to change over following a plan*: PPCs easily accept changes by adding or removing features and/or aspects and they are connected between them to configure working architectures.

With regard to the twelve agile principles, next we detail those that could be enriched with our proposal.

- *(P1). Our highest priority is to satisfy the customer through early and continuous delivery of valuable software*: PPCs help get closer and closer to customer needs over iterations, and by extension the working architecture.
- *(P2). Welcome changing requirements, even late in development. Agile processes harness change for the customer's competitive advantage*: PPCs are plastic. They are ready to be extended or modified at any moment.
- *(P3). Deliver working software frequently, from a couple of weeks to a couple of months, with a preference to the shorter timescale*: Working architectures are part of the delivery.

- *(P4). The most efficient and effective method of conveying information to and within a development team is face-to-face conversation*: The architecture team participates in every meeting of the project and is welcome to the new customer needs. The architecture team shares architectural information among its members and with all others in every scheduled meeting. The architecture team is open minded to the changes that their feedback may imply. This is thanks to the adaptation facilities that PPCs and working architectures provide.
- *(P5). Working software is the primary measure of progress*: the working architecture is part of the working software that is delivered in each iteration.
- *(P6). Continuous attention to technical excellence and good design enhances agility*: PPCs supports to intuitively modularize and scale software by using its variability mechanisms, which can be advantageously used for adding or removing pieces of software throughout the different iterations that comprise the development of a working product. In addition, PPCs help us to easily apply a major technique used in Agile to cope changes: refactoring. Refactoring is a process and a set of techniques to reorganize code while preserving the external behavior of a working system [31]. PPCs help us to extend and reorganize code by its encapsulation into features and aspects, which avoids the inherent tangled-code that crosscutting concerns generate.

# 5  Applying PPC for the Agile Development of a Testing Framework for Biogas Plants

In this section, we illustrate the use of PPCs in Agile through our experience of developing a framework for monitoring, testing and operating biogas power plants. This development has been performed following SCRUM [18] and in cooperation with the software company Answare-Tech, which is operating in the software and system engineering arena. This industrial collaboration has taken place within *FLEXI ITEA2 project*, in which both UPM and Answare-Tech have worked closely together.

## 5.1  A Test and Operation Framework for Biogas Plants

Biogas power plants produce electric energy from the anaerobic digestion of the animal meat/vegetable waste. The process of biogas production is composed of four main stages: shredding, pasteurization, homogenization, and anaerobic digestion. Each stage is performed in tanks that must be monitored, tested and controlled.

It is common that customers monitor and control several biogas plants distributed in a geographical area. In addition, they require that the language and framework to monitor, test and operate the plant will be specific of the biogas domain. To satisfy these needs, we decided to evolve an existing domain-specific framework for testing and operating environments, called TOPENprimer [32]. TOPENprimer is devised for testing and operating systems from various domains. Therefore, UPM and Answare-Tech work together to update TOPEN-Primer to test biogas plants, i.e. TOPEN Biogas.

## 5.2    Developing a Flexible Architecture for TOPEN Biogas

TOPEN Biogas was developed through 6 SCRUM *sprints* during 15 weeks (see P3, section 4.3). The Scrum Team was composed of 10 engineers: a Product Owner, a Scrum Master, two architects (architecture team), and six developers (development team). During Pre-game phase, we created the *Product Backlog* with the USs identified by the customer (see P4, section 4.3). Later in the process, the USs were prioritized in each sprint in a Sprint Backlog. The development results of 3 sprints are described below.

- **Sprint 1:** The Sprint 1 was focused on the TOPEN Biogas main functionalities. Following, some selected USs from the Sprint Backlog:

   **(US1).** *Test engineers specify a test case utilizing a user interface and with the biogas plant specific language.*
   **(US2).** *Test engineers compile and execute a test case from the user interface. The results of the test case executions must be shown to them.*
   **(US3).** *Test engineers remotely test/monitor the biogas plant.*

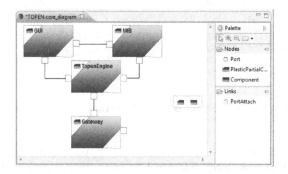

**Fig. 3.** Topen Biogas Working Architecture of the First Sprint

From these USs, the architecture team identified some non-functional requirements with regard to the distribution, security and the critical nature of the data. The architecture team decided on a distributed architecture and identified 4 PPCs, i.e. 4 incomplete components that had to be completely defined in following sprints. These PPCs are: kernel functions (TopenEngine), graphical user functions (GUI), data management (MIB), and the communication with the biogas plant (Gateway), as shown in Figure 3[3] (see P1 and P6, section 4.3). From now on, our focus will be the PPC *TopenEngine* to illustrate how a PPC can be iteratively updated by considering each sprint working architecture. In the first sprint, to support distributed communication among components, the use of Java Remote Method Invocation (RMI) was decided. As a result, the architecture team defined a crosscutting feature (aspect), which implemented a distribution concern based on RMI. In addition, it was implemented an AVP, which hooked the aspect to the *TopenEngine* (see Figure 4.a).

---

[3] Figures 3 and 4 are snapshots of Flexible-PLA tool.

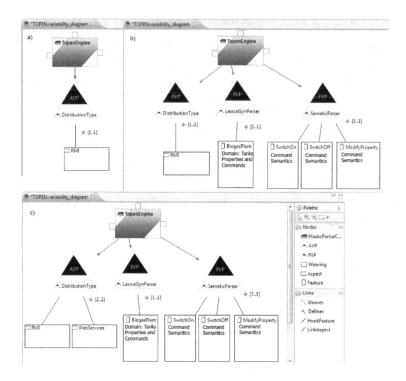

**Fig. 4.** Topen Engine PPC Adaptation through Sprints

- **Sprint 2:** The Sprint 2 was focused on supporting the operation of the
  biogas plant. Below, some selected USs from the Sprint Backlog:

**(US4).** *Test engineers operate biogas tanks and modify the value of their
properties.* As a result of this US, the properties and operations supported by
each tank were developed. This US was divided into sub-USs as:

**(US42).** *Test engineers switch on/off a tank, and/or modify the tank properties value by sending commands.*

**(US44).** *Test engineers be notified about temperature excess in tanks by means
of alarm reception.*

From these USs, the architecture team decided to add two features to the
TopenEngine PPC. One feature implements the lexical-syntactic parser to analyze the commands/alarms that test engineers send/receive to/from the tanks
of a biogas plant (e.g. parsing of references to tanks, properties and operations).
The other feature implements the semantic parser to provide of meaning to these
commands/alarms (see Figure 4.b). These parsings validate both lexically and semantically the commands and alarms that test engineers send or receive to/from
the tanks of a biogas plant. Adding these new User Stories by means of adding
new features that hook the TopenEngine PPC implies more effort in specifying
the pointcuts and the weaving operators. However we gain in code modularity,

scalability and reusability because these fragments of code are unaware of the linking context (see P5 and P6, section 4.3).

- **Sprint 3:** The Sprint 3 was focused on the physical communication with the biogas plant.

Since the Gateway had a Service Oriented Architecture based on Web Services technology, TopenEngine had to be changed to support Web Services (see P2, section 4.3) . Therefore, the TopenEngine supported both RMI communication with the GUI and MIB, and Web Services communication with the Gateway (see Figure 4.c). This new requirement was solved by hooking a new distribution aspect, which provided Web Services technology. It is important to emphasize that this aspect was not only hooked to the PPC TopenEngine, but also to all the PPC components that needed to communicate with the Gateway. As a result, the distribution of our application was modified just by adding a new single fragment of code. We did not need search in all the components the scattered distribution capabilities of the components previously implemented to modify them. The incremental design of the architecture in subsequent sprints by means of the use of PPC allowed us to flexibly modify the distribution capabilities with the minimum impact both in cost and effort, and to inherently refactor the distribution code (see P5 and P6, section 4.3).

# 6   Conclusions and Further Work

The deployment of PPCs is an attempt to provide a solution for architectural design of large software systems in Agile. They are malleable components that we have advantageously used for adding or removing pieces of software throughout the different iterations that comprise the development of our *working product*. As a result, we realized that PPCs were *working components* of a *working architecture* that was designed in time to our working framework for testing and operating biogas power production plants.

In cooperation with our industrial partners we have managed to show that it is possible to focus on architecture without suffering from practices that move away the customer from the architecture and development teams. In addition, we realized that non functional requirements can be allocated into the architecture while the discussion/communication with the customer is mainly focused on the set of functional requirements. Therefore, the impact of introducing non-functional requirements in Agile is minimized. From an architectural technical point of view, scaling up can be achieved and, as important, the need of refactoring was sized down: the impact of introducing new features was often less dramatic thanks to the flexibility and reusability provided by PPCs.

As future work, we plan to work in larger size projects to understand what is still missing and to obtain measures and empirical results. Systematization of use of PPCs and automation are two issues that will have to be faced for the approach deployment. Together with Answare-tech we intend to use PPCs in a project for security and safety of intelligent buildings and IT for energy management systems. In addition, it is necessary to analyze how the use of PPCs can facilitate the maintenance and evolution of software architectures.

## Acknowledgments

The work reported here has been partially sponsored by the Spanish MEC (DSDM TIN2008-00889-E), MICINN (INNOSEP TIN2009-13849), and MITYC (FLEXI ITEA2 6022 FIT-340005-2007-37 TSI-020400-2009-066) and by UPM (Researcher Training program). Authors are indebted to Answare-tech and BiogasFuelCell SA for their participation and support during the development of the project.

## References

1. Perry, D.E., Wolf, A.L.: Foundations for the study of software architecture. SIGSOFT Softw. Eng. Notes 17(4), 40–52 (1992)
2. Garlan, D.: Software architecture. In: Wiley Encyclopedia of Computer Science and Engineering (2001)
3. Beck, K., et al.: The Agile Manifesto (2001), http://www.agilemanifesto.org (accessed July 2010)
4. Bowers, J., May, J., Melander, E., Baarman, M., Ayoob, A.: Tailoring xp for large system mission critical software development. In: Proceedings of the Second XP Universe and First Agile Universe Conference on Extreme Programming and Agile Methods - XP/Agile Universe 2002, London, UK, pp. 100–111. Springer, Heidelberg (2002)
5. Dybå, T., Dingsøyr, T.: Empirical studies of agile software development: A systematic review. Inf. Softw. Technol. 50(9-10), 833–859 (2008)
6. Babar, M.A., Abrahamsson, P.: Architecture-centric methods and agile approaches. In: Agile Processes in Software Engineering and Extreme Programming (XP 2008), pp. 242–243 (2008)
7. Cockburn, A.: Agile Software Development. The Cooperative Game, 2nd edn. Addison-Wesley Professional, Reading (2006)
8. Kruchten, P.: On software architecture, agile development, value & cost. Keynote SATURN, Pittsburgh, Pennsylvania, USA (2008), http://www.sei.cmu.edu/architecture/saturn/2008/keynotes.html
9. Boehm, B., Turner, R.: Balancing Agility and Discipline: A Guide for the Perplexed. Addison-Wesley, Reading (2004)
10. McMahon, P.: Extending agile methods: A distributed project and organizational improvement perspective. CrossTalk: The J. Defense Software Eng. 18(5), 16–19 (2005)
11. Babar, M.A., Ihme, T., Pikkarainen, M.: An industrial case of exploiting product line architectures in agile software development. In: Software Product Lines Conference, SPLC (2009)
12. Pérez, J., Díaz, J., Costa-Soria, C., Garbajosa, J.: Plastic partial components: A solution to support variability in architectural components. In: WICSA 2009: Joint Working IEEE/IFIP Conference on Software Architecture and European Conference on Software Architecture, ECSA (2009)

13. Pohl, K., Böckle, G., Linden, F.: Software Product Line Engineering: Foundations, Principles and Techniques. Springer, Germany (2005)
14. Shore, J., Warden, S.: The Art of Agile Development. O'Reilly Media, Inc., Sebastopol (2007)
15. Vilki, K.: Juggling with the paradoxes of agile transformation. Flexi Newsletter 2(1), 3–5 (2008)
16. Beck, K., Andres, C.: Extreme Programming Explained: Embrace Change, 2nd edn. Addison-Wesley Professional, Reading (November 2004)
17. Poppendieck, M., Poppendieck, T.: Implementing Lean Software Development: From Concept to Cash. Addison-Wesley Professional, Reading (2006)
18. Schwaber, K., Beedle, M.: Agile Software Development with Scrum. Prentice-Hall, Englewood Cliffs (2002)
19. Assmann, U.: Invasive Software Composition. Springer, New York (2003)
20. Bachmann, F., Bass, L.: Managing variability in software architectures, pp. 126–132. ACM Press, New York (2001)
21. Kiczales, G., Hilsdale, E., Hugunin, J., Kersten, M., Palm, J., Griswold, W.G.: An overview of aspectj, pp. 327–353. Springer, Heidelberg (2001)
22. Beydeda, S., Book, M., Gruhn, V.: Model-Driven Software Development. Springer, Heidelberg (2005)
23. Schmidt, D.C.: Guest editor's introduction: Model-driven engineering. In: Model-Driven Engineering (2006)
24. Steinberg, D., Budinsky, F., Paternostro, M., Merks, E.: EMF: Eclipse Modeling Framework 2.0. Addison-Wesley Professional, Reading (2009)
25. Ambler, S.W.: Agile architecture: Strategies for scaling agile development, http://www.agilemodeling.com/essays/agileArchitecture.htm (accessed July 2010)
26. Kruchten, P.: Software architecture and agile software development an oxymoron? Keynote Software Architecture Challenges in the 21st Century, USC (June 8, 2009)
27. Erdogmus, H.: Architecture meets agility. IEEE Software 26(5), 2–4 (2009)
28. Madison, J.: Agile architecture interactions. IEEE Software PP(99), 41–48 (2010)
29. Kornstadt, A., Sauer, J.: Tackling offshore communication challenges with agile architecture-centric development. In: WICSA 2007: Proceedings of the Sixth Working IEEE/IFIP Conference on Software Architecture, Washington, DC, USA, p. 28. IEEE Computer Society, Los Alamitos (2007)
30. Andrade, L.F., Fiadeiro, J.L.: Architecture based evolution of software systems. In: Bernardo, M., Inverardi, P. (eds.) SFM 2003. LNCS, vol. 2804, pp. 148–181. Springer, Heidelberg (2003)
31. Fowler, M., et al.: Refactoring: Improving the Design of Existing Code. Addison-Wesley, Reading (1999)
32. Magro, B., Garbajosa, J., Perez, J.: A software product line definition for validation environments. In: Software Product Lines Conference (SPLC), pp. 45–54 (2008)

# Lightweight and Continuous Architectural Software Quality Assurance Using the aSQA Technique

Henrik Bærbak Christensen[1], Klaus Marius Hansen[2], and Bo Lindstrøm[3]

[1] Department of Computer Science, Aarhus University, Aarhus, Denmark
hbc@cs.au.dk
[2] Department of Computer Science, University of Iceland, Reykjavík, Iceland
kmh@hi.is
[3] Systematic A/S, Aarhus, Denmark
blm@systematic.com

**Abstract.** In this paper, we present a novel technique for assessing and prioritizing architectural quality in large-scale software development projects. The technique can be applied with relatively little effort by software architects and thus suited for agile development in which quality attributes can be assessed and prioritized, e.g., within each development sprint. We outline the processes and metrics embodied in the technique, and report initial experiences on the benefits and liabilities. In conclusion, the technique is considered valuable and a viable tool, and has benefits in an architectural, technical, context, as well as in a business and people context.

## 1 Introduction

Software architecture is a major concern in any large scale software development and therefore a central concern for successful IT companies. One particular task that rests heavily on a software architect's shoulder is *architectural quality assessment, prioritization, and conformance checking*. It is well established that different architectural qualities often compete, the classic trade-off between performance and maintainability being one example, and that implementations of architecture may drift away from the architect's stated design due to, e.g., misunderstandings, communication problems, and developers' skill sets. Software architects are thus in need of models, techniques, and tools to help in facing these challenges. Researchers and practitioners have responded by developing different architectural quality frameworks and evaluation techniques, a short outline is presented in the related work section of this paper. However, most of these techniques are characterized by being rather heavyweight and costly to perform (e.g. scenario-based techniques such as the Architecture Trade-off Analysis Method (ATAM; [17]) and/or resulting in quality measurements that are difficult to compare and thus form a poor basis for prioritizing effort (e.g. specific measurements as defined by ISO/IEC 9126 [13]). Thus they are less than

M. Ali Babar and I. Gorton (Eds.): ECSA 2010, LNCS 6285, pp. 118–132, 2010.

optimal for software architects to apply continuously in agile development as well as less than optimal for prioritizing components and qualities to focus on during the next iteration.

The *architectural Software Quality Assurance* technique (aSQA), has been developed by software architects in Systematic A/S as a lightweight technique for continuous quality assessment and prioritizing in software architecture and development work. Systematic A/S [21] is a privately owned software development company in Denmark, employing approximately 500 people, 50 of these in the UK, Finland, and USA. Systematic is certified with respect to process maturity at Capability Maturity Model Integration (CMMI; [11]) level 5 and combines CMMI with lean development [19,14], specifically the Scrum method [20].

The main contribution of this paper is the description and presentation of aSQA as a novel and viable technique for continuously assessing, controlling, and balancing quality attributes in a development project. A second contribution is experience reports from using the technique, primarily in the company in which it was developed, with additional comments from two other companies that have made initial tests of it. Though we cannot claim a rigorous evaluation, the experience reports generally support the claims of the method as a lightweight and effective way of assessing and prioritizing software quality.

The paper is organized as follows. In section 2 we describe the aSQA technique, presenting experience from using aSQA in Systematic, and Section 3 presents initial observations from two other companies. Section 4 compares with alternative software architecture evaluation techniques. We discuss our findings in section 5 before we conclude in section 6.

## 2   The aSQA Technique

Systematic combines CMMI with the Scrum method for agile development of its software systems. Scrum is inherently a feature-oriented method focusing on adding user-oriented functionality in each iteration (or "sprint") for the customer to evaluate. Nevertheless, the quality of the software architecture is essential in the products of Systematic in order to support both customer-dictated quality requirements (typically performance and reliability) as well as more engineering-related quality requirements (such as maintainability). This is basically a conflict: a feature-oriented process that measure success and progress in terms of functionality on one hand, and the wish for a sound architecture that to a large extend is orthogonal to functionality on the other [8].

The aSQA evolved as a software architect's technique to support an architectural focus even in the face of a feature-oriented process. A central requirement of the technique was therefore that it should *allow continuous quality assessment*. It should be *lightweight* meaning efficient to perform in terms of spent person hours for the software architect as well as central stakeholders of the project. The technique should be efficient enough to be performed at the end of each sprint to ensure architectural issues and tasks can be added to the sprint backlog for handling during the next or future sprints.

Another requirement was that it should *allow software architecture quality attributes to be quantified.* In projects much focus is on easy quantifiable and measurable parameters such as cost, schedule and functionality. However, many architectural aspects of quality are much more difficult to measure, like testability or maintainability. This makes it difficult to manage quality not only with respect to defining and communicating a goal for the quality of the product but also with respect to controlling if the intended quality goal is obtained. This necessitated defining a way of quantifying quality attributes as well as championing a set of quality attributes to consider.

The third and final requirement was that aSQA should *allow software architecture quality attributes to be prioritized.* During development the software architect has to prioritize certain quality attributes in certain components before others to ensure costly development time is invested wisely. However, the metrics used for quality attributes vary greatly and this makes comparisons highly difficult: is achieving 5,000 transactions per second better than lowering estimated time to introduce a new taxation policy to 16 staff hours? This necessitated defining a uniform scale across quality attributes.

The latter two requirements are indirect consequences of the wish for a lightweight technique. By mapping relevant software architecture quality attributes into a consistent and uniform scale, they can be documented and traced using a spreadsheet or similar tools (see Figure 3), which again lowers the effort spent on documentation and tracking evolution.

## 2.1   The aSQA Steps

The activities of aSQA are shown in Figure 1 and outlined below. The first two steps are preparation steps while steps 3–7 are iteration steps that are considered or performed as part of each sprint. While the full seven steps of the aSQA technique rigorously speaking are carried out for each new project much of the work associated with the preparation steps can be reused across projects once the technique is mastered.

*Step 1:* A central aspect of aSQA is to get stakeholders to agree on which software architecture quality attributes to consider for the project as well as agree on what they mean. An obvious way is to choose an existing quality framework like the ISO/IEC 9126 standard [13] or Bass et al. [4]. Systematic has chosen the ISO/IEC 9126 standard for all projects and have internal introductory courses on the standard as well as on the aSQA to ensure a common understanding of its quality attributes between internal stakeholders (architects, testers, developers, business, etc.) For external stakeholders the experience is that quality attributes are too abstract and definitions are therefore translated to concrete cases and scenarios to be discussed. Then the conclusions of these discussions are then mapped back into the ISO qualities.

*Step 2:* A crucial step in aSQA is to define a mapping of quality measurements to *aSQA levels.* In aSQA an ordinal scale of values ranging from 1 to 5 (a reference interval scale) is used ubiquitously to measure all quality attributes as this allows a coarse and manageable comparison of values across quality attributes.

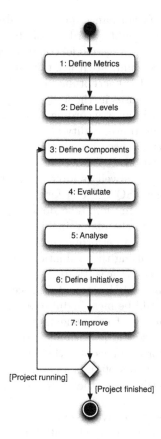

**Fig. 1.** Steps of the aSQA Technique

On this scale level 1 is always "worst" (or "least") and level 5 is always "best" (or "most") to avoid confusion. At Systematic levels have been uniformly defined across all projects and are defined in terms of stakeholders' perception. This is exemplified below showing levels 1, 3 and 5:

1: *Unacceptable:* Important stakeholders find the system unacceptable because of the value of the quality attribute in question.
3: *Acceptable:* No relevant stakeholder finds the system unacceptable because of the value of the quality attribute in question.
5: *Excellent:* All relevant stakeholders are highly satisfied by the value of the quality attribute in question

As an example, consider the performance quality attribute of some component of a system, and that around 20,000 transactions per second is required by some system stakeholder for the given component. Measurements or analyses by the software architects indicate the performance to be around 25,000 transactions per second, which would lead to an aSQA value of 3 (acceptable) or perhaps 4 (above acceptable) for the performance quality attribute. As another example, consider the maintainability quality attribute of the same component. If some stakeholder requires that the storage model could be changed in 15 person days but estimates by the architects indicate it will take about 30 person days then the aSQA value would be set to 1 (unacceptable) or perhaps 2 (below acceptable).

In the way that Systematic uses it, the aSQA technique can be classified as a metrics-based measuring technique according to the framework of Clements et al. [9], but it is also possible to use quality attribute scenarios [4] as a basis for evaluation, though this has not been pursued by Systematic.

Note how the two preparation steps force stakeholders to agree both on which quality attributes to consider as well as force a uniform scale across attributes which supports comparisons. aSQA level 4 for performance is fine while level 2 for maintainability calls for attention. The obvious conclusion of the software architect would be to focus on the maintainability quality in the next iteration while to waste no more effort on performance tuning.

*Step 3:* A prerequisite for using the evaluation part of aSQA is the existence of (a design of) components for a software system. This definition is usually made in an iterative and possible incremental process in which the set of components may change. It should be meaningful to assign a level of quality to that component—if the granularity of components gets too small it is difficult to assign a quality attribute, like e.g. performance, to it, and the number of components to assess quality for becomes overwhelming. At Systematic, experience has shown that 5–10 components often is a good number. Furthermore, to ease historical comparisons of evaluations, the component structure and scope should preferably be stable.

*Step 4:* The evaluation step involves assessing target and current aSQA levels for all components for all considered quality attributes and results in a table that

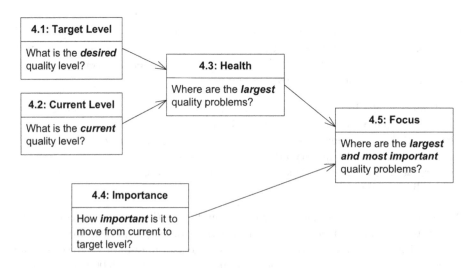

**Fig. 2.** aSQA Evaluation Sub-steps

highlight architectural issues that require attention by the software architects. It is carried out in several sub-steps (cf. Figure 2). These sub-steps are carried out for each component and for each considered quality attribute. In Step 4.1 a *target* level is set for each component. The target is set according to what is currently seen as the needed quality level for the specific component for the specific quality attribute. In Step 4.2 the *current* quality level is measured/assessed (using the criteria set up in Step 2). Step 4.3 is a computation step as the current *health* is calculated using the following formula:

$$health = 5 - max(0, (target - current))$$

This formula assigns health from 1 to 5 with 5 being excellent *health*, i.e. the *target* level has been achieved. Once the *health* has been calculated for all components and all quality attributes the architects can readily overview which architectural aspects are sound (those at level 5) and which aspects may require more attention (below level 5). However, no priority has been assigned between those components and quality attributes that require attention: which issues are the most important to address in the next sprints and which issues may be postponed or even neglected? Therefore aSQA adds two more sub-steps.

In Step 4.4 the *importance* levels are defined i.e. stakeholders' assessment of which quality attributes of which components should be prioritized. Returning back to the initial example, stakeholders may consider performance much more important (giving it importance level 5) than maintainability (giving it importance level 2) for the given component.

The last step is Step 4.5 that again is a pure computation step that combines *health* and *importance* to determine the *focus* level of each quality attribute of each component. The focus level is calculated as:

$$focus = ceil((6 - health) \times importance/5)$$

Thus the lower the *health* level is and the more higher the *importance* level is, the higher the *focus* level will be, and thus highlighting that raising the level of the quality attribute for the component is important.

The cumulative result of step 4 is a table or spreadsheet showing *target, current, health, importance,* and *focus* levels for each quality attribute for each component. Figure 3 shows an example of calculating levels for an imaginary Point-of-Sales architecture containing three components, Terminal, Scanner, and Application Server, and using the six system quality attributes defined by Bass et al. [4].

In the example, the table warns the architects that particular focus should be put on performance for the Application Server (since its focus level is 5), followed by focus on performance in the Terminal component (focus level 4), etc. Thus the resulting table of aSQA levels for target, current, health, importance, and focus, provides a compact overview of quality levels as well as a prioritization of components and quality attributes that need attention.

Note that for the *health, importance,* and *focus* levels, the scale is just an ordinal scale where level 5 is "important/best" and level 1 is "unimportant/worst".

| | Terminal | | | | | Scanner | | | | | App Server | | | | |
|---|---|---|---|---|---|---|---|---|---|---|---|---|---|---|---|
| | t | c | h | i | f | t | c | h | i | f | t | c | h | i | f |
| Availability | 4 | 4 | 5 | 1 | 1 | 3 | 3 | 5 | 1 | 1 | 4 | 4 | 5 | 1 | 1 |
| Performance | 5 | 2 | 2 | 5 | 4 | 5 | 3 | 3 | 5 | 3 | 5 | 1 | 1 | 5 | 5 |
| Modifiability | 4 | 4 | 5 | 2 | 1 | 3 | 4 | 5 | 2 | 1 | 5 | 5 | 5 | 2 | 1 |
| Testability | 4 | 4 | 5 | 2 | 1 | 3 | 4 | 5 | 2 | 1 | 5 | 4 | 4 | 2 | 1 |
| Security | 4 | 4 | 5 | 2 | 1 | 3 | 3 | 5 | 2 | 1 | 5 | 2 | 2 | 3 | 3 |
| Usability | 5 | 1 | 1 | 2 | 2 | 5 | 2 | 2 | 2 | 2 | 3 | 3 | 5 | 2 | 1 |

**Fig. 3.** aSQA Levels Example. Shown are target (t), current (c), health (h), importance (i), and focus (f) levels.

It is only the *target* and *current* levels that are defined in terms of the stakeholder metrics defined in step 2 of the technique. Note also that once the project is under way, the *target* and *importance* levels are usually rather stable and as *health* and *focus* are computed values, the only real assessment that demands some effort from the software architects are finding the *current* level. As sprint objectives are clearly defined in terms of stories or features to implement, even this assessment can be made fast as all untouched components and postponed architectural tasks most often do not influence on *current* levels.

*Step 5:* The analysis step is basically to overview the table, and based on that define initiatives to improve quality. In *Step 6*, these initiatives will typically lead to items being added to the product backlog and planning these for later sprints. Finally *Step 7* is the improving step which is the concrete work by the team to increase the quality attributes in the particular components.

The computation sub-steps and the spreadsheet nature of the evaluation step of course calls for a tool, and Systematic has developed one that presents overview in tabular format as exemplified by figure 3, and moreover keeps track of the evolution keeping snapshots of the spreadsheet for each iteration.

## 2.2   Discussion

In this section we will argue why the aSQA technique is viable for software architects in agile development. Its viability is further argued by the experience reports, described in the next section.

The three main requirements of the aSQA technique were:

– *Allow continuous quality assessment* which is essentially that the technique must not be demanding in terms of invested person hours.
– *Allow quality to be quantified* which is essentially that the technique must allow all architectural quality attributes to be measured and represented by numerical values.
– *Allow quality to be prioritized* which is essentially that all numerical values can readily be compared.

The two latter requirements, quantification and prioritization of quality, are fulfilled by Step 2 and Step 4 of the technique. Step 2 introduces a suitable, common, metric across all quality attributes, in Systematic's case by means of the aSQA levels 1 to 5 which is a grading based on stakeholders' perceptions. Step 4 results in the calculation of *health* and *focus* levels which directly defines a prioritization of both quality attributes and components to address.

Regarding requirement one, that the technique should be lightweight in terms of invested person hours, we have to draw upon the experiences from Systematic in general and the author who is presently software architect at Systematic in particular.

Step 1 and 2 are preparation steps and potentially performed for every project. In practice this is neither cost-efficient nor necessary. At Systematic these steps are now part of the internal and required training to become software architect. The quality metrics and aSQA level definitions are thus standardized across the organization. However, special needs of a particular project may require tailoring ISO definitions to stress a specific aspect of a system. Thus an estimated two hours is spent on average for a project at reviewing the quality framework and the levels and potentially tailor these.

Regarding the effort invested in steps 3–7 (performed once in each sprint) the by far most demanding task is finding the *current* values of the architecture in step 4. An estimated 80% of the effort invested in aSQA during a sprint is invested here. It mainly just involves the software architects but other stakeholders may be consulted.

The *target* level is only revisited if the scope of the project has changed which in fixed-scope projects happens rarely. However, in projects where the concrete scope of the project is defined during the project, the *target* level may change slightly more often. When changing the target the architect will typically involve consultance with the project manager—in order to discuss the trade-offs among quality, project costs, schedule, and functionality.

*Importance* is adjusted periodically when priorities changes in the project. For example, it may become more important to reach the target level of the ISO *time behaviour* quality attribute than obtaining better maintainability in a release if this issue has political focus by the customer. This attribute will typically be adjusted by the achitect, possibly based on an agreement with the project manager.

Regarding Step 3: Define Components, the experience is that effort is invested in the first sprint to define approximately 5–10 components (this effort does of course not include designing the architecture). It takes approximately two hours for a full project to decide and define components. The architect is typically the only person involved in this step. When using components corresponding to subsystems it is rare that new components are defined during a project and thus this step impose little effort in the following sprints.

Steps 5 and 6, Analyse and Define Initiatives, are performed by the architect and the invested time depends on severity of issues, approximately one to two hours. These issues are sent to the project manager which includes the issues in the next or following sprints.

The total time for completing steps 3–7 for the full project is typically less than five hours if the architect has experience with aSQA, bases the evaluation on his existing knowledge, and makes the evaluation no more frequent than once a month. However, if the evaluation is made more frequently the time per evaluation will be lower as fewer aspects change between evaluations.

Thus we conclude that once the learning curve has been climbed, the aSQA is a lightweight technique as the required effort per sprint is usually below five hours and aSQA can thus keep up with the pace of agile development.

## 3 Experience Outside Systematic

Systematic A/S participated in the research project, *Software Architecture at Work* (SA@Work) [7], a one and a half year research collaboration between two of the authors and four Danish IT companies, focusing at software architects work in the respective companies. Two of the participating companies in the SA@Work project made initial tests of the aSQA technique within their own context. The two companies were:

1. *Bang & Olufsen (BeO)*. BeO produces high-end audio products, television sets, and telephones.
2. *Jyske Bank (JB)*. JB is the second largest independent Danish bank, employing some 4,000 people in 119 Danish branches.

Due to resource constraints on behalf of the researchers, the two companies tested the aSQA technique on a project on their own choosing with little guidance and their evaluations were concluded by qualitative interviews, see [6] for further details.

Both companies chose to test aSQA on only a single component, only had time for a single "iteration" of the technique steps, and both simply used the quality framework (ISO 9126) and metric definitions (aSQA levels 1–5) of Systematic. Thus Step 1 and 2 were largely avoided simply by adoption. This was, however, only partially successful. BeO reported that assessment of *current* level for the component in question lead to very different assessed levels by different developers and architects and next to heated discussions amongst these people concerning how to interpret the ISO quality definitions as well as how to use the aSQA levels. We conjecture that the preparation steps of aSQA require a substantial investment in order to get a common understanding of quality framework as well as the aSQA levels. On the other hand BeO reported these intense discussion as being highly important to ensure a common understanding within the team and with stakeholders. Thus it can be seen as an investment to ensure architectural conformance between *as-designed* and *as-built* architecture.

JB reported an interesting application of the technique. The bank was in the process of buying a third party banking system and had two competing systems to choose from. Architecturally, the two systems were very different, one being SOA based and open which was valued high, the other being "black-box" but cheaper and with a better graphical user interface. The lead architect used a modified aSQA to structure the architectural assessment of the two systems. In Step 4 of aSQA, the *current* level was reinterpreted as the "supplied" level from the third party system, while *target* level was reinterpreted as the "ideal" level as seen from JB. Technical staff from the two companies collaborated with the JB architect to determine the "supplied" values of the quality attributes. Then the architect could calculate the *health* for each quality attribute to provide a basis for make a sound choice of system as seen from the software architect's perspective.

## 4   Related Work

Much work has been done on techniques for evaluation of software architecture [12,10]. Dobrica and Niemelä [12] surveyed eight software architecture analysis methods all focusing on predicting the effects on software quality on choosing a specific software architecture design. They categorize evaluation methods as (following [1]) either being "questioning techniques", based on qualitative, often software quality-independent questions to be asked of an architecture, or "measuring techniques", based on quantitative, often software quality-dependent measurements to be made on an architecture. In this spectrum, aSQA is somewhat agnostic in that it focuses on software qualities, but allows for both questioning and measuring techniques in analyzing a software architecture/system under development with respect to a given quality. In practical use, aSQA has typically been used with qualitative techniques.

Arguably, the most prominent techniques for software architecture evaluation are scenario-based following or based on SAAM [16] and ATAM. Babar and Gorton [2] compare four such methods and present a framework for comparing evaluation methods. The framework contains the components of context (e.g., goal of the method, quality attributes covered, development phase), stakeholders (e.g., stakeholders involved, process support, resources required), contents (e.g., activities and approaches), and reliability (maturity and validation). The aSQA technique has as a goal to make decision makers aware of the quality status of a software system throughout development, focusing on the quality attributes of a chosen quality framework. In particular, the focus on continuous assessment distinguishes it from other architecture evaluation methods. The technique is supported by a defined set of activities, a database-backed tool, and requires few resources to perform (see Section 2). Finally, the technique has been used for several years at Systematic and has matured in that way and has been evaluated through studies at other companies (see Section 3).

Comparing aSQA and ATAM have resemblence to comparing agile to more traditional development methods. aSQA focuses on an iterative and evolving evaluation within each sprint while ATAM in the onset focuses on an early and thorough evaluation and not on constant follow up during development and is as such necessarily time-consuming ([5], e.g., reports on time consumption of around 100 hours excluding preparation and follow-up). ATAM uses a (drilled-down) version of system wide quality attribute scenarios and uses stakeholder voting for prioritization of quality attributes. aSQA does not assess individual scenarios but focus on quality attribute statements on a per-component basis and computes prioritization based upon the assigned *target* and *importance* levels. Stakeholders' influence is thus indirect through the value they put on these levels. ATAM puts emphasis on discussing and analyzing architectural decisions, in aSQA this is captured in Step 5 and 6: Analyse and Define Initiatives. As such, aSQA complements ATAM, especially for agile projects. ATAM can fruitfully evaluate an initial architecture, and aSQA used to monitor architectural evaluation during development. We envision that aSQA could be tailored to use metrics and levels closer to those proposed by ATAM (utility tree scenarios, and simple prioritization) in the Step 1 and 2 of aSQA, but this has not been explored so far.

The Cost Benefit Analysis Method (CBAM; [15]) provides an economic-based approach for prioritizing architectural design decisions. The prioritization is based on the "return on investment" (in CBAM ratio of benefit and cost) for the selection of each available design decision. In aSQA, focus levels are decided in an analogous way: the attribute (and component) for which the health level can potentially be improved the most (subject to importance), is suggested to be the focus of the next iteration. Furthermore, CBAM couples stakeholder prioritization with utility improvement to derive benefits of applying a decision whereas aSQA uses importance levels to produce focus levels. While aSQA has a different goal than CBAM, this suggests that Step 4 of the aSQA technique could be supplemented (or replaced) by a CBAM-like step, taking potential architectural decisions into account.

Recently, focus has been put on the ability for architecture evaluation methods to scale [22,3] particularly in the context of Ultra-Large-Scale systems [18]. Zhu et al. [22] describe how to scale methods by combining process components from existing methods and Babar et al. investigate distributed evaluation (through distributed involvement of stakeholders). The aSQA technique is, first, lightweight and can, secondly, be applied in a hierarchical manner, both of which contribute to scalability. Furthermore, the technique has been validated (and developed) in the context of large systems in the health-care and military domains.

## 5    Discussion

Concerning the cost of applying the method, it is important to define an appropriate granularity of the selected components. Too fine-grained components implies that the cost of the evaluation is too high compared to the overall effect of the evaluation. Too coarse-grained components implies that it is difficult to use the information for adjusting focus on a given quality attribute during software development process in a sufficiently precise manner. The granularity also depend on the size of the system that is being developed and what the evaluation results and insights will be used for. For high-level management, coarse-grained components will often be sufficient, e.g. sub-systems of a large solution, while developers need information on a finer granularity, e.g. sub-components constituting a sub-system. In other words, the granularity of the components will depend on what level the system is managed. A solution architect who is responsible for a portfolio of systems will most likely not be interested in internal components within each system, but only consider the dominant components of each system. A system architect who is responsible for a single system (or application) will need to divide the system into relatively fine-grained components which gives sufficient information to make him able to lead the developers to focus on small parts of the system. At Systematic, the experience is that around five to ten components seems to be a reasonable number of components which keeps the application of aSQA manageable with respect to the cost-benefit balance.

It is necessary for the parties being involved in analysing and understanding the results of aSQA to have a common agreement on the complete scope of the components. For example, a product or project being developed over several years may change its scope over time. As the scope of the project (and thereby the components) may gradually be redefined it is often necessary to redefine the goals periodically in order to be aligned with the changing scope. This may lead to some confusion on what functionality is actually within the scope of the components. Essentially, it is a matter of change management – but in practice it turns out to be difficult to grasp changing scope during quality assessments.

The external companies reported benefits from Step 1: *define metrics*. The very premise of aSQA is to force stakeholders to evaluate and prioritize a set of quality attributes in some quality model, like ISO 9126 or similar frameworks. In the external studies this process led stakeholders into heated discussions about "what quality attribute X really means!" If stakeholders have different perceptions of a quality (and often they have) they will assign different levels. Getting to an agreement on a specific current, target, or importance level, simply force stakeholders into deep discussions on how to understand qualities and force a common understanding. This common understanding is vital in a team and important to avoid *architectural mismatch*.

Another aspect of the technique that all the software architects reported and valued high (even though it is more of a people issue than purely technical issue) is the *compelling argument of numbers in spreadsheets*. Business decision makers are used to convincing arguments in the arena of economy, budgets, and project management in the form of spreadsheet accounts. Software architects primarily communicate by other means, whether it is graphical design diagrams, quality attribute scenarios, or similar. However, aSQA's output is a scoring of quality attributes and prioritizing in the form of spreadsheets like that shown in figure 3. This communication medium is simply much more similar to the language of business decision makers. Though unintentional, architects within Systematic report this a major benefit of the technique as their opinions simply are given much more weight when deciding resources. Furthermore, a low number of components, coupled with the spreadsheet representation of results, also enable management to get a quick overview of project quality status. In particular, at Systematic, a strategy of colour-coding (with green, yellow, red) has proved effective in communicating quality status and issues.

Regarding the future, Systematic is currently investigating if it is better to consider functionalities (or services) as the ones being monitored instead of the inner architectural components in the context of projects using Scrum and feature-driven development (where functionality is added as vertical slices to a system). Focusing on end-user functionality may make it easier to communicate and discuss quality aspects with non-technical stakeholders than if the basis is the more technical components.

# 6   Conclusions

This paper has described a new lightweight and continuous architecture-software quality assurance technique called *aSQA*. The technique is defined in terms of a seven-step, iterative process in which software architects select a set of components whose quality attributes are considered important to assess and control. The technique is based upon selecting a quality model, such as ISO/IEC 9126, and defining a uniform, coarse-gained metric for evaluating quality based upon stakeholder perception. Within each iteration and thus assessment, architects evaluate each component's current level for each quality attribute in question, and the aSQA model then yields a prioritization of which quality attributes for which components should receive the most attention.

The paper has outlined experiences with the aSQA technique both from within the company that invented the technique, Systematic A/S, as well as two other Danish companies. This data suggests that the technique is a viable and valuable tool for software architects; that it can be executed with a relatively low investment in time, especially if the selection of components and their granularity is made with care; that it support getting a common understanding between stakeholders of architectural quality issues; and that it helps in making the inevitable prioritizing of which quality attributes that should receive the greatest attention.

This said, it would be highly interesting to get more data from other companies and/or research institutions testing the technique. We therefore invite the research community to try it out and thereby explore further aspects and refinements of the technique.

# Acknowledgments

The aSQA technique was a team effort and many people have contributed. However, the principal designers are Bo Lindstrøm, Dennis Pedersen, Henrik Kjær, and Søren Skovsen from Systematic A/S.

The research presented in this article has been funded by Systematic A/S and the ISIS Katrinebjerg competency centre, Aarhus, Denmark (http://www.isis.alexandra.dk). We thank the companies and software architects that participated in the SA@Work project.

# References

1. Abowd, G., Bass, L., Clements, P., Kazman, R., Northrop, L., Zaremski, A.: Recommended best industrial practice for software architecture evaluation. Software Engineering Institute Technical Report, CMU/SEI-96-TR-025 (1996)
2. Babar, M.A., Gorton, I.: Comparison of scenario-based software architecture evaluation methods. In: 11th Asia-Pacific Software Engineering Conference 2004, pp. 600–607 (2004)
3. Babar, M.A., Kitchenham, B., Jeffery, R.: Comparing distributed and face-to-face meetings for software architecture evaluation: A controlled experiment. Empirical Software Engineering 13(1), 39–62 (2008)
4. Bass, L., Clements, P., Kazman, R.: Software Architecture in Practice, 2nd edn. Addison-Wesley, Reading (2003)
5. Boucké, N., Weyns, D., Schelfthout, K., Holvoet, T.: Applying the ATAM to an architecture for decentralized control of a transportation system. Quality of Software Architectures, 180–198 (2004)
6. Christensen, H.B., Hansen, K.M., Lindstrøm, B.: aSQA: Architectural Software Quality Assurance. Technical report, Computer Science Department, Aarhus University (2010)
7. Christensen, H.B., Hansen, K.M., Schougaard, K.R.: SA@Work - A Field Study of Software Architecture and Software Quality at Work. In: Proceedings of Asia-Pacific Software Engineering Conference, APSEC 2008, Beijing, China, December 2008, pp. 411–418 (2008)
8. Christensen, H.B., Hansen, K.M., Schougaard, K.R.: An Empirical Study of Software Architects' Concerns. In: Proceedings of the 16th Asia-Pacific Software Engineering Conference, APSEC, pp. 111–118 (2009)
9. Clements, P., Kazman, R., Klein, M.: Evaluating software architectures: methods and case studies. Addison-Wesley, Reading (2002)
10. Clements, P., Kazman, R., Klein, M.: Evaluating software architectures: methods and case studies. Addison-Wesley, Reading (2006)
11. CMMI Product Team. Cmmi for development. version 1.2. Technical report, CMU/SEI (2006)
12. Dobrica, L., Niemelä, E.: A survey on software architecture analysis methods. IEEE Transactions on software Engineering, 638–653 (2002)
13. ISO/IEC. Software engineering – Product quality – Part 1: Quality model., ISO/IEC 9126-1:2001 (2001)
14. Jakobsen, C.R., Johnson, K.A.: Mature Agile with a Twist of CMMI. In: AGILE Conference, pp. 212–217 (2008)
15. Kazman, R., Asundi, J., Klein, M.: Quantifying the costs and benefits of architectural decisions. In: ICSE, pp. 297–306. IEEE Computer Society, Los Alamitos (2001)
16. Kazman, R., Bass, L., Webb, M., Abowd, G.: SAAM: A method for analyzing the properties of software architectures. In: Proceedings of the 16th international conference on Software engineering, pp. 81–90. IEEE Computer Society Press, Los Alamitos (1994)
17. Kazman, R., Klein, M.H., Barbacci, M., Longstaff, T.A., Lipson, H.F., Carrière, S.J.: The architecture tradeoff analysis method. In: ICECCS, pp. 68–78. IEEE Computer Society, Los Alamitos (1998)

18. Northrop, L., Feiler, P., Gabriel, R., Goodenough, J., Linger, R., Longstaff, T., Kazman, R., Klein, M., Schmidt, D., Sullivan, K., et al.: Ultra-large-scale systems: The software challenge of the future. Software Engineering Institute (2006)
19. Poppendieck, M., Poppendieck, T.: Software Development: An Implementation Guide. Addison-Wesley, Reading (2006)
20. Sutherland, J., Jakobsen, C.R., Johnson, K.: Scrum and CMMI Level 5: The Magic Potion for Code Warriors. In: AGILE Conference, pp. 272–278 (2007)
21. Systematic A/S Web site, http://www.systematic.com/ (accessed, June 2010)
22. Zhu, L., Staples, M., Jeffery, R.: Scaling Up Software Architecture Evaluation Processes. In: Wang, Q., Pfahl, D., Raffo, D.M. (eds.) ICSP 2008. LNCS, vol. 5007, pp. 112–122. Springer, Heidelberg (2008)

# An Architectural Approach to Composing Reputation-Based Distributed Services

Suronapee Phoomvuthisarn[1,3,4], Yan Liu[2,3], and Liming Zhu[1,3]

[1] National ICT Australia (NICTA), Australia
[2] Pacific Northwest National Laboratory, USA
[3] School of Computer Science and Engineering, University of New South Wales, Australia
[4] Mahanakorn University of Technology, Bangkok, Thailand
{suronapee.phoomvuthisarn,liming.zhu}@nicta.com.au,
yan.liu@pnl.gov

**Abstract.** Reputation-Based Trust (RBT) model with embedded incentive mechanisms provides an accurate quantitative measurement for services choosing their partners based on fair ratings accumulated from users. These mechanisms stimulate services to offer ratings truthfully, otherwise they lose their gains or even receive penalties. However, leveraging such mechanisms in distributed environments is a challenging task by its centralized nature. In this paper, we propose a new architecture development that combines relevant architectural components to make trust systems highly scalable with the auction mechanisms' capability to prevent lie. In this architecture we define an auction-based trust negotiation protocol that guides the interactions of distributed services and realize it in the distributed trust framework. Our architecture scales efficiently for increasing numbers of services interacting with the system, while still achieving protection against untruthful incentives even when a majority of ratings are unfair. An example of a supply chain is devised with empirical evidence collected.

## 1 Introduction

Service oriented applications are highly distributed and loosely coupled with less central authority over participating for services. Such decentralized architectures are given a high degree of autonomy [13] and hence are susceptible to potential attacks caused by malicious services[1]. As a result, other services within the same architecture are at risks for being affected with quality degradation or even failure. Trust helps services to minimize the risk of future interactions, especially when services have no prior interaction with others. One of the trust mechanisms commonly used is the Reputation-Based Trust (RBT) [1]. Such mechanism assumes that services can provide ratings for others. These ratings are then aggregated into a meaningful reputation that can assist services to choose other services for their cooperation.

However, acquiring such reputation is not robust against cheating behavior. This is because the reputation itself relies on each rating given by an individual service. Rational services might behave strategically to provide ratings based on how they can

---

[1] We assume that all services follow common rationality and irrational behavior is not considered.

M. Ali Babar and I. Gorton (Eds.): ECSA 2010, LNCS 6285, pp. 133–149, 2010.

benefit from rating others. For example, a service might rate other services negatively since its own reputation would be increased with respect to the average of others, or purposely overstate the ratings of members within the group of their own interest. Hence, the reputation gathered from these ratings can be compromised and not correctly use to determine the trustworthiness of individual services.

In [17], we utilized the Vickrey Auction Mechanism (VAM), which has been widely accepted to help eliciting truthful information from participants, by incorporating it into the trust framework [5]. In a nutshell, our approach allows services to retrieve other services' reputation through auctions. Once receiving an enquiry about a service's reputation, the trust framework generates an auction service to elicit ratings from raters (i.e., services providing ratings for others). These ratings submitted can be aggregated into a reputation, which is returned to the enquiring service. By utilizing the VAM capability, the trust framework can manipulate the auctions so that all raters would not deviate from reporting ratings truthfully. Our approach ensures truthful incentives for raters even when the majority of them lie.

Leverage such technique within distributed systems is challenging due to several issues. One is to achieve high scalability. In [17], the existing technique relies on the centralized trust system taking care of all auctioning computation. Such a system provides a common interface by which raters can issue their bids through auctions. Consequently, concurrent raters are either blocked when they issues their bids simultaneously or cannot process other tasks until the auctioning process is completed. As a result, such system cannot scale up to handle the increased load of raters. Hence, this method is not suitable for ultra-large scale distributed environments where the number of potential services is huge [18]. This necessitates the need for distributed trust systems that can handle bids from multiple raters independently and asynchronously so that raters are not blocked while their bids are executed in the auctioning process. The second issue is to capture the VAM's truth-telling property in the deployed trust-based scenario. Since raters can participate in multiple auctions, and such a distributed environment lacks of the overall knowledge of individual's budgets, services may take underbidding strategies to gain remote resources. As a result, the auction property to prevent lying may be broken. Finally, to report the VAM outcome, explicit polling by the VAM for notification is not feasible since raters are dynamic, i.e., not known a priori or changing their identities over time.

In this paper, we describe our new architecture development in distributed systems to prevent cheating behavior. Extending our previous work [17], we introduce new architectural components to facilitate the integration of the VAM in distributed systems that enforce participants to reveal their budget information. Our approach involves defining an auction-based trust negotiation protocol that guides the interactions of distributed services, each of which is integrated with the VAM. This protocol is further realized by relevant components of the distributed trust framework.

We evaluate the overall architecture using an example on a supply chain scenario. Unlike other preventive mechanisms that prevent cheating behavior, our architecture demonstrates that distributed services will not gain their own benefits when they lie about their ratings, especially when the majority of ratings are unfair. Our approach also scales well for a very large number of raters interacting with the system. Our approach enables efficient trust-based communication among services, especially when it is hard to detect cheating behavior.

The structure of this paper is as follows: Section 2 discusses the background and introduces the motivating case study that the VAM is applied. Section 3 proposes the architecture that supports the VAM in distributed environments. Section 4 demonstrates our approach via an example on a supply chain and evaluates the overall architecture with experiments. Section 5 describes related works. The paper concludes in Section 6.

## 2  Background

### 2.1  Trust Level Calculation

The degree of trust is usually represented as the trust level, which is a collective measure of an entity's trustworthiness. The trust level can be calculated from the summation of the weighted direct trust (i.e., *Beta* value $\varepsilon$ [0..1] (a real number between 0 and 1) [6]) that one entity has on a targeted entity and the targeted entity's reputation as shown in Eq.1.

$$Trust\ Level = (\alpha \times Direct\ trust) + (\beta \times Reputation) \tag{1}$$

where $\alpha$ and $\beta$ represent weights $\varepsilon$ [0..1], which is subjectively determined by the entity depending on how important each source of trust is ($\alpha + \beta = 1.0$).

One entity can acquire the reputation of a targeted entity by collecting ratings from other entities that have previously interacted with the targeted entity. The reputation of one targeted entity can be calculated by aggregating all values of ratings submitted into one percentage measure *Reputation* $\varepsilon$ [0..1], each of which is weighted by its rater's reputation as shown in Eq.2.

$$Reputation = \sum_{i=1}^{n} w_i \times rating_i \tag{2}$$

where $w_i$ represents a weighted reputation $\varepsilon$ [0..1] of a rater, $rating_i$ represents a rating rated by a rater $i$, and $n$ represents a number of raters.

### 2.2  The VicKrey Auction Mechanism (VAM)

The VAM is a specific type of auction and known as the second-price sealed-bid auction in which bidders place their bid on the items and hand them to the auctioneer [4]. The winner of the auction is the individual who places the highest bid, and pays a price equal to the exact amount of the second-highest bid. The utility gain for each bidder is the difference between the true value each bidder places on an item and his payment (i.e., a monetary value each bidder gains after auction) as follows:

$$u_i = \begin{cases} v_i - Max_{\ j \neq i} b_j & if \ \ b_i > Max_{\ j \neq i} b_j \\ o & otherwuse \end{cases} \tag{3}$$

where $v_i$ represents bidder $i$ 's true value for an item, $b_i$ represents bidder $i$ 's bid for an item.

According to Eq.3, the winner gets a utility which is equal to the difference between its true valuation and the second highest bid, while the losers gain nothing (i.e., utility = 0). This VAM rules govern the interaction of self-interested participants with preferences to obtain limited resources through auction and guarantee that individuals not telling the truth would not gain [4]. This principle ensures that bidding something other than the bidder's true value is never beneficial and sometimes was detrimental with penalties.

### 2.3 Motivating Example

In this section, we illustrate the problem of unfair ratings in distributed environments, which motivates the need for the VAM within distributed services' architecture.

Consider the case of a supply chain, where a consumer submits an order consisting of line items to a retailer service. Each line item identifies a product and the corresponding quantity to be ordered. To fulfill orders, the retailer goes through each line item and finds a warehouse service with sufficient stock to ship them. The warehouse then ships the line item to the customer. To manage stock levels in the warehouse, each warehouse needs to restock from the relevant manufacturer service's inventory whenever inventory levels fall below the minimum of inventory levels for a particular product. To enable the exchange of information, as well as fast propagation of services offered, each service is connected with others in a peer-to-peer fashion. A key challenge lies in how to choose the best deals available among all retailers, warehouses and manufacturer services offering the same function.

Quality of service (QoS) is a major factor of making decisions in service oriented environments [1]. It helps services to differentiate the best candidate service from others that meets their requirements in terms of performance, reliability, and availability. In this decentralized scenario, the customer encounters unknown retailers, each of which is often established dynamically with warehouses which are also unknown. Moreover, each warehouse needs to manage its inventory level with unknown manufacturers. Hence, each service's interaction has some risk of failure, such as not reaching customer satisfaction in terms of not providing a service in a promised time, or failing to provide a service at all. Therefore, the overall QoS attributes including delivery time and availability can be used by all requesting services (or requesters) including customers, retailers, and warehouses to select relevant providing services (or providers) including potential retailers, warehouses, and manufacturers offering comparable functions.

The QoS properties advertised by the providers are then used as a selection factor for the requesters. To ensure that these QoS properties are delivered as described, the trust level of each provider can be used to determine the probability that they will fulfill its guaranteed QoS [1]. Each provider's trust level can be based on the requesters' past personal experience (or historical records) with them. However, in distributed systems where the requesters do not have much history interacting with all the providers, the requesters need additional advice from other services that can provide their opinion about these providers' QoS information. To acquire such opinion, the requesters collect QoS ratings from others that have previously interacted with the providers into a collective evaluation of a group opinion called *reputation*.

For simplicity without losing generality, we nominate the term "*QoS rating*" ε [0..1] to represent the average value of QoS attributes submitted by each rater, including delivery time ε [0..1] and availability ε [0..1], such that a quality of 1 denotes the best possible service as shown in Eq.4.

$$QoS\ rating = (delivery\ time + availability) / 2 \qquad (4)$$

The problem then arises when the reputation relies on the aggregation of each QoS rating given by an individual rater. Some raters might provide unfairly high or low QoS ratings for their own benefits (e.g., boosting their partners), resulting in the reputation compromised due to the unfair ratings captured. This unreliable reputation would lead the requesters to interact with some providers, which indeed are completely untrustworthy. Hence, the requesters might experience some unexpected QoS (e.g., slow response time), which itself leads to an unwanted service or even failure. To solve this problem, some mechanisms need to be integrated with each requester's trust manager to ensure the robustness and accuracy of the ratings accumulated. The integrated mechanisms should force raters to gives only fair ratings.

The VAM comes into play in this context. The VAM can motivate each rater to reveal its fair rating. In the supply chain (see Fig. 1), the customer would invoke its trust manager to evaluate each retailer's trustworthiness before sending the list of line items. Once having taken a decision for choosing one retailer, the chosen retailer then invokes its trust manager to evaluate each warehouse's trustworthiness before ordering a shipment from a warehouse. If a warehouse's stock is needed to be refilled, the warehouse then invokes its trust manager to evaluate each manufacturer's trustworthiness before ordering a product from the manufacturer. To ensure that each requester selects a trustworthy provider to interact with, a requester's trust manager is integrated with the VAM in order to acquire truthful QoS ratings from raters through auctions. To acquire such ratings, the trust managers generates auction services (one per each provider requested) to get fair ratings from others that have previously interacted with them. The QoS ratings submitted can be interpreted as the resources in terms of current bidding reputation (measured as credits) of each rater. These QoS ratings accumulated are then used to calculate the reputation of providers. By utilizing the VAM capability, trust managers can manipulate auctions so that raters would not deviate from reporting truthful ratings for the providers. This is achieved by using a reputation as the measure of gains. At the end of the auction, the winning rater will enhance (or degrade) his reputation proportional to the utility gain/loss, which is accumulated with the winning rater's existing reputation stored in the reputation repository as a reference for future encounters.

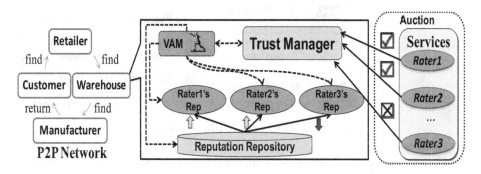

**Fig. 1.** The Problems of Unfair Ratings

However, integrating the VAM with trust managers in distributed environments poses a number of challenges from the architecture point of view as previously mentioned in the introduction section. In the next section, we discuss the architectural solutions as well as their relevant components that address those challenges.

## 3   The Architecture

This section presents the architecture with key components designed to accommodate the VAM in a distributed peer to peer environment. An auction-based trust negotiation protocol is proposed that guides the interactions amongst these key components. Through our architecture design experience, the challenges of integrating the VAM with the rest of distributed services' architecture are discussed at the end of this section.

### 3.1   Architecture Layers

The overall architecture consists of distributed services built on top of the P2P network as depicted in Fig. 2. This P2P network stores trust data across the network and thus the communication requires *the trust manager* for each service to (1) aggregate relevant trust data in order to make their decisions on a calculated trust level and (2) to submit its feedback when other services enquire about specific services' ratings. Consequently, the trust manager's architecture has four layers, namely *application layer, queuing layer, trust layer* and *service metadata layer*.

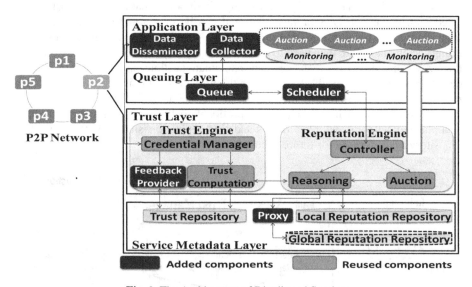

**Fig. 2.** The Architecture of Distributed Services

The application layer interacts with other services for feedback submission through the *data disseminator* and feedback aggregation through the *data collector*.

The queuing later mediates the communication between the application layer and the trust layer. It consists of the *queue list* and the *scheduler engine*. The queue list stores the ratings of raters when the application cannot process them immediately, while the scheduler engine schedules the execution of these ratings according to a specific set of constraints, such as priorities or deadline.

The trust layer incorporates components that enable the prevention of unfair ratings accumulated. This layer is composed of two key components: the *trust engine* to calculate a trust level and the *reputation engine* to produce a robust reputation. The trust engine employs the *credential manager* to check the existence and validity of raters' credentials, such as whether it has sufficient trust to provide ratings to others. The trust engine also computes the trust level of certain services (using Eq.1) requested through the *trust computation*. Finally, it encapsulates the feedback submission's functionalities to retrieve ratings from the trust repository through the *feedback provider*.

In the trust layer, the reputation engine computes the reputation (using Eq.2) and outputs it to the trust engine. The function of the reputation engine uses the *reasoning manager* to provide a reputation and updates the newly raters' reputations to the reputation repositories. The VAM logic is encapsulated by *the auction engine*. The *controller* captures the ratings provided by raters as well as to dispatch the monitoring service for monitoring the true value of the rating submitted by the winning rater, which is required to calculate the utility function (see Eq. 3).

The service metadata layer stores trust data in the system. The *trust repository* stores a calculated trust level and historical ratings of services. The reputation repositories store a rater's reputation, which represents the reward and punishment made to raters. Without a central coordinator in distributed environments, each service itself needs to calculate and share services' reputation to others. Hence, the reputation repositories consist of both the *local reputation repository* and the *global reputation repository*. The local reputation repository stores the reputation of raters in which itself is responsible for these raters' reputations, while the global reputation repository stores the reputation of other raters organized by its set of trusted neighbors. The global reputation repository provides an interface for services to either store or retrieve raters' reputations from their trusted neighbors globally.

## 3.2 Key Components

The key elements to support distributed environments are structured in the queuing layer and the service metadata layer. The components in the queuing layer make the application scalable in terms of a number of interacting raters, while the components in the service metadata layer coordinate with others to store and retrieve raters' global reputations. The architecture also has new helper components in the application layer and the trust layer to enable each distributed service to both calculate and share services' reputation to others when a central coordinator in distributed environments does not exist. The details of each component are shown in the architecture (see Fig. 2).

The data disseminator is an application's interface for submitting application messages such as ratings to others. It routes the data to appropriate services in the network. It works with the feedback provider to submit specific services' ratings upon request. Without a central coordinator to evaluate a service's trust level, services need to pay their participation by contributing feedback to each other. To report such feedback to others, the credential manager component is first used to authenticate a requester whether it has sufficient trust to elicit requested services' trust level. After the authentication process is completed, the feedback provider queries the requested services' rating from its trust repository and reports back to the requester.

The data collector is a publicly accessible interface for collecting data from others. In particular, it receives ratings from raters to conduct auctions for evaluating a certain service's trustworthiness. To receive ratings simultaneously, the data collector interface is exposed its corresponding implementation of the trust manager to each rater's thread. As a result, each rater can invoke the trust manager's service within its own thread without blocking itself or others. Therefore, raters can issue their ratings simultaneously without blocking, process with other tasks such as submitting ratings in another auction, and access results whenever the auctioning process is completed. The data collector works with the queue list to stored submitted ratings that arrive faster than they can be processed as pending ratings. The queue list is structured with appropriately sized queue to buffer submitted ratings. To process pending ratings in the queue, the scheduler engine schedules the execution of these ratings received according to a set of given constraints. The scheduler engine also monitors the queue list to identify raters' ratings that become executable, remove the ratings submitted from underbidding strategies, and send all excluded ratings to the auction engine through the controller.

The database proxy serves as the explicit interface of the global reputation repository to separate the repository's public contract from its realization. It performs accessing and manipulating raters' budget (e.g. reputations measured as credits) shared by all services. It also supports the coherent integration of applications that operate on the same data. To propagate changes among shared data, the database proxy offers an observer-based changes notification mechanism in which the global reputation repository is the subject and each requester's trust manager as the observer. The database proxy also supports trust managers to detect underbidding strategies. By maintaining the state of each rater's budgets within the global reputation repository, the database proxy can trigger the trust manager to be notified about the changes of raters' budget when they participate in multiple auctions through the reasoning manager.

### 3.3 Auction-Based Trust Negotiation Protocol

To enable this architecture to prevent cheating behavior from unfair raters, the steps of the VAM are embedded in the trust negotiation protocol, which guides the interactions between layers in this architecture. This protocol is realized by key components across four service layers. The protocol consists of the following four stages: *initiation, interrogation, negotiation,* and *interaction* that realize the interaction of a requester to choose its partner to interact with. Each requester in the line of distributed applications uses the same protocol correspondingly.

At stage one *initiation*, a requester broadcasts a query message to a set of services it is directly linked in the network for requested services. When a service receives a query message, it first checks whether its offered services can meet the requester's functional requirements contained in the query message. If yes, the service then sends the requester a respond message for its acknowledgement to provide the required services. Otherwise, it forwards the query to other services it is directly linked.

At stage two *interrogation,* once receiving the answer messages, the requester can get a list of potential services that can offer the service requested. If the requester has enough experience with those services, it can choose one or a set of services that it trusts most. Otherwise, the requester requests raters their opinions about these potential services' reputations. To compute these reputations, the reasoning manager instructs the auction engine to initialize auction services to gather all values of ratings from raters. Upon receiving an auction request, if a rater has past history of these services and such a rater wants to participate in auctions, it then sends an acknowledgement message containing ratings to the requester. These ratings submitted are stored in the queue list waiting for the execution of the auctioning process.

To exclude unfair ratings from underbidding strategies, the reasoning manager first instructs the controller to dequeue pending ratings from the queue list. These ratings are then checked with corresponding raters' reputations whether the credits' condition of these raters is limited. Since raters can participate in multiple auctions and each distributed service lacks of the overall knowledge of individual's budgets, the database proxy thus helps the reasoning manager to check for the raters' spending credits in their currently active auctions. The database proxy deducts the raters' credits a priori whenever they put their bids in auctions. If a rater submits his rating as exactly the same as the credit they actually have in the repository, the reasoning manager is then notified by the database proxy to verify suspicious ratings using the controller's monitoring services. If the monitored rating's true value is not the same as the rating the rater put in the auction, this rating is removed from the queue list by the scheduler engine. After terminating auctions, all the rest of the ratings in the queue list are sent to the auction engine for computing the auction's results through the controller.

The auction-based calculation steps (see Fig. 3) are as follows: (1) the auction engine initiates a new auction round (for each potential service) by setting an auction time and aggregating ratings from raters; (2) the auction engine terminates auction; (3) the reasoning manager sends all values of ratings already excluded to the auction engine; (4) the auction engine finds the winning rater and instructs the controller to monitor the winner's true value; (5) the controller then monitors the winning rater's true value; (6) the auction engine instructs the VAM component to perform utility computation; (7) the auction engine announces the winning rater and its utility through the reasoning manager; (8) the reasoning manager perform the reward and punishment process and update the newly raters' reputations to the local or global reputation repository; (9) the reasoning manager then calculates a service's reputation.

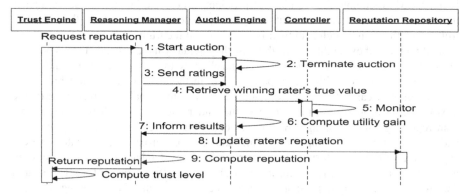

**Fig. 3.** Auction-based Trust Negotiation Protocol

After calculating potential services' reputations, the trust engine then uses these reputations to calculate the services' trust level, which is used to determine whether each service's trust level exceeds the requester's trust threshold to further negotiate with.

At stage three *negotiation*, once having taken the decision of choosing services, the requester then establishes a trust negotiation with the chosen providers directly to get their services. At this stage, the chosen provider is in turn a requester's role to broadcast a query message to all services it is directly linked as in stage 1.

At stage four, *interaction*, after the trust negotiation is established, the requester then gets the chosen providers' services. Once terminating the service, the requester evaluates the service's rating it has experienced and updates it in its trust repository.

## 3.4 Discussion

The architecture is designed to address the integration of the VAM within the distributed trust framework. The VAM is encapsulated in the auction engine, which interacts with the rest of the architecture through the reputation engine. The main advantages of our architectural design are threefold.

First, the separation of each requesting service's interface through data collector enables a scalable architecture handling a large amount of raters interacting with the distributed systems. The cooperation of these services follows a divide and conquer model, in which each service is specialized for solving a particular part of the overall task and all works together on the solution. With the use of structured peer-to-peer overlays as the service repository network, this solution can be built by integrating a result of each service, which in turn sends back to an initiating service (e.g., customer) that floods the request. Hence, the architecture is highly scalable in terms of huge raters involved in the system. In addition, the decoupling between service invocation and service execution makes it possible for each requester to handling multiple requests simultaneously. By using the queue list and the scheduler engine, the raters and its interacting trust manager can interact asynchronously using them as the mediator to store and manipulate raters' ratings. As a result, raters can issue their ratings on the distributed application without blocking itself or other raters.

Second, the architecture makes it possible for the reasoning manager to capture underbidding strategies so that the desired property of the VAM is maintained. Traditional VAM is suitable for the class of problems where the budget of each bidder is unlimited. Without worrying about their money, bidders always submit the bids they truly value the item, which lead their behavior to tell the truth. However, if raters have limited budgets, they might submit the bids they actually have instead. This is because all bidders' bids are strictly tracked and controlled by the auctioneer which they have to register themselves with before participating in the auction. To submit bids more than the bidders can actually afford would result in some penalties. Consequently, the VAM desired property is violated since the underbidding is much more preferable than reporting truthful ratings. By loosely coupling between the reasoning manager and the global reputation repository using the database proxy as a mediator, the encapsulation of the repository variation behind the proxy database makes it possible to notify the corresponding reasoning manger about the state changes of a set of shared data without becoming dependent on each other. As a result, the reasoning manager can dynamically detect underbidding strategies at runtime and therefore react immediately to exclude ratings from raters who have scarce resources before starting auctions. Also, the application is simplified by using the database proxy as a modular component that shields them from the details of their application's functionalities making it reusable when porting to another distributed environment.

Finally, the architecture delivers the VAM's desired property through the auction engine, which interacts with other components according to the VAM logic embedded in a trust negotiation protocol. The VAM outcome is communicated by the reasoning manager in the publisher-subscriber model, which uses asynchronous message communication to send out the result to a number of subscribers (e.g., raters). This asynchronous communication makes our architecture much more efficient when performing an auction amongst dynamic raters whose availability might not be known.

## 4 Case Studies and Evaluation

In this section, the supply chain scenario derived from section 2.3 is used to demonstrate our architecture. The architecture and the key components presented in section 3 are now applied to process ratings to ensure (1) the *effectiveness* of the VAM to prevent the benefits gained by unfair raters when they simply lie, and (2) the *scalability* of the VAM approach in terms of the performance overhead it incurs when the number of raters interacting with distributed systems is huge.

### 4.1 Testbed Setup

The architecture of the supply chain application has been implemented as a set of Web services (see Fig.4) deployed on JXTA distributed environment, which includes a set of open peer-to-peer protocols. All services including customers, retailers, warehouses, manufacturers are built using nodes from JXTA, each having its own trust manager hosted by the Apache AXIS 1.0 Web Server. These services interact with a rater's service through auctions processed by their associated trust managers that receive ratings or any service requests, and sends responses from the application.

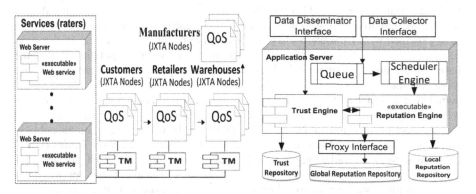

**Fig. 4.** Supply Chain Deployment          **Fig. 5.** Trust Manager (TM)

The components of the trust managers (TM) in Fig. 5 are developed as Java EJBs and deployed as the single trust-based applications hosted by the Tomcat Application Server. This Application Server processes requests from the Web Server and sends responses back to the Web Server. The Application Server implements the auction-based trust negotiation protocol. It communicates with services using SOAP messages and connects to all repositories using the JDBC driver. The reputation repositories implements LDAP components to support service registration. The test environment includes two identical Windows XP machines with 3GHz Core 2 Duo processors. One is used for hosting raters' services, and the other hosts the rest of the applications.

## 4.2  The Experimental Results

**The VAM Property Test.** The purpose of this experiment is to examine how practical usage of the architecture can effectively prevent benefits gained by unfair raters when they lie about their ratings. Unfair raters should gain nothing or even get a penalty, especially when the majority of ratings are unfair. The gain can be measured by the effect of changes in the average reputation of unfair raters when they constantly provide unfairly high or low ratings to potential services. We then observe and compare the results of changing in all raters' reputation when the number of the services being rated increases.

We build a simulation operating with our prototype. We performed a series of experiments by varying the number of unfair raters from 10% to 90%, with 10% incremental per experiment. Each experiment involved 100,000 raters, each of which had to rate QoS ratings of providing services including retailers, warehouse, and manufacturers (i.e. delivery time and availability) requested by requesting services (i.e., customers, retailers, and warehouse respectively). The credit that a rater can spend for the auctions can be calculated by the multiplication of the rater's current reputation (i.e., a percentage measure between 0 and 1) stored in the reputation repository and its total number of transactions previously conducted. To simplify our problem, we consider the case where all raters have past experience with a certain providing service with 70% probability. Each of them has to rate each provider with 50% probability. A fair rater offers QoS ratings to a providing service exactly the same as it perceived while an unfair rater randomly offers QoS ratings above or below it perceived. A total of 10, 300, and 500 auction rounds (equal to the number of the providers rated) have been executed with 1 minute per auction to observe the effect of changes in the average reputation of raters. At the end of each auction, a rater's reputation is updated based on the utility gain/loss calculated by Eq.3. To update a rater's reputation with these calculated utility gains, a rater's newly updated reputation is calculated by accumulating the rater's utility gain with the rater's current reputation, each of which is weighted by their total number of previous transactions (The number of transactions for one auction is equal to 1). To make these newly updated reputations publicly known to others in distributed environments, we use *Distributed Hash Tables* (DHT) techniques to store index reputation [1] amongst a set of trusted services (or neighbors). This method uses multiple hash functions to map a single service ID to several positions where corresponding services will calculate and store this service 's reputation individually. DHT also provides a basic operation for retrieving a specific service's reputation. When other services need some services' reputation, they can retrieve them using DHT operation with service ID as a parameter.

In our setting, we initially set the reputation of unfair raters to any random numbers between 5 to 15 percents while for the fair raters is between 10 to 20 percents based on 100 transactions previously conducted. To make a trust decision, each requesting service chooses one of the providing services whose reputation is the highest to interact with. Fig. 6 shows that the unfair raters' reputation decreases when the number of raters lying increases. This is because when the majority of raters are unfair, the unfair raters have more chance to win the auction, however their gains of reputation are impaired by the punishment made to these unfair winning raters by the VAM. In contrast, we can see that the reputation of fair raters increases as the result of the reward granted by the VAM process.

The results clearly demonstrate that The VAM can help preventing cheating behavior by ensuring that unfair raters would not gain any benefits when they simply lie. This is evident by the significantly decrease in the reputation of unfair raters, especially when the majority of ratings are unfair. These VAM-based rating results are in clear contrast to existing preventive mechanisms that fail to motivate raters to report truthful ratings when the majority of raters lie. Also, our approach promotes a direct incentive for fair raters participating in an auction due to the increasing of reputation when they give fair ratings.

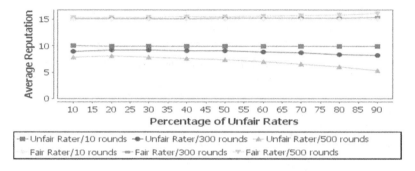

**Fig. 6.** The Effect of Changes in the Average Reputation of Raters

**Scalability Test.** In this experiment, we intend to observe what extent the decentralized supply chain can scale when integrating with the VAM. We measured the performance overhead in terms of application response time (second) with and without the VAM by varying a number of raters from 10 to 1,000,000. Experiments were performed with 5 auction rounds conducted by each requesting service. The results show that no significant performance overhead for 1,000,000 raters (see Fig. 7) regardless of using the VAM.

We also compared our result with the equivalent centralized supply chain as shown in Fig. 8. From the graph, we can notice that the response time is initially identical between both infrastructures when a number of customer's requests are at the early stage. This can be linked to the sequential chain of applications. Each requesting service needs to choose one of the providing services first before delegating these services to conduct auctions. Hence, each service's task cannot be performed in parallel because they have to call others until completing the overall process. Nevertheless, the response time of the decentralized supply chain is still slightly better than the corresponding centralized one due to the separation of design for the explicit interface that is exposed to each rater's thread making the system receive ratings simultaneously.

When the number of customer's requests increases, the centralized supply chain's performance overhead is approximately 3 times higher than the decentralized one with the performance without the VAM as a benchmark. This is due to the fact that all services in the line of supply chain can serve different requests from different services. Hence, these services can have an opportunity to perform their tasks separately at the same time without only waiting for specific sequential lines of orders.

The plot demonstrates that the distributed trust framework is more much scalable handling a very large number of raters compared to the centralized infrastructure.

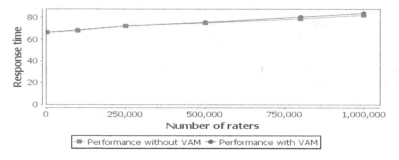

**Fig. 7.** Performance Variation

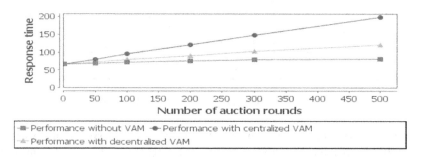

**Fig. 8.** Scalability Variation

## 5  Related Work

Much previous research in P2P communities has been applied statistical methods to handle the problems of unfair ratings. These approaches detect and exclude unfair ratings based on the analysis of statistical data from former transactions. Aberer et al. [13] propose the reputation model that allows peers to file a complaint to other malicious peers after each transaction. This model takes a majority of accumulated complaints to identify malicious peers. Kamvar et al. [14] proposed EigenTrust that can uniquely identifies each peer's global trust value, which is calculated from the experience of other peers in the network. EigenTrust takes into account the majority of voting from pre-trusted peers to check fake reputation scores reported. Peertrust [15] evaluates the trustworthiness of a peer by considering the quality of feedbacks based on five important parameters. This framework can eliminate dishonest feedback using the similarity between two different groups.

Although these detective techniques provide a promising approach to predict the trend of unfair ratings, they still suffer from one major drawback – lack of sufficient ratings. The main reason is that the raters might not have a direct incentive to provide ratings for others. This is because providing ratings for others requires some effort, which might end up with losing business profits due to wasting time or decreasing the bandwidth of raters' running services. As a result, the trends of untruthful behavior cannot correctly be used to detect unfair ratings or even can misrepresent one service's reputation due to insufficient ratings captured.

The limitations of detective mechanisms have thus drawn intensive research activities on developing incentive techniques to either eliminate or prevent incentives to lie. Such mechanisms are devised and embedded into a reputation model to stimulate services to not only provide ratings but truthfully offer ratings. Unlike statistical approaches to detect unfair ratings, preventive approaches aim to make sure *'lie does not gain'*. This property makes it in the best interest of one participant to report the truth so that truthful reporting maximizes their expected revenue. However, no incentive mechanisms can claim their victory. They still have some limitations.

Payment mechanisms offer side payment to raters that fairly rate others. These mechanisms guarantee that lying is not in the best interest of the raters. Dellarocas [12] proposes "Goodwill Hunting" mechanism that encourages sellers to truthfully reveal their qualities of product by rebating some payment to sellers based on the similar quality of transactions among the whole communities. Jurca et. al. [11] describes incentive compatible payment scheme organized through a set of distributed broker agents. These agents buy feedback and sell reputation information aggregated from the feedback. The author makes faithful reporting an optimal strategy by devising a payment scheme that pays a submitted report if it has the same value of randomly chosen report.

However, the side payment scheme cannot ensure truthful reporting when the majority of raters lie. This is because these approaches assume the majority of ratings provided must be fair, and unfair ratings are in the minority as outliers and reward a rater a side payment only if its rating is the same as the next rating of the same rated service provided by another rater. Therefore, if the majority of ratings are unfair, this opens up the possibility for dishonest raters to gain benefits from the payment given to similar ratings as many others, which is unfair. Hence, embedding such mechanisms into distributed systems could lead to ineffective solutions to prevent cheating behavior.

In addition to the limitations of the mechanisms itself, very little attention has been devoted to the exploration of how these mechanisms can be composed in distributed systems. This is because these approaches either assume the existence of an infrastructure or some trusted centralized party that maintains the digital currency or reputation of participants for rewarding or charging. As a result, computation is all centralized in the trust framework, which imposes the research questions in terms of their extension to support distributed environments.

# 6 Conclusion

In this paper, we presented the trust-based architecture with the Vickrey Auction Mechanism (VAM) integrated in distributed environments. The VAM is encapsulated with each distributed service's architecture and embedded in an auction-based trust negotiation protocol realized in relevant components. These components interact with trust components in our architecture to prevent cheating behavior. An example on a supply chain is implemented to validate our approach when raters give unfair ratings.

Our architecture integrating with the VAM induces an effective trust negotiation by preventing the distributed trust framework from being exploited by unfair raters, especially when the majority of them lie about their ratings. Our architecture also ensures that the system is highly scalable compared to the centralized infrastructure.

One drawback, however, is that when a number of participating services involved in distributed systems is very high, a lot of flooding searches might induce a large volume of traffic overhead. This imposes the research questions in the architectural design that leverages the VAM's benefit of preventing cheating behavior with optimized search efficiency. Future work involves optimizing architectural solution to support a hybrid trust framework with the VAM capability. The resulting architecture will be optimized using centralized registries as super peers to maintain a global resource index of distributed services' group to reduce traffic overhead significantly.

**Acknowledgments.** NICTA is funded by the Australian Government as represented by the Department of Broadband, Communications and the Digital Economy and the Australian Research Council through the ICT Centre of Excellence program.

# References

1. Jøsang, A., Ismail, R., Boyd, C.: A Survey of Trust and Reputation Systems for Online Service Provision. Decision Support Systems (2005)
2. Dellarocas, C.: Immunizing Online Reputation Reporting Systems Against Unfair Ratings and Discriminatory Behavior. In: Proceedings of the 2nd ACM Conference on Electronic Commerce (EC), Minneapolis, MN (2000)
3. Sen, S., Sajja, N.: Robustness of Reputation-based Trust: Boolean Case. In: Proceedings of the 1st International Joint Conference on AAMAS. ACM, New York (2002)
4. Klemperer, P.: Auctions: Theory and Practice. Princeton University Press, Princeton (2004)
5. Phoomvuthisarn, S.: Trust and Role Based Access Control for Secure Interoperation ("TracSI"). In: ISCIT (2007)
6. Withby, A., Jøsang, A., Indulska, J.: Filtering Out Unfair Ratings in Bayesian Reputation Systems. In: Proceedings of the Third International Joint Conference on Autonomous Agents and Multi Agent Systems, New York, pp. 106–117 (2004)
7. Sicard, S., Boyer, F., Palma, N.D.: Using Components for Architecture-Based Management: the self-repair case. In: Proceeding of the 30th International Conference on Software Engineering, Leipzig, Germany (May 2008)
8. Wang, Y., Vassileva, J.: Toward Trust and Reputation Based Web Service Selection: A Survey. In: 5th The International Social Work & Society' Academy, Italy (2007)

9. Braynov, S., Sandhome, T.: Incentive Compatible Mechanism for Trust Revealation. In: Proceedings of the 1st International Joint Conference on AAMAS, Italy (2002)
10. Liu, J., Issarny, V.: An Incentive Compatible Reputation Mechanism for Ubiquitous Computing Environments. International Journal of Information Security (2007)
11. Jurca, R., Faltings, B.: An Incentive-Compatible Reputation Mechanism. In: Proceeding of the IEEE Conference on E-Commerce, Newport Beach, CA, USA (2003)
12. Dellarocas, C.: Goodwill Hunting: An Economically Efficient Online Feedback Mechanism for Environments with Variable Product Quality. In: Padget, J.A., Shehory, O., Parkes, D.C., Sadeh, N.M., Walsh, W.E. (eds.) AMEC 2002. LNCS (LNAI), vol. 2531, pp. 238–252. Springer, Heidelberg (2002)
13. Aberer, K., Despotovic, Z.: Managing Trust in a Peer-2-Peer Information System. In: Proceedings of the 10th international Conference on information and Knowledge Management, Atlanta, Georgia, USA (October 2001)
14. Kamvar, S.D., Schlosser, M.T., Garcia-Molina, H.: The Eigentrust Algorithm for Reputation Management in P2P Networks. In: Proceedings of the 12th international Conference on World Wide Web, Budapest, Hungary (2003)
15. Xiong, L., Liu, L.: PeerTrust: Supporting Reputation-Based Trust for Peer-to-Peer Electronic Communities. In: Knowledge and Data Engineering (July 2004)
16. Vu, L.-H., Hauswirth, M., Aberer, K.: QoS-Based Service Selection and Ranking with Trust and Reputation Management. In: Meersman, R., Tari, Z. (eds.) OTM 2005. LNCS, vol. 3760, pp. 466–483. Springer, Heidelberg (2005)
17. Phoomvuthisarn, S., Liu, Y., Hun, J.: An Architectural Approach to Composing Reputation-based Trustworthy Services. In: ASWEC, Auckland, New Zealand (2010)
18. Zhu, L., Staples, M., Tosic, V.: On Creating Industry-Wide Reference Architectures. In: 12th IEEE International EDOC Conference, Munich, Germany (2008)

# Automated Detection of Least Privilege Violations in Software Architectures

Riccardo Scandariato, Koen Buyens, and Wouter Joosen

IBBT-DistriNet
Katholieke Universiteit Leuven
3001 Leuven, Belgium
first.last@cs.kuleuven.be

**Abstract.** Due to the lack of both precise definitions and effective software engineering methodologies, security principles are often neglected by software architects, resulting in potentially high-risk threats to the systems. This work lays the formal foundations for the understanding of the least privilege (LP) principle in software architectures and provides a technique to identify LP violations. The proposed approach is supported by tools and has been validated in four case studies, one of which is presented in detail in this paper.

**Keywords:** security, least privilege, architectural analysis.

## 1 Introduction

Security design principles, like least privilege and complete mediation, have survived the test of time since they have been introduced by the seminal work of Saltzer and Schroeder [16]. Their value in secure engineering processes is now widely acknowledged, e.g., in Microsoft's Security Development Lifecycle [9]. However, the concrete implementation of these principles in a software design is often problematic due to the lack of a precise definition. This is particularly true for the architectural design [5]. Because of the key role played by the architecture in the development process, failing to support sound security principles at this level could jeopardize the entire software project and could result in severe costs to fix the vulnerabilities afterwards. Therefore, ways of expressing and reasoning about security principles in software architectures are needed [21].

The main goal of this paper is to improve the support for the least privilege (LP) security principle in software architectures by providing a precise definition of LP violations. Such definition enables formal, automated analysis of architectural design models.

As highlighted in a previous study, LP is a well recognized principle [5]. In the literature (e.g., [19]), least privilege is given the following informal definition. In a particular abstraction layer of a computing environment, every *principal* (i.e., a user or a computer process executing on behalf of a user) must be able to access only those computing resources and information that are necessary to complete its *tasks*. A task is generally comprised by a sequence of smaller steps,

M. Ali Babar and I. Gorton (Eds.): ECSA 2010, LNCS 6285, pp. 150–165, 2010.

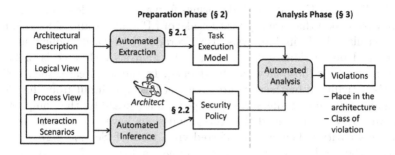

**Fig. 1.** Overview of the proposed approach

namely *actions*. In this context, a *permission* represents the right for a principal to execute an action.

As an example of LP violation, consider a Unix utility program (e.g., kill) that might need elevated privileges to execute. One strategy is to give the "root" password to the users that need to use that utility program. This way, the users can execute the program via the su command. Clearly, this is a violation of the least privilege principle, as the users have too many, unnecessary rights. A better strategy is to use sudo, which allows to assign finer-grained permissions. This work addresses the same concern, although at the level of software architectures.

The correct enforcement of the LP principle prevents popular vulnerabilities related to elevation of privilege and task interference. The former are vulnerabilities that can be exploited by an attacker to gain access to resources that would have normally been shielded. The latter are vulnerabilities that can be exploited by an attacker to subvert the planned outcome of a task.

*Approach.* As depicted in Figure 1, the approach presented in this paper consists of two phases: preparation and analysis. As shown in the left-hand side of the figure, the approach uses a conventional architectural description to identify violations. Indeed, the architecture is expected to be documented via a logical view, a process view, and the interaction scenarios, e.g., in UML. In an architectural description, the *logical view* typically decomposes the system into a set of key abstractions, called components. Every component can be described in terms of the actions (commonly known as operations) of its interfaces. The *process view* specifies which runtime element (thread or process) executes the components identified in the logical view. The view also relates these runtime elements to the principals that execute them. These principals can be end users (e.g. John) or system accounts (e.g. the web server). The *scenarios* show how the architectural elements work together by means of tasks (commonly known as use cases), which consist of a sequence of temporally ordered invocations of actions. This minimal documentation set can be safely assumed to be available in all software projects where an explicit architectural design effort has been carried out.

In preparation for the analysis step, a so-called Task Execution Model is automatically derived from the above documentation and thence used for formal analysis. The Task Execution Model brings forward all the elements of an architecture (like tasks) that are key for the sake of LP analysis and hides the unnecessary details. The formal analysis also leverages the security policy describing the assigned permissions in the system. The analysis technique is orthogonal to the many ways the policy can be defined. In the ideal case, such policy is explicitly articulated by the software architect based on input from the relevant stakeholders (including the security expert) and, possibly, the company-wide rules. Alternatively, provided that the permissions have not been documented, a realistic security policy can be inferred via a tool (cf. Section 2.2).

During the analysis phase, a tool leverages a formally-based technique to analyze both the Task Execution Model and the security policy. The analysis technique identifies three important classes of violations and pinpoints the places in the architecture where each violation occurs (cf. Sections 3.1 and 3.2). More potential violations can be detected by applying heuristics-based techniques (cf. Section 3.3).

The identified violations can be tackled by means of architectural refactoring rules, which are part of previous work and are not covered here [4]. However, this paper provides a theoretical framework that enables a more informed selection of the appropriate refactoring rule depending on the class of LP violation that has been identified.

*Contribution.* The contribution of this work is twofold: (i) this paper provides a precise definition of least privilege in a software architecture and (ii) describes a formal analysis technique to identify three classes of LP violations. In this work, a collection of views are jointly interpreted. Further, the analysis uses a model that realistically captures important aspects of real world-systems, e.g., the delegation relationships among principals cooperating in the completion of a task. Finally, a complete tool chain is provided.

The rest of this paper is structured as follows. The preparation phase is described in Section 2 while the analysis phase is presented in Section 3. Section 4 describes the validation of the presented approach by means of four case studies, one of which is illustrated in detail. Finally, Section 5 compares the approach to the related work and Section 6 presents the concluding remarks.

## 2   Preparation Phase

This section presents the formal definition of the Task Execution Model and describes the type of security policy that is expected to be documented for the system under analysis. The definitions given here are then used in Section 3.

### 2.1   Task Execution Model

The Task Execution Model can be derived from three established architectural views. As an example, consider the simple architecture of a software maintenance system documented in Figure 2. Figure 2(a) contains the logical view (components, interfaces, connectors) and the processes (see the dashed circles). Due to space limitations, the two views have been overlaid. Figure 2(b) depicts three

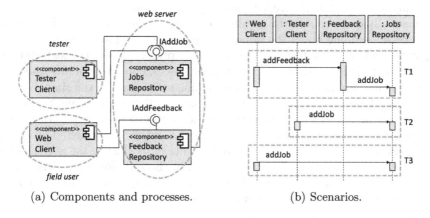

(a) Components and processes.              (b) Scenarios.

**Fig. 2.** Sample architectural description

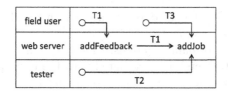

**Fig. 3.** Sample Task Execution Model

scenarios. The system allows the field users of a given software package to provide feedback to the developers, e.g., in order to request new features (task T1). The feedback is stored in the Feedback Repository via the addFeedback action of the IAddFeedback interface. Feedback reports are processed internally within the Feedback Repository component and whenever many similar reports have been submitted, e.g., requesting the same feature, a maintenance job is added to the Jobs Repository component via the addJob action of the IAddJob interface. Testers also add maintenance jobs to the repository whenever they discover a bug (task T2). This functionality is also enabled for the bugs discovered by field users (task T3). Each front-end client runs in a separate process. The Web Client is executed by the field user and the Tester Client by the tester. The back-end components run as a single process under the web server server principal (i.e., the back-end is a web application).

Note that the above example is not meant to describe a real-world system. It is introduced for illustrative purposes only. As such, it is very small and the functionality has been decomposed in an ad-hoc way so that violations can be visible at a glance. More sophisticated examples are presented in Section 4.

The Task Execution Model relates the architectural concepts (e.g., components, processes, and so on) to LP concepts (e.g., principals, tasks, delegation relationships, and so on). This model is partially inspired by the Business Process

Modeling Notation [20]. Figure 3 depicts the Task Execution Model that has been automatically derived from the architectural description of Figure 2. In general, all processes running under the same principal are merged and represented as a single "swim lane" (the term is borrowed from process flow diagrams). Actions that belong to (the interfaces of) the components executed by the processes of a given principal are placed in the corresponding swim lane. In the simple example presented above, there are only two actions and they both belong to the web server swim lane. Tasks are represented as flows of actions by means of labeled arrows. Furthermore, tasks have a starting event, which is considered an action as well. From the Task Execution Model, it is easy to identify the actions each principal completes personally (they are within the corresponding swim lane), the actions it delegates to other principals (arrows across swim lanes), and the dependencies between actions (arrows between actions).

**Formal Definition.** More formally, the following sets are defined:

- A countable set $\mathcal{P}$ of named principals, which are denoted by $p_i$. These correspond to the swim lanes.
- A countable set $\mathcal{A}$ of named actions, which are denoted by $a_i$. Actions (including the start events) are associated with the corresponding swim lanes via the $\mathcal{PA}$ relationship, which is introduced later on.
- A countable set $\mathcal{T}$ of named tasks, which are denoted by $t_i$. Tasks are represented as directed graphs. Nodes are actions and they are interconnected in the order they are performed. Tasks are represented as graphs so that the parallel execution of multiple sequences (of actions) can be modeled. Tasks are associated with the principals that initiate them via the $\mathcal{PT}$ relationship, which is introduced later on.

The principal-action relationship is introduced to associate a principal $p$ to any action $a$ that is in a component that runs in a process executing under that principal. It is defined as follows: $\mathcal{PA} \subseteq \mathcal{P} \times \mathcal{A} \mid (p, a) \in \mathcal{PA} \Leftrightarrow p \in \mathcal{P} \ offers$ $a \in \mathcal{A}$. The above relationship can be derived via the principal-process and process-component relations (process view) combined with the component-action relations (logical view). This is intuitive and is not shown here. For conciseness, the start events are not mentioned in the above definition.

The principal-task relationship is introduced to associate a principal $p$ to any task $t$ that is initiated by that principal. It is defined as follows: $\mathcal{PT} \subseteq \mathcal{P} \times \mathcal{T} \mid$ $(p, t) \in \mathcal{PT} \Leftrightarrow p \in \mathcal{P} \ initiates \ t \in \mathcal{T}$.

The set of actions in a task can be obtained via the operator actionsOf(t). Concerning the actions, two additional operators are defined:

- follows returns true when an action is immediately invoked after another in a task.
$follows : \mathcal{A} \times \mathcal{A} \times \mathcal{T} \rightarrow \{true, false\} :$
$follows(a_i, a_j, t) \mapsto true \Leftrightarrow \exists$ directed edge from $a_i$ to $a_j$ in $t$

– **after** returns true when an action is eventually invoked after another in a task.

$after : \mathcal{A} \times \mathcal{A} \times \mathcal{T} \rightarrow \{true, false\}$ :

$after(a_i, a_j, t) \mapsto true \Leftrightarrow \exists$ path from $a_i$ to $a_j$ in $t$

With respect to the above definitions, a principal is directlyResponsible for an action if it "must execute" that action to complete a task or if it "must delegate" the execution of that action to another principal (1 hop) who completes a part of the task. I.e.:

$directlyResponsible(p, a) : \mathcal{P} \times \mathcal{A} \rightarrow \{true, false\}$ :

$(p, a) \mapsto true \Leftrightarrow mustExecute(p, a) \lor mustDelegate(p, a)$

A principal mustExecute an action if that action is part of a task and it is executed in one of the processes that run under that principal. I.e.:

$mustExecute(p, a) : \mathcal{P} \times \mathcal{A} \rightarrow \{true, false\}$ :

$(p, a) \mapsto true \Leftrightarrow a \in \mathcal{PA}_p \land ( \exists t \in \mathcal{T} \mid a \in actionsOf(t) )$

The set of actions a principal $p$ must execute is represented by $mustExecute_p$ $= \{a \in \mathcal{A} \mid mustExecute(p, a)\}$

Note that the relationship $mustExecute_p \subseteq \mathcal{PA}_p$ holds, as there could be actions that are not used in any task.

A principal mustDelegate the execution of an action to another principal if that action is part of a task he must complete and it is executed by another principal (1 hop). I.e.:

$mustDelegate(p, a) : \mathcal{P} \times \mathcal{A} \rightarrow \{true, false\}$ :

$(p, a) \mapsto true \Leftrightarrow a \notin \mathcal{PA}_p \land ( \exists a' \in \mathcal{A} , \exists t \in \mathcal{T} \mid a' \neq a \land a' \in \mathcal{PA}_p \land follows(a', a, t) )$

The set of actions a principal $p$ must delegate is represented by $mustDelegate_p$ $= \{a \in \mathcal{A} \mid mustDelegate(p, a)\}$

**Definition 1.** *The set of actions a principal $p$ is directly responsible for is represented by $\mathcal{D}_p = \{a \in \mathcal{A} \mid directlyResponsible(p, a)\}$*

Further, a principal is indirectlyResponsible for an action if that action is after another action (in the same task) that the principal has delegated. I.e.:

$indirectlyResponsible(p, a) : \mathcal{P} \times \mathcal{A} \rightarrow \{true, false\}$ :

$(p, a) \mapsto true \Leftrightarrow a \notin \mathcal{PA}_p \land ( \exists a' \in \mathcal{A} , \exists a'' \in \mathcal{A} , \exists t \in \mathcal{T} \mid a \neq a' \neq a'' \land a' \notin \mathcal{PA}_p \land a'' \in \mathcal{PA}_p \land follows(a'', a', t) \land after(a', a, t) )$

**Definition 2.** *The set of actions a principal $p$ is indirectly responsible for is represented by $\mathcal{I}_p = \{a \in \mathcal{A} \mid indirectlyResponsible(p, a)\}$*

### 2.2   Security Policy

Together with the tasks, the permissions are the second pillar of the architectural analysis of LP violations. The permissions represent the right for a principal to invoke the interface actions. The assigned permissions embody the access control policy of the system. Many policy models and languages can be used to specify the assigned permissions. For instance, permissions can be assigned directly to principals as it happens in Access Control Lists (ACLs, [12]). Alternatively, additional levels of indirection can be used to make the permissions assignment more manageable, e.g., by using Role-Based Access Control (RBAC [17]). In order to preserve the generality of the approach, this paper does not assume any advanced feature of the policy language. Hence, this work focuses on a minimal policy model (similar to ACLs) where a permission is granted to a principal (subject) to invoke an action on a component (resource). Permissions that are specified via more advanced policy languages can be mapped to the model adopted here [1].

**Formal Definition.** A policy can be represented as a set of principal-action tuples:
$\mathcal{AUTH} \subseteq \mathcal{P} \times \mathcal{A} \mid (p,a) \in \mathcal{AUTH} \Leftrightarrow p \in \mathcal{P}$ is allowed to invoke $a \in \mathcal{A}$.

Access to the starting event is considered to be implicitly granted to the principal initiating the corresponding task. In general, a function is defined to determine whether a principal is granted permission for an action:
$canCall(p,a) : \mathcal{P} \times \mathcal{A} \to \{true, false\} : (p,a) \mapsto true \Leftrightarrow (p,a) \in \mathcal{AUTH}$

**Definition 3.** *The set of actions a principal $p$ can call is represented by $\mathcal{C}_p = \{a \in \mathcal{A} \mid canCall(p,a)\}$*

The key question of the LP analysis is to determine whether this set is too large with respect to defined tasks. The answer to that question is provided in Section 3.

**Inferring the Permissions Assignment.** In general, the permissions should be documented and available to the analysis technique. The architect (or the security specialist) should provide the principals with an initial set of permissions. However, if the permissions assignment is not explicitly documented, an automated procedure can be used to assign permissions to the principals in a sensible way. The algorithm (and the supporting tool) assigns each principal $p$ with the permission to execute the actions in the set resulting from the union of $\mathcal{PA}_p$ (the start events and the actions of the principal's components) and mustDelegate$_p$ (the actions the principal delegates).

## 3   Analysis Phase

From a helicopter view, there are two broad situations that must be detected. First, assuming that the tasks structure defined by the architect is correct, no principal should be able to call more actions than it is minimally necessary in order to carry out its tasks. Second, the structure of the tasks itself must be questioned. In particular, no principal must be able to use the permissions coming from one task to interfere with the execution of other tasks – its own or, worse, those of other principals. From a methodological perspective, the analysis technique follows two steps. First, the principals are considered in isolation, and then, further violations are spotted by considering groups of principals.

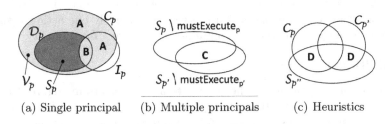

(a) Single principal    (b) Multiple principals    (c) Heuristics

**Fig. 4.** Least privilege analysis

## 3.1  Single Principal

For each principal, the intersections of the sets in Figure 4(a) are computed. $\mathcal{D}_p$ represents the set of actions a principal must have permission to call in order to complete its tasks, given the tasks structure in the Task Execution Model. $\mathcal{C}_p$ represents the set of actions a principal can call, according to the security policy. If $\mathcal{C}_p$ is not a super-set of $\mathcal{D}_p$, the principal does not have sufficient rights to execute the tasks it is assigned to. Although this is not a LP violation, such inconsistency in the security policy is detected by the analysis technique as well.

The set of actions that can be safely granted to a principal in isolation ($\mathcal{S}_p$, in dark gray) is defined as the difference between the sets of directly responsible and indirectly responsible actions ($\mathcal{S}_p = \mathcal{D}_p \setminus \mathcal{I}_p$). Any action in the light gray area ($\mathcal{V}_p = \mathcal{C}_p \setminus \mathcal{S}_p$) is considered a violation. As shown in the picture, violations are classified as type A or B according to the place they may occur.

*Type A: One principal is assigned unnecessary permissions.* A principal is allowed to call an action, but it is not required to do so in order to complete its tasks. For instance, consider the example introduced in Figure 3. Suppose that the architect assigned the tester with the permissions to call the addFeedback and the addJob actions. The former action represents a violation, because addFeedback is not required for its task (see T2 in Figure 3). A cause for this type of violation (beside inadvertence) could be the incorrect granularity of the assigned permissions. For instance, given that a role-based access control model is used, the permissions assigned to some role could be too coarse-grained for the existing tasks. In order to solve the violations of this type, the unnecessary permissions must be removed from the security policy, e.g., by using finer-grained access rules.

*Type B: One principal can shortcut the planned sequence of actions in a task.* Actions in $\mathcal{D}_p$ are necessary in order to complete the tasks a principal is responsible for (by definition). However, actions that are both in $\mathcal{D}_p$ and in $\mathcal{I}_p$ are dangerous, because they enable the principal to circumvent the planned interaction with an action that is meant to be invoked via an indirect execution path only. For instance, consider the example in Figure 3. The addJob action of the field-user principal represents a violation, because it is an indirect action for task T1 and a direct action for task T3. Hence, the field user can skip the processing logic of addFeedback (a feature is added when enough requests are received) and demand for a new feature directly via the addJob action. Violations of this type can be solved by splitting the action in two parts, namely one action with the direct functionality and one other containing the indirect functionality.

## 3.2  Multiple Principals

For each couple of principals, the intersections of the sets in Figure 4(b) are computed. Plainly, $S \setminus$ mustExecute represents the mustDelegate part of $S$.

*Type C: Two principals are responsible for interacting tasks.* A violation exists if an action in the mustDelegate part of $S_p$ is also in the mustDelegate part of $S_{p'}$ (with $p' \neq p$), but for different tasks. This violation enables a principal to call an action of another principal's task and, thus, partially complete a task it is not responsible for. For instance, consider the example described in Figure 3. The addJob action belongs to the mustDelegate part of $S$ of both the tester (for task T2) and the field user (for task T3). Therefore, the field user is able to complete task T2, which was intended for the tester only. Violations of this type can be solved by splitting the action in two parts, namely one action for each task.

## 3.3  Heuristic-Based Techniques

The types of violation mentioned above are most likely going to be sources of flaws in the end system if they are not resolved, e.g., via the transformations described in [4]. These violations are sharply identified by means of the formally-based techniques described so far.

More *potential* violations can be identified by means of heuristic-based techniques. However, this type of violations should be handled warily. Rather than being crisp indicators of architectural weaknesses, they represent attention points for the architect and the implementers.

For instance, the names of the actions and their parameters can be used to conjecture whether two actions of the same component use some internal shared state and, therefore, can cause unplanned interactions. E.g., modifyFeedback and getFeedback will probably access the same attribute. This heuristic estimates whether the result of an action can be influenced by an external principal that tampers with the shared state. Violations of this type can be solved by splitting the component into smaller (segregated) parts and executing each part by independent processes (i.e., under different principals).

However, in order to be certain that a real interaction exists, additional information must be provided. In case the architecture of an existing system is being evaluated, the code of the two actions can be analyzed. Alternatively, a formal specification of the pre- and post-conditions of the two actions must be present. Unfortunately, this kind of documentation is hardly available for real-world software architecture artifacts and, hence, it is not assumed to exist in the context of this work.

The analysis tool implements heuristics similar to the one mentioned above and the formal model is used to direct the analysis. The "corners" of the architectural design where potential (shared state) interactions can take place are scoped by means of the model, as shown in Figure 4(c). The actions belonging to the intersections marked as D are screened against the heuristic-based rules. This reduces the number of false positives that might be produced if the entire architecture were evaluated.

### 3.4 False Positives

It is hard to conceptually assess the number of wrongly detected violations (false positives) and unidentified violations (false negatives) until the system has been implemented. However, as a rule of thumb, violations of type C and D are more likely to contain false positives and, hence, deserve special attention. Indeed, the implementation logic of the actions causing a violation of type C can ensure that the principals only follow their legitimate execution path. Hence, the violation will not become manifest as a flaw in the implemented system. Further, violations of type D can be false positives if the necessary controls are enforced to prevent any influence between the actions causing the violation.

## 4   Validation

The approach presented in this paper has been validated by means of four case studies, one of which is more extensively presented in this section. The case studies are, in order of increasing size, (i) a modified version of the chat system delivered with ArchStudio [6], (ii) a conference management system [13], (iii) a digital publishing system [11], and (iv) a banking system [7]. The size of the case studies, in terms of components, actions and tasks is summarized in Table 1. Note that each component is executed in a stand-alone process running under a different principal.

Table 2 summarizes the results obtained by analyzing the case studies. Later in this section, the banking case study is elaborated upon in order to appreciate the type of problems that can be encountered in practice. However, we first draw some general observations about the overall trends in the numbers. The authors have screened the results obtained from the tool and no false positives were

**Table 1.** Size of the case studies

|            | Chat System | Conference System | Publishing System | Banking System |
|------------|-------------|-------------------|-------------------|----------------|
| Components | 3           | 8                 | 13                | 18             |
| Actions    | 6           | 27                | 82                | 106            |
| Tasks      | 2           | 11                | 22                | 22             |

**Table 2.** Number of detected violations for the case studies

|        | Chat System | Conference System | Publishing System | Banking System |
|--------|-------------|-------------------|-------------------|----------------|
| Type A | 0           | 0                 | 1                 | 28             |
| Type B | 2           | 0                 | 7                 | 9              |
| Type C | 0           | 2                 | 6                 | 13             |
| Type D | 2           | 15                | 90                | 6              |

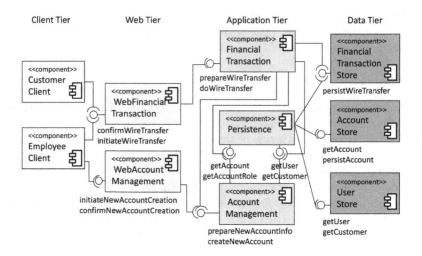

**Fig. 5.** Excerpt of the banking system's architecture

detected. In general, formally-based violations (type A, B, and C) tend to grow with the size of the case study, which is not surprising. As far as heuristic-based violations (type D) are concerned, this pattern has not been observed.

Type A violations (unnecessary permissions) represent the low-hanging fruit. Therefore, they are a strong indicator of poor architectural coherence, which becomes manifest with larger case studies. In particular, the violations in the banking system are caused by the assignment of permissions that are too coarse-grained, while the violation in the publication system is due to an action that is not used by any of the defined tasks. Type B violations (shortcut in a task) are an indicator of missteps made by the architect, typically because a complex system has evolved over time. Type C violations (interacting tasks) are often due to "fat" actions that implement multiple functional requirements, or by tasks interacting with a general-purpose component (e.g., a database). For instance, the number of these violations is higher in the banking system, because many tasks use the same data access actions.

## 4.1   Banking System: Architecture and Permissions

The banking system case study has been chosen because the documentation contains the required views for our analysis, including a partial mapping between permissions and actions. The system supports two major scenarios: banking employees use the system in their everyday operations (20 tasks), while customers can connect from home (2 tasks). The system is able to handle accounts management and financial transactions such as wire transfers.

As shown in Figure 5, the logical view decomposes the system into four tiers. The client tier consists of components used by a customer or employee to interact with the web tier (CustomerClient and EmployeeClient, respectively). The web tier relays user requests to the application logic tier. The application is

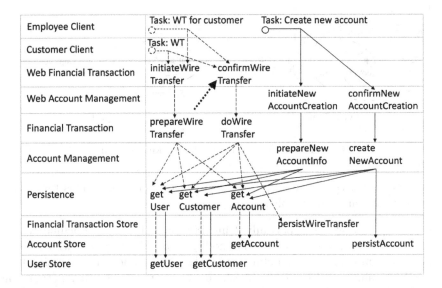

**Fig. 6.** Task Execution Model for a subset of the banking system

responsible for processing the incoming transactions, while the data tier stores the results of these transactions. The application tier consists of an Authorization component handling access control decisions (not shown in the figure), an AccountManagement component handling account information, and a Financial-Transaction component providing the logic for processing financial transactions. The Persistence component is used as proxy for the data tier.

The process view was not defined in the architectural documentation. Hence, we assume that every component runs in its own process and with its own principal. The results are comparable to the case of separate principals per tier.

Figure 6 shows a small subset of the complete Task Execution Model. The figure only contains the following tasks:

- *Wire transfer*: a customer wants to add a wire transfer to a list of pending transactions. This task (dashed arrows) is executed in two phases. In a first phase, the CustomerClient initiates the wire transfer by accessing the initiateWireTransfer action of the web tier. This tier forwards the request to the application tier via the prepareWireTransfer action. By interacting with the Persistence component, the application logic retrieves information about the customer executing the wire transfer, the customer the money should be wired to, and the account details for both. In a second phase, the validated order is presented to the user for the final approval (via the confirmWire-Transfer).
- *Wire transfer for customer*: a bank employee executes a wire transfer on behalf of a customer. This is similar to the previous task and, therefore, dashed arrows are used.

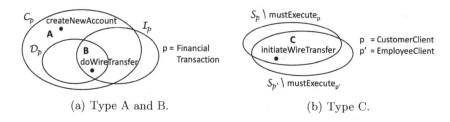

(a) Type A and B.                    (b) Type C.

**Fig. 7.** Violations of LP in the banking system

- *Create new account*: an employee creates a new customer. This task (solid arrows) executes in two phases as above.

The security view was only partially defined in the architectural documentation. The defined permissions included the modify account permission, which allows principals to modify account details or pending transactions by accessing both the doWireTransfer and the createNewAccount actions. Some other permissions were defined in the documentation, but no mapping to the corresponding architectural actions was provided. In this case, the mapping has been manually added. This was straightforward, as the permission name indicated its relation to the architectural actions. Finally, the principal-permission assignments were missing. These have been inferred via the algorithm in Section 2.2.

### 4.2 Banking System: Analysis

The analysis technique identified all types of violations. However, we dwell on the formally defined violations only (A, B and C), which represent the core contribution of this paper.

A first set of violations (type A) is related to the permission granularity (28 violations). For instance, consider the FinancialTransaction principal in Figure 6. It can call the createNewAccount action but need not to access that action to complete its tasks. This happens because the modify account permission is too liberal. This is illustrated in Figure 7(a), where the createNewAccount action is a violation for the FinancialTransaction principal. As a consequence, an attacker penetrating into a component running as this principal can create an employee account and perform the actions an employee is allowed to do. This problem can be solved by splitting the permission as described earlier.

A second type of violations (type B) is related to shortcuts (9 violations). For instance, consider the FinancialTransaction principal in Figure 6. The principal is supposed to ask the CustomerClient for confirmation via the WebFinancial-Transaction (see the dotted arrow). However, it can skip this step and invoke the doWireTransfer action directly, as it is responsible for this action itself. This is illustrated in Figure 7(a), where the doWireTransfer action is a violation for the FinancialTransaction principal. This violation can be solved by splitting the FinancialTransaction principal in two principals.

A third type of violations (type C) is related to the action granularity (13 violations). For instance, consider the CustomerClient principal in Figure 6. It violates LP because the system cannot refrain the CustomerClient from executing wire transfers on behalf of customers (employee's task) via the initiateWire-Transfer web action. As a consequence, a customer and an employee are able to perform wire transfers on behalf of each other. This is illustrated in Figure 7(b), where the initiateWireTransfer action is a violation for the CustomerClient and the EmployeeClient principals. To solve this violation, one could introduce different actions (and permissions) for wire transfers executed by the employee and the customer, respectively. Alternatively, one could transform the task by introducing a third party (e.g. a manager) that manually verifies whether the transaction is allowed.

### 4.3   Discussion

A number of observations driven by the results of our experiments are worthy to be discussed further.

*Applicability.* The class of systems that can be analyzed by the presented approach are (distributed) systems with support for action level security. Indeed, the approach depends on the notion of permission as the right to invoke an operation provided by a component. Applications depending on OS-level permissions (e.g., for files and sockets), are analyzable at the architectural level on condition that the list of the used permissions is provided. However, often such list remains implicit until the system is actually implemented.

*Extensions.* The presented approach is suitable to analyze the correct enforcement of (static) separation of duty policies at the architectural level. A SoD policy can be specified as (or mapped to) a desired Task Execution Model instance where the task is split over different swim lanes, corresponding to the different, to-be-separated responsibilities. The analysis tool can be used to check whether the architecture enforces the SoD policy, as specified.

*Limitations.* One should carefully interpret the violations identified by the analysis technique before attempting to solve them. An architect often makes a trade-off between LP and other security properties (as well as other non-security qualities). For instance, some security-specific components, like an Audit Interceptor or a Single Access Point, can be purposely used to implement a full-mediation strategy. Hence, all tasks are forced to interact with those components. As a consequence, several (intended) violations of type C are produced. A LP-specific transformation meant to solve these violations could break the overall architectural integrity.

## 5   Related Work

Related work focusses on (i) program separation, (ii) model checking, and (iii) execution monitoring.

Program separation, a technique to split a program in multiple processes, has been successfully applied in applications such as qmail to minimize trust [2].

Our least privilege approach provides a systematic and automated means for program separation at architectural level. Another more general approach is privilege separation, which partitions an existing program into two processes: a privileged monitor and an unprivileged slave [3]. Our approach enhances this technique by optimizing the number of privileged processes.

Model checking techniques are used to verify whether a design meets certain security properties. Rubacon is a tool that checks whether an application model (in UML) and its configuration data (such as security permissions specified as RBAC rules over SAP transactions) comply to the security policies that arise from business regulations, like separation of duty [8]. These policies are specified via a custom GUI and the tool verifies whether the permissions actually implement the policies. Our work shares a similar spirit (automating the architectural analysis) but takes a more general perspective. Our goal is to check the compliance vis-a-vis the security principles. The techniques presented here can be adapted to the special case of checking compliance to business polices, as outlined in the discussion section. Jürjens mentions that UMLSec can be used to formulate LP requirements and verify the system specifications with respect to them [10]. However, no further details are given about the method to be used. Secure xADL is a connector-centric approach for architectural access control, which extends xADL with access control concepts [15]. Our tool chain could be adapted to process secure xADL descriptions in order to identify authorized accesses that violate LP.

Execution monitoring is a technique that limits the privileges assigned to a program. Based on policies, these techniques block system calls, access to file, and the use of network resources. An examples is Systrace [14]. These mechanisms have two drawbacks. First it is hard to specify policies in terms of application-specific resources and functions, because these do not always map to files and system calls, as illustrated in [18]. Second, these mechanisms limit the number of privileges at run-time (impacting the run-time performance), while our work ensures that the privileges are limited by construction.

## 6    Conclusions and Future Work

This paper proposes a technique that automates the identification of least privilege violations in software architectures. To this aim, the concept of architectural-level least privilege has been modeled formally. This model has been leveraged to create a technique that analyzes an architecture for violations starting from conventional documentation. The approach has been validated by means of four case studies, one of which has been presented in detail.

In future work, the authors plan to apply the same formal approach to other security principles and study the interplay (and trade-offs) among the principles.

**Acknowledgements.** This research is partially funded by the Interuniversity Attraction Poles Programme Belgian State, Belgian Science Policy, and by the Research Fund K.U. Leuven.

# References

1. Barkley, J.: Comparing simple role based access control models and access control lists. In: ACM Workshop on Role Based Access Control, RBAC (1997)
2. Bernstein, D.J.: Some thoughts on security after ten years of qmail 1.0. In: ACM Workshop on Computer Security Architecture (2007)
3. Brumley, D., Song, D.: Privtrans: Automatically partitioning programs for privilege separation. In: USENIX (2004)
4. Buyens, K., De Win, B., Joosen, W.: Resolving least privilege violations in software architectures. In: Workshop on Software Engineering for Secure Systems, SESS (2009)
5. Buyens, K., Scandariato, R., Joosen, W.: Process activities supporting security principles. In: International Workshop on Security in Software Engineering, IWSSE (2007)
6. Dashofy, E., Asuncion, H., Hendrickson, S., Suryanarayana, G., Georgas, J., Taylor, R.: Archstudio 4: An architecture-based meta-modeling environment. In: ICSE Companion (2007)
7. Debie, E., De Ryck, P.: Non-repudiation middleware for web-based architectures. Master's thesis, Katholieke Universiteit Leuven (2009)
8. Höhn, S., Jürjens, J.: Rubacon: automated support for model-based compliance engineering. In: ICSE (2008)
9. Howard, M., Lipner, S.: The Security Development Lifecycle. Microsoft Press (2006)
10. Jürjens, J.: Secure Systems Development With UML. Springer, Heidelberg (2005)
11. Van Landuyt, D., Grégoire, J., Michiels, S., Truyen, E., Joosen, W.: Architectural design of a digital publishing system. Technical Report CW465, Katholieke Universiteit Leuven (2006)
12. MSDN Library. Access control lists, http://msdn.microsoft.com
13. Morandini, M., Nguyen, D.C., Perini, A., Siena, A., Susi, A.: Tool-supported development with tropos: The conference management system case study. In: Luck, M., Padgham, L. (eds.) AOSE 2007. LNCS, vol. 4951, pp. 182–196. Springer, Heidelberg (2008)
14. Provos, N.: Improving host security with system call policies. In: USENIX Security Symposium (2003)
15. Ren, J.: A connector-centric approach to architectural access control. PhD thesis, University of California Irvine (2006)
16. Saltzer, J.H., Schroeder, M.D.: The protection of information in computer systems. Proceedings of the IEEE 63(9), 1278–1308 (1975)
17. Sandhu, R.S., Coyne, E.J., Feinstein, H.L., Youman, C.E.: The protection of information in computer systems. IEEE Computer 29(2), 38–47 (1996)
18. Schneider, F.B.: Enforceable security policies. ACM Transactions on Information and System Security 3(1), 30–50 (2000)
19. Viega, J., McGraw, G.: Building Secure Software. Addison-Wesley, Reading (2002)
20. White, S.A.: Business process modeling notation. BPMI.org (2004)
21. Wing, J.: A call to action: Look beyond the horizon. IEEE Security & Privacy 1(6), 62–67 (2003)

# Architecting a Model-Driven Aspect-Oriented Product Line for a Digital TV Middleware: A Refactoring Experience

Diego Saraiva, Lucas Pereira, Thais Batista, Flávia C. Delicato, Paulo F. Pires,
Uirá Kulesza, Rodrigo Araújo, Tássia Freitas, Sindolfo Miranda,
Ana Liz Souto, and Roberta Coelho

Computer Science Department, Federal University of Rio Grande do Norte (UFRN),
59072-970, Natal – RN, Brazil
{diegosaraiva,lucasilpe,thaisbatista,fdelicato,paulo.f.pires,
uirakulesza,fenrrir,tassiafreitas,
sindolfo.miranda.filho,analiz,souzacoelho}@gmail.com

**Abstract.** In this paper, we present the experience of refactoring the architecture of Ginga, the Brazilian Terrestrial Digital TV System (SBTVD) middleware. The main goal of the Ginga refactoring was to increase its configurability, through the automatic management of its variabilities. The resultant middleware, named GingaForAll, is based on a software product line (SPL) architecture, which encompasses both the middleware commonalities and its specific functionalities. Aspect-oriented techniques were used to improve the modularization of crosscutting mandatory and variable features from the Ginga SPL architecture. A model-driven based process was developed to allow the automatic management of the common and variable features in a high abstraction level that supports the management of code assets in terms of configurable models. The integration of such software engineering techniques have contributed to provide a flexible and configurable Ginga architecture, which allows the automatic generation of middleware customizations driven by the devices constraints and applications needs.

**Keywords:** architecture refactoring, software product lines, model-driven development, aspect-oriented development, configurable middleware.

## 1 Introduction

The development of middleware systems to support digital TV applications has been facing challenges due to the heterogeneity and resource constraints of the execution platforms, as well as different requirements of applications that may run in such platforms. In this scenario, the middleware has to be highly configurable in order to be tailored to meet both the application needs and the constraints of the underlying platform or specific target devices. For instance, if the underlying hardware does not have an enabled network board, the middleware does not need to include functionality to receive video via IP (IPTV). In order to adapt the middleware to fit the needs of the

M. Ali Babar and I. Gorton (Eds.): ECSA 2010, LNCS 6285, pp. 166–181, 2010.

target customer, platform or device in which it will be deployed, it is necessary to define different service configurations to the same (base) middleware.

This problem can be addressed by using the software product line approach (SPL) [9] that supports the creation of a portfolio of similar products using a common software infrastructure to assembly and configure parts designed to be reused across products. SPL approaches identify *commonalities* of all family members, as well as features that vary among members of the family, the *variabilities*. Thus, members of a family have a basic set of common functions with many variants. A fundamental challenge in this context is to manage the variabilities by defining the variation points and the dependencies between them. Aspect-oriented software development (AOSD) [10] has been recently explored in the development of SPLs since many common and variable concerns has a crosscutting nature and cannot be suitably modularized with conventional variability mechanisms, such as conditional compilation or inheritance [2]. Therefore, AOSD can be used to support improved modularity of crosscutting concerns, expressing them as aspects that can be added/removed to/from the middleware architecture according to the different underlying platform or application requirements.

In this paper, we present the experience of refactoring the architecture of Ginga, the Brazilian Terrestrial Digital TV System (SBTVD) middleware, in order to build a family of products, named *GingaForAll*. Such refactoring was built based on the SPL and AOSD approaches and its main goal was to increase the *Ginga* middleware configurability, through the automatic management of variabilities. In order to increase the abstraction level of the SPL development, we developed a *model-driven based approach* [11] to allow the automatic management of the common and variable features at the modelling level, thus supporting the management of assets in terms of configurable models. Therefore, models are first-class reusable assets in the Ginga-ForAll development lifecycle.

Initially, this paper presents the Ginga-CC architecture (Section 2) and its main drawbacks. Next, it presents the GingaForAll architecture (Section 3) composed of different models that address the middleware commonalities and variabilities. We also present (Section 4) the model-driven (MDD) process developed to the automatic variability management. It is implemented by a tool designed to configure and assembly the architectural middleware components to generate a specific product (an instance of the GingaForAll middleware). This tool provides a systematic way to automate the process of generating a specific product. A case study is briefly illustrated in Section 5. Section 6 contains the related work and Section 7 presents the final remarks and lessons learned.

## 2   Ginga Common Core Architecture

As in all major terrestrial Digital TV (DTV) Systems, Ginga middleware supports the execution of both declarative and imperative applications. Ginga architecture is composed of three main modules: (i) Ginga-NCL provides an execution environment for declarative applications; (ii) Ginga-J provides an execution environment for Java applications; and (iii) Ginga Common Core (Ginga-CC) provides a set of common digital TV services for both Ginga-NCL and Ginga-J execution environments, allowing such applications to run on a Digital TV set-top box. Since our work aims at refactoring Ginga-CC, the remaining of this section will focus on its architecture. Figure 1 shows the main elements of Ginga-CC architecture.

The *Tuner* component offers an API for TV channels management and it is responsible for selecting a specific source of Transport Stream (TS). When such stream is selected, it is sent to the *TSParser* component. *TSParser* demultiplexes the content of the selected TS in elementary flows, and sends such flows to the *DataProcessing* component. *DataProcessing*, then, properly processes the information from such elementary flows, according to the type of the information sent. If such information comprises an application flow, for instance, *DataProcessing* may load and run such application. The *Player* component comprises content decoder/players for some media formats such as H264 video and AAC Audio.This component depends on the System component, which is in charge of managing every data storage requested by applications. The *UpdateManager* is responsible for downloading and executing middleware updates. It establishes the connection to the Internet through the *Interaction Channel* component. Finally, the *ComponentManager* component implements the Abstract Factory *design pattern*, and it is in charge of creating every other component that composes the Ginga-CC architecture.

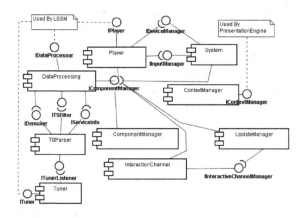

**Fig. 1.** The Ginga-CC architecture

The current **Ginga-CC** architecture presents the following shortcomings: (i) it is multi-use and designed to satisfy a broad range of DTV applications. A manual customization is needed to adapt it to platforms with more stringent resources or specific applications that do not need a plethora of functionalities. The manual customization is a time-consuming and error-prone activity; (ii) the presence of crosscutting concerns and a strong coupling between the classes that compose the middleware makes the customization even harder and after the customization process the resulting architecture can contain remnants crosscutting concerns; (iii) this architecture is based on components, but the customization process requires the manual modification of fine-grained code inside these components. This low level specialization process requires a lot of reimplementation of the functionality of the original component; and (iv) there is no high level representation of the architecture, as a consequence customizations relies on tailoring the middleware code.

The set of shortcomings aforementioned motivated the refactoring of the original architecture in order to isolate crosscutting concerns, as well as to define a SPL-based architecture. SPL provides mechanisms to efficiently manage the variability of an application domain. However, this technique does not eliminate the problems arising from the presence of crosscutting concerns. Thus, the aspect-oriented development was applied to separate and compose crosscutting concerns in terms of features, allowing to (un)plug these features of the SPL core architecture, and providing the architecture with a higher capacity for adaptation and better modularization. In addition, model-driven development (MDD) techniques were used to manage the customizations at the modeling level, avoiding manual modifications at code level, thus improving the traceability and documentation of commonalities and variabilities of the middleware.

## 3   Refactoring the Ginga Architecture

In this section, we detail the refactoring of Ginga architecture. Such refactoring was organized into three activities: (i) identification of the features that appear in Ginga in order to define the feature model of the GingaForAll SPL (Subsection 3.1); (ii) definition of the base and the crosscutting models (Subsection 3.2); and (iii) definition of the variability model to SPL (Subsection 3.3). The definition of the base, crosscutting and variability models was necessary to provide the automatic management of the Ginga variabilities, allowing the generation of different customizations (products) according to the user and plataform needs.

The first activity of the refactoring process was the specification of the *feature model*, defining the common and variable features of a family of related products. This model allows the identification of variabilities as well as dependency and exclusion relationships between the features. The second activity of the process was composed of two steps: (i) the design of the base model - composed of elements that are common to all products generated by the SPL (in particular for the Ginga-CC, the base model contains all mandatory features for the reception of TV signals with no optional feature); and (ii) the *aspect-oriented* refactoring of the base model – addressed the modularization of the crosscutting concerns, such as synchronization and security, which are tangled with other features of the middleware. Finally, the third activity of the refactoring process received as input the base and the feature model and produced, as output, the *variability model*. This activity was divided into two steps: (i) building the variability model for Ginga – presenting how the optional and alternatives features identified in the feature model are addressed in the SPL architecture; and (ii) the aspect-oriented refactoring of the variability model in order to modularly manage the variable features. The use of aspects, therefore, allows the flexible adaptation of the Ginga architecture to particular requirements of each product. The ability to extend and adapt the Ginga-CC SPL architecture is directly related to the flexibility offered by the variation points, since the various combinations and configurations of these points determine the creation of SPL products Therefore, it is essential that the variation points to be generic, extensible and well modularized. The following sections detail the models created during the refactoring process.

## 3.1 Feature Model

The first step when using a SPL approach to create a family of products is to perform *the domain analysis*, where commonalities and variabilities are specified in terms of *features*. A *feature* is a concept that is prominently visible to any stakeholder involved in the development of applications [1]. Features are organized in *feature models*, in order to explicit the different configuration options of the products.

The specification of variabilities for Ginga starts with the identification of features of this domain, which are represented by a feature model. In this model, three types of relationships are found : (i) composed of, when a feature is composed of several sub-features, (ii) generalization or specification, when a feature is a generalization of sub-features and (iii) implemented by, when a sub-feature is needed to implement a feature. Figure 2 illustrates a partial view of the Ginga-CC feature model. Next we detail the most relevant features raised by the Ginga architecture refactoring.

The Tuner feature is responsible for selecting the physical channel of signal transmission. The transport stream (TS) reception can occur through Terrestrial signal (Terrestrial feature), Satellite signal (Satellite feature) and over IP (Internet Protocol) by the IPTV, InternetTV and P2PTV features. InternetTV consists on the retrieval of the transport stream through the Internet infrastructure. The Application Manager mandatory feature is responsible for loading, instantiating, configuring, and executing applications. In addition, it controls the life cycle of applications, and manages the use of resources and access control. The Resident Applications mandatory feature and its different optional features represent application platform that can run in the middleware, such as GEM (Globally Executable MHP), JavaDTV and NCL/Lua.

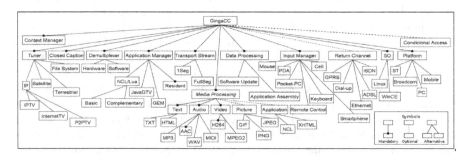

**Fig. 2.** Ginga-CC's Feature Model

The *Media Processing* mandatory feature manages the processing of multimedia data and makes them available to other components of the middleware. The *Video* feature has mandatory support to H.264 (video compression standard) and, optionally, to MPEG2. The *Audio* feature has mandatory support to AAC Feature (Advanced Audio Coding, audio compression standard), MP3, WAV, MIDI. *Application*, other optional feature, is responsible for interpreting applications implemented in XHTML (XHTML feature), NCL (NCL feature), etc. *Data Processing* is the feature responsible for accessing, processing and providing elementary data streams to other middleware components. Additionally, it is also responsible for notifying other components on the occurrence of events, such as updating of applications, synchronization, etc. The *Input Manager* mandatory feature has Remote Control (RC), Keyboard, Mouse, Cell phone, PDA, Smartphone, Pocket-PC as alternative features, requiring the choice of at least one. The *Return Channel* feature is optional and refers to the technology used in the return channel to connect to the Internet.

In the ISDB-T system (*Integrated Services Digital Broadcasting Terrestrial*), each channel has 13 segments. *Transport Stream* (TS) mandatory feature represents the type of the selected transport stream. The one-segment stream (1Seg Feature) consists of a TS stream with low resolution video, filling only one segment. The middleware can be developed to play only the 1Seg or to play all streams of the channel, represented by the *FullSeg* Feature.

**Table 1.** Features relationships

| Feature | Sub-feature | Relationship | Feature |
|---|---|---|---|
| Application Manager | JavaDTV, GEM ou NCL/Lua | Dependence | Data Processing,Application Assembly |
| | NCL/Lua Complementary | Dependence | NCL/Lua Basic |
| | NCL/Lua Basic + Complementary | Dependence | All the formats specified in the Media Processing |
| Platform | Mobile | Exclusion | Return Channel Dial-up, ADSL, Ethernet, ISDN |
| | | Exclusion | Input Manager Mouse, RC |
| | | Dependence | Flow 1Seg |
| | | Exclusion | Application Manager JavaDTV e GEM |
| | | Dependence | Return Channel GPRS |

Besides the three types of relationships previously mentioned, the feature model can also be used to represent two types of relationship constraints: (i) *dependence*– the selection of a feature implies the selection of features on which it depends; and (ii) *exclusion*– the selection of a feature automatically excludes the selection of other ones. Table 1 shows the dependency and exclusion constraints among the features.

### 3.2 Base Model

The base model defines the aspect-oriented (AO) reference architecture of the Ginga SPL. It consists of the core reusable assets (packages, classes, aspects) that are common to all products of the product line. In the case of Ginga-CC, the base model contains all the core assets that address the mandatory features for the reception of the TV signal. Therefore, the base model has no optional feature. Figure 3 depicts the GingaForAll base model, showing the packages that compose the base model and their main classes. Packages containing classes crosscutted by aspects (Synchronization, Distribution/Transmission and Resource Manager) include the correspondent aspect name as stereotypes. The base model encompasses all Ginga-CC components that support the mandatory set of functionalities.

In order to discover the crosscutting concerns present in Ginga-CC, we combine two strategies. Initially, we used the Feature-Oriented Analysis proposed in [8] - to discover the main features of the product family including both common and variable assets - and identify the crosscutting concerns [8]. The details of the process of identifying the requirements is out of scope of this work. Secondly, we have adopted a strategy based on the use of code level metrics. As we only had the source code of Ginga-CC, the use of well-known software metrics has revealed to be an effective way to find out the crosscutting concerns. In our analysis, we applied the following code level metrics: CBO (*Coupling Between Objects classes*), MPC (*Messaging Passing Coupling*) and DAC (*Data Abstraction Coupling*). CBO is defined as the number of classes to which a class is coupled (a class is coupled to other if it uses variables or operations of another class). For a given class, MPC is the number of invocations of static methods that are not implemented in this class. DAC is the number of attributes in a class that have another class as their type. The results obtained from the coupling metrics confirmed the existence of a strong coupling between some Ginga entities due to the presence of crosscutting concerns in the Ginga-CC source code. The complete description of metrics and their results can be found in http://www.dimap.ufrn.br/gingaforall. From the analysis of the existing Ginga-CC code, we identify the following concerns as being crosscutting: (i) synchronization, (ii) resource management and (iii) transmission / distribution of information. The presence of these crosscutting concerns decreases the system modularity and makes reuse more difficult in the middleware architecture. In general, crosscutting concerns increases the coupling between entities. Therefore, we applied AO techniques to modularize the crosscutting concerns of Ginga-CC.

In the new system architecture (Fig. 3), produced as result of the AO refactoring, we defined the crosscutting concerns from the original architecture as *aspects* that crosscut the Ginga-CC classes. We implemented the three aforementioned crosscutting concerns. In this paper, we detail the *Synchronization* aspect since it is the more spread and tangled concern identified in the Ginga-CC components.

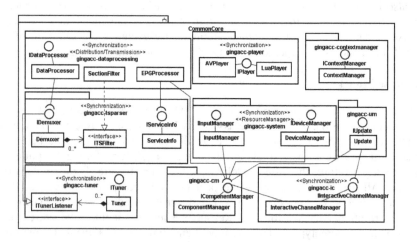

**Fig. 3.** Packages and classes affected by the synchronization aspect

**Synchronization aspect.** Ginga uses concurrent programming for properly managing the execution of multiple threads. The synchronization mechanism is based on mutexes. From the source code analysis, we detected its implementation as a tangled and spread concern in several system components. The analysis of the synchronization concern showed a strong coupling between the components of the *gingacc-player* package and the *Thread* class, which defines synchronization methods using commands from the *pthread* library. This coupling is due to the need for synchronization during the execution of various types of players defined in this package. Results of applying the coupling metrics shown that 9 of 15 classes of the *gingacc-player* package were coupled to the *Thread* class. To reduce this coupling, we characterized synchronization as a crosscutting concern. There was a strong coupling between *gingacc-ic*, *gingacc-player*, and *gingacc-system* packages and the *pthread* library due to the invocation of synchronization commands. Modeling the synchronization concern as an aspect is straightforward: the aspect must intercept the specific fragments of code that need to be protected by synchronization mechanisms. After the interception, the aspect injects the synchronization code into the intercepted elements. The modularization of the synchronization crosscutting concern as an aspect improves the middleware modularity. It also contributes to a better readability of the source code, as the classes will contain only the application logic, the synchronization is handled by aspects.

### 3.3 Variability Model

The variability model defines extension points on the base architecture to adapt the SPL to the requirements of each product. The main goal of this model in our approach is to allow a better management of existing variability in the GingaForAll product family. We applied the methodology proposed by Braga [3] to determine the modularization approach to be used in the development of features. Optional features are natural candidates to be modeled as aspects since they can be easily inserted to and removed from the code. The modularization of optional features depends on the core SPL architecture and therefore it requires an individual analysis of each optional feature for determining the best programming paradigm to be applied.

In the implementation of the Ginga-CC variations, the AO approach was employed with different purposes: (i) to extend the product line core classes to include additional behavior, such as 3G authentication and persistence; and (ii) to redefine the behavior of classes in the core product line to adapt them to new requirements that were not planned during the design phase.

Figure 4 shows the class diagram with the aspects that add optional features to the core of Ginga-CC. Our variability model is composed by classes and aspects.

The variation points implemented as inheritance and polymorphism were: (i) *Demux* and *Platform* since their variations depend on the hardware APIs; and (ii) *MediaProcessing* since its code is well modularized and is easy to extend. In MediaProcessing, each media player extends the iPlayer interface. Thus, to support new media formats, we can extend the current MediaProcessing architecture just implementing new classes that inherit from the IPlayerinterface or any of its subclass. We detail the *Tuner* and *InputManager* variation points. The others variations follow the same approach.

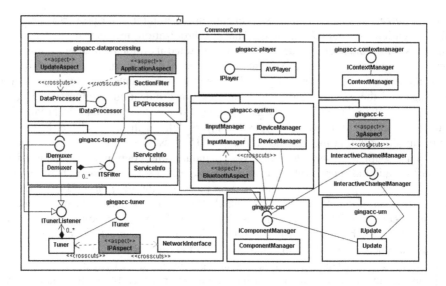

**Fig. 4.** Class diagram of Ginga-CC representing variability as aspects

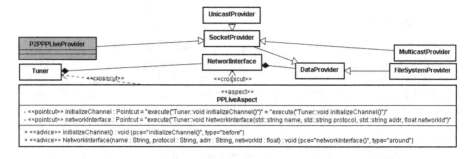

**Fig. 5.** Modeling the Tuner variation point

**Tuner Variation Point.** This variation point refers to the selection of the physical transmission channel. It was mapped to the *Tuner* component. Figure 5 shows the design of features related to the Tuner. New classes of data providers should be implemented to provide support to the addition of new features. For example, in Figure 5, *PPLiveProvider* class was added to implement the *PPLive* feature. This new class could be able to retrieve streams using the protocol adopted by the PPLive network [4]. Obviously, if more than one peer-to-peer protocol is supported, new Provider classes needed to be implemented. Thus, *PPLiveProvider* performs adaptation in the middleware to support different types of peer-to-peer. To allow the easy runtime activation of the features associated with this variation, one aspect was created for each associated feature, which acts on the method *initializaInterfaces()* of the *Tuner* class. In Figure 5, the PPLive feature is represented as the PPLiveAspect.

The *open-closed* principle states that software architecture should be open for extension, but closed for modification; that is, an entity can allow its behaviour to be modified without changing its source code. In the specific case of the *Tuner* architecture, the opening for extension is supplied by the data provider class hierarchy whose base class is *DataProvider*. We decided to keep the original code closed for modification, so that only the aspects need to be modified to implement and deal with new features. Thus, the addition of a new provider will require the implementation of a new aspect for each new feature, without modifying the base code previously developed. Figure 5 shows the definition of a new feature called *PPLiveAspect*.

The *Tuner* class instantiates and keeps track of all channels created at runtime. It implements the *initializeChannels()* method for instantiating the different kinds of channels supported by the middleware (for example, a file system channel, an IP channel, etc). Each channel is represented by a different *NetworkInterface* object, which is responsible for creating an internal *DataProvider* object that implements the data retrieving mechanism for that channel. The method responsible for the creation of data providers is the *createProvider()* method of *NetworkInterface*. It works as a factory method for different kinds of data providers. The operation of *PPLiveAspect* is quite simple. It defines the *initializeChannels()* pointcut specifying the methods that performs the channel initialization process. *PPLiveAspect* acts before the *initializeChannel()* method to advise it to instantiate a *NetworkInterface* responsible for creating a given channel type, in this example, a P2P channel. In addition, it defines the *createProvider* pointcut in order to intercept the *createProvider()* method execution, allowing this method to create a specific kind of data provider, in this case, *PPLiveProvider*. The approach adopted for the PPLive aspect is generic enough to modularize other alternative features planned for the Tuner variation point (H323, SIP, Joost, SopCast and HTTP).

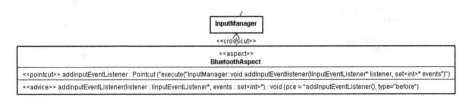

**Fig. 6.** Modeling the input manager variation point

**InputManager Variation Point.** It supports different mechanisms to receive user events. We also applied AO modeling to modularize this feature allowing its easy (de)activation from the Ginga-CC core architecture. Figure 6 shows an aspect that handles bluetooth input devices. It intercepts the input manager to capture input events sent by the Bluetooth device. It acts before the *addInputEventListener()* method call, where it adds the listener specified in the parameter as its own listener, through the specification of the pointcut and advice *addInputEventListener*. Thus, the call before registering the listener on an InputManager keyboard, now connects the listener via bluetooth and keyboard. As previously mentioned, each feature should be implemented as an aspect and if more than one feature is selected, more than one aspect will act on the *addInputEventListener()* method adding the listener on their own listeners list.

## 4  Automatic Variability Management

In this section, we present an overview of the MDD approach developed to support the automatic management of variabilities in the GingaForAll product line architecture. Our approach encompasses a MDD based process composed of systematic activities that are used to automatically transform and refine the models that define the GingaForAll architecture. This approach automatically interconnects features and core assets (classes and aspects) of the architecture. It supports the product derivation from the set of models previously presented (Section 3) in order to automatically customize and derive specific instances of the Ginga middleware.

Figure 7 illustrates the main activities of the proposed process and the different artifacts (models, metamodels) and transformations used to allow the automatic derivation of middleware instances (products). The activities presented in Figure 7 are supported by the GingaForAll tool. It implements the functionalities to create all models and transformations comprised in the process using the metamodels, which are also provided by the tool.

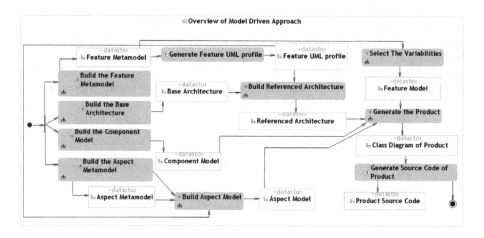

**Fig. 7.** Overview of the Model-Driven Approach

In the first activity - ***Build the Feature Metamodel*** two metamodels are produced: **(i)** the **Feature metamodel** that is an Ecore model specified by the domain engineers using EMF (*Eclipse Modeling Framework*); (ii) a **feature UML profile** generated by a model-to-model (M2M) transformation from the feature metamodel in order to allow the creation of different stereotypes that represent all the features in the ***build the referenced architecture*** activity. The **feature metamodel** contains all possible features of Ginga-CC with their respective constraints and relationships. It is used in a further activity (***Generate the product*** activity) for the definition of the GingaCC **feature model**. The feature metamodel allows the instantiation of different feature model instances, each one describing the configuration of a specific product. The feature model instance is called *product configuration*. It is further used by the ***Generate the Product*** activity to select entities (classes, aspects, interfaces, methods, and so on) from the referenced architecture related with the selected product. The **feature UML profile** allows the use of UML stereotypes in the architectural units (classes and interfaces) in order to indicate the features that these architectural units are associated to. This profile is an UML 2.1 diagram composed of all features specified in this model.

The **Build the Base Architecture** activity consists of modeling the GingaForAll architecture. The artifacts produced in this step are the UML class diagrams that represent the specification of the architecture for the purpose of generating the base architecture (presented in Section 3.2) with all elements. The **Build the Referenced Architecture** activity consists of annotating the elements of the architecture model, using the UML profile produced as result of the **Build the Feature Metamodel** activity. Each stereotype of the UML profile specified inside an element (class and interfaces) indicates the direct relationship between a feature (stereotype) and the element. The application of the feature UML profile stereotypes in the base architecture generates a class diagram, called the *referenced architecture*. This architecture is afterward used in the **Generate the Product** activity to identify the desired features for each product. This artifact is also used by a model transformation (M2T) to generate the Ginga-CC source code. Futhermore, the **Generate the Product** activity performs an aspect weaving over the elements of this model. The weaving integrates the aspects (of the aspect model) in the referenced architecture.

The **Build the Aspect Metamodel** activity consists of defining and modeling the aspects (crosscutting concerns) identified in Ginga-CC. The aspect metamodel is used to specify the aspect model (aspects and pointcuts). An aspect metamodel specifies the aspects and pointcuts of a SPL architecture. The **Build the Aspect Model** activity consists of defining the aspects pointcuts. The aspect model is built here and it is an instance of the aspect metamodel. The aspects can also be annotated using UML stereotypes - in the same way the elements of the architecture model are – indicating which feature(s) an aspect is related to. The aspect models are used by the **Generate the Product** activity to perform aspect weaving over the referenced architecture.

The **Build Component model** activity consists of selecting the specific deployment platform to a given product and it includes the instantiation of the platform specific metamodel (PSM), the component model. **The component model** is a UML Profile defining stereotypes to represent concepts of the employed component model. This profile provides additional information about the component implementation, allowing the automatic generation of the component source code. The **Select the variabilities** activity consists of a product configuration process in which the optional and alternative features are selected in order to make explicit the specific product of GingaForAll that an engineer is interested to generate. The selection of variabilities consists of the instantiation of elements from the feature metamodel - built on **Build the feature metamodel** - by selecting features from this metamodel for the generated product. In this activity, a product configuration is produced. The elements of the feature model are in accordance with the requirements of the product to be generated.

Finally, the last activity – **Generate the Product** - consists of generating a product. This activity receives as input: (i) the platform specific models (PSM) generated as output of the **Build component model** activity; (ii) the referenced architecture produced in the **Build the Referenced Architecture** activity; (iii) the feature model instance produced in the **Select the variabilities** activity; and (iv) the aspect models from the **Build Aspect Model** activity. The GingaForAll tool generates, as result, the Ginga-CC model of the selected product and also the C++ code. The complete specification of the tool can be found in: http://www.dimap.ufrn.br/gingaforall

## 5  Case Study: Ginga IPTV and Ginga Zapper Products

This Section illustrates our approach by presenting two possible software products (the middleware itself) that can be built using GingaForAll. The first product is called Ginga IPTV. It includes support for IPTV tuner and for running NCL and Java applications. The second product, called *zapper*, includes only basic functionalities and is not able to execute applications transmitted by the TV broadcasters. Such product is targeted to low cost set-top box and to limited hardware capabilities, and the underlying middleware needs to be tailored to such constrained environment. Table 2 shows the features selected for Ginga IPTV and for Zapper.

**Table 2.** Features for the Ginga Zapper product

| | Ginga Zapper | Ginga IPTV |
|---|---|---|
| *Variation Points* | *Variant* | *Variant* |
| *Tuner* | Terrestrial | Terrestrial, IPTV |
| *Demultiplexer* | Hardware | Hardware |
| *Application Manager* | Missing | NCL/Lua Basic + Complementary and JavaDTV |
| *MediaProcessing* | H264 and AAC | All |
| *Data Processing* | Software Update | Software Update and application builder |
| *Input Manager* | RC Control | RC Control |
| *Return channel* | Missing | Ethernet |
| *Plataform* | ST ou *Broadcom* | ST ou *Broadcom* |

As previously mentioned, our MDD approach is supported by the GingaForAll tool that offers a graphical interface where user can require the creation of GingaForAll artifacts. Using the tool the following steps are needed to generate a product: (i) to create the four input models (feature model, referenced architecture, aspect model, and component model) based on the Ginga architecture; (ii) to select the desired features of the feature model – the specific configuration of the product; (iii) to execute the transformations for generating the GingaForAll product.

It is worthwhile to mention that the referenced architecture, the aspect model, and the component model are developed once, and then reused through the generation of any other product. Regarding the Tuner component, the Ginga IPTV product model contains two different stereotypes – <<Tuner>> and << IP >> - representing how the different modeling elements (classes) are related to the Ginga-CC features. On the other hand, the Zapper Tuner has only the Tuner class.

In short, using GingaForAll, the process to generate the Zapper product from Ginga IPTV consists in modifying the feature model to reflect the product configuration. The GingaForAll tool automatically generates the Ginga Zapper source code. In contrast, with the original Ginga architecture, adaptations must be manually done and it is necessary to change up to 45% relevant classes and also the Ginga-CC configuration file. For instance, to remove the support for IPTV transmission and maintain the Terrestrial transmission, it would be needed to remove, from the Tuner package, the following classes: `UnicastProvider`, `MulticastProvider`, and `Socket-Provider`. Moreover, it would be necessary to change the implementation of several methods of the `Tuner` class. Other packages also needed to be manually changed.

## 6  Related Work

In this section, we present a set of research work directly related to our work. It is organized in three categories: (i) approaches for AO refactoring; (ii) approaches for MDD-based refactorings; (iii) approaches for SPL-based refactorings;

**AO Refactoring of Middleware Platforms.** The work described in [7] was the first to perform an AO refactoring of middleware platforms. The authors applied an aspect mining approach in some middleware platforms and identified a set of crosscutting concerns. They mentioned that middleware architectures inherently suffer from coordinating crosscutting concerns. Our work differs from [7] in the way how the crosscutting concerns were identified. The approach used in our work to identify crosscutting concerns was twofold. Firstly, some crosscutting concerns were identified by applying the methodology described in [8] that uses Feature-Oriented Analysis - to discover the main features of the product family including both common and variable assets as well as non-functional requirements - and identifies the crosscutting concerns by means of a traceability matrix [8]. Secondly, additional crosscutting concerns were discovered through the application of a set of code level metrics (e.g. coupling and cohesion metrics).

**SPL Refactoring.** In [6], the traditional notion of refactoring was extended to a SPL context, focusing on refactoring the feature model (FM). We used refactoring to improve the modularity of Ginga. However, in contrast with [6], that addresses only the process of building FM, we performed all steps of an SPL development, from the domain engineering to the application engineering, generating the final product.

**MDD-based Refactoring.** In [5], a refactoring based on patterns and metamodeling techniques was proposed. They proposed a rigorous approach to define refactorings as OCL contracts between meta-patterns, MOF-metamodels that describe families of instances of refactoring patterns and also identify refactorings by a formal specification matching. The main contribution of the work was the definition of refactorings from metamodel-based transformations that are expressed as OCL contracts. The formalization ensures that each refactoring maintains the consistency between models. In contrast, our proposal is not just about using models refactoring techniques. We created a SPL to customize Ginga according to the resources constraints and platform needs. For this, MDD allows working in a high abstraction level, through the management of code assets in terms of configurable models.

As we can see, none of the aforementioned approaches combine MDA, AOSD and SPL as we did. We used refactoring in Ginga in order to increase its configurability, through the automatic management of its variabilities. We addressed this challenge by using a SPL architecture, which encompasses both the middleware commonalities and its specific functionalities. Our AO refactoring approach was based in the methodology described in [8] to identify crosscutting concerns in Ginga and modularizing them in aspects. We also adopted MDD as the vehicle for mapping architectural abstractions to implementation.

## 7   Final Remarks and Lessons Learned

This paper presented our experience on applying SPL, MDD and AOSD concepts in a refactoring of the Ginga architecture. Some relevant discussion topics are discussed in the next paragraphs.

**MDD Management of Variabilities.** We adopted MDD technologies with two main aims: (i) to allow the automatic variability management of the GingaForAll architecture; and (ii) to enable the automatic generation of source code of different Ginga-ForAll products through the refinement of models from different abstraction levels without requiring manual interference of developers. The variability management was addressed by two strategies: (i) by directly annotating, with *feature* stereotypes, the classes and aspects that modularize the commonalities and variabilities of the middleware architecture in the class diagram model (PIM); and (ii) by defining MDA transformation rules that assure the different software artifacts are correctly bound according to each product specification. This strategy has revealed to be easy to implement and enough to the variability management of UML models.

In this work we made extensive use of all the MDA standard mechanisms, such as metamodeling, UML profiling and transformations. Besides the well-known MDD benefit of increasing the abstraction level in the building of software systems, the use of such mechanisms also has proved to be a powerful tool for managing SPL assets, such as the feature model, the reference architecture and the specification of product configurations. The use of metamodels along with their implementation support provided by tools such as *EMF* provides a common framework for the definition, verification and documentation of the diferent models needed in a SPL process. Moreover, the use of MDA transformation rules assures that such models are correctly synchronized to each other. Finally, since the profiling mechanism is a standard implemented by any UML compliant tool, our proposed solution can be used in any UML development environment.

**AO Model-Driven Development.** One interesting point that we noticed during the architecture refactoring of the Ginga middleware is that two different transformation strategies can be used to generate PSM instances from the PIM instances: (i) the object-oriented strategy, that processes the base and aspect models and weaves them to produce a unique UML class diagram model; and (ii) the aspect-oriented strategy that maps the aspect abstractions from the PIM instances to aspects implemented in any existing AO programming language. The weaving between classes and aspects in this case is directly supported by the aspect weaver of the adopted AO language. The first strategy was adopted in our work, since we are not interested in forcing Ginga developers to use AspectC++ programming language.

**AO Modeling.** In our work, we have explored the adoption of AO techniques to address the existing crosscutting variations during the refactoring of the Ginga architecture. The modeling of variabilities as aspects have contributed to increase: (i) the understanding and maintenance of the architecture core, mainly because most of variabilities are addressed isolately; and (ii) the understanding of the intrinsic relationships between the aspects (variabilities) and the core, which are fundamental to analyze and address future evolution and maintenance scenarios. Thus, the benefits of the adoption of AO modeling in the Ginga architecture were not restricted only to improve the modularization of the existing crosscutting concerns and variations but also to better understand how each of these elements is coupled to the base code.

**AO Architecture Refactoring.** The refactoring of the Ginga architecture was preceded by the early analysis and identification of crosscutting concerns and variations. Coupling metrics were collected in the original implementation of Ginga. They were useful to discover crosscutting concerns and features that are strongly coupled to the base classes. We identified the synchronization concern, for example, by analyzing all the classes strongly connected to the Thread class.. After refactoring, we used the methodology presented in [8] to analyze the modularization of each middleware component. We basically built a matrix that shows the relationships between the Ginga features and components. It allowed us to compare the results obtained with the previous Ginga implementation, whose implementation of common/variable features and crosscutting concerns are completely diffuse and tangled along the classes of the system core.

**Acknowledgments.** This work is partially funded by CTIC - Centre for Research and Development in Digital Technologies for Information and Communications within the National Network of Education and Research (RNP), project GingaForAll.

# References

1. Linden, L.F., Schmid, K., Romes, E.: Software Product Lines in Action: The Best Industrial Practice in Product Line Engineering. Springer, New York (2007)
2. Muthig, D., et al.: Generic Implementation of Product Line Components. In: Aksit, M., Mezini, M., Unland, R. (eds.) NODe 2002. LNCS, vol. 2591, pp. 313–329. Springer, Heidelberg (2003)
3. Braga, R., et al.: AIPLE-IS: An Approach to Develop Product Lines for Information Systems Using Aspects. In: Proc. of the Brazilian Symp. on Comp., Arch. and Software Reuse, SBCARS (2007)
4. PPLive, http://www.pplive.com/en/
5. Favre, L., et al.: Improving MDA-based Process Quality through Refactoring Patterns. In: Proc. of the 1st International Workshop on Software Patterns and Quality (2007)
6. Alves, et al.: Refactoring product lines. In: Proceedings of the 5th Int. Conf. on Generative Programming and Component Engineering, pp. 201–210 (2006)
7. Zhang, C., et al.: Refactoring Middleware with Aspects. IEEE Transactions on Parallel and Distributed Systems, 1058–1073 (November 2003)
8. Conejero, J., Hernandez, J., Jurado, E., Clemente, P.J., Rodríguez, R.: Early Analysis of Modularity in Software Product Lines. In: 21st International Conference on Software Engineering and Knowledge Engineering (SEKE), Boston, USA (2009)
9. Clements, P., et al.: Software Product Lines Practices and Patterns. Addison-Wesley, Reading (2002)
10. Filman, R., et al.: Aspect-Oriented Software Development. Addison-Wesley, Reading (2005)
11. Frankel, D.: Model-Driven Software Development. Business Process Trends Journal in MDA (2004)

# Impact Evaluation for Quality-Oriented Architectural Decisions regarding Evolvability

Stephan Bode and Matthias Riebisch

Ilmenau University of Technology
P.O. Box 10 05 65, 98684 Ilmenau, Germany
{stephan.bode,matthias.riebisch}@tu-ilmenau.de

**Abstract.** Quality goals have to be under a special consideration during software architectural design. Evolvability constitutes a quality goal with a special relevance for business critical systems. Architectural patterns can significantly contribute to the satisfaction of quality goals. But architectural design decisions regarding these goals have to be made in a systematic, methodical way and concerning the patterns' influence on quality properties. Unfortunately, pattern catalogs do not well support quality goal-oriented design decisions. This paper presents a systematic refinement and mapping of the quality goal evolvability to properties for good architectural design. A set of architectural patterns is evaluated regarding these properties. Furthermore, a calculation scheme is provided that enables the evaluation of the patterns to support design decisions. The results have been developed, revised, and evaluated in a series of applications based on industrial expertise.

## 1 Introduction

For the development of many types of software systems, the satisfaction of quality requirements and the appropriate options for future changes are among the major goals of software architectures, even more important than functional requirements [12]. Business critical systems demand for the constant provision of the business services and for a long lifetime for the return of the investment, while changes have to be performed with a high frequency. As a consequence, the rank of evolvability often is higher compared to many other quality goals. Quality attributes have been considered by recent architectural design methods and approaches, for example QASAR [7], Siemens' 4 Views [23], ADD [4], and QADA [28]. Their activities can be classified to the phases architectural analysis, synthesis, and evaluation [22], of which synthesis creates the candidate solutions balancing the quality and functional requirements.

According to the importance of quality goals for architectural design, a high risk is related to them. As a consequence, an effective guidance is needed during the development, especially for the implementation of goals such as evolvability, flexibility, and variability. Quality goals often compete or even conflict with each other and with functional requirements. A refinement of quality goals to

M. Ali Babar and I. Gorton (Eds.): ECSA 2010, LNCS 6285, pp. 182–197, 2010.

quality properties eases the resolution of conflicts and the identification of compromises [25]. For balancing between functional and quality requirements, the utilization of patterns [20] or tactics [4] for architectural structuring constitute an effective way. Architectural decisions between the several solutions have to be made according to their impact on the quality properties. This shall result in a goal-oriented way of selecting patterns and tactics.

The architect's set of solution elements is usually contained in a toolbox representing a knowledge base of design knowledge. There are suggestions to structure a toolbox into two parts [30]: *(a)* a catalog of approved methods and solution templates (e.g. patterns), as well as *(b)* a catalog of fundamental technologies and tools (e.g. frameworks). To enable the intended goal-oriented way of selecting solution elements, the impact of the toolbox elements on quality properties is required as a decision criteria. Usually, pattern catalogs (e.g. [13,18]) provide descriptions for context, problem, and solution. Influences on quality properties of the resulting architecture are considered to a lesser extent, and qualitatively rather than quantitatively. Classification is related to pattern types instead of quality properties. Therefore, the catalogs do not sufficiently guide the architect in a pattern selection related to quality goals. Unfortunately, to the best of our knowledge there is no quantitative evaluation nor classification of architectural patterns regarding their impact on quality attributes, which is required for a goal-oriented pattern selection process. This is especially the case for the goal evolvability.

This paper presents an approach for the quantitative evaluation of the impact of architectural solution elements on quality goals, which provides all necessary means for a goal-oriented decision-making for architectural design. As described in prior works [5,8], we refine quality goals to subcharacteristics to facilitate conflict resolution. The quality subcharacteristics are mapped to properties for good architectural design. Architectural solution elements such as patterns are then related to these properties, based on evaluations of their impact on the latter. We utilize our concept of the Goal Solution Scheme [5] to structure these relations and to form a knowledge base. A sequence of evaluations of the approach has lead to revisions of previous schemes, thus, achieving a higher degree of maturity. The results provide the means for the different steps of a goal-oriented design process, such as refining the goals, prioritizing the quality subcharacteristics, and providing a ranked list of candidate solution elements during architectural synthesis. The presented work is focused on the quality goal evolvability, however, it is intended for other quality goals as well.

The results have been developed, revised, and evaluated in a series of applications based on industrial expertise. Here we explain them with a case study of a software system for collective orderers, which additionally confirmed and improved our evolvability model from an earlier work [8].

The rest of the paper is organized as follows. We introduce the fundamentals for our evaluation in Section 2: the evolvability model with the subcharacteristics and the quality properties. Section 3 describes our procedure for the evaluation of the impact of architectural patterns. Then, in Section 4 the results of the evaluation are discussed. Section 5 deals with related work. Finally, Section 6 concludes the paper and gives an outlook on further work.

## 2   Evolvability Subcharacteristics and Design Properties

This section provides the fundamentals for our approach. Three elements form the base for our approach of goal-oriented decision support on architectural solutions: (1) A quality model with a refinement of quality goals to subcharacteristics and properties, (2) a process for selecting architectural solutions, and (3) an evaluation of solutions regarding their impact on quality goals—in this case evolvability. We use a definition of evolvability based on Breivold et al. [9] and Rowe et al. [32]:

**Definition.** *Evolvability is the ability of a software system throughout its lifespan to accommodate to changes and enhancements in requirements and technologies, that influence the system's architectural structure, with the least possible cost while maintaining the architectural integrity* .

**Table 1.** Evolvability subcharacteristics

| Subcharacteristic | Description |
|---|---|
| Analyzability, Ease of comprehension, (Understandability)* | The capability of the software product to be diagnosed for deficiencies or causes of failures in the software and to enable the identification of influenced parts due to change stimuli (based on [24] and [9]). |
| Changeability/ Modifiability* | The capability of the software product to enable a specified modification to be implemented quickly and cost-effectively (based on [24] and [27]). |
|     Extensibility* | The capability of a software system to enable the implementation of extensions to expand or enhance the system with new capabilities and features with minimal impact to existing system [9]. |
|     Variability* | The capability of a software system or artifact to be efficiently extended, changed, customized, or configured for use in a particular context by using preconfigured variation points (based on [34]). |
|     Portability* | The capability of the software product to be transferred from one environment or platform to another [24]. |
| Reusability* | The system's structure or some of its components can be reused again in future applications [27]. |
| Testability* | The capability of the software system to enable modified software to be validated [24]. |
| Traceability* | The capability to track and recover in both a forwards and backwards direction the development steps of a software system and the design decisions made during on-going refinement and iteration in all development phases by relating the resulting artifacts of each development step to each other (based on [19]). |
| Compliance to standards* | The extent to which the software product adheres to standards or conventions relating to evolvability (based on [24]. |
| Process qualities | Additional process quality characteristics are for example Project Maturity and Community Quality, which are recognized as characteristics that influence the evolvability of open source software projects [17]. |

## 2.1   The Evolvability Model

Evolvability of a software system is a property referring to the effort concerning different aspects of its evolution. This effort can be determined by the help of several subcharacteristics of evolvability, which we define by a quality model. This model is an extension of the works of Breivold et al. [9,10] and Cook et al. [15] and was introduced earlier in [8].

For a goal-oriented way of decision-making during architectural synthesis, the impact of a decision on the quality goal has to be determined or predicted. Expert estimations constitute an effective way of impact determination. An expert in this regard should have experience with the implications of architectural patterns on quality properties in a certain class of software systems. The subjective

**Table 2.** Properties of good architectural design

| Property | Description |
|---|---|
| Low complexity* | The extent to which the amount/number of elements and their interdependencies are reduced. |
| Abstraction* | The extent to which unnecessary details of information are hidden to build an ideal model and the extend to which a solution is generalized (based on [6]). |
| Modularity* | The property of a software system to be decomposed into a set of coherent and loosely coupled elements with subsumption of abstractions (based on [6]). |
| Cohesion* | The strength of the coupling between the internals of an element (based on [6]). |
| Loose coupling* | The extent to which the interdependencies between elements are minimized (based on [6]). |
| Encapsulation* | The extent of hiding the internals of an element for example by separation of interface and implementation (based on [6]). |
| Separation of Concerns* | The extent to which different responsibilities are mapped onto different elements with as little as possible overlap, at which ideally one responsibility is assigned to exactly one specific element. The violation of this property is called tangling and scattering. |
| Hierarchy* | The arrangement or classification of related abstractions ranked one above the other according to inclusiveness and level of detail (based on [6] and [29]). |
| Simplicity* | The quality or condition of being easy to understand or do [29]. |
| Correctness | The property of an element to be complete and consistent resulting in a fulfillment of its responsibilities. |
| Consistency | The absence of contradictions and violations between related elements. |
| Completeness | The coverage of all relevant responsibilities by an element without lacking any necessary detail. |
| Conceptual integrity | The continuous application of ideas throughout a whole solution, preventing special effects and exceptions (based on [11]). |
| Proper granularity* | The size and complexity of an element is appropriate to its responsibilities and to the particular situation. |
| Coherent mapping to concepts* | The way to map elements to ideas and mental pictures so that they are easy to understand, for example by proper names. |

character of expert estimations can be reduced by performing them on a detailed level and then aggregating the results.

We discovered that properties for good architectural design provide a proper refinement of the quality subcharacteristics to determine the impact of architectural elements on the different aspects of evolution effort. We modeled the refinement by a mapping between subcharacteristics and properties.

The subcharacteristics of evolvability are described in Table 1. These subcharacteristics are based on the ISO 9126 [24] and other works on evolvability [9,10,15]. They also strongly correlate to what Matinlassi et al. [27] call evolution qualities and additional characteristics (e.g. traceabiliy, variability) for specifying the quality goal maintainability.

The design properties used for refinement are listed in Table 2. The mapping between subcharacteristics and design properties is shown in Figure 1 and Table 3. In the figure we left out some direct dependencies and show the aggregated ones for a better visualization. In Table 3 an existing influence relation is represented by 1 if positive and by -1 if negative. Indentations in the tables express the refinements of subcharacteristics and properties. For example modularity aggregates cohesion and loose coupling. The indentations correspond to the refinement links in Figure 1.

Many evolvability subcharacteristics can be influenced by the architectural structure and behavior. However, there are important influence factors on evolvability as for example qualification and motivation of the team members, process

**Table 3.** Mapping of subcharacteristics to properties

| Property \ Subcharacteristic | Analyzability | Changeability | Extensibility | Variability | Portability | Testability | Reusability | Traceability | Compliance |
|---|---|---|---|---|---|---|---|---|---|
| Low complexity* | | | | | | | 1 | | |
|   Abstraction* | 1 | 1 | 1 | 1 | | | 1 | | 1 |
|   Modularity* | | | | | | | | | |
|     Cohesion* | 1 | 1 | 1 | 1 | 1 | 1 | | | |
|     Loose coupling* | 1 | 1 | 1 | 1 | 1 | 1 | | | |
|   Encapsulation* | 1 | 1 | 1 | 1 | -1 | 1 | | | |
|   Separation of concerns* | 1 | 1 | 1 | 1 | 1 | 1 | 1 | | |
|   Hierarchie* | 1 | 1 | 1 | 1 | 1 | | | | 1 |
|   Simplicity* | 1 | 1 | 1 | 1 | 1 | 1 | | | |
|   Correctness | | | | | | | | | |
|     Consistency | 1 | 1 | 1 | 1 | 1 | 1 | 1 | | |
|     Completeness | | 1 | | | | 1 | 1 | 1 | |
|   Conceptional integrity | 1 | 1 | 1 | 1 | | | | | 1 |
| Proper granularity* | | 1 | 1 | 1 | | | 1 | | |
| Coherent mapping to concepts* | 1 | 1 | 1 | 1 | 1 | 1 | 1 | 1 | 1 |

1 – Positive influence; -1 – Negative influence

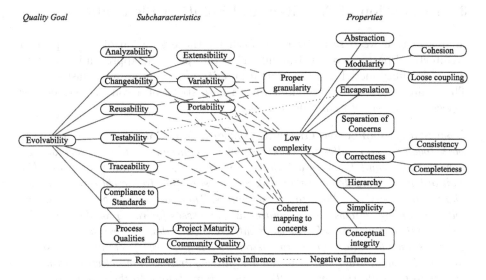

**Fig. 1.** Graphical representation of the evolvability model

maturity, or quality management activities. The development process with roles, phases, communication paths, and traceability has a large influence as well. Architectural structures cannot control these factors; they will be considered partly in the calculation scheme in Section 3.3. For the subcharacteristics (Table 1) and the design properties (Table 2) we marked the ones with a direct influence from architectural patterns by an * in the first columns. They are applied as evaluation criteria for the architectural patterns in the sequel.

The mapping relations have been developed in an iterative way, starting with hypotheses [8] and multiple steps of revision during application in case studies [31,33]. Meanwhile, the relations and the way of calculating impact values can be considered as rather mature. As an additional benefit of the evolvability model the refinement of the quality goals by mapping to properties enables a conflict resolution between competing quality goals, as discussed earlier in [5].

## 2.2   The Selection Procedure for Architectural Decisions

Architectural decisions concern design changes or the introduction of architectural solution elements, for example from the architect's toolbox. In order to implement a goal-oriented development we embed our approach into a two step procedure of selecting architectural solutions: (1) Architectural constraints are used to determine the set of applicable solutions by eliminating all unsuitable ones. (2) All solutions in the set are evaluated and ranked regarding the relevant quality goals. According to the ranking the architect selects and implements a solution. The evaluation needed for step 2 is presented in the next chapter.

# 3    Evaluation of Architectural Solution Elements

In this section we describe our approach for the evaluation of the impact of architectural patterns on evolvability. The concept of the approach is based on the evolvability model and the evaluation criteria presented in the last section. The evaluation itself is presented with a case study of a software system for collective orderers of mail order companies.

**Case Study: Collective Ordering System.** *Mail order companies prefer to work together with collective orderers, who accumulate orders of several customers and submit them as a collective order to the mail order company. The mail order company delivers the goods in one shipment to the collective orderer, who in turn distributes them to the customers. There are several advantages: The collective orderer knows the formalities and processes for rare procedures such as reshipment, complaint, deferred payment, etc. better than the average customer. The personal, familiar contact to customers has positive effects on the business volume. The mail order company can delegate communication activities with customers to the collective orderer. These procedures belong to the core business in the domain and are affected by frequent changes. Therefore, they were chosen for this case study.*

The software system of the company shall enable collective orderers to submit orders, manage their customers, and deal with complaints. We applied our approach for the task of enhancing this system. First, we selected some architectural patterns as explained in Section 3.1. Second, we determined the impact of the patterns on the properties for good architectural design (Section 3.2). For evaluation purposes, a suitable part of the collective ordering software was designed for each of the considered architectural patterns. This architectural design was used for the impact determination. Based on the results, the impact on the subcharacteristics was determined as discussed in Section 3.3. Finally, we aggregated the values to determine the impact on the quality goal evolvability (Section 3.4). The resulting values are stored together with the patterns in the architect's catalog. They can be used for future design decisions regarding this quality goal.

## 3.1    Selection of Patterns

For the impact determination regarding the quality goal evolvability, architectural and design patterns with an influence on the software architecture constitute interesting candidates. There is a high number of patterns available. For the evaluation with this case study we selected a set of patterns from the entirety which have an influence on the architecture, which are well documented, and which are expected to have an impact on evolvability. According to step 1 of our decision procedure, they have to fulfill the constraints of the software system of the case study. The selected patterns are listed in Table 4.

**Table 4.** Selected architectural patterns

| Name | Sources |
|------|---------|
| Client-Server | see Avgeriou&Zdun [1] |
| Layers/Tiers | |
| Repository | |
| Blackboard | |
| Pipes and Filters | |
| Model View Controller (MVC) | |
| Presentation Abstraction Control (PAC) | |
| Event-Based, Implicit Invocation | |
| Broker | |
| Micro Kernel | |
| Reflection | |
| Facade | Gamma et al. [18] |
| Adapter | |
| Proxy | |
| Plug-in | Manolescu et al. [26] |

## 3.2   Determination of the Impact on the Properties

This section explains the determination of the impact values for the selected patterns in the case study. First, we applied the patterns in an exemplary architectural design for the case study. The resulting pattern-based design was rated regarding the impact on the properties for good architectural design. The ratings were gained through an assessment of the impact for each property by experts. The value of the impact is expressed by values of -2 (strong negative), -1 (weak negative), 0 (neutral), 1 (weak positive) and 2 (strong positive).

*Case study example for impact discussion.* A collective orderer has to enter orders into the software system, and then the orders have to be transmitted to the mail order company. Usually this is done via phone but should be supported by the new software system. As a possible solution in the case study, we utilized the Client-Server pattern (see Figure 2(a)). The server at the mail order company is connected to the collective orderer's client via internet. It provides an interface for the transmission of orders. The client is structured in three layers as shown in Figure 2(b). The presentation layer is responsible for the graphical user interface (GUI). It uses the application layer, which provides functions as calculations for deferred payment, a search for ordered but not delivered goods, or a reminder for the deadline for returning the goods. The data layer is responsible for the data persistence in a databank.

Now we discuss the evaluation of the patterns Client-Server and Layers regarding their impact on the properties for good architectural design. They both have a strong positive impact on several properties. For example they provide a good abstraction of internal details (rating 2). The resulting architecture is simple to understand (2). They provide good modularity due to high cohesion

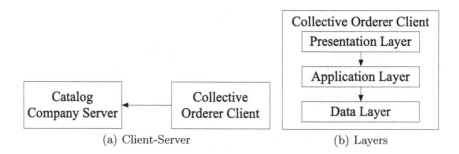

(a) Client-Server                    (b) Layers

**Fig. 2.** Pattern application in the case study example

inside the layers, client, and server (2), as well as a loose coupling between the elements (2) for example for the deferred payment. Unnecessary details are hidden behind interfaces between the layers. Therefore, the encapsulation is improved (2). Regarding separation of concerns Client-Server and Layers have a positive impact, but they cannot completely prevent mixing different concerns (rating 1). Regarding the Hierarchy criteria the two patterns differ in their impact. The Layers pattern supports the ranking and grouping of abstractions on different levels very well due to the different layers (2). For the Client-Server pattern this cannot hold to this extend resulting in a lower rating (1). The same applies for the coherent mapping to concepts criteria. The Layers pattern has a weak positive impact on a proper granularity of an architectural design by structuring into layers instead of one big structural element (1). Overall, the Client-Server pattern and the Layers pattern reduce the complexity of an architecture through structuring.

Inside the client's presentation layer, the Model View Controller (MVC) pattern can be used to separate the data to be presented (e.g. a customer or order), from the different views and control mechanisms. For example there are views for editing the customers' contact information or for collecting and managing the orders.

The support for abstraction and cohesion as well as separation of concerns of MVC is very good (rating 2) as a result of the strict separation of model, view, and controller. This improves the simplicity of the design as well (1), although it is not so easy to use MVC with modern GUI libraries. The encapsulation is also good because the internals of each element are hidden behind interfaces (1). To build a hierarchy with MVC is not so well supported (0)—here Presentation Abstraction Control (PAC) would be better. Regarding coupling MVC is evaluated slightly negative (-1). Of course, the views can be decoupled from the model via a change-propagation mechanism, however, view and controller are coupled very tightly. Summed up, the complexity resulting from MVC is good but not excellent. The granularity that results from MVC can be quite good (1) if the models and views are properly designed. However, MVC's real strength is to provide a coherent mapping of concepts for the user interaction through the GUI (2).

For the rest of the patterns the evaluation concerning the properties was done in the same way. It cannot be explained here in detail due to space limitations.

**Table 5.** Values for the patterns' impact on the properties

| Property \ Pattern | Client-Server | Layers/Tiers | Repository | Blackboard | Pipes&Filters | MVC | PAC | Impl. Invoc. | Facade | Adapter | Broker | Proxy | Micro Kernel | Reflection | Plug-in |
|---|---|---|---|---|---|---|---|---|---|---|---|---|---|---|---|
| Low complexity | 1,7 | 1,8 | 0,8 | 0,3 | 1,7 | 1,1 | 1,4 | 0,8 | 1,3 | 1,4 | 1,5 | 1,5 | 2 | 0,3 | 1,6 |
| Abstraction | 2 | 2 | 0 | 0 | 2 | 2 | 2 | 1 | 2 | 2 | 2 | 2 | 2 | 2 | 2 |
| Modularity | 2 | 2 | 0 | 0,5 | 0 | 0,5 | 0,5 | 1 | 1,5 | 1,5 | 2 | 2 | 2 | 1 | 1,5 |
| Cohesion | 2 | 2 | 1 | 1 | 2 | 2 | 2 | 0 | 1 | 1 | 2 | 2 | 2 | 0 | 2 |
| Loose coupling | 2 | 2 | -1 | 0 | -2 | -1 | -1 | 2 | 2 | 2 | 2 | 2 | 2 | 2 | 1 |
| Encapsulation | 2 | 2 | 1 | 2 | 2 | 1 | 1 | 1 | 2 | 2 | 2 | 2 | 2 | 0 | 2 |
| Separation of concerns | 1 | 1 | 2 | 0 | 2 | 2 | 2 | 0 | 0 | 1 | 1 | 1 | 2 | 0 | 2 |
| Hierarchie | 1 | 2 | 0 | 0 | 2 | 0 | 2 | 0 | 0 | 0 | 0 | 0 | 2 | 0 | 0 |
| Simplicity | 2 | 2 | 2 | 2 | 2 | 1 | 1 | 2 | 2 | 2 | 2 | 2 | 2 | -1 | 2 |
| Proper granularity | 0 | 1 | 0 | 0 | 2 | 1 | 1 | 0 | 2 | 1 | 0 | 0 | 1 | 0 | 2 |
| Coherent mapping to concepts | 1 | 2 | 1 | 0 | 2 | 2 | 2 | 0 | 1 | 1 | 2 | 0 | 2 | 0 | 2 |

Table 5 shows the determined impacts of all selected patterns on the properties for good architectural design. The ratings of the aggregated properties modularity and low complexity are calculated by arithmetic mean of the subordinates.

### 3.3 Calculation of the Impact on Evolvability Subcharacteristics

The patterns' impact on the quality subcharacteristics is primarily determined from the impact on the properties, as discussed above. They are considered in the first step of the calculation. Additional influences on the subcharacteristics—for example from efforts not related to the properties of good design—are considered by introducing adjustments in a second step.

We calculated the results in the following way. Let $R$ be the matrix of the impact ratings for the properties (Table 5) and $r_p$ be a column vector of this matrix for one element $p$ of the set of patterns $P$. Let $M$ be the mapping matrix of Table 3 and $M^*$ be $M$ reduced by the rows for which the properties were not evaluated (and are not marked with *). Further, let $m_s$ be a column vector of $M^*$ for one element $s$ of the set of subcharacteristics $S$. Moreover, let $V$ be the matrix with the impact values of the patterns on the subcharacteristics. Then, each element $v_{sp}$ of $V$ is calculated by

$$v_{sp} = r_p \cdot m_s / \|m_s\|_1 .$$

Finally, the matrix $V'$ in the top of Table 6 is obtained from $V$ by calculating the impact values for changeability in row 2 by the arithmetic mean of the values for extensibility, variability, and portability. In this way we determine the patterns' impact values on the subcharacteristics from the direct ratings for the properties (Table 5) by evaluating and normalizing the influences of the interdependencies described by the mapping in Table 3.

However, through the calculation there is no discrimination regarding the subcharacteristics of changeability. The Reflection pattern for example contributes to extensibility and variability but reduces portability if the base technology does not support reflection. Furthermore, testability is decreased due to possible dynamic changes at runtime.

These effects are not represented by the aggregated impact values in $V'$ of the first step. Therefore, we considered offset values $o_{sp}$ shown in the middle of Table 6 for the determination of the patterns' impact on the subcharacteristics. To determine these offset values we also incorporated knowledge about conse-

**Table 6.** Impact values for subcharacteristics and evolvability

| Subcharacteristic \ Pattern | Client-Server | Layers/Tiers | Repository | Blackboard | Pipes&Filters | MVC | PAC | Impl. Invoc. | Facade | Adapter | Broker | Proxy | Micro Kernel | Reflection | Plug-in |
|---|---|---|---|---|---|---|---|---|---|---|---|---|---|---|---|
| **Calculated Rating** | | | | | | | | | | | | | | | |
| Analyzability | 1,6 | 1,9 | 0,8 | 0,1 | 1,5 | 1,1 | 1,4 | 0,8 | 1,3 | 1,4 | 1,6 | 1,4 | 2,0 | 0,4 | 1,6 |
| Changeability | 1,4 | 1,8 | 0,7 | 0,2 | 1,6 | 1,1 | 1,3 | 0,7 | 1,3 | 1,3 | 1,4 | 1,2 | 1,9 | 0,3 | 1,7 |
|   Extensibility | 1,4 | 1,8 | 0,7 | 0,2 | 1,6 | 1,1 | 1,3 | 0,7 | 1,3 | 1,3 | 1,4 | 1,2 | 1,9 | 0,3 | 1,7 |
|   Variability | 1,4 | 1,8 | 0,7 | 0,2 | 1,6 | 1,1 | 1,3 | 0,7 | 1,3 | 1,3 | 1,4 | 1,2 | 1,9 | 0,3 | 1,7 |
|   Portability | 1,4 | 1,8 | 0,7 | 0,2 | 1,6 | 1,1 | 1,3 | 0,7 | 1,3 | 1,3 | 1,4 | 1,2 | 1,9 | 0,3 | 1,7 |
| Testability | 1,4 | 1,8 | 0,8 | -0,2 | 1,2 | 1,0 | 1,4 | 0,6 | 0,8 | 1,0 | 1,4 | 1,0 | 2,0 | 0,2 | 1,4 |
| Reusability | 1,5 | 1,8 | 0,8 | 0,3 | 1,5 | 1,3 | 1,3 | 0,8 | 1,5 | 1,5 | 1,6 | 1,4 | 1,9 | 0,4 | 1,9 |
| Traceability | 1,2 | 1,6 | 1,3 | 0,8 | 1,9 | 1,7 | 1,8 | 0,3 | 0,8 | 1,1 | 1,5 | 0,8 | 2,0 | 0,1 | 1,9 |
| Compliance to standards | 1,3 | 2,0 | 0,3 | 0,0 | 2,0 | 1,3 | 2,0 | 0,3 | 1,0 | 1,0 | 1,3 | 0,7 | 2,0 | 0,7 | 1,3 |
| **Offset** | | | | | | | | | | | | | | | |
| Analyzability | | | 0 | -1 | | | | -1 | 2 | 0 | 1 | | 0 | | |
| Changeability | | | | | | | | | | | | | | | |
|   Extensibility | 1 | 1 | 2 | -1 | | 2 | 2 | 2 | 2 | 2 | 2 | | | 2 | 2 |
|   Variability | 1 | 1 | | | | 2 | 2 | 2 | | 2 | | | | 2 | 2 |
|   Portability | 2 | 2 | | | | 2 | 2 | | | 2 | 2 | 2 | | -1 | |
| Testability | | | | -2 | | | | -2 | -1 | | | 2 | 0 | -1 | 2 |
| Reusability | | | | | | | | 2 | 2 | 2 | | | | 1 | |
| Traceability | | | | | | | | 2 | | | | | | | |
| Compliance to standards | | | | | | | | | | | 2 | | 0 | | 2 |
| **Final Values** | | | | | | | | | | | | | | | |
| Analyzability | 1,6 | 1,9 | 0,4 | -0,4 | 1,5 | 1,1 | 1,4 | -0,1 | 1,6 | 0,7 | 1,3 | 1,4 | 1,0 | 0,4 | 1,6 |
| Changeability | 1,4 | 1,6 | 0,9 | 0,0 | 1,6 | 1,6 | 1,7 | 1,1 | 1,4 | 1,7 | 1,6 | 1,4 | 1,9 | 0,7 | 1,8 |
|   Extensibility | 1,2 | 1,4 | 1,3 | -0,4 | 1,6 | 1,6 | 1,7 | 1,3 | 1,7 | 1,7 | 1,7 | 1,2 | 1,9 | 1,2 | 1,8 |
|   Variability | 1,2 | 1,4 | 0,7 | 0,2 | 1,6 | 1,6 | 1,7 | 1,3 | 1,3 | 1,7 | 1,4 | 1,2 | 1,9 | 1,2 | 1,8 |
|   Portability | 1,7 | 1,9 | 0,7 | 0,2 | 1,6 | 1,6 | 1,7 | 0,7 | 1,3 | 1,7 | 1,7 | 1,6 | 1,9 | -0,3 | 1,7 |
| Testability | 1,4 | 1,8 | 0,8 | -1,1 | 1,2 | 1,0 | 1,4 | -0,7 | -0,1 | 1,0 | 1,4 | 1,5 | 1,0 | -0,4 | 1,7 |
| Reusability | 1,5 | 1,8 | 0,8 | 0,3 | 1,5 | 1,3 | 1,3 | 1,4 | 1,8 | 1,8 | 1,6 | 1,4 | 1,9 | 0,7 | 1,9 |
| Traceability | 1,2 | 1,6 | 1,3 | 0,8 | 1,9 | 1,7 | 1,8 | 1,1 | 0,8 | 1,1 | 1,5 | 0,8 | 2,0 | 0,1 | 1,9 |
| Compliance to standards | 1,3 | 2,0 | 0,3 | 0,0 | 2,0 | 1,3 | 2,0 | 0,3 | 1,0 | 1,0 | 1,7 | 0,7 | 1,0 | 0,7 | 1,7 |
| **Evolvability** | 1,4 | 1,8 | 0,7 | -0,1 | 1,6 | 1,3 | 1,6 | 0,5 | 1,1 | 1,2 | 1,5 | 1,2 | 1,5 | 0,3 | 1,8 |

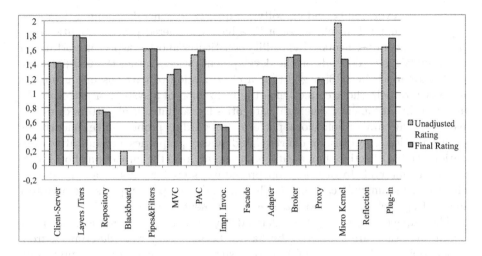

**Fig. 3.** Resulting Impact of Patterns on Evolvability

quences of the pattern application regarding quality properties mentioned in the literature (e.g. Buschmann et al. [13]). The final impact values are calculated as follows. Let $F$ be the matrix for the adjusted impact values. Then each element $f_{sp}$ of $F$ is calculated by

$$f_{sp} = \begin{cases} v_{sp} & \text{if } o_{sp} \text{ is undefined} \\ (v_{sp} + o_{sp})/2 & \text{otherwise.} \end{cases}$$

The final impact values $F'$ for the subcharacteristics including changeability shown in the bottom of Table 6 again are obtained as for $V'$ before.

### 3.4  Determining the Impact on Evolvability

As the last step the overall impact of the patterns on the quality goal evolvability is to be determined by aggregating all subcharacteristics with equal weights. The resulting values of the patterns' impact on evolvability are shown in Figure 3 and in the lowermost row of Table 6. The experts gave feedback on the results. This feedback led to a minor revision of the offset values discussed in the last section. The changes resulting from the offset values can be seen by comparing the unadjusted and the final values shown in Figure 3. As a consequence of the evaluation, a plug-in-based architecture was selected as the best solution.

## 4  Discussion of the Results

The final results of the impact evaluation are illustrated by Figure 3. The chart shows that the patterns in general do have a positive impact on the quality goal evolvability. Some patterns turned out to be excellent, for example Layers, Plug-in, or Pipes and Filters; others are less supportive. However, the impact of the patterns on evolvability and on software quality in general is limited if process aspects are not taken into account. We have considered process qualities only partly by the adjustments. Traceability constitutes another aspect important for evolvability which depends on the development process rather than on patterns.

Buschmann et al. [13] argue that a classification of patterns into groups is necessary to help the architect with the utilization of a system of patterns. We agree to this argument for general categories like architectural pattern or design pattern, structural or behavioral pattern, or regarding problems like concurrency or distribution. However, for effort-related quality properties a quantitative evaluation is more effective than a categorization because the impact on effort varies within an interval. In our decision procedure, step 1 results in a very similar effect as Buschmann's categories. The ranking of step 2 supports the architect in selecting the most appropriate solution element.

The impact values have been derived from a concrete case study. We must admit that they are subjective by nature because they were determined from expert opinion. The results of an expert survey also depend on the application conditions as the experience of the development teams. However, an improvement regarding objectivity is possible by including several experts. The values shall be applicable and applied in further projects. The degree of universality of the impact values can be improved by revising them in a series of projects.

The presented results have been developed as hypotheses, later revised, and evaluated in a series of applications based on industrial expertise. They can be considered as rather mature. Even if forthcoming revisions might result in smaller modifications of the impact values, the revisions of the relations for refinement and mapping (Fig. 1) can be expected to be minor ones.

## 5   Related Work

There is a lot of literature with works about patterns and their classification in pattern catalogs, some of which were already mentioned in the preceding sections. A good start to read are Avgeriou and Zdun [1], Buschmann et al. [13], or the seminal work of Gamma et al. [18]. Unfortunately, there is no catalog of patterns for evolvability. For security such a thing exists already for a quite long time [35].

A similar work to ours is the one of Harrison and Avgeriou [21]. They give an overview about the strengths and liabilities of a set of common architectural patterns regarding their impact on the qualities of the ISO 9126. They also present a design method for architectural design, which describes how to select the appropriate patterns for balancing quality and functional requirements in [20]. However, they do not discuss the impact of the patterns on the properties for good architectural design as we do. Furthermore, our work has a strength in focussing on evolvability.

Architectural tactics discussed in several works by the SEI (e.g. [3], [2]) can be other means for a proper selection of patterns during architectural design. They are used for example in the Attribute Driven Design (ADD) method [4]. The tactics give some qualitative hints for choosing patterns concerning several quality attributes as e.g. modifiability or performance. But they do not consider design principles either, only partly deal with evolvability through modifiability, and cannot be interpreted quantitatively as the ratings in our approach.

POSAAM [16] is a method for quantitative architectural evaluation that relates patterns to quality attributes and design principles in an ontology. In this it is akin to our approach, though not for architectural synthesis.

Furthermore, the NFR-Framework of Chung et al. [14] has some similarities to our evolvability model. They link quality goals, so-called softgoals, and their subgoals via contribution links and operationalize them with solutions to perform an evaluation of the quality goals' satisfaction. However, the NFR-Framework has a requirements-oriented viewpoint, and therefore, does not consider architectural design principles or properties important for architectural synthesis.

# 6   Conclusion and Further Work

In this paper as the major contribution we presented an approach for the quantitative selection of architectural elements regarding quality goals. It consists of a quality model for evolvability as a basis for the evaluation of architectural patterns regarding their impact on the quality goal evolvability. We defined subcharacteristics of evolvability and mapped them to properties for good architectural design in order to be able to determine the impact on evolvability. Additionally, we presented our calculation scheme for the evaluation together with the results of the evaluation. The evaluation is embedded in a decision procedure on architectural elements in a toolbox. With a case study we explained how to determine the patterns' impact on the properties, to calculate the impact on the subcharacteristics through our mapping, then to consider additional influences by offset values to fit expertise knowledge, and finally, to aggregate the ratings to the final impact values on evolvability. The results show a considerable impact of architectural patterns on evolvability, although this quality goal cannot be addressed by merely using architectural patterns.

Another contribution of this work consists in a quantitative evaluation of architectural patterns regarding their impact on the quality goal evolvability and its subcharacteristics. In our opinion this is a valuable mean for supporting the decision-making process of a software architect. Using the patterns' impact values, a software architect can enrich his toolbox and rank the patterns according to their quality impact. This eases the search and selection of appropriate solutions for quality goals during architectural design. Furthermore, the mapping of quality goals on subchararcteristics facilitates the resolution of conflicts between competing quality goals.

In further works, the mapping relations between properties and subcharacteristics will be investigated in more detail, to elaborate a weighting of the mapping relations. Moreover, the results can be combined with knowledge on patterns' impact on other quality attributes, in addition to evolvability. Furthermore, with our approach additional solution concepts of an architect's toolbox can be evaluated, for example architectural refactorings or frameworks. Tool support for the approach is currently developed.

# References

1. Avgeriou, P., Zdun, U.: Architectural patterns revisited – a pattern language. In: 10th European Conf. on Pattern Languages of Programs (EuroPlop 2005), Irsee, pp. 1–39 (2005)
2. Bachmann, F., Bass, L., Nord, R.: Modifiability tactics. Tech. Rep. CMU/SEI-2007-TR-002, CMU/SEI (September 2007)
3. Bachmann, F., Bass, L., Klein, M.: Deriving architectural tactics: A step toward methodical architectural design. Tech. Rep. CMU/SEI-2003-TR-004, CMU/SEI (March 2003)
4. Bass, L.J., Klein, M., Bachmann, F.: Quality attribute design primitives and the attribute driven design method. In: van der Linden, F.J. (ed.) PFE 2002. LNCS, vol. 2290, pp. 169–186. Springer, Heidelberg (2002)
5. Bode, S., Fischer, A., Kühnhauser, W., Riebisch, M.: Software architectural design meets security engineering. In: Proc. 16th Int. Conf. and Workshop on the Engineering of Computer Based Systems (ECBS 2009), pp. 109–118. IEEE, Los Alamitos (2009)
6. Booch, G.: Object Oriented Analysis and Design. With Applications. Addison-Wesley, Longman (October 1993)
7. Bosch, J.: Design and use of software architectures: Adopting and evolving a product-line approach. ACM Press/Addison-Wesley, New York (2000)
8. Brcina, R., Bode, S., Riebisch, M.: Optimization process for maintaining evolvability during software evolution. In: Proc. 16th Int. Conf. and Workshop on the Engineering of Computer Based Systems (ECBS 2009), pp. 196–205. IEEE, Los Alamitos (2009)
9. Breivold, H.P., Crnkovic, I., Eriksson, P.: Evaluating software evolvability. In: Proc. of the 7th Conf. on Software Engineering Research and Practice in Sweden (SERPS 2007), Göteborg, Sweden, pp. 96–103 (2007)
10. Breivold, H.P., Crnkovic, I., Land, R., Larsson, S.: Using dependency model to support software architecture evolution. In: 23rd IEEE/ACM International Conference on Automated Software Engineering - Workshops, 2008. ASE Workshops 2008., pp. 82–91. IEEE, Los Alamitos (September 2008)
11. Brooks, F.P.: The Mythical Man-Month: Essays on Software Engineering. Addison-Wesley, Reading (1995)
12. Brown, A.W., McDermid, J.A.: The art and science of software architecture. In: Oquendo, F. (ed.) ECSA 2007. LNCS, vol. 4758, pp. 237–256. Springer, Heidelberg (2007)
13. Buschmann, F., Meunier, R., Rohnert, H., Sommerlad, P., Stal, M.: Pattern-Oriented Software Architecture: A System of Patterns. John Wiley & Sons, Chichester (1996)
14. Chung, L., Nixon, B.A., Yu, E., Mylopoulos, J.: Non-functional Requirements in Software Engineering. Int. Series in Software Engineering, vol. 5. Kluwer, Dordrecht (2000)
15. Cook, S., Ji, H., Harrison, R.: Dynamic and static views of software evolution. In: 17th IEEE International Conference on Software Maintenance (ICSM 2001), November 2001, pp. 592–601. IEEE, Los Alamitos (2001)
16. da Cruz, D.B.: POSAAM – Eine Methode zu mehr Systematik und Expertenunabhängigkeit in der qualitativen Architekturbewertung. Ph.D. thesis, TU München (2009)

17. Deprez, J.-C., Monfils, F.F., Ciolkowski, M., Soto, M.: Defining software evolvability from a free/open-source software perspective. In: Proceedings of the Third International IEEE Workshop on Software Evolvability, October 2007, pp. 29–35. IEEE, Los Alamitos (2007)
18. Gamma, E., Helm, R., Johnson, R., Vlissides, J.M.: Design Patterns: Elements of Reusable Object-Oriented Softwaresystems. Addison-Wesley, Reading (November 1994)
19. Gotel, O.C.Z., Finkelstein, A.C.W.: An analysis of the requirements traceability problem. In: Proceedings of the First International Conference on Requirements Engineering, Colorado Springs, CO, USA, April 1994, pp. 94–101. IEEE, Los Alamitos (1994)
20. Harrison, N., Avgeriou, P.: Pattern-driven architectural partitioning: Balancing functional and non-functional requirements. In: ICDT 2007, IEEE, Los Alamitos (2007)
21. Harrison, N., Avgeriou, P.: Leveraging architecture patterns to satisfy quality attributes. In: Oquendo, F. (ed.) ECSA 2007. LNCS, vol. 4758, pp. 263–270. Springer, Heidelberg (2007)
22. Hofmeister, C., Kruchten, P., Nord, R.L., Obbink, H., Ran, A., America, P.: A general model of software architecture design derived from five industrial approaches. Journal of Systems and Software 80(1), 106–126 (2007)
23. Hofmeister, C., Nord, R., Soni, D.: Applied software architecture. Addison-Wesley, Boston (2000)
24. ISO/IEC: ISO/IEC 9126-1 International Standard. Software Engineering - Product quality - Part 1: Quality models (June 2001)
25. van Lamsweerde, A.: From system goals to software architectures. In: Bernardo, M., Inverardi, P. (eds.) SFM 2003. LNCS, vol. 2804, pp. 25–43. Springer, Heidelberg (2003)
26. Manolescu, D., Voelter, M., Noble, J.: Pattern Languages of Program Design, vol. 5. Addison-Wesley Professional, Reading (2006)
27. Matinlassi, M., Niemelä, E.: The impact of maintainability on component-based software systems. In: Proc. 29th Euromicro Conf., 2003, pp. 25–32. IEEE, Los Alamitos (2003)
28. Matinlassi, M., Niemelä, E., Liliana, D.: Quality-Driven Architecture Design and Quality Analysis Method. A Revolutionary Initiation Approach to a Product Line Architecture. Tech. Rep. 456, VTT Technical Research Centre of Finland (2002)
29. McKean, E.: The New Oxford American Dictionary, 2nd edn. Oxford University Press, Oxford (2005)
30. Posch, T., Birken, K., Gerdom, M.: Basiswissen Softwarearchitektur: Verstehen, entwerfen, wiederverwenden. dpunkt.verlag, 1 edn (2004)
31. Riebisch, M., Bode, S.: Software-Evolvability. Informatik-Spektrum 32(4), 339–343 (2009)
32. Rowe, D., Leaney, J., Lowe, D.: Defining systems architecture evolvability - a taxonomy of change. In: Proceedings of the 11th International Conference on the Engineering of Computer Based Systems (ECBS 1998), pp. 45–52. IEEE, Los Alamitos (1998)
33. Stollberg, R.: Klassifikation von Architekturstilen und -mustern hinsichtlich qualitativer Ziele für den Softwarearchitekturentwurf. Bachelor thesis, Ilmenau University of Technology, Ilmenau, Germany (2010)
34. Svahnberg, M., van Gurp, J., Bosch, J.: A taxonomy of variability realization techniques. Software: Practice and Experience 35(8), 705–754 (2005)
35. Yoder, J.W., Barcalow, J.: Architectural patterns for enabling application security. In: 4th Conf. on Patterns Languages of Programs, PLoP 1997 (1997)

# Functional Architecture Modeling for the Software Product Industry

Sjaak Brinkkemper and Stella Pachidi

Department of Information and Computing Sciences
University of Utrecht
P.O. Box 80.089, 3508 TB Utrecht, The Netherlands
{S.Brinkkemper,s.pachidi}@cs.uu.nl

**Abstract.** Although a lot of research has been carried out on the technical architecture of software systems, the domain of Functional Architecture in the software product industry lacks a formalization of the related concepts and practices. Functional Architecture Modeling is essential for identifying the functionalities of the software product and translating them into modules, which interact with each other or with third party products. Furthermore, the Functional Architecture serves as a base for mapping the functional requirements and planning the product releases. In this paper, we present the Functional Architecture Diagrams, a powerful modeling tool for the Functional Architecture of software products, which comprises: a modular decomposition of the product functionality; a simple notation for easy comprehension by non-specialists; and applicability in any line of business, offering a uniform method for modeling the functionalities of software products.

**Keywords:** software product, functional architecture modeling, modularity.

## 1 Towards Functional Architecture Modeling Attuned to Software Products

The discipline of software architecture, developed mainly during the last 20 years, is considered to be fundamental for the successful development of software products. According to Bass, Clements & Kazman [5] software architecture: constitutes a common language for the stakeholders −architects, product managers, software engineers, consultants, customers, marketing department− to communicate; captures design decisions in the early stages of a software product, which enable or inhibit implementation attributes and are used as reference in the future for managing change; consists of generalized constructs that can be transferred and reused in other product lines.

According to IEEE Standard 1471 [14], architecture is defined as "the fundamental organization of a system embodied in its components, their relationships to each other and to the environment and the principles guiding its design and evolution". A lot of definitions for software architecture have been developed [25], among which we find interesting the view of Johnson [10], who considers architecture as "the set of design decisions that must be made early in a project".

M. Ali Babar and I. Gorton (Eds.): ECSA 2010, LNCS 6285, pp. 198–213, 2010.
© Springer-Verlag Berlin Heidelberg 2010

Architecture viewpoints in software products provide guidelines to describe uniformly the total system and its subsystems. In the sense that the architecture should address the concerns of the stakeholders of the system [14][15], a viewpoint can be understood as a frame that identifies the modeling techniques that should be used to describe the architecture in order to address a defined subset of these concerns. Following the categorization of concepts by Broy et al. [8], we suggest that architecture viewpoints could be divided into three abstraction layers: The functional architecture describes the system by its functional behavior and the interactions observable with the environment. The logical architecture describes the system's internal structure, represented as a network of logical components that implement the system's functionality. The technical architecture describes how the system is realized, its software behavior, and its hardware structure.

A view represents the content of a viewpoint applied to a particular system. According to IEEE Standard 1471 description, view is defined as "a representation of the whole system from the perspective of a related set of concerns" [14]. Numerous sets of views have developed since 1990, amongst which we distinguish Kruchten's "4+1" view model of software architecture [17], the Siemens Four View model [23] and the model proposed by Herzum and Sims [12] in their book Business Component Factory. Furthermore, frameworks from the area of Enterprise Architecture such as Zachman's Framework [28] and TOGAF [9] include sets of architectural views that could also be applied in software architecture.

According to Van Vliet [26], the phase of designing the architecture of a software product is placed in the product lifecycle between the requirements engineering phase and the design phase. During the architecture design phase the architectural views are developed and relevant design decisions are taken with respect to all stakeholders' concerns and interests [15]. Hence, considering the requirements as triggers and input for the architecture design phase, we look for a method of capturing the requirements into the software product architecture. Although many well known techniques have evolved at a low level (e.g. use case diagrams), we have observed that there is no formal way of modeling the Functional Architecture at a high level, such that it can comprise all requirements addressed to the product's functions, and it can be communicated from product managers and architects to non-technical stakeholders (consultants, marketing, customers, end-users) in an efficient and effective way, and constitute a basis for the product design and planning. In this context, we have developed and present here a technique for *Functional Architecture Modeling*.

We define *Functional Architecture (FA)* as an architectural model which represents at a high level the software product's major functions from a usage perspective, and specifies the interactions of functions, internally between each other and externally with other products.

The *Functional Architecture Model (FAM)* includes all the necessary modules and structures for the visualization of the Functional Architecture of a software product and its relevant applications in the business domain. Consequently, it constitutes a standard arrangement of all the product's functional requirements positioned in modules, which correspond to functionalities. The Functional Architecture should be designed together with product managers, architects, partners and customers, and should be expressed in easy to understand diagrams. Referring back to the definition of viewpoints, we clarify that Functional Architecture addresses mainly the concerns of stakeholders like customers, marketing and sales employees, end-users, i.e. stakeholders with no technical expertise.

The Functional Architecture Model that we propose, can be used by software product managers to show the product roadmap to their customers and can constitute a reference base for the architecture design phase in the software product lifecycle. Consequently, it can also be used as a basis for managing the product vision for subsequent releases, registering incoming functional requirements and dividing work amongst development teams [10].

Many organizations already tend to design intuitively the functional architecture of their software systems. A practical example is the effort to model the functional architecture of Baan ERP, the main product of Baan, a vendor of enterprise resource planning software that is currently owned by Infor Global Solutions. In [11], the case studies indicate an effort to model the product's functionalities, but from a more technical perspective. Also, in this context, we have noticed the use of reference architectures during the design phase of enterprise solutions [21][3], which provide generic templates for the functional architecture of applications in a particular line of business, such as the IBM Insurance Application Architecture [13] and the Supply Chain Operations Reference [24].

However, we do not find a scientifically supported way to design the functional architecture of a software product irrespective of its domain. Furthermore, we do not consider the use of other modeling techniques sufficient to serve the aforementioned usage of Functional Architecture Modeling in software product management processes. Although Reference Models [2] include the division of functionality combined with data flow, they are "a characteristic of mature domains" [5] i.e. they model the functionalities on the level of a particular industry, while their notation varies according to the domain. Data Flow Diagrams focus on the flow of data in order to illustrate the related data stores, and are commonly used for lower levels of abstraction. Component Diagrams also focus on lower abstraction levels, by visualizing the interconnections between the components of a software system. In addition, sometimes UML models are not easily readable by stakeholders with no technical background such as customers or the marketing department. [4]

In this paper we intend to formalize the existing practices in a uniform modeling technique that can be used in all domains for the communication of the functionalities of a software product to the non-specialist stakeholders. This technique has been followed in the FA design of approximately 40 software products developed by the students of ICT Entrepreneurship course in Utrecht University for the last four years [19].

In the following sections of this paper, we present the structures of the Functional Architecture, provide guidelines for modeling the functional architecture of a software product, and finally illustrate this process through an example.

## 2 Functional Architecture Modeling: Design Principles and Structures

On our way of modeling the functional architecture of a software product, we get to notice that architecture is a premier key to the success of the product. A look at well known software products that have met huge commercial success over the years, such as the Google search engine, SAP R3 or Linux OS, gives us an insight that a robust and well designed architecture constitutes a significant factor for the development, maintenance, usability and performance of a software product. A well designed functional architecture enables the usability of a software system, and should be able to survive many releases, so that new functionalities can easily be incorporated without making fundamental changes. These observations lead us to the search of structures that will enable the design of a high-quality Functional Architecture. Bass et al. [5] suggest that there is no scientific evidence to decide whether an architecture design is good or bad, but there are several rules that should be applied in the architecture design. In table 1, we mention their recommendations adjusted for the construction of a functional architecture.

**Table 1.** Principles for Functional Architecture Modeling

| Principles for the FA design process | Principles for the structure of a FA |
|---|---|
| One single architect or else a group of a few architects with an appointed leader to design the architecture | Featuring of unambiguous modules following the principles of hiding information and separating concerns, with well-defined interfaces |
| Existence of a list of requirements and prioritized qualities | Modules should be developed as much independently from one another as possible |
| Documentation with notation understandable by all stakeholders | Architecture independent of technical changes |
| Involvement of all stakeholders in the review of FA | Architecture independent of particular commercial products |
| Early inspection for quantitative measures and qualitative properties that should be followed | Separation of modules that "produce data" from modules that "consume data" |
| Forming of a "skeletal system'" that will be used for the incremental growth and expansion of the software product | Small number of simple interaction patterns, in order to increase performance and enhance reliability and modifiability |

The design of a functional architecture is influenced by four main factors[5]: First of all the requirements set by the stakeholders, functional and non-functional, determine what kind of functionalities are going to be incorporated, as also technical restrictions that have to be taken under consideration. Secondly, the developing organization affects the architecture, with regard to earlier versions of the product, or available design patterns to be used, or already known data such as an existing database, etc. But also the customer organization has a strong opinion in the division of functionalities, since they might also be affected by the architectural decisions later on. Furthermore, the technical environment, which includes software engineering techniques or industry standards available, available design tools and development platform, can influence the architectural decisions. Finally, the background and expertise of the architect influence the selection of architectural techniques to be followed.

Based on the aforementioned principles and the influences on architecture, we distinct three design structures for the functional architecture:

- *Modularity*: According to Anderson [1], modular design is "a design technique in which functions are designed in modules that can be combined in subsequent designs". Modularity is related to the decomposition of the software products in several components, their positioning in the system and their connectivity. Modularity in functional architecture has to be given a robust structure, so that each module incorporates a well-defined functionality and can be developed independent of other modules [20]. Flexibility is also an important aspect of modularity, in the sense that the structure should not change often in subsequent releases of the product, but should easily direct new requirements to its current modules or a new functionality in a new module.
- *Variability* deals with the fact that the product might need to run in different organizational settings and cooperate with multiple products. Consequently, variability is related to the extent to which the various components can differ. Functional variability includes the product's modules that need to interact with different functional components; for example an ERP system used in multiple customer organizations might interact with different products in each organization. We also recognize technical variability, in the sense that technical features may need to differ on different platforms.
- *Interoperability* defines the interfaces that need to be placed between the product's features and external products. The product should have interfaces adapted to the specifications of external products in order to enable interaction with them. Care should be taken to design standard interfaces for optimal flexibility [1]. Furthermore, the decision of positioning these interfaces in the software product needs to be taken within the interoperability structure.

In the following section, we elaborate the presented design principles and structures in our suggested approach for modeling the Functional Architecture.

## 3  Modeling the Functional Architecture of Software Products

The purpose of this paper is to emphasize the need for a uniform technique to model the Functional Architecture of Software Products. In this section we present the concepts related to Functional Architecture and we propose the Functional Architecture Model and its corresponding views, which are designed through the Functional Architecture Diagrams. In the second part of the section, we elaborate on the modular decomposition of the Functional Architecture.

### 3.1  Functional Architecture Model

As we mentioned earlier, the Functional Architecture reflects a software product's architecture from a usage perspective. Evidently, such a model should resemble the functions performed in the individual user context, or −when we have to do with a corporate customer− the enterprise functions of the customer organization that are supported by the software product.

In figure 1 we can see an example of the functional architecture of Baan ERP Product [6]. Following the principle of modularity, each module in the FA represents

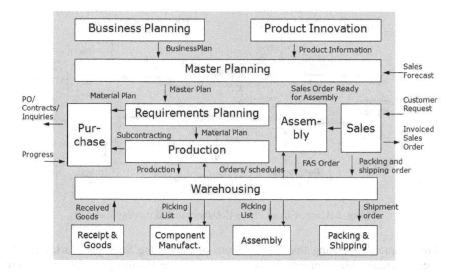

**Fig. 1.** Functional Architecture of an ERP product

a function in the customer domain (e.g. Requirement Planning, Production, etc). The flows represent interactions between functions or with external products. The principle of variability is also reflected in the functional architecture of the ERP Product, as it should easily run in different operating systems and platforms (technical variability) and in different customer organizations (functional variability). Finally, the interactions with other products or with the user indicate the interfaces that need to be built so that the product can interoperate with external factors.

We define the *Functional Architecture Model (FAM)* as the representation of the primary functionality of a software product, consisting of its main functions and supportive operations. The purpose of designing the FAM is to identify the main functionalities performed by the software product; show the interactions of these functions between each other and with external products; and create a clear overview of how the product should operate to satisfy the user's functional requirements.

In order to model the FA of a software product we borrow the notation and rules of Enterprise Function Diagrams, which are used in the domain of Enterprise Architecture to model the primary process of an enterprise, its physical and administrative functions [16]. Consequently, a *Functional Architecture Diagram (FAD)* will contain modules that resemble the functions of a software product. A *function* is defined as a collection of coherent processes, continuously performed within a software system and supporting its use. Functions are implemented in a software product by modules. The interactions between modules are represented in the function diagrams by *flows*.

In figure 2, we can see the FAD of a collaborative authoring tool. This diagram visualizes the product's usage context,  and could be useful for the phase of product roadmapping [27] as it indicates which modules need to be developed for each functionality of the product, thus the management can plan the development of the product releases. Furthermore, such a diagram could be useful for modeling domain components of the software product in the context of core assets development in the software product line [18].

**Fig. 2.** Usage Context for a Collaborative Authoring Tool

For instance, supposing that the functions of Publishing Strategy, Market Intelligence, Reference Management, Reviewing and Image Handling are left out of the first release, we can see the product usage scope of the collaborative authoring tool in figure 3. The boxes (Authoring, Version Management, Templates Management, Publishing, etc) are called modules, and correspond to the software product parts that implement the respective functions. In the diagram, we can also see how the modules interact with each other through information flows, by sending and receiving requests, documents etc. An interface needs to be implemented in a module, for each information flow with other modules or external products.

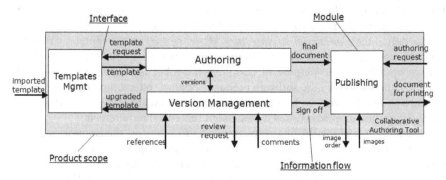

**Fig. 3.** Product scope

## 3.2  Modular Decomposition

The Functional Architecture of a software product is not limited in the product scope level. Instead, it can be modeled in more layers, supporting the functional decomposition of the product. A module of the software product represents a set of sub-modules which correspond to lower level functions that interoperate to implement the corresponding functionality. On a second FA layer, we could consequently model the functional architecture on the module level. In figure 4 we can see the FAD that visualizes

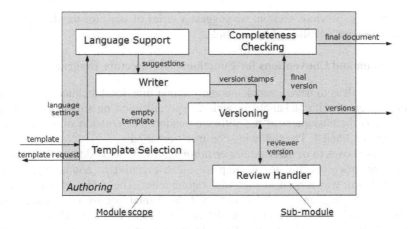

**Fig. 4.** FAD of the module *Authoring*

the module scope for the function Authoring. We strongly encourage preserving the consistency between FADs on different levels. For example, in figure 4 we can notice the same external interactions for the module Authoring, as the internal flows between this module and other modules in the FAD of the product scope in figure 3.

From our experience, we have noticed that the functional architecture is usually modeled in two to three layers. The FADs are designed following the same notation and rules, which we will see in the next section. On the lowest level, each module is supported by features, which represent the processes that constitute the respective function that the module implements. We remind here that functions were defined as collections of processes. A *process* is defined as an activity, the start and end of which are clearly defined and its execution can be described in terms of needed and delivered data. The features indicate what the software system does and not how it realizes it. They include lower level of details than the module.

The names of features usually start with a verb, to indicate the process they correspond to. Examples are: "open template", "send template to", "select rules", etc. Processes are modeled by *Feature Models*, which constitute a modeling tool for the process support functionality in a software product. Riebisch [22] has elaborated on defining feature models for supporting processes in software product lines. The feature models are considered as a criterion for ending the modular decomposition of the functional architecture, as we know that by reaching the process level we have created a sufficient number of views of the functional architecture model.

In this section we presented the Functional Architecture Model, which is reflected in the different views, visualized by Functional Architecture Diagrams, on different layers of decomposition. In the next section we will suggest a technique for creating the FAM in simple and uniform diagrams, applicable for any product domain.

## 4   An Approach for Designing Functional Architecture Diagrams

We now propose a technique for modeling the Functional Architecture of software products; we introduce a notation and some conventions for designing the FADs presented in the previous section; we suggest a series of steps for the design; and we illustrate our approach through an example.

## 4.1 Notation and Conventions for Functional Architecture Diagrams

One of our goals is to have a simple notation so that functional architecture can easily be communicated with stakeholders with no specialization on software architecture [14], such as the customers of the software vendor. The notation of a FAD can be seen in figures 3 and 4. The following constructs are used:

a) We use boxes to model *modules* or *sub-modules* of the product, which represent functions or processes. For the naming we use substantivized nouns (e.g. Planning instead of Plan), which need to start with capital letter. The choice of names is critical: since the diagram will constitute a fundamental means of communication amongst the stakeholders, precise and determining terms that are well known in the business domain are preferred. Finally, coloring can be used to categorize the modules hierarchically or according to their use.

b) Arrows are used to model interactions between modules in the form of *information flows*. Typical examples of information flows include notifications, requests, feedback to requests, and documents. The names of information flows are all written in lower case.

c) A rectangle is used to cover the modules of the product (or the sub-modules of the modules) to indicate the *product (or module) scope*. The module name should be stated in the lower-right corner of the rectangle.

It is a convention to position the modules hierarchically in the FADs. Vertically, we position the modules according to their control, i.e. in a hierarchical order, from high to low:

- *Strategic modules*, which implement management related functions, such as Business Planning, Product Innovation.
- *Tactical modules*, which are related to control items, e.g. Requirements Planning.
- *Operational modules*, which have to do with execution functions, such as Production, Assembly.
- *Supportive modules*, which are related to platform issues, e.g. Warehousing.

Horizontally, we position the modules from left to right according to the flow of execution:

- Modules that implement *input functions* (e.g. Purchase) are positioned on the left side.
- Modules related to *processing functions* (e.g. Production, Assembly) are placed in the middle.
- Modules related to *output functions* (e.g. Sales) are positioned on the right side of the diagram.
- *Third party products* are positioned outside the product scope: External products that provide input to the product's modules are placed on the left side, while external products that receive the output of the product's modules are placed on the right side.

## 4.2  Creating a Functional Architecture Diagram

In this section we present the basic steps for modeling the Functional Architecture of a software product with a Functional Architecture Diagram. We illustrate the process with the example of a Dining Room Management Application. The usage context of the product consists of all the functions that need to be performed in a restaurant, from the handling of a reservation, the processing of an order, up to the customer's payment.

*Determine the scope*

At first, we need to decide upon the product scope: the scope constitutes the functionalities of the software product. All external products in the usage environment need to be identified, with which the product will interact. Furthermore, products with which the product will possibly be interfaced in the future need to be defined at this stage. The Product Context Diagram [7] can be a starting point for identifying the third party applications that will interact with the software product.

For example, if we are architecting a software application for dining room management in restaurants, the external products would be a labor management application, the ERP system of the restaurant, a book keeping application, and possibly in the future it could also interface with an e-commerce application for restaurant reservations (figure 5a).

*Define request-feedback flows*

After determining the scope, we need to define the functional interactions between the modules of the product and the external products. Most of the times, the interactions appear in a pair of a request flow and a return arrow that represents the feedback of the result. This construction is called a request feedback loop. We focus on the main interactions that are related to the primary functionality of the product.

Referring to the restaurant application example, the defined request-feedback loops between the product and the third party applications are defined in figure 5b.

(a) Product Scope and external products          (b) Request-feedback flows with external applications

**Fig. 5.** Steps i and ii

*Model the operational module flow*

The next step consists in modeling the operational module flow, i.e. the flow of the modules that constitute the implementation of the main functionality of the product. The operational module flow usually shows the input, the primary process and the output. We identify the steps as module boxes, which are separated by flows that are usually information flows or waiting queues.

Figure 6 includes the operational modules that are needed for the Dining Room Management application. The Table Arrangement module includes the related processes for finding an available table for a new customer request. The Ordering module consists of the processes related to a customer's meals order. The module Order Processing corresponds to the processing of orders in the kitchen and updating the status of each order. The Inventory Control module contains the processes of checking whether there is enough inventory for preparing a meal and thus realizing the corresponding order. The Order Fulfillment box refers to the functionalities of arranging the processed orders and delivering them to the tables. The Pricing module is related to arranging the menu prices. Finally, the Payment Processing module corresponds to arranging a payment method, executing the payment and printing the invoice. Apart from these operating modules, we can also see in the diagram the supportive module Wireless Communications Management, which ensures that all wireless communications between the PDAs and the central component are functioning correctly. For reasons of readability we have not added the flows of the supportive module, which needs to interact with all the operating modules.

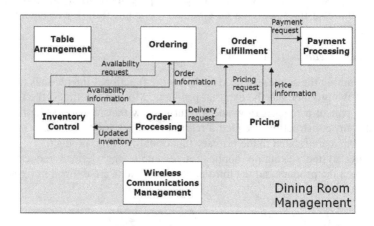

**Fig. 6.** The operational modules

*Add control and monitoring modules*

Usually, the operational module flow is controlled by one or more control modules, which in turn are controlled by planning modules. We add the control module that corresponds to each operational module. The interaction between an operational and a control module is a request-feedback loop. On top of the control modules, we add the appropriate planning modules.

In our restaurant application example we can only identify control modules, which are added in the diagram. The module Reservations Management is handling the reservations request, while the waitlist management arranges all requests that are queued, either from new reservations or from new customers that have visited the restaurant directly. The Order Management module schedules and prioritizes the handling of orders. Finally, the Financial Management module corresponds to the financial management processes, e.g. registering payments, storing the invoices, etc.

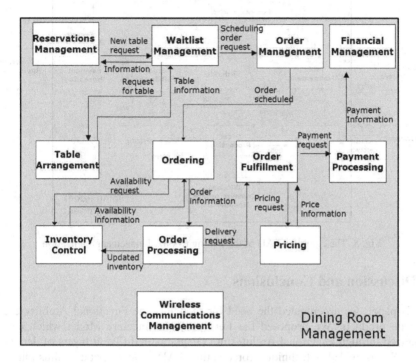

**Fig. 7.** Adding control and monitoring modules in the Dining Room Management application

*Specify external to/from internal interactions*

This step is related to the second step, where we had to identify the interactions between the product and external products. At this point we need to perform further analysis, to identify which of the modules will need to be interfaced with the external product for each request-feedback flow. It is possible that we may discover new modules at this stage which we had ignored in the previous steps. Also, for the sake of certain interaction we may need to add more interactions also amongst the internal modules of the product.

In figure 8 we can see the final FAD of the Dining Room Management application. All interactions from the external third party applications to the product's modules and vice versa are modeled in this step. The functions are triggered either by a new table request, which corresponds to a request of a customer who visits the restaurant without reservation, or by a new reservation request, which can be performed either by a customer directly or through a related e-commerce application.

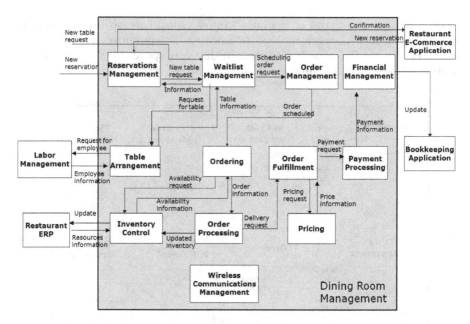

**Fig. 8.** The complete FAD of the Dining Room Management application

## 5 Discussion and Conclusions

In this paper, we accentuated the need for modeling the Functional Architecture of software products. We proposed the Functional Architecture Model which can be visualized through Functional Architecture Diagrams in different layers of decomposition. We provided a technique for creating FADs and in parallel illustrated the design process through an example.

The Functional Architecture Model has been introduced in a manner that supports the design principles and structures for FA discussed in section 2. As far as the principles for the FA design process are concerned: The FA can be designed by one or few architects, based on the existing requirements, which can be mapped on the product's modules. The notation is easily understandable by non-specialists, thus all stakeholders (product managers, architects, developers, customers, marketing and sales, end-users) can be involved in the review of FA. The visualization of FA through FADs contributes to the identification of bottlenecks and the inspection of qualitative and quantitative measures. Finally, the suggested modular decomposition supports the creation of a "skeletal system" that can be expanded in the future by adding new modules.

Regarding the principles for the structure of FA, first of all the modules in our FAM separate concerns and support the hiding of information, while the interfaces are placed only when request-feedback flows between modules and/or external products are needed. Evidently, since each module corresponds to different functionality, it is possible to develop modules quite independently from one another, while the focus on functionalities makes the architecture independent of technical changes and of particular commercial products, and enables the introduction of few and simple inter-action patterns that increase performance and enhance modifiability and reliability. The suggested convention of positioning the modules hierarchically and according to the flow of execution separates the modules that "produce data" from those that "consume data".

The suggested design structures for the FA were followed in our FAM approach. Modularity is supported by the creation of modules which correspond to different product functionalities and are later on decomposed in lower levels of abstraction. In section 3, we inspected the modules of the product scope for a Collaborative Author-ing Tool and the decomposition of its "Authoring" module into sub-modules. The FADs are structured in a way that the FA can be adapted in different organizational settings. For example, the FAD for a Dining Room Management application in figure 8 was constructed for a restaurant environment. However, it could easily be adapted in other similar environments: certain modules (Ordering, Inventory Control, Order Processing, Pricing, Payment Processing, Financial Management) are standard for all organizational settings while the remaining modules are variant according to the envi-ronment. If we wanted to create the FAD for a fast food restaurant, we could remove the modules Reservations Management, Waitlist Management, Order Management and Table Arrangement and insert the module Order Forecasting. Finally, the inspec-tion of the request-feedback flows enables the identification of all possible interfaces that will need to be designed so that the product can flexibly interact with different external products, confirming the interoperability structure.

The Functional Architecture Model can facilitate the system design by describing the inherent functional structure of the system's modules and their interactions, as well as the interactions with external applications. The modular decomposition offers a separation of the system's functionalities, thus it reduces complexity, eases the com-munication and collaboration among stakeholders, enables managing the product development by partitioning work into independent tasks, and set off transferrable and reusable elements of the product.

We suggest that FADs constitute a useful tool for modeling the Functional Archi-tecture of software products. The notation is simple thus they can easily and quickly be designed [4], leaving space to the manager to deal with planning the functionalities of the product in an optimal way and easing the communication with the non-specialist customers, who can recognize the models without formal training.

FADs can be used to determine the modules of the software product. Although certain programming languages like Java support hierarchical module structure, other languages (e.g. PHP) have not developed modularity sufficiently. A module structure is useful in the design process for a software product, in order to plan and organize the development work [20].

Moreover, FADs indicate the interactions between the product's modules and the environment. This is convenient from a development point of view, since we have a visualization of which interfaces will need to be implemented for the software prod-uct, as also from a management point of view, to have an indication of which third party products will interact with the software product.

Finally, our proposed approach for Functional Architecture Modeling can be ap-plied in any type of business: public sector (healthcare, governmental) and private sector (manufacturing, financial, services, food and beverage, project industries) [19].

In our future research we intend to describe the semantics of FAD formally and add details to out method. Furthermore, we plan to inspect the incorporation of scenarios with the Functional Architecture Diagrams, in order to visualize on a high level the flow between the product's modules and third party applications for the implementation of the system's functionalities.

# References

1. Anderson, D.M.: Design for Manufacturability. In: Optimizing Cost, Quality and Time-to-Market. CIM Press, Cambria (2001)
2. Angelov, S., Grefen, P.W.P.J., Greefhorst, D.: A classifcation of software reference architectures: Analyzing their success and effectiveness. In: Proceedings Joint Working IEEE/IFIP Conference on Software Architecture & European Conference on Software Architecture 2009, pp. 141–150 (2009)
3. Arsanjani, A., Zhang, L.J., Ellis, M., Allam, A., Channabasavaiah, K.: Design an SOA solution using a reference architecture (2007),
   http://www.ibm.com/developerworks/library/ar-archtemp/
4. Bajaj, A.: The effect of the number of concepts on the readability of schemas: an empirical study with data models. Requirements Engineering 9(4), 261–270 (2004)
5. Bass, L., Clements, P., Kazman, R.: Software architecture in practice. Addison-Wesley Longman Publishing Co., Inc., Boston (1998)
6. Brinkkemper, S.: Dynamic enterprise innovation: Establishing continuous improvement in business. In: van Es, R. (ed.) Baan Business Innovation, pp. 4–15 (1998)
7. Brinkkemper, S., van Soest, I., Jansen, R.L.: Modeling of product software businesses: Investigation into industry product and channel typologies. In: Proceedings of the Sixteenth International Conference on Information Systems Development (ISD 2007), Springer, Heidelberg (2007)
8. Broy, M., Gleirscher, M., Merenda, S., Wild, D., Kluge, P., Krenzer, W.: Toward a holistic and standardized automotive architecture description. Computer 42, 98–101 (2009)
9. Buckl, S., Ernst, A.M., Matthes, F., Ramacher, R., Schweda, C.M.: Using enterprise architecture management patterns to complement TOGAF. In: EDOC 2009: Proceedings of the 13th IEEE international conference on Enterprise Distributed Object Computing, Piscataway, NJ, USA, pp. 32–39. IEEE Press, Los Alamitos (2009)
10. Fowler, M.: Who needs an architect? IEEE Softw. 20(5), 11–13 (2003)
11. van Gurp, J., Brinkkemper, S., Bosch, J.: Design preservation over subsequent releases of a software product: a case study of baan erp: Practice articles. J. Softw. Maint. Evol. 17(4), 277–306 (2005)
12. Herzum, P., Sims, O.: Business Components Factory: A Comprehensive Overview of Component-Based Development for the Enterprise. JohnWiley & Sons, Inc., New York (2000)
13. IBM Insurance Application Architecture, http://www-07.ibm.com/solutions/sg/insurance/enterprise_aa/summary.html
14. Ieee std 1471-2000, recommended practice for architectural description of software-intensive systems. Technical report, IEEE (2000)
15. Koning, H.: Communication of IT Architecture. Thesis Dutch Research School for Information and Knowledge Systems (2008),
    http://igitur-archive.library.uu.nl/dissertations/2008-0908-200828/koning.pdf

16. Koning, H., Bos, R., Brinkkemper, S.: A lightweight method for the modeling of enterprise architectures. In: Feuerlicht, G., Lamersdorf, W. (eds.) ICSOC 2008. LNCS, vol. 5472, pp. 375–387. Springer, Heidelberg (2008)
17. Kruchten, P.: The 4+1 view model of architecture. IEEE Softw. 12(6), 42–50 (1995)
18. Moon, M., Yeom, K.: An Approach To Developing Core Assets in Product Line In: 11th Asia-Pacific Software Engineering Conference (APSEC 2004), pp. 586–588 (2004)
19. Nab, J., Pilot, A., Brinkkemper, S., ten Berge, H.: Authentic competence-based learning in university education in entrepreneurship. International Journal of Entrepreneurship and Small Business 9(1), 20–35 (2010)
20. Parnas, D.L.: On the criteria to be used in decomposing systems into modules. Commun. ACM 15(12), 1053–1058 (1972)
21. Reed, P.: Reference Architecture: The best of best practices (2002),
    http://www.ibm.com/developerworks/rational/library/2774.html
22. Riebisch, M.: Towards a more Precise Definition of Feature Models – Modelling Variability for Object-Oriented Product Lines, pp. 64–76. BookOnDemand Publ. Co., Norder-stedt (2003)
23. Soni, D., Nord, R.L., Hofmeister, C.: Software architecture in industrial applications. In: ICSE 1995: Proceedings of the 17th international conference on Software Engineering, pp. 196–207. ACM, New York (1995)
24. Supply Chain Council: What is SCOR? (2010), http://www.supply-chain.org/about/scor/what/is (Retrieved March 10, 2010)
25. Software Engineering Institute: How Do You Define Software Architecture? (2005), http://www.sei.cmu.edu/architecture/definitions.html
26. van Vliet, H.: Software engineering: principles and practice, 2nd edn. John Wiley & Sons, Inc., New York (2000)
27. van de Weerd, I., Brinkkemper, S., Nieuwenhuis, R., Versendaal, J., Bijlsma, L.: Towards a reference framework for software product management. In: IEEE International Conference on Requirements Engineering, pp. 319–322. IEEE Computer Society, Los Alamitos (2006)
28. Zachman, J.A.: A framework for information systems architecture. IBM Syst. J. 26(3), 276–292 (1987)

# Experiences from Scenario-Based Architecture Evaluations with ATAM

Ville Reijonen, Johannes Koskinen, and Ilkka Haikala

Institute of Software Systems
Tampere University of Technology
PL 553, 33101 Tampere, Finland
{vilre,jomppa,ijh}@cs.tut.fi

**Abstract.** Software architecture may go through many changes during its existence. Architecture evaluation can point out current problems, help to anticipate some of the future changes, and also show the absolute limits of a design. This paper presents experiences from eleven scenario based architecture evaluations with ATAM. The evaluations were completed on a tight two day evaluation schedule. This limited time forced to search for alternative scheduling options. The evaluated system designs had relatively long life cycle up to 30 years and all the designs were evaluated for the first time. We have learnt that in evaluations current issues often overshadow the long view of the future. We suggest that architecture evaluations should be integrated to the development process as a tool not only for today but also for tomorrow.

## 1 Introduction

Software architecture in a product with long life cycle will go through many changes. New requirements, regulations and laws as well as changing hardware will push the old architecture to the limits, often slowly breaking it and making later modifications even more difficult and costly. With architecture evaluation one can try to peek the near and distant futures of an architecture and see how well it can fulfill expected and unexpected changes. This information can be then used to guide the design to an evolutionally sound path. A good design might be the essential part in reducing overall costs and extending systems lifespan.

An architecture evaluation involves many stakeholders, often takes multiple days and is therefore costly. Often in business, work that does not immediately produce results, or profit, is hard to justify. Therefore, extensive amounts of time cannot be used. After doing eleven scenario based architecture evaluations with tight schedules, we have gained knowledge how to squeeze as much effective work as possible into a two day period. The evaluations were done for four target companies in Finnish machine industry for distributed control systems with expected life cycle between 20 to 30 years.

We used Architecture Tradeoff Analysis Method (ATAM) as a base for our evaluations. ATAM is presented in reference [4]. It uses one terse form of scenarios as a tool for inspecting architectures. Unfortunately, there is a steep learning curve between reading about ATAM and applying it [12]. For example, the

M. Ali Babar and I. Gorton (Eds.): ECSA 2010, LNCS 6285, pp. 214–229, 2010.

description of ATAM in reference [4] omits many details which probably had became "obvious" by the time of writing to the authors. Unfortunately, few of the other experience reports available fill up these holes, usually due to the limited knowledge gained with analysis of one or two systems. Therefore, the main purpose of this paper is to fill out this void and help to disseminate knowledge to diminish the threshold between reading and doing.

Scenario based techniques are one of the oldest, most popular and widely used tools from futures studies methodology toolbox [2]. For example, scenarios are regularly used in business as a tool for strategic planning and preparation. Still, the same level of planning is rare when it comes to software design and architecture. When software is under construction it is not usual to think its demise, unlike in our case where the expected life cycle of a whole system is well known. The strong future studies background of scenario techniques could be used when architectures are evaluated for long term view. A typical time frame for future studies is between 15 and 30 years.

This paper proceeds as follows. Section 2 summarizes the ATAM method and dissects it into more detailed steps. Section 3 discusses the first contact, the evaluation team, and the first meeting for Phase 0. Section 4 presents an example evaluation schedule for two day ATAM. In Section 5 presentations and work steps are summarized for Phase 1. Section 6 discusses Phase 2 and experiences on utility tree generation, brainstorming and prioritization. Section 7 summarizes found benefits of architecture evaluations. Section 8 discusses the related work and finally in Section 9, the experiences are summarized.

## 2   ATAM Steps Deciphered

In this section, the phases and steps of ATAM are described. This work builds upon the previous work in references [4,7,8,9,10,11]. For a beginner it would be advisable to start from Chapter 6 of reference [4] as it contains a good case study and checklists that are helpful when preparing for the first evaluation along with this paper.

ATAM, as it is presented by SEI after year 2000, consists of nine steps. These steps cover the main activities of the ATAM, but as a simplified list, it is also incomplete and somewhat misleading. The most concerning problem is the omission of preparation and post-work. To be able to discuss our experiences, a more dissected list of steps and phases is presented. When referencing to this list later on, a combination of step group letter and step number is used, e.g. A1. If the list is compared to the content of Chapter 6 of reference [4], the steps are similar but more detailed, only the repetition of Phase 1 is dropped and the preparation phase is more condensed.

**Phase 0:** Preparation
  **A** Preparation
    1. First contact
    2. Evaluation team
    3. First meeting

    4. Pre-check of presentations

**Phase 1:** Evaluation

**B** Presentations (mainly) for architecture team

    1. Evaluation method presentation
    2. Business drivers presentation
    3. Architecture presentation

**C** Work with architecture team

    1. Identifying architectural decisions
    2. Generating utility tree with scenarios
    3. Prioritization of scenarios
    4. Analyzing scenarios

**Phase 2:** Verification

**D** Presentations for stakeholders

    1. Evaluation method presentation
    2. Business drivers presentation

**E** Work with stakeholders

    1. Brainstorming scenarios
    2. Prioritization of scenarios

**F** Work with architecture team and stakeholders

    1. Analyzing scenarios

**G** Instant feedback

    1. Present findings & discussion
    2. Collect immediate feedback

**Phase 3:** Follow-up

**H** Follow-up and report

    1. Retrospective and process improvement
    2. Deliver report
    3. Experiences from the customer

**I** Post-report

    1. Review the changes introduced by the evaluation
    2. Examine the need for re-evaluation

To make sure that presentations are prepared and right people are able to attend, there should be at least two weeks between Phases 0 and 1. A week between Phases 1 and 2 has proven to be convenient as it provides time for additional preparations such as architectural clarifications. In Phase 3, the report can be delivered as soon as it is finished, which usually takes at least a few weeks. Need for re-evaluation can be examined, for example, after half an year or when it is a convenient time for it as a part of iterative software development process.

## 3    Phase 0: Preparation

### A1: First Contact

Everything starts from the first contact. The most important task during this step is to set a preliminary schedule with required participants for each phase. The architecture team and someone aware of the business requirements is required for Phase 1. Additionally, a wide range of stakeholders and the architect team should be available for Phase 2. For the first meeting the project management and the architecture team is required so that both management and technical knowledge is present.

During the first contact some general details should be revealed to the evaluators, so that they can decide if an area specialist could provide assistance. For example, in one evaluation we had an expert on digital systems bridging the gap in our knowledge. For the first meeting the company personnel has to prepare an introduction to the domain, the design and the current level of documentation.

## A2: Evaluation Team

The evaluation sessions can be managed with just two people but for active participation at least three evaluators are needed. There can be more active participants in the evaluation team, but the team members should not be the ones predominantly discussing. It is important to remember that the evaluation team works as a catalyst; over time most of the risks would be found even without evaluation. The evaluation team brings in evaluation process guidance, outside view and expertise that can help to find risks before they emerge and cause problems. The architecture team cannot evaluate their own architecture alone as they are blind to the decisions and their implications.

*A scribe* is the most important team member. The scribe writes the discussion down so that it can be viewed from screen by all participants. The record should be understandable and all participants should agree with recorded details. It is a bad idea to use company personnel as a scribe or replace the scribe with a recording equipment. The most important function of the scribe is to prevent vague explanations from being accepted as is. If the scribe is not able to write the explanation then the issue has not been explained well enough. Additional roles should not be set on the scribe as record keeping is often the bottleneck during the analysis step. We noticed that a custom spread sheet with macros is helpful in reducing copy-pasting and rewriting. The sheet has its own page for each work step in Phases 1 and 2. This way architectural decisions, scenarios, prioritization and analysis are logically separated. Data from previous steps is readily available from a drop-down menu.

*A process enforcer* is another required member in a team. The process enforcer's task is to keep the process on schedule by stopping parallel or off-topic discussions. This is important as the scribe cannot follow multiple discussions at the same time and off-topic talk cannot be recorded in a systematic way.

*A proceedings scribe* writes down all the non-architectural problems, issues, that are discovered during the evaluation. Additionally, the proceedings scribe can record all questions asked, ask for explanation for unclear abbreviations and record the general flow of the discussion. To back up the transcript a recording can be made, if allowed.

Additional roles, which let the people participate in the discussion are *evaluation leader*, *questioner* and *process observer* roles. The questioner's job is to demand detailed explanations and to dig deep to verify sound design - how and why the design decision supports the scenario in question. The process observer takes timed notes on the process flow and records encountered problems within the process. This is important data for process improvements.

### A3: First Meeting

On agreed date, a couple of members from the evaluation team will meet with the company representatives. We have sent the evaluation leader and a scribe to the first meeting. The meeting usually takes between two and four hours. During the meeting the evaluation method is presented concentrating on possible goals, schedule and stakeholder participation. For some of our evaluations it has been difficult to get stakeholders present for Phase 2. We have found out that it is important to emphasize that we need the stakeholders, even if only for brainstorming and prioritization steps (E1 and E2). If both of the evaluation days are done with the same crew, it is not possible to see if the views of the architecture team are in alignment with views of the stakeholders. This is the most beneficial check in ATAM. It will show how well the architecture team is aware of the issues which are important to those who, for example, sell, use, or maintain the system. If no stakeholders will be available, Phase 2 will be waste of time and it might be reasonable to just extend Phase 1 analysis over Phase 2. In any case, architecture team members are needed the whole time.

The first meeting is a opportunity to get to know the system a bit informally. This will help the scribe as the terminology and the domain will become more familiar. Sometimes a draft of the architecture presentation is shown, otherwise suitable questions should be asked to gather domain knowledge and probe boundaries of the design. Presenters for the architecture and business drivers presentation should be agreed upon. We have given slide templates on paper to the presenters, so there should not be any excuses for not following the template.

There should be at least a two-week break between the preliminary meeting and the first phase so that the presentations can be finalized and additional participants can be still summoned. If there are problems with the presentations or participants, a no-go decision can be made to prevent a failure.

### A4: Pre-check of the Presentations

We have usually demanded that the slides are sent us for pre-check one week before the presentation. This way we made sure that presentations are done in time focusing on right issues. This is important as a bad architecture presentation can prevent from evaluating the design. By forcing an additional deadline, the quality of the presentations has vastly risen. This is probably because the additional deadline "creates" additional time when the presentations can be thought over. Another issue we observed before the deadline-rule was that the presentations did not follow the templates. Often it looked like that some older existing material had been used at the last moment to whip up a presentation.

## 4   Efficient Two Day Schedule

To carry out the evaluations efficiently, we had to compress the traditional ATAM into two days. We have found out that by streamlining the ATAM presentation step, considerable time savings can be gained. The saved time should be spent for analysis, which has the highest importance for the information gathering.

The morning of the first day begins with a short opening where the company people introduce themselves and the evaluation team leader presents the evaluation team and their tasks. This is followed by the evaluation method presentation. We suggest that instead of speaking about the finer details of the method, only a quick introduction is given and the daily schedule shall keep the participants aware of the following steps and their time limits. An example schedule for the first evaluation day is shown is Table 1.

**Table 1.** Example schedule handout (1st day)

| First evaluation day | |
|---|---|
| 8.30 | Opening |
| 8.45 | Evaluation method presentation (**B1**) |
| 9.00 | Business drivers presentation (**B2**) |
| 9.45 | Architecture presentation (**B3**) |
| 11.15 | Lunch |
| 12.00 | Identifying decisions (**C1**) |
| 12.30 | Utility tree creation (**C2**) |
| 13.30 | Scenario prioritization (**C3**) |
| 13.45 | Break |
| 14.00 | Scenario analysis (**C4**) |
| 16.30 | Free discussion and closing |

After the evaluation method presentation, financial incentives are explained during the business drivers presentation as ATAM suggests. When the participants are familiar with the business requirements, the architecture is presented to show the actual design. These presentations are also good for stakeholders and, in general, to distribute knowledge, so this could be arranged on a larger venue. After the presentations it is good to have a lunch break. We have noted that this creates a natural interruption that allows the stakeholders following the presentation to leave before the afternoon program. As the evaluation days are exhausting for the evaluation team and for the company participants, at least one break should be scheduled during the afternoon.

A proposed schedule for the second day is shown in Table 2. The second evaluation day follows quite much the same path as the first day. The main difference is that the stakeholders have a large influence on the second day outcome. The first evaluation day is more to see what the architect and the team had planned whereas the second day is to find out how the stakeholders see the future of the system and does it match with the visions and ideas of the architecture team. We have learnt that the second day morning (E1) creates the most of the experienced customer value. It provides a perfect opportunity for guided discussion, which there seems to be lack of, especially in larger organizations.

**Table 2.** Example schedule handout (2nd day)

| Second evaluation day | |
|---|---|
| 8.30 | Opening |
| 8.45 | Evaluation method presentation (recap) (**D1**) |
| 8.50 | Business drivers presentation (recap) (**D2**) |
| 9.00 | Scenario brainstorming (**E1**) |
| 10.45 | Scenario prioritization (**E2**) |
| 11.15 | Lunch |
| 12.00 | Scenario analysis (**F1**) |
| 15.30 | Break for summary preparation |
| 16.00 | Summary and Feedback (**G1 & G2**) |
| 16.30 | Free discussion and closing |

As the afternoon on the second day consists mainly of technical discussions, the stakeholders and busy managers might not be so interested to follow the discussion, at least in our experience. We suggest that the architecture is not presented again as it would cause havoc with the schedule. This might make it difficult for new people to participate in the analysis (F1), if they do not know the architecture beforehand. Therefore, it is better if people are directed from the beginning of the process to participate in steps B2 and B3 for general knowledge sharing. For many participants, brainstorming gave the opportunity to share their thoughts. The awareness that the most important scenarios elicited by the prioritization will be evaluated, is satisfactory for many stakeholders.

The speed in which the evaluation proceeds depends on the amount of people present and especially on the amount of people who are active and taking part in the conversation during utility tree generation (C2), brainstorming (E1) and analysis phases (C4 & F1). The amount of time available for the analysis depends entirely on how well the schedule is kept. With the presented schedule, there are six hours for analysis when other parts of the process take ten hours - the overhead is still quite large. However, the overhead is less than with the traditional ATAM schedule (e.g. [11, p. 43], which contains about the same time for analysis in three full days). The lower overhead for shorter time ties less personnel to the process.

The best cost benefit ratio can be gained when the analysis time is maximized. Still, an adequate amount of time for knowledge sharing and discussions should be given. Hence, it could be very useful, if the analysis phase could be extended. We would not recommend extending the evaluation day schedule as the days are already quite exhausting as is. Instead a better option would be using one more day for the evaluation. Additional day would more than double the time used in analysis. Still, three day evaluation might be difficult idea to sell when even two evaluation days are hard to accept. Instead, if the company personnel has a feeling that more could or should be done after the second day, additional analysis day could be suggested. As additional day would only involve architect and evaluators, it would not require much from the target company.

# 5   Phase 1: Evaluation

### B1: Evaluation Method Presentation

We have found out that a detailed method presentation is not necessary for a successful evaluation. Our short presentation slide set consists from the following slides: evaluation etiquette, schedule, possible goals for an evaluation, evaluation phases and stakeholder participation, example utility tree, scenario types and as last an evaluated example scenario. The presentation does not take more than 15 minutes.

Instead of a detailed walkthrough, a schedule for the day gives people something they can actually remember for a while. When the daily schedule is first shown, a basic division to morning and afternoon sessions is explained: in Phase 1, the morning is for presentations and the afternoon is for analysis. In Phase 2, the morning is for brainstorming and the afternoon is again for analysis. Before each step a short introduction is given to inform what will be done next.

The etiquette, or "general instructions" as we have labeled them, tries to guide how people should behave. For example, we tell the people to close their laptops while we work, as an open laptop is a distraction and it isolates the person from the discussion. Additionally, just one person should talk at a time. At last, the spirit of the evaluation is explained; we are not grading the design, we are here to help them to improve it.

### B2: Business Drivers Presentation

During this step the system and domain are viewed through business drivers. There is no point of creating features, which nobody pays for, so it is important to have the business support behind the design. When the presentation follows a template such as [4, p. 46], the presentation should give a good outlook on the major business aspects. We have allocated 45 minutes in the schedule for this presentation. This has been noted to be sufficient time for the presentation on every evaluation. It is also the same what is recommended by reference [4].

### B3: Architecture Presentation

The architect presents the product architecture at an appropriate level of detail. This step is important, as it will directly affect the depth of the analysis and the quality of this analysis. The architecture presentation is time-wise the most volatile step. In few cases the business drivers presentation has been shorter than the allocated time slot, so there has been more time for the architecture presentation. It has never occurred that the architecture presentation would have been shorter than the time allocated for it.

In reference [4], 60 minutes are allocated for the presentation. We have used 1.5 hours for it and we feel that this additional 30 minutes is worthwhile especially when non-native speakers are giving presentations. If the audience has a lot of questions and comments, the time might run out even when the presentation does not proceed. The process enforcer should be observant and stop discussions which analyze the design or which do not benefit the architecture presentation. It is good to know the architecture as well as possible, but all the extra time spent here will be taken away from the analysis time.

## C1: Identifying Architectural Decisions

Identifying architectural decisions has usually taken in our evaluations less than twenty minutes. Decisions can be either unconscious or deliberate; hacks forced by the existing architecture, solutions known to work or designs based on patterns. During the architecture presentation, the evaluation team records noticed solutions and patterns. During this step the architect is guided to identify decisions made within the architecture. The architect may first be unsure what is meant by a decision. When some examples are given by the evaluation team, the architect will soon pick up the lead. If the evaluation team member feels that something is missing, it can be added when the architect starts to slow down. After a while some of the decisions might feel unfamiliar if they are made up from just word or two. Therefore, it might be a good idea to expand and/or explain the approaches a bit more to cover "what" and "where" and even "why".

A listed architectural decision should not be too general such as a pattern name, especially if used more than once in the architecture. A decision should be concrete. A too general decision may prevent deeper analysis and therefore the decisions should be more or less on the same level of magnitude. A too general decision can be noticed quite easily during the analysis, as it is vague and difficult to grasp. If such a decision is noticed, the decision should be revised immediately. It is good to remember that the list is not static, it will change and grow also during the analysis when new decisions are identified.

## C2: Generating Utility Tree with Scenarios

During this step a utility tree is created. Quality attributes, such as performance, form the base of the tree. Each quality attribute is refined by the participants. For example, a system could have refinement such as latency of the network under performance. The concrete scenarios are formed under the refinements. Especially during scenario creation, the discussion easily wanders and turns to analysis, which cannot be captured systematically during this step. Therefore, this phase needs strong process enforcement. In our evaluations, the creation of scenarios has taken three to five times as much time as the creation of the base of the tree with quality attributes and their refinements. The whole tree can be constructed in one hour with strong guidance. The tree easily expands exponentially in those places, which are under longer exposure. It is important to remember that quantity is not quality.

In the first few evaluations, we did show the quality attribute list from the ISO 9126-1 standard [6] to help the company personnel to identify the essential quality attributes. This caused a problem with too many selected attributes. Consequently, the utility tree was loaded with attributes and this made the development of the utility tree time consuming. Therefore, it would be better if most of the quality attributes are taken from the business drivers presentation. The team should take note of any missing quality attribute, which they think as essential for this system. It is best to let the company personnel use their own terms as quality attributes. The terminology does not need to match with any standard. It is up to the evaluation team to understand and write down what each term means. A discussion on the correct terminology is waste of time.

Often when the quality tree is developed, the people have already some example case in mind when the quality attribute is presented. It is a good idea to write the example down as a stub, as otherwise it will probably be forgotten. Later on, it can be refined when that particular level of the tree is under work. Scenario outlines should be well formed – they should have at least a stimulus and a response. As a result the scenario stubs can be understood even if they need more elaboration later on. The best way to make sure that everybody tries to create proper scenarios is to explain beforehand the scenario structure. To tackle this problem, we have given to all participants a paper with scenario templates and examples of use-case, growth and exploratory scenarios.

In true journalist fashion, a good scenario should be able to answer some of questions: "who, what, where, when, why and how" (W5H). Simple, fast to use and well understandable way to write scenarios outlines is the three part format proposed in reference [4]. Short outline is made out of *stimulus, environment* and *response* parts. Stimulus defines the change causing input to the system; by "who" and "why" something happens. Environment describes "where" or "when" the scenario takes place, for example during normal operation or performance peak. Response explains "what" measures are taken to respond to the stimulus. There are other longer, detailed and more complex formats available as, for example, six part scenario presented in reference [1, p. 76]. We did not see that any benefits could be attained from more complex or detailed format, only more time would be used per scenario outline. The most important thing for a scenario outline is that when it is much later re-read, it can still be understood and it is unambiguous. The most important question "how" will only get answered during the analysis.

## C3: Prioritization of Scenarios

The prioritization phase takes ten to twenty minutes, if done systematically. We have used two way prioritization with High-Medium-Low scale for the rating. This prioritization system is quite simple and so far, it has been accepted without any questions. The business owner, often the person who presented business drivers, announces first her opinion for the business value of the scenario (e.g. "High") and after that, the lead architect expresses her view on the difficulty of achieving the scenario (e.g. "Medium"). After this short, one-word conversation the next scenario can be rated.

After votes has been given, the scenarios are ordered emphasizing on the business value when the scales are the same. If a manual system is used to order the scenarios, you need to have free time in the schedule to do this work. The risk in the prioritization lies in the architect's opinion, as some scenarios might be more difficult to attain than thought. Especially, if the original architect has left the project, there might not be suitable persons available who could tell the difficulty of the work needed to make a scenario possible.

The most evident problem in the prioritization method is that the business value is often rated higher on scenarios that are closer to the sales. This excludes exploratory scenarios which might have more impact in the long run. In many cases, a futuristic scenario often reveals similar problems as a scenario based on a sales case. This myopia can only be truly cured when the current issues are first taken care of and there is no further need to put out fires. The future of the system can then be adequately prioritized in the business view.

### C4: Analyzing Scenarios

The highest ranked scenario is taken first under analysis. For every scenario, a set of related architectural decisions and sensitivity points are selected. Change in a sensitivity point is likely to affect the quality attribute, which is the scenario's parent in the utility tree. For example, for a scenario under performance, the sensitivity point could increase or decrease performance. During the analysis, additional architectural approaches might be identified and added to the list.

The right mindset during analysis is that your job is to break the system. The architect has to be assumed guilty until proven innocent. It is the job of the architect to explain how her decisions will help the scenario and the quality attribute at hand. Every detail in the scenario should be probed and explained. This is the main task for the questioner. When the first scenario under evaluation is both important on business value and difficult to attain, it should have several risks. One guideline which was given to us is to analyze the first scenario until at least five risks emerge, this could take long, a figure of 1.5 hours was given as an example [12]. In general, a successful scenario analysis usually takes between half an hour and an hour.

When a larger quantity of scenarios is created than evaluated, for some people it might be worrisome that only some of those scenarios are evaluated. This is easy to understand when one thinks the scenarios as test cases and is thinking of test coverage. The test metaphor is an easy way to explain the process in familiar terms – scenario tests if the architecture can meet its demands. The difference is that the scenarios are just vehicles that allow us to probe the architecture; the actual target is the discussion and analysis of whatever thoughts and ideas the scenario brings up, not the scenario itself. In testing there is no discussion, the code is the target and it either passes or fails.

## 6    Phase 2: Verification and Phase 3: Follow-Up

### D1: Evaluation Method Presentation

On the second day the evaluation method is presented shortly. We have mainly focused on possible goals, what can be gained from the analysis and how the process provides a constructive venue where ideas can be exchanged. The daily schedule can be presented in the same way as in step B1 explaining the division to morning and afternoon work. It is good to emphasize that scenarios created and voted topmost, will be the ones that will be analyzed during the afternoon. The rest are left for the architecture team to handle as they wish.

### D2: Business Drivers Presentation

A terse business drivers presentation is sufficient for Phase 2, but a short presentation has been included in the program to make sure that the participants understand the business constraints.

## E1: Brainstorming Scenarios

When Phase 1 results were presented during our evaluations, we felt that it directed the stakeholders too much to the same direction which was taken during Phase 1. Therefore, we have diverted a bit from mainline ATAM by not presenting Phase 1 results to the stakeholders before brainstorming. Additionally, this way Phase 2 really is a verification for Phase 1. If Phase 1 and Phase 2 scenario focus has a large discrepancy, a mismatch between stakeholder needs, assumed business goals and architecture team's views will be found.

There are many ways to do brainstorming. As an example, we have used a pair working based method. It does not require any other equipment than pens and paper. The brainstorming is done in three rounds. For the first round all participants are given a paper with scenario types (use-case, growth and exploratory) and basic scenario structure (stimulus-environment-response). Everyone has roughly five minutes of silent time to think alone and write ideas on the paper. For the second round adjacent participants are paired up. Their task is to discuss on existing ideas and generate new ideas for ten minutes. For the third round, the pairing should be made so that pairs do not know each other too well to stimulate more diverse idea exchanging for another ten minutes.

After the pair work, scenarios are gathered in round-robin style. One by one, each participant presents one undiscussed scenario idea, always presenting the the most important idea for her. The presented idea is written down as a preliminary scenario. The other participants are asked if they have similar ideas, which could be combined into the same scenario. If there is, a combined scenario is written down. After a valid scenario has been written, the next scenario is elected from the next person in the round robin. This is done as long as there are scenarios left or time runs out. When a large group of stakeholders is present, more time has to be allocated. The stakeholders might feel left out if they cannot present all the scenarios, which they feel as important. The round-robin collection style makes it possible to gather for each participant the most important scenarios first, so it softens the pain if the time runs out. For the stakeholders this creates a possibility to share their views with the architecture team and other stakeholders. As such, it makes most of the stakeholders satisfied even if they do not participate to the actual analysis step.

## E2: Prioritization of Scenarios

Different kinds of voting methods are discussed in reference [4, pp. 192-193]. One method given in the book as one with quite balanced results has two voting rounds where the second round done in reverse order. We noticed that with a large group it is too time consuming as only one person at a time is active. As an alternative, we would suggest similar but a bit disorganized procedure. The scenarios are printed on paper and taped on the wall. For example, five pens are available for marking the votes and people go and mark their points freely when a pen is free. After the participants have voted for one time, the tally is presented. After this the second round is run. The vote can be run on the average in half of the time compared to one-at-a-time two round voting.

Another voting method we have used is a simultaneous voting using High-Medium-Low cards. For every scenario, everyone selects privately a paper with her selection of grade or empty vote. The grades are then revealed at the same time to all and the tally is counted. The good thing in this is that this method proceeds almost the same speed even with a large group and all the participants will be active all the time during the voting. As one can give as many high votes as she wants, there will not be any accumulation problem as in a completely blind voting. When H/M/L is used the set is quite small and therefore the total scale is quite narrow - but still sufficient for this use.

As during Phase 1 prioritization, in this phase the immediate needs often overshadowed the future. This was especially true when evaluating a new system that was going to replace an older dysfunctional system. There were often scenarios that covered aspects which were fixed in the new architecture. In these cases, if not always, it might be beneficial to remind the stakeholders that the problems are well known, but now you as stakeholders have a possibility to point out what you could think to be important in the distant future.

### F1: Analyzing Scenarios

The scenarios that were brainstormed and prioritized high are analyzed in the same way as in the earlier in step C4. As this time there might be stakeholders present during the analysis, it will probably add new flavor to the conversations. If there are new participants, it is important that they were present during the architecture presentation during Phase 1, otherwise they might feel lost during the analysis.

### G1, G2: Present Findings, Discussion and Immediate Feedback

At the end of Phase 2, preliminary results are presented. The evaluation team needs some private space to prepare the slides. This can be done in half an hour if the slide template is ready and the evaluation leader has prepared the result from Phase 1. While the evaluation team prepares, the participants can prepare to go home after the summary presentation. At this point, it is good to give feedback forms for the participants to be filled up while they are waiting. The summary presentation should start, as all feedback, with some positive points. After this, the risk themes are processed and finally other found issues are presented. After the presentation, the participants can discuss on the findings and the team can collect the feedback forms back.

### Phase 3: Follow-Up

After the evaluation, the evaluation team holds a retrospective meeting where the process observer's notes are gone through and the process improvements are considered. After the report is finished, it is delivered to the company. We have visited the company to return the report. This has made it possible to find out if there is need for clarifications. After returning the report, a query can be sent to find out what kind of changes the evaluation and the report had with the target design.

# 7  Benefits of Evaluation

After evaluations, we have gathered feedback from the participants. Most of the benefits we have noticed are the same as reported already in reference [4, pp 37-38] such as articulation on quality goals, prioritization of goals, explication of the architecture, improved documentation and improved practices. What we found as most beneficial was that the evaluation gave the excuse to get architects and stakeholders together to discuss and present their own views on what is important. For the architects this also gave a lot of material in form of scenarios, which can be used to aid the further architecture design.

In all the companies which we evaluated, the hardware design was handed down to the software team. In all the companies, competition was told to be the reason for cheap hardware designs. The cost analysis rarely reached to the level of software. As a result, a few cents might be saved on hardware, but tens or hundreds of thousands of Euros could be spent on the compromised software design. As the size of the series in the evaluated systems do not run in millions, the life cycle is tens of years with demands for additional features, one can see why this can be a problem.

Our evaluations targeted distributed embedded control systems. It should not be surprising that the embedded nature also made the systems often invisible as a whole. As one person reported: "they would be shocked to know that the system is run by software". Due to the evaluation and stakeholder participation, the knowledge of the architecture and its limitations also spread outside of the software team. As an interesting side effect, the evaluation report was also used in some cases as a tool in corporate politics. This went from "see we do good work here!" to "now proven bad, can we finally fix it?".

# 8  Related Work

Scenario based analysis is not so well known, studied and used on the software area as for example in futures studies. The most cited and used book for the area is "Evaluating Software Architectures: Methods and Case Studies" from year 2002 [4]. The book discusses on scenario based methods such as SAAM, ATAM and ARID. Three sections have been used for describe ATAM from which the last, Section 6, is the best documentation for ATAM freely available. Section 5, an experience story, has contradictions with the other two sections and presents an older version of ATAM. Section 5 has been also released previously as technical report [7].

One of papers sharing more than a few lines of experiences of ATAM based architecture evaluations in industry is reference [3], where ATAM was applied to evaluate decentralized control of a transport system. This is quite close to our domain where we did evaluations. In the paper, applying ATAM provided a course to finalize the architectural documentation. This is one of the goals which some of our evaluated companies shared. The modified ATAM described in the paper was one day Phase 1 with stakeholders. Still it provided valuable in-depth discussion with the stakeholders and distributed knowledge. They noted that ATAM could not be carried out in one day, whereas we have demonstrated that it can be carried out in two days when prepared well. As the utility tree was their way to create scenarios, it was also found important, but the team had problems when building the tree as first timers. It consumed a lot of time and good preparation and a chairman was suggested as a remedy.

ATAM was used to review a product line architecture in reference [5]. Quality attributes were noted to be too vague for analysis whereas scenarios express important aspects of quality attributes better. They found out that the most important benefit of ATAM is the stakeholder's awareness of architectural decisions, tradeoffs and risks. Later on in the paper they note that marketing and sales did not use the opportunity to participate and only three stakeholders took part in the process. We have noticed the same issue in many of our evaluations. It might be that the software department may have difficulties to reach out to other departments unless the command comes from the top. The ATAM process increased the quality of architectural documentation and distributed knowledge. Architecture presentation in a workshop was said to be much more effective than any documentation can be. Communicating the results to non-participants was seen difficult.

In [13] Svahnberg et al. present their experiences on a lightweight software architecture evaluation method derived from SAAM and ATAM. The method is primarily used in student projects, but they have also used the method together with industry partners. Even though an evaluation using the method described in the paper will take only a couple of hours, the experiences and evaluation guidelines presented can be extended, at least to some extent, to longer evaluations like ours.

## 9   Conclusions

Running the evaluation in two days is tough, especially when a large group of stakeholders is present on the second day and when it seems that everybody has much more to say than there is time. Sometimes flexibility is needed, even if it is lost in the analysis time. Nevertheless, a tight schedule demands strong process enforcement and a good writing tool for the scribe. A spread sheet with some macros proved to be quite helpful in utility tree, prioritization and evaluation steps, reducing the need for copy-pasting and rewriting. When the tool and the text are shown on the screen, it is also easy to guide the discussion. The structured way of analyzing scenarios is a powerful tool in ATAM. It makes it easier to concentrate on the scenario at hand and it will yield in better analysis and in the end a better report.

Within two evaluation days, six hours on average were spend for analysis work. Based on our experiences, six hours are not that much for analysis, especially when compared to the ten hour of work which has to be done before analysis on the evaluation days. Still, an adequate amount of time for knowledge sharing and discussions should be given. Thus, even from the cost perspective, it would be reasonable to dig bit deeper. For a deep analysis, a third evaluation day would be recommendable, as additional eight hours could be used for analysis and other discussions. This would be still relatively cheap as only members of the evaluation and architecture teams would be required.

When an architecture is evaluated for the first time, it is very difficult to think about the future as the immediate needs shadow the needs of the future. This is understandable especially when an older product is replaced with a newer one and all the problems with the older product are still well in mind. Typically this is visible as low number of exploratory far reaching scenarios voted for evaluation. When the life cycle of a product is long, also the boundaries of the design have to be probed and questioned, therefore architecture evaluations should be a part of a software development toolbox. The best way to gain competitive edge is to go from reactive to proactive. An evaluation can be the tool to make this happen.

# References

1. Bass, L., Clements, P., Kazman, R.: Software Architecture in Practice. Addison-Wesley Longman Publishing Co., Inc., Boston (1998)
2. Bell, W.: Foundations of Futures Studies, Human Science for a New Era. Transaction Publishers (1997)
3. Bouck, N., Weyns, D., Schelfthout, K., Holvoet, T.: Applying the ATAM to an architecture for decentralized control of a transportation system. In: Hofmeister, C., Crnković, I., Reussner, R. (eds.) QoSA 2006. LNCS, vol. 4214, pp. 180–198. Springer, Heidelberg (2006)
4. Clements, P., Kazman, R., Klein, M.: Evaluating Software Architectures: Methods and Case Studies. Addison-Wesley Professional, Reading (January 2002)
5. Ferber, S., Heidl, P., Lutz, P.: Reviewing product line architectures: Experience report of ATAM in an automotive context. In: van der Linden, F.J. (ed.) PFE 2002. LNCS, vol. 2290, pp. 194–197. Springer, Heidelberg (2002)
6. International Organization for Standardization: Software engineering - product quality - part 1: Quality model, ISO/IEC 9126-1:2001(E) (2001)
7. Jones, L., Lattanze, A.: Using the architecture tradeoff analysis method to evaluate a wargame simulation system: A case study. Tech. rep., Software Engineering Institute, Carnegie Mellon University (2001)
8. Kazman, R., Klein, M., Barbacci, M., Longstaff, T., Lipson, H., Carriere, J.: The architecture tradeoff analysis method. In: IEEE International Conference on Engineering of Complex Computer Systems, p. 68. IEEE Computer Society, Los Alamitos (1998)
9. Kazman, R., Barbacci, M., Klein, M., Carriere, S.J., Woods, S.G.: Experience with performing architecture tradeoff analysis. In: Proceedings of the 1999 International Conference on Software Engineering, pp. 54–63 (May 1999)
10. Kazman, R., Klein, M.: Performing architecture tradeoff analysis. In: ISAW 1998: Proceedings of the third international workshop on Software architecture, pp. 85–88. ACM, New York (1998)
11. Kazman, R., Klein, M., Clements, P.: ATAM: Method for architecture evaluation. Tech. rep., Software Engineering Institute, Carnegie Mellon University (2000)
12. Reijonen, V., Eloranta, V.P., Leppänen, M., Bachmann, F.: Discussion on ATAM at Tampere University of Technology (August 2009)
13. Svahnberg, M., Mårtensson, F.: Six years of evaluating software architectures in student projects. Journal of Systems and Software 80(11), 1893–1901 (2007)

# Feature-Based Composition of Software Architectures

Carlos Parra, Anthony Cleve, Xavier Blanc, and Laurence Duchien

INRIA Lille-Nord Europe, LIFL CNRS UMR 8022,
Université des Sciences et Technologies de Lille, France
{carlos.parra,anthony.cleve,xavier.blanc,laurence.duchien}@inria.fr

**Abstract.** In Software Product Lines variability refers to the definition
and utilization of differences between several products. Feature Diagrams
(FD) are a well-known approach to express variability, and can be used
to automate the derivation process. Nevertheless, this may be highly
complex due to possible interactions between selected features and the
artifacts realizing them. Deriving concrete products typically involves
the composition of such inter-dependent software artifacts. This paper
presents a feature-based composition approach to automatically derive
a product architecture from a given feature configuration. The proposed
approach relies on the combination of Model-Driven Engineering (MDE)
and Aspect-Oriented Modeling (AOM) techniques. We introduce a metamodel to reify each feature as a high-level aspect model. Product derivation is achieved by weaving the set of aspect models corresponding to a
particular feature configuration. The weaving strategy is derived from an
in-depth cross-analysis of both the feature interactions and the aspect
model dependencies.

## 1 Introduction

One of the most important challenges of Software Product Line Engineering
concerns variability management, i.e., how to describe, manage and implement
the commonalities and variabilities existing among the members of the same
family of software products. A well-known approach to variability modeling is by
means of Feature Diagrams (FD) introduced as part of Feature Oriented Domain
Analysis (FODA) [1] back in 1990. An FD typically consists of (1) a hierarchy
of *features*, which may be *mandatory* (commonality) or *optional* (variability),
and (2) a set of *constraints* expressing inter-feature dependencies. Nevertheless,
deriving a concrete software product from an FD remains a highly complex
process. The latter starts with the *feature configuration* step, which aims at
selecting the features to include in the desired product, in strict conformance to
the specified constraints. The product derivation process then necessitates the
*composition* of the *software artifacts* corresponding to the selected features. This
second step may be very challenging, since the fact of selecting a single feature
may impact several several places in the product itself.

In order to enable the automated derivation of a product in an SPL, it is
necessary to specify the corresponding artifacts that reify each feature. One way

M. Ali Babar and I. Gorton (Eds.): ECSA 2010, LNCS 6285, pp. 230–245, 2010.
© Springer-Verlag Berlin Heidelberg 2010

to develop such artifacts is by means of *software components*. Given a particular configuration, the artifacts associated with the selected features are to be *composed* in order to obtain the desired product. In the context of Component-Based Software Engineering (CBSE) the typical unit of composition is the *software component* [2]. Ideally, all components are independent from each other. Nevertheless, in SPLs, each feature may be supported by *several components* which means that feature interactions may translate as dependencies and conflicts between components implementing them.

In this paper we propose an approach for feature-based architecture composition in component-based software product lines. To fill the gap between features and software components, we rely on the definition of aspect-like composition models that link every particular feature with several software components. Every model contains the information required for the composition including: (1) the locations modified by the feature, (2) the elements to be added and (3) the set of modifications to perform in order to add such elements. Their definition relies on Aspect Oriented Modeling (AOM), that consists in using the Aspect Oriented Programming (AOP) principles as part of the Model-Driven Engineering (MDE) development process [3]. We present an aspect metamodel to define the aspect models, and the mappings that enable such models to be composed by means of model transformations. Furthermore, our approach includes the combined analysis of the inter-feature constraints of the FD and the dependencies between the corresponding aspect models. We argue that such an analysis may significantly improve the composition process by allowing (1) the verification of the constraints explicitly defined in the FD, (2) the identification of implicit dependencies between the aspect models that are not defined in the FD, and (3) the derivation of a conflict-free composition strategy. The constraint analysis and composition are performed at the model level. Afterwards, the composed model is transformed into software components. We use Service-Component Architecture (SCA) [4] as target platform. SCA proposes a reconciliation between the Service Oriented Architecture (SOA) and CBSE, by defining a framework for describing the composition and the implementation of services using software components.

The main advantages of the proposed architecture composition approach as a whole are: (1) a clear separation of concerns achieved by defining independent aspect models, (2) the possibility to identify inconsistencies both in the FD and in the aspect models, (3) the definition of a feature-driven order to prevent conflicts in the process of architecture composition, and finally (4) the platform independence guaranteed by aspect models that are agnostic to the underlying technologies used for implementation.

The remainder of this paper is organized as follows. Section 2 presents a motivating example and a set of challenges for feature-based composition. Section 3 illustrates our approach in detail. In Section 4 we give some results of our experimentation and revisit the challenges identified in Section 2. Section 5 provides a related work discussion. In Section 6 we conclude the paper and anticipate future work.

## 2    Motivation and Challenges

In this section, we present an illustrative example and define a set of challenges for feature-based software composition.

### 2.1    Motivating Scenario

Let us consider the feature diagram of Figure 1. It defines a family of products with the essential functionality for an e-shopping scenario where a client connects to a server in order to find and buy items. The FODA terminology distinguishes three types of features: (1) *mandatory* features (dark circles) which are always selected (e.g. Notification and Payment), (2) *optional* features (white circles), which can be chosen or not (e.g. Location), and (3) *alternative* features (inverted arc), a special kind of optionality where the selection is realized among a limited set of alternatives, it can be non-exclusive (e.g. CreditCard and Discount) or exclusive (e.g. SMS and Call). In addition to that, the diagram introduces two types of constraints among features: *requires* and *excludes*. The requires constraint states that for a given feature to be selected, the required feature has to be selected before. The excludes constraint states that for a given feature to be selected, the excluded feature has to be deselected. In the feature diagram of Figure 1 there is one constraint indicating that location-filtered catalog needs one type of location to work.

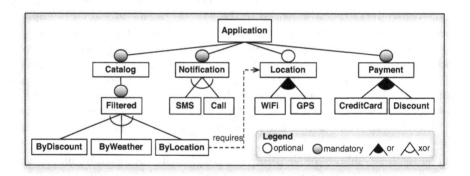

**Fig. 1.** A sample feature diagram

### 2.2    Challenges

The main idea with a feature diagram like the one in Figure 1 is to enable software architects to derive their products based on (1) the selection of features, (2) the existence of dependencies between the selected features, and (3) the mapping between the selected features and the supporting software artifacts. In order for software composition to fully benefit from the information contained in the feature diagram (variabilities, commonalities, and constraints), several challenges have to be faced:

1. **Ensure a clear separation of concerns:** Although feature diagrams enable the clean specification of software variability as a feature hierarchy, the mapping that holds between the features and the corresponding software artifacts may prove much more difficult to define. This is especially the case in the presence of *crosscutting* features, i.e., features that are materialized at multiple places in the final product. Possibly complex interactions between features on the one hand, and between artifacts on the other hand, further complicate the definition of the composable elements.

2. **Identify inconsistencies:** When composing multiple artifacts to form a software product, it is possible that two or more of those artifacts have conflicts regarding the elements where they are going to be composed and the requirements for the composition to take place. It may happen that implicit dependencies exist between artifacts that support independent features in the FD, and conversely. Such *inconsistencies* do not necessarily lead to composition problems but they have to be made explicit.

3. **Derive a suitable composition strategy:** This challenge corresponds to use the information at the feature and also at the artifact level to obtain the composition strategy. For example if two features have a dependency, like in the example ByLocation depends on any kind of Location, it is necessary to first compose the artifacts related to Location so that, ByLocation can reference parts of the Location artifacts. In other words, features have to be used to define partial orders in the composition of artifacts.

4. **Use multi-platform artifacts:** Finally, it is desirable that the artifacts that implement the features are platform-independent, this allows the SPL to have multiple targets and postpone the decision of a particular platform until later steps of the product derivation.

# 3  From Features to Aspect Composition

In order to obtain a software product from a set of features, we define a product derivation process with three main phases as illustrated in Figure 2: (1) *feature and aspect modeling* concerning to the language used to define both feature diagrams and aspect models, (2) *constraint analysis* dealing with the analysis of constraints at both the feature and aspect level, and finally (3) *model composition* that introduces a process to derive a single product using aspect model composition.

## 3.1  Feature and Aspect Modeling

In our approach, both the software variability and the composable software artifacts are represented as *models*. Here below, we present the two metamodels used to define feature and aspect models.

**Feature Metamodel.** Several works on feature modeling have proposed multiple extensions to the FDs initially introduced in [1]. In [5] Schobbens *et al.* survey different approaches to feature modeling and define an abstract syntax

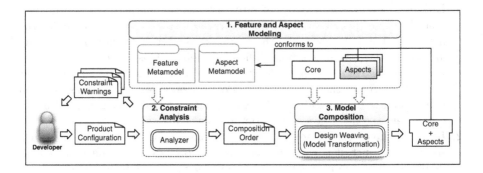

**Fig. 2.** Variability and Product Derivation

for feature diagrams that eliminate the ambiguity occurring in earlier proposals. They employ a mathematical notation to define the inter-feature relationships. A different approach to deal with ambiguity in FDs is by defining a metamodel like the one proposed by Pohl *et al.* [6]. This metamodel presents two main concepts: *variation points* and *variants*. A variation point is a representation of a variability subject, for example, the type of user interface that an application provides. A variant identifies a single option of a variation point. Using the same example, every single user interface that can be chosen for the application (e.g., rich, thin, web-based, mobile) is represented by a variant. The metamodel presented in [6] further specializes the relationships between variation points and variants, by classifying the types of relationships that may exist. They define dependencies (*optional* and *mandatory*) and constraints (*requires, excludes*). In this paper we define a feature metamodel inspired from the concepts that Pohl *et al.* have identified. In our metamodel, we define the same concepts and relationships using the Eclipse Modeling Framework (EMF) [7], but we change the way they are modeled, since EMF does not support the specialization or inheritance of relationships between two different meta-classes. Our feature metamodel is shown in Figure 3(Part a).

**Aspect Metamodel.** The aspect metamodel (see part b of Figure 3) is essential in our approach, it allows us to link the three different methodologies (SPL, SCA, and AOSD) into one single model. First, the root of the metamodel is the `Aspect` which implements a `Variant` from the SPL. Second, an `Aspect` introduces the concepts needed to model a component and service based application (`Model`), and third, the `Aspect` also defines the two essential elements of any AOSD approach: the places where the weaving is realized (`Pointcut`), and the set of modifications to be performed (`Advice`).

*Modeling the elements to be weaved* (`Model`): The `Model` part of the metamodel is used to define the *core*. It is inspired by the SCA, our target platform, and describes the structure of applications as a set of components (meta-class `Element`) that provides services (meta-class `Service`) and requires references (meta-class `Reference`). An element can contain other elements. This is expressed using the

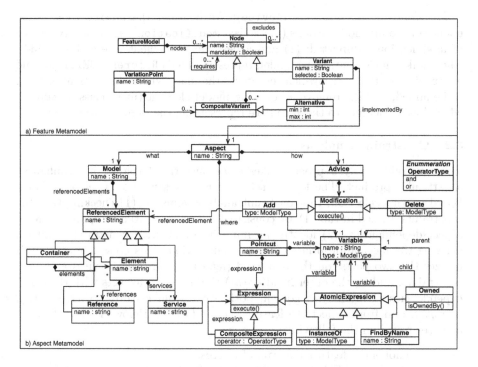

**Fig. 3.** Feature and aspect metamodels

composite pattern of the meta-class `Container`. Additionally, to fully describe the architecture, the metamodel also introduces concepts like contracts, operations, objects, activities, connections, etc. Nevertheless, for space reasons, we show a reduced version of the metamodel making emphasis on the aspect information which is used in the constraint analysis. Every aspect uses the meta class `ReferencedElement` as an entry point to the `Model` part. As it can be noticed, every meta-class in the `Model` inherits from `ReferencedElement` which makes them accessible from the `Pointcut` and `Advice` definitions.

*Modeling the place* (`Pointcut`): We consider the `Pointcut` to be a query that returns all the model elements that have to be present in the model in order for an aspect to be weaved. A pointcut (meta-class `Pointcut`) is composed of expressions (meta-class `Expression`) and variables (meta-class `Variable`). An expression can be either composite (meta-class `Composite`) or atomic (meta-class `Atomic`). A composite expression has an operator (meta-attribute `operator`) that defines the semantics of the composition (e.g., `and`, `or`). An atomic expression can be specialized in three different forms. `InstanceOf`, `FindByName` and `Owned`. `InstanceOf` is used to find an element using its type as a parameter. `FindByName` returns the elements whose name equals the `name` attribute of the expression. Finally the `Owned` expression looks for couples of elements where one of the elements (`parent`) owns the other (`child`). A variable represents a place where the elements obtained by executing an expression are stored.

*Modeling the modifications* (`Advice`): We consider the `Advice` to be a sequence of atomic modifications (meta-class `Modification`). There are two types of modifications supported: (1) add a new model element (meta-classes `Add`), which links an element of the model, represented as a `ReferencedElement`, and a `Variable` of the query, which represents the place where the element is going to be added, and (2) remove an existing model element (meta-classes `Remove`), which has a reference to the `Variable` representing the elements to be removed.

## 3.2   Constraint Analysis

The constraint analysis process takes place once the developer has configured a particular product. The feature selection is represented as a set of variants. Based on this selection, the constraint analysis aims at: (1) checking that the constraints defined in the FD are consistent with respect to corresponding inter-aspect dependencies, (2) identifying implicit composition constraints, and (3) deriving the most appropriate order of composition. This cross-model analysis utilizes the two parts: on the one hand (*left*) there are the features and their constraints, and on the other hand (*right*) there are the aspects with their own dependencies. The analysis goes in both ways: from features to aspects (*left to right*), and from aspects to features (*right to left*). Below, we specify both analyses based on the following notations:

- $FD$ denotes the feature diagram of interest;
- $\mathcal{F} = \{F_1, F_2, \ldots, F_n\}$ denotes the set of features of $FD$;
- $\mathcal{P}$ denotes the set of valid products that can be derived from $FD$;
- $\mathcal{R} = \{(F_1, F_2) \in \mathcal{F} \times \mathcal{F} : F_1 \text{ requires } F_2\}$ denotes the set of *requires* constraints of $FD$;
- $\mathcal{E} = \{(F_1, F_2) \in \mathcal{F} \times \mathcal{F} : F_1 \text{ excludes } F_2\}$, denotes the set of *excludes* constraints of $FD$;
- $A_F$ denotes the aspect model associated with a feature $F$;
- $\mathcal{A} = \bigcup_{F \in \mathcal{F}} A_F$ denotes the set of aspect models associated with the features of $FD$;
- $A.\texttt{Model}$ denotes the `Model` part of an aspect $A \in \mathcal{A}$;
- $A.\texttt{Pointcut}$ denotes the `Pointcut` of an aspect $A \in \mathcal{A}$;

**Left to right analysis.** The *left to right* analysis, concerns the constraints (*requires* or *excludes*) that are *explicitly* specified in the FD. Given a valid feature configuration, the analysis (1) checks that the related FD constraints actually translate as equivalent inter-aspect dependencies, (2) takes such dependencies as a basis to derive a correct weaving order, and (3) returns a warning for each FD constraint that has no "equivalent" at the aspect level.

- A "$F_1$ *requires* $F_2$" constraint in the FD usually implies that the pointcut of aspect $A_{F_1}$ references some model element(s) introduced by aspect $A_{F_2}$. If it is the case, $A_{F_2}$ must be woven *before* $A_{F_1}$ when deriving the product.
- A "$F_1$ *excludes* $F_2$" constraint in the FD usually implies that the pointcuts of $A_{F_1}$ and $A_{F_2}$ references common model elements.

Algorithm 1 summarizes the *left to right* analysis process, which takes as inputs (1) the feature diagram $FD$, (2) the associated aspect models $\mathcal{A}$, and (3) a valid feature configuration $p$. Each *requires* constraint relative to $p$ is analyzed (lines 2–8). If the constraint translates as a Pointcut-Model dependency, the weaving order is adapted accordingly (line 6). If such a dependency is not found, a corresponding warning is returned. The analysis of *excludes* constraints (lines 9–12) is similar, except that (1) it is based on Pointcut-Pointcut dependencies and (2) it does not impact the weaving order. Indeed, the feature configuration is supposed to be valid with respect to the explicit FD constraints.

**Right to left analysis.** The second part of the analysis is intended to find *implicit* inter-feature constraints. Such dependencies are not specified in the FD, but hold between the corresponding aspects and, thus, may cause a conflict when realizing the composition. Similarly to the *left to right* analysis, two types of constraints are considered:

- A *requires* constraint indicates that an aspect pointcut refers to parts of the model of other aspect.
- An *excludes* constraint indicates that there are at least two pointcuts in distinct aspects with equivalent expressions. If such a situation occurs, then it is necessary to verify whether the corresponding advices are interfering with each other. Generally, aspects can be classified with respect to the interferences with each other in three categories: (1) *independent*, when their pointcuts and modifications do not affect other aspects, (2) *partially dependent*, when pointcuts may involve previously woven aspects but advices are independent, and (3) *totally dependent*, when pointcuts are dependent on previous aspects and advices may impact other aspects. In our case, it is the third category that may lead to composition conflicts. Consequently, aspects that exhibit such dependencies should not be weaved within the same product derivation. In order to determine whether the aspects are totally dependent, one must check if the modifications introduced by one aspect have a negative impact on the other. This is similar to *critical pair analysis* [8] in the domain of graph rewriting. Since there are only two types of modifications in our aspect metamodel: *add* and *delete*, the analyzer has to make sure that one aspect is not deleting an element referenced in the other aspect. If it does, the developer is warned about an implicit *excludes* constraint missing in the FD.

The *right to left* analysis is formalized in Algorithm 2. In case an implicit *requires* constraint is detected (lines 2–14), the behavior of the analyzer varies depending on whether the product configuration includes the required feature $F_2$ or not. If $F_2$ is selected, a warning is returned and the composition can be achieved according to an appropriate weaving order (line 8). If, in contrast, $F_2$ is not part of the configuration, then the composition is aborted (lines 10–11). Regarding the detection of implicit *excludes* constraints, the analyzer behaves in the other way around. In this case, indeed, the *presence* of excluded features $F_2$ in the configuration causes the composition to be aborted (lines 20–21), while their absence leads to a warning only (line 18).

---

**Algorithm 1.** Left to right analysis

---

**Require:** A feature diagram $FD$, the associated aspect models $\mathcal{A}$, a valid feature configuration $p = \{F_1, F_2, \ldots, F_k\} \in \mathcal{P}$
**Ensure:** A weaving order $\mathcal{O}$ and a set of warnings $\mathcal{W}$
1. $\mathcal{O} \leftarrow \texttt{toList}(p)$
2. **for all** $(F_1, F_2) \in \mathcal{R}$ such that $F_1 \in p$ **do**
3.    **if** $A_{F_1}.\texttt{Pointcut} \cap A_{F_2}.\texttt{Model} = \emptyset$ **then**
4.       $\mathcal{W} \leftarrow \mathcal{W} \cup \{F_1 \text{ does not require } F_2 \text{ at the architectural level}\}$
5.    **else**
6.       $\mathcal{O} \leftarrow \texttt{switchPositionIfNeeded}(\mathcal{O}, F_2, F_1)$
7.    **end if**
8. **end for**
9. **for all** $(F_1, F_2) \in \mathcal{E}$ such that $F_1 \in p$ **do**
10.    **if** $A_{F_1}.\texttt{Pointcut} \cap A_{F_2}.\texttt{Pointcut} = \emptyset$ **then**
11.       $\mathcal{W} \leftarrow \mathcal{W} \cup \{F_1 \text{ does not exclude } F_2 \text{ at the architectural level}\}$
12.    **end if**
13. **end for**

---

---

**Algorithm 2.** Right to left analysis

---

**Require:** A feature diagram $FD$, the associated aspect models $\mathcal{A}$, a valid feature configuration $p = \{F_1, F_2, \ldots, F_k\} \in \mathcal{P}$, an initial weaving order $\mathcal{O}$
**Ensure:** A flag $\texttt{compositionAllowed}$, a possibly adapted weaving order $\mathcal{O}$ and a set of warnings $\mathcal{W}$
1. $\texttt{compositionAllowed} \leftarrow \textit{true}$
2. **for all** $F1 \in p$ **do**
3.    **for all** $F_2 \in \mathcal{F}$ such that $A_{F_1}.\texttt{Pointcut} \cap A_{F_2}.\texttt{Model} \neq \emptyset$ **do**
4.       **if** $(F_1, F_2) \notin \mathcal{R}$ **then**
5.          $\mathcal{W} \leftarrow \mathcal{W} \cup \{F_1 \text{ implicitly } requires\ F_2 \text{ at the architectural level}\}$
6.       **end if**
7.       **if** $F_2 \in p$ **then**
8.          $\mathcal{O} \leftarrow \texttt{switchPositionIfNeeded}(\mathcal{O}, F_2, F_1)$
9.       **else**
10.          $\texttt{compositionAllowed} \leftarrow \textit{false}$
11.          $\mathcal{W} \leftarrow \mathcal{W} \cup \{F_1 \text{ implicitly requires a non-selected feature } (F_2)\}$
12.       **end if**
13.    **end for**
14. **end for**
15. **for all** $F1 \in p$ **do**
16.    **for all** $F_2 \in \mathcal{F}$ such that $A_{F_1}.\texttt{Pointcut} \cap A_{F_2}.\texttt{Pointcut} \neq \emptyset$ **do**
17.       **if** $(F_1, F_2) \notin \mathcal{E} \wedge \texttt{totallyDependent}(A_{F_1}, A_{F_2})$ **then**
18.          $\mathcal{W} \leftarrow \mathcal{W} \cup \{F_1 \text{ implicitly } excludes\ F_2 \text{ at the architectural level}\}$
19.          **if** $F_2 \in p$ **then**
20.             $\texttt{compositionAllowed} \leftarrow \textit{false}$
21.             $\mathcal{W} \leftarrow \mathcal{W} \cup \{F_1 \text{ implicitly excludes a selected feature } (F_2)\}$
22.          **end if**
23.       **end if**
24.    **end for**
25. **end for**

---

**Defining the composition order.** The composition order is derived from the analysis in both ways. To obtain it, the analysis tool traverses the list of features in the same order as they were selected, and, whenever a feature requires (implicitly or explicitly) other feature, it is moved in the list to the position right after the feature being required. This is done in both the *left to right* algorithm (line 6) and the *right to left* algorithm (line 8). This order guarantees that the pointcuts of features requiring other features are correctly executed during the composition.

### 3.3    Composition of Aspects

In general terms, the aspect composition consists of successive calls to a single generic model transformation (*weaver*). This transformation takes as inputs the *core* model $M$ and an aspect $A$ to be weaved, and returns a single model representing the composition of the core and the aspect. The transformation itself relies on the metamodel of Figure 3 (Part b). It consists in iterating over the set of modifications specified in the *Advice* of $A$ in order to execute each of them.

The places where each modification takes place are defined by the associated `Pointcut`. The execution of this pointcut on the core model iterates over its `Expressions`, which can be either atomic or composite. Atomic expressions correspond to `FindByName`, `InstanceOf` and `Owned`. Each atomic expression returns the collection of *core* model elements that match their conditions. A composite expression is evaluated by accumulating and combining the result of each atomic expression. The way the resulting elements are combined depends on the composite operator. The `AND` operator is interpreted as the *intersection* of the model elements, whereas the `OR` operator translates as their *union*.

At the end of the pointcut execution, all the places impacted by the aspect have been identified. Then the modifications specified by the aspect can be applied. In the case of an `Add` modification, the elements of the aspect are added to the *core* model. Applying a `Delete` consists in removing the elements found in the pointcut from the *core* model.

The transformation finishes when all modifications specified in the advice have been performed. The global weaving process repeats until all the aspects corresponding to the variants selected in the feature configuration have been composed with the core model.

## 4    Experimentation and Discussion

In order to test the constraint analysis introduced in the previous section, we have implemented the sample SPL introduced with the FD in Section 2 and applied our constraint analysis. There are in total 9 variants (`ByDiscount`, `ByWeather`, `ByLocation`, `SMS`, `Call`, `Wifi`, `GPS`, `CreditCard`, and `Discount`) which are realized with individual aspect models. The total number of valid products that are derivable from such diagram is 66, that is 72 in total minus 6 that do not respect the requires constraint. In Table 1 we have selected a subset of 10 products to illustrate the result of the analysis. For each product we

Table 1. Constraint Analysis Results

| Product | v1 | v2 | v3 | v4 | v5 | v6 | v7 | v8 | v9 | L2R | R2L | Result | Time(ms) |
|---|---|---|---|---|---|---|---|---|---|---|---|---|---|
| 1 | ✓ | – | – | ✓ | – | – | – | ✓ | – | – | – | {v1,v4,v8} | 242 |
| 2 | – | ✓ | – | – | ✓ | – | – | – | ✓ | – | HI(v9,v4) | Not allowed | 229 |
| 3 | – | – | ✓ | ✓ | – | ✓ | – | ✓ | – | Order | – | {v6,v3,v4,v8} | 240 |
| 4 | – | – | ✓ | – | ✓ | ✓ | – | ✓ | – | Order | – | {v6,v3,v5,v8} | 236 |
| 5 | – | – | ✓ | – | ✓ | – | ✓ | – | ✓ | Order | HI(v9,v4) | Not allowed | 231 |
| 6 | – | ✓ | – | ✓ | – | ✓ | – | ✓ | – | – | – | {v2,v4,v6,v8} | 234 |
| 7 | ✓ | – | – | – | ✓ | – | ✓ | ✓ | – | – | – | {v1,v5,v7,v8} | 242 |
| 8 | – | ✓ | – | ✓ | – | – | ✓ | ✓ | – | – | – | {v2,v4,v7,v8} | 270 |
| 9 | – | – | ✓ | – | ✓ | – | – | ✓ | – | Order | HI(v9,v4) | Not allowed | 255 |
| 10 | ✓ | – | – | ✓ | – | – | – | ✓ | ✓ | – | HI(v9,v4) | {v1,v4,v9,v8} | 244 |

present the list of selected variants (v1-v9), the results of the *left2right* (l2r) and *rigth2left* (r2l) algorithms, the order of composition (Result), and the execution time (Time) in milliseconds.

As it can be seen from the results, the analysis for each product takes slightly short times for this small FD. Nevertheless, the more variants there exist, the more aspects to verify for each product with consequences in performance, but such an overload is related to the nature of the product family itself. Additionally, since this process is executed during the design phase, time and performance are less critical than correctness and conflict-free composition.

Regarding the results of the analysis, we notice that the *left to right* algorithm modifies the *order* of composition of the products 3,4,5, and 9. On the other side, the *requires* constraint between the variant ByLocation and the variation point Location has an equivalent dependency in the aspect level. However, as previously stated, even if there was no equivalent dependencies, the constraint does not necessarily represent an error since it may come from a business rule.

On the other side, the *right to left* analysis shows that the aspect for the variant 9 (Discount) has a dependency (presented in the table as HI for *Hidden Includes*), with the aspect realizing the variant 4 (SMS). As a result, products 2,5 and 9 are not allowed for composition. In the case of product 10, the analysis shows the same dependency, but the composition is allowed since the variant 4 (SMS) is selected. Additionally, the order does not need to be changed since the variant 4 (SMS) is already placed before the variant 9 (Discount).

Regarding the implementation, we have used the tools provided by EMF. There are four metamodels in total: the feature and aspect metamodels introduced in Section 3, and additionally, there are two metamodels for SCA and Java respectively. The constraint analysis algorithms as well as the model transformations are written in Java and use the EMF API to import and manipulate the models. We have made this choice over other model platforms for two main reasons: first, we wanted to let the aspect developers to decide how the aspect has to be composed. Our weaver is generic and allows aspects to define any combination of advices and pointcuts. This gives aspects great expressivity and at the same time, we guarantee that every aspect, modeled with the metamodel presented in Figure 3, can be processed by the weaver. And second, by using our own definition and semantics for the modification operations (Add and Remove), we are able to generate equivalent reconfiguration scripts that can be executed at runtime. With this property we aim at defining a dynamic product derivation using the same aspect models.

## 4.1   Discussion

Let us now revisit the feature-based architecture composition challenges identified in Section 2 for discussing the tool-supported approach proposed in this paper. Regarding challenge 1, our modeling approach contributes to a clear separation of concerns at three levels: variability expression, architecture definition, and feature-architecture mapping specification. We benefit from the complementary capabilities of Feature Modeling, Component-Based/Service-Oriented Architecture and Aspect-Oriented Modeling. The constraint analysis algorithms allows the detection of inconsistencies (challenge 2) in the FD as well as in the aspect models. This prevents the composition from taking place unless all the constraints are respected. Additionally, the algorithms take explicit and implicit features interactions as a basis to derive a conflict-free composition strategy (challenge 3) that ensures that aspects are weaved in the appropriate order for any given configuration. Finally, our aspects are platform-independent models (challenge 4). In our case, model transformations have been implemented towards a particular platform (SCA and Java) to enable the SPL to deal with dynamic product derivation as explained in [9]. Nevertheless, such aspect models can be transformed towards different component-based platforms, in which case, the analysis and composition processes remain valid.

## 5   Related Work

This section discusses the complementarity of our approach with respect to previous work on feature-based software composition, aspectual feature modeling and aspect-oriented model composition.

**Feature-based software composition.** In   [10] van der Storm presents a generic approach to feature-based software composition, with a particular focus on the feature configuration phase. Feature descriptions are mapped to related software artifacts through a formal model. This mapping indicates which artifact(s) should be included in the product if a feature is selected. A scalable configuration technique, based on binary decision diagrams (BDDs) [11], is developed. The BDDs, derived from the feature interactions specified in the feature model, aim to lead to valid configurations only. Several possible methods are identified for the composition process itself, each supporting a different level of granularity. In contrast, we assume that a valid product configuration is available, and we contribute to the subsequent feature composition process.

Voelter and Groher [12] present an approach based on the combination of aspect-oriented and model-driven software development. This approach supports the explicit separation and modeling of variability in feature models. In the implementation of this approach, an AOP framework enables product derivation to be performed using a weaving process described in a workflow. Kuhlemman *et al.* [13] presents a tool-supported approach to support safe composition of *non-monotonic* features, i.e., features that *add* and *remove* code. In particular, the authors verify that all valid combinations of features can be composed without errors. Considering each feature implementation as an increment in program functionality, software composition is seen by the authors as the application of successive *feature transformations* that add features to a program (by adding and/or removing code). The authors use SAT technologies to check *configurable sequences* of feature transformations. They show that automated support is indispensable due to the rapidly growing complexity of the analysis.

Our approach also enables the automated composition of (non-monotonic) features, but it considers the architecture level rather than the code level. Furthermore, in contrast with Kuhleman *et al.*, we do not assume that the feature composition order is encoded in the feature model by reading from right to left. Our analysis technique aims at deriving an adequate composition order based on both explicit and implicit feature interactions.

Lee *et al.* [14] addresses the challenge of software composition in the presence of feature dependencies. They suggest the use of *aspect-oriented* implementation patterns for such dependencies. This approach allows a clear separation of feature dependencies from feature implementations, thereby increasing the reusability of the latter. The authors mainly focus on *dynamic* feature interactions as those identified in [15], whereas we consider *structural* dependencies between features. Czarnecki *et al.* [16] present an automated procedure for verifying that a given feature configuration will lead to a *correct* product model. The notion of correctness they consider is *well-formedness*: they verify that the resulting product model conforms to the meta-model of the target modelling language. In constrast, we aim to check that the configured product can be composed. When possible, we derive a conflict-free composition strategy allowing all the selected features to be correctly supported. The analysis of implicit feature dependencies is essential in this context. For instance, failing to identify an implicit *requires* constraint may lead to an incomplete, yet well-formed, product model.

**Aspectual feature modeling.** Griss [17] presents a conceptual framework for feature-based and aspect-oriented product line engineering. The key idea is to use aspects for implementing the features identified as common and variable in a product line. Lee *et al.* [18] go a step further by proposing a set of detailed guidelines on how feature-oriented programming and aspect-oriented programming can be combined in order to enhance the reusability, adaptability and configurability of software product line artifacts. They aim at addressing the so-called *invasive change* problem. This problem is due to the fact that the code implementing a particular feature may be scattered across multiple components, and consequently adding or removing a feature may have an impact on several source code locations. Our work also aims at addressing this problem by considering both inter-feature dependencies and inter-aspect dependencies.

More recently, Apel *et al.* [19] introduce the notion of *aspectual feature module* (AFM), which constitutes a proposal of the symbiosis of Feature-Oriented Programming and Aspect-Oriented Programming. An AFM encapsulates the roles of collaborating classes and aspects that together contribute to implementing a feature. According to this view, a feature implementation regroups a collection of artifacts among which classes, class refinements and aspects. The use of aspects in an AFM brings the benefit from AOP's modularization capabilities. In our approach, we also from aspect modularization, but in our case we do not mix aspects and classes to implement a feature. We aim at defining independent aspects that are woven with a core. Since our aspects are self-contained, they include a model part, which defines the components and services that are latter transformed into configuration files and classes.

**Aspect-oriented model composition.** Zhang *et al.* [20] show that the explicit specification of aspect precedence at the modeling level allows to mitigate the problem of aspect interference in AOM. The precedence declarations enable the composition mechanism to automatically derive an appropriate weaving order. Our approach relies on this principle and also takes into account the mutual dependency between feature interactions and related aspect precedence.

Morin *et al.* [21] consider the introduction of variability at a higher level of abstraction. They present a generic approach to weaving variability in metamodels, by means of a reusable variability aspect. This aspect allows the description of the variability concepts and the relationships between them, in a metamodel-independent manner. Such an aspect can then be woven using standard AOM techniques in order to include variability in a given domain-specific metamodel. The authors then show how to compute a feature diagram from an instance model with variability. In contrast, our approach takes feature diagrams as input for aspect-based architecture composition.

# 6   Conclusion

This paper presented a comprehensive approach to feature-driven composition of software architectures. This approach allows the automated derivation of product architectures from feature configurations, by combining MDE and AOM techniques. The composition process is realized through transformation-based model weaving and is guided by the explicit and implicit dependencies that exist between the selected features. Our proposal relies on a clear separation of concerns enabled by the underlying variability and aspect metamodels. Our method allows to identify implicit dependencies and conflicts between features, and takes such feature interactions as a basis to derive an appropriate architecture composition strategy. The overall approach is implemented in a generic SPL framework that enables the composition and deployment of both component-based and service-oriented architectures on various platforms. In the near future, we intend to consolidate the promising results obtained so far, following two main directions.

First, we want to explore the reusability of our approach in the context of *dynamic* feature (de)selection. We believe that it could be extended to support the derivation of context-aware, self-adaptive systems. Second, we intend to evaluate the application of our feature-based composition techniques to larger software systems. We already identified FraSCAti [22], a configurable SCA platform, as a good candidate for such an experiment.

**Acknowledgments.** The CAPPUCINO project is funded by the Conseil Régional Nord-Pas-de- Calais, Oseo/ANVAR, and the Fonds Unique Interministériel. This work was also supported by Ministry of Higher Education and Research, *Nord-Pas de Calais* Regional Council and FEDER through the *Contrat de Projets Etat Region* (CPER) 2007-2013. This research was carried out during the tenure of an ERCIM *"Alain Bensoussan"* Fellowship.

# References

1. Kang, K.C., Cohen, S.G., Hess, J.A., Novak, W.E., Peterson, A.S.: Feature-oriented domain analysis (foda) feasibility study. Technical report, Carnegie-Mellon University Software Engineering Institute (November 1990)
2. Szyperski, C.: Component Software: Beyond Object-Oriented Programming, 2nd edn. Addison-Wesley Professional, Reading (2002)
3. Jézéquel, J.M.: Model driven design and aspect weaving. Software and System Modeling 7(2), 209–218 (2008)
4. Open SOA: Service component architecture specifications (November 2007), http://www.osoa.org/display/Main/Service+Component+Architecture+Home
5. Schobbens, P.Y., Heymans, P., Trigaux, J.C.: Feature diagrams: A survey and a formal semantics. In: 14th Int. Requirements Engineering Conference (RE 2006), pp. 136–145 (2006)
6. Pohl, K., Böckle, G., van der Linden, F.J.: Software Product Line Engineering: Foundations, Principles and Techniques. Springer, Heidelberg (2005)
7. The Eclipse Foundation: Eclipse Modeling Framework Project, EMF (2010), http://www.eclipse.org/modeling/emf/
8. Plump, D.: Hypergraph rewriting: critical pairs and undecidability of confluence, pp. 201–213 (1993)
9. Parra, C., Blanc, X., Duchien, L.: Context Awareness for Dynamic Service-Oriented Product Lines. In: Proceedings of the 13th International Software Product Line Conference (SPLC 2009), pp. 131–140 (2009)
10. der Storm, T.V.: Generic feature-based software composition. In: Lumpe, M., Vanderperren, W. (eds.) SC 2007. LNCS, vol. 4829, pp. 66–80. Springer, Heidelberg (2007)
11. Bryant, R.E.: Symbolic Boolean manipulation with ordered binary-decision diagrams. ACM Computing Surveys 24(3), 293–318 (1992)
12. Voelter, M., Groher, I.: Product line implementation using aspect-oriented and model-driven software development. In: 11th Int. Software Product Line Conference (SPLC 2007), pp. 233–242. IEEE CS, Los Alamitos (2007)
13. Kuhlemann, M., Batory, D., Kästner, C.: Safe composition of non-monotonic features. In: 8th Int. Conference on Generative Programming and Component Engineering (GPCE 2009), pp. 177–186. ACM, New York (2009)

14. Lee, K., Botterweck, G., Thiel, S.: Aspectual separation of feature dependencies for flexible feature composition. In: 33rd Annual IEEE Int. Computer Software and Applications Conference, pp. 45–52. IEEE CS, Los Alamitos (2009)
15. Lee, K., Kang, K.C.: Feature dependency analysis for product line component design. In: Bosch, J., Krueger, C. (eds.) ICOIN 2004 and ICSR 2004. LNCS, vol. 3107, pp. 69–85. Springer, Heidelberg (2004)
16. Czarnecki, K., Pietroszek, K.: Verifying feature-based model templates against well-formedness ocl constraints. In: 5th Int. Conference on Generative Programming and Component Engineering (GPCE 2006), pp. 211–220. ACM, New York (2006)
17. Griss, M.L.: Implementing product-line features by composing aspects. In: 1st Conference on Software Product lines: experience and research directions (SPLC 2000), pp. 271–288. Kluwer Academic Publishers, Dordrecht (2000)
18. Lee, K., Kang, K.C., Kim, M., Park, S.: Combining feature-oriented analysis and aspect-oriented programming for product line asset development. In: 10th Int. Software Product Line Conference (SPLC 2006), pp. 103–112. IEEE CS, Los Alamitos (2006)
19. Apel, S., Leich, T., Saake, G.: Aspectual feature modules. IEEE Transactions on Software Engineering (TSE) 34(2), 162–180 (2008)
20. Zhang, J., Cottenier, T., van den Berg, A., Gray, J.: Aspect composition in the motorola aspect-oriented modelling weaver. Journal of Object Technology 6, 89–108 (2007) (Special issue on Aspect-Oriented Modelling)
21. Morin, B., Perrouin, G., Lahire, P., Barais, O., Vanwormhoudt, G., Jézéquel, J.M.: Weaving variability into domain metamodels. In: Schürr, A., Selic, B. (eds.) MODELS 2009. LNCS, vol. 5795, pp. 690–705. Springer, Heidelberg (2009)
22. Seinturier, L., Merle, P., Fournier, D., Dolet, N., Schiavoni, V., Stefani, J.-B.: Reconfigurable sca applications with the frascati platform. In: 6th IEEE International Conference on Service Computing (SCC 2009), September 2009, pp. 268–275 (2009)

# Linking Design Decisions to Design Models in Model-Based Software Development

Patrick Könemann[1] and Olaf Zimmermann[2]

[1] Informatics and Mathematical Modelling, Technical University of Denmark,
2800 Kgs. Lyngby, Denmark
pk@imm.dtu.dk
[2] IBM Research – Zürich, Säumerstrasse 8, 8803 Rüschlikon, Switzerland
OLZ@zurich.ibm.com

**Abstract.** Numerous design decisions are made in model-based software development which often are not documented explicitly. Hence, the design knowledge is 'in the designers mind' and communicated orally, if at all, and the rationale behind the decisions is lost. Existing tools tackle this problem for architectural decisions which refer to the higher level architecture of a system. However, these decisions are separate artifacts and not linked to individual design model elements. Hence, there is no automatic check whether the design models comply with made decisions.

This paper presents concepts for explicitly linking design decisions and design model elements. As first class artifacts, design decisions can be used for documentation, consistency checking, and reuse. In case consistency constraints are violated, the user is notified that the design models no longer comply with the decisions made. Reuse is realized by extracting design model changes as reusable patterns for recurring decisions.

## 1 Introduction

Development of software systems is done in teams today, and models improve the communication within the teams and help to develop such systems. Model-based software development increases the productivity because the level of abstraction rises and models (e.g. in the *Unified Modeling Language*, UML [1]) are first class artifacts: the models are used for documentation, discussion, and to some extent also for code generation [2].

One way of documenting design decisions in such projects is the use of decision management systems. Decisions might either be specific to one particular project or generic, and thus reusable in similar contexts [3]. Reusable decisions, e.g. the use of design patterns [4] to solve a particular design issue, can be stored as best practices and reused in other projects. This makes design decisions valuable artifacts for expressing and sharing design knowledge.

The state-of-the-art decision management systems are only used for documentation, analysis, and for sharing architectural design knowledge [5,11,16], and are isolated from the actual models in model-based software development. All of these tools store the information semi-formally, i.e. structured by decisions.

M. Ali Babar and I. Gorton (Eds.): ECSA 2010, LNCS 6285, pp. 246–262, 2010.

Current modeling tools, on the other hand, have only limited or no capabilities for documenting design decisions. Hence, formal design models and semi-formal design decisions are separated. Our previous work already introduced decision enforcement as a proof-of-concept which is the first step to update design models according to made design decisions [6].

The concepts in this paper introduce an explicit link between design models and design decisions in model-based software development. Our vision is to treat design decisions as first-class artifacts and to exploit them to integrate design models and semi-formal documentation: an explicit link between design model elements and design decisions will allow keeping the design models consistent with the decisions made. Moreover, we propose concepts for automating redundant work on design models with the use of model differences—the latter are used to store reusable design model changes that realize recurring design decisions.

All concepts are tool-independent; to integrate another modeling or decision management tool, the other tool has to realize the interface specified in [7]. In essence, a modeling tool must offer reflection (e.g., as EMOF [8] provides) and design decisions must be mapped to the decision meta model of the interface.

The main benefits of our contributions are reuse of design decisions and the corresponding changes in the design models as well as automated recognition of consistency violations between these artifacts. The goals is to make the development of model-based software faster and less error-prone (because of reuse).

The remainder of the paper is structured as follows. Sect. 2 introduces an example, Sect. 3 states the state of the art as well as our goals, Sect. 4 defines our central concept of a binding and its use, Sect. 5 sketches the prototypic implementation, Sect. 6 discusses related work, and Sect. 7 concludes the paper.

## 2  Example

In this section, we introduce a running example to illustrate our concepts. It is small on purpose in order to focus on relevant properties. It consists of two decisions, taken from a case study in [7], that describes the development of a web application with respect to made design decisions. Here we assume that the design decisions to make (described by design issues and their solutions, called alternatives) are already known and available in a decision management tool.

The first issue, *Session Awareness*, concerns an existing class *Controller* in the UML design model (which was created due to a previous design decision) and deals with the issue whether or not to introduce session support in the web application. Possible solutions are *Yes* and *No*, as sketched informally in a simplified decision model in Fig. 1. Here we make the decision to pick the alternative *Yes* which induces another issue *Session Management*. Note that although this particular choice does not affect the design models directly, subsequent decisions in fact can have impact on the design models as explained next.

The second issue, *Session Management*, concerns *how* the session management will be realized. The choice will be the *Server Session State* pattern (as defined by Fowler [9]) describing a controller, a session manager, and a session object. Other

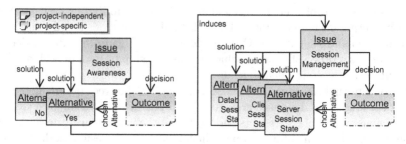

**Fig. 1.** Design decisions *Session Awareness* and *Session Management*

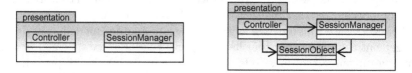

**Fig. 2.** Parts of the design model before and after the decision *Session Management*

alternatives are *Client Session State* and *Database Session State*. As depicted on the left-hand side of Fig. 2, a session manager already exists – for instance, due to previous work on the design model.

The next step is the realization of the server session state in the design model, i.e. adding design model elements according to the chosen pattern (the result is shown on the right-hand side of Fig. 2). That work is usually tedious and error-prone although it varies with the complexity of the selected solution. There might also be variations of how a particular solution can be realized in the design models. Moreover, the very same solution could have been realized before in another project, and, hence, its realization in design models is recurring work.

We use this example in the next sections to illustrate our approach that adds support for automatic consistency checking (whether the design models comply with made design decisions) and reuse of realizations of design decisions. Thus, design decisions are not lost but captured explicitly.

Although the example is dealing with a web application, all model-based software development processes are supported in which design decisions can be documented and recur in similar projects.

## 3   Requirements

This section gives an overview of the state-of-the-art of decision management, introduces model differences, and states the goals of our contributions.

### 3.1   Current Situation

Design knowledge in terms of design decisions consists mostly of informal information (text) structured as follows. A design decision in terms of the system's

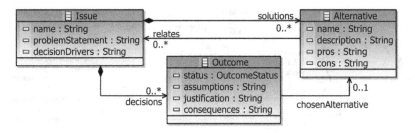

**Fig. 3.** A typical design decision metamodel in existing work

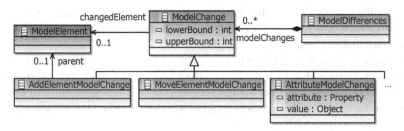

**Fig. 4.** An excerpt from a typical metamodel for model differences in existing work

architectural design consists of a design *issue* or *problem*, several *constraints* and *assumptions*, one or many *solutions*, and a *rationale*, amongst others [10]. The solutions describe *how* they shall be applied; in case of design patterns it might refer to its definition and/or informally describe its realization in the context of the issue. Moreover, we distinguish between *project-independent* and *project-specific* decisions, at which the former are reusable decisions and the latter are only documented for one particular project [11].

A typical design decision metamodel is shown in Fig. 3 which can be mapped to multiple decision management tools: a design decision addresses a particular design problem (*Issue*), considering one or many solutions (*Alternatives*), and the rationale why a particular alternative was chosen (*Outcome*). Attributes like *problemStatement* and *justification* describe the properties mentioned before. The association *relates* between alternatives and issues allows relating decisions to each other; the reference *induces* in Fig. 1 is an instance of it. This metamodel is based on the one specified in [6], in particular concerning the distinction between project-independent parts (issues and alternatives) and project-specific parts (outcomes). Design model changes are, however, not included in any existing work of decision management we are aware of.

Model differences describe changes in a design model, e.g., adding a class and three associations (cf. decision 2 in the example in Sect. 2). Hence, they can be used for describing design model changes for a particular realization of a solution of a design decision. Here it is sufficient to know that model differences consist of several *ModelChanges* as shown in Fig. 4. Concrete changes are, for instance, addition or movement of elements or change of attributes ([12] discusses

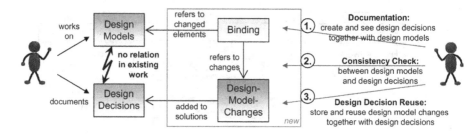

**Fig. 5.** Binding and design model changes enable our goals

selected differencing approaches in more detail). *lowerBound* and *upperBound* of *ModelChange* are specific for our differencing technology [13] and define how often a particular change may be applied.

We require our solution to be independent of particular tools. That is to say, the metamodels for design models and design decisions shall not be modified. This ensures that the concepts for the binding are tool-independent and are thus applicable to many modeling tools and decision management systems.

## 3.2   Goals

This section states the goals of our contributions. The left-hand side of Fig. 5 sketches the situation without our extensions: design decisions are isolated from the design model. Adding a *Binding* and *DesignModelChanges*, as shown in the center of the figure, enables our goals to *ease documentation*, to *check consistency*, and to *reuse design model changes of design decisions*.

**Goal: Documentation.** Almost every change in design models can be seen as a design decision. However, most decisions, even if they are made consciously, are not documented because of lacking tool support and developers lacking discipline. To overcome that problem, our goal is to explicitly link design models to the design knowledge stored in a decision management system. That is, related design decisions can be retrieved for each element in the design model. For instance, if the developer selects the class *SessionObject* (cf. Sect. 2), the tool shall return a list of design decisions containing the decision *SessionManagement*.

**Goal: Consistency.** Another goal is to validate whether design decisions and their induced changes in the design models are consistent with each other. That is, for the decision *Session Management* in the example, the class *SessionObject* and the three associations between that class, the *Controller*, and the *Session-Manager* must prevail in the design model. If any of these classes or associations are removed later on, the design model is not consistent anymore with the result of the decision and the developer shall be notified.

**Goal: Design Decision Reuse.** The last goal addresses reuse of design decisions in the same or in a similar context, e.g. in another project. Realizing the same solution multiple times in one or several projects is recurring and error-prone work. Design model changes of a particular design decision, in the form of model differences, can be extracted from one design model and applied to another design model the next time that decision is made. That will not happen fully automatically but the developer has to revise (and, if necessary, refine) the application of design model changes. That said, there might be similar design model changes which realize the same solution, depending on the scenario and context; there are, for instance, multiple realizations of the server session state pattern. Hence, our goal is to support multiple realizations per solution.

# 4 Concepts: Binding Design Knowledge to Design Models

Next, existing and new components are introduced, the binding is defined, and finally we explain how to use the binding for documentation, consistency checking, and reuse of design decisions.

## 4.1 Relevant Components

This section lists all relevant existing components before defining a formal link between design decisions and design models. The link has to connect the particular decision, more precisely the *Outcome* of a decision and its chosen *Alternative* (cf. design decision metamodel in Fig. 3), with the design model elements the decision affects. A design model element can be any part of the design model; in case of UML it would be instances of *Element*, that are, for example, classes, associations, attributes, actors for use cases, or messages in a sequence chart [1].

*ModelDifferences*, which describe *how* a model should be changed when a design decision is made, contain a set of individual *ModelChanges* (cf. metamodel for model differences in Fig. 4).

## 4.2 Binding between Design Decisions and Design Models

This section defines a new artifact, the *DecisionModelBinding*, to achieve our goals listed in Sect. 3.2. We first sketch it informally with the help of the running example before we define it. Its purpose is to map each change from the model differences to the design model elements the particular design decision affects.

In case of the design decision *Session Management* from the example in Sect. 2, the binding consists of a couple of *ModelElementBindings*, one for each design model element. Fig. 6 sketches the overall picture for that decision. The design model on the left-hand side and the design decisions on the right-hand side are already known from Sect. 2. The center part shows the project-independent *ModelDifferences* and the project-specific *DecisionModelBinding*. That is, the *ModelDifferences* describe *how* the design model is changed for that specific alternative (this is the reusable realization of the alternative). The *DecisionModelBinding* links these changes to the actual design model elements. We made this separation because the *ModelDifferences* are reusable and, thus, project-independent (required for *Goal: Design Decision Reuse*) whereas the *DecisionModelBinding* is only used for one particular design model and is project-specific.

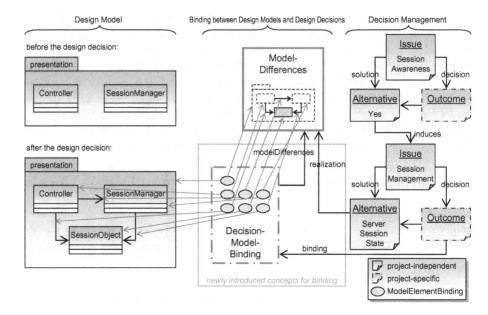

**Fig. 6.** Example binding between design decisions and design model

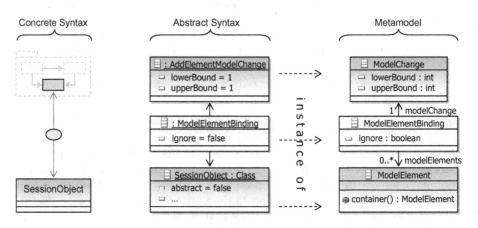

**Fig. 7.** One *ModelElementBinding* in concrete and abstract syntax and its metamodel

Figure 7 shows one of the binding elements in detail, namely the binding for the added class *SessionObject*. The left-hand side shows the concrete syntax whereas the abstract syntax (UML object diagram) of that binding is shown in the middle. The *ModelElementBinding* contains references to both, the change *AddElementModelChange* in the model differences and to the *SessionObject* in the design model. Furthermore, the figure shows the metamodel elements for this scenario on the right-hand side. The *lowerBound* and *upperBound* define how many design model elements are allowed for a particular binding.

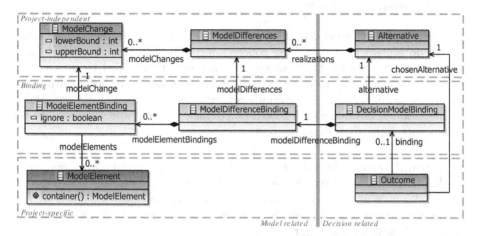

**Fig. 8.** Metamodel of the binding between design decisions and design model

The definition of the binding is given as a metamodel in Fig. 8. The classes in the middle row define the binding; the *DecisionModelBinding* and *ModelElementBindings* in Fig. 6 are their instances, respectively. The classes are vertically divided into being design model-related and decision-related. The other components in the figure (already introduced in Sect. 4.1) are horizontally divided into being project-independent and project-specific. They are explained next.

- An *Alternative* is a solution in a design decision and may contain several realizations. An *Outcome* is the result of a particular decision and points to the chosen alternative.
- A *ModelChange* defines an individual change in the design model, *Model-Differences* groups them logically as a realization for an alternative.
- A *ModelElement* is an arbitrary element in the design model.
- A *ModelElementBinding* links a *ModelChange* to the affected *ModelElement* (if *ignore* is true, this binding is not validated); a *ModelDifferenceBinding* groups the binding logically; a *DecisionModelBinding* connects the *Model-DifferenceBinding* to the outcome, that is, to the result of the decision.

Note that the design model does not know about the binding because we do not want to modify the modeling tool. Moreover, *Alternative* and *Outcome* are just wrapper classes for alternatives and outcomes in a decision management system. Thus, the references *Alternative.realizations* to *ModelDifferences* and *Outcome.binding* to *DecisionModelBinding* belong to these wrapper classes. This level of indirection keeps all decision related classes independent of the binding.

Since the explicit binding links design model elements and design decisions, the rationale and other documentation can directly be annotated to the design model (Goal: Documentation).

### 4.3   Consistency Check

It is easily possible to check the consistency between design models and made design decisions with the binding concepts introduced in Sect. 4.2. We defined a set of constraints for that purpose, for instance that added elements must prevail in the design model. A violated constraint produces either a warning or an error, specified by the constraint's severity. In case of constraint violations, the developer is notified with a description of the constraint and the cause. These constraints apply to design-time only.

**Constraint Levels.** In order to check that the design model corresponds to a made design decision, two criteria have to be checked. Firstly, all related design model elements must exist. Secondly, all design model changes defined by the model differences must prevail. Starting with these two criteria, we identified three levels with increasing granularity.

1. *Element level: all design model elements linked to the binding must exist.*
   This level is independent of design decisions and concrete changes in the design model but concerns only the relation between the binding and the existence and cardinality of design model elements.
   Example: the class *SessionObject* is referenced by a *ModelElementBinding* and, thus, must exist in the design model (if *ignore* is false).
2. *Change level: all changes must prevail in the design model.*
   This level is specific for changes which are made due to a design decision.
   Example: if a class is changed to being abstract, that change must prevail in the design model.
3. *Decision level: additional custom constraints for a particular decision.*
   Constraints in this level are specific for decisions and do not necessarily relate to model differences. They are specified manually by the developer during design-time.
   Example: the classes *Controller* and *SessionObject* must be located in the same package in the design model.

Constraints for the first two levels are static—we defined them once and for all. Custom constraints (decision level), on the other hand, can be specified by the developer and concern individual decision-related properties in the design model. Two examples from the element and the change level follow. We use the *Object Constraint Language* (OCL) [14] to define them as invariants.

**Constraints Excerpts.** The element level contains exactly the three invariants shown in Listing 1. They apply to all *ModelElementBinding*s (**context**) and ensure that the correct number of design model elements is bound. The cardinality is defined in the attributes *lowerBound* and *upperBound* of the class *ModelChange* (cf. binding definition in Fig. 8) and is checked in lines 4–5. The third invariant (line 8) checks that all referenced design model elements are defined which includes the check that added elements prevail in the design model.

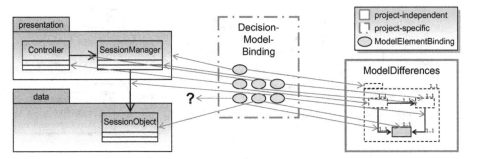

**Fig. 9.** Example scenario with constraint violations

```
1   context ModelElementBinding
2
3   -- the binding contains links to the correct number of model elements
4   inv lowerBound: modelChange.lowerBound <= modelElements->size()
5   inv upperBound: modelChange.upperBound >= modelElements->size()
6
7   -- all model elements exist and are defined
8   inv modelElements: modelElements->forAll(e | not e.oclIsUndefined())
```

**Listing 1.** Three constraints for the element level (severity: error)

In contrast to the element level, change level constraints check design model-specific properties, for instance whether a class is abstract or not. Thus, the constraints have to access properties which are design model specific. The constraint in Listing 2 checks whether added elements are contained in their expected containers. It uses the reflective call container()[1] (line 6) to retrieve the actual container and compares it with the expected value *AddElementModelChange.parent* (cf. metamodel in Fig. 4) in line 7. The invariant is only relevant for *AddedElementModelChange*s, hence the implication in line 5.

```
1   context ModelElementBinding
2
3   -- all added elements are contained in the expected parent
4   inv addedElementContainedInExpectedParent:
5     modelChange.oclIsTypeOf(diff::AddElementModelChange) implies
6       modelElements->forAll(e | e.container() =
7         modelChange.oclAsType(diff::AddElementModelChange).parent)
```

**Listing 2.** A constraint for the change level (severity: warning)

**Example.** The following example illustrates the consistency check. The left-hand side of Fig. 9 shows a modified design model: *SessionObject* was moved to another package and the association between *Controller* and *SessionObject* was removed. Consequently, not all design model changes induced by the design decision *Session Management* prevail. Using the constraints, we can automatically detect these violations: the upper and lower bounds of each *ModelChange* (denoted with *1..1* for model changes in Fig. 9) match the number of referenced

---

[1] This constraint requires an EMOF-compliant [8] metamodel because EMOF provides facilities for reflection like the operation container() : ModelElement.

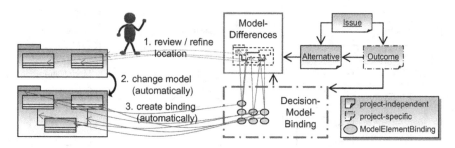

**Fig. 10.** Reusing Design Decisions by applying model differences

design model elements, so we are safe here. However, one *ModelElementBinding* has a dangling reference, i.e. it points to a design model element that does not exist anymore (invariant in line 8 of Listing 1). This violation is presented to the developer with the severity *error*. Moreover, the parent for the added element *SessionObject* differs from the one defined in the model change (invariant in Listing 2). This violation, in contrast, is presented with the severity *warning* because the added element still exists.

These constraints ensure that for each design decision all relevant design model elements exist (element level) and that all changes prevail in the design model (change level). Hence, it is now automatically possible to verify that design decisions are realized in the design model (Goal: Consistency).

### 4.4   Reusing Design Decisions

Up to now, we defined the binding and explained its use for consistency checking. The question is how to create these bindings. Similar to having the design knowledge already predefined in some decision management system, we assume that the model differences representing design model changes have been created and attached to an alternative in advance. At this point, one can think of these model differences as a design template extracted from a sample model, a previous project, or a pattern repository.

Next, we explain how a binding is created as a result of a made design decision (sketched in Fig. 10). Once the decision *Session Management* is made, i.e. the developer selects a particular alternative, she/he chooses one of the attached realizations (in form of model differences):

1. The developer has to review/refine the location for applying the changes to the design model. In the example, the package *presentation* and the two classes *Controller* and *SessionManager* must be selected.
2. The design model is (automatically) changed according to the model differences. As for any automatic step, it is recommended to review all changes.
3. Then the binding is (automatically) created and contains one *ModelElement-Binding* for each changed design model element.

Overall, the only manual work for realizing a design decision in the design model is to define the correct location where to apply the design model changes and to review them afterwards (instead of manually changing the design model). The binding can then be used for the goals *Documentation* and *Consistency Checking*.

## 5 Realization

This section gives some insight into the realization (architecture and some parts of the GUI) of our prototype. All concepts presented in Sect. 4 are implemented.

**Architecture.** Here we briefly outline the architecture of the prototype. We have chosen Eclipse as the base platform because many technologies already exist for reuse and because it is easily extendable. Figure 11 informally sketches the dependencies between used and new components. Their purpose in the prototype is explained on the website `http://imm.dtu.dk/~pk/decisions`.

One can easily see that the component setup conforms to the binding definition in Fig. 8. We decided to keep the *Difference Binding* and the *Decision Binding* separate because the *Difference Binding* is independent of any design decision—it can be stored after applying model differences to a model and can also be exploited for other things, for instance, model synchronization.

In order to create the binding, we extended the algorithm for difference application in the component *Model Differencing*. The extension is straightforward: every time a change is made to the design model, e.g. an element was added or moved, corresponding *ElementBinding*s (cf. Fig. 8) are created.

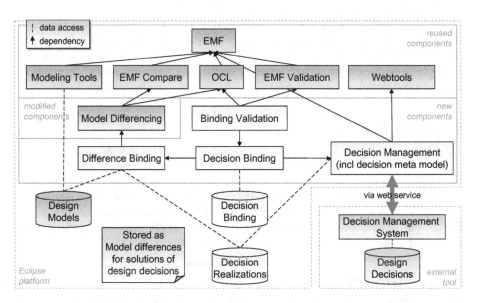

**Fig. 11.** The architecture of the prototype

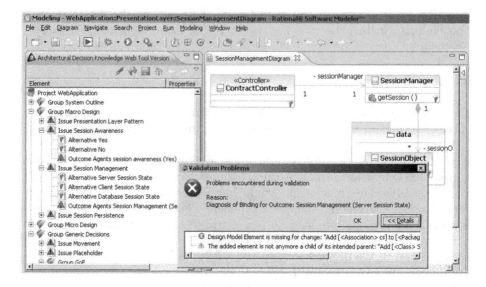

**Fig. 12.** Design Decision view and validation results

**User Interface.** This section sketches the realization of the user interface for the presentation of design decisions within Eclipse and for consistency checking.

The left-hand side of Fig. 12 shows all design decisions of the current project in the design decision view. Actions are available for browsing through design decisions, creating new, or modifying existing decisions.

The right-hand side of Fig. 12 shows a dialog as the result of a consistency check of the bindings between the design decisions shown on the left and the design model on the right. The dialog shows the same two violations from the example in Sect. 4.3 with their severity (error and warning) and a description. The affected design model elements are also marked in the graphical editor.

## 6 Related Work

There are many tools for documenting decisions and capturing architectural knowledge. None of the existing research prototypes and commercial tools provides the integration between design decisions and design models we motivated and specified in a previous publication [15] and in previous sections of this paper. Hence, our documentation goal has only been partially met so far; the consistency and reuse goals have not been addressed sufficiently yet.

**Documentation Goal.** There are several systems and approaches which support developers in capturing and making decisions during a software development process. ADDSS [5], for instance, is a web-based tool to collect and store architectural knowledge including, but not limited to, architectural decisions.

ADDSS supports after-the-fact decision capturing; the captured information can be studied retrospectively, for instance on a subsequent project phase or different project. However, ADDSS does not support a tight, use case-driven design model integration such as the one we introduced in the previous sections. For instance, it is not possible to create outcome instances via the modeling tool to record the rationale behind a design model change while or immediately after performing the change. To do so, it is required to switch to the decision management tool.

AREL [16] is another system for the documentation of architectural decisions based on their rationale. It specifies a UML profile for modeling architectural design decision rationale and traces them back to the architectural elements; a single tool can be used to work with UML design models and with design decisions. However, AREL does not allow the user to capture and reuse changes in the design models, and to synchronize this information with decision decisions on the fly; these two artifacts merely coexist in the tool.

The Architectural Decision Knowledge Web Tool (formerly known as Architectural Decision Knowledge Wiki) [11], which we extended in our prototype, allows architects to capture, store, and share design rationale. Its base version supports the user in making and reusing decisions but does not integrate design decisions with design models. This support is provided by the prototype described in Sect. 5.

Other tools [17,18] have similar characteristics as the ones discussed so far.

**Consistency Goal.** The consistency goal is not met by any of the existing research prototypes; ensuring consistency remains a manual task. In practice, informal, human-centric techniques such as coaching, architectural templates, and code reviews dominate. For instance, software engineering processes like RUP [19] advise architects to enforce decisions by refining the design in small and therefore actionable increments. The agile community emphasizes the importance of face-to-face communication and team empowerment [20]. Maturity models such as the Capability Maturity Model Integration[2] recommend rigid approaches to ensure that decision outcome materializes, e.g., formal reviews. Applying these techniques takes time and their success depends on the architects' coding and leadership skills.

We are not aware of any model-based software development tools that respect design decisions. OpenArchitectureWare[3] is a framework for model-driven development allowing the developer to define and use model transformations. However, architectural decisions are not a genuine modeling concept in OpenArchitectureWare. Modeling tools like the IBM Rational Software Modeler[4] and Borland Together[5] provide pattern authoring capabilities which are similar to the intention of the realizations of design decisions. However, a metamodel for expressing relations between them as well as tool supported guidance, i.e. proposing

---

[2] Available at: http://www.sei.cmu.edu/cmmi/
[3] Available at: http://www.openarchitectureware.org
[4] Available at: http://www.ibm.com/software/awdtools/modeler/swmodeler/
[5] Available at: http://www.borland.com/us/products/together/

subsequent patterns, is missing. Other commercial modeling tools allow the user to make simple decisions, for instance regarding model element naming, but use fixed defaults for architectural concerns, e.g. system transaction management boundaries [21]. Consequently, development resources have to be invested to change the defaults to the settings required in a particular application design and implementation.

**Design Decision Reuse Goal.** In the past, the design decision rationale and architectural knowledge communities have focused on documenting decisions that have already been made (following a retrospective, after-the-fact decision capturing approach). As a consequence, there is no notion of reusing knowledge about decisions required (i.e., issues and alternatives); few concepts exist for bringing required decisions into the original design process or into the model-driven development transformation chain. For instance, ADDSS and AREL do not support a reuse strategy which automatically updates the design models according to a decision made. In our previous work, we have developed a framework for architectural decision modeling with reuse which includes an explicit decision enforcement step [6]. The integration concepts introduced in this paper provide an advanced, partially automated form of decision enforcement for the framework.

# 7    Conclusion and Future Work

In this paper, we presented concepts for connecting design models in model-based software development with semi-formal design knowledge (design decisions) to automate tedious and error-prone, recurring work. The proposed concepts make use of existing technologies (decision management systems and model differences) and introduce a formal binding between design models, design decisions, and model differences. We defined three goals for our contributions: easier documentation is achieved by exploiting the binding and showing the information in an additional view; consistency checking is achieved by validating formal constraints on bindings; reuse of design decisions is partially automated by attaching design model changes to solutions of design issues.

The concepts are implemented in a prototype[6] and its technical feasibility is proven with a case study [7]. Decision reuse has been validated in our previous work [6,21]. Moreover, we evaluated reuse of model differences with all 23 design patterns from [4] and 25 refactorings from [22] (the other refactorings are not applicable to UML models): 8 design patterns and 14 refactorings are generically applicable right away. Although the other 15 design patterns are also applicable, they rather produce a draft which must be adjusted. The other 11 refactorings are not applicable generically because the current prototype only allows to reuse precisely those realizations which have been made before. In other words, if the design model does not contain the context specified in the model differences,

---

[6] Information about the prototype is available at `http://imm.dtu.dk/~pk/decisions`

that particular realization cannot be used. Work in progress is a generalization of model differences which aims to overcome this problem. Moreover, we demonstrated the prototype to leading software architects and developers of a commercial modeling platform. An evaluation on a real project is in preparation.

Future work includes to improve the presentation of the consistency check results and to exploit causal relations between design decisions to propose subsequent decisions—e.g. via the relation *induces* in Fig. 1.

# References

1. Object Management Group: UML Superstructure, V2.2 (November 2007)
2. Object Management Group: MDA Guide V1.0.1 (June 2003)
3. Nowak, M., Pautasso, C., Zimmermann, O.: Architectural Decision Modeling with Reuse: Challenges and Opportunities. In: 5th SHARK, South Africa (May 2010)
4. Gamma, E., Helm, R., Johnson, R., Vlissides, J.: Design Patterns: Elements of Reusable Object-Oriented Software. Addison-Wesley, Reading (January 1995)
5. Capilla, R., Nava, F., Duenas, J.C.: Modeling and Documenting the Evolution of Architectural Design Decisions. In: 2nd SHARK-ADI, Minneapolis, USA, pp. 9–15. IEEE Computer Society, Los Alamitos (May 2007)
6. Zimmermann, O.: An Architectural Decision Modeling Framework for Service-Oriented Architecture Design. Dissertation, University of Stuttgart (2009)
7. Könemann, P.: Integrating a Design Decision Management System with a UML Modeling Tool. IMM-Technical Report-2009-07, Technical University of Denmark (April 2009)
8. Object Management Group: MOF Core Specification, Version 2.0 (January 2006)
9. Fowler, M.: Patterns of Enterprise Application Architecture. Addison Wesley, Reading (November 2002)
10. Shahin, M., Liang, P., Khayyambashi, M.R.: Architectural Design Decision: Existing Models and Tools. In: WICSA/ECSA Working Session. IEEE Computer Society, Los Alamitos (September 2009)
11. Zimmermann, O., Gschwind, T., Küster, J.M., Leymann, F., Schuster, N.: Reusable Architectural Decision Models for Enterprise Application Development. In: Overhage, S., Szyperski, C., Reussner, R., Stafford, J.A. (eds.) QoSA 2007. LNCS, vol. 4880, pp. 15–32. Springer, Heidelberg (2008)
12. Förtsch, S., Westfechtel, B.: Differencing and Merging of Software Diagrams–State of the Art and Challenges. In: ICSOFT, Setubal, Portugal, pp. 90–99 (July 2007)
13. Könemann, P.: Model-independent Differences. In: ICSE Workshop on Comparison and Versioning of Software Models, pp. 37–42. IEEE Computer Society, Los Alamitos (May 2009)
14. Object Management Group: OCL Specification, Version 2.0 (May 2006)
15. Könemann, P.: Integrating Decision Management with UML Modeling Concepts and Tools. In: WICSA/ECSA Working Session. IEEE Computer Society, Los Alamitos (September 2009)
16. Tang, A., Jin, Y., Han, J.: A Rationale-based Architecture Model for Design Traceability and Reasoning. Journal of Systems and Software 80(6), 918–934 (2007)
17. Bachmann, F., Merson, P.: Experience Using the Web-Based Tool Wiki for Architecture Documentation. Technical Report CMU/SEI-2005-TN-041, Carnegie Mellon University, Software Engineering Institute (September 2005)

18. Liang, P., Jansen, A., Avgeriou, P.: Knowledge Architect: A Tool Suite for Managing Software Architecture Knowledge. Technical Report RUG-SEARCH-09-L01, University of Groningen (February 2009)
19. Kruchten, P.: The Rational Unified Process: An Introduction. Addison-Wesley, Reading (2003)
20. Beck, K.: Extreme Programming Explained: Embrace Change. Addison-Wesley, Reading (1999)
21. Zimmermann, O., Grundler, J., Tai, S., Leymann, F.: Architectural Decisions and Patterns for Transactional Workflows in SOA. In: Krämer, B.J., Lin, K.-J., Narasimhan, P. (eds.) ICSOC 2007. LNCS, vol. 4749, pp. 81–93. Springer, Heidelberg (2007)
22. Fowler, M.: Refactoring: Improving the Design of Existing Code. In: Object Technology Series. Addison-Wesley, Reading (June 1999)

# Customer Value in Architecture Decision Making

Ana Ivanović and Pierre America

Philips Research, High Tech Campus 37
5656 AE Eindhoven, The Netherlands
{Ana.Ivanovic,Pierre.America}@philips.com

**Abstract.** This paper focuses on the business aspects of architecture decision making – in particular how to quantify the customer value of quality improvements to support architecture investment decisions. We developed concepts for quantifying the impact of quality improvements on customer value, customer value-in-use, and customer segments. In two real-life case studies we present (1) how the concept for quantifying customer value was used, (2) how the customer value relates to the existing value indicators in the organization, and (3) how the importance of customer value for architecture decision making was assessed by practitioners in the organization.

**Keywords:** architecture investment, decision making, customer value.

## 1 Introduction

The aim of any architecture improvement is fulfilling quality attribute requirements aligned with the business goals [1]. Since implementing such an improvement typically requires a large investment of time and effort, an organization that makes an architecture decision wants to be confident that the value created justifies the investment. The existing approaches for supporting architecture investment decisions focus on proposing business cases [2] based on cost savings, e.g., in product lines [3-5], or quantified benefits of quality attributes [6] to justify the architecture investments.

According to Kotler and Keller [7] the task of any business is to deliver customer value at profit. This becomes also apparent in an increasing number of organizations that follow a market-differentiation strategy to satisfy customers' needs and create the value derived from the customer benefits. In such circumstances the old economy model organized by product units, focused on profitability and transactions, looking primarily at financial scorecards is shifting to the new economy model organized by customer segments, focused on customer life-time value, and looking at marketing scorecards [7].

Therefore, any approach for supporting architecture investment decisions will need to incorporate the customer value to adapt to the new economy model. The most used concept of customer value refers to the to the price customer is willing to pay for a product offering in terms of the set of perceived benefits that the product offering provides to the customer. In the context of this paper, we broaden this definition to the value that drives decisions about product development and modification, pricing, and

M. Ali Babar and I. Gorton (Eds.): ECSA 2010, LNCS 6285, pp. 263–278, 2010.
© Springer-Verlag Berlin Heidelberg 2010

marketing communication. The literature refers to market scoping [8] or coarse benefit functions for assessing the market benefits [4] as examples of using customer value in architecture decision making. These models are primarily used in making business cases and do not include structured guidelines on how to determine and quantify the customer value of the quality improvements.

To accommodate the existing approaches and at the same time satisfy the urgent need for making the customer value explicit in decision making, we address the question: *How to quantify the customer value of quality improvements to support architecture decision making in practice?*

To answer this question, we propose to use the well-known marketing concepts customer value-in-use and customer segments [7] in the architecture context. Depending on the business goal of the architecture improvements, these concepts can be used alone or together to estimate the customer value. In two real-life case studies, we applied these concepts for quantifying the customer value derived from architecture improvements in the imaging systems organization in Philips Healthcare [9]. The customer value concepts were compared to the existing value indicators in the organization and evaluated by decision makers.

The rest of this paper is organized as follows. Section 2 describes the study design that we have used for conducting research. Section 3 describes the first study for quantifying the customer value–in-use. Section 4 describes the second study for quantifying customer segments. Finally, Section 5 elaborates on applicability of the customer value in architecture decision making in practice and concludes with recommendations for improvements.

## 2  Methodology

We have been conducting a large-scale study[1] in cooperation with Philips Healthcare [9] to support architecture decision making aligned with a customer-centric and market-driven strategy. During the last four years we have conducted several real-life case studies realizing that the economics of architecture is necessary but not sufficient for architecture decision making [10] and further improvements should propose linking quality improvements to customer value indicators explicitly [11].

Because so far in the literature little attention has been paid to quantifying the customer value of architecture and our aim was a practice-oriented approach, the descriptive practice-oriented case study [12] was chosen as the appropriate research strategy for this investigation. We used a step-by-step process for conducting our case studies as shown in Figure 1.

The first step proposes a concept to quantify the customer value by adopting established marketing techniques to the architecture context. We elaborate on this step in each study in more detail.

The second step focuses on selecting the case. We selected the cases in which the quality improvements were directly observable by the customers and were the main

[1] This work has been carried out as a part of the Darwin project at Philips Healthcare under the responsibility of the Embedded Systems Institute. This project is partially supported by the Dutch Ministry of Economic Affairs under the BSIK program.

drivers of customer value creation (rather than the introduction of new functionality). With the fact that the quality/price ratio rather than price is the main determinant of the purchase decision in the professional (business-to-business) market, we deliberately selected the architecture decision making cases from the professional market.

The third step focuses on collecting the data to identify the existing value indicators used in the organization and to quantify the customer value using the proposed concept. In this step we also collected the time spent on quantifying the customer value, which is relevant for the evaluation session.

The fourth step is about analyzing data by comparing the elicited customer value with the existing value indicators. According to Rogers [13] any change in the organization can only be accepted if it is based on small incremental changes. Thus, understanding the relation between the customer value and the existing value indicators in the organization can help us to better understand the acceptance of the customer value concept for decision making in the organization.

Finally, the concept of quantifying customer value was evaluated with respect to the cost involved in collecting the data and the importance of the quantified customer value in architecture decision making in practice. The evaluation was done by initiating and observing a discussion between business decisions makers about the study findings at an hour review meeting. The two authors of the paper shadowed the discussion and cross-checked their observations immediately after the meeting.

We envision that improvements of each concept require repeating the study. Since this study focuses on how and whether customer value can be used, we decided to conduct a single case study for each customer value concept.

The two case studies following this study design were conducted in Philips Healthcare using internal and external documentation, interviews, meetings, and observations as the main source of evidence.

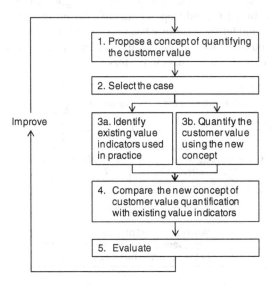

**Fig. 1.** Study design

## 3   Study 1: Customer Value-in-Use

A state-of-practice study about customer value assessment in business markets high-lights that business decisions about product modification and redesign apply different techniques such as internal engineering assessment, field value-in-use assessment, focus group value assessment, or importance rating [14]. Among those techniques, the value-in-use assessment was the most frequently used technique for supporting new investments. Therefore, we selected value-in-use as a suitable technique for architecture decision making. Adapted to the scope of our study we define the value-in-use as differential cash flow generated in using the product with improved quality in the customer business.

Knowing the customer-value-in-use would offer a twofold benefit to the organization. First, the value-in-use can be used to demonstrate the added value of the new product with quality improvements to the customer and as a value indicator for the architecture. Second, the value-in-use can be used to estimate the customer's willingness to pay for such improvements, and therefore to define the potential cash flow of quality improvements that can be compared to the architecture investment.

In this study we investigate *how the customer value-in-use of quality improvements can be quantified and used in architecture decision making.*

### 3.1   Step 1: Concept of Quantifying Customer Value-in-Use

To quantify the customer value-in-use we need to understand the customer business, in particular how the quality improvements impact the business indicators in the customer business. We propose the concept for quantifying the value-in-use of quality improvements in Figure 2.

In the first step, we identify the customer business goals in the context of using a particular product. In the second step, we identify the business indicators in the customer business and model the customer business to better understand how the product in use affects the business indicators. Finally, we analyze conceptually the impact of quality improvements on the business indicators.

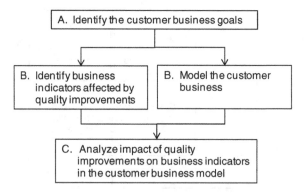

**Fig. 2.** Concept: Customer value-in-use

## 3.2  Step 2: Explorer Case[2]

*Explorer* is a workstation consisting of dedicated hardware and clinical applications used for viewing medical images acquired by a scanner and post-processing of these images to support radiologists and cardiologists in making a diagnosis.

Using Explorer in a hospital can take up an hour per patient. One of the reasons is that the user needs to delineate manually up to 3,500 myocardial contours to make a diagnosis. Therefore, although Explorer was proven to be clinically beneficial, it has been used mainly for research purposes by academic hospitals and rarely for routine use in community hospitals where the throughput has the highest priority.

Philips Healthcare, in cooperation with clinical partners, decided to do an architecture redesign to improve the usability and simplify the use of Explorer [15]. No new clinical application areas were added. The usability redesign involved (1) minimizing the amount of interaction needed for post-processing, through judicious use of automation and (2) introducing new viewing protocols that better reflect the users' way of working. The validation study of the redesign in a laboratory setting has shown significant efficiency improvements described in more detail in the following section. Despite strong evidence that the quality improvements were significant, the main question in the business was whether such improvements make a difference once the product is in use in hospital.

We were asked to assess the value-in-use of usability improvements in the BEST hospital. BEST was selected as a preferred customer of Philips Healthcare because of the strong cooperation and the most efficient use of Explorer in a clinical workflow among all customers. Thus, if the customer value-in-use would show sufficient contribution to the BEST business, all other hospitals would have higher benefits of using Explorer with improved usability.

The study question was *how usability improvements impact the customer business when Explorer is being used in hospitals.* This study was conducted using several sources of evidence, such as scientific publications, internal documentation, expert interviews, and observing users while working with Explorer in the BEST hospital.

## 3.3  Step 3: Data Collection

This step involves two activities: (1) to identify existing value indicators used in the organization in the given case and (2) to quantify the customer value-in-use applying the concept proposed in Section 3.1.

### 3.3.1  Existing Value Indicators
As we have seen, automation in image post-processing and the new viewing protocol were the two main improvements in Explorer. The value of these improvements was assessed using technology assessment techniques and expert opinion.

**Technology assessment.** The validation study in a lab setting had shown that users need significantly less time to verify and correct fully automatically detected contours

---

[2] The major identifying details for this case, such as product name and hospital name have been replaced with pseudonyms for confidentiality reasons.

than they need for drawing these contours manually in the four main procedures as shown in Table 1 [15].

**Table 1.** Time required delineating an exam manually and with automation

|  | Images | Contours | Manual (minutes) | Auto (minutes) |
|---|---|---|---|---|
| Procedure 1 | 500 | 1500 | 90 | 5 |
| Procedure 2 | 420 | 6 | 6 | 3 |
| Procedure 3 | 20 | 40 | 10 | 1 |
| Procedure 4 | 600 | 1800 | 120 | 10 |

**Expert opinion.** Furthermore, the senior doctor from the BEST hospital estimated that new viewing protocols will result in time gains in the clinical workflow:

- o   10-15% for experienced cardiologists
- o   50-60% for novice cardiologists

Thus, the efficiency improvement in the procedure completion from the technology assessment and the experts' first order estimates about productivity improvements were the two value indicators used for demonstrating the value of usability improvements of Explorer in the organization.

### 3.3.2  Customer Value-in-Use

In the Explorer case the main quality improvements were in usability. To identify usability measures we used the established concept of measuring usability in context obtained by measuring the user's satisfaction, effectiveness, and efficiency [16]. In the Explorer case most benefits were expected in the efficiency improvements, therefore we simplify our investigation to understand the impact of Explorer efficiency improvements in the BEST hospital business. Further, we will follow the concept of quantifying the customer-value-in-use presented in Figure 2.

**A. Identify customer business goals.** To identify the BEST business goals we interviewed the head of the cardiology department. The global trend of improving quality of care and reducing cost was also apparent in BEST. The quality of care improvements are seen in reducing the patient waiting list with increased productivity to gain enough time for making an additional exam per day. Such an improvement would also affect the BEST business as each exam would be reimbursed for about € 800.

To achieve the business goal of increasing the number of exams, the most urgent issue in the department was to shorten the time needed from the scan start to the final report without compromising the quality of image analysis. To get an overview of the current business in BEST at the moment of the study: Yearly 2000 imaging exams were performed per scanner with an average time from scan start to report ready of 15-25 minutes.

**B. Identify business indicators and model the customer business.** From the interview with the department head we learned that examination volume per modality was the main business indicator monitored regularly in BEST. That agrees with the literature about the most frequently used productivity indicators [17].

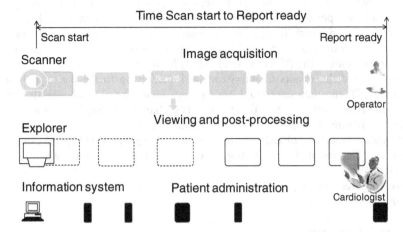

**Fig. 3.** Explorer in the clinical workflow in BEST hospital

To understand how Explorer is used we shadowed an experienced cardiologist in the clinical workflow. We identified three parallel activities in the clinical workflow: Image acquisition from the scanner, image viewing and post-processing using Explorer, and patient administration done on the cardiology information system, see Figure 3.

We model the clinical workflow as time spent on parallel activities (rectangles) in the hospital to address the potential contribution of usability improvements of Explorer towards minimizing the time from the scan start to report ready, therefore towards achieving the customer business goal. The clinical workflow can be described as follows. The image acquisition begins with "scan start" initiated from the console by the operator, who is sitting next to the cardiologist. It takes some time until the acquired images are available for viewing and post-processing on Explorer. That gap time the cardiologist usually uses for checking old exams (dashed rectangles) or administrating patient data on the information system such as writing a report (black rectangles). Once the scan is available at Explorer the cardiologist starts viewing and post-processing images. If he notices some irregularity in the images, he might request from the operator to repeat the image acquisition or look at the console to help the operator to define the right acquisition parameters. We observed that the ends of all three activities, image acquisition, image viewing and post-procession, and reporting almost coincide. When the patient leaves the scan room the report is ready. Typically, this clinical workflow will be followed for all routine exams. In such a highly-efficient workflow, improvements in efficiency of image viewing and post-processing during scanning were critical to shorten the scan start to report ready time, in order to fit in another exam.

**C. Analyze the impact of quality improvements.** We analyzed the different exams in the clinical workflow to identify when and how usability improvements of Explorer would achieve the most time gain. We realized that different exams in the exam portfolio benefit differently from usability improvements. Regarding viewing improvements, all exams would benefit from a time saving of 1.5 minutes in average. On the other side, automation improvements would make a significant contribution only to one exam, which was performed every second day and the gain would be approximately 7 minutes per exam considering the technology assessment of task efficiency improvements in Section 3.3.1. In other exams delineation was performed rarely or never because of the tedious manual work. Thus, automation would not make significant improvements in the BEST hospital except for the one exam type.

We presented the results of interviews and shadowing to the participants in the study in BEST and they confirmed our findings about the clinical workflow model and productivity improvements due to usability changes of Explorer. Since the 1.5 minutes improvements were too short to schedule the new exam, only the automation improvements were considered for potential scheduling of an additional exam every second day. This resulted in 2 additional exams for 50 weeks amounting to the value of 80K€ per year.

This study required 1 person-month for a researcher to quantify the customer value-in-use.

### 3.4  Step 4: Comparison

We realized that the expert opinion about productivity improvements (10-15%) for the new viewing protocol closely relates to the estimated time savings in the clinical workflow (1.5 minutes in the 15-25 minutes exam). On the other side, estimates about task efficiency of automation (see Table 1) in the lab setting did not relate directly to the improvements in clinical practice. This difference can be explained with the fact that procedures which required manual delineation of many contours were used only a few times, therefore automation improvements would not be observed directly in the existing clinical workflow. Nevertheless, once the automation becomes available the cardiologist may start using these procedures more frequently.

Furthermore, we can conclude that the task efficiency and expert opinion indicators have to be correlated to the real-life clinical workflow to understand the potential customer value created in a real-life setting. The concept of quantifying the customer value-in-use provides this information. However, it became apparent that only by understanding the hospital workflow the relationship between usability improvement and customer value-in-use can be established.

### 3.5  Step 5: Evaluation

An evaluation of the Explorer case findings was conducted with the product marketer and a clinical scientist responsible for estimating the efficiency improvements in the organization. We presented our findings and asked the review team to discuss how the proposed framework for quantifying the customer value-in-use can possibly support the decision making process in the organization. Two themes emerged from the discussion: the cost of applying the concept of quantifying the customer value and the importance of such a concept for the organization.

Regarding the time spent on quantifying the customer value-in-use the organization has to account for an additional effort of 1 person-month if the efficiency indicators are already available. This time spent could be shorter for an expert knowing the domain or having already modeled the workflow of the hospital.

In the Explorer case the practitioners found the customer value-in-use promising and at the same time incomplete for decision making. Making the value of quality improvements in the hospital business explicit was perceived positively. However, analyzing a high diversity of hospitals and their workflows would be very labor-intensive.

Nevertheless, if improving the business of existing customer is the main strategic goal of the organization, this analysis can be used for selected representative hospitals to support the right architecture changes. Another use is envisioned in the case when quality improvements are so large that details of the hospital workflow do not impact the customer value-in-use. Then the customer value-in-use can be used generically for all hospitals and therefore become a relevant value indicator.

## 4   Study 2: Customer Segments

According to Kotler and Keller, the new economy is organized by customer segments grouping customers by their needs and their value to the organization [7]. In this section we develop the concept to link the quality improvements to the customer segments, exemplified by a real-life case and evaluated by the decision makers.

### 4.1   Step 1: Concept of Quantifying Customer Segments

The first step of analyzing any architecture investment is to identify the business goals of architecture changes, as shown in Figure 4. If the business goals involve addressing new customer segments or addressing existing segments in a new way, then it makes sense to identify the customer segments affected by the architecture changes, which is done in the second step. In the same step, several possible architecture scenarios to meet the business goals are proposed. Finally, the third step, analyses the impact of proposed quality improvements on the identified customer segments for different scenarios.

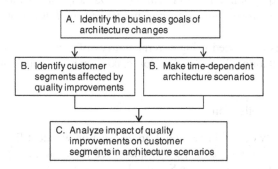

**Fig. 4.** Concept of quantifying customer segments

### 4.2   Step 2: Tricorder Case[3]

*Tricorder* is a product line consisting of dedicated hardware and clinical applications to make a diagnosis and prepare treatment. Over the last years, with an increasing market pressure to release new applications quickly, the Tricorder architecture has

---

[3] The major identifying details for this case, such as product names and data have been replaced with pseudonyms for confidentiality reasons.

been eroding, resulting in increased development effort and difficulties to predict time-to-market of new application releases. Furthermore, the newest market research about customer insights has shown opportunities for improvement in:

- *Usability:* The system should be *easier to use*; i.e. the user interfaces of the various applications should be harmonized
- *Accessibility:* The applications should be *accessible from any workplace*
- *Multi-modality:* The system should offer *viewing of images from other product lines*

To meet these challenges, it has been decided to migrate all Tricorder applications to the architecture of a successful existing product line. This decision of merging product lines was made also to strengthen the competitive advantage of Tricorder by offering applications from another product line.

The architects selected two potential architectures from existing product lines, *LabTricorder* and *ViewAll*. Regardless of the architecture choice, the marketers requested phased development to offer a few market releases of the new Tricorder to incrementally meet the customer needs during the migration. It was estimated that in both scenarios the migration process would last for two years.

At the moment of this study the business had already made the first multi-attribute ratings of scenarios and favored the LabTricorder scenario. To support this informal decision to invest in the LabTricorder scenario, the product marketer was asked to make a business case for the LabTricorder investment.

At the same time, we were asked to estimate how the customer segments will be affected by the LabTricorder and ViewAll scenarios during the migration as an input for evaluating the ongoing architecture investment decision making process. Thus, the study question was: *How will Tricorder's quality improvements impact customer segments during the migration process in the LabTricorder and ViewAll scenarios?*

This study was conducted using several sources of evidence such as internal and external documentation, observing decision making meetings, and interviewing practitioners.

### 4.3  Step 3: Data Collection

Following our study design in Section 2, in this section we identified value indicators used for modeling the business case and quantified the customer segments using the customer value concept proposed in Section 4.1.

#### 4.3.1  Existing Value Indicators

As we already mentioned the business case was made only for the LabTricorder scenario conforming to the informal decision that has already been made. The total sales of the LabTricorder and Tricorder product was used for estimating the present value (PV) of the difference in the cash flow facilitated with migrating to the LabTricorder or keeping the existing Tricorder architecture over four years as shown in Figure 5. The positive business case confirmed the LabTricorder informal decision.

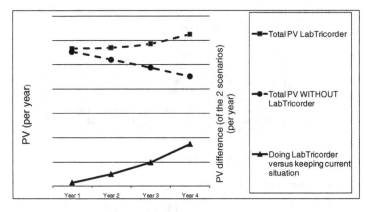

**Fig. 5.** Present value difference upon introduction of Tricorder

### 4.3.2 Customer Segments
Although the decision to invest in the LabTricorder scenario was already made, it was not clear to decision makers how the quality improvements made a difference in generating the customer value in the LabTricorder and ViewAll scenarios.

**A. Identify the business goals of the architecture changes.** In multiple one-to-one interviews with the program manager of Tricorder, the system architect, and product marketer we spent a significant time to identify the business goal. We realized that the Tricorder project had a large impact across several business units resulting in diverse business incentives of the project such as quicker time-to-market, improved maintenance by reducing the number of lines of codes, meeting customer needs, and improving customer satisfaction. Finally, a consensus was reached on the business goal to *increase the number of customers with met imaging needs,* including not only Tricorder customers but also customers using LabTricorder or ViewAll.

**B. Identify customer segments and architecture scenarios.** Based on the business goals we identified two customer segments that would be affected by the architecture changes (shown in Figure 6).

As expected, the Tricorder customers would benefit from access to the applications from anywhere and from the harmonized user interface. At the same time LabTricorder or ViewAll customers would benefit from being able to use Tricorder applications on their respective products. Thus, we needed to understand the impact of the quality improvements on the number of Tricorder and LabTricorder/ViewAll customers in meeting their imaging needs in different scenarios.

Since the marketer requested phased development to maximize the customer value before all applications are migrated to the new architecture, we needed to make two time-dependent scenarios to understand how customer segments would be affected by the products offered in different phases. We interviewed 20 stakeholders involved in this project and read product documentation to reconstruct the time-dependent LabTricorder and ViewAll scenarios shown in Figure 7.

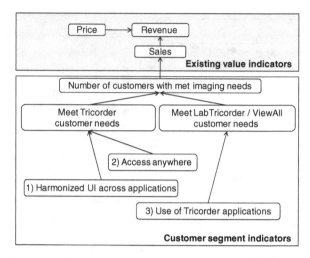

**Fig. 6.** Existing value indicators (top) and customer segments (bottom)

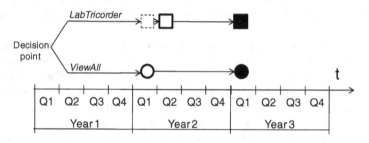

**Fig. 7.** Scenarios used for quantification of customer segments

The LabTricorder scenario was envisioned in three phases. Phase 0 (dashed square) enables viewing but not post-processing of all Tricorder images on the LabTricorder platform in a year. Phase 1 (square) offers a few Tricorder applications with harmonized user interface while the remaining applications would be still available on the existing Tricorder in the next quarter. Finally, in Phase 2 (filled square) the remaining Tricorder applications would be available on the LabTricorder architecture in the two years from the moment of this study. All applications would be accessible from any PC in the hospital (thin client).

The ViewAll scenario was envisioned in two phases. Phase 1 (circle) enables migration of all Tricorder applications to the ViewAll architecture in a year. Tricorder would not be available on the market anymore. In Phase 2 (filled circle), the Tricorder applications can be used on multiple dedicated hardware terminals (thick client) in two years. The Tricorder applications become available for ViewAll customers.

**C. Analyze the impact of quality improvements on customer segments in architecture scenarios.** As we have seen, in both scenarios the customer needs are met but with different solutions (thin vs. thick client) and different timing of releases (phases), which satisfy different customer segments. To quantify the customers whose imaging needs are met we used sales of Tricorder and LabTricorder/ViewAll products from the previous year as proxies for number of customers, see Table 2.

**Table 2.** Number of customers with met imaging needs over time in LabTricorder and ViewAll scenarios

| LabTricroder scenario | | | | | | | | | |
|---|---|---|---|---|---|---|---|---|---|
| | | Phase 0 | Phase 1 | | | Phase 2 | | | |
| | Y0 | ↓ | ↓ Year 1 | | | ↓ | | Year 2 | |
| Segmented customers | Q4 | Q1 | Q2 | Q3 | Q4 | Q1 | Q2 | Q3 | Q4 |
| Tricorder | 66 | 68 | 75 | 75 | 77 | 79 | 80 | 80 | 80 |
| LabTricorder | 30 | 34 | 34 | 34 | 34 | 34 | 34 | 34 | 34 |
| Total | 96 | 102 | 109 | 109 | 111 | 113 | 114 | 114 | 114 |
| **View All scenario** | | | | | | | | | |
| Tricorder | 66 | 66 | 69 | 71 | 71 | 71 | 72 | 73 | 73 |
| ViewAll | 38 | 38 | 38 | 38 | 38 | 40 | 40 | 40 | 40 |
| Total | 104 | 104 | 107 | 109 | 109 | 111 | 112 | 113 | 113 |

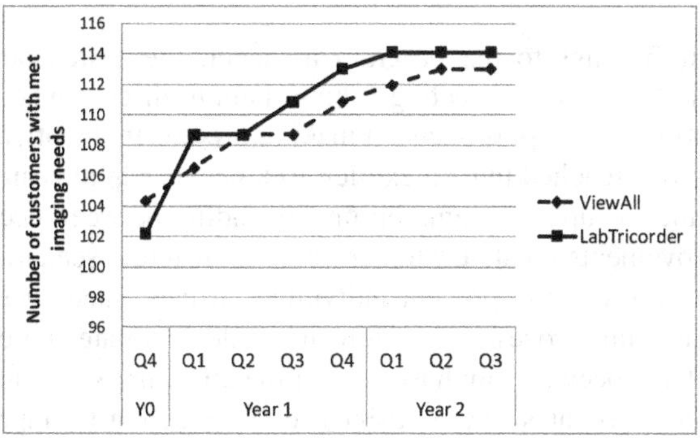


**Fig. 8.** Total number of customers whose imaging needs are met over time

The estimates were made by the architect, who corrected the individual quarterly sales using information from Figure 6 and Figure 7, resulting in the total number of customers whose imaging needs are met in both scenarios (see Figure 8).

The total effort to quantify the customer segments affected by the architecture changes was 3 person-month for a researcher.

### 4.4 Step 4: Comparison

According to Figure 8, the LabTricorder scenario offers a higher number of customers whose imaging needs are met, averaged over the in migration period. That can be used as a value indicator for the LabTricorder investment, which was consistent with the business case analysis. With the fact that the organization estimated only the present value for the business case in the LabTricorder scenario, we compared the customer segment analysis and the present value in the LabTricorder scenario resulting in the following observations:

- The customer segments analysis did not consider the negative effect on meeting the customers' needs if the investment were not made
- The customers with met imaging needs estimates were estimated only during the migration process without considering the long-term effect that was the part of our assignment
- The increase of the number of customers with met imaging needs (Figure 8) is related to the increase in the present value generated in the LabTricorder scenario in the first two years (Figure 5).
- The maximum number of customers with met imaging needs was a predictor of making a decision in favor of the LabTricorder scenario (Figure 8) that was aligned with the business case findings

As we have seen large similarities between the concept of customer segments and present value used for making the business cases, we expect that customer segments can be used in architecture decision making.

### 4.5  Evaluation

We presented our findings to the program manager, the system architect, and the marketers in a one-hour review meeting asking them to discuss whether and how the customer segments could support decision making process in the organization.

The consensus was reached that an explicit link between quality improvements and the customer segments supports common understanding between decision makers on how quality improvements create customer value in different scenarios. Furthermore, such structured analysis would prevent individual business incentives from dominating the decision making process. Therefore it would facilitate more objective decisions. The marketer especially emphasized that the customer segments analysis could be used to fine-tune estimates in the business case modeling to improve accuracy of the existing data. Regarding the time spent for collecting the data, the practitioners were not concerned as they envision that quantifying customer segments would be part of the existing business case modeling process, so this time would pay off and even potentially shorten the whole decision process.

Although the importance of customer segments was recognized the practitioners still wished to translate quality improvements directly to the financial (sales) data to have a direct comparison of the monetary value to the architecture investments to support architecture decision making.

## 5  Discussion and Conclusion

In this paper we proposed the two concepts of quantifying customer value for particular customer-centric business strategies and we applied these concepts in real-life architecture decision making projects.

We made two main observations about the proposed concepts. First, the proposed customer value concepts increased understanding on how quality improvements contribute to the customer value creation. Second, the proposed customer value concepts established more suitable input for architecture decision making than the existing value indicators in the organization.

Regarding the first observation, it became apparent that a systematic approach of quantifying customer value helped the practitioners to discuss the architecture changes in the context of customer value. We also realized that understanding and acceptance of the customer segment concept (Tricorder case) was higher than the customer value-in-use concept (Explorer case). This can be explained with the fact that the customer segment concept was closer to the business case concept already used in the organization, which is consistent with the diffusion of innovation theory stating that people are only able to accept small incremental changes [13].

In the second observation, it became apparent that the proposed customer value concept was better tailored to the architecture decision making than the existing indicators in the organization. In the Explorer case, the technology assessment of efficiency did not provide the sufficient knowledge of the hospital's actual usage of Explorer; therefore the architecture redesign could be overlooking the main customer needs reflected in the value-in-use. This observation is consistent with findings about low percentage of judged success using technology assessments in business decisions [14]. On the other side, the customer segments provided more accurate data, which can be used as fine-grained input for making the business case (Tricorder case).

With respect to the time involved in data collection, we observed that additional labor would be spent in quantifying the particular customer value only if this became important to the business strategy of the organization. For example, if the organization has the business goal to retain customers by demonstrating the value of product improvements in the customer business, value-in-use would be used.

Drawing upon the findings of our study, some ways to advance the concept of quantifying customer value can be suggested. Our results indicate that practitioners most easily accept concepts similar to their existing concepts. A challenge for researchers is to identify the practitioners' way of working and propose a customer value concept with small incremental changes compared to practice to increase acceptability of the concept. One useful approach would be to make an inventory of customer value concepts used in practice for assessing the architecture changes as a starting point in developing this research domain further.

By themselves, the studies described in this paper do not prove absolutely that quantifying customer value via these concepts really supports architecture decision making. However, confidence in our findings is increased [18] by several other case studies indicating that cost data are necessary but not sufficient for decision making [10] and that there is a need for customer-related information linked to quality attributes [11]. Furthermore, those findings suggest that customer value concepts need to be broadened to include the other concepts as well.

We conclude this paper with the proposition that quantification of customer value linked to quality improvements should be used for architecture decision making when the customer value is closely aligned with the business strategy of the organization and the time spent on data collection is acceptable.

**Acknowledgments.** We would like to thank the people at Philips Healthcare and our colleague Rob van Ommering for their comments on earlier versions of this paper.

# References

1. Bass, L., Kazman, R., Clements, P.: Software Architecture in Practice, 2nd edn. Addison Wesley, Reading (2003)
2. Boehm, B.W.: Value-Based Software Engineering: Seven Key Elements and Ethical Considerations. In: Biffl, S., Aurum, A., Boehm, B., Erdogmus, H., Grünbacher, P. (eds.) Value-Based Software Engineering. Springer, Heidelberg (2006)
3. Böckle, G., Clements, P., McGregor, J.D., Muthig, D., Schmid, K.: A Cost Model for Software Product Lines. In: van der Linden, F.J. (ed.) PFE 2003. LNCS, vol. 3014, pp. 310–316. Springer, Heidelberg (2004)
4. Clements, P., McGregor, J.D., Cohen, S.G.: The Structured Intuitive Model for Product Line Economics (SIMPLE). Technical Report CMU/SEI-2005-TR-003, Carnegie Mellon University (2005)
5. Schmid, K.: A Quantitative Model of the Value of Architecture in Product Line Adoption. In: van der Linden, F.J. (ed.) PFE 2003. LNCS, vol. 3014, pp. 32–43. Springer, Heidelberg (2004)
6. Kazman, R., Asundi, J., Klein, M.: Making Architecture Design Decisions: An Economic Approach. Technical Report CMU/SEI-2002-TR-035, Carnegie Mellon University (2002)
7. Kotler, P., Keller, K.: Marketing Management, 13th edn. Prentice Hall, Englewood Cliffs (2008)
8. van der Linden, F., Schmid, K., Rommes, E.: Software Product Lines in Action. Springer, Heidelberg (2007)
9. Philips Healthcare,
   http://www.philips.com/about/company/businesses/healthcarehighlights
10. Ivanovic, A., America, P.: Economics of Architectural Investments in Industrial Practice. In: 2nd International Workshop on Measurement and Economics of Software Product Lines. SPLC proceedings, vol. 2, pp. 273–276 (2008)
11. Ivanovic, A., America, P.: Information Needed for Architecture Decision Making. In: 1st International Workshop in Product LinE Approaches in Software Engineering, PLEASE 2010 (2010)
12. Dul, J., Hak, T.: Case Study Methodology in Business Research. Elsevier, Amsterdam (2008)
13. Rogers, E.M.: Diffusion of Innovation, 5th edn. Free Press, New York (2003)
14. Anderson, J.C., Jain, D.C., Chintagunta, P.K.: Customer Value Assessment in Business Markets: A State-of-Practice Study. Institute for the Study of Business Markets (1993)
15. Breeuwer, M., Hautvast, G., Higgins, S., Nagel, E.: Simplifying cardiac MR analysis. MedicaMundi 52(2), 68–76 (2008)
16. Bevan, N., Macleod, M.: Usability measurement in context. Behaviour and Information Technology 13, 132–145 (1994)
17. Ondategui-Parra, S., Bhagwat, J.G., Zou, K.H., Nathanson, E., Gill, I.E., Ros, P.R.: Use of Productivity and Financial Indicators for Monitoring Performance in Academic Radiology Departments: U.S. Nationwide Survey. Radiology 236(1) (2005)
18. Yin, R.K.: Case study research: design and methods. Applied Social Research Methods Series, vol. 5. SAGE Publications, Thousand Oaks (2003)

# A Formal Approach to Enforcing Consistency in Self-adaptive Systems

Najla Hadj Kacem[1], Ahmed Hadj Kacem[1], and Khalil Drira[2,3]

[1] ReDCAD Laboratory - University of Sfax
B.P.1088, 3018 Sfax, Tunisia
najla.hadjkacem@isimsf.rnu.tn, ahmed.hadjkacem@fsegs.rnu.tn
[2] CNRS, LAAS, 7 Avenue du Colonel Roche,
F-31077 Toulouse, France
[3] Université de Toulouse; UPS, INSA, INP, ISAE, LAAS,
F-31077 Toulouse, France
khalil@laas.fr

**Abstract.** The ability of systems to adapt is increasingly seen as a necessary underlying capability for modern software systems. The resulting self-adaptive systems are not only supposed to cope with changes, but must also preserve their consistency. To deal with such challenges in a systematic way, the design of self-adaptive systems needs to be put on a formal basis. In this paper, we argue for the benefits of a formal yet extensible approach to behavioural adaptations of component-based system architectures. This approach provides the usage of alternative adaptation processes rather than being limited to a single one. The application of Coloured Petri Nets for modelling and analysing the adaptation processes proves to be useful to trust consistency preservation.

## 1 Introduction

Adaptability is emerging as a key feature of modern software systems, particularly long running distributed systems (e.g., web servers, application servers for E-business). Such systems inevitably have to adapt themselves at run-time to shifting requirements, changing environments and resource variability. The resulting self-adaptive systems are supposed to keep most of their complexity hidden from the user, and more importantly to be able to behave correctly.

In component-based systems the basic building block is the component, and applications are built as component compositions. Self-adaptation at the architectural level of these systems can be performed through structural or behavioural adaptation actions [1]. Structural adaptation is defined as the ability to change the compositional topology by adding/removing components and/or their connections. In contrast, behavioural adaptation refers to the ability to not only replace individual components, but also adjust their parameters. Of particular interest to us is behavioural adaptation, and especially how to safely adapt component-based system architectures.

M. Ali Babar and I. Gorton (Eds.): ECSA 2010, LNCS 6285, pp. 279–294, 2010.

As the adaptability required by systems increases, so does the need for rigorous techniques to design, build and analyse systems and thereby avoid unnecessary flaws [2]. Such flaws would generate undesirable transient behaviour and subsequently would compromise system consistency. The application of formal methods has proved to be useful at the early stages of the development process. This can greatly increase the understanding of the system by revealing ambiguities and incompleteness that might otherwise go undetected [3]. Therefore, it is a fact that for a systematical engineering of self-adaptive systems modelling and early analysis is required [4]. In this perspective, a significant amount of effort is invested in formal approaches to structural adaptations [5]. Behavioural adaptations, in contrast, have received little attention (e.g., [6], [7], [8]).

In this paper, we propose a Coloured Petri Nets based approach to model behavioural adaptations of component-based system architectures. The essence of our approach is to provide the usage of alternative adaptation processes rather than being limited to a single one. Towards preserving consistency, these processes efficiently manage dependencies between components even if they are cyclic. Coloured Petri Nets (CPN) [9] as supported by CPN Tools [10] are used to model and analyse the adaptation processes.

This paper is structured as follows. Section 2 presents a typical example to illustrate the applicability. Section 3 introduces fundamental concepts used throughout the paper. Section 4 describes the alternative adaptation processes. Section 5 gives the basic concepts of CPN. Section 6 provides some insight into the constructed model. Sections 7 and 8 detail the description of some modules constituting the model. Section 9 shows the analysis results. Section 10 summarizes related work. Finally, some conclusion remarks are drawn.

## 2   Motivating Example

In this section, we briefly present a simple example of a real world system that we use throughout the paper to illustrate our proposition. As shown in figure 1, the example is a typical web based system built as a composition of components. In a given interaction, a component can provide services to other components and consume services provided by other ones. The same component can either play the role of a *provider*, a *requestor*, or even both of them in case of processing a *dependent* request. A request is said to be dependent if its completion depends on the completion of another consequent request by another component. Otherwise, it is said *independent*. Dependent requests create a call-path which may include the same component more than once. This implies the presence of a *cycle*.

Fig. 1. Example system

Our example system serves as a suitable abstraction of many real world systems. For illustration, consider a medical system. Doctors, nurses, paramedical practitioners and even patients may issue requests to a local health center in order to access to electronic patient records. A request is then serviced according to specific access rights of the requestor. To illustrate dependent requests, assume an example in which a doctor issues a request for specialized care services to the local health center which in turn issues a request to a remote health center as part of processing the request of the doctor.

As another illustration, consider a travel planning system used to make travel bookings. A traveller issues to a travel agency a trip order together with the information about the credit card to be charged for the ordered tickets. To actually make the ticket orders, the travel agency issues a request to a flight booking company. If the requested seats are available, the flight booking company initiates a request to the travel agency in order to get the information about the credit card. Hence, this leads to a cycle. Upon receipt of the reply, the credit card will be charged and a confirmation of the flights is sent back to the travel agency. This information is completed into an itinerary which is sent to the traveller.

The above examples illustrate the importance of understanding and managing component dependencies. Obviously, replacing a component, subsequently referred to as target, cannot be achieved at any arbitrary time. What if it is processing requests; or it is waiting for a reply to a request it sent? This will inevitably lead to inconsistencies. Therefore, the system must be placed in a safe sate before adaptation can take place.

# 3   Fundamental Concepts

This section develops a model of a self-adaptive component that we adopt in the paper. Our model aligns with the autonomic computing initiative [11]; it is split up into two parts: a *core functionality* part and an *adaptor* part. The core functionality part provides the alternate usage of multiple algorithms with equivalent functionality, each one optimized for a different execution environment. If a component has a state which is required to be preserved in adaptation, the component is said to be *stateful*. Having no such state, the component is said to be *stateless* and lacks the need for a state preservation. A component interacts with its environment through well-defined *ports*. It exports functions through *input* ports and imports its dependencies via *output* ports. A connector binds an output port of a component to an input port of another component to resolve a component dependency. A port dependency however is defined between ports of the same component. An input port is said to be *dependent* on an output port, if the component issues a request through the output port as a direct result of a request it received through the input port. Based on port dependencies, dependent requests are thus easily derived.

The adaptor part acts as a unit of autonomy for making decisions about when and how to perform adaptations. It additionally imposes control over a component's interactions. A very straightforward method for an adaptor to manage interactions of a component via its ports is interception. Beyond its interception capability, an adaptor can fine tune parameters of a component and even impose control on its internal behaviour, including suspending and resuming activity and also transferring its state. State transfer operation is only applied to stateful components. To safely carry out adaptation, an adaptor might interact with other adaptors. Hence, two categories of messages must be distinguished: *cross-components* and *cross-adaptors*.

The facility of interception is exploited to monitor the requests going into or out of the component and also to restrict them. The essential purpose of monitoring is to ensure that a component is not actively processing a request or waiting for a reply. One way to ensure monitoring is by means of a counter located at each port. Furthermore, rather than merely blocking requests, an adaptor should selectively restrict them. This selective restriction is based on inspection of so-called *tag* of a request. A tag refers to the call-path traversed by a sequence of requests and is added to a request as follows. Whenever an adaptor intercepts an incoming request on a dependent port, it recognises this request as dependent request and checks whether it is tagged or not. If untagged, the adaptor adds to the request as an implicit parameter the identity of the requestor component followed by the identity of the current component. Otherwise, it only adds to the request the identity of the current component. Upon generating a consequent request, the tag will be copied and extended for the request. The selective restriction can be applied using either a blocking algorithm or a queuing algorithm. These two algorithms will be described later in the following section.

# 4    Adaptation Processes

In [12], we distinguish four ways to adapt a component referred to as *full-blocking* (FB), *passive partial-blocking* (PPB), *active partial-blocking* (APB) and *non-blocking* (NB) adaptation processes. The FB, PPB and APB processes apply when replacing a component algorithm whereas NB process only applies to parameter-tuning adaptation.

## 4.1    Full-Blocking Process

During this process, the target evolves incrementally from its current algorithm to a new algorithm in three steps: the *deactivation* step, the *switch* step and the *reactivation* step. In the deactivation step, the target is driven from its original running state to the safe state. This state change is possible as soon as all interactions involving the target are finished. For this purpose, the adaptor of the target prevents requestor components, referred to as *affected*, from generating further requests to the target. This is achieved by sending Block_Requests messages to the adaptors of all affected components. In response to this message, an adaptor selectively blocks requests to the target. That is, if the target's identity is included in the tag of the request, then the request will be passed. Otherwise, the request is blocked and an exception is subsequently returned back to the component. Further requests issued from the target are selectively blocked. Any untagged request, i.e., newly initiated by the target and is not part of processing another request, is blocked. An exception is returned back to the target. Otherwise, the request is allowed to proceed. The reachability of the safe state is delayed until the target (i) has processed all incoming requests and (ii) has received replies of all outgoing requests.

At the beginning of the switch step, the adaptor loads the new algorithm of the target. Then, if the target is stateful, state transfer operation has to retrieve the internal state contained in the current algorithm and set it back to the new algorithm. No state preservation has to be taken for a stateless target. Subsequently, the target is moved from the safe state to the adapted state.

In the reactivation step, the target proceeds from the adapted state to the resuming state. At this state, the adaptor of the target sends Unblock_Requests messages to the adaptors of affected components. After that, it allows resuming operation with the new algorithm. Finally, when the target resumes its normal execution it returns to the original running state.

## 4.2 Passive Partial-Blocking Process

Similarly to the former adaptation process, this process is three-step and comprises the *deactivation, switch* and *reactivation* steps. The deactivation step moves the target from its original running state to the safe state. When compared to the former deactivation step, the reachibility of the safe state is relatively less disruptive to the running system. The affected components are not prevented from initiating requests to the target. They can interact as normal during adaptation. Incoming requests to the target will be selectively queued. Only tagged requests in which the target's identity is included are allowed to proceed. The others are kept queued and will be served after adaptation. Further requests issued from the target are selectively blocked in a similar way to the former process. The target is considered to be in the safe state when it (i) has completed all ongoing requests and (ii) has received replies to all outgoing requests.

Similarly to the previous switch step, the target is driven to the adapted state after loading the new algorithm and initialising it with the transferred internal state, if available.

The transit of the target from the adapted state to the resuming state makes the adaptor allow fetching out queued requests and resuming normal execution. At the end, the target returns to the running state.

## 4.3 Active Partial-Blocking Process

Unlike the FB and PPB processes, this process allows for the current and new algorithms of the target to coexist. Although the process could significantly reduce delays in adaptation, it does not provide any facilities for state preservation, thus limiting its use to stateless components. Two steps are involved in the process: the *preparation* step and the *switch* step. During the preparation step, the adaptor drives the target to the prepared state in parallel with normal execution of the current algorithm. It first loads the new algorithm. Next, at each input port, it puts an additional counter in order to control incoming requests to the new algorithm. The idea is to incrementally limit the interactions of the current algorithm.

After the preparation step, all new requests made by the current algorithm are selectively blocked. As such, untagged requests are blocked and tagged ones are allowed to proceed. Given an incoming request, if the request is tagged and includes the target's identity, then it is passed to the current algorithm. Otherwise, it will be forwarded to the new algorithm to be serviced. The current algorithm gets the chance to finish processing requests and waiting for replies. Meanwhile, the new algorithm can be partially operational; it can begin the processing of requests. All its output would be queued and delivered as long as the current algorithm completes. If so, the target is said to be in the adapted state. The counters controlling incoming requests to the current algorithm can be subsequently removed since the control will be in charge of the added counters. When the new algorithm is fully operational, the target transits from the adapted state to the running state.

### 4.4    Non-blocking Process

This process comprises a single *adjustment* step in which the adaptor of the target is required to have ready "read/write" access to a parameter. Once changing the value of a parameter finishes, the target is considered to be in the adapted state. From this state, it can directly proceed to the running state.

## 5    Background on Coloured Petri Nets

A CPN consists of two types of nodes, *places* (drawn as ellipses) and *transitions* (drawn as rectangles). *Arcs* connect places to transitions and transitions to places. A place is typed by a *colour set* and contains multi-sets of markers called *tokens*. The state of a CPN is called a *marking* and consists of the number of tokens positioned on each place. A transition represents an action. An incoming arc of a transition indicates that the transition may remove tokens from input places while an outgoing arc of a transition indicates that the transition may add tokens to output places.

The colours of the tokens removed and added are determined by evaluating the *arc expressions* (positioned next to the arcs). A transition is *enabled* if the multi-set of tokens obtained by evaluating each incoming arc expression is a subset of the tokens present on the corresponding input place. Any enabled transition may *occur* and change the distribution of tokens on the places. Simple boolean expressions, called *guards*, can be associated with a transition and enforce constraints on its occurrence.

In CPN Tools, CPN models can be hierarchically structured into a set of modules, referred to as *pages*, to handle large models. The pages are related to each other in a well-defined way. *Fusion places* are duplicates of places to make the places accessible at different pages or different locations on one single page.

## 6    CPN Model Overview

The purpose of this section is to provide some insight into the constructed CPN model. The model makes it possible to carry out adaptation using FB, PPB or APB adaptation processes. The reason behind not considering the NB adaptation process is that it is intuitive and quite easy to realize parameter-tuning adaptation. In the model, we make sufficient abstraction of implementation details, but still deal with the behaviour of interest. Hence, processing that is irrelevant for analysis is abstracted away. This makes the model simpler and the analysis easier due to restricted state space size.

The complete CPN model is hierarchically structured in 36 pages. The topmost level page in the CPN model is the SelfAdaptiveSystem page shown in figure 2. This page is organised such that it reflects the model of a component, basic building block of the system. On this page, there are six substitution transitions modelling the adaptor part (DecisionMaker, LifeCycleController, Interceptor), the core functionality part (Requestor, Provider), and the transport medium over which the components communicate as well as the adaptors (Transport). We assume that the underlying transport medium is reliable.

The states of the components making up the system are modelled by the place ComponentsState. Typed by the colour set CPTxStCPT, this place contains the components identity along with their states (Running, Safe, Adapted, Resuming). The initial marking of this place states that all the components are in the original Running state.

Similar to ComponentsState, the place AdaptorsState contains the states of all the adaptors of the components. The core set of states an adaptor can go through are defined by the colour set StADP. There are three possible states to be in with respect to the corresponding component: ExcNrm if the component is in its normal execution; AdpTrgCpt if the component is the target; AdpAffCpt if the component is affected. The initial marking of the AdaptorsState place defines that all the adaptors are initially in the state ExcNrm.

When a component sends a request or receives a reply, it will appear as a token on the place OutPort. Because every message going into or out of the

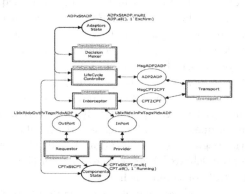

**Fig. 2.** Top-level page

component is intercepted, we need to associate the request/reply with the adaptor's identity. Hence, the colour set of the OutPort place is defined as the product of the following colour sets:

1. Lbl models the label of a message indicating if it is a request (REQ, Nw_REQ), a reply (REP, Nw_REP) or an exception (EXCP). Note that the prefix Nw is used when the current and new algorithms of the target coexist while APB is the actual process, in order to specify the messages of the new algorithm.
2. Rid models the identity of the requestor.
3. OutP models an output port of the requestor.
4. Tag is declared as a union colour set (colset Tag=union Path: LstCPT + None). The first constructor Path models a call-path as a list of components identity, and is only added to requests. In contrast, the second constructor None is only added to replies since replies are evidently not tagged.
5. Pid models the identity of the provider.
6. ADP models the identity of the adaptor of the corresponding requestor.

The colour set of the InPort place is defined in a similar way as the colour set of the OutPort place, except that InP models an input port of the provider and ADP represents the identity of the adaptor of the corresponding provider.

The two places ADP2ADP and CPT2CPT are used to contain the messages cross-adaptors and cross-components respectively.

## 7    Modelling the Core Functionality Part

According to figure 2, the core functionality part splits the operation of a component into two subparts: one is responsible for requiring services (Requestor), and the other for providing services (Provider).

### 7.1    Requestor Page

Figure 3 shows the Requestor page. In this page, the requests of components are abstractly modelled and collected in the ComponentsRequests fusion place. A token is removed from the ComponentsRequests place when the component sends a request, or put on this place if the component generates a consequent request to process a dependent one. Any request contained in the initial marking of this place consists of a label REQ (of colour LblREQ, subset of Lbl), a requestor, an output port of the requestor, an empty list as tag, and a provider.

When a component in the Running state requires a service, a request whose requestor corresponds to that component will be picked non-deterministically from the ComponentsRequests place. By default, the label of a request to be sent is REQ. But after the beginning of adaptation, if the actual adaptation process is APB then the function IsNwREQ determines whether the label of each target's request becomes Nw_REQ or is left unchanged.

Upon sending a request, either one of the two counters recorded in the fusion places REQ_Counter and NwREQ_Counter is incremented by one. The purpose of

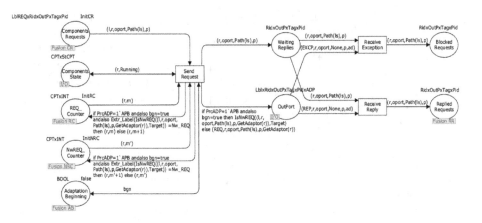

**Fig. 3.** Requestor page

these counters is to keep track of the number of requests each component has sent. More precisely, the first counter keeps track of those requests only whose label is REQ. The second counter records the number of the requests whose label is Nw_REQ. This allows us to ensure that all requests will be inevitably intercepted. A request being sent by a component is represented by a token put in the place OutPort. The place WaitingReplies keeps track of the requests being sent. The reception of an exception or a reply is abstractly modelled by the transitions ReceiveException and ReceiveReply respectively.

## 7.2 Provider Page

The Provider page shown in figure 4 models the processing of incoming requests assigned by an adaptor to the corresponding component. There are two cases in processing a request. First, if the request is independent (as specified by the function IsInPDpd), the transition ProcessInDpdReq is enabled. When it occurs, (i) a token representing the reply will be put on the place InPort. The function placed on the outgoing arc sets the label of the reply to REP or Nw_REP depending on the label of the processed request (REQ or Nw_REQ), and (ii) a token representing the request is added to the ProcessedRequests place.

Second, if the request is dependent, the transition ProcessDpdReq is responsible for processing the request. But a request having a Nw_REQ label could not be completed in a similar way to how this is done for requests with a REQ label. The completion of a request with a REQ label (modelled by the transition CompleteDpdReq) is possible once its consequent request is completed, i.e., a token representing this request is placed on the fusion place RepliedRequests. However, if the actual adaptation process is APB then the completion of a request with a Nw_REQ label could be postponed temporarily since its consequent request will be queued.

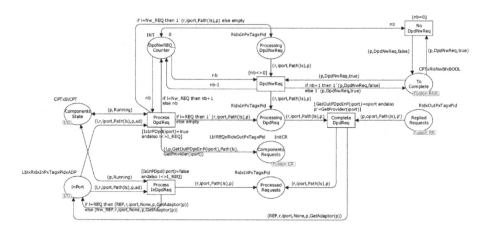

**Fig. 4.** Provider page

## 8  Modelling the Adaptor Part

As shown in figure 2, the description of the adaptor part is organised such that
it reflects how an adaptor (i) acts as a unit of autonomy for making decisions
(DecisionMaker), (ii) manages all the interactions of the component (Interceptor),
and (iii) manages the component life cycle (LifeCycleController).

### 8.1  DecisionMaker Page

As previously stated, we do not care about processing that is irrelevant for the
analysis. Hence, the procedure of making decisions about when to begin adaptation and how to select the adaptation process that better fits to the current
execution environment is abstracted away. In figure 5(left), adaptation beginning is abstractly modelled by the BeginAdaptation transition. This transition is
initially enabled and can occur at any time, thus making adaptation *at random*.

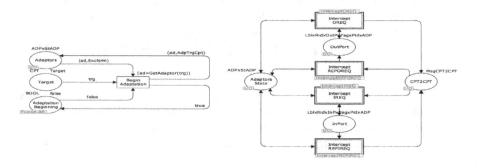

**Fig. 5.** DecisionMaker (left) and Interceptor (right) pages

## 8.2   Interceptor Page

The Interceptor page depicted in figure 5(right) consists of four substitution transitions modelling the interception of: outgoing requests (InterceptOREQ), replies to outgoing requests (InterceptREPOREQ), incoming requests (InterceptIREQ) and replies to incoming requests (InterceptREPIREQ). Due to lack of space, we only consider the InterceptOREQ and the InterceptIREQ pages.

The InterceptOREQ page structures the process of intercepting outgoing requests into three substitution transitions depending on the current state of the adaptor (IntOREQ_ExcNrm, IntOREQ_AdpTrg, IntOREQ_AdpAff). We only consider the IntOREQ_AdpTrg page. On this page, there are three substitution transitions modelling the behaviour of an adaptor (in the AdpTrgCpt state) with respect to each adaptation process. As a representative example, we consider the IntOREQ_AdpTrg_FB page shown in figure 6. This page models how an adaptor manages the requests initiated by the target in case the actual adaptation process is FB. Any request placed on the OutPort place as a part of processing another request (specified by the guard of the PassIntReq transition) will be transmitted over the transport medium. Conversely, any request newly initiated by the target as not a part of processing another request will be blocked and an exception will be returned back to the target.

After a request goes through the transport medium and reaches the provider, it has first to be intercepted by the adaptor of this provider. There are essentially two cases for intercepting incoming requests, modelled by the substitution transitions IntIREQ_NrmExcOrAdpAff and IntIREQ_AdpTrg on the InterceptIREQ page. Similarly to the IntOREQ_AdpTrg page, the page IntIREQ_AdpTrg is organised into three substitution transitions. We consider the IntIREQ_AdpTrg_PPB page (figure 7). By the predefined function mem, an adaptor checks whether the identity of the target is included in the list representing the call-path. If so, the request is assigned to the target. The assignment of a dependent request differs from the assignment of an independent one in that the update of the call-path.

In contrast, if the identity of the target is not included in the list representing the call-path the request will be queued. A counter maintained in the place BuffREQ_Counter records the number of queued requests and serves to releasing them. The transition BuffReq takes care of fetching out queued requests and deposits them in the InPort place.

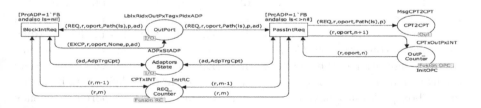

**Fig. 6.** IntOREQ_AdpTrg_FB page

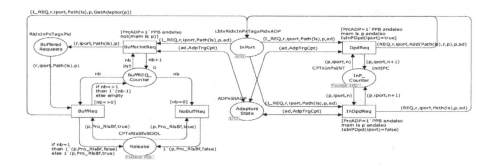

**Fig. 7.** IntIREQ_AdpTrg_PPB page

## 8.3   LifeCycleController Page

The LifeCycleController page has two substitution transitions modelling how an adaptor manages the life cycle of the target (LCC_AdpTrg) and an affected component (LCC_AdpAff). As a representative example, we only consider the LCC_AdpTrg_FB page which is organised such that it reflects the three steps of the FB process. The first deactivation step is abstractly represented by the FB_Deactivation page that is not shown here due to space limitation. On this page, the reachability of the Safe state is delayed until:

1. A BlkReq message is sent to the adaptors of affected components. To ensure that these adaptors have effectively received the BlkReq message, the adaptor of the target collects BlkReqDone messages.
2. The value of the counters located at the output ports and input ports of the target is equal to zero. As such, it can be ensured that the target has processed all incoming requests and has received replies of all outgoing requests.
3. The value of the counter recorded in the place REQ_Counter is equal to zero.

## 9   Model Analysis

In this section, focus changes from modelling to state space analysis. The purpose of state space analysis is to conduct investigation of the operation of the modelled system, including verification of its key properties. The first step in CPN Tools towards state space analysis is to initialise the CPN model according to a specific configuration. Consider in figure 8 one representative component-based configuration of the above-described example system. On this figure, there are five components (a, b, c, d, e) interconnected through their ports indicated in the box positioned next to them (for example, outx1). A port dependency between an input port and an output port is represented by a dashed line. The adaptors (A, B, C, D, E) of the components can be recognised by the grey bar around each component.

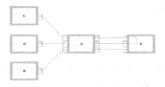

**Fig. 8.** Initial configuration

**Table 1.** Initial tests

| | 1 | 2 | 3 | 4 | 5 | 6 |
|---|---|---|---|---|---|---|
| Target | a | a | a | a | a | a |
| PrcADP | FB | PPB | APB | FB | PPB | APB |
| M(CR) | 1`(REQ,c,outx1,Path([]),a) | 1`(REQ,c,outx1,Path([]),a) | 1`(REQ,c,outx1,Path([]),a) | 1`(REQ,c,outx1,Path([]),a)++ 1`(REQ,e,outx3,Path([]),a) | 1`(REQ,c,outx1,Path([]),a)++ 1`(REQ,d,outx2,Path([]),a)++ 1`(REQ,e,outx3,Path([]),a) | 1`(REQ,c,outx1,Path([]),a)++ 1`(REQ,d,outx2,Path([]),a) |

Table 1 shows the chosen values to set the target (**Target**), the actual adaptation process (**PrcADP**) and the initial marking of the **ComponentsRequests** place
(**M(CR)**), in order to carry out six representative tests.

The state space analysis is done by first generating the state spaces for the
considered tests. State space generation is followed by generation of the state
space report which provides some statistical information about the state space
and contains answers to a number of standard behavioural properties of Petri
nets. Table 2 shows part of the generated state space reports. In the following,
we interpret selected analysis results.

**Table 2.** Analysis results

| | 1 | 2 | 3 | 4 | 5 | 6 |
|---|---|---|---|---|---|---|
| State Space Nodes | 15193 | 180 | 704 | 233467 | 60968 | 19815 |
| State Space Arcs | 58289 | 275 | 1748 | 1085428 | 197169 | 65981 |
| Secs | 48 | 1 | 0 | 13032 | 521 | 65 |
| Scc Graph Nodes | 15193 | 180 | 704 | 233467 | 60968 | 19815 |
| Scc Graph Arcs | 58289 | 275 | 1748 | 1085428 | 197169 | 65981 |
| Dead Markings | [9722,15193] | [180] | [704] | [131350,176900, 232009,233467] | [60968] | [19815] |
| Dead Transition Instances | 31 | 41 | 37 | 31 | 41 | 37 |
| Live Transition Instances | none | none | none | none | | none |

**Property1: Absence of Deadlocks.** This property can be formulated as the
absence of unexpected *dead markings*. A dead marking is a marking in which no
transition is enabled. With respect to the CPN model, the only acceptable dead
markings would be the states in which the components end up being adapted
properly and correctly resume normal execution. In the considered tests, the
analysis reveals dead markings. By transferring the dead markings into the simulator, we inspect the markings and observe these as desired terminal states of the
system. Common for all dead markings we have all adaptors in the ExcNrm state
(AdaptorsState place); all components in the Running state (ComponentsState

place) and all requests are either replied (RepliedRequests place) or blocked (BlockedRequests place).

**Property2: Absence of Livelocks.** This property states that the model should be free from livelocks. A livelock is revealed when the state space contains a cycle that once entered will repeat forever and within which no progress is made. Absence of livelocks can be determined by examining the Scc graph. In table 2, common result for all tests is that the Scc graph has the same number of nodes and arcs as the state space. This implies that there are no cycles in the state space and the system will always terminate correctly. Proper termination is further acknowledged by the absence of *live transitions*, as is shown in table 2. A live transition is a transition which always can become enabled once more.

**Property3: Absence of Unexpected Dead Transitions.** This property states that every transition is enabled by at least one reachable marking. As expected, the analysis shows a number of dead transitions with respect to each test. They are caused by transitions being modelled but not enabled due to the initially considered adaptation process. For example, consider the test 1 where FB is the actual process. There are 31 dead transitions. Inspection of these transitions shows that dead transitions are related to the PPB and APB processes.

Even though the state space report proves to be useful to investigate a set of standard behavioural properties, some properties which are particular for the CPN model need to be verified. For example, an interesting property (**Property4**) to check states that each request will be eventually replied or blocked whatever the considered adaptation process. Checking this property boils down to check that in all terminal markings, the addition of the multisets of tokens on places RepliedRequests and BlockedRequests is identical to the multi-set of tokens on place ComponentsRequests (without considering the label). The query function PredAllNodes is used to list all nodes violating this property. As shown in figure9(left), there are no such nodes when the actual process is FB. The property is consequently satisfied, and so is for the PPB and APB processes.

Another property (**Property5**) to investigate states that when the considered process is FB, the target in the Safe state will neither receive nor initiate requests. That is, once the target is driven in the Safe state the number of tokens on the place OutPort whose requestor is the target and the number of tokens on the place InPort whose provider is the target should be equal to zero. In the query, we negate this condition and hence the function PredAllNodes checks the state

**Fig. 9.** Checking results of Property4 (left) and Property5 (right)

space for nodes which satisfy it. The result in figure9(right) shows that there are no such nodes, therefore the property is satisfied.

# 10    Related Work

The work by Kramer and Magee [6] presents one of the earliest approaches for dynamic adaptation. In this approach, a system is seen as a directed graph consisting of nodes and connections between the nodes. Nodes can only affect each other through transactions, thus limiting the use of the approach to transactional systems. During adaptation, node quiescence is defined as a state in which the node is not within a transaction and will neither receive nor initiate any new transactions. However, the offered solution to reach quiescence is coarse-grained. That is, any adaptation of a node can suspend completely its adjacent nodes, where some activities are unnecessarily suspended.

More fine-grained approach is used by Wermelinger [13] which argues that the passivation of links needs to be dealt with instead of the passivation of nodes. A novelty of this approach is that each node must be supplied with a description of internal port dependencies, which relate input ports and output ports. Dependencies between transactions are derived from port dependencies. Cycles are not allowed since transactions cannot be interleaved.

Zhang and Cheng [14] propose an approach to create formal models for the behavior of adaptive systems. In this approach, an adaptive system is modeled as the composition of a finite number of programs and the adaptations among these programs. The properties of each program are assumed to be specified with a Linear Temporal Logic (LTL) formula. To specify an adaptation from one program to another, Zhang and Cheng introduce the A-LTL, an extension to LTL. This approach does not only require from the developer expertise of A-LTL, but also substantial effort to describe the relative temporal ordering among events and program states that occur during the adaptation process.

Recently, in [8], Rasche and Polze introduce an algorithm for dynamic adaptation. They model a system configuration together with the adaptation algorithm using Petri Nets. To prove some important properties of the algorithm, such as the absence of deadlocks and progress, they use model checking. The algorithm is however limited to adding or removing a component, and changing its attributes. No support for replacing a component is provided.

# 11    Conclusion and Future Work

In this paper, we investigate the use of CPN for modelling and analyzing self-adaptive systems in order to ensure consistency. First, we present an abstract model of alternative adaptation processes that an adaptor can apply to adapt a component. In the model, the multi-threaded nature of a component is taken into account as it must deal with dependent requests and even cycles. Furthermore, the chosen level of abstraction excludes implementation details, but still deals with the behaviour of interest. Second, for the values of parameters considered in the tests, we analyse the model and show that it terminates correctly. We prove that there are no deadlocks or livelocks, and the terminal states show that the components end up being adapted properly and resume normal execution in a correct manner. This helps us to give further confidence in the constructed model and thereby in the self-adaptive system which is assured to preserve consistency.

Future work will include modelling of systems with timing constraints. Beyond preserving consistency, these systems must ensure that adaptation is carried out in such a way that all timing constraints are satisfied. CPN include a time concept that makes it possible to capture the time taken to execute activities in the system.

# References

1. Oreizy, P., Medvidovic, N., Taylor, R.: Architecture-Based Runtime Software Evolution. In: Proc. of the 20th International Conference on Software Engineering, pp. 177–186. IEEE CS, Los Alamitos (1998)
2. Kramer, J., Magee, J.: Towards robust self-managed systems. Progress in Informatics (5), 1–4 (2008)
3. Clarke, E.M., Wing, J.M.: Formal methods: state of the art and future directions. ACM Computing Surveys 28(4), 626–643 (1996)
4. Becker, B., Giese, H.: Modeling of Correct Self-Adaptive Systems: A Graph Transformation System Based Approach. In: Proc. of the 5th International Conference on Soft Computing as Transdisciplinary Science and Technology (CSTST 2008), pp. 508–516. ACM, New York (2008)
5. Bradbury, J., Cordy, J., Dingel, J., Wermelinger, M.: A survey of self-management in dynamic software architecture specifications. In: Proc. of the 1st ACM SIGSOFT Workshop on Self-managed Systems, pp. 28–33. ACM, New York (2004)
6. Kramer, J., Magee, J.: The Evolving Philosophers Problem: Dynamic Change Management. IEEE Trans. on Soft. Eng. 16(11), 1293–1306 (1990)
7. Zhang, J., Yang, Z., Cheng, B.H., McKinley, P.K.: Adding safeness to dynamic adaptation techniques. In: Proc. of ICSE 2004 Workshop on Architecting Dependable Systems, WADS 2004 (2004)
8. Rasche, A., Polze, A.: ReDAC - Dynamic Reconfiguration of Distributed Component-based Applications with Cyclic Dependencies. In: Proc. of the 11th IEEE International Symposium on Object-Oriented Real-Time Distributed Computing (2008)
9. Jensen, K., Kristensen, L., Wells, L.: Coloured Petri Nets and CPN Tools for Modelling and Validation of Concurrent Systems. International Journal on Software Tools for Technology Transfer 9(3), 213–254 (2007)
10. CPN Tools (2007), http://www.daimi.au.dk/CPNTools
11. Kephart, J.O., Chess, D.M.: The Vision of Autonomic Computing 36(1), 41–50 (2003)
12. Hadj Kacem, N., Hadj Kacem, A., Drira, K.: Orchestrating Safe Behavioural Adaptations of Component-based Systems. In: Proc. of the Sixth International Conference on Autonomic and Autonomous Systems, pp. 37–46. IEEE CS, Los Alamitos (2010)
13. Wermelinger, M.A.: Specification of software architecture reconfiguration. Ph.D, Thesis, Universidade Nova de Lisboa (1999)
14. Zhang, J., Cheng, B.: Using Temporal Logic to Specify Adaptive Program Semantics. Journal of Systems and Software 79(10), 1361–1369 (2006)

# Architecture-Centric Component-Based Development Needs a Three-Level ADL

Huaxi (Yulin) Zhang, Christelle Urtado, and Sylvain Vauttier

LGI2P / Ecole des Mines d'Alès, Nîmes, France
{Huaxi.Zhang,Christelle.Urtado,Sylvain.Vauttier}@mines-ales.fr

**Abstract.** Architecture-centric, component-based development intensively reuses components from repositories. Such development processes produce architecture definitions, using architecture description languages (ADLs). This paper proposes a three step process. Architecture specifications first capture abstract and ideal architectures imagined by architects to meet requirements. Specifications do not describe complete component types but only component roles (usages). Architecture configurations then capture implementation decisions, as the architects select specific component classes from the repository to implement component roles. Finally, architecture assemblies define how components instances are created and initialized to customize the deployment of architectures in their own execution contexts. This development process is supported by a three-level ADL which enables the separate definition of these three representations. The refinement relationships between these architecture representations are also discussed.

## 1 Introduction

Component-based software development (CBSD) consists in two activities: the development of software components for reuse and the development of software applications by the reuse of components. The first activity can be managed by classical software development processes, with an analysis, a design and then a coding phase. The produced software modules, encapsulated as component classes, are then stored and indexed in repositories to be reused later on. The second activity corresponds to a more specific and still scarcely studied development processes. We propose an architecture-centric development process that aims at defining the structure of an application as a set of reused components and a set of connections between them, using a dedicated language called an Architecture Description Language (ADL). This process is structured in three steps, through which architecture definitions are gradually refined, from abstract to concrete representations. After a classical analysis step, architecture specifications first capture design decisions as ideal architectures imagined by architects to meet the requirements. Specifications do not describe complete component types but only component roles (usages). These roles are used to search for matching component classes in repositories. Specification and roles are thus key concepts to integrate component reuse effectively in the development process.

M. Ali Babar and I. Gorton (Eds.): ECSA 2010, LNCS 6285, pp. 295–310, 2010.

Second, architecture configurations capture implementation decisions, as the architects select specific component classes to implement component roles. Finally, architecture assemblies define how components instances are created and initialized to customize the deployment of architectures in different execution contexts. Our process is supported by an three-leveled dedicated ADL, called Dedal, which enables the explicit and separate definitions of architecture specifications, configurations and assemblies. This way, a single abstract architecture definition can be refined into many concrete architecture definitions, to foster not only the reuse of components but also of architectures. The refinement relationships between these separate architecture representations — i.e. the relationship between the component roles, classes and instances they are composed of — are proposed to control and verify the global coherence of these multi-level architecture definitions.

The remaining of this paper is organized as follows. Section 2 introduces our proposed architecture-centric, reuse-based development process. It studies how existing ADLs are suitable for it. Section 3 presents the different component description levels supported in Dedal, our proposed ADL to support this development process. Section 4 presents the different architecture description levels which can be expressed in Dedal, along with the refinement relations between them. Section 6 concludes with future work directions.

## 2    Software Architectures in CBD

### 2.1    A Development Process for Component Reuse

Component-based software development is characterized by its implementation of the "reuse in the large" principle. Reusing existing (off-the-shelf) software components therefore becomes the central concern during development. Traditional software development processes cannot be used as is and must be adapted to component reuse [1, 2]. Figure 1 illustrates our vision of such a development process which is classically divided in two:

- the component development process (sometimes referred to as component development *for* reuse), which is not detailed here. This development process is the producer of components that are stored in repositories for later consumption by the component reuse process.
- and, the component-based software development process (referred to as component-based software development *by* reuse) that describes how previously developed software components can be used for software development (and how this reuse process impacts the way software is built).

The proposed component-based software development process deliberately focuses on the produced artifacts (architecture descriptions, as models of the software) for each development step. For simplicity's sake, it is also exclusively "reuse-centered" and does not describe how components should be developed

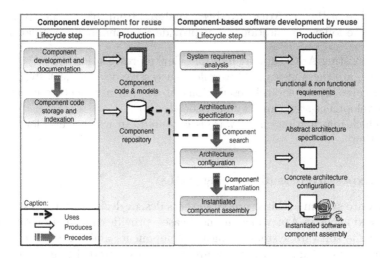

**Fig. 1.** Component-based software development process

from scratch if no component is found that matches or closely matches specifications, adapted if no existing component type perfectly matches specifications, tested and integrated or, physically deployed.

In this component-based software development process, software is considered to be produced by the reuse of components that have previously been stored and indexed in a component repository. It decomposes in three steps each of which produces a description that models the view of the architecture at this development step:

1. *Model of requirements.* After a classical requirement analysis step, architects establish the abstract architecture specification. They define which functionalities should be supplied by components, which interfaces should be exported by components, and how interfaces should connect to build a software system that meets the requirements.
2. *Model of design.* In a second step, architects create architecture configurations that define the sets of component implementations (classes) by searching and selecting from the component repository. Abstract component types from the architecture specification then become concrete component types in architecture configurations.
3. *Model of runtime.* In a third step, configurations are instantiated into component instance assemblies and deployed to executable software applications.

The claim of this paper is that an architectural description should correspond to each of the three steps of the component-based software development process. In other words, architectures should be described from all specification (model of requirements), configuration (model of design) and assembly (model of runtime) point of views. These three descriptions should reflect the architect's design decisions at each step of the development cycle and be expressed using an adequate

ADL. State-of-the-art ADLs have been analyzed from this perspective, trying to answer the following questions (that provide a taxonomy for comparison):

- Do existing ADLs support multiple view representations?
- If so, are these views used to reflect successive development steps?
- In cases where several descriptions of a given architecture coexist, which development step can they be associated to?
- Which information on software is captured? In which view / level representation?

## 2.2   Expressiveness of Existing ADLs

A software system architecture [3] gathers design decisions on the system. It is expressed using an ADL which, in most cases, provides information on the structure of the software system listing the components and connectors the system is composed of. Quality attributes are sometimes provided (*e.g.* xADL [4]). The dynamic behavior of systems is often described (*e.g.* C2SADEL [5], Wright [6], SOFA [7]) but their descriptions are not homogeneous as various technologies (*e.g.* message-based communication, CSPs, regular expressions) are used.

When systems are too complex to easily be described, two classical mechanisms can be used to split descriptions into smaller ones. *Hierarchical decomposition* enables to view the system at various granularities (*e.g.* Darwin [8], SOFA [7] or Fractal ADL [9]). Systems are composed of sub-systems that can further be described at a finer level. *Thematic decomposition* amounts to consider the system from distinct viewpoints (*e.g.* syntactic and behavioral diagrams of UML [10]). Whole systems are seen from several partial viewpoints that make each description focus on some system attributes.

Systems can also be described at various steps of their life-cycles. To our knowledge, no ADL really includes this "time" dimension. Some works such as UML [10] or Taylor *et al.* [3] implement or describe close notions. UML makes it possible to describe object-oriented software at various life-cycle steps but this capability is not transposed in their component model. Taylor *et al.* [3] distinguish two description levels for architectures at design and programming time, respectively called perspective (or as-intended) and descriptive (or as-realized) architectures. However, as far as we know, they do not propose any ADL or metamodel to concretely implement these two architecture descriptions. Garlan *et al.* [11] propose a three-layer framework (task, model and runtime layers) and points out the importance of three levels for dynamic software evolution management. Beside their having close notions, these existing works do not propose such descriptions that would follow the three identified steps of component-based software development.

We then examine the representative ADLs to see which levels of architecture descriptions are supported (as shown in Tables 1 and 2). As far as we know, the studied ADLs unfortunately do not enable the three levels that correspond to lifecycle steps to be all described. This analysis results in requirements for the language presented in this paper:

**Table 1.** Expressiveness of existing ADLs — Modeling of the three lifecycle steps

| ADL | Specification | Configuration | Assembly |
|-----|---------------|---------------|----------|
| C2SADEL | ✓ | ✓ | ✗ |
| Wright | ✗ | ✓ | ✗ |
| Darwin | ✗ | ✓ | ✗ |
| Unicon | ✗ | ✓ | ✗ |
| SOFA 2.0 | ✗ | ✓ | ✗ |
| FractalADL | ✗ | ✓ | ✗ |
| xADL 2.0 | ✗ | ✓ | ✓ |

**Table 2.** Expressiveness of existing ADLs — Component representations

| ADL | Abstract component type | Concrete component type | Component class | Component instance |
|-----|-------------------------|-------------------------|-----------------|--------------------|
| C2SADEL | ✗ | ✓ | ✓ | ✗ |
| Wright | ✗ | ✓ | ✓ | ✗ |
| Darwin | ✗ | ✓ | ✓ | ✗ |
| Unicon | ✗ | ✓ | ✓ | ✗ |
| SOFA 2.0 | ✗ | ✓ | ✓ | ✗ |
| FractalADL | ✗ | ✓ | ✓ | ✗ |
| xADL 2.0 | ✗ | ✓ | ✓ | ✓ |

1. No ADLs presented in Table 1 is tailored to CBD. Switching to such a reuse-centered development process shall impact the description language.
2. No ADLs presented in Table 1 models component types in an abstract way in order to support the search and selection of concrete component in component repositories. Concrete components in architecture configurations should not be strictly identical to abstract component types described in their architecture specification. As components pre-exist, the specification should define abstract (ideal) and partial component types while configurations describe concrete (satisfying) components that are going to be used (as claimed by Taylor *et al.* [3]).
3. Connectors should not necessary be explicit but the architect should have the possibility to explicit them when needed. Explicit connectors model specific connection types and can be reused from one design to another. However, in most situations, connectors can be system-generated and thus remain implicit for simplicity's sake.
4. Most ADLs do not model the running system (assembly level) or component instances, except xADL 2.0. ADLs should include some description on how components classes are instantiated and what are the characteristics of the running assemblies (constraints on component state values).
5. Components should possibly be primitive (implemented by an implementation class) or hierarchically composed of components (implemented by a configuration).

6. Component types should be reusable. This implies that their description is modularized (outside architectures).
7. Both structural and behavioral viewpoints should be provided for both components and architectures.

### 2.3 Example of a Bicycle Rental System

Figure 2 shows the example used throughout the paper: the architecture specification of a bicycle rental system (BRS). A *BikerGUI* component manages a user interface. It cooperates with a *Session* component which handles user commands. The *Session* component cooperates with the *Account* and *Bike&Course* components to identify the user, check the balance of its account, assign him an available bike and then calculate the price of the trip when the rented bike is returned. In the following sections, we will use a part of this system to illustrate our concepts and ADL syntax.

The two following sections present Dedal, the proposed ADL which spans the three levels of architecture descriptions. Dedal enables the description of abstract architecture specifications, concrete architecture configurations and instantiated component assemblies. It also supports a controlled architecture evolution process the description of which is out of the scope of this paper (see [12] for this aspect).

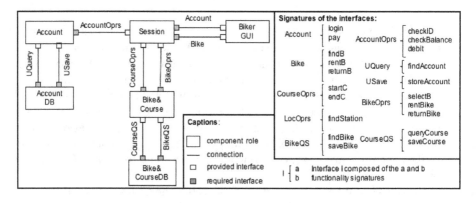

**Fig. 2.** BRS abstract architecture specification

## 3    Component Descriptions in the Three Levels of Dedal

Dedal models architectures at three separate abstraction levels, each of which contains different forms of components and connectors. For now, Dedal mainly focuses on modeling components. At the specification level, components are modeled as roles which are requirement models for concrete component search. These specifications thus are abstract and partial. At the configuration level, components are modeled as (whole) component classes which realize the specifications.

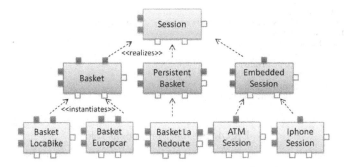

**Fig. 3.** The *Session* component role, some possible concrete realizations and some of their instantiations

Several component classes might correspond to a single component role as there might exist several concrete realizations of a single specification. At the assembly level, concrete component classes are instantiated into component instances that represent runtime components and their parameterizations. Figure 3 shows a complete example of components at three levels.

### 3.1 Components in Abstract Architecture Specifications

*Component roles* model abstract component types in that they describe the roles components should play in the system. A component role lists the minimum list of interfaces (both required and provided) the component should expose and the component behavior protocol that describes the behavior of the component in the architecture (dynamics of the architecture). As they define the requirements of the architect (its ideal view) to guide the search for corresponding concrete components, component roles are abstract and partial component representations (*e.g. Session* component role on Fig. 3). Dedal uses the protocol syntax of SOFA [7] to describe component behavior as regular expressions[1]. Other formalisms could have been used instead; the notation chosen is interesting as it is compact and is implemented as an extension of the Fractal component model we used for or experimentation, with companion verification tools. Component protocols capture the behavior of components in their context describing all valid sequences of emitted function calls (emitted by the component and addressed to neighbor components) and received function calls (received by the component from neighbor components). As component roles are abstract component specifications, Dedal modularly describes them outside architecture specifications, so as they can be reused from a specification to another (which would not be possible if they were embedded). Figure 4 shows the description of the *Session* component role. This description contains (a part of) the SOFA-like description of its behavior.

---

[1] !i.m (*resp.* ?i.m) denotes an outgoing (*resp.* incoming) call of method m on interface i. A+B is for A or B (exclusive or) and A;B for B after A (sequence).

```
component_role Session
 required_interfaces BikeOprs; CourseOprs; AccountOprs
 provided_interfaces Account; Bike
 component_behavior
 (!Session.Bike.findB,
 ?Session.BikeOprs.findB;)
 +
 (!Session.Account.login,
 ?Session.AccountOprs.checkID;)
 . . .
```

**Fig. 4.** *Session* component role

## 3.2    Components in Concrete Architecture Configurations

At configuration level, components are modeled in two ways with *component types* and *component classes*. Figure 5 provides a close-up view of the relationships between a component role (that model an abstract and partial view of a required component), a component type that models the complete type of some existing concrete implementation, a component class that represent the concrete component implementation and a parameterized component instance.

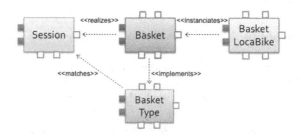

**Fig. 5.** *BikeCourseDBClass* composite component

*Component types* represent the full types of at least one (maybe several) existing component implementations. They are defined by describing the interfaces and behavior of these component classes. Component types are reusable as they can be implemented by multiple component classes which possess the same interfaces and component behavior. The *BasketType* component type description of Fig. 6 is an example of component type description.

*Component classes* represent concrete component implementations. Each component class points to the component type it implements. Component classes can either be primitive or composite.

Primitive component classes (*e.g. Basket* as described in Fig. 7) define the reused components by describing their interfaces, behavior, version[2] and implementing class. Existing models usually do not include links to the implementaing

---

[2] This information (as well as all the versioning information included in other descriptions later on) serves evolution management purposes that are not described in this paper. For more information, the interested reader might refer to [12].

```
component_type BasketType
  required_interfaces BikeOprs; CourseOprs; AccountOprs; CampusOprs;
AccessoryOprs
  provided_interfaces Account; Bike
  component_behavior
    (!BasketType.Bike.findB,
    ?BasketType.BikeOprs.findB;)
    +
    (!BasketType.Account.login,
    ?BasketType.AccountOprs.checkID;)
    . . .
```

**Fig. 6.** Description of the *BasketType* component type

```
component_class Basket
  implements BasketType
  using fr.ema.locaBike.Basket
  attributes string company; string currency
```

**Fig. 7.** The *Basket* (primitive) component class description

```
component_instance BasketLocaBike
  instance_of Basket (1.0)
    initiation_state company="LocaBikecurrency"; currency=="Euro."
```

**Fig. 8.** The *BasketLocaBike* component instance description

class as they assume there is a single implementation. In Dedal, components can thus have several implementations (which can be useful to have implementations versioned in such cases as software product lines management).

Composite component classes will be introduced in Sect.4.2. Both primitive and composite component classes can export an attribute list (as exemplified on Fig. 7 and 11). Attributes are not mandatory but can be declared as observable / visible properties for component classes so as to be able to set assembly constraints on attribute values in the instantiated component assembly level.

### 3.3   Components in Instantiated Software Component Assemblies

Component instances document the real artifacts that are connected together in an assembly at runtime. They are instantiated from the corresponding component classes. They might define constraints on components' attributes that reflect design decisions impacting component states (attribute values) over time. They also set the initial component state by initializing attributes values.

## 4   Three Levels of Architecture Description in Dedal

### 4.1   Abstract Architecture Specifications

Abstract architecture specifications (AASs) are the first level of software architecture descriptions. They provide a generic definition of the global structure and behavior of software systems according to previously identified functional requirements. They model the requirements expressed by the architect to serve as a basis to search for concrete component to create concrete architecture configurations. These architecture specifications are abstract and partial: they do not identify concrete component types that are going to be instantiated in the software system. They only describe the "ideal" component types from the application point of view. Types of concrete components need not be identical to abstract types. As CBD processes favors component reuse, component type compatibility should be more permissive than strict identity but still guarantee safety of use. Compatible concrete component types can, for example, provide more functionalities than strictly specified (extra functionality will remain unused) or provide more generic functionalities (use of polymorphism of object-oriented languages)[3].

```
specification BRSSpec
component_roles
  BikeCourse; BikeCourseDB
  ...
connections
 connection connection1
  client BikeCourse.BikeQS
  server BikeCourseDB.BikeQS
 connection connection2
  client BikeCourse.CourseQS
  server BikeCourseDB.CourseQS
  ...
architecture_behavior
  (!BikeCourse.BikeOprs.selectBike;
  ?BikeCourse.BikeQS.findBike;
  !BikeCourseDB.BikeQS.findBike;)
  +
  (!BikeCourse.CourseOprs.startC;
  ?BikeCourse.CourseQS.findCourse;
  !BikeCourseDB.CourseQS.saveCourse;)
  ...
version 1.0
```

**Fig. 9.** AAS of the BRS (partial)

In Dedal, an AAS is composed of a set of component roles, a set of connections and its architecture behavior. Figure 9 provides an example of the AAS for the BRS. For readability reasons, this description represents only a small part of the BRS AAS depicted in Fig. 2. **Connections** make interactions between two components possible. They define which component interfaces are bound together. *connection1* and *connection2* from Fig. 9 are such connections. **Architecture behaviors** describe the protocols of complete architectures – meaning all possible interactions between their constituent components. As for component protocols, the syntax used is that of SOFA protocols[4]. Compatibility

---

[3] The reader further interested about component compatibility can refer to authors' work on component repositories [13] and component substitution [14].

[4] !c.i.m (*resp.* ?c.i.m) denotes an outgoing (*resp.* incoming) call of method m on interface i of component c.

between individual component protocols and the protocol of their containing architecture as well as compatibility between the protocols of two connected components is not studied in this work as we interface our language with corresponding mechanisms (trace inclusion) from SOFA. Figure 9, that describes the BRS architecture specification, contains the BRS architecture protocol. The reader can intuitively check that the protocol of the *BikeCourse* component role is compatible with ("included" in) the protocol of the BRS architecture.

## 4.2   Concrete Architecture Configurations

Concrete architecture configurations (CACs) are the second level of system architecture descriptions. They result from the search and selection of real component types and classes in a component repository. These component types must match abstract component descriptions from the architecture but need not be identical; compatibility is sufficient. Component classes must be valid implementations of their declared component type. CACs describe the architecture from an implementation viewpoint (by assigning component roles to existing component types). Architecture configurations thus list the concrete component and connector classes which compose a specific version of a software application. The architecture of a given software is thus defined by a unique AAS and possibly several CACs. For a given software, each architecture configuration must conform to the architecture specification. This means that each component or connector class used in an architecture configuration must be a legal implementation of the corresponding component role or connection in the architecture specification. Figure 10 describes the architecture configuration of the BRS. The explicit description of **connector classes** is possible (as exemplified on Fig. 12) but not mandatory. In cases where they are implicit, we consider connectors as generic entities which are provided by containers (execution environments) in which configurations are deployed. Connections are automatically administered by containers at runtime to manage the instantiation of configurations. In cases where connectors are explicitly added, their descriptions define the specific connector classes that reflect design choices and that must be used to manage special communication, coordination, and mediation schemes. **Composite component classes** are components the implementation of which is not a simple class but a complete configuration that differ from the above described configurations in that it has some unconnected interfaces. The composite component class concept enables hierarchical composition of architectures which has been identified

```
configuration BRSConfig
 implements BRSSpec (1.0)
 component_classes
  BikeTrip (1.0) as BikeCourse;
  BikeCourseDBClass (1.0) as BikeCourseDB
 version 1.0
```

**Fig. 10.** A possible CAC for the BRS

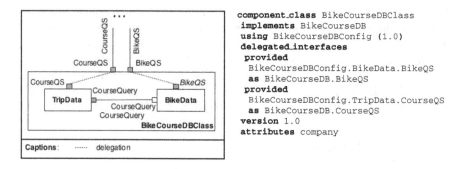

```
component_class BikeCourseDBClass
implements BikeCourseDB
using BikeCourseDBConfig (1.0)
delegated_interfaces
 provided
  BikeCourseDBConfig.BikeData.BikeQS
  as BikeCourseDB.BikeQS
 provided
  BikeCourseDBConfig.TripData.CourseQS
  as BikeCourseDB.CourseQS
version 1.0
attributes company
```

**Fig. 11.** The *BikeCourseDBClass* composite component class and its description

```
specification BikeCourseDBSpec
component_roles
 BikeDB; CourseDB
connections
 connection ConnectionCourseQuery;
 client BikeDB.CourseQuery
 server CourseDB.CourseQuery
version 1.0
```

```
configuration BikeCourseDBConfig
implements BikeCourseDBSpec (1.0)
component_classes
 BikeData (1.0) as BikeDB;
 TripData (1.0) as CourseDB
connector_classes
 CourseQuery (1.0) as
ConnectionCourseQuery;
 version 1.0
```

**Fig. 12.** Descriptions of the *BikeCourseDBSpec* abstract specification and of the *BikeCourseDBConfig* inner configuration

as an effective means to manage system complexity and concretely implement reuse (as whole configurations can be considered as coarser grained components). Composite component classes further define how unconnected interfaces from the inner configuration can be delegated to interfaces of the composite component. As for provided and required interfaces in primitive components, delegated interfaces are implementations of the corresponding provided and required interfaces in the corresponding component role. Figures 11 and 12 give the example of the composite component class *BikeCourseDBClass* that implements the *BikeCourseDB* role where the *BikeQS* provided interface of the *BikeData* component inside the *BikeCourseDBConfig* configuration is delegated as a provided interface of the composite component that implements the *BikeQS* interface of the *BikeCourseDB* component role. Figure 11 shows a graphical representation of the same *BikeCourseDBClass* component.

**Conformance between an AAS and a CAC** is a matter of conformance between component roles and the component classes that supposedly implement them. Many conformance relations could be defined, from stricter to very loose ones. On the one hand, we defend that reused components need not be exactly identical to specifications because being too strict in this matter might seriously decrease the number of reuse opportunities. On the other hand, it is expected from a conformance relation that it enables verifications that guarantees good chances that the thought component combination will execute. The rule of the thumb that can be used is that concrete components must provide at least what is the specification declare it provides and require less than what the specification already requires. This translates into rules for interfaces and rules for behavior protocols:

- the provided interfaces list of the concrete component class must contain all the interfaces specified in the component role,
- all the required interfaces of the concrete component class must be specified in the component role,
- the behavior of a component class includes (in the sense of trace inclusions) the behavior specified in the component role.

Variations on these rules can further consider interface specialization rules as in [13]. Figure 7 shows an example of a concrete component class (*Bike Trip*) that has a required interface (*LocOprs*) that is not in the specification (*Bike-Course* component role) it conforms to. In the case of composite components, delegated interfaces of provided (*resp.* required) direction are considered exactly as if they where provided (*resp.* required) interface of primitive components. Indeed, when considered externally, composite components can be seen as if they where primitive. Figure 7 provides an example of the *BikeCourseDBClass* composite component class, that conforms to the specification of the *BikeCourseDB* component role.

## 4.3   Instantiated Software Component Assemblies

Instantiated software component assemblies (IsCAs) are the third level of system architecture descriptions. They result from the instantiation of the component classes from a configuration. They provide a description of runtime software systems and gather information on their internal states. Indeed, this description level enables the record of state-dependent design decisions [15]. IsCAs list the component and connector instances that compose a runtime software system, the attributes of this software system, and the assembly constraints the component instances are constrained by. Figure 13 gives the description of a software assembly that instantiates the Brs architecture configuration of Fig. 10.

```
assembly BRSAss
 instance_of BRSConfig (1.0)
 component_instances
  BikeTripC1; BikeCourseDBClassC1
 assembly_constraints
  BikeTripC1.currency="Euro.";
  BikeCourseDBClassC1.company=
   BikeTripC1.company
 version 1.0
  component_instance BikeTripC1
   instance_of BikeTrip (1.0)
  component_instance BikeCourseDBClassC1
   instance_of BikeCourseDBClass (1.0)
```

**Fig. 13.** Component assembly description of the Brs

The explicit description of **connector instances** is possible but not mandatory. In cases where they are implicit, we consider them as generic entities which are provided by containers (execution environments) in which configurations are deployed. In cases where connector instances are explicitly added, their descriptions define the specific attributes that reflect implementation choice to meet different situation. By default, component classes can be instantiated into multiple component instances. When more precise **cardinality** information is needed, it is expressed in component role descriptions using *minInstances* and *maxInstances* that define the minimum and maximum numbers of component instances that are permitted to instantiate from the component class which implements this component role. By this means, component classes do not include this configuration-dependent information and remain reusable. In the assembly level, assembly constraints that restrain the valid number of instances will be checked against the cardinality information defined in the component role (in the specification level). There is no rule to constrain the name of component instances of a given component class. **Assembly constraints** define conditions that must be verified by attributes of some component instances of the assembly, to enforce its consistency. Such assembly constraints are not mandatory. For now, Dedal only permits to list several constraints that must all be enforced and that either:

- limit the possible values for an attribute to a given constant,
- restrain the cardinality of some connection end (*i.e.,*the number of instances of the component class that stands at the end of the connection in the configuration) to a given constant,
- or, enforce equality of the values of two distinct attributes that pertain to two distinct component instances of a given component assembly.

Such assembly constrains are illustrated on Fig. 13 where the value of the *currency* attribute of component *BikeTripC1* is fixed to *Euro* and where the value of the attribute *company* of the *BikeCourseClassDBC1* component must be maintained identical to the value of attribute *company* of component *BikeTripC1*. Another example that involves cardinalities would be expressed as the assembly constraint *InstanceNbr(BikeTrip)=2* that mean that exactly two component instances of the *BikeTrip* component class should be instantiated in this system. The cardinality of the *BikeTrip* component class is recorded in the *BikeCourse* component role specification. These constraints are very simple and do not yet enable the expression of alternatives, negation, nor the resolution of possible conflicts. Such extended assembly constraint management is one of the perspectives for this work for which we plan to take inspiration from systems that manage architectural styles as constraints sets [6, 16].

**Conformance between a CAC and an ISCA** is quite straightforward. All component instances of the assembly must be an instance of a corresponding component class from its source configuration (and reciprocally). Conformance also includes the verification that attribute names used in an assembly constraint of some component assembly pertain to the component classes the components of the assembly are instances of. For example, the assembly constraint *BikeTripC1.currency="Euro."* of Fig. 13 has the conformance process check whether the *BikeTrip* component class (from which *BikeTripC1* is instantiated) possesses a *currency* attribute.

# 5 Implementation of Dedal in the Arch3D Tool Suite

The Dedal ADL presented in this paper has been implemented in the Arch3D tool suite. The language has been implemented twice: as an XML-based ADL and as a Java-based ADL. The tools also propose a component model which enables to instantiate and manipulate corresponding assemblies at runtime which is extended as an extension of Julia, the open-source java implementation of the Fractal component platform[5]. Our extension of the Fractal platform tools has two purposes: to support the explicit and separate representation of specifications and configurations and, to embed these representations in the component model. The three architecture representations are then available and manipulable at runtime, also providing a full support for evolution management. The *Arch3D Editor* tool provides a graphical console to create, view and modify Dedal-based Fractal architectures. Architects can simultaneously display the different representations of an architecture and work on them.

# 6 Conclusion

Dedal enables the explicit and separate representations of architecture specifications, configurations and assemblies. Architecture design decisions can thus be precisely captured and traced throughout the development process. The three-level syntax of Dedal supports the expression of requirements by the means of abstract and partial component roles that are used as the main conceptual support for the search of reusable components to be included in configurations. The model of the runtime system (the instanciated component assembly) is rich enough to serve as the baseis of a full evolution process [12]. A perspective for this work is to experiment the use of Dedal to manage component-based software product lines.

# References

1. Crnkovic, I., Chaudron, M., Larsson, S.: Component-based development process and component lifecycle. In: Proc. of the Intl. Conf. on Software Engineering Advances, Papeete, French Polynesia, October 2006, p. 44 (2006)
2. Chaudron, M., Crnkovic, I.: Component-based Software Engineering. In: Software Engineering; Principles and Practice, pp. 605–628. Wiley, Chichester (2008)
3. Taylor, R., Medvidovic, N., Dashofy, E.: Software Architecture: Foundations, Theory, and Practice. Wiley, Chichester (January 2009)

---

[5] http://fractal.ow2.org/

4. Dashofy, E., van der Hoek, A., Taylor, R.: A highly-extensible, XML-based architecture description language. In: Proc. of 2nd WICSA Conf., Amsterdam, The Netherlands, pp. 103–112 (2001)
5. Medvidovic, N., Rosenblum, D., Taylor, R.: A language and environment for architecture-based software development and evolution. In: Proc. of ICSE Conf., Los Angeles, USA, May 1999, pp. 44–53 (1999)
6. Allen, R., Garlan, D.: A formal basis for architectural connection. ACM Trans. Softw. Eng. Methodol. 6(3), 213–249 (1997)
7. Plasil, F., Visnovsky, S.: Behavior protocols for software components. IEEE Trans. Softw. Eng. 28(11), 1056–1076 (2002)
8. Magee, J., Kramer, J.: Dynamic structure in software architectures. SIGSOFT Softw. Eng. Notes 21(6), 3–14 (1996)
9. Bruneton, E., Coupaye, T., Leclercq, M., Quéma, V., Stefani, J.B.: The Fractal component model and its support in Java: Experiences with auto-adaptive and reconfigurable systems. Softw. Pract. Exper. 36(11-12), 1257–1284 (2006)
10. Booch, G., Rumbaugh, J., Jacobson, I.: Unified Modeling Language User Guide, 2nd edn. Addison-Wesley, Reading (2005)
11. Garlan, D., Schmerl, B., Chang, J.: Using gauges for architecture-based monitoring and adaptation. In: Proc. of Working Conf. on Complex and Dynamic Systems Architecture, Brisbane, Australia (December 2001)
12. Zhang, H. Y., Urtado, C., Vauttier, S.: Architecture-centric development and evolution processes for component-based software. In: Proc. of 22nd SEKE Conf., Redwood City, USA (July 2010)
13. Aboud, N.A., Arévalo, G., Falleri, J. R., Huchard, M., Tibermacine, C., Urtado, C., Vauttier, S.: Automated architectural component classification using concept lattices. In: Proc. of the Joint WICSA/ECSA Conf., Cambridge, UK (September 2009)
14. Desnos, N., Huchard, M., Tremblay, G., Urtado, C., Vauttier, S.: Search-based many-to-one component substitution. J. Softw. Maint: Res. Pract. 20(5), 321–344 (2008)
15. Shaw, M., Garlan, D.: Software architecture: perspectives on an emerging discipline. Prentice-Hall, Englewood Cliffs (1996)
16. Cheng, S.W., Garlan, D., Schmerl, B., Sousa, J.P., Spitznagel, B., Steenkiste, P.: Using architectural style as a basis for system self-repair. In: Proc. of 3rd WICSA Conf., Montreal, Canada, August 2002, pp. 45–59 (2002)

# Dynamic Architectural Constraints Monitoring and Reconfiguration in Service Architectures

Jose John, MingXue Wang, and Claus Pahl

School of Computing, Dublin City University
Dublin, Ireland
jose.john2@mail.dcu.ie, {mwang,cpahl}@computing.dcu.ie

**Abstract.** Service-oriented architecture is an architectural approach that can be applied for building autonomous service systems dynamically to satisfy on-demand business requests. During the execution of service compositions, architectural constraint violations relating to functional and non-fucntional system properties need to be handled intelligently and autonomously, possibly requiring architectural reconfigurations. We propose integrated architectural constraint violation handling to deal with architectural quality problems through dynamic reconfiguration. We concentrate on service replacement selection as a remedial strategy for a possible quality violation requiring architectural remedies.

## 1 Introduction

Service-oriented architecture (SOA) allows us to build interoperable distributed systems. Service processes are build using orchestration languages like WS-BPEL. Composing processes dynamically is a solution for on-demand requests. Dynamic reconfiguration is often the consequence of faults (e.g., caused by the violation of architectural constraints). The severity of some faults might not allow a service to be used further. BPEL provides fault handling mechanisms, but no remedial mechanisms. A solution is to dynamically select a remedial strategy. Architectural constraint violations indicating quality problems are important faults that can occur during execution [12].

Our solution is an operationalisation of dynamic service architecture through an architectural quality monitoring instrumentation of processes using the WS-BPEL fault handling mechanism. Fault and violation handling based on dynamically available architectural knowledge in the form of quality-oriented service annotations acts here as a framework for dynamic architectural decision making:

- A dynamic remedial strategy selection mechanism. In [11], remedial strategies are proposed for business constraint violations and runtime faults, which are mapped to architectural remedial strategies for reconfiguration. This paper focuses on the service replacement remedial strategy.
- Service replacement selection based on a service quality annotation scheme. The annotation scheme captures different architectural properties for each replacement service. When a quality constraint violation occurs, the annotation scheme will be searched for a suitable replacement.

M. Ali Babar and I. Gorton (Eds.): ECSA 2010, LNCS 6285, pp. 311–318, 2010.

We focus on the operationalisation of dynamic selection techniques. Based on an empirical study, we have identified a number of properties that can be used for the annotation scheme of recomposable services. We introduce a similarity metric based on an aggregated distance, which is used for selecting a suitable replacement. We also use a history-based success ranking heuristics as a weighting mechanism to further discriminate between replacement candidate services.

Section 2 introduces service fault handling. In Section 3, we outline our architecture. We define the annotation scheme in Section 4, the selection mechanism in Section 5, and the monitoring and violation handling implementation in Section 6. Finally, we discuss our implementation and conclusions are given.

## 2   Service-Oriented Architecture and Service Composition

*Constraint Violation and Fault Monitoring.* If we compose services dynamically based on on-demand user requests, we can customise services based on user profiles or remedy requirements validation [9]. BPEL process instances interact with the constituent web services through invoking various activities. Normally, the process ends its execution with a reply activity. During the execution of a process, faults can occur. One category of faults are technical runtime exceptions which are thrown by the BPEL engine itself. There are also business or requirements constraint violations. The faults can be the consequence of violations of architectural quality constraints or can impact on these. Quality constraints need to be monitored and faults need to be handled appropriately so that the composed process do not fail. Fault monitoring detects faults and records data for analysis. We use BPEL fault handlers for architectural constraints monitoring and fault handling. BPEL has fault handlers for handling specific faults ($<catch>$) and for handling all kinds of faults ($<catchAll>$). We will use a constraint monitoring and fault handling framework to monitor architectural quality (expressed as architectural constraints) and handle violations by recomposing the service process.

*Fault Analysis.* Used for finding the best remedial strategy for a fault instance, it takes fault data as input and outputs a strategy. Pre-defined remedial knowledge is used for fault analysis. Defining remedial knowledge involves three steps: defining a fault taxonomy, defining remedial strategies, and matching each fault category with remedial strategies. The types of faults that can occur define a fault taxonomy [1],[4]. In order to deal with business constraint validations, a fault taxonomy is derived from the context model which is used for constraint validation services. Remedial strategies like process goal-preserving retry, replace, ignore or recompose [1],[11] are selected and applied dynamically:

- Ignore: this strategy completely ignores the fault occurred. This is suitable for faults that do not have any effect on the overall architectural goal.
- Retry: this strategy tries to execute the faulted service again. Maximum retries and the retry interval can be defined.
- Replace: this strategy replaces the faulty service with a suitable one with same the business functionality.

– Recompose: this strategy discards the entire faulty process and establishes a new process with the same architectural goal.

Non-goal preserving strategies identified are log (the fault data is recorded), alert (concerned parties will be alerted) and suspend (suspends the faulty process based on a threshold value of past failure ratio). The fault taxonomy is mapped to the strategies. We can have two kinds of constraint violation faults, pre-condition constraint violation faults and post-condition constraint violation faults, which are validated before or after service execution, respectively.

## 3   Fault Handling Architecture

We focus on the replacement strategy in particular as it is the core activity in architectural reconfiguration – recomposition creates specific problems in terms of planning techniques [10] that go beyond the focus of this paper. Replacement requires additional supporting infrastructure for discovering alternatives. We can implement it in two ways: pre-assign a replacement service so that the strategy can be instantly applied or discover alternative services dynamically. This discovery can be based on functional and/or non-functional architectural annotations. We select an alternative service from a service repository, which may have multiple services which match the functionality of the faulty service. A decision which one to select is made by a selection mechanism.

We use BPEL fault handling to implement annotation and remedial activities. This avoids the overhead of BPEL engine-dependent modifications and additional monitoring components in order to reduce monitoring and fault handling overhead. We add validation services for business constraint validations. Constraint violations are thrown from these constraint services as service faults. This allows us to catch the architectural constraint violation faults in the BPEL fault handlers. Fig. 1 shows the architecture. Main layers identified are process execution layer, fault tolerance layer and database layer. The fault-tolerance layer contains monitoring, analysis (selection mechanism) and a service wrapper component. The database layer stores all available services to be considered for a possible replacement in a service repository. The annotation is stored in an annotation scheme database. The wrapper handles the invocation of the replacement service. The execution of the process happens at the process execution layer.

## 4   Service Quality Annotation Scheme

The annotation scheme is a central component that enables dynamic alternative service selection. Annotations of replacement services are kept in a dynamically accessible and updatable repository. The annotation scheme works based on operational (QoS) properties of services. The values of these architectural quality properties play a crucial role in the selection of a replacement service. We choose here three architecturally important properties which can be measured - all suitable for easy operationalisation:

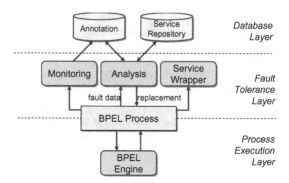

**Fig. 1.** Fault Handling Architecture

- Response Time (Latency): This property measures the difference between the time a service request takes between the request and response. It can be calculated as follows: *Response Time = Response Completion Time - User Request Time*. Response Completion Time is the time when all data for a response arrives at the user. User Request Time is the time when the user sends a request. This is a measure of the performance of a web service.
- Availability: It is the time period in which the service is ready for use or the service is maintained. If the time when a system is not available is 'Down Time' and when its is available is 'Up Time', then availability is the average uptime. It can be measured using *Availability = 1 - (Down Time / Up Time)*.
- Accessibility: Accessibility represents the degree that a system is normatively operated to counteract request messages without delay. In some cases, a service system could be accessible for external users to try accessing its resources even if its services are not available. We can determine whether a web service system is accessible by just ensuring that the system can return an acknowledgment for a request message. Thus, accessibility can be calculated as the ratio of number of acknowledgments received to the number of request messages: *Accessibility = Number of Acknowledgments Received / Number of Request Messages*.

Other properties such as throughput and reliability, but also integrity, compliance and security are also considered to be important, but have not been addressed in our framework yet. We focus on selection based on operational criteria of architectural relevance, which capture classical quality-of-service properties in the first category (such as response time or accessibility). Maintaining architectural quality through quality monitoring and remedy is our objective.

## 5   Analysis and Selection Mechanism

The selection mechanism that we use here is based on the concept of an aggregated distance (AD). An aggregated distance is the sum of distances of all the annotated properties for a service. For each annotated property there is some threshold value for the running process. A distance is the difference between this threshold value and the actual property value of the service. Let $P_{i_j}$ be the value of the $j$-th property of the $i$-th replacement service $P_i$. $T_j$ as the threshold value is defined for the $j$-th property in order to normalise the values. Then, the aggregated distance, a simple additive weighting, for the $i$-th service is

$$AD_i = \sum_{j=1}^{n_i} \frac{P_{i_j} - T_j}{max(P_{i_j}) - min(P_{i_j})}$$

for all properties $j$ where $max$ and $min$ refer to the maximal and minimal values of each property in order to normalise each property in comparison to the other properties. $AD_i$ shall be defined 1 where $max(P_{i_j}) - min(P_{i_j}) = 0$. The service with the least aggregated distance is the best replacement candidate.

In addition to the AD, we use a heuristic function to support the selection. A history-based success ranking system shall support the decision. The heuristic is in this case an approximation of the expected reliability of a service. If the post-constraint evaluation finishes without any exception, we increase the rank of the service by one. If the execution flow reaches the fault handler, the service has generated some fault and we decrease the rank by one. While selecting the replacement service, we take the service with highest rank into account as a weighting to discriminate between similarly valued services based on AD. We adjust the distance measure using the rank for service $i$, $rank(i)$, with 1 being the best and $\|rank\|$ denoting the total number of ranked services:

$$AD_i^{norm} = AD_i \times (1 + \frac{rank(i)}{\|rank\|})$$

This ranking-based weighting works as a passive recommendation system as it gives up-to-date feedback on each service. The normalised $AD_i^{norm}$ value that is closest to the original $AD_i$ is considered the best (lower ranked services would create a greater distance to $AD_i$).

## 6   Architectural Constraint Monitoring and Handling

Two aspects need to be distinguished: monitoring in order to keep the service annotations up to date and architectural constraint monitoring and handling.

*Annotation Monitoring and Updating.* The annotation scheme is kept up to date. The advantage of dynamic monitoring is that the selection mechanism can make decisions based on the latest information to increase the accuracy of selections. We monitor the response time of a service, measured as the time between the end of pre-condition validation to the start of post-condition validation. This time is updated for that service in the annotation scheme as the new response time. We are working on a constraint monitoring instrumentation that can be applied to provide measurement for the suggested quality properties.

*Instrumentation Template for Constraint Handling.* The implementation of the violation handling needs a BPEL process instrumentation that integrates

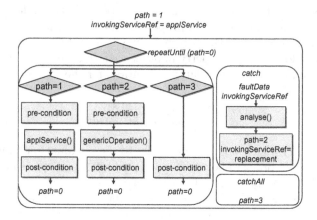

**Fig. 2.** Instrumentation Template

fault handling and monitoring capabilities. To achieve this, we use constraint services. The instrumentation also applies the selected remedial strategies. We use a modified version of the instrumentation template which is used in [11]. Fig. 2 shows this modified instrumentation template. Two important variables are used in the instrumentation template, invokingServiceRef and path. invokingServiceRef holds a reference to the current activity which is invoked. invokingServiceRef is passed to both pre- and post-constraint services so that they can inspect the properties of the invoking service to see whether constraints are satisfied. Whenever there is a fault, the invokingServiceRef will be passed to the fault handlers for further analysis along with the fault data. There are two main execution paths in the template. In the default path (path=1), the original service is invoked along with the pre- and post-constraint services. If there is a fault, then the path variable is changed so that the execution follows the second path (path=2). Once an execution path is completed without faults, the path variable is assigned to 0 (path = 0) and the repeatUntil construct finishes.

*The Replacement Strategy.* Faults caused by pre-condition constraint violation are caught by the <catch> fault handler. It passes fault data as well as the invokingServiceRef variable to the analyse() service. Since the replacement strategy is applied, the analyse operation sets path=2. It also assigns a new service found by the selection to invokingServiceRef. This alternative service is called by the genericOperation() wrapper. Faults caused by the invoking service are caught by a <catchAll> handler. It sets path to 3. This path has a post-constraint validator which converts this fault into a constraint validation fault. This is caught by the <catch> and analyse() will run as in case 1.

## 7   Discussion

Our evaluation focus was on the effectiveness and performance of the monitoring and fault handling system. Performance is critical as the context is dynamic architectural reconfiguration. Effectiveness and reliability are equally important in an autonomous setting.

The aggegrated distance approach essentially creates an attribute vector of normalised values (threshold), which based on a manual validation determines good candidate replacements. We have used the success ranking to have a second analysis stage to remove unsuitable cases. 35 test cases were designed for a payment process, which involves four business services (requestBill; payBill; updateRecords; infoProvider) to evaluate the remedial strategy as a whole. We developed three alternative services for each service to test the replacement remedies with alternative services. Test cases cover architectural constraint violations and runtime faults in the context of all proposed remedial strategies.

The overhead created for monitoring and updating annotation attributes did not exceed 9% of the overall execution time and the overhead for the violation was in average between 3 and 4% due to the embedding of the instrumentation into the BPEL fault handling. Only the access to the database for replacement selection was a significant element in the 9% figure. Each process was composed of a different number (2 to 10) of application services. We instrumented each process and created pairs of processes to compare their performance. The performance evaluation results show that the instrumented processes does not introduce any significant overhead (in average less than 1%). The instrumented processes do not delay the overall execution unless a fault needs to be handled.

Effectiveness, performance and reliability shall also be looked at in the context of related work. In [10], a solution using various planning techniques for dynamic service composition is provided. However, they lack comprehensive fault-tolerance mechanisms. Constraint integration and monitoring platforms has been looked at. In [2], a constraint language is proposed for the Dynamo monitoring platform. We use a simpler and more efficient standard BPEL fault handling without requiring additional execution monitoring subsystems.

Different remedial strategy selections have been proposed. An interesting approach [5] is to invoke all alternative services in parallel and select the one which gives back the first response. It allows to select the best service quickly, but causes computational and network overheads and has the risk of multiple transactions, which is avoided in our annotation repository-based solution.

Our selection approach is based on aggregated distances and heuristics as a basic recommendation mechanism. Recommendation system are based on the learning done by the system from user or system feedbacks [7]. While aggregated distances seem to perform well as a similarity measure in terms of determining effective replacements, agglomerative clustering algorithms (e.g. association coefficient based similarity measures) can also be used.

## 8   Conclusions

We have introduced an integrated constraint monitoring and violation handling mechanism for dynamic service compositions. Flexible service process orchestrations at runtime form the problem setting [8],[3]. We used replacement as the basis of our remedial architecture strategy. We provided an instrumentation template to support the integrated fault monitoring and handling for architectural quality constraints. A quality-oriented selection mechanism has been implemented to select from the available replacement services. Architectural reconfiguration is a problem of technical fault-tolerance, but also the consideration of architectural compliance with respect to business rules.

An extension is a more intelligent selection strategy based on machine learning. We will also address access performance improvements for the selection mechanism. Storage of the annotation scheme is another point of improvement.

## Acknowledgment

The authors would like to thank the Science Foundation Ireland for their support for the CASCAR project.

## References

1. Ardagna, D., Cappiello, C., Fugini, M., Mussi, E., Pernici, B., Plebani, P.: Faults and recovery actions for self-healing web services. In: World Wide Web Conf. (2006)
2. Baresi, L., Guinea, S., Pasquale, L.: Towards a unified framework for the monitoring and recovery of bpel processes. In: Workshop on Testing, analysis, and verification of web services and applications (2008)
3. Barrett, R., Patcas, L.M., Murphy, J., Pahl, C.: Model Driven Distribution Pattern Design for Dynamic Web Service Compositions. In: International Conference on Web Engineering, ICWE 2006, Palo Alto, US, pp. 129–136. ACM Press, New York (2006)
4. Chan, K.M., Bishop, J., Steyn, J., Baresi, L., Guinea, S.: A fault taxonomy for web service composition. In: 3rd Intl. Workshop on Engineering Service Oriented Applications, WESOA (2007)
5. Dobson, G.: Using ws-bpel to implement software fault tolerance for web services. In: 32nd EUROMICRO Conf. on Software Eng. and Adv. Applications (2006)
6. Liu, A., Li, Q., Huang, L., Xiao, M.: A declarative approach to enhancing the reliability of bpel processes. In: IEEE Intl. Conf. on Web Services (2007)
7. Manikrao, U., Prabhakar, T.: Dynamic selection of Web services with recommendation system. In: Next Generation Web Services Practices (2005)
8. Pahl, C.: A Formal Composition and Interaction Model for a Web Component Platform. In: Proc. ICALP Workshop on Formal Methods and Component Interaction FMCI 2002. Electronic Notes on Computer Science, ENTCS, vol. 66(4) (2002)
9. Pahl, C.: Layered Ontological Modelling for Web Service-oriented Model-Driven Architecture. In: Hartman, A., Kreische, D. (eds.) ECMDA-FA 2005. LNCS, vol. 3748, pp. 88–102. Springer, Heidelberg (2005)
10. Pistore, M., Barbon, F., Bertoli, P.: Planning and monitoring web service composition. In: Workshop on Planning and Scheduling for Web and Grid Services (2004)
11. Wang, M., Bandara, K.Y., Pahl, C.: Integrated Constraint Violation Handling for Dynamic Service Composition. In: IEEE International Conference on Services Computing, SCC 2009 (2009)
12. Zeng, L., Benatallah, B., Ngu, A.H., Dumas, M., Kalagnanam, J., Chang, H.: Qos-aware middleware for web services composition. IEEE Transactions on Software Engineering 30(5), 311–327 (2004)

# Using Domain Knowledge to Boost Software Architecture Evaluation

Veli-Pekka Eloranta and Kai Koskimies

Department of Software Systems,
Tampere University of Technology, Finland
{firstname.lastname}@tut.fi

**Abstract.** Benefits of scenario-based software architecture evaluation such as ATAM are widely recognized. However, full-scale software architecture evaluation is resource and time consuming. In this paper we propose a technique to facilitate the creation of scenarios in a particular domain using a conceptual model especially targeted for architecture evaluation. The technique supports the finding of general, system-independent scenarios and the use of general scenarios in new evaluations. If the model is annotated with a (domain-specific) pattern language, the approach also supports the identification of solutions and the analysis of the architecture. The potential benefits of the technique in terms of semi-automatically produced scenarios are analyzed in the context of an industrial architecture evaluation.

## 1 Introduction

The benefits of software architecture evaluation have been widely recognized (e.g. [4]), and especially scenario-based evaluation methods [11] have become popular. However, a major problem of scenario-based evaluation methods is their need of resources, often hindering their usage especially in smaller development projects. For example, a full-scale ATAM evaluation of an average-sized system may easily take from 200 up to 400 manhours [7], which can be hard to justify in many cases. We need techniques to make software architecture evaluation more efficient without losing its benefits and accuracy. This is particularly required in agile development.

The main idea of scenario-based evaluation methods is to identify the architectural solutions of the target system, refine and concretize the quality requirements of the system as scenarios, and analyze the prioritized scenarios against the architectural solutions. The problem of efficient scenario elicitation has been studied by several authors. In particular, the concept of a general scenario was introduced in [3] for the purpose of expressing reusable scenarios in a system-independent fashion. General scenarios are abstracted from previous evaluations and specialized for a particular system. The main contribution of this paper is a technique that supports the creation and specialization of general scenarios in the context of a particular domain. In contrast to general frameworks (e.g. [10]) or scenario categories ([1], [5]), we propose the use of a conceptual model of a system category as the basis of scenario elicitation. The main benefits of this approach are that the model provides a vehicle to relate scenarios with the basic concepts of the system, making it possible to derive and specialize general scenarios in

M. Ali Babar and I. Gorton (Eds.): ECSA 2010, LNCS 6285, pp. 319–326, 2010.

a systematic way, and that the coverage of the scenarios can be evaluated in terms of the system concepts.

On the other hand, the identification of architectural solutions of a given system during evaluation can be hard as well. Often the architecture is poorly documented at the time of evaluation, or the documentation does not explicitly identify the architectural solutions. We demonstrate that the same conceptual model can be enriched with generic solutions (patterns) as well, supporting the identification and analysis of architectural solutions during the evaluation.

The domain we have investigated is mobile working machine control systems; however, it seems plausible that the proposed techniques are applicable to other domains as well. Our study is based on four full-scale ATAM-like architectural evaluations we have carried out in two Finnish companies manufacturing large industrial working machines: mining machines and forest harvesters. Additionally, the potential benefits of this approach were studied in a fifth evaluation.

## 2   System Concept Model for Architecture Evaluation

### 2.1   System Concept Model (SCM)

A central artifact in our approach is a conceptual model of a system or system category, called a *system concept model* (SCM). Essentially, SCM describes the basic concepts required to communicate about a system during the architecture evaluation. As such, the concepts in SCM can be related to the software architecture (e.g. archetypes [6]), hardware in an embedded system, input and output devices, domain concepts, system resources and external artifacts relevant for the system etc. The scope of SCM can vary, and we deliberately leave it open: SCM should serve as a pragmatic description of the conceptual world of architecture evaluation, rather than as a formal specification. SCM differs from a traditional domain model in that it contains technical concepts as well; on the other hand it describes the logical relationships between concepts rather than system architecture. Minimally, SCM should contain the system-related concepts appearing in the scenarios and the core concepts of the system architecture, i.e. archetypes. SCM can be given for a single system, or (more usefully) for a system category. We assume here that SCM is given as a UML class diagram.

### 2.2   Process of Scenario Elicitation Using SCM

Our process for exploiting general scenarios in architecture evaluation is illustrated in Fig. 1. The first step in our technique is to carry out an architecture evaluation (e.g. ATAM), which produces a set of concrete scenarios. SCM is assumed either to exist before the evaluation or to be constructed after (or during) the evaluation. If SCM exists before the evaluation, it can be used to facilitate the communication between stakeholders during the evaluation, providing the evaluators and stakeholders with the same domain-specific vocabulary.

The second step is to annotate SCM with concrete scenarios. This means that keywords that can be found from SCM are searched from the scenario descriptions and the

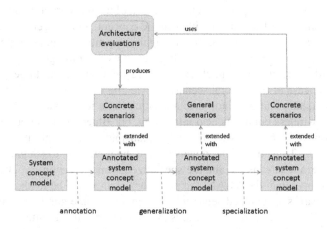

**Fig. 1.** Process to produce general scenarios and new concrete scenarios using SCM

scenario is linked with the corresponding classes in SCM. Often it is useful to mark implicit relationships as well, that is, even if a concept is not mentioned in the scenario but is known to be closely related with the scenario, the corresponding link can be added for the scenario. The scenarios are presented as UML collaborations in SCM. In principle, it should be possible to attach every scenario with some concepts in SCM; in case there is a scenario with no links, it is a sign that SCM lacks concepts that are essential for understanding the system, and it should be completed with such concepts.

Once SCM is annotated with concrete scenarios, general scenarios can be derived in the third step (Fig. 1). For each concrete scenario that is linked with certain specialized concepts, the generalization relationships of these concepts are followed upwards until a suitable level of abstraction is reached, and a new general scenario is created and linked with those higher-level concepts. Naturally, a scenario can be associated with arbitrary many concepts.

For example, assume that a concrete scenario is "The joystick can be operated via Bluetooth, the necessary change can be made in a month". This scenario involves two specific concepts: the joystick and Bluetooth. Both are specific kinds of more general concepts, namely a user control device and a wireless communication protocol. Thus, a general scenario could be "A user control device can be operated via a wireless communication protocol, the necessary change can be made in x months". Note that the response part cannot be generalized in the same manner, but it has to expressed for example using variable names for specific numbers or using a template list for responses.

This process is by no means fully mechanical, since there can be several levels of more general concepts in SCM, or possibly none. In the former case, it may be possible and useful to create several general scenarios at different levels of abstraction. In the latter case, the lack of a generalization relationship may indicate that SCM needs new generalized concepts. It is also quite possible that some concrete scenarios simply cannot be generalized in a sensible manner. If a concrete scenario is linked only with the subclasses of a single concept (say, "changing CAN bus to Ethernet"), the corresponding general scenario will be linked with a single concept, and the general scenario has to be formed in a different way (e.g. "changing the communication bus type").

In the fourth step scenarios are specialized by traversing the generalization hierarchy downwards, selecting the subclasses that are relevant for the target system. For example, in the case of the general scenario above, the new target could be the control system of a machine that does not have a joystick but a touch pad. In the case of the new machine, wireless control is also interesting, but Bluetooth is not an option since the remote control is too far away. Instead, a plausible option might be a wireless internet connection. Thus, traversing downwards in the hierarchy, touch pad and WLAN are seen as relevant subclasses, and the specialized scenario becomes "The touch pad control can be operated via WLAN, the necessary change can be made in 3 months". The response part is specialized separately, assigning suitable numbers in the place of the variables. The new concrete scenario is then included in the architecture evaluation in the normal way, prioritized and possibly analyzed. The relevant quality attribute for the scenario is readily available as the general scenario is already mapped to the quality attribute through the original concrete scenario.

Besides scenario elicitation, SCM can be used also for estimating scenario coverage. SCM can be divided into major subareas, and ideally the scenarios should be fairly evenly associated with the different subareas. If the scenarios are mainly attached to only certain subareas, or if one subarea is without any scenarios, it is possible that the scenario set is somewhat misaligned and new scenarios should be elicited for the empty or scarse subareas. For example, in the domain studied in this work, SCM was divided into 9 subareas (e.g. Messaging, User interfaces, Remote access etc).

### 2.3    Annotating SCM with Solutions

On the solution side, the counterpart of a general scenario is a pattern: a pattern describes a solution in a system-independent manner. In the same way as a concrete scenario is an instance of a general scenario, a solution in the architecture is often (although not always) an instance of a pattern documented as part of a pattern language. Similarly to general scenarios, patterns can be and often are domain-specific.

Assuming that SCM is available, patterns can be linked to the concepts in the model in the same way as general scenarios: if a pattern refers to a concept in SCM, it is linked to the corresponding class. We have used UML collaborations also for denoting patterns in SCM. This kind of model annotation can be useful for the pattern language itself, as it provides a domain-oriented structuring for the pattern language, but it makes sense also from the viewpoint of architecture evaluation. In particular, the representation of both the problem domain (general scenarios) and the solution domain (patterns) in the same model together with the essential system concepts facilitates discussions about the relationships of problems and solutions. We will present concrete examples in the next section.

Since patterns describe general solutions in a system-independent way, they will be typically linked to the base classes in the inheritance hierarchies. For example, if a pattern describes a solution to create an abstraction for a bus, it is linked to the Bus class; if a pattern describes a communication mechanism between nodes based on a bus, it is linked with Bus and Node classes etc. Basically, the nouns in the context and solution parts of the pattern description are potential concepts to be linked with the pattern in SCM. This process can also lead to the observation that new classes need to be added to SCM.

SCM, annotated with scenarios and patterns, can be utilized in the analysis phase of ATAM in particular for more accurate solution identification. When a scenario has been proposed in such a way that it is linked with the same concepts as a pattern, an instance of the pattern may exist in the architecture. This may have been overlooked in the identification of architectural solutions: either the solution has not been recognized at all or it has been recognized but not seen as an instance of a pattern. In both cases, recognizing a solution as an instance of a pattern makes the analysis faster and more reliable, as the potential non-risks and risks are readily available as positive and negative consequences in the documentation of the pattern, respectively.

## 3   Applying the Approach

We have applied the proposed techniques in the domain of mobile working machine control systems. Based on four full-scale ATAM-like architectural evaluations carried out in Finnish machine industry, SCM was created, and the elicited scenarios were generalized and attached to SCM. During those evaluations, patterns were identified, documented and organized into a pattern language, and the patterns were attached to the SCM as well.

After that, a fifth evaluation was carried out. In this evaluation, the aim was to evaluate the potential usability of SCM enriched with general scenarios and patterns. However, since the primary purpose of the evaluation was to produce normal analysis results for the company, we could not risk the evaluation process by trying entirely new techniques in the elicitation of scenarios. Instead, scenarios were created in the conventional way during the evaluation, and compared afterwards against a set of concrete scenarios that was created before the evaluation on the basis of the general scenarios and SCM refined according to the specialized concepts of the target system.

A part of the resulting SCM annotated with patterns for mobile working machine control systems is depicted in Fig. 2. A basic source of information for SCM was the set of scenarios elicited during the four evaluations. Essentially, SCM was created by gathering first a list of generally known basic concepts for the domain such as bus, node, controller etc. After that all scenarios were studied and more concepts were found in the phrasing of the scenarios. Additionally, the list of concepts was augmented with concrete examples of the existing concepts. We decided to leave attributes out from SCM as they are not required in our context. The entire SCM comprises of 71 classes.

Once we had created SCM, we annotated it with concrete scenarios from previous architecture evaluations. The concrete scenario (Scenario 1) has been attached as a UML collaboration to classes Boom Control Algorithm and Boom Controller in Fig. 2 as the scenario is related to the control algorithm of the boom, residing in the boom controller. Scenario description is as follows:

> *Boom's control algorithm geometry (spherical, cartesian, etc) can be changed by changing only one parameter.*

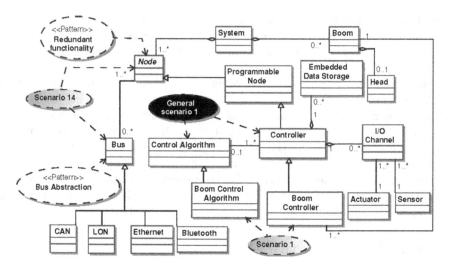

**Fig. 2.** Part of SCM with example scenario and some of the domain-specific patterns

Note that here we have used an implicit relationship between a scenario and a concept: the controller is not explicitly mentioned in the scenario, but the location of the control algorithm is considered essential from the viewpoint of the scenario.

Next, general scenarios were developed using SCM. For example, we can see from SCM that Boom Control Algorithm is inherited from Control Algorithm and Boom Controller is inherited from Controller. By following this generalization hierarchy and applying little rephrasing we can form a general scenario for Scenario 1 as follows:

> *A control algorithm in a controller can be changed to another algorithm version by changing x parameters.*

The resulting general scenario is linked with Control Algorithm and Controller, as shown in Fig. 2. We created in this way 52 general scenarios from the concrete scenarios elicited in the evaluations.

The fifth evaluation was carried out as a normal ATAM-like evaluation. Scenarios were elicited by the stakeholders only, without any influence from our side. After the evaluation sessions we verified how many of the scenarios in the fifth evaluation could have been actually "guessed", at least approximately, before the evaluation sessions using the general scenarios developed earlier.

We created 57 concrete scenarios as specializations of the general scenarios before the fifth evaluation and compared these to the 22 well-formed concrete scenarios which were elicited during the evaluation. We found out that 17 of the concrete scenarios created during the evaluation were essentially the same that we have generated beforehand. This means that 77 percent of the correctly formed scenarios could have been created, in a more or less accurate form, prior to the evaluation. Bass et al. [3] reports that as much as 91 percent of created concrete scenarios could be mapped to general scenarios extracted from five evaluations, suggesting that we can reach a fairly good level of coverage of general scenarios with our technique.

During the four evaluations we gathered a pattern language of 45 patterns for the domain of distributed embedded control system [8]. These patterns were linked to the domain concepts in SCM using (general) scenarios, resulting in general scenarios and patterns linked with the classes of SCM. When annotated both with scenarios and patterns, SCM provides useful information about the interplay of scenarios and patterns during the evaluation. For example, in Fig. 2 scenario 14 describes a situation where the bus is changed from CAN to Ethernet in a week. If this scenario is analysed, evaluators can look if there is a solution described by BUS ABSTRACTION or REDUNDANT FUNCTIONALITY pattern. If the solution provided by the pattern is not used, evaluators can ask whether this was intentional or not, and if not, why. In some cases, the architect just may have ignored such a solution.

## 4   Related Work

Babar and Biffl [1] divide the techniques to steer scenario creation into two main types: top-down elicitation is guided by a predefined classification of scenario categories, while bottom-up techniques aim at extracting the scenarios directly from stakeholders using queries, interviews and brainstorming. Our technique falls clearly in the former category. In that category, the approaches that come near to ours are the idea of general scenarios discussed previously ([2], [3]), the use of various (domain-independent) matrix forms like [10] or [12], and the use of change categories (e.g. [5]). In addition, slightly similar approach than ours has been taken in [9] to share architectural knowledge of quantitative analysis. Another way to classify scenario elicitation techniques is the level of domain independence: domain-specific techniques build an instrument guiding the scenario elicitation on the basis of a particular domain, while domain-independent techniques rely on generic guiding instruments. Our technique belongs obviously to the top-down domain-specific category. Basically, the techniques in this category require some additional work to build the domain-specific instrument, but they can provide stronger support for scenario elicitation. This has been actually empirically verified by Babar and Biffl [1] in the case of change categories: they have shown that domain specific categories of software changes can help stakeholders to generate better quality scenarios.

According to Bengtsson et al [5], a classification of change categories can guide the scenario elicitation process towards high quality scenarios. The classification of change categories is derived from the target domain. Change categories also help to decide scenario coverage: when there are scenarios in each category, the amount of scenarios can be regarded sufficient [5] [12]. When compared to our technique, change categories are more focused, addressing quality attributes like maintainability and modifiability. Our technique is in principle independent of quality attributes.

## 5   Conclusions

In this paper we have shown how to take advantage of domain knowledge in a scenario-based architecture evaluation process using SCM, a model that captures the conceptual world of architecture evaluation. The approach is particularly suitable if a number of evaluations is carried out for a well-understood domain. Our work leaves a number of open research questions. A practical problem is related to architectural knowledge management (e.g. [13]): how to support the collecting and management of the large amount of information pertaining to our approach, including SCM, scenarios, and patterns in a particular domain or company context? Another related problem is how to manage both architectural knowledge management and the actual architectural evaluations in an agile project context with minimal effort, without losing the benefits? These topics will be on our future research agenda.

# References

1. Babar, M.A., Biffl, S.: Eliciting better quality architecture evaluation scenarios: a controlled experiment on top-down vs. bottom-up. In: ISESE 2006: Proceedings of the 2006 ACM/IEEE international symposium on empirical software engineering, pp. 307–315. ACM Press, New York (2006), http://dx.doi.org/10.1145/1159733.1159779
2. Bachmann, F., Bass, L., Klein, M.: Deriving architectural tactics: A step toward methodical architectural design (March 2003)
3. Bass, L., Klein, M., Moreno, G.: Applicability of General Scenarios to the Architecture Tradeoff Analysis Method (2001)
4. Bass, L., Nord, R.L., Wood, W., Zubrow, D., Ozkaya, I.: Analysis of architecture evaluation data, vol. 81 (2008),
   http://dblp.uni-trier.de/db/journals/jss/jss81.html#BassNWZO08
5. Bengtsson, P., Bosch, J.: An experiment on creating scenario profiles for software change, vol. 9, pp. 59–78. Springer, Netherlands (2000)
6. Bosch, J.: Design and use of software architectures: adopting and evolving a product-line approach. ACM Press/Addison-Wesley Publishing Co., New York (2000)
7. Clements, P., Kazman, R., Klein, M.: Evaluating Software Architectures: Methods and Case Studies. Addison-Wesley Professional, Reading (January 2002)
8. Eloranta, V.P., Koskinen, J., Leppänen, M., Reijonen, V.: A pattern language for distributed machine control systems. Tech. rep., Tampere University of Techology (2010) ISBN 978-952-15-2319-9
9. Jansen, A., Vries, T., Avgeriou, P., Veelen, M.: Sharing the architectural knowledge of quantitative analysis. In: Becker, S., Plasil, F., Reussner, R. (eds.) QoSA 2008. LNCS, vol. 5281, pp. 220–234. Springer, Heidelberg (2008)
10. Kazman, R., Carriére, S.J., Woods, S.G.: Toward a discipline of scenario-based architectural engineering (2000)
11. Kazman, R., Klein, M., Clements, P.: ATAM: Method for Architecture Evaluation (2000)
12. Lassing, N., Rijsenbrij, D., van Vliet, H.: The goal of software architecture analysis: Confidence building or risk assessment (1999)
13. Peng, L.: Paris, Avgeriou. In: Muhammad, A.B., Torgeir, D., Patricia, L., Hans, v.V. (eds.) Tools and Technologies for Architectural Knowledge Management, Springer, Heidelberg (2009)

# Independently Extensibile Contexts

Martin Rytter and Bo Nørregaard Jørgensen

The Maersk Mc-Kinney Moller Institute, University of Southern Denmark,
Campusvej 55, 5230 Odense M, Denmark
{mlrj,bnj}@mmmi.sdu.dk
http://www.sdu.dk/mmmi

**Abstract.** Building and maintaining non-trivial software systems that
are independently extensible is a difficult task. This is because the combination of independent extensions tends to produce conflicts that are
difficult to anticipate, and to which no general resolution strategy exists.
In this paper, we show how some of these conflicts can be avoided if
domain-specific contexts are modeled using a representation that is open
for extension and safe for sharing among independent extensions.

**Keywords:** Independent extensibility, openness, sharing, context.

## 1 Introduction

The creation of software systems that are *independently extensible* is a difficult
but important challenge [14]. To be independently extensible, it must be possible
to combine independently developed extensions of a system without performing
a global integrity check.

Independent extensibility would be easy to achieve, if system designers were
able to anticipate dimensions of extension that would be needed in the future.
Unfortunately, this is often not the case:

- It is difficult for a programmer to anticipate *extension points* required by
  future extensions. Whenever the programmer fails to do so, and the required
  extension point cannot be introduced, the system fails to be extensible.
- It is difficult for a programmer to anticipate *interactions* among mutually
  unaware extensions developed independently of each other. When the combination of extensions may lead to undesirable interactions, the system fails
  to be independently extensible.

In other words, the combination of requirements for independent extensibility
and *unanticipated extensibility* is difficult to achieve.

We suggest that the above problems may be minimized, if we improve our
ability to model independently extensible contexts. Specifically, the representation of domain-specific contexts must be open to extension and yet safe to share
among independent extensions.

The rest of the paper is organized as follows. Section 2 presents the state of the
art of independent extensibility mechanisms. Section 3 motivates the importance
of context representations that are open and suitable for sharing. Finally, section
4 concludes the paper.

M. Ali Babar and I. Gorton (Eds.): ECSA 2010, LNCS 6285, pp. 327–334, 2010.
© Springer-Verlag Berlin Heidelberg 2010

## 2   State of the Art

Independent extensibility cannot be achieved when the means of extensibility violate the mutual independence of extension providers [14]. In the context of this observation, we now provide an overview of approaches for achieving extensibility.

When dimensions of extension can be anticipated, it is possible to constrain interaction using a component framework approach [17]. In this approach, existing systems ensure that all supported dimensions of extension are coordinated in such a way that independent extensibility can be guaranteed. Such coordination generally relies on high-level contracts among components [1]. Modern operating systems are examples of component frameworks. They work by letting the subject of extension (the operating system core) coordinate shared resources (processor, memory, etc.) through which independent extensions (programs, drivers, etc.) interact [11].

The difficulty of anticipating the future may be used to advocate mechanisms that support unanticipated extensibility. Two categories of unanticipated extensibility exist: i) Invasive in-place modification, and ii) non-invasive refinement that leads to client migration. Unfortunately, both categories of solutions lead to independent extensibility problems [12].

With *invasive in-place modification*, an extension provider modifies the existing system in order to allow for extension. Since modification is performed in place, changes become globally visible to all extensions. Modifications may be performed directly in source code, i.e. traditional evolutionary pressure [9], or on an intermediate representation of the system, e.g. using open classes [3] or aspects [7]. Invasive in-place modification techniques suffer from the problem that some conflicts are not detectable during development of the individual extensions, but first when extensions are combined. Such conflicts may be due to the introduction of similar members, overlapping invariants, or the need for an order in which to advice, or overwrite methods [13].

*Non-invasive refinement* is an extension strategy where modifications are performed on copies. This approach avoids conflicts that may emerge from in-place modification. Instead, we encounter the problem of *client migration*, i.e. the task of making existing clients refer to a newly refined version of a source file, module, or class. The ability to migrate a client may itself be unanticipated, and thus lead to the need for migration of clients-of-clients [12]. In the extreme case, the user is "migrated" to use a new version of the entire system. The oldest and most basic non-invasive refinement strategy is the practice known as copy-and-paste reuse. Other examples include Hyper/J [16] and object-based wrappers [4,2].

Lasagne/J [6] is an example of a hybrid approach where the primary extension mechanism is object-based wrappers, i.e. a non-invasive technique, but it also supports adherent methods, i.e. an invasive technique similar to aspect-oriented advices.

# 3   Independently Extensible Contexts

We now proceed to discuss independently extensible contexts. First, we discuss what a context is, and how it is usually represented in mainstream software systems. Subsequently, we discuss the role of openness and sharing in making contexts independently extensible.

## 3.1   Context

In general terms, a *context* is a setting in which statements may be interpreted or claims verified [10]. E.g. "a letter" is a context in which we can interpret statements such as "read it", "write it", "send it", and so on.

There are *constraints* on which statements can be meaningfully interpreted in a context. In context of "a letter" we can meaningfully interpret statements such as "send it", while other statements such as "drive it" has no obvious meaning.

A context may change. What this really means is that we maintain the perception of a context's identity, while we allow its state or constraints to change. E.g. given "a letter" we may change its state by "writing it", or we may change its constraints by discovering meaningful semantics for a statement such as "shred it". Despite these changes the identity of the letter remains the same. It is possible to see the state of a context as a simple constraint that must always be true, e.g. "the letter must be blank". However, we use the word "state" because it is extremely intuitive.

Our motivation for discussing contexts' ability to change is to highlight how modeling of contexts using networks of objects often constrains this process. We may do so by outlining three levels of context openness:

- A *closed* context never changes. E.g. a `String` object never changes. This is also known as immutability.
- A *restricted* context may change in well-defined *anticipated* ways. E.g. a `Letter` object may change the value of its `address` field, but only because the developer of the `Letter` class anticipated this scenario by introducing an appropriate set method.
- An *open* context may change in *unanticipated* ways. In a statically-typed language this level is difficult to achieve because every object is constrained by its class, i.e. an explicit definition of the forms of change that can occur. A `Letter` cannot suddenly have a return address if no `setReturnAddress()`-method was anticipated.

In order to achieve openness of any context, one must be able to modify its representation – in case of the inability to do so, the context is effectively closed.

## 3.2   Open Context

The openness of a software system relies on our ability to modify networks of objects. We now discuss how such modification is constrained in statically-typed

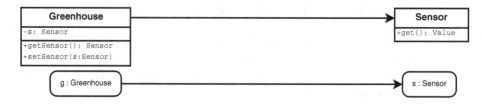

**Fig. 1.** A restricted network of objects

object-oriented languages, and we outline a simple modeling technique that may increase openness.

The modification of a network of objects is closely related to the concept of *object composition*. Object composition is traditionally seen as the combination of simple objects into more complex ones – i.e. composing a network of objects. However, a widely accepted benefit of object composition lies not in the ability to create, but in the ability to modify, a composition at runtime [4].

In order to understand how a network of objects is restricted by classes we will introduce a trivial example. The example is focusing on only two objects, a `Greenhouse` object, g, and a `Sensor` object, s. The diagram in figure 1 shows a class view and an object view of the example.

Now let us consider the openness of this object network, i.e. which modifications are possible without imposing change on existing classes. Below we consider openness with respect to the g object – a similar analysis can be made for the s object.

- It is possible to set the existing link outgoing from g to i) null, ii) a new object of class `Sensor`, or iii) a new object of a subtype of class `Sensor`.
- Without invasive change it is impossible to modify g to i) have a link to an object of a class that is not a subclass of `Sensor`, or ii) have a new number of outgoing links.

Given this analysis we may say that the object, g, is constrained by its class, `Greenhouse`. We may also say that the specific object-level link, g.s, is constrained by the class-level association, `Greenhouse.s`. While it is possible to introduce an object with an unanticipated implementation, e.g. a `Specific-Sensor`, it is not possible to introduce an object with an unanticipated interface, i.e. an object that is not a subtype of `Sensor`.

Figure 2 demonstrates how the lack of openness can be avoided by using the lookup pattern [8]. The idea is that a class, e.g. `Greenhouse`, by associating a `Lookup` at the class level, may allow for links to objects with unanticipated interfaces, e.g. `Actuator` objects.

By introducing the lookup pattern [8] when designing `Greenhouse`, the developer can facilitate openness with respect to unanticipated interfaces. E.g. an independent extension may decide to compose g with an `Actuator` object, a, using the `Lookup`:

```
g.getLookup().addLink(Actuator.class, new Actuator());
```

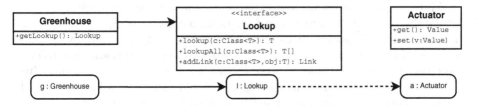

**Fig. 2.** An open network of objects

The openness offered in our example is not specific to a single extension. Another extension may navigate the link from **g** to **a** indirectly through the Lookup:

```
Actuator a = g.getLookup().lookup(Actuator.class);
if(a != null) { /* use actuator */ }
```

The increased openness comes from the idea that links can be qualified by a `Class` object. In Java, the `Class` object can be obtained through the special class-field, e.g. `Actuator.class`.

The lookup pattern has helped us to create a network of objects that is open to unanticipated changes. Specifically, a network of objects is not just open to objects with unanticipated implementations but also objects with unanticipated interfaces.

### 3.3  Shared Context

In addition to being open, the representation of a context must also be designed to be shared among multiple independent clients. An object is shared when more than one *alias* refer to it [5]. The owner of an alias may be called a *client* of the object to which the alias refers.

To illustrate a simple case of sharing, we will now consider two independently developed extensions being clients of the `Actuator`, **a**, in figure 2. For this example, we will assume that **a** controls the position of a window in the Greenhouse, **g**.

Extension 1 attempts to prevent condensation in the Greenhouse by ventilating when humidity becomes critically high:

```
// Extension 1: Prevent condensation.
if(humidityCriticallyHigh) { a.set(Value.OPEN); }
```

Extension 2 attempts to prevent loss of heat by closing all windows when the Greenhouse is being heated up:

```
// Extension 2: Prevent heating energy loss.
if(heatingValveOpen) { a.set(Value.CLOSED); }
```

While the code snippets from extension 1 and extension 2 work fine in isolation, their combination may lead to undesirable behavior. Specifically, it may happen that condensation takes place when extension 2 runs after extension 1, or a loss of heating energy may happen when extension 1 runs after extension 2. Note that this problem emerges even though both extensions are non-invasive.

In a monolithic system, the sharing of a would merely be a bug that should be fixed. However, in an independently extensible system the problem is more severe, because no extension developer can be blamed for the undesirable behavior that emerges from sharing [14,15]. If someone is to blame, it is the developer of Actuator, who has published an interface that allows a conflict to emerge at a point in time where no general resolution strategy applies. For this reason we hold that:

> The interface of an object, o, shared among independent extensions, must ensure that any contract offered to a client, c1, cannot be violated by any other client, c2.

In the example outlined above, no explicit contract is stated for Actuator.-set(Value) above the language level. However, traditionally programmers expect the effects of a client invoking a set method to persist until the same client invokes the same method again. In a non-sharing scenario this contract would hold, but not always in a sharing scenario.

Note that the formal specification of a contract may facilitate detection of undesirable interactions [1]. However, a formal specification does not ensure that independent clients will actually find the offered contract useful – i.e. independent extensibility is limited by the nature of contracts, and not merely by the lack of formal specification.

A set method is one of the most common examples of an idiom that does not support sharing and thus hinders independent extensibility. The solution to this problem is to assign state using a *protocol* that supports multiple clients.

In our example we may substitute a traditional assignment for a simple priority-based protocol. Figure 3 demonstrates how this can be done. Instead of invoking a set method, a client can influence state by adding a ValueProvider.

A ValueProvider provides not only a desired value but also a priority. The protocol ensures that a value of higher priority will always be preferred over one of lower priority. Thus, instead of being arbitrary, the conflict resolution is now handled using a high-level protocol known to all extensions. The core protocol behavior is implemented in Actuator.get() that statically depends on the ValueProvider interface:

```
Value get() {
  List<ValueProvider> l = getValueProviders();
  sort(l, DESC_PRIORITY);
  return (l.size() > 0) ? l.getValue(0) : null;
}
```

In figure 3 all interfaces, i.e. Actuator and ValueProvider, support sharing. This has been achieved by promoting the desire to modify a shared state

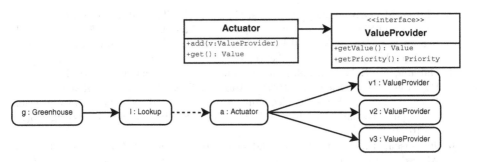

**Fig. 3.** A network of objects suitable for sharing

to an object, i.e. `ValueProvider`. In doing so, we have eliminated the method `Actuator.set(Value)` which, as we have seen, does not support sharing. Instead we have introduced `Actuator.add(ValueProvider)`. An extension invoking this method does not cause any undesirable interactions with other independent extensions – thus, this method is safe in sharing scenarios.

## 4  Conclusion

Our inability to model independently extensible contexts poses a threat to the design of software systems, for which not all dimensions of extension can be anticipated. To remedy this problem, we have emphasized two techniques, which we believe offer a pragmatic approach to improve the situation.

First, by using the lookup design pattern, it is possible to model fine-grained domain-specific contexts as networks of objects that allow for non-invasive introduction of links to objects with unanticipated interfaces. The technique is useful when it is possible to anticipate the existence of an open context, but not specific interfaces required by future extensions that must be used in that context.

Second, we suggest that interfaces of objects representing an open context must be carefully designed in order to support sharing. Specifically, a shared interface must ensure that a contract offered to a specific client cannot be violated by any other client. This can be achieved by accepting the selection of high-level coordination protocols to be an integral part of interface design.

Improved modeling of independently extensible contexts is essential in order to achieve independent extensibility of non-trivial software systems.

## References

1. Beugnard, A., Jézéquel, J., Plouzeau, N., Watkins, D.: Making Components Contract Aware. Computer 32(7), 38–45 (1999)
2. Büchi, M., Weck, W.: Generic Wrappers. In: Bertino, E. (ed.) ECOOP 2000. LNCS, vol. 1850, pp. 201–225. Springer, Heidelberg (2000)

3. Clifton, C., Leavens, G., Chambers, C., Millstein, T.: MultiJava: Modular Open Classes and Symmetric Multiple Dispatch for Java. In: OOPSLA 2000 – Proceedings of the 15th ACM SIGPLAN Conference on Object-Oriented Programming, Systems, Languages, and Applications, pp. 130–145 (2000)
4. Gamma, E., Helm, R., Johnson, R., Vlissides, J.: Design Patterns: Elements of Reusable Object-Oriented Software. Addison-Wesley Professional, Reading (1994)
5. Hogg, J., Lea, D., Wills, A.: deChampeaux, D., Holt, R.: The Geneva Convention – On The Treatment of Object Aliasing. ACM SIGPLAN OOPS Messenger 3(2), 11–16 (1992)
6. Jørgensen, B.: Integration of Independently Developed Components through Aliased Multi-Object Type Widening. Journal of Object Technology 3(11), 55–76 (2004)
7. Kiczales, G., Hilsdale, E., Hugunin, J., Kersten, M., Palm, J., Griswold, W.: An Overview of AspectJ. In: Knudsen, J.L. (ed.) ECOOP 2001. LNCS, vol. 2072, pp. 327–354. Springer, Heidelberg (2001)
8. Kircher, M., Jain, P.: Pattern-Oriented Software Architecture. Patterns for Resource Management, vol. 3. Wiley, Chichester (2004)
9. Lehman, M.: Programs, Life Cycles, and Laws of Software Evolution. Proceedings of the IEEE 68, 1060–1076 (1980)
10. McGregor, J.: Context. Journal of Object Technology 4(7), 35–44 (2005)
11. Oreizy, P., Taylor, R.: Coping with Application Inconsistency in Decentralized Software Evolution. In: International Workshop on the Principles of Software Evolution (1999)
12. Ostermann, K., Kniesel, G.: Independent Extensibility – An Open Challenge for AspectJ and Hyper/J. In: ECOOP 2000 – Workshop on Aspects and Dimension of Concerns (2000)
13. Steimann, F.: The Paradoxical Success of Aspect-Oriented Programming. In: OOPSLA 2006 – Proceedings of the 21st Annual ACM SIGPLAN Conference on Object-Oriented Programming Systems, Languages, and Applications, pp. 481–497 (2006)
14. Szyperski, C.: Independently Extensible Systems – Software Engineering Potential and Challenges. In: Proceedings of the 19th Australasian Computer Science Conference (1996)
15. Szyperski, C.: Component Software – Beyond Object-Oriented Programming, 2nd edn. Addison-Wesley Professional, Reading (2002)
16. Tarr, P., Ossher, H., Sutton, S.: Hyper/J$^{TM}$: Multi-Dimensional Separation of Concerns for Java$^{TM}$. In: Proceedings of the 24th International Conference on Software Engineering, pp. 689–690 (2002)
17. Weck, W.: Independently Extensible Component Frameworks. Special Issues in Object-Oriented Programming, pp. 177–183 (1997)

# Mediating Connector Patterns for Components Interoperability[*]

Romina Spalazzese and Paola Inverardi

Università degli Studi dell'Aquila
via Vetoio I-67100 L'Aquila, Italy
{romina.spalazzese,paola.inverardi}@di.univaq.it

**Abstract.** A key objective for ubiquitous environments is to enable system interoperability between system's components that are highly heterogeneous. In particular, the challenge is to embed in the system architecture the necessary support to cope with behavioral diversity in order to allow components to coordinate and communicate. In this paper we present the design building blocks for the dynamic and on-the-fly interoperability between heterogeneous components. Specifically, we describe an Architectural Pattern called *Mediating Connector*, that is the key enabler for communication. In addition, we present a set of *Basic Mediator* Patterns, that describe the basic mismatches which can occur when components try to interact, and their corresponding solutions.

**Keywords:** Heterogeneous Components Interoperability, Mediating Connector Architectural Pattern, Basic Mediator Patterns.

## 1 Introduction

A multitude of heterogeneous networked devices are today embedded in the Ubiquitous networked environment [2] where a key objective is to enable system interoperability. Tremendous work has been done in the middleware field while the application-layer interoperability remains an open problem calling for *mediating connectors* or *mediators*. The mediator concept was initially introduced to cope with the integration of heterogeneous data sources [13] and as design pattern [17]. In the field of software architectures ad hoc wrappers have been proposed to address communication problems [8]. Mediators and automated mediation have received attention within the Web Services and Semantic Web contexts [6,3,4]. Recently, the challenge is to provide general solutions to the behavioral diversities at runtime and on-the-fly, to respond to the continuous evolution of the environment[1]. An approach to protocol mediation is to categorize the types of protocol mismatches that may occur and that must be solved in order to provide corresponding solutions to these recurring problems. This immediately reminds of patterns [18,1,12,17] and of pattern-based works [15,16,20,21,22].

---

[*] The work is partly supported by the CONNECT European Project No 231167.
[1] CONNECT European project, http://connect-forever.eu/

M. Ali Babar and I. Gorton (Eds.): ECSA 2010, LNCS 6285, pp. 335–343, 2010.

In this paper we present a set of design building blocks for the interoperability between heterogeneous components which would certainly facilitate the solution. The contributions of this paper are: (1) an Architectural Pattern called *Mediating Connector*, that is the key enabler for communication; (2) a set of *Basic Mediator* Patterns that describe: (i) the basic mismatches which can occur while components try to interact, and (ii) their corresponding solutions. The paper is organized as follows: in Section 2, we sketch a pattern-based approach for the automatic synthesis of Mediating Connector. In Section 3, we illustrate the Mediating Connector Architectural Pattern for the ubiquitous networked environment. In Section 4, we show the Basic Mediator Patterns and we conclude, in Section 5, by outlining future work.

## 2   A Pattern-Based Approach for Interoperability Mismatches

In this section we describe our proposal for an automated pattern based approach, whose details are in [9]. For the sake of this paper, we make some assumptions and we investigate the related underling research problems as part of CONNECT. We assume to know the interaction protocols run by two networked components as Labeled Transition Systems (LTS) [14] and the components' interfaces with which to interact as advertised or as result of learning techniques [5,19]. We also assume a semantic correspondence between the messages exchanged among components exploiting ontologies. The first step is to establish whether the components are *potentially compatible*, i.e., if it makes sense for them to *interoperate* through the Mediating Connector. This amounts to understand if the components share some *intent* (trace), i.e., if they have some complementary sequences of messages visible at interface level. To do this we define (1) a decomposition strategy/tool to decompose the whole components' behavior (LTS) into *elementary behaviors* (traces) representing *elementary intents* of the components and then (2) an automatic analyzer to identify mismatches between elementary behaviors of the different components. Once discovered the components compatibility, solving their interoperability means solving the behavioral mismatches that they exhibit. Then it is necessary to: (3) define a mismatches manager to solve the identified mismatches between elementary behaviors; (4) define a composition approach to build elementary mediating behaviors (mediating traces) based on the identified mismatches and their relative solutions; (5) define a composition strategy to build a mediating connector's behavior starting from the elementary mediating behaviors.

The above described approach is far from trivial, especially to achieve automatically. However, in the following we show its feasibility. To address steps (1) and (5) the approach makes use of a compositional strategy to decompose components interaction protocols into traces and compose mediating connectors interaction protocol from mediating traces respectively. Furthermore, we describe six Basic Mediator Patterns that are the building blocks on which the steps (2), (3), and (4) can be built upon.

## 3   Mediating Connector Architectural Pattern

We characterize the interoperability problem between diverse components populating the ubiquitous environment and its related solution as a *Mediating Connector Architectural Pattern* basing on the template used in [1]. The Mediating Connector is a behavioral pattern. Being an architectural building block embedding the necessary support, it should be used to dynamically cope with components' behavioral diversity.

**Name.** Mediating Connector.

**Also Known As.** Mediator.

**Example.** We describe the example used in [10] where we have been studying the problem and where appeared first results on the theory underlying our approach. An extended and more complete version of the theory can be found in [9]. We consider the simple yet challenging example of instant messaging. Various instant messaging systems are now in use. However, although those systems implement similar functionalities, end-users need to use the very same system to communicate due to behavioral mismatches of the respective protocols. For instance, consider Windows Messenger[2](WM), now called Windows Live Messenger, and Jabber Messenger[3](JM). Figure 1 models their behavioral protocols using LTSs. We

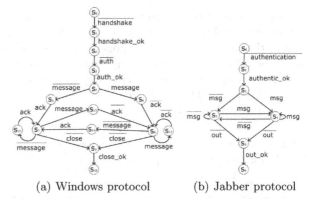

(a) Windows protocol          (b) Jabber protocol

**Fig. 1.** Behavioral models of two instant messengers

use the usual convention that actions with overbar denote output actions while the ones with no overbar denote input actions. These systems should be able to interoperate since they both amount to supporting authentication with their servers and then message exchanges among peers. However mediating their respective protocols to achieve interoperability is far from trivial, especially if one wants to achieve a general solution. An effort has been done in [11] requiring the implementation of the translation from any client protocol to a reference exchange protocol, and vice versa. Unfortunately this affects the generality and the automation of the approach.

**Context.** The environment is distributed and changes continuously. Heterogeneous mismatching systems require seamless coordination and communication.

**Problem.** In order to support existing and future systems' interoperability, some means of mediation is required. From the components' perspective, there

---

[2] Windows Live Messenger, http://www.messenger.it/

[3] Jabber Software Foundations, http://www.jabber.org/

should be no difference whether interacting with a peer component, i.e, using the very same interaction protocol, or interacting through a mediator with another component that uses a different interaction protocol. The component should not need to know anything about the protocol of the other one while continuing to "speak" its own protocol. Using the Mediating Connector, the following *forces* (aspects of the problem that should be considered when solving it [1]) need to be balanced: (a) the different components should continue to use their own interaction protocols. That is, components should interact as if the Mediating Connector were transparent; (b) the following *basic interaction protocol mismatches* should be solved in order for a set of components to coordinate and communicate (cfr. Section 4): 1) Extra Send/Missing Receive Mismatch; 2) Missing Send/Extra Receive Mismatch; 3) Signature Mismatch; 4) Ordering Mismatch; 5) One Send-Many Receive/Many Receive-One Send Mismatch; 6) Many Send-One Receive/One Receive-Many Send Mismatch.

**Solution.** The introduction of a Mediating Connector to manage the interaction behavioral differences between potentially compatible components. The idea behind this pattern is that components that would need some interaction protocol's adaptation to become compatible, and hence to interoperate, are able to coordinate and communicate achieving their goals/intents without undergoing any modification. The Mediating Connector is one (or a set of) component(s) that manage the behavioral mismatches. It directly communicates with each component by using the component's proper protocol. The mediator forwards the interaction messages from one component to the other by making opportune translation/adaptation of protocols when/if needed.

**Structure.** The Mediating Connector Pattern comprises three types of participating components: communicating components, potentially compatible components and mediators. Figure 2 shows the objects involved in a mediated system. The *communicating components* implement already compatible components, i.e. able to interact and evolve following their usual interaction behavior. The *potentially compatible components* implement application level entities that want to reach some of their intents by interacting with other components able to satisfy their needs, i.e. required/provided functionalities. However those components are unable to directly interact because of protocol mismatches and can only evolve following their usual interaction behavior, without any change. The *mediators* are entities responsible for the mediated communication between the components. This means that the role of the mediator is to make compatible components that are mismatching. That is, a mediator must receive and properly forward requests and responses between potentially compatible components.

**Fig. 2.** Entities involved in a mediated system

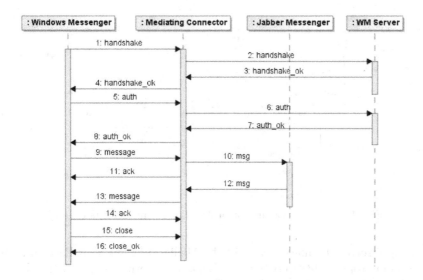

**Fig. 3.** Scenario on the relevant operation of a Mediator

**Dynamics.** Figure 3 illustrates the interactions between three components and one mediator belonging to the messengers example. Triggered by a user, the Windows Messenger protocol (Figure 1(a)) performs one of its possible behavior: it authenticates after an handshake, sends/receives several messages, and closes. The mediator should: (1) forward the handshake and authentication messages as they are between the Windows Messenger and its authentication server (communicating components), (2) translate and forward messages between the Windows and Jabber Messengers (potentially compatible components)[4] (3) forward the closing messages as they are between the Windows Messenger and its server (communicating components).

**Implementation.** The implementation of this pattern implies the definition of an approach/tool (we have proposed one in Section 2) to automatically synthesize the behavior of the Mediating Connector which allows potentially compatible components to interoperate mediating their interactions.

**Example Resolved.** The Mediating Connector's concrete protocol for the example is shown in Figure 4. Once established that the two messengers are potentially compatible, i.e., they have some complementary portion of interaction protocols, the mediating connector manages the components' behavioral mismatches allowing them to have a mediated coordination and communication.

**Variants.** Distributed Mediating Connector. It is possible to implement this pattern either as a centralized component or as distributed components. This latter introduces a synchronization issue that has to be taken into account.

---

[4] With "translation" we refer to a "behavioral translation" (see Section 4).

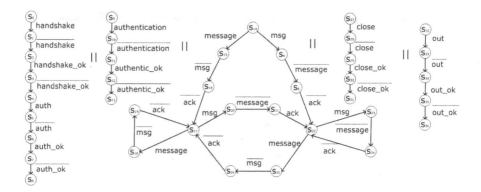

**Fig. 4.** Mediating Connector protocol of the messengers example

**Consequences.** The main *benefit* of the Mediating Connector Pattern is that it allows interoperability between components that otherwise would not be able to do it because of their behavioral differences.

The main *liability* that the Mediating Connector Pattern imposes is that the systems using it are slower than the ones interacting directly because of the indirection layer introduced. However the severity of this drawback is mitigate and made acceptable by the fact that such systems, without mediator, are not able at all to interoperate.

## 4   Basic Mediator Patterns

The *Basic Mediator Patterns* include the above mentioned basic interoperability mismatches together with their corresponding solutions. These patterns are: (1) Message Consumer Pattern, (2) Message Producer Pattern, (3) Message Translator Pattern, (4) Messages Ordering Pattern, (5) Message Splitting Pattern, (6) Messages Merger Pattern.

Figure 5 shows, for each Basic Mediator Pattern: (i) two traces (left hand-side and right hand-side), showing the basic interoperability mismatch coming from two potentially compatible components, and (ii) its related basic solution trace (in the center). All the considered traces are the most elementary in terms of messages exchanged and only their visible messages are shown. The mismatches, inspired by service composition mismatches, refer to send/receive problems that can occur while synchronizing two traces. In real cases, the traces may also contain portions of behavior already compatible (abstracted by dots in the figure) and may amount to any combination of the presented mismatches. Then an appropriate strategy to detect and manage this is needed. The basic patterns, share the context considering two traces (left and right) expressing similar complementary functionalities and focusing on one of their semantically

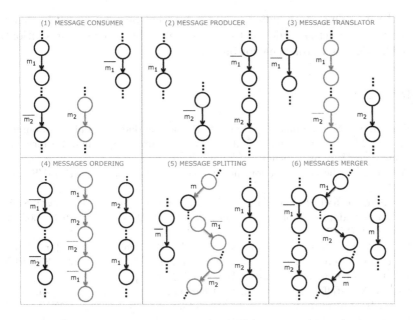

**Fig. 5.** Basic Mediator Patterns

equivalent elementary actions. Moreover the patterns have the same intent: to allow synchronization between the two traces letting them evolve together which otherwise would not be possible because of behavioral mismatches. Due to the lack of space, we do not give here further details that can be found in [7].

## 5 Conclusion

The Ubiquitous environment, embedding a big number of heterogeneous system's components, puts forward an ever growing need of mediation entities for component's interoperability purpose. The challenge is to embed *mediators* components into the system architecture allowing mismatching components to coordinate and communicate. Another challenge is to find dynamic and on the fly approaches to cope with component's behavioral diversities. To respond to these two challenges, we illustrated the Mediating Connector Architectural Pattern which, encapsulating the necessary support, is the key enabler for the communication between mismatching components. We also proposed an automatic pattern based approach describing a set of Basic Mediator Patterns, including basic mismatches and respective solutions, which represent the basic building blocks on which an automatic approach can build upon.

As future works, we intend to define a theoretical compositional strategy to allow reasoning on mismatches and to build the mediating connector behavior. Moreover we also aim at providing the "concrete" Basic Mediator Patterns, i.e., the skeleton code corresponding to the "abstract" ones presented in this work and present the actual code for the component's behavior decomposition and the mediating connector behavior building.

# References

1. Buschmann, F., Meunier, R., Rohnert, H., Sommerlad, P., Stal, M., Sommerlad, P., Stal, M.: Pattern-Oriented Software Architecture. A System of Patterns, vol. 1. John Wiley & Sons, Chichester (August 1996)
2. Weiser, M.: The computer for the 21st century. Scientific American (September 1991)
3. Motahari Nezhad, H.R., Benatallah, B., Martens, A., Curbera, F., Casati, F.: Semi-automated adaptation of service interactions. In: WWW 2007, pp. 993–1002. ACM, New York (2007)
4. Williams, S.K., Battle, S.A., Cuadrado, J.E.: Protocol mediation for adaptation in semantic web services. In: Sure, Y., Domingue, J. (eds.) ESWC 2006. LNCS, vol. 4011, pp. 635–649. Springer, Heidelberg (2006)
5. Issarny, V., Steffen, B., Jonsson, B., Blair, G., Grace, P., Kwiatkowska, M., Calinescu, R., Inverardi, P., Tivoli, M., Bertolino, A., Sabetta, A.: CONNECT Challenges: Towards Emergent Connectors for Eternal Networked Systems. In: ICECCS 2009, pp. 154–161 (2009)
6. Vaculin, R., Neruda, R., Sycara, K.P.: An Agent for Asymmetric Process Mediation in Open Environments. In: Kowalczyk, R., Huhns, M.N., Klusch, M., Maamar, Z., Vo, Q.B. (eds.) SOCASE 2008. LNCS, vol. 5006, pp. 104–117. Springer, Heidelberg (2008)
7. Spalazzese, R., Inverardi, P.: Mediating Connector Patterns for Components Interoperability. Tech. Rep., University of L'Aquila (2010)
8. Spitznagel, B., Garlan, D.: A compositional formalization of connector wrappers. In: ICSE 2003, pp. 374–384. IEEE Computer Society, Washington (2003)
9. Spalazzese, R., Inverardi, P., Issarny, V.: A Theory of Mediators for the Ubiquitous Networking Environment - Version 2. Tech. Rep. TRCS 002/2010 (2010)
10. Spalazzese, R., Inverardi, P., Issarny, V.: Towards a formalization of mediating connectors for on the fly interoperability. In: WICSA/ECSA 2009, pp. 345–348 (2009)
11. Motoyama, M.A., Varghese, G.: Crosstalk: scalably interconnecting instant messaging networks. In: WOSN 2009, pp. 61–68. ACM, New York (2009)
12. Avgeriou, P., Zdun, U.: Architectural Patterns Revisited – A Pattern Language. In: EuroPLoP 2005, Irsee, Germany, 139 Pages (2005)
13. Wiederhold, G.: Mediators in the architecture of future information systems. IEEE Computer 25, 38–49 (1992)
14. Keller, R.M.: Formal verification of parallel programs. Commun. ACM 19(7), 371–384 (1976)
15. Benatallah, B., Casati, F., Grigori, D., Nezhad, H.R.M., Toumani, F.: Developing adapters for web services integration. In: Pastor, Ó., Falcão e Cunha, J. (eds.) CAiSE 2005. LNCS, vol. 3520, pp. 415–429. Springer, Heidelberg (2005)
16. Cimpian, E., Mocan, A.: Wsmx process mediation based on choreographies. In: Bussler, C.J., Haller, A. (eds.) BPM 2005. LNCS, vol. 3812, pp. 130–143. Springer, Heidelberg (2006)

17. Gamma, E., Helm, R., Johnson, R., Vlissides, J.: Design Patterns: Elements of Resusable Object-Oriented Software. Addison-Wesley Professional, Reading (1995)
18. Alexander, C., Ishikawa, S., Silverstein, M.: A Pattern Language. Center for Environmental Structure Series, vol. 2. Oxford University Press, New York (1977)
19. Bertolino, A., Inverardi, P., Pelliccione, P., Tivoli, M.: Automatic synthesis of behavior protocols for composable web-services. In: Proc.ESEC/FSE, pp. 141–150 (2009)
20. Li, X., Fan, Y., Jiang, F.: A classification of service composition mismatches to support service mediation. In: GCC, pp. 315–321 (2007)
21. Li, X., Fan, Y., Wang, J., Wang, L., Jiang, F.: A pattern-based approach to development of service mediators for protocol mediation. In: WICSA 2008, pp. 137–146. IEEE Computer Society, Los Alamitos (2008)
22. Jiang, F., Fan, Y., Zhang, X.: Rule-based automatic generation of mediator patterns for service composition mismatches. In: Proc. of GPC-WORKSHOPS 2008, pp. 3–8. IEEE Computer Society, Washington (2008)

# Assessing the Impact of AOSD on Layered Software Architectures

Juliana Saraiva, Sérgio Soares, and Fernando Castor

Centro de Informática - Universidade Federal de Pernambuco (UFPE), Recife – PE, Brazil
{jags2,scbs,castor}@cin.ufpe.br

**Abstract.** Software structuring techniques aim to make software systems easier to develop and maintain, increasing their quality. Aspect-Oriented Software Development (AOSD) and Software Architectural Styles are examples of such techniques. In spite of all the benefits of structuring techniques, both actual and intended, it is not always easy or even advantageous to integrate two or more of these techniques. For example, the effects of combining AOSD and Layered Software Architectures are still not well understood. This might be detrimental to system quality and can be a decisive factor when deciding whether or not to employ AOSD, specially considering the pervasiveness of layered architectures. This paper presents a study aiming to assess the impact of AOSD on software architectures adopting the layered style. To better account for the influence of aspects on the layered structure of the system, we have extended existing approaches to measure dependencies and layering violations in software architectures.

**Keywords:** Aspect-Oriented Software Development, Layering Software Architectures, Layering Structuring Violations, Coupling.

## 1 Introduction

The complexity of software is one of the major problems encountered in software development. When this problem is not dealt with, software quality decreases, costs increase, delays in delivery occur and, in some cases, the project is canceled completely [8]. However, there are techniques for structuring software that can reduce this complexity, such as software architecture. The software architecture adheres to one or more architectural styles. Architectural styles define families of software systems in terms of their organization [9]. This paper focuses on the study of the Layered Architectural Style. In this architectural style, software systems are structured in groups of subtasks, so that each group is implemented at a certain level of abstraction and groups at higher levels of abstraction are clients of the groups at lower levels of abstraction [2]. Although software architecture is an important discipline for software development, it can and should be complemented by other approaches such as, Design Patterns and Aspect-Oriented Software Development (AOSD)[1].

AOSD is a software development approach where the basic development activities (requirements, design, coding, testing, and deployment) are conducted starting

---

[1] http://www.aosd.net

M. Ali Babar and I. Gorton (Eds.): ECSA 2010, LNCS 6285, pp. 344–351, 2010.
© Springer-Verlag Berlin Heidelberg 2010

from the assumption that the system will be implemented in an aspect-oriented programming (AOP) language. AOP languages provide constructs to structure the so-called crosscutting concerns - concerns whose implementation is scattered throughout system modules, tangled with code pertaining to other concerns. Another assumption of AOSD is that proper use of AOP languages makes the system more modular. Since AOSD is a recent approach, it is necessary to conduct empirical studies that demonstrate the benefits and/or drawbacks of its use with respect to object-oriented programming (OOP), the current dominant software development approach. Hence, some important research questions remain unaddressed:

- How does the use of AOSD to modularize crosscutting concerns affect the coupling between the layers of object-oriented systems?
- Do layered architectures whose crosscutting concerns are modularized by means of AOSD respect the basic principles of the layered architectural style?

This paper presents a study aiming to assess the impact of AOSD on systems that adopt a layered organization. We intend to assist developers in making decisions about which concerns are worth modularizing with aspects in a layered software system. In addition, we propose adaptations to existing metrics to take the effect of aspects into consideration since they introduce new dependencies that are not covered by existing metrics to assess layered software architectures. These extensions are another contribution of the paper. This paper is organized as follows. Section 2 presents the target application of our study, our approach to counting dependencies and violations in layered software architectures, and the employed metrics suite. The results of the study are presented in Section 3. Section 4 discusses the conclusions and future work.

## 2   Setting of the Study

This section presents the setting of our study. Section 2.1 briefly describes Health Watcher, the target system of our study. Section 2.2 describes the ways in which we have identified and computed the dependencies and violations in layered software architectures. Finally, Section 2.3 presents the group of metrics that we employed in this study.

### 2.1   Our Case Study

Health Watcher[2] (HW) is a Web-based information system that receives and manages requests and notifications about the public healthcare system. It is also used to expose important healthcare information to patients. Health Watcher is implemented in Java and leverages a number of well-known design patterns and technologies. The architecture of the system consists of four layers: Data Management, Business, Communication and User Interface. For more information, access the HW website. HW has ten releases, each one with an object-oriented version and an aspect-oriented version.

---

[2] http://www.comp.lancs.ac.uk/~greenwop/ecoop07/

Each release stems from maintenance activities aiming to improve the structure of the system or to add new functionality.

## 2.2 Dependencies and Violations Counting

This section explains how we have counted dependencies between layers in our study, for both object-oriented and aspect-oriented versions of HW. To the best of our knowledge, this is the first work to extend existing approaches to count dependencies between layers that also consider dependencies caused by aspects. In this section we also explain some of the basic principles that govern the structure of layered software architectures. These principles are among the factors responsible for the desirable properties that layered architectures. As a consequence, violations of these principles partially negate the benefits of layering and should be avoided.

**Dependencies.** Before explaining the dependency counting process, we need to clarify some basic definitions. Methods, *pointcuts*, advice, and attributes are considered internal entities of a module. A module (class, aspect) is a structure with a defined purpose, which has one or more entities, described above. It is important to note that the presence of all kinds entities in the modules is not required. A layer comprises a set of modules. This work considers only dependencies between modules pertaining to different layers. In this scenario, dependencies between modules located within the same layer are less relevant.

In this work, we consider 5 groups of dependencies: (i) Method Call; (ii) Attribute Access; (iii) Inheritance; (iv) Pointcut Interception; and (v) Exception Handling. A high number of dependencies between system layers indicate a problem: either the code was not implemented in accordance with the architecture design or the architecture did not reflect the best solution for the problem at hand. We consider that a dependency caused by a method call occurs when a method declared in a module (class/aspect) that is in layer $B$ is called by a method declared by a module in a different layer $A$. We also include in this group dependencies that stem from a module in layer $B$ being instantiated by a method declared in a module in a different layer $A$. In this case, the method from layer $A$ is calling the constructor of the module from layer $B$. On the other hand, attribute access dependencies occur when the entities of a **module** (class/aspect) belonging to layer $A$ access/update any attribute declared in a module (class/aspect) of a different layer $B$.

Inheritance dependencies are different from Attribute Access and Method Call dependencies because they are not associated with the entities in a module. A layer $A$ has an inheritance dependency on a different layer $B$ if a **module** (class/aspect) of layer $A$ extends (inherits from) a different module (class/aspect) belonging to layer $B$. The fourth group of dependencies identified in this study comprises dependencies caused by pointcuts defined in aspects that intercept Java and AspectJ join points. We consider that there is a pointcut dependency between two different layers $A$ and $B$ if a module in layer $A$ specifies a pointcut that explicitly refers to a module in layer $B$ or one or more of its entities. The last group of dependencies comprises the dependencies caused by exception handling code. There is an exception handling dependency between two different layers $A$ and $B$ if a module (class/aspect) or entity (methods/advices) from layer $A$ catches or throws some exception defined by a module (class) belonging to layer $B$.

**Violations.** To assess the impact of a structuring technique such as AOSD in layered software architectures, it is first necessary to understand the basic principles that direct the design of these architectures. These principles, when combined with the principles of modular software development [1], yield the expected benefits of layered software architectures. To enjoy these benefits, the structure of a software system must follow three basic principles [6]:

- **Back-Call Principle:** A top layer should depend only on a lower layer, but lower layers should not depend on the upper layers;
- **Skip-Call Principle:** Each layer should depend only on the layer located immediately below it;
- **Cyclic-Call Principle:** Cycles of dependencies between layers should not exist because they make a set of layers monolithic and inseparable.

These violations indicate that the architecture of the system does not faithfully reflect the intention of its architect. They also partially cancel out the expected advantages of a layered structure. In addition, these violations are measurable, which makes it possible to compare the quality of different versions of the same release of our case study.

### 2.3 Metrics Suite

As cited above, all these metrics were collected automatically, using a tool that was developed in Java language. This tool collects metrics from Java and AspectJ programs. In this work, the metrics implemented were divided into three groups: **Vocabulary Size**, **Coupling between Layers** and **Violations**. Vocabulary Size Metrics provide a sense of the complexity of a system. The second group of collected metrics is the Coupling between Layers. The coupling metric was first proposed by Zhao [5] and measures the coupling between aspects and classes. The results of this group of metrics were computed by adding the dependencies that exist between one layer and another.

**Table 1.** Metrics collected from ArchE Meter

| Group | Metrics | Description |
|---|---|---|
| Vocabulary Size | NC | Number of Classes. |
| | NM | Number of Methods. |
| | NAs | Number of Aspects. |
| | NAd | Number of Advices. |
| CBL (*Coupling between Layers*) | MCD | *Method Call Dependencies.* |
| | AAD | *Attribute Access Dependencies.* |
| | ID | *Inheritance Dependencies.* |
| | PID | *Pointcut Interception Dependencies.* |
| | EHD | *Exception Handling Dependencies.* |
| Violation Metrics | SCV | *Skip Call Violation.* |
| | BCV | *Back Call Violation.* |
| | CCV | *Cyclic Call Violation.* |

Table 1 shows all the metrics that are collected automatically by the ArchE Meter tool, where the first column indicates which group is the metric, the second column indicates the name of the metric and the third column provides a description of the metric. For the metrics belonging to Coupling Between Layers and Violation Metrics, the lower the value the better. The Vocabulary Size group includes additional metrics, i.e. it helps just in understanding the structure of the systems evaluated.

# 3  Study Results

In this section, we present and analyze the results of the three groups of metrics that were collected in this study. We have collected these metrics for each one of the ten releases of the two versions of HW. The values for the Vocabulary Size group and a discussion about these values are presented in Section 3.1. Section 3.2 presents and analyzes the results for the Coupling Between Layers metrics. Section 3.3 focuses on the Layering Violation Metrics.

## 3.1  Vocabulary Size

We obtained values of the Vocabulary Size metrics for all the releases of HW in its two versions, aspect-oriented and object-oriented. It could be observed from these results that throughout the evolution of HW, all the values of the Vocabulary Size metrics increased. Comparing the first release of the system with the last, the following additional values were obtained: for the object-oriented versions, the NC increased 51.13% and NM showed an increase of 66.8%. In the aspect-oriented versions, the NC grew by 47.7%, the NM increased 43.9%, the NAs by 127% and the NAD by 193%. Furthermore, if size metrics can be considered a proxy to the system complexity, we can say that the aspect-oriented releases of HW were more complex than their object-oriented counterparts.

## 3.2  Coupling between Layers Result

This section shows the results obtained in the collection of the Coupling Between Layers metrics. The analyses of the results can be used to assist developers in making decisions about how to model their layered architectures. A qualitative analysis of these values can also be used to aid developers in making decisions regarding the use or absence of AOSD in the construction of systems adhering to this layered architectural style.

Table 2 exhibits all the values of the Coupling Between Layers metrics obtained for the twenty releases of HW. The first column is the name of the system. The second, third, fourth, fifth, and sixth columns are the coupling metrics, represented by the names **MCD**, **AAD**, **ID**, **PID**, and **EHD**, respectively. The seventh column of Table 3.1 represents the total of relationships and dependencies between the layers of the system. We use **boldface** to indicate the version with the higher overall coupling between layers for a given release. The eighth and last column shows the percentage difference between the two versions of the same HW release. This percentage refers to the value of the object-oriented version. Therefore, a positive percentage means that the aspect-oriented version of a given release had stronger overall coupling between layers than its object-oriented counterpart. In the same vein, a negative value indicates a lower coupling between the layers of the aspect-oriented version.

Note that in Table 2 there is a radical change in the percentage differences between releases 4 and 5. The reason for this growth has not yet been detected and needs further examination. May have been caused by the Adapter Pattern implementation in release 5, or may have been because of aspectization some specific concern, which was not examined separately in this study. The tendency in the evolution of the MCD metric is also an interesting result. With these results is possible to infer that, at least from the viewpoint of MCDs, the aspect-oriented releases seem to better accommodate the evolution scenarios than the object-oriented ones. This has a cost, however, the number of PIDs of HW_AO_10 is almost 41,7% greater than HW_AO_02's. Combining MCD and PID it is possible to get a better picture of how well the aspect-oriented releases fare, when compared with the object-oriented releases, after a number of evolution scenarios (ID and AAD do not seem to change significantly between the two versions).

**Table 2.** Coupling Between Layers Metrics

| Systems | MCD | AAD | ID | PID | EHD | Total | Percentage Difference |
|---------|-----|-----|-----|-----|-----|-------|----------------------|
| HW_OO_01 | 317 | 22 | 22 | 0 | 213 | 591 | |
| HW_AO_01 | 465 | 54 | 22 | 1 | 132 | 674 | 14% |
| HW_OO_02 | 314 | 29 | 26 | 0 | 213 | 582 | |
| HW_AO_02 | 456 | 22 | 27 | 113 | 132 | 750 | 28% |
| HW_OO_03 | 308 | 29 | 34 | 0 | 213 | 584 | |
| HW_AO_03 | 458 | 22 | 35 | 129 | 132 | 776 | 32.8% |
| HW_OO_04 | 312 | 29 | 34 | 0 | 221 | 596 | |
| HW_AO_04 | 458 | 22 | 36 | 132 | 132 | 780 | 30.8% |
| HW_OO_05 | 339 | 29 | 34 | 0 | 382 | 784 | |
| HW_AO_05 | 457 | 22 | 36 | 132 | 132 | 779 | -0.63% |
| HW_OO_06 | 355 | 29 | 36 | 0 | 382 | 802 | |
| HW_AO_06 | 456 | 22 | 38 | 136 | 132 | 784 | -2.29% |
| HW_OO_07 | 356 | 29 | 36 | 0 | 382 | 803 | |
| HW_AO_07 | 445 | 22 | 38 | 140 | 132 | 777 | -3.23% |
| HW_OO_08 | 359 | 28 | 37 | 0 | 386 | 810 | |
| HW_AO_08 | 444 | 22 | 40 | 142 | 132 | 780 | -3.7% |
| HW_OO_09 | 424 | 25 | 47 | 0 | 632 | 1128 | |
| HW_AO_09 | 520 | 22 | 50 | 148 | 193 | 933 | -17.28% |
| HW_OO_10 | 427 | 27 | 50 | 0 | 634 | 1138 | |
| HW_AO_10 | 530 | 23 | 53 | 160 | 197 | 963 | -15.37% |

It can be observed in Table 2 that the number of dependencies is higher in aspect-oriented versions for the first, second, third, and fourth releases. This is intuitive, since aspects normally affect classes and other aspects in a number of layers, due to the kind of concern that aspects aim to modularize. Overall, this result indicates that, for the first few releases of the systems, AOSD results in more strongly coupled layers. Nevertheless, starting from the fifth release, the level of coupling between layers became consistently lower in the aspect-oriented versions. For example, HW_AO_10 had more than 15% less dependencies between layers than HW_OO_10. This result must be analyzed with care, however. If we remove EHDs from the calculations, the overall number of dependencies of HW_AO_10 is 52% greater than the number of dependencies of HW_OO_10. Again, it is important to stress that the difference was even greater in the initial: 67%.

### 3.3 Violations Result

This section presents the results for the Layering Violation metrics. The greater the number of violations, the less the system complies with this style. In Table 3 we can see all the values of the Layering Violation metrics. The first column represents the system **names**, similarly to Tables 2 The second, third and fourth columns present the values of the metrics: **BCV**, **SCV**, and **CCV**, respectively. The fifth column of Table 3 represents the total of violations of the layered style. Remember that the higher the number of violations occurring in the system, the less the system is in accordance with its intended architecture. The last column represents the percentual difference between the numbers of violations exhibit by the two versions of the same release of HW.

Note that from release four there was a huge change in the percentage difference between versions. This happened because the Adapter Pattern was implemented only in the object-oriented version. There was thus, an increase in Skip-Call and Back-Call violations in those versions. As a consequence, with this increase and stagnation in the numbers of violations of the aspect-oriented releases, the percentage difference between them has decreased considerably across subsequent releases.

**Table 3.** Violation Metrics

| System | BCV | SCV | CCV | Total | Percentage Difference |
|--------|-----|-----|-----|-------|----------------------|
| HW_OO_01 | 108 | 226 | 1 | 335 | |
| HW_AO_01 | 228 | 271 | 0 | 499 | 48.9% |
| HW_OO_02 | 110 | 209 | 1 | 320 | |
| HW_AO_02 | 233 | 234 | 0 | 467 | 45.9% |
| HW_OO_03 | 84 | 229 | 1 | 314 | |
| HW_AO_03 | 217 | 250 | 0 | 467 | 48.7% |
| HW_OO_04 | 89 | 225 | 1 | 315 | |
| HW_AO_04 | 232 | 247 | 0 | 479 | 52% |
| HW_OO_05 | 116 | 333 | 1 | 450 | |
| HW_AO_05 | 232 | 246 | 0 | 478 | 6.22% |
| HW_OO_06 | 117 | 332 | 1 | 450 | |
| HW_AO_06 | 209 | 247 | 0 | 456 | 1.33% |
| HW_OO_07 | 116 | 334 | 1 | 451 | |
| HW_AO_07 | 209 | 248 | 0 | 457 | 1.33% |
| HW_OO_08 | 119 | 318 | 1 | 438 | |
| HW_AO_08 | 208 | 246 | 0 | 454 | 3.65% |
| HW_OO_09 | 140 | 444 | 0 | 584 | |
| HW_AO_09 | 215 | 216 | 0 | 511 | -12.5% |
| HW_OO_10 | 143 | 455 | 1 | 589 | |
| HW_AO_10 | 255 | 298 | 0 | 553 | -6.11% |

The values of the object-oriented versions of releases 9 and 10 are much greater than the previous releases because of the increase in the number of dependencies caused by EHDs. This result is intuitive, since layering violations are dependencies that violate the Back Call, Skip Call, and Cyclic Call Principles, and the number of dependencies generated by handling exceptions grew sharply in the object-oriented versions after the eighth release. HW_AO_10 has 9,44% more BCVs than HW_AO_02, while HW_OO_10 has 30% more BCVs than HW_OO_02.

Overall, it is difficult to say whether AOSD has a negative or positive impact on the layered architecture of a system. In spite of the better results, these results stem to a great extent from a specific kind of dependency that cannot be considered as representative as, e.g., MCDs. Moreover, it is not easy to determine how much EHDs affect maintenance and comprehension tasks. After analyzing the study results, our conclusion is that, at least in the specific context of this study, aspects are more of an obstacle than a facilitator.

## 4   Conclusion and Future Work

This paper presents a study aiming to assess the impact that AOSD has on the architecture of software systems that employ the layering architecture style. To produce a realistic evaluation, we have extended existing notions of dependencies between architectural layers with a new kind of dependency that stems from the use of aspects.

Two adaptations to count dependency metrics were performed. The first one, unlike Zhao's study [5], considers that the level of abstraction is the layer, while Zhao considered the abstraction level to the modules (classes and aspects) of the system. Thus, in this present paper, the dependencies between modules of the **same** layer were not computed. The second adjustment made for this approach was motivated by limitations of the study conducted by *Monteiro et al.* [10], where aspects were allocated to a specific layer, orthogonal to the system layer. Due to this organization, they decided to ignore the dependencies created by the aspects. According to the presented results, the use of AOSD to structure crosscutting concerns in layered software systems has mixed results to say the least. Perhaps the negative impact of AOSD in some cases is due to the fact that specific concerns, such as *logging, persistence*, and *exception handling*, were not evaluated separately. Therefore, a natural thread for future work is the exploration of the effects of aspects on the quality of specific concerns that appear in layered systems.

**Acknowledgment.** This work was partially supported by the National Institute of Science and Technology for Software Engineering (INES), funded by CNPq and FACEPE, grants 573964/2008-4 and APQ-1037-1.03/08. Juliana is supported by FACEPE. Sérgio is partially supported by CNPq and FACEPE, grants 309234/2007-7 and APQ-0093-1.03/08. Fernando is partially supported by CNPq, grants 308383/2008-7, 481147/2007-1, and 550895/2007-8. We would like to thank the anonymous referees, who helped to improve this paper with insightful comments and suggestions.

# References

1. Parnas, D.L.: On the Criteria for Decomposing Systems into Modules (1972)
2. Albin, T.S.: The Art of Software Architecture: Design Methods and Techniques, pp. 85–111. Wiley Publishing, Chichester (2003)
3. Kweku, E.-M.: Technical Factors and Abandoned Projects. In: Software Development Failures: Anatomy of Abandoned Projects. MIT Press, Cambridge (2003)
4. Sant'Anna, C., Garcia, A., Chavez, C., Lucena, C., Staa, A.: On the Reuse and Maintenance of Aspect-Oriented Software: An Assessment Framework. In: SBES 2003 (2003)
5. Zhao, L.: Measuring Coupling in Aspect-Oriented Systems. In: 10th International Software Metrics Symposium. EUA, Chicago (2004)
6. Sangal, N., Jordan, E., Sinha, V., Jackson, D.: Using Dependency Models to Manage Complex Software Architecture. In: OOPSLA 2005, California, USA (2005)
7. Sarkar, S., Rama, G.M., Shubha, R.: A method of detecting and measuring architectural layering violations in source code. In: XIII Asia Pacific Software Engineering Conference (APSEC 2006), Bangalore, India (2006)
8. Booch, G., Maksimchuk, R.A., Engel, M.W., Young, B.J., Conallen, J., Houston, K.A.: Object oriented analysis and design with applications (2007)
9. Buschman, F., Meunier, R., Rohnert, H., Sommerlad, P., Stal, M.: Pattern- Oriented Software Architecture, pp. 31–52. Wiley Publishing, Chichester (2008)
10. Monteiro, M., Moura, M., Soares, S., Castor, F.F.: Towards an Analysis of Layering Violations in Aspect-Oriented Software Architectures. In: 3rd International Workshop on Aspects, Dependencies and Interactions (2008)

# Explaining Architectural Choices to Non-architects

Diego Bernini and Francesco Tisato

D.I.S.Co., University of Milano-Bicocca, Viale Sarca, 336
20126 Milano, Italy
{bernini,tisato}@disco.unimib.it

**Abstract.** Explaining and motivating architectural choices are crucial points both in real system development and in computer scientists education. Stakeholders and students should fully understand from a high level perspective the rationale behind basic architectural choices. The paper proposes a communication approach that is complementary to established design processes and can be exploited in workshops that involve the "non-architects" at the end of each phase of an iterative development process. Starting from a problem analysis focused on the significant aspects of data, activities and information flows, a logical architecture is defined by grouping activities into logical components. Different logical architectures are rated according to several conceptual dimensions, in order to highlight their specific rationale and benefits. Finally, deployment solutions are considered to weight the ratings according to costs and constraints of different deployment architectures and of the underlying technologies.

**Keywords:** requirements analysis; architectural design; components; architecture teaching.

## 1 Introduction

Many methods and approaches have been proposed to drive the architectural design [1]: among them Rational Unified Process methods [2] and Kruchten's 4+1 views [3], the Siemens Four Views model [4] and the Architecture Tradeoff Analysis Method [5]. Most methods rely on an iterative approach and highlight the relevance of frequent workshops [6] to assess the achievements of each iteration and to draw the guidelines for the next ones. Workshops involve "non-architects", be they stakeholders in a business context or undergraduate students in an educational context; they play a crucial role but are often flooded with trendy buzzwords including, during the last decades, client-server, three-tier, grid, SOA, cloud computing and so on. Though these terms denote significant technological opportunities, they are often misused and presented as silver bullets in a marketing perspective.

The risk is the premature elaboration [6] of key architectural aspects (e.g., distribution issues) that are improperly biased by scarcely motivated technological choices and do not rely on a clear understanding and assurance that the architecture meets the business needs [7]. This risk is especially high at early stages of the process,

M. Ali Babar and I. Gorton (Eds.): ECSA 2010, LNCS 6285, pp. 352–359, 2010.

(e.g., at the end of the inception and of the initial elaboration phases in RUP), both because key choices about coarse-grained architectural aspects can be hardly modified later and because non-architects playing strategic roles are involved in these stages.

The aim of the paper is to suggest a *communication* process that is complementary to the overall design process and can support the explanation of architectural choices to non-architects when they are involved in critical decisions. The explanation should present in understandable and linear way the rationale of the choices, not the history of the underpinning process; this can be subsumed by the sentence "fountain process, waterfall explanation".

First, the *problem architecture* is introduced. It includes, as one can expect, actors, use cases and domain model. It provides insights about the conceptual activities the system must perform by sketching the major information flows in a Data Flow Diagram style [8]. The problem architecture also summarizes the major Non-Functional Requirements (NFRs), whereas it carefully excludes technological issues.

Then the *logical architecture* is defined by grouping activities into *logical components* according to two well-established criteria, Low Coupling and High Cohesion [9]. Coupling and cohesion are rated according to dimensions that correspond not only to functional, but mainly to non-functional requirements. The ratings are synthesized by Kiviat charts allowing alternative architectural solutions to be roughly compared "at-a-glance". Technological issues are still kept out of scope.

Finally the *deployment architecture* shows how the components of a logical architecture can be deployed into a distributed system. Technological platforms enter the scene. The ratings are weighted by considering costs and criticalities in different deployment scenarios.

Section 2 introduces a simple case study and the problem architecture. Section 3 presents two logical architectures and discusses how they can be compared. Section 4 sketches some deployment architectures and exemplifies the impact of technological constraints. Finally, Section 5 highlights lessons learned from the application of the approach.

## 2  Problem Architecture

A simple example will be used as reference in the following. A shop chain has several shops and one central warehouse. Each shop has a local warehouse. The goal is to manage the demand chain. Sold goods are recognized at each POS via RFID (or via code bar or keyboard). Product stocks are managed at three levels: shelf (to notify an operator about the need for replenishment), local shop inventory (to require the delivery of goods from central to local warehouse) and global inventory (to plan purchases or production).

The aim of the Problem Architecture is to communicate the key elements of the problem by answering a few basic questions: *Who* actors are, *Where* they are located, *What* the interesting information is, *How* it is generated and processed, *When* activities have to be performed and *Why* they are triggered.

Every question leads to the identification of properties of information and activities on the basis of both functional and non-functional requirements. Properties correspond to *problem dimensions* that will provide a conceptual framework for the comparison of alternative logical architectures, as we shall discuss later.

Answering the *"Who" and "Where"* questions means to identify actors and where they are physically located. In the example, there are four actors: POS, located at the shop; Operator, mobile inside the shop; Shop manager, located at the shop and Purchase manager, located at the central site.

*"What"* we are talking about is answered by a domain model in terms of class diagrams. In the example the basic concept is that of good, characterized by an identifier and by a number of items (sold or on a shelf or in the shop warehouse or in the central warehouse). This can be modeled in a straightforward way by an abstract Goods class with several subclasses corresponding to different views of the general concept of Goods. Subclasses may exhibit significant NFRs: for example, the required precision, which is different for different subclasses.

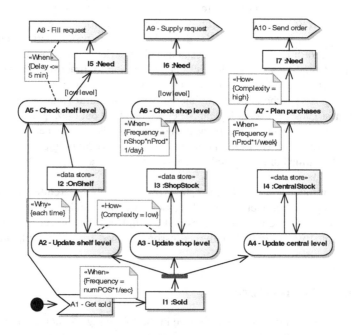

**Fig. 1.** "How", "When" and "Why"

*"How"* information are generated and flow among computational activities is sketched by the data flows in the activity diagram of Fig. 1. A relevant intrinsic property of the activities is their computational complexity. Adornments dealing with "When" and "Why" issues would be better presented in separate diagrams to highlight that "How" just defines necessary conditions (i.e., the availability of information) for the execution of the activities. Defining *"When"* they are performed implies to identify frequencies and timing constraints. Finally, answering the *"Why"* question implies to identify those, and only those, control constraints that are explicitly stated by the specifications.

## 3  Logical Architectures

The next step is to describe the *Logical Architecture*, i.e. how to group activities into *logical components*. A logical component conceptually identifies a coarse-grained software entity which encapsulates computations and state in a self-contained whole that can be utilized through well-defined interfaces [10][11].

Activities can be grouped into logical components in many ways. Architects often choose a dominant dimension as driver and check the resulting architecture against other dimensions. Choosing different dimensions as drivers may lead to dramatically different logical architectures. For example, Fig. 2 a) sketches a grouping driven by the "What" question i.e., the goods a component manages. Fig. 2 b) sketches a grouping driven by the "Where" question i.e., the location of devices and actors.

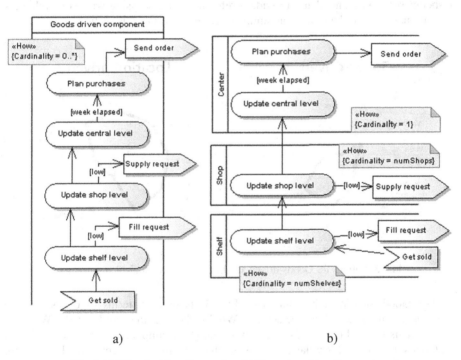

a)                                              b)

**Fig. 2.** a) "Goods-driven" grouping; b) "Location-driven" grouping

<<How>> adornments deal with the multiplicity of component instances. The assumption is that the Goods-driven component is dynamically instantiated for each sold item, whereas the Location-driven components are statically instantiated according to the locations they deal with; of course, they have a cyclic behavior, not shown for simplicity.

The presented solutions are naive and extreme, but they are useful to stress how the choice of a driving dimension influences the logical architecture. The solutions are named "Goods-driven" and "Location-driven" respectively to help non-architects identifying the driving problem dimensions, though the solutions correspond to well-known composition criteria (e.g., functional grouping and user/device oriented grouping [12]).

The question is: how to compare the effectiveness of different logical architectures by considering *all* the problem dimensions? Key criteria are *low coupling* and *high cohesion* [9], which should be evaluated over all the dimensions of the problem, including NFRs. This can be done via Kiviat charts (see Fig. 3) where axes correspond to problem dimensions. The "What" issue is refined to consider how many data types are exploited by a component (Types), how may object instances are managed by a component instance (Instances), data flows across components (Flows) and data sharing among components (Sharing). The effectiveness on each dimension is rated from 1 to 10 by assigning crisp "rule-of-thumb" values; this may suffice in a workshop discussion aimed at providing a broad comparison of different solutions.

The footprint of a chart provides a rough but impressive "at-a-glance" feeling about the effectiveness of different logical architectures: wider footprints correspond to better solutions. The charts provide a reference for discussing with non-architects the rationale behind the ratings, as summarized in the rest of this section.

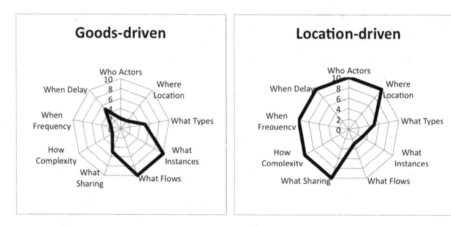

**Fig. 3.** Ratings for Goods-driven and Location-driven logical architectures

The Goods-driven architecture (see Fig. 3) is poor in terms of cohesion. The component interacts with all the actors ("Who") wherever they are located ("Where"). It also deals with all the Goods types; in this simple example there are few subclasses of Goods that perform similar functions, so that this dimension gets a medium rating, though in more complex situations this aspect might be more critical. The cohesion is also poor regarding "How" and, in particular, the complexity, because the component intermixes very simple and computationally intensive activities (Plan purchases). Finally, the component exhibits scarce cohesion in the "When" dimension, regarding both the frequency of the activities it includes and the timing constraints.

Things are not so bad when looking at coupling. There is only one component, which obviously is fully uncoupled if its static structure is considered. However, the component is multi-instantiated; therefore the coupling among different instances must be rated by considering the dynamic behavior. Each instance of the component manages an individual Goods item, so that different instances do not explicitly communicate and are fully uncoupled in the "What-Flows" dimension. They sometimes interact over the data stores, so that there is a moderate coupling in the "What-Sharing" dimension.

The Location-driven architecture can be rated in a similar way (see Fig. 3). Just note that component manages several instances of Goods ("What-Instances"). There are several information flows among components ("What-Flows"). Information sharing ("What-Sharing") is negligible because the data stores exploited by the components contain disjoint information.

The comparison of the two charts in Fig. 3 shows that the ratings of the two logical architectures are somehow complementary. The Location-driven one looks better, but this preliminary conclusion will be refined in the following.

## 4  Deployment

At last platforms and technologies enter the stage. The *deployment architecture* defines how logical components can be deployed into computational nodes. A natural deployment for the Goods-driven architecture is to rely on a centralized server farm, where instances of the unique logical component can be dynamically created each time items are sold. On the opposite, a natural deployment for the Location-driven architecture is to rely on a distributed infrastructure where computational nodes are associated with shelves, shops and central site. Again, these are naive solutions, presented here to exemplify how technological issues can be exploited to tune the ratings deriving from the logical architecture.

**Fig. 4.** Weighted ratings for Goods-driven and Location-driven logical architectures

The straightforward idea is that the rating of a logical architecture on each dimension must be weighted according to the advantages it produces in a specific deployment scenario. For example, if a low-cost and reliable broadband network is available, computing power is not a problem and an efficient DBMS is available, the ratings of the cohesion on the "Where", "How-Complexity", "What-sharing" and "When" dimensions get a low weight (say 0.3). On the opposite, the presence of complex inter-component data flows may imply high development and management costs; therefore the rating of the "What-Flows" gets a high weight (say 0.8). The result is shown in Fig. 4, highlighting that the Goods-driven logical architecture might be more cost-effective than the Location-driven one. Of course, the result can be very different under different technological assumptions, for example if connectivity problems are foreseen.

## 5  Lessons Learned and Conclusions

The proposed approach focuses on "how to communicate to non-architects the criteria underlying architectural choices". The idea is that the communication process cannot mirror the development process, because the explanation must follow a waterfall pattern even if the real development process is iterative. Therefore the approach should be viewed as complementary, not alternative to established design and development processes.

The approach borrows some central ideas from the Model Driven Architecture (MDA) approach [13]. Moreover it strong related with the Use-Case driven architecture design [14]. The Krutchen 4+1 views [3]   and the Rational Unified Process [2] pay particular attention to the identification of use cases, business and problem analysis to validate the final architecture. The term "Logical Architecture" is used there to identify the functionalities that the system has to provide. However, our approach is more focused on how the component organization can be conceptually defined and motivated in term of clusters of functionalities and properties. Similar remarks apply to the Conceptual Architecture view proposed by [4].

The approach stems from experiences in real-life projects and, in particular, from the participation in project reviews involving high-level stakeholders which "want to understand" (and to decide) in half an hour and are often biased by up-to-date buzzwords. The problem here is to focus on key issues and to avoid discussions shifting from vague philosophical principles to technological tricks. The separation between problem, logical and deployment architectures might seem pedantic, but it helps enforcing the attitude towards abstraction and separation of concerns, without neglecting technical aspects and constraints.

The approach has been also successfully tested in several introductory courses on software architecture. What the authors learned is that presenting to students one or more systems is reasonably easy; what is difficult is to communicate the rationale underlying the choices and the conceptual process that led to a specific architecture. Not surprisingly, students with an "algorithm-oriented" culture started with solutions like the "goods-driven" one, whereas students with a "web-oriented" culture started with the "location-driven" one. The comparison of the solutions by relying on the impressive, though naive, presentation of the footprints, together with the "what-if" discussion of what happens if different dimensions have different weights, have been the basis for highly effective classroom discussions.

Ultimately, our goal was to support fruitful discussions, to raise doubts, to stimulate a critical attitude and to warn against the unconscious adoption of a-priori solutions.

Further research will deal with a more precise formalization of the communication process and, in particular, on metrics supporting the rating of the architectures over the problem dimensions.

# References

1. Wieringa, R.: A survey of structured and object-oriented software specification methods and techniques. ACM Comput. Surv. 30, 459–527 (1998)
2. Kruchten, P.: The Rational Unified Process: An Introduction. Addison-Wesley Professional, Reading (2000)
3. Kruchten, P.: The 4+1 View Model of Architecture. IEEE Softw. 12, 42–50 (1995)
4. Hofmeister, C., Nord, R., Soni, D.: Applied Software Architecture. Addison-Wesley Professional, Reading (1999)
5. Kazman, R., Barbacci, M., Klein, M., Carrière, S.J., Woods, S.G.: Experience with performing architecture tradeoff analysis. In: Proceedings of the 21st international conference on Software engineering, pp. 54–63. ACM, Los Angeles (1999)
6. Larman, C.: Applying UML and Patterns: An Introduction to Object-Oriented Analysis and Design and Iterative Development, 3rd edn. Prentice Hall PTR, Englewood Cliffs (2004)
7. Tyree, J., Akerman, A.: Architecture Decisions: Demystifying Architecture. IEEE Softw. 22, 19–27 (2005)
8. DeMarco, T.: Structured Analysis and System Specification. Prentice Hall PTR, Englewood Cliffs (1979)
9. Stevens, W.P., Myers, G.J., Constantine, L.L.: Structured design. IBM Systems Journal 13, 115–139 (1974)
10. Shaw, M., Garlan, D.: Software architecture: perspectives on an emerging discipline. Prentice-Hall, Inc., Englewood Cliffs (1996)
11. Heineman, G.T., cur Councill, W.T.: Component-based software engineering: putting the pieces together. Addison-Wesley Longman Publishing Co., Inc., Boston (2001)
12. Wieringa, R.J.: Design Methods for Reactive Systems: Yourdon, Statemate, and the UML. Morgan Kaufmann, San Francisco (2003)
13. Mellor, S.J., Kendall, S., Uhl, A., Weise, D.: MDA Distilled. Addison Wesley Longman Publishing Co., Inc., Amsterdam (2004)
14. Tekinerdogan, B., sit, M.A.: Classifying and Evaluating Architecture Design Methods. In: sit, M.A. (cur.) Software Architecture and Component Technology, pp. 3–28. Kluwer Academic Publishers, Dordrecht (2001)

# Reference Models and Reference Architectures Based on Service-Oriented Architecture: A Systematic Review

Lucas Bueno Ruas de Oliveira, Katia Romero Felizardo,
Daniel Feitosa, and Elisa Yumi Nakagawa

Dept. of Computer Systems
University of São Paulo - USP
PO Box 668, 13560-970, São Carlos, SP, Brazil
{buenolro,katiarf,fdaniel,elisa}@icmc.usp.br

**Abstract.** Service-Oriented Architecture (SOA) has received increasing attention by providing low coupling, reuse, productivity, and a better understanding of the business domain. However, there are challenges in creating quality solutions using services. Based on SOA, reference models and reference architectures have been proposed to support the understanding, development, and standardization in the development of service-oriented systems. Considering the relevance of SOA, as well as the lack of a complete panorama about these models and architectures, this paper aims at presenting a detailed view about the establishment and use of these models and architectures. For this, we conducted a systematic review. As main results, we observed a recent increase in the number of work regarding reference models and reference architectures based on SOA, including for different domains. Furthermore, based on the presented view, we identified interesting and important perspectives for future research.

## 1 Introduction

SOA has arisen as a new architectural style to develop software systems. It has been recently focus of considerable attention of the academy and industry. In SOA, software functionalities are packaged in independent, self-contained and well-defined modules, called services, that are the basis to compose more complex service-oriented systems. SOA intends to contribute with low coupling systems and, as a consequence, it can promote reuse and productivity in software development [1]. However, in spite of the relevance of SOA, there is still challenges to create efficient solutions using this architectural style [2].

In another perspective, Software Architecture has received increasing attention as an important research area of Software Engineering. Software architectures play a major role in determining system quality, since they form the backbone to any successful software-intensive system. In this context, reference models and reference architectures have emerged as elements that aim at facilitating and systematizing the development of software systems. In this work, we have adopted reference model as an abstract framework that presents a minimal set of unifying concepts, axioms and relationships within a particular problem domain, independently of specific standards, technologies, implementations,

M. Ali Babar and I. Gorton (Eds.): ECSA 2010, LNCS 6285, pp. 360–367, 2010.

or other concrete details [3]. Otherwise, the reference architecture aggregates knowledge of a domain, identifying abstract solutions of a problem and promoting reuse of design expertise by achieving solid, well-recognized understanding of a specific domain. In other words, while reference model is usually in a higher abstraction level, reference architecture intends to provide more details. In order to contribute to development of service-oriented software systems, service-oriented reference model and service-oriented reference architecture (i.e., models and architectures that are based on SOA) can also be found; for instance, the OASIS reference model [3] and Service-Oriented Solution Stack (S3) reference architecture [2]. In this context, a complete and detailed view about these models and architectures seems to be very relevant, considering the impact that they can have to the service-oriented system development.

The main objective of this paper is to present a detailed panorama about how reference models and reference architectures based on SOA have been recently proposed and used. For this, we have adopted and applied the systematic review technique [4] that makes possible to have a complete and fair evaluation about a topic of interest. As main results of our systematic review, we have observed that in the last years there is an increase in the number of work involving reference models and reference architectures based on SOA, showing a real interest by both academy and industry. Furthermore, this panorama makes possible to identify interesting and important research topics that could be investigated yet[1].

The remainder of this paper is organized as follows. In Section 2, we present the conducted systematic review. In Section 3, we discuss results, lessons learned and limitations of this work. Finally, in Section 4, we present our conclusions.

## 2   Systematic Review Application

Our systematic review was conducted aiming at identifying relevant primary studies related to service-oriented reference models and service-oriented reference architectures. It was conducted from Sep/2009 to Dec/2009 and was carried out by four people (one software architecture researcher, one systematic review specialist and two graduate students). To conduct our systematic review, we followed the process proposed by Kitchenham [4]. In short, this process presents three main phases: (i) **Phase 1 - Planning:** the research objectives and the review protocol are defined. The protocol constitutes a pre-determined plan that describes the research questions and how the systematic review will be conducted; (ii) **Phase 2 - Conduction:** the primary studies are identified, selected and evaluated according to the inclusion and exclusion criteria established previously. For each selected study, data are extracted and synthesized; and (iii) **Phase 3 - Reporting:** a final report is formatted and presented. In next subsections, we present how these phases were conducted in our systematic review.

---

[1] Detailed information about our systematic review is available in a technical report found in http://www.icmc.usp.br/~biblio/BIBLIOTECA/rel_tec/RT_353.pdf

## 2.1    Phase 1: Planning

In this phase, we established the review protocol. For this, we specified: (i) research questions; (ii) search strategy; (iii) inclusion and exclusion criteria; and (iv) data extraction and synthesis methods.

(i)**Research Questions:** Aiming at finding all primary studies to understand and summarize evidences about reference models and reference architecture based on SOA, the following research questions (RQ) were established:

**Table 1.** Research Questions

| RQ | Description |
|---|---|
| 1 | Which SOA characteristics have been considered during the design and development of reference models and reference architectures? |
| 2 | How reference architectures and reference models can enhance the development of service-oriented systems and which are the main benefits of their use? |
| 3 | In which contexts (academy or industry) service-oriented reference architectures and service-oriented reference models have been applied? |
| 4 | Which is the evaluation and use level of the service-oriented reference architectures and service-oriented reference models, considering their use to implement service-oriented systems? |
| 5 | What are the "inputs" (set of information) that support the development of service-oriented reference architectures and service-oriented reference models? |

(ii)**Search Strategy:** Considering the research questions, we identified the main keywords: "Reference Architecture" and "Service Oriented Architecture". Following, we found related terms for these keywords: "Reference Model", "Service based", "Service Oriented", and "SOA". The keywords chosen must be simple enough to bring many results and, at the same time, rigorous enough to cover only the desired research topic. We used the boolean OR operator to link the main terms and their related terms. Finally, all these terms were combined using the boolean AND operator. The final search string was: *(("Reference Architecture" OR "Reference Model") AND ("Service Oriented Architecture" OR "Service based" OR "Service Oriented" OR SOA )).*

The selected databases to our systematic review are: *ACM Digital Library, IEEE Xplore, ScienceDirect, Scopus, Springer, Web of Science.* According to Dybå et. al [5], these databases are efficient to conduct systematic review in the context of software engineering. Furthermore, *Scopus* was added, since it is considered the largest database of abstracts and citations [4].

(iii)**Inclusion and Exclusion Criteria:** Another important element is to define the Inclusion Criteria (IC) and Exclusion Criteria (EC). These criteria make possible to include primary studies that are relevant to answer the research questions and exclude studies that do not answer them. The inclusion and exclusion criteria are presented in Table 2.

(iv)**Data Extraction and Synthesis Method:** In order to extract data, we plan to build data extraction tables related to each research question. These tables must synthesized results to obtain conclusions. To summarize and describe the set of data, statistical synthesis method will be used.

**Table 2.** Inclusion Criteria and Exclusion Criteria

| Criterion | Description |
|---|---|
| IC1 | The primary study presents a service-oriented reference architecture or a service-oriented reference model. |
| IC2 | The primary study presents some experience involving a service-oriented reference architecture or service-oriented reference model. |
| EC1 | The primary study presents a reference architecture or reference model; however, it involves a specific characteristic or a part of SOA (for instance, reference architecture for systems that support *Enterprise Service Bus* (ESB) or systems that manage *Service Level Agreement* (SLA)). |
| EC2 | The primary study presents a reference architecture or a reference model to other types of systems that do not contain features related to service. |
| EC3 | The primary study is related to SOA, but it does not propose or discuss about reference architectures or reference models. |

## 2.2 Phase 2: Conduction

The search by primary studies was conducted according to previously established plan. This identification was done by looking for all primary studies that match with the search string in the search sources. This phase is defined by three steps. In Step 1, we identified primary studies in the databases, following the systematic review plan established previously. As result, 181 studies were identified. In the next step (Step 2), we selected the primary studies, through reading of titles and abstracts and application of the inclusion and exclusion criteria. Thus, a total of 38 studies were selected. In Step 3, the 38 papers were read in full and inclusion and exclusion criteria were again applied. Finally, 21 studies were considered as the most relevant to our systematic review. Table 3 summarizes our findings. It is important to observe that Scopus indexes studies of other databases, such as IEEE xplore and Springer. Thus, it can cause an increase in the number of repeated studies; among 36 studies, 15 were therefore repeated. However, Scopus was the most efficient source, since 66.7% of all included papers were obtained in this source. Otherwise, ACM contributed with only 4.8% of papers.

**Table 3.** Search sources, obtained and included primary studies

| Database | Obtained | Included | Rate Index[2] | Date |
|---|---|---|---|---|
| ACM Digital Library | 7 | 1 | 0.048 | 10/27/2009 |
| IEEE Xplore | 41 | 7 | 0.333 | 09/29/2009 |
| Science Direct | 4 | 1 | 0.048 | 10/29/2009 |
| Scopus | 67 | 14 | 0.667 | 10/30/2009 |
| Springer | 19 | 5 | 0.238 | 10/28/2009 |
| Web of Science | 43 | 8 | 0.381 | 10/27/2009 |

Table 4 presents the 21 primary studies included. Column "Type" indicates if the study is related to a service-oriented reference model (RM) or a service-oriented reference architecture (RA). Column "Doc. type" indicates if the study

---

[2] Ratio between the total of included studies of a database and the total of primary studies obtained.

**Table 4.** Included primary studies

| Study | Authors | Year | Type | IC | Doc. type |
|---|---|---|---|---|---|
| S1 | Arsanjani, A. et al. | 2007 | RA | IC1, IC2 | JA |
| S2 | Brehm, N. and Gomez, J. | 2007 | RA | IC1 | CP |
| S3 | Choi, H. et al. | 2009 | RA | IC1 | CP |
| S4 | Costagliola, G. et al. | 2008 | RM | IC1 | JA |
| S5 | Costagliola, G. et al. | 2006 | RM | IC1 | CP |
| S6 | Dillon, T. et al. | 2008 | RA | IC2 | CP |
| S7 | Duro, N. et al. | 2005 | RA | IC2 | CP |
| S8 | Fioravanti, F. et al. | 2007 | RA | IC2 | CP |
| S9 | Futo, I. | 2007 | RM | IC1 | CP |
| S10 | Hemalatha, T. et al. | 2008 | RA | IC1 | CP |
| S11 | Lan, J. et al. | 2008 | RA | IC1, IC2 | CP |
| S12 | Leppaniemi, J. et al. | 2009 | RA | IC1 | CP |
| S13 | Liu, L. et al. | 2008 | RA | IC1, IC2 | CP |
| S14 | Murakami, E. et al. | 2007 | RA | IC1 | JA |
| S15 | OASIS | 2006 | RM | IC1, IC2 | TR |
| S16 | Peristeras, V. et al. | 2009 | RA | IC1, IC2 | JA |
| S17 | Ramanathan, S. | 2008 | RA | IC2 | JA |
| S18 | Reiff-Marganiec, S. et al. | 2008 | RA | IC1 | CP |
| S19 | Zheng, Q. et al. | 2008 | RA | IC1 | CP |
| S20 | Zimmermann, O. et al. | 2009 | RA | IC2 | BC |
| S21 | Zirpins, C. et al. | 2008 | RM | IC1 | JA |

was published in a Journal Article (JA), Conference Paper (CP), Technical Report (TR) or a Book Chapter (BC). Moreover, almost all studies were included by criteria 1 (i.e, the primary study presents a service-oriented reference architecture or a service-oriented reference model). Following, a more detailed analysis was conducted on the 21 primary studies included in our systematic review and data were extracted.

### 2.3    Phase 3: Reporting

In this phase, we present analytical results of our systematic review. Only studies published until Oct/2009 were considered. It is observed an increase in the number of primary studies related to service-oriented reference models and service-oriented reference architectures. This seems to indicate an increasing interest on this topic of research. The data extraction and synthesis of knowledge arisen considering each research question are discussed below.

**RQ1:** Regarding RQ1 (i.e., SOA characteristics in reference models and reference architectures), we have identified five main characteristics that have been more widely treated in the primary studies. Table 5 summarizes these characteristics and presents the studies that address each characteristic. Definition for these characteristics can be found in [2]. In some studies, we had to infer about the SOA characteristics that the studies were dealing with, since they was not explicitly indicated. Among these characteristics, "service publication" and "service composition" have had more attention.

**Table 5.** SOA characteristics in the reference architectures and reference models

| Characteristic of SOA | Total | Percentage | Primary Studies |
| --- | --- | --- | --- |
| Service publication | 16 | 76.19% | S1, S2, S3, S4, S5, S6, S8, S10, S14, S15, S16, S17, S18, S19, S20, S21 |
| Quality of service | 11 | 52.38% | S1, S2, S7, S9, S11, S13, S15, S16, S17, S18, S20 |
| Polices and governance | 8 | 38.10% | S1, S2, S9, S11, S13, S18, S19, S20 |
| Service composition | 12 | 57.14% | S1, S3, S6, S9, S10, S11, S16, S17, S18, S19, S20, S21 |
| Enterprise service bus | 7 | 33.33% | S1, S3, S11, S14, S17, S19, S20 |

**RQ2:** This research question addresses the support that reference architectures and reference models have provided to the service-oriented system development. We have concluded that these architectures and models have been mainly used to provide facilities to the development of systems related to a specific domain. Moreover, the primary studies have pointed out that a common "basis" to develop a set of systems is interesting. We identified also the main benefits by using these architectures and models: inter-operability, better comprehension of the domain, establishment of a common vocabulary, architectural reuse, consistence in the system representation, and a better time-to-market.

**RQ3:** This research question refers to the context in which service-oriented reference architectures and service-oriented reference models have been applied. We have observed that these architectures and models have been applied in different domains. Table 6 summarizes our findings. Domains that involve governmental systems, collaborative work environments, and e-learning have been investigated. We have also identified efforts to establish architectures and models that are independent of a specific domain. For instance, S3 reference architecture [2] and OASIS reference model [3] are two initiatives widely known, cited, and used as basis of other reference architectures and reference models. However, in spite of these efforts, there are still several other domains that could be considered.

**RQ4:** This research question addresses the *evaluation and level* of the service-oriented reference architectures and service-oriented reference models. Table 7 presents how these architectures and models have been applied. It is observed that, on the one hand, 61.90% (4.76% + 14.28% + 42.86%) of the studies have presented an instantiation and/or implementation based on the proposed architecture or model; on the other hand, eight studies (38.10%) have presented only the architecture or the model. It is important to observe that none study has explicitly treated evaluation of reference architectures and reference models. According to Clements et. al [6], the application of evaluation methods in software architectures can improve the success of systems built from these architectures. Thus, it seems to be interesting to concentrate efforts to investigate the evaluation of architectures and models based on SOA.

**RQ5:** The RQ5 refers to the "inputs" that support the development of service-oriented reference architectures and service-oriented reference models. The inputs to the reference architectures and reference models involved in our sys-

**Table 6.** Application domains of the primary studies

| Application domain | Total | Percentage | Context Academy | Industry |
|---|---|---|---|---|
| Generic (domain independent) | 6 | 28.57% | S6, S11, S13 | S1, S15, S20 |
| Governamental system | 3 | 14.29% | S3, S9, S12 | |
| E-learning | 3 | 14.29% | S4, S5, S19 | |
| Collaborative work | 2 | 9.52% | S16, S18 | |
| Enterprise resource planning (ERP) | 1 | 4.76% | S2 | |
| Multimedia | 1 | 4.76% | | S8 |
| Image processing | 1 | 4.76% | S10 | |
| Precision agriculture | 1 | 4.76% | S14 | |
| Telecommunication | 1 | 4.76% | | S17 |
| Collaborative network organization | 1 | 4.76% | S21 | |
| Ground software system | 1 | 4.76% | S7 | |

**Table 7.** Evaluation and use of the reference architectures and reference models

| Evaluation and use level | Total | Percentage | Primary Studies |
|---|---|---|---|
| Evaluate | 0 | 0% | – |
| Architectural instantiation (a) | 3 | 14.28% | S2, S11, S21 |
| Implementation (b) | 1 | 4.76% | S10 |
| Both (a) and (b) | 9 | 42.86% | S3, S4, S5, S14, S16, S17, S18, S19, S20 |
| None | 8 | 38.10% | S1, S6, S7, S8, S9, S12, S13, S15 |

**Table 8.** Inputs used to design the reference architectures and reference models

| Input | Total | Percentage | Primary Studies |
|---|---|---|---|
| Existing systems and concrete architectures | 5 | 23.81% | S1, S6, S19, S20, S21 |
| Other reference architectures or reference models | 5 | 23.81% | S4, S5, S7, S8, S14 |
| Knowledge and experience of the domain expert | 11 | 52.38% | S2, S3, S9, S10, S11, S12, S13, S15, S16, S17, S18 |

tematic review are: existing systems, concrete architectures, similar reference architectures, and knowledge coming from domain experts. These inputs were also pointed by Angelov et. al [7] to establish reference architectures and reference models. Table 8 summarizes the inputs that we have found through the 21 primary studies considered. For instance, the most of studies (53.38%) have used knowledge and experience coming from domain experts. Five studies (23.81%) used other reference architectures and reference models as input; however, these architectures and models are not based on SOA.

# 3   Discussion

Results of our systematic review point out that reference architectures and reference models based on SOA have recently received increasing attention from both academia and industry. We have also observed that there is not a consensus about how to represent service-oriented reference models and service-oriented reference architectures. Some of them have used UML; however, the most of them have used particular and informal way to represent them. Thus, different understanding can be obtained, disturbing the real purposes of these models and architectures. We also observe that the included studies have been published in different conferences and periodicals. In other words, they are not concentrated, for instance, in only software architecture or SOA events. Thus, the conduction of systematic review seems to be an adequate choice, aiming at finding possibly all primary studies in this context. In spite of positive results, relevant primary studies written in other languages can have been ignored, it was considered only papers in English. Our review could be conducted again, aiming at inserting studies published from Sep/2009 until now. Although the databases used in our systematic review are usually considered efficient sources to Software Engineering area, other databases, such as Compendex[3], could be included.

## 4    Conclusion

The main contribution of this work is to present a detailed panorama about proposal, use and evaluation of reference models and reference architectures based on SOA. For this, we have conducted a systematic review. As main result, we can conclude that these models and architectures have been focus of increasing attention in the last years. Another important contribution of this work is to make possible identification of new research lines; for instance, evaluation of service-oriented reference architecture and establishment of architectures and models for other domains that have not been considered yet. Thus, there are still different perspectives that could be investigated, aiming at improving reuse, productivity and quality of service-oriented systems.

## References

1. Papazoglou, M.P., Traverso, P., Dustdar, S., Leymann, F.: Service-oriented computing: a research roadmap. Int. Journal of Cooperative Information Systems 17(2), 223–255 (2008)
2. Arsanjani, A., Zhang, L.J., Ellis, M., Allam, A., Channabasavaiah, K.: S3: A service-oriented reference architecture. IT Professional 9(3), 10–17 (2007)
3. OASIS: Reference model for service oriented architecture 1.0. Technical report, OASIS Standard (October 2006)
4. Kitchenham, B., Charters, S.: Guidelines for performing systematic literature reviews in software engineering. Technical Report EBSE 2007-001, Keele University and Durham University Joint Report (2007)
5. Dybå, T., Dingsoyr, T., Hanssen, G.K.: Applying systematic reviews to diverse study types: An experience report. In: ESEM 2007, pp. 225–234. IEEE Computer Society, Los Alamitos (2007)
6. Clements, P., Kazman, R., Klein, M.: Evaluating Software Architectures: Methods and Case Studies. Addison-Wesley, Boston (2002)
7. Angelov, S., Grefen, P.W.P.J., Greefhorst, D.: A classification of software reference architectures: Analyzing their success and effectiveness. In: WICSA 2009, Cambridge, UK, Sep 2009, pp. 141–150 (2009)

---

[3] http://www.engineeringvillage.com

# A Classification of Value for Software Architecture Decisions

Ulrik Eklund and Thomas Arts

Department of Applied IT
Chalmers Univ. of Technology/Göteborg University, Sweden
ulrik.eklund@ituniv.se

**Abstract.** This paper introduces a classification for decisions originating from work performed by architects. With the creation of a new architecture, all observed decisions were documented using an existing taxonomy extended with the introduced classification. In the first four months, 80 decisions were documented. Not all decisions have the same value for the architecture and one needed a classification to reason about importance of decisions. After realization of the first increment of the architecture a sanity check was performed: The architects showed how the six most important design artefacts and the fifteen most important architectural constraints and prerequisites were related. The relationship was via decisions and the classification helps to reduce the work to make and maintain this connection over time. The classification is dynamic and over time decisions can be classified differently. This enables architectural learning by pointing out which decisions were taken too early or had little impact.

## 1 Introduction

The classification introduced in this paper originates from a practical problem a group of architects was confronted with. In their preparation of a software architecture for a new product, they have to take a large number of decisions. Design artefacts such as specifications, models and code remain, but the 'why' is lost over time. In the lifetime of a product, but in particular when an architecture for a new product is created, an answer to the 'why' question is of utmost importance; "Did we base this decision on technology that now is replaced?"; "Did we take this decision because the company decided for a specific business unit to implement it?". If the reasons for a decision has been invalidated, then it would be wise to revisit that decision, but one can only do so, if the reasoning around the decision is documented.

The architects were in particular interested in the relationship between design artefacts and the prerequisites for the architecture, which includes business and technical requirements, and design constraints. During the work we noticed a demand among the architects to discuss and understand more in detail how prerequisites and artefacts were related, especially as a rationale for the architecture as a whole. This lead to a new classification of decisions supporting reasoning about the value or usefulness of a decision, also over time.

M. Ali Babar and I. Gorton (Eds.): ECSA 2010, LNCS 6285, pp. 368–375, 2010.
© Springer-Verlag Berlin Heidelberg 2010

We aim to aid in answering questions like "do the architects spend their time on the right/best decisions?", "Are there some decision the architects should *not* make?" and "which decisions could be reused?". Our contribution is a classification of decisions and show that this helps architects to:

- detect possible decisions that need to be elaborated on,
- detect decisions that need discussion with stakeholders,
- detect over time whether the architects spend their time on taking the right decisions, those that create true value for the organisation. These are the decisions that would be impossible, less efficient or more costly if they would be made by an other stakeholder, for example an acquirer or programmer.

The focus on the vital decisions become even more necessary if architects are a limited resource or one has a lean perspective on software development, i.e. eliminate spending time on issues not creating value.

**Related Work.** Kruchten et al. [1] have noticed the need of explicitly documenting design decisions and recognize that this is often omitted in practice. They present an ontology to help documenting and analysing design decisions. In our case the architects build upon this existing ontology. Tang et al. [2] focus much on the relation between prerequisites, decision and artefacts and have tool support for documenting this by means of a UML model profile [3]. This approach would support a change impact analysis of the architecture, e.g. [4].

A difference between the two mentioned approaches is that Tang et. al. only describes relationship between prerequisites and design outcomes and not between decisions themselves. If such relations need to be expressed, then a design outcome from one decision must be modelled as a prerequisite for another. Kruchten et al. on the other hand give no extra status to prerequisites; these are decisions at the beginning of the chain of relations and one may use a decision attribute to document their special rationale.

## 2   The Case of Documenting Decisions

How can one help the architect to make a limited set of decisions, and still do a proper job? We expect that each "architectural requirement" or prerequisite relates via a number of decisions to at least one design artefact, most likely a few. Similarly we would expect each design artefact to be traceable to at least one prerequisite. If we consider the software architect to be the link between the requirement owners (stakeholders) and the software design, then part of the job of the software architect is to take decisions such that the set of architectural artefacts is a smallest set covering the prerequisites.

In our case a team of software architects is appointed to deliver a new software architecture, but one of them has the extra task as an industrial PhD student to document all decisions taken. This is communicated to the team and everyone agrees on the usefulness of that extra task being carried out. The decisions were documented in a systematic way with attributes[1] similar to the ones by Kruchten et al. [1]. Additional notes were taken describing how the decision was taken, e.g. was it made by the lead architect, by consensus after discussion, or if alternatives were not even discussed?

In the first four months, 80 decisions were documented relating to both the process of defining the architecture and the resulting artefacts. After first increment of the software architecture a sanity check on the work was to be performed. In order to do so, the architects showed how the six most important design artefacts and the fifteen most important architectural prerequisites and constraints were related by various decisions.

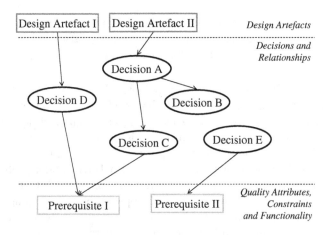

**Fig. 1.** The relationship between decisions and other elements in a simple graphical notation. The relationships to other architectural artefacts are inspired by [2].

When documenting decisions care was taken to relate them. Whenever a new decisions was added, it was related to already existing decisions if possible. Kruchten et. al. have a rather elaborate categorisation of different relationships [5], [1], but in practice this richness of relations is a bit overwhelming; the simplest thing to determine is whether a decision depends upon another. We propose a very simple relationship of "is influenced by"[2]. If decision B is influenced by decision A then decision B must be re-evaluated if decision A is removed or changed. This simple relationship would make it possible to evaluate how far the influence of a single decision reaches. The link between artefacts and decisions and between decisions and prerequisites were made as part of the documentation process (Fig. 1), sometimes within the team of architects, sometimes by the PhD student alone. These relations are also characterized as "influenced by".

Future work involves evaluation of this classification together with an analysis of the benefits at Volvo Cars.

---

[1] Epitome (or decision itself), Rationale, Scope, Authors, State, and Category.

[2] Note that the relation 'influenced by' is the inverse of Kruchten's 'depends on'.

# 3    Classes of Architectural Design Decisions

We now want to talk about the decisions by characterizing the decisions based upon how valuable the decisions are for the organization. Our point of view is that each design artefact should be based upon a decision taken and that decisions are taken to meet some prerequisite.

If we consider for simplicity the prerequisites and design artefacts as decisions as well, then in this way one obtains a directed graph of decisions. When the Ph.D. student studied this graph, it was observed that certain relations were missing, since it was believed that two nodes were related, but no path existed between them. In those cases it turned out that an implicit decisions was taken they were added to the graph (similar to "Implicit and undocumented decisions" mentioned in [1][3]. Obviously, there may still be implicit decisions not recognized this stage and therefore not made explicit, hence undocumented. The implicit decisions are the first we want to define a name for in order to talk about them.

**Oblivious Decisions** are the decisions that the architects are not aware that they are making and at best are documented in hindsight. Examples include earlier experience, implicit company policies to use certain approaches, standards, and the like. These were the most difficult decisions to observe since the observer was native to the setting he observed, i.e., he was as accustomed to the 'of course' knowledge as the other architects. The existence of them is based on a theoretical reasoning rather than empirical observation.

*Example:* Typical examples are decisions where there is only one alternative. This can be due to technical limitations, but also that the consensus is so strong or the decisions was taken so long ago that no-one is aware of any alternatives.

## 3.1    Classification by Relations in the Decision Graph

We base our terminology on the directed graph, of which Fig. 1 is an example, obtained by relating all decisions and including prerequisites and design artefacts as nodes in the graph. We first divide the decisions in four main classes, corresponding to the following relation with the decision graph:

**Exterior Decision.** A node in the graph that has a path to a prerequisite.
**Interior Decisions.** A node in the graph that has no path to a prerequisite.
**Effectual Decisions.** A node in the graph for which there exists a path from a design artefact to this node.
**Ineffectual Decisions.** A node in the graph for which there exists no path from a design artefact to this node.

**Exterior decisions** have a clear stakeholder that drives the decision and the decisions give value to the organization by bringing the requirements of a stakeholder closer to the design artefacts. Decision A, C and D in Fig. 1 are typical Exterior decisions.

---

[3] "The architect is unaware of the decision, or it concerns 'of course' knowledge."

**Table 1.** Example of a decision directly affecting the design outcomes driven by a number of business concerns

| Name: | #35 AUTOSAR Basic Software |
|---|---|
| Epitome: | The basic software of the electronic control units (ECU) in the electrical system shall follow the AUTOSAR standard. |
| Rationale: | |
| Scope: | All software in the electrical system |
| History: | Director nn, 200x-xx-xx, 1st version |
| Category: | Exterior Effectual decision |
| Note: | This is an assumption that the architects have worked on since the project start in 2008 and was observed as a decided fact rather than when the actual decision was made by management. |

*Example:* A typical example of an exterior decision is the use of the AUTOSAR standard [6], which supports a number of business decisions and defines a number of standardized software components that are part of the design outcomes (cf. Table 1 for the documented observed decision).

**Interior decisions** are decision necessary for the architecture to progress. Decision B in Fig. 1 is a typical Interior decision. Within this class of decisions, we discriminate two kinds of decisions: *Imposed Decisions* and *Supporting Decisions*.

**Imposed decisions.** Decisions that are imposed on the architects and need to be resolved for the design of the architecture to progress. There is no stakeholder that drives the decision, but a choice needs to be made in order to progress. Normally the choice made limits certain future business cases. An experienced architect will need a solid knowledge about the system and what needs to be resolved in order to have a finished product.

*Example:* For a connected car [7] it is important to know if the car manufacturer will offer all services or if 3rd parties also shall have a possibility to offer services (in some sort of open innovation scenario). This is really a business decision which acts as an architectural prerequisite but if it is not known the architects need to make an assumption to progress the work with the technical solution in the car anyway.

**Supporting Decisions.** A supporting decision is a decision necessary for the architects to progress, but not discernible for other stake holders than the architects themselves.

*Example:* An architecture team is tasked with developing both a product line architecture and the architecture for the first instance. They can then decide between first developing the product line architecture and use that as a basis for the product architecture. Or they can first define a product architecture and then generalise that to a product line. Either way it is not discernible for any stakeholders which decision they made if they are both delivered at the same time.

**Table 2.** Example of a decision directly affecting the design outcomes

| Name: | #25 Choice of deployment views |
|---|---|
| Epitome: | The logical architecture components will have three deployments: 1. Logical architecture components onto hardware (ECUs) 2. Logical architecture components onto systems 3. Logical architecture components onto organisation The deployment will be modelled separately from the logical package structure in the UML model. |
| Rationale: | |
| Scope: | The entire logical architecture, the entire life-span |
| History: | Architect nn1, 2009-06-08, 2nd version |
| Category: | Exterior Effectual decision |
| Note: | Consensus decision after several discussions. Original decision observed at working meetings of the logical architecture team. |

**Effectual decisions** result in a visible Design Outcome. In a design document driven organization, these are typically the decisions that the software architects are expected to make and document the outcomes in various views. An example of an effectual decision is seen in Table 2 stating how the design outcome will be presented. However, the software architect should obey to the principle of "an architect should make as few decisions as possible, deferring the rest until later in the lifecycle" [8].

**Ineffectual Decisions** are those decisions that address a prerequisite but are never visible in a design artefact.

We have not found any examples of Ineffectual decisions in our study but an analysis of design decisions and their relationship to Concerns and Outcomes shows that these types of decisions can also exist if the classification should be considered complete. Decision E in Fig. 1 is a typical Ineffectual decision.

## 4    Value of Decisions

By defining classes of decisions as above, one can determine by the position in the graph what kind of decision is taken (Exterior or Interior, Effectual or Ineffectual) and for those that are Interior, one can determine by studying the decisions whether it is an Imposed decision or a Supporting decision. This can then help to determine the value of a decision or to detect decisions that need elaboration or more discussion with stakeholders. The value depends on the organizational context. In the context of Volvo Cars, some guidelines can be formulated for decisions that probably need more attention than other decisions. For example, interior imposed decisions are most important to document, since they indicate that a technical decisions is made before the business stakeholders have made up their mind. In other words, further discussion with stakeholders is required; either immediately for the software release under development or at a later stage when the business propositions are clearer.

Ineffectual decisions may in the case of Volvo Cars indicate that the architects are not yet ready with their work, since the rôle of the software architect is seen to produce the initial top-level design and Volvo Cars is a design artefact-driven organization. In other organizations it may be the other way around, where many effectual decisions may indicate overambitious software architects that deal too much with details.

Exterior and effectual decisions are, of course, also important to document, since the "why" will be forgotten when the Design Outcome is fixed, but these decisions are relatively easy to trace in the organization and can potentially be reconstructed.

## 5    Classifying Decisions over Time

The classes of decisions we described before are statically determined. However it was observed that decisions change over time for various reasons and this needs to be addressed when evaluating the value or usefulness of them. Two classes emerged after the involved architects analysed the 80 observed decisions in our case. In order to asses the value of the decisions over time the analysis needs to be iterated.

**Unstable decisions** are those decisions that change over time due to added or changed prerequisites, given that these prerequisites were hard to foresee. At the moment of this analysis, we have not yet been able to identify such decisions, but since our study only lasted four months and the products based on the architecture are manufactured in more than seven years this is not unexpected.

**Premature decisions** are decisions that show to be erroneous over time. They had to be changed without new prerequisites emerging, because they were based upon incorrect interpretation of prerequisites or forgotten prerequisites.

*Example:* A decision on what to include in the architecture description was changed from: Items/headings that are known to be included in the reference architecture description with a comment that future information will be included in future versions of the document, to: There will not be any empty headings with TBD (to be defined) in the architecture description. This decision was changed by the lead architect after three months. Because of too little contextual information available at the moment that the decision was taken, this precise decision had to be adjusted quickly after.

**Expedient decisions** are those decisions that do not change over time (thus it depends upon when in time one determines their status whether they are expedient or not). Expedient decisions are unchanged when prerequisites are added or changed.

## 6    Conclusion

With the proposed classification of decisions it should be possible to reason about the value of decisions, as seen from the architects perspective, both when the decisions are are made and later in retrospective. The classification should support post-mortem analysis if the architects spend their time on the most useful issues, especially in the view of the architects being a limited resource.

A software architect should observe and take care of Interior Imposed decisions, since they form a potential risk for the architecture. If one is to re-use decisions in a next project, then the Interior Imposed and Interior supported decisions need to be evaluated thoroughly. Exterior decisions also need to be re-evaluated, but the situation of having a stakeholder for them eases that task.

When gaining experience from working with software architecture it is important to observe which decisions become unstable, premature or stay expedient throughout the product lifetime. In particular premature decisions indicate a learning opportunity for software architects.

In practice it seems impossible to document all architectural decisions in the lifetime of a car, in particular to maintain the documentation of these decisions. A learning organization starting to document decisions will become better in choosing which decisions to maintain.

If an organisation is interested in re-using architectural knowledge from previous projects and systems, it should also be interested in what subset of this knowledge that is *useful* for the architects to re-use. We believe this paper presents a classification and an associated in-depth terminology to use in such analyses.

**Acknowledgements.** This work has been financially supported by the Swedish Agency for Innovation Systems (VINNOVA) as part of the FFI program. We are grateful for all the time fellow architects have contributed in discussions.

# References

1. Kruchten, P., Lago, P., van Vliet, H.: Building up and reasoning about architectural knowledge. In: Hofmeister, C., Crnković, I., Reussner, R. (eds.) QoSA 2006. LNCS, vol. 4214, pp. 43–58. Springer, Heidelberg (2006)
2. Tang, A., Han, J., Vasa, R.: Software architecture design reasoning: A case for improved methodology support. IEEE Software 26(2), 43–49 (2009)
3. Tang, A., Jin, Y., Han, J.: A rationale-based architecture model for design traceability and reasoning. Journal of Systems and Software 80(6), 918–934 (2007)
4. Jansen, A., Avgeriou, P., van der Ven, J.S.: Enriching software architecture documentation. Journal of Systems and Software 82(8), 1232–1248 (2009)
5. Kruchten, P.: An ontology of architectural design decisions in software intensive systems. In: 2nd Groningen Workshop on Software Variability, pp. 54–61 (2004)
6. AUTOSAR: AUTomotive open system ARchitecture, AUTOSAR (2009)
7. Automotive technology: The connected car. The Economist (June 2009)
8. Tyree, J., Akerman, A.: Architecture decisions: demystifying architecture. IEEE Software 22(2), 19–27 (2005)

# Beeeye: A Framework for Constructing Architectural Views

Hervé Verjus[1], Sorana Cîmpan[1], Azadeh Razavizadeh[1], and Stéphane Ducasse[2]

[1] University of Savoie, LISTIC Lab, France
[2] INRIA Lille-Nord Europe, RMoD Team, France
{firstname.lastname}@univ-savoie.fr, stephane.ducasse@inria.fr

**Abstract.** We believe that offering means for defining and building multiple architectural views of a given system enhances the understanding of the system as a whole. BeeEye is a *generic and open framework for architecture reconstruction*, which allows to construct architectural views using different (possibly combined) viewpoints and perspectives. The framework follows a model-driven approach where viewpoints and views (abstract and concrete) are models that are defined, constructed and used.

## 1 Introduction

Software systems need to *evolve* over time. They get modified to improve their performance or change their functionality in response to new requirements, detected bugs, *etc.* Some changes are part of the system maintenance; others evolve the system, generally by adding new functionalities, modifying its architecture, *etc..* To successfully evolve a complex system, it is essential to *understand* it. The understanding phase is time and effort consuming, due to several reasons, among which: the system size, lack of overall views of the system, its previous (undocumented) evolutions, *etc.* Software architectures are valuable assets during software evolution; they improve the system understanding, by providing abstract representations of it. This motivates us on supporting the software system understanding phases, by constructing for an existing system different architectural representations, at different abstraction levels, called *architectural views.*

It is widely accepted that multiple architectural views are useful when describing the architecture of a software system [11,4,1]. Architecture relevant information can be found at different granularity levels of given systems and needs to be studied from different perspectives. A viewpoint is a collection of patterns and conventions for constructing one type of views. It reflects stakeholders concerns and guides the construction of views [9]. This paper presents the BeeEye framework, dedicated to the construction of architectural views according to different, possibly composed, viewpoints. The framework proposes several viewpoints related to both business and software engineering domains. It also provides the means for defining new viewpoints. The next section presents an overview of the BeeEye approach. Then we zoom on architectural views (Section 3), architectural viewpoints (Section 4), and view construction (Section 5). Section

M. Ali Babar and I. Gorton (Eds.): ECSA 2010, LNCS 6285, pp. 376–383, 2010.
© Springer-Verlag Berlin Heidelberg 2010

6 presents related work and section 7 briefly addresses the BeeEye framework implementation. The paper closes in section 8 with concluding remarks.

## 2 BeeEye: Goal and Overall Approach

Current propositions highlight the importance of taking into account multiple viewpoints in both the engineering of the system, and in the maintenance phase. Several viewpoints were proposed to be used during the different phases of the software process [11,18,7]. Software architecture recovery aims at extracting architectural representations for existing systems. Ducasse and Pollet [6] propose an exhaustive process-oriented taxonomy of existing architecture reconstruction approaches. Such approaches are classified according to their goal, processes employed, inputs used, techniques and outputs. Given the wide range of propositions, we identified the need for *a unifying architecture recovery framework*, where processes, techniques and views can be combined in different ways, depending on the user expectations. The main constraints on such a framework are: *(1) genericity*: set and structure the main concepts to cover as much as possible the existing techniques; give system representations from different (possible user-defined) perspectives; *(2) flexibility, openness*: provide different construction processes and means to combine them; give the possibility to define user-specific construction processes. None of the existing approaches is generic enough to provide such a framework: they either limit to some specific viewpoints and/or representations, either the process is fixed, either the techniques employed are limited: they are not adapted as a basis for a generic framework, as their intended goal was not to provide such a framework.

BeeEye is a first proposal for a *generic architecture recovery framework*. BeeEye deals with the above mentioned contraints on genericity, flexibility and openness throughout the use of:

- *views*, and *viewpoints*: as the main artefacts for architecture representation and recovery, where views are system representations from a given perspective defined in a viewpoint;
- *composable construction processes*: different basic operators (construction techniques) are provided and can be combined in a flexible manner to obtain user-defined construction processes;
- *different abstraction levels*: architectural representations (views) are considered at different abstraction levels; different kinds of relations exist among constructed views; abstraction and refinement relations concern views situated at different abstraction levels; composition relations concern views situated at the same abstraction level; these relations are inferred either by construction, either by analysis of existing views.

Figure 1 presents an overview of the possibilities offered by the framework in terms of view construction, relations among views and viewpoints. Each construction step corresponds to a framework recursion [16] where an output view is constructed from an input view using a given viewpoint. The viewpoint entails

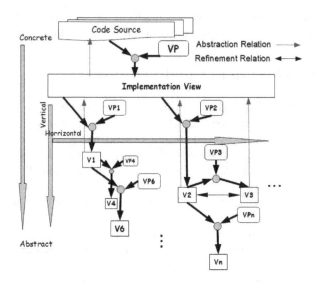

**Fig. 1.** An overview of the BeeEye Framework

the technique used to construct the view. Such construction steps can be chained horizontally and/or vertically. An architectural view construction process can combine multiple construction steps. A vertical application of a construction step leads to output views representing the system from the same perspective as the input view. It induces a change in the abstraction level: the output view is either an abstraction, either a refinement of the input view. Horizontal applications of construction steps lead to composed output views in which the system is represented from multiple perspectives. This translates in a representation which details elements of the input view using a different perspective on the system: the concerned elements are represented as composite elements.

## 3    Architectural Views

An *architectural view* represents a system in terms of interconnected *architectural elements* from a given (possibly composed) perspective. Such a perspective is related to particular stakeholders concerns [9], and conditions the representation elements and their relationships. A view is generally part of a set of views representing the system using different perspectives. Several views may represent the system from the same perspective, but at different abstraction or detail levels. Relations exist among views, generally related to the framework recursions that constitute the view construction process (Section 5). We consider two kinds of architectural views: *abstract views* and *concrete views*.

An *abstract view* represents a possible (intuitive) model for a system within a considered perspective. Each element of the abstract view is supposed to be an abstraction of a part of the system, but the relation with the system's elements is not explicit. Abstract views are means for representing *a priori* knowledge on the system architecture. Different inputs, architectural or not [6], can be considered when defining abstract views, such as previous architectures, documentation, expertise on the system, *etc.*

A *concrete view* gives a concrete representation for a software system: the relation between this view and the system is explicit, generally by abstraction relationships among view and system elements. Concrete views are considered at different abstraction levels. Elements of a concrete view are either directly, either transitively connected to system elements via abstraction relations. An implementation view is considered for the system, where for each system element a corresponding architectural element is defined and connected by an abstraction relationship. Concrete views are always issued from a construction process (section 5) which employs one or several viewpoints (section 4).

## 4   Viewpoints

[9] defines a viewpoint as a collection of patterns and conventions for constructing one type of view. It reflects stakeholders concerns and guides the construction of views. BeeEye uses viewpoints in each framework recursion where starting from an entry concrete view another concrete view is constructed (see Section 2). BeeEye proposes two general classes of viewpoints: *(a) matching viewpoints*: are used to verify whether the system is compliant (in terms of established criteria) to a given architectural representation (abstract view); the user has thus representation expectations which are tested against the system; *(b) discovery viewpoints*: are used as means for discovering representations of the system in the absence of particular representation expectations; elements are grouped using generic *similarity criteria*.

The two intuitive definitions given above can be refined in terms of *user concerns representation* and *kind of construction process* employed. Thus, user concerns can be represented in terms of *abstract views* (*matching viewpoints*) or/and in terms of a *similarity criteria* to be used and an associated *threshold* (*discovery viewpoints*). In *matching viewpoints* the construction process maps the elements of the system[1] against architectural elements of the abstract view. In *discovery viewpoints* the construction process makes use of clustering techniques; it compares among them elements of the entry concrete view using the chosen similarity criteria (reflecting user concerns). Elements with a degree of similarity above the established threshold are grouped and association relations are defined between them and a corresponding architectural element introduced in the constructed concrete view.

Our framework formalizes thus the [9] definition by separating the concerns reflected in the viewpoint (in an abstract view for mapping viewpoints and similarity criteria for discovery viewpoints) on the one hand, and rather generic construction primitives that make use of this information when constructing a

---

[1] We use the term system elements here to make reference to elements of the view used as an entry view for the construction process.

new view on the other hand. The separation of the viewpoint definition in these distinct, yet related descriptions, has several benefits: *(i) reusability* and *maintenance flexibility*: each part of the framework (abstract and concrete views, viewpoints, construction process) can be maintained and reused independently; *(ii) accessibility* and *security*: this separation gives the ability to use the framework for different categories of users with different levels of knowledge about a system.

Examples of matching viewpoints are *business domain*-based mapping viewpoints which consider the principal business domain concepts and their relationships, and *software pattern*-based viewpoints [8] which identify architectural elements conform to a given pattern. Examples of discovery viewpoints are the *activity*-based viewpoint which identifies the architectural elements according to their level of interaction with their environment, and the *business domain*-based discovery viewpoint which identifies business domain concepts. The framework can easily integrate other viewpoints.

# 5   View Construction

Concrete views are always constructed using framework recursions, or construction steps 1. Such a step takes an existing concrete view as input and produces another concrete view using a viewpoint. The specificity of concrete views relies in their relations with the system they represent (dashed arrows in Figure 1). They provide abstract representations of the system, from a given perspective entailed implicitly in the viewpoint definition. This relation can be direct, if the view was constructed directly from the system. Otherwise, it can be obtained by transitive closure, as each concrete view posses relations towards the view from which it was constructed. So at each framework recursion the view constructed is linked to the input view. The nature of this relation depends on the technique employed: construction by *refinement, composition* or *abstraction.*

Construction steps can be chained, combining vertical and horizontal recursions, and concrete views are issued from a succession of construction steps. We employ the term *construction process* to make reference to this combination of construction steps. As each step employs a different viewpoint each of which can be related to a different perspective, a view can represent the system from a combined perspective.

*Construction by Abstraction.* The elements of the constructed view are at a higher abstraction level than their related elements of view given as input. Elements of the input view sharing a particular characteristic are grouped. Characteristics used for grouping elements are either provided by the abstract view (matching viewpoint), either they are provided by generic algorithms ( *i.e.* detecting elements' naming similarities - discovery viewpoint). The elements of the constructed view have abstraction relationships towards elements of view given as input.

*Construction by Refinement.* This technique is the counterpart of the previous one. The output view represents the system from the same perspective, but at a lower abstraction level. It consists a more detailed representation of the system.

*Construction by Composition.* This technique is employed to obtain multiple perspective views and corresponds to horizontal framework recursions. The viewpoint *V* employed in a construction by composition step corresponds to a perspective that differs from the one in which the input view represents the system. Thus, for each element *E* in the entry view, the associated abstracted elements are considered and grouped according to the viewpoint *V*. The elements thus obtained and their relationships are considered as a representation of the element *E* and bare composition relationships to it.

# 6 Related Work

Various contributions concern architecture recovery for object-oriented systems [6]. The inputs used by extraction approaches are various. Most often the source code is used, but also alternative sources of information such as: developer knowledge [13,10]; bug reports and external documentation [2]; or an ontology of the software system's domain [3]. In our approach we use viewpoints to guide the extraction from the source code of a system. Viewpoints are generic and can be related to a software pattern, a business model or cohesion metric, *etc.*. Separating user concerns and construction process in viewpoint definition increases their genericity, reuse and maintainance.

There are several techniques to reconstruct architecture of an existing system. Approaches like [12] and [15] consider external constraints (represented as queries) to be checked against the reality of source code or recovered architectural elements. [13,10,17] propose an automatic reconstruction technique based on reflexion models, starting with a structural high-level model. In Murphy et al. proposition, users iteratively refine a structural high level view model to gain information about the source code. The technique is based on the definition of a set of mappings between this high level model and the source code. Our technique is a reflexion model; the main difference is that we propose a framework to apply this reflexivity. This framework leads in define multiple views from any generated (or existing) view.

# 7 Implementation

Conceptually, the BeeEye framework entails all reconstruction steps starting from the source code. Nevertheless, the initial steps correspond to reverse engineer the system. The BeeEye implementation (in Smalltalk) uses the Moose re-engineering environment [14] for the construction of the implementation view (the first BeeEye framework recursion) which is represented using the FAMIX meta-model [5]. The current framework implementation supports part of the proposed techniques. Although not complete, the implementation allowed us to test both vertical and horizontal view construction. The paper [16] details and further analyses the results obtained in a case study using the BeeEye framework.

# 8   Concluding Remarks

We propose in this paper BeeEye, a *generic architecture recovery framework*. The architecture is defined here as a set of *architectural views* representing the system from different perspectives and at different abstraction levels. In building this framework we tried as much as possible to cover existing propositions and to build an open framework that eases the integration of new means for view construction. Thus, BeeEye provides generic enough concepts to cover as much as possible the existing extraction techniques and to support system representations from different (possible user-define) perspectives. It equally provides different construction processes and means to combine them, giving the possibility to define user-specific construction processes. None of the existing approaches in software architecture recovery is generic enough to provide an open and generic framework for architecture recovery: they either limit to some specific representations, either the extraction process is fixed, either the techniques employed. Using the BeeEye framework, viewpoints related to both business and software engineering domains are defined. It also provides means for defining new viewpoints.

## References

1. Clements, P., Bachmann, F., Bass, L., Garlan, D., Ivers, J., Little, R., Nord, R., Stafford, J.: Documenting Software Architectures: Views and Beyond. Addison-Wesley Professional, Reading (2002)
2. Cubranic, D., Murphy, G.: Hipikat: Recommending pertinent software development artifacts. In: Proceedings 25th International Conference on Software Engineering (ICSE 2003), pp. 408–418. ACM Press, New York (2003)
3. Deissenboeck, F., Ratiu, D.: A unified meta-model for concept-based reverse engineering. In: Proceedings of the 3rd International Workshop on Metamodels, Schemas, Grammars and Ontologies, ATEM 2006 (2006)
4. Deursen, A., Hofmeister, C., Koschke, R., Moonen, L., Riva, C.: Symphony: View-driven software architecture reconstruction. In: Proceedings of the Fourth Working IEEE/IFIP Conference on Software Architecture (WICSA), pp. 122–134 (2004),
   http://csdl.computer.org/comp/proceedings/wicsa/2004/2172/00/21720122abs.htm
5. Ducasse, S., Gîrba, T., Greevy, O., Lanza, M., Nierstrasz, O.: Workshop on FAMIX and Moose in software reengineering (FAMOOSr 2008). In: 15th Working Conference on Software Maintenance and Reengineering (WCRE 2008), October 2008, pp. 343–344 (2008),
   http://scg.unibe.ch/archive/papers/Duca08bFAMOOSr2008.pdf
6. Ducasse, S., Pollet, D.: Software architecture reconstruction: A process-oriented taxonomy. IEEE Transactions on Software Engineering (2009),
   http://scg.unibe.ch/archive/external/Duca09x-SOAArchitectureExtraction.pdf
7. Finkelstein, A., Goedicke, M., Karmer, J., Niskier, C.: Viewpoint oriented software development: Methods and viewpoints in requirements engineering. In: Algebraic Methods II: Theory, Tools and Applications (1991)

8. Guo, Y., Atlee, Kazman: A software architecture reconstruction method. In: Working Conference on Software Architecture (WICSA), pp. 15–34 (1999)
9. IEEE Architecture Working Group: IEEE P1471/D5.0 Information Technology — Draft Recommended Practice for Architecural Description (August 1999)
10. Koschke, R., Simon, D.: Hierarchical reflexion models. In: Proceedings of the 10th Working Conference on Reverse Engineering (WCRE 2003), p. 36. IEEE Computer Society, Los Alamitos (2003)
11. Kruchten, P.B.: The 4+1 view model of architecture. IEEE Software 12(6), 42–50 (1995)
12. Mens, K., Kellens, A., Pluquet, F., Wuyts, R.: Co-evolving code and design with intensional views — a case study. Journal of Computer Languages, Systems and Structures 32(2), 140–156 (2006),
http://prog.vub.ac.be/Publications/2005/vub-prog-tr-05-26.pdf
13. Murphy, G., Notkin, D., Sullivan, K.: Software reflexion models: Bridging the gap between source and high-level models. In: Proceedings of SIGSOFT 1995, Third ACM SIGSOFT Symposium on the Foundations of Software Engineering, pp. 18–28. ACM Press, New York (1995)
14. Nierstrasz, O., Ducasse, S., Gîrba, T.: The story of Moose: an agile reengineering environment. In: Proceedings of the European Software Engineering Conference (ESEC/FSE 2005), pp. 1–10. ACM Press, New York NY (2005), (invited paper)
http://scg.unibe.ch/archive/papers/Nier05cStoryOfMoose.pdf
15. Pinzger, M., Fischer, M., Gall, H., Jazayeri, M.: Revealer: A lexical pattern matcher for architecture recovery. In: Proceedings of the 9th Working Conference on Reverse Engineering (WCRE 2002), pp. 170–178 (2002)
16. Razavizadeh, A., Cîmpan, S., Verjus, H., Ducasse, S.: Software system understanding via architectural views extraction according to multiple viewpoints. In: 8th International Workshop on System/Software Architectures, Algarve, Portugal (November 2009)
17. Robillard, M.P., Murphy, G.C.: Concern graphs: finding and describing concerns using structural program dependencies. In: ICSE 2002: Proceedings of the 24th International Conference on Software Engineering, pp. 406–416. ACM Press, New York (2002)
18. Woods, S.G., Carrière, S.J., Kazman, R.: The perils and joys of reconstructing architectures. SEI Interactive, The Architect 2 (September 1999)

# Facilitating the Selection of Architectural Patterns by Means of a Marked Requirements Model

Javier Berrocal, José García-Alonso, and Juan Manuel Murillo

Escuela Politécnica, University of Extremadura,
Av. Universidad S/N, 10071, Cáceres, Spain
{jberolm,jgaralo,juanmamu}@unex.es

**Abstract.** Architecture definition requires architects who are highly qualified in both the use of architectural patterns and the analysis of the application's requirements. This is because they have to identify what patterns satisfy the application's functional requirements (FR) and quality attributes (QA), and the interrelationships between them. However, since QAs and FRs are usually addressed separately, their interrelationships are not detailed in full. This situation means that the architect has to expend considerable effort on their identification, with the risk of misinterpretations that lead to an inappropriate choice of patterns. We here present a model that allows the FRs to be marked with the constraints imposed by the QAs. The marks are conceived to be re-used during the architecture definition. The model brings knowledge of the requirements and their relationships closer to the architect, allowing patterns aligned with the requirements to be identified with less effort.

**Keywords:** Requirements Engineering, Quality Attributes, Software Architecture.

## 1 Introduction

Companies are undertaking software projects that are ever more complex, with more features, and with stricter quality attributes. In this context, software architecture has moved from pure research to occupying a crucial place in the development life cycle [1]. The architecture specifies the structure of an application, the relationships between its subsystems, the requirements they cover, and how each QA is to be satisfied [2], [3]. This allows the architect to establish a basis on which to design and implement the system as well as facilitating its maintenance and reuse [5], [6].

Creation of the architecture involves a complex decision-making process in which the architect structures the application to meet both the FRs and the QAs [7]. To facilitate this work, catalogues have been defined of the architectural patterns and tactics applied in the commonest situations [1]. Also, approaches such as ADD (attribute-driven design) [11] or quality-driven architecture development [13] assist the architect in choosing and applying the most suitable patterns to meet the system's requirements.

All these techniques assume that the architect has a profound knowledge of the requirements and their relationships. The architect usually extracts this knowledge from

M. Ali Babar and I. Gorton (Eds.): ECSA 2010, LNCS 6285, pp. 384–391, 2010.
© Springer-Verlag Berlin Heidelberg 2010

an in-depth analysis of the requirement artefacts. However, although the QAs and the FRs are usually properly documented, they are often specified separately [16]. This is an obstacle to the full specification of the relationships between FRs and QAs. The result is not only that the architect's work is more difficult, but it also exposes him to making errors of interpretation that can lead to defects being introduced into the architecture which eventually will have to be found and corrected.

Approaches such as IESE-NFR [15] focus on the architects' re-use of the aforementioned information in order to check whether a requirement has been met. However, they do not indicate how architects can use this information to create a more precise architecture. The architect still has to perform a complex analysis of the detailed information. Moreover, both the requirements and the relationships are defined in natural language, which makes it difficult to re-use them in applications to assist the architect in generating the architecture.

The focus of the present work is the reduction of the effort and expertise required to create the architecture. To that end, this paper describes a marked requirements model. This model allows the functional requirements to be marked with the relationships and constraints imposed by the QAs. Thus, it brings the knowledge of the requirements and their relationships closer to the architect. Also, the marks were designed to be re-used both by the architect to manually detect which pattern to apply at each moment, and by tools that assist the architect in selecting the most appropriate pattern. The result is that architecture patterns aligned with the requirements can be identified with less effort by architects who are less specialized.

The paper is organized as follows. Section 2 details different approaches to architecture definition. Section 3 presents the marked requirements model. And Section 4 gives some conclusions and describes future work.

## 2  Background

Software architecture allows the architect to structure an application to satisfy both the FRs and the QAs. Designing an architecture is a very complex task [8], [9]. It requires the architect to make an in-depth analysis of the requirements to obtain the information that will show which patterns or tactics will allow them to be met. For the analysis to be successful and to avoid misunderstanding, the requirements have to be correctly detailed and the architect has to be highly experienced in their analysis.

Several methods have been proposed to reduce the complexity of this task. Some of them provide a requirement model especially designed to facilitate the architect's work. For example, IESE-NFR [15] proposes artefacts and templates which act to guide the elicitation of the non-functional requirements (NFRs). They even define how to document and interlink each NFR with the FRs that have to satisfy them. The aim of this approach is to refine the QAs until they reach a level at which pattern and metrics can be specified. From this information, the architect can evaluate whether the QAs are correctly achieved by the architecture. However, this approach gives no indication on how to re-use this information to generate the architecture, or how to choose the most appropriate pattern.

Other proposals define activities that guide the architect during the analysis of the requirements and the selection of patterns. For example, Quality-Driven Architecture

Development [13] details each pattern and its variations in a model based on feature modeling [14]. Among other things, this model is used to specify the relationship between patterns, indicating how they should be combined. The architect uses it to identify the patterns that can achieve the QAs of the system, and can also consider the relationships modeled to select those which are most appropriate. However, this approach does not indicate how to consider the relationships between QAs or with the FRs. Also, the selection is done entirely by the architect based on his knowledge.

Attribute-Driven Design (ADD) [11] is one of the best known approaches. It defines a recursive process guiding the architect in selecting *system elements*, in identifying the *architectural driver* within each system element, and in applying patterns to satisfy them. In order to reduce the effort of the selection of patterns, it proposes the use of *reasoning frameworks* [12], [8]. A reasoning framework is an application implementing mechanisms to evaluate which patterns achieve some of the architectural drivers of a QA. However, these frameworks are unable to evaluate the effect of the patterns on the rest of the QAs. Furthermore, selecting the architectural driver requires the architect to conduct a thorough analysis of the requirements.

Therefore, approaches which define activities to model more of the requirements' information do not show how to re-use this information to create the architecture. Approaches guiding the selection of patterns require a major effort on the part of skilled architects to avoid misinterpretation during the analysis of the requirements and their relationships. The present work is intended to contribute to overcoming the drawbacks of these two kinds of approach, bringing the knowledge of the requirements closer to the architect. In particular, it describes a marked requirements model. This model marks which FRs are constrained by each QA. The marks are conceived to be re-used both by the architect to identify which pattern to apply in each situation, and by tools to assist the architect in the selection of patterns.

## 3   Marked Requirements Model

Architecture definition requires the analysis of the QAs and the FRs. Through this analysis the architect identifies the NFRs that have to be satisfied, and gains information on the subsystems, their interconnections, and their size. This information is later used to identify which patterns to apply. However, choosing the most appropriate pattern also requires the architect to analyze the relationships between requirements. He must know which part of the system is constrained by each QA and how. For example, if an application has to be maintainable and portable, it can be split into layers using the Layer Pattern [4]. But if only a part should achieve these QAs, the architect should evaluate the possibility of applying other patterns.

However, although the requirements are usually perfectly detailed in the requirements model, this is not the case for their relationships. The reason is that each kind of requirement is addressed separately. OpenUP [10], for instance, defines different artefacts for each class of requirement. Thus, the architect has to analyze these artefacts carefully to identify the relationships between requirements. This requires great experience to avoid making mistakes of interpretation.

The present section describes a marked requirements model. The objective of this model is to convey more information to the architect about the quality restrictions of each subsystem or FR. The following subsections will describe the process[1] of identifying and marking requirements, and how the architect re-uses this information.

## 3.1 The Process of Marking Requirements

This model proposes marking the FRs influenced by some QA with the notation <<*QA*>> + *attributes to satisfy*. In this way, the relationships between FRs and QAs can be modeled. This notation has been defined as a stereotype in a UML profile[2].

The process of marking requirements begins with their identification. Like other processes, this identification starts by analyzing the business processes and the stakeholders' objectives. From the former, one extracts the application's subsystems and the functional requirements of each subsystem. Each functional requirement is detailed with the use case nomenclature, and the sequencing of its steps/actions is modeled with Interaction Diagrams. These diagrams will later be used to mark the relationships between requirements.

From the latter, one identifies the QAs comprising the stakeholders' objectives and which business processes and subsystems will have to satisfy them. This information is used to bind the subsystems to the QAs to create a first approximation to their relationships. Then, the QAs are refined to detail the NFRs that conform them. If possible, the NFRs have to be refined until measurable values are extracted. Besides the stakeholders' NFRs, the NFRs set by the software company also have to be specified. Examples might be the need for distributed development, or the use of a specific technology.

As the NFRs are detailed, one must refine the relationships between subsystems and QAs. To that end, the FRs and NFRs involved in each relationship have to be identified. Once identified, the actions of the functional requirement Interaction Diagrams have to be marked to indicate which NFRs they must satisfy. This marking process can be performed using a purpose-designed UML profile that defines the stereotype <<QA>> + *restrictions to satisfy*. This stereotype allows the requirements engineer to indicate which actions or group of actions are constrained by a given QA. In this way, these diagrams can convey a fuller picture of the requirements and their relationships, and can even reflect the actions involved in each relationship.

Figure 1 shows a marked activity diagram. This diagram models a use case of a web-shop. This use case indicates how the seller checks that a customer's order is correct. In this diagram, there are two marked groups of actions. The first indicates that the whole use case should be maintainable and developed by multiple teams, and the second that the communication between the actor and the use case should be secure.

Once the requirements have been modeled, the analysis discipline commences. As in other processes, one of the first tasks of this discipline is to identify the analysis classes. As well as being included in a Class Diagram, each class identified is also included in the Interaction Diagrams of the requirements in which it has some kind of responsibility, similar to the indications given in [18]. For this, each class is modeled as a lane encompassing the actions for which it is responsible. Thus, the actions are

---

[1] A brief outline will be given of the activities related to the discipline of the requirements so as to deal in some depth with the activities of architecture generation.

[2] The formal specification of the UML profile is not given in this paper because we think that it falls beyond the scope of the conference.

first grouped into classes, and second, knowing which QAs constrain each action, the architect can infer which QAs affect each class. This information can be re-used to identify what pattern to use and in which classes to apply it. For example, Figure 1 shows two levels of lanes. The first indicates that the Sales subsystem is responsible for all the actions. And the second indicates that, within this subsystem, the Orders class is responsible for these actions. Therefore, this subsystem and this class have to achieve the QAs of security, maintainability, and development by multiple teams.

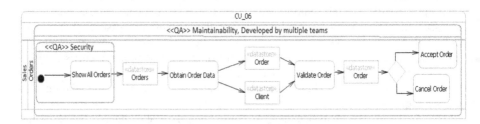

**Fig. 1.** Use case of a web-shop

After these classes have been identified, the architect can define the system architecture. As discussed above, to create the architecture the architect has to analyze the use cases, the analysis classes, and the restrictions imposed by the QAs on each element. In this case, the architect can use the marked Interaction Diagrams to access this information without needing to perform an in-depth analysis of the requirements. In particular, architects with less experience in methods of analysis and requirement processing can access these data with less effort. Also, the architect can re-use these marks to evaluate which QAs impact each part of the system and how. This information can be used to decide which pattern to apply. For example, if a system's diagrams are marked with the QAs of maintainability, but not with the efficiency QA, the layer pattern could be applied.

Furthermore, these marked diagrams can also be re-used by tools that assist the architect in the selection of patterns. This kind of tool usually defines an ontology detailing a company's architectural criteria. These criteria may be related to the stereotype <<QA>>, defining which criteria apply depending on the QAs that are marked. Thus, the use of these tools together with the marked requirements model reduces the effort and expertise needed to define the architecture.

## 3.2   Using the Marked Requirements Model to Select and Apply Patterns

This section details how the *layer pattern* is selected from the marked requirements model and how it is applied. Only one pattern is presented due to space limitations. This pattern was chosen because it satisfies some of the QAs marked in the activity diagram of Figure 1. For this pattern, the following data is detailed (similarly to [17]): intent, consequences, motivation, and structure and necessary transformations.

*Intent.* The layer pattern helps to structure applications that can be decomposed into groups of subtasks. If these groups are based on responsibility (*responsibility-based layering*), the grouping is into layers called tiers. The number of tiers will differ from one application to another depending on the complexity.

*Consequences.* Table 1 lists, ordered by relevance, the QAs affected positively and negatively by the implementation of this pattern.

**Table 1.** Benefits and liabilities of the Layer pattern

| Benefits | Liabilities |
|---|---|
| Maintainability | Inefficiency |
| Developed by multiple teams | Development complexity |
| Portability (adaptability) | |

*Motivation.* The Interaction Diagrams can be used to easily identify whether this pattern can be applied. To this end, the architect has to check whether all or almost all the diagrams are marked with the QAs affected positively, and not with those affected negatively. For example, all of the actions of the activity diagram of Figure 1 are marked with the QAs of maintainability and development by multiple teams. If the rest of the diagrams are also marked with these QAs, this pattern can be implemented.

Without these diagrams the architect would have to do the following: analyze the artefact in which the QAs are documented; for each QA, e.g., maintainability, evaluate the FRs to identify which of them have to be maintainable; re-analyze all the QAs to identify which other attributes constrain the same requirements, e.g., development by multiple teams or efficiency; check for conflicts; and finally identify the patterns that satisfy the QAs and resolve the conflicts.

*Structure and necessary transformations.* To implement this pattern the following steps are taken. First, by analyzing the class diagram, the architect has to identify the number of tiers into which the application will be divided. If the diagram has no more than four classes[3], the application will have one tier. If the diagram has between five and ten classes, the application will have two tiers (*presentation and data*). If the diagram has more than ten classes, the application will be divided into three tiers (*presentation, business logic, and data*). Due to lack of space, only the transformations for the three-tier case will be detailed.

Second, the architect has to assign responsibilities to the tiers. This involves the following steps:

- Create the *presentation* tier in the class and interaction diagrams.
- Create a new class in the *presentation* tier, and add a new action responsible for communication to this class.
- If the previous action is not the last of the use case, the sequence of actions has to be followed, so that a flow between this action and the next has to be created.
- Interactions between actions and actors that exchange data need a document detailing the data exchanged to be associated with them.

---

[3] These numbers will be based on an architect's knowledge and experience of his or her company and team. They may differ from company to company.

The actions of the interaction diagram which require data to be read/written must obtain them through the *data* tier. This involves the following steps:

- Create the *data* tier in the class and interaction diagrams.
- For each group of data read/written, a value object (VO) is created.
- For each VO, a data access object (DAO) managing it is created.
- Every action reading/writing data must be included in the responsible DAO.

The remaining operations will be part of the *business logic* tier. Figure 2 shows the diagram resulting from applying this pattern to the use case specified in Figure 1.

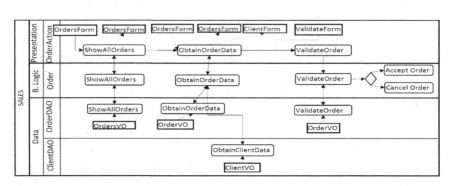

**Fig. 2.** The use case of Figure 1 after applying the Layer Pattern

# 4  Conclusions and Future Works

We have presented a marked requirements model which provides the architect with more information on the requirements and their interrelationships.

Architecture definition requires architects who are highly experienced in methods of dealing with requirements. Even experienced architects who join a new company have to go through an adaptation period to understand how requirements are defined. Today, there are techniques such as MDA that automate some development activities. Architecture definition is another activity that needs to be automated to reduce its complexity and the dependence on highly skilled architects. The marked model presented here was designed to be re-used by tools that assist the architect in his work.

We are currently working on developing a tool based on an ontology describing a company's development criteria. This tool analyzes the marked requirements model to assist the architect in defining an architecture. Also, we are analyzing the relationships between FRs and QAs to identify further situations in which patterns are applied, and how these situations are marked in the requirements model.

**Acknowledgments.** This work was funded by PDT08A034, TIN2008-02985, GRU09137, PRE09156, and Fundación Valhondo Calaff.

# References

1. Clements, P., Shaw, M.: The golden age of software architecture. Revisited. IEEE Software 26(4), 70–72 (2009)
2. Bengtsson, P.: Towards Maintainability Metrics on Software Architecture: An Adaptation of Object-Oriented Metrics. In: 1st Nordic Workshop on Software Architecture (1998)
3. Bass, L., Clements, P., Kazman, R.: Software Architecture in Practice. Addison-Wesley, Boston (2003)
4. Avgeriou, P., Zdun, U.: Architectural Patterns Revisited - A Pattern Language. In: 10th European Conference on Pattern Languages of Programs, Germany, pp. 1–39 (2005)
5. Clements, P., Kazman, R., Klein, M.: Evaluating Software Architectures: Methods and Case Studies. Addison-Wesley, Boston (2002)
6. Lung, C.H., Kalaichelvan, K.: An Approach to Quantitative Software Architecture Sensitivity Analysis. J. Software Eng. and Knowledge Eng. 10(1), 97–114 (2000)
7. ISO/IEC 9126,
   http://www.iso.org/iso/catalogue_detail.htm?csnumber=39752
8. Bachmann, F., Bass, L., Klein, M., Shelton, C.: Designing software architectures to achieve quality attribute requirements. IEE Proc., Softw. 152(4), 153–165 (2005)
9. Bosch, J.: Design and use of software architectures adopting and evolving a product-line approach. Addison-Wesley, Boston (2000)
10. OpenUP, http://epf.eclipse.org/wikis/openup/index.htm
11. Wojcik, R., Bachmann, F., Bass, L., Clements, P., Merson, P., Nord, R., Wood, B.: Attribute-Driven Design (ADD), Version 2.0. Technical Report, Software Engineering Institute, CMU/SEI-2006-TR-023 (2006)
12. Bachmann, F., Bass, L., Klein, M.: Moving from quality attribute requirements to architectural decisions. In: 2nd International Software Requirements to Architectures Workshop, Portland, Oregon, USA (2003)
13. Kim, S., Kim, D., Lu, L., Park, S.: Quality-driven architecture development using architectural tactics. J. Systems and Software 82(8), 1211–1231 (2009)
14. Czarnecki, K., Eisenecker, U.: Generative Programming: Methods, Tools, and Applications. Addison-Wesley, Boston (2000)
15. Doerr, J., Kerkow, D., Koenig, T., Olsson, T., Suzuki, T.: Non-Functional Requirements in Industry - Three Case Studies Adopting an Experience-based NFR Method. In: 13th IEEE Int. Conference on Requirements Engineering, pp. 373–384 (2005)
16. Xu, L., Ziv, H., Richardson, D., Liu, Z.: Towards Modeling Non-Functional Requirements in Software Architecture. In: Workshop on Early-Aspect (2005)
17. Buschmann, F., Henney, k., Schmidt, D.C.: Pattern-Oriented Software Architecture: On Patterns and Pattern Languages. John Wiley & Sons, England (2007)
18. Meszaros, G., Doble, J.: A Pattern Language for Pattern Writing. In: Pattern Languages of Program Design, vol. 3, pp. 529–574. Addison-Wesley, Boston (1998)

# Modelling Changes and Data Transfers for Architecture-Based Runtime Evolution of Distributed Applications

An Phung-Khac, Jean-Marie Gilliot,
Maria-Teresa Segarra, Antoine Beugnard, and Eveline Kaboré

Department of Computer Science, Télécom Bretagne
Technopôle Brest-Iroise - CS 83818 - 29238 Brest Cedex 3 - France
{an.phungkhac,jm.gilliot,mt.segarra,antoine.beugnard,eveline.kabore}
@telecom-bretagne.eu

**Abstract.** Architecture-based approaches for runtime evolution enable
software systems to dynamically move between consistent architectural
variants. Successful runtime evolution must enable the new, replacement
variant to be initialized with the data of the replaced one. In distributed
systems, however, the initialization is complex and may be time-consuming
due to data transfers across sites. Identifying systems' components subject
to change is then critical for planning evolution and reducing replacement
actions, avoid unnecessary data transfers, and then, reduce downtime of
system services. Addressing this issue, this paper presents an approach to
runtime evolution of distributed applications. We present how a development process allows to 1) specify architectural variants of an application
and 2) identify components subject to change and operations for transferring data managed by these components. Moreover, the design information is used at runtime to automatically plan evolution.

## 1 Introduction

An important class of software systems needs to evolve at runtime in order to
adapt to changing executing environments. Moreover, during evolution, they
are expected to be continuously available which require the software system to
modify its own architecture at runtime [1]. Such runtime modifications include
1) replacement, addition, and removal actions to achieve the target variant, and
2) initialization of the replaced variant with data of the replacement one.

As the above tasks may disrupt collaboration among components, coordination is needed when performing modification actions. Such coordination is even
more difficult when considering distributed software. Furthermore, initializing
the replacement variant with data of the replaced one may be time-consuming
due to data transfers across sites. Such data transfers make continuous availability difficult or even impossible to achieve. Therefore, planning evolution,
including identifying components subject to change and operations for transferring data managed by these components, becomes a critical task in order to

M. Ali Babar and I. Gorton (Eds.): ECSA 2010, LNCS 6285, pp. 392–400, 2010.

avoid unnecessary replacement of components and data transfers, thus reducing downtime of system services.

In our previous work [2], we have proposed an architecture-based approach, called *adapt-medium* approach, for runtime adaptation and evolution of distributed applications. The approach is based on a model-based development process that allows to generate consistent architectural variants of a distributed application, and then, embed the variants into an adaptive distributed component. However, although an adapt-medium component is able to evolve at runtime without recompilation, the whole running variant must be replaced when performing evolution.

This paper extends our previous work by allowing identification, through the model-based development process, of the variants' components subject to change and operations for manipulating their data. Therefore, when performing evolution, instead of replacing the whole running variant, only the necessary components are replaced. Moreover, we describe how the system can exploit design information of the model-based process in order to automatically plan evolution.

The remainder of the paper is organized as follows. Section 2 briefly presents the adapt-medium approach that was presented in [2]. Section 3 describes the basics when applying this approach to develop an adaptive publish/subscribe system. Section 4 presents the main contribution of this paper, i.e., how our approach allows identifying components subject to change and operations for manipulating their data. Section 5 discusses related work and Section 6 concludes the paper.

## 2   Adapt-Medium Approach Overview

To cope with distribution complexity and manage evolution we adopt the *adapt-medium approach* when developing a distributed software system. This approach is mainly defined by (see Figure 1) :

- **A high-level abstraction** of the system with a set of fixed services. As defined by [3], these services define the functional properties of the system and is represented by the dotted-line oval on top of Figure 1, called *medium*.
- **A distributed architecture** for implementing the system. As the system should allow distributed collaborations among services, its internals are implemented as a set of distributed components, called managers. Managers collaborate to provide the specified services.
- **A development method** proposed in [4] which consists in a set of refinements successively applied. Each refinement considers a particular design concern and each concern has several alternative solutions. The refinement process can be described and automated by using reusable model transformations.

In [2], we reused the refinement process in order to build architectural variants of a software system. The process was extended to allow evolution and completed with a composition step enabling to embed all variants of a manager into an *adapt-manager* (see Figure 2). Moreover, *adapt-managers* include Buisson's framework [5] (*Decider, Planner, Executor* in the figure) to perform transitions between variants.

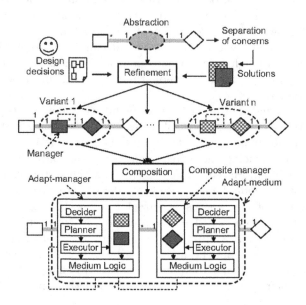

**Fig. 1.** Adapt-medium development approach

# 3    Example: A Publish/Subscribe Adapt-Medium

We have recently been working in the Compagnym@ges project[1] that aims at deploying services to help elderly people stay at home. In this project, we used a publish/subscribe (P/S) system for developing a news service and an events sharing service. Because of the many faces of P/S systems [6] and different data storage strategies, there is a large number of possible variants. In order to develop (a subset of) these variants and be able to switch between them, we used the adapt-medium approach for both services.

## 3.1    High-Level Abstraction

Consider a P/S system managing resources published by different publishers. Subscribers subscribe to events they are interested in and will be notified about new events matching their demands. A publisher can remove the resources he has published. Likewise, a subscriber can unsubscribe from event(s) he has subscribed to.

Based on this description, the P/S high-level abstraction should propose five services: *subscribe, unsubscribe, notify,* and *publish, unpublish.*

---

[1] www.companymages.eu

## 3.2   Refinement Process

Figure 2 shows the refinement process of the adapt-medium approach applied to a P/S system. Each level in the figure corresponds to a refinement step which considers a particular design concern. Each node represents a model of the system. An edge from node *A* at level *i* to node *B* at level *i+1* represents the transformation that introduces a particular solution model for the design concern considered at level *i* into the system model at node *A*. The result is the model represented by node *B*.

Therefore, the first transformation introduces managers for managing the *resources* and *events* sets (nodes *1a, 1b*). From these nodes, two corresponding refinement subtrees are created. As an example, the model at node *1a* is step by step transformed into several resources-implementation models at the leafs (nodes *2, 7, 8, 9*) which include solutions to all the considered concerns. Likewise, the refinement subtree of the *events* data will lead to different events-implementation models. An implementation variant will be derived by merging two models, one from each subtree.

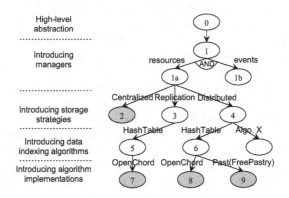

**Fig. 2.** Refinement process for resources data management

The refinement of the resources (and events) management contains three steps corresponding to three design concerns:

- Introducing *storage strategies*: three solutions, centralized, distributed, and replicated are the considered solutions for this design concern.
- Introducing *data indexing algorithms*: when the functional data are not managed by the centralized strategy, the P/S system needs to use data indexing algorithms for indexing and locating data. For example, the system can use hash table to index resources.
- Introducing *algorithm implementations*: each algorithm for indexing data may have different implementations. For example, the system can use two design solutions for a hash table: OpenChord DHT [7] or Past DHT [8].

# 4   Facilitating Runtime Evolution

Our approach to facilitate runtime evolution consists of enabling the identification of 1) variants' components subject to change and 2) operations for manipulating data managed by these components.

The main idea of our approach is to 1) modularize solutions into components and 2) model the refinement process. By analyzing the refinement process model, the components implementing the concern solution subject to change and operations for manipulating their data can be identified. This section presents the basics of the modularization principle and the refinement process model.

## 4.1   Modularization

At each refinement step, the introduced solution may be modularized into components located in different (distributed) adapt-managers. Realizing an evolution that replaces one solution by another one thus relies on replacing all the constituent components of the former solution. The set of interfaces implemented by the components forms a *change point*. If a component implements data management, read-/write-operations of the change point interfaces will be used for transferring data between the components.

Although an important goal of the separation of concerns is to modularize software, implementations of a design concern are not always completely represented by individual components because a design concern may interleave other ones [9]. The solution introduced for such a design concern may require modifying components modularized by previous transformations of the refinement process. In this case, we modularize the independent parts, if any, of the solution into components and create new variants of all the interleaved concerns' components modularized previously. Moreover, constraints among these components are also defined for constraining evolutions, i.e., replacing components of the interleaving concern requires replacing those of the interleaved one.

## 4.2   Modelling Refinement Process

We extend the refinement process by providing an explicit process model. The model describes the steps of the process, the modularized components, and change points referring to components' interfaces and their read-/write-operations. This model is used by the planner at runtime to automatically plan evolution.

Figure 3 shows the refinement process model. Each design decision (*DesignDecision*) corresponds to a branch of the tree in Figure 2. A design decision contains a solution model (*SolutionModel*) describing a solution (its set of components) of the considered design concern, and a solution introduction model (*SolutionIntroduction*). The latter describes how to introduce the solution model into the current model (*MediumModel*) by indicating a change point (*ChangePoint*). Together with a model (*MediumModel*), a change point is included in a decision point (*DecisionPoint*) which corresponds to a node in Figure 2. As previously mentioned, a change point includes the interfaces (*Interface*) implemented by

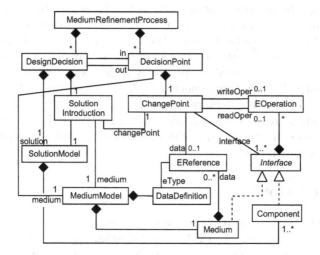

**Fig. 3.** Description of the adapt-medium refinement process model

the introduced solution and, if it corresponds to data management services, the change point indicates the data set and read-/write-operations of the interfaces for manipulating the data. The process model can be considered as a variability model whose variation points correspond to the decision points.

This explicit refinement process model allows to identify the components implementing a solution of a design concern and its interfaces, including data management operations. Therefore, evolutions can be automatically planned at runtime by using this model.

### 4.3   Planning Evolution

In order to explain how automatic planning can be achieved, we use the example of the P/S system and its variants presented in Section 3. By using the refinement process model, the planning of the evolution from variant *V2* (centralized-resources) to variant *V8* (OpenChord-resources), resp. nodes *2* and *8* in Figure 2, is realized as follows:

– Identifying components to be replaced: all the components corresponding to interfaces identified by the change point related to node *1a* in Figure 2 will be replaced.
– Identifying replacement components: all the components corresponding to refinements in the righthand branch from node *1a* to node *8* will be replacement components.
– Identifying operations for transferring data: evolution from *V2* to *V8* requires transferring resources between the variants. The required operations are then the read-operation provided by the to-be-removed components and the write-operation provided by the to-be-added components.

When running, the process model is replicated and managed by the *MediumLogic* component presented in Figure 1. By using the model, the *Planner* component of a particular adapt-manager, called the coordinator, plans the actions to be executed to perform evolutions. These actions are executed by the *Executor* component of each concerned adapt-manager. Moreover, when data transfers are needed, each *Executor* component reads local data managed by the replaced component and writes the data into the replacement one through the identified interfaces. Depending on the functional implementation of the replacement component, the data will be placed in this component or sent across sites to other replacement components.

## 5   Related Work

Automatic planning of component-based adaptation has been addressed mainly in architecture-based and/or SPL-based adaptation approaches.

In the first type of approaches, variants of an adaptive software system can be built by using architecture description languages (such as Darwin ADL [10] or ArchWare-ADL [11]), specific architectural styles (such as C2 in ArchStudio [12]), or multiple architectural styles (such as Rainbow [13] or ArchWare [11]). Adaptation plans can then be generated by analyzing models of source and target system variants.

Considering automatic adaptation planning as a consequence of modelling commonality and variability (CVM) of adaptive software, approaches employing techniques in the domain of software product lines are particularly relevant. In these approaches, a system variant is considered as a software product. Commonality and variability of system variants can be modelled by relying on variation points of the corresponding product line (such as MADAM [14]), by using feature models (such as DIVA [15] or the approach by Cetina *et. al.* [16]), or by using orthogonal variability models (such as Genie [17]).

None of the existing approaches supports automatic planning of distributed evolutions including data transfers across sites. This issue is addressed in our approach by 1) using a high-level abstraction (for specifying distributed applications) and its model-based refinement process, and 2) describing the process as a variability model. Moreover, unlike existing CVM approaches, our variability modelling does not assume that features can be directly mapped to (a set of) components, which allows us to model interleaved concerns.

## 6   Conclusion

In this paper, we have introduced an architecture-based approach to support runtime evolution of distributed applications, addressing the challenges of identifying applications' components subject to change and supporting data transfers between variants when performing evolution.

In our approach, the target distributed application is first specified by using an abstraction that represents the functional communication between distributed client components. This initial abstraction is then refined by an iterative process that considers one design concern at a time and introduces different solutions for it. Moreover, a model for the process has been proposed so that components implementing solutions and their interfaces can be identified and, thus, be used for automatic planing on evolution.

We have automated the development process by using model-based techniques including Eclipse Modelling Framework [18] and Kermeta [19] and used it for developing to P/S system based services: a news and an event sharing services.

Our future work include supporting an explicit model of modularity and variability. Feature models could be employed for organizing variation points, that correspond to decision points of the process model. We expect to build an integrated environment that support the adapt-medium development process.

# References

1. Cheng, B.H.C., et al.: Software engineering for self-adaptive systems: A research roadmap. In: Software Engineering for Self-Adaptive Systems, pp. 1–26 (2009)
2. Phung-Khac, A., Beugnard, A., Gilliot, J.M., Segarra, M.T.: Model-driven development of component-based adaptive distributed applications. In: SAC 2008 DADS Track, ACM Press, New York (2008)
3. Cariou, E., Beugnard, A., Jézéquel, J.M.: An architecture and a process for implementing distributed collaborations. In: EDOC 2002, Lausanne, Switzerland (2002)
4. Kaboré, E., Beugnard, A.: Implementing a data distribution variant with a meta-model, some models and a transformation. In: Meier, R., Terzis, S. (eds.) DAIS 2008. LNCS, vol. 5053, pp. 224–237. Springer, Heidelberg (2008)
5. Buisson, J., André, F., Pazat, J.L.: A framework for dynamic adaptation of parallel components. In: ParCo 2005 (2005)
6. Eugster, P.T., Felber, P.A., Guerraoui, R., Kermarrec, A.M.: The many faces of publish/subscribe. ACM Computing Surveys 35(2), 114–131 (2003)
7. Bamberg University, Distributed System Group: Openchord, http://www.uni-bamberg.de/projects/openchord
8. Druschel, P., Rowstron, A.: PAST: A large-scale, persistent peer-to-peer storage utility. In: HOTOS 2001. IEEE Computer Society, Los Alamitos (2001)
9. Tarr, P., Ossher, H., Harrison, W., Sutton, S.: N degrees of separation: Multidimensional separation of concerns. In: ICSE 1999. ACM Press, New York (1999)
10. Magee, J., Dulay, N., Eisenbach, S., Kramer, J.: Specifying distributed software architectures. In: PESEC 1995. Springer, Heidelberg (1995)
11. Oquendo, F., Warboys, B., Morrison, R., Dindeleux, R., Gallo, F., Garavel, H., Occhipinti, C.: ArchWare: Architecting Evolvable Software. In: Oquendo, F., Warboys, B.C., Morrison, R. (eds.) EWSA 2004. LNCS, vol. 3047, pp. 257–271. Springer, Heidelberg (2004)
12. Oreizy, P., Gorlick, M.M., Taylor, R.N., Heimbigner, D., Johnson, G., Medvidovic, N., Quilici, A., Rosenblum, D.S., An, A.L.W.: Architecture-Based Approach to Self-Adaptive Software. IEEE Intelligent Systems 14, 54–62 (1999)
13. Garlan, D., Cheng, S.W., Huang, A.C., Schmerl, B., Steenkiste, P.: Rainbow: Architecture-based self-adaptation with reusable infrastructure. Computer 37(10), 46–54 (2004)

14. Floch, J., Hallsteinsen, S., Stav, E., Eliassen, F., Lund, K., Gjorven, E.: Using architecture models for runtime adaptability. IEEE Software 23(2), 62–70 (2006)
15. Morin, B., Barais, O., Jézéquel, J.-M., Fleurey, F., Solberg, A.: Models@run.time to support dynamic adaptation. IEEE Computer 42(10), 44–51 (2009)
16. Cetina, C., Giner, P., Fons, J., Pelechano, V.: Autonomic computing through reuse of variability models at runtime: The case of smart homes. Computer 42(10), 37–43 (2009)
17. Bencomo, N.: Supporting the Modelling and Generation of Reflective Middleware Families and Applications using Dynamic Variability. PhD thesis, Lancaster University (2008)
18. The Eclipse Foundation: Eclipse modeling framework (EMF), http://www.eclipse.org/modeling/emf/
19. IRISA Triskell: Kermeta, http://www.kermeta.org/

# Mining Relationships between the Participants of Architectural Patterns

Ahmad Waqas Kamal and Paris Avgeriou

Department of Mathematics and Computing Science,
University of Groningen, The Netherlands
a.w.kamal@rug.nl, paris@cs.rug.nl

**Abstract.** Architectural patterns are often combined with other, relevant architectural patterns during software architecture design. However, combining patterns effectively remains a challenging task: first because the integration of any two architectural patterns can take several forms; second because existing pattern languages only mention generic pattern-to-pattern relationships and do not go into the details of their combination. In this paper, we propose to address this problem by discovering and defining a handful of recurring pattern relationships at the level of the participants of patterns. We have studied 32 industrial case studies and mined a number of relationships between participants of different patterns. We present a few of these relationships and outline some examples of their appearance.

**Keywords:** Architectural Patterns, Pattern relationships, Pattern Languages.

## 1 Introduction

Over the last decade, architectural patterns have increasingly become an integral part of software architecture design practices [1]. Architectural patterns are seldom applied in isolation within a software architecture: individual architectural patterns can only solve specific parts of the design problem; it takes a combination of patterns to cover all the requirements. For instance, the Client-Server and Broker patterns are often used in combination to design distributed systems architectures [2]. Architectural patterns are characterized of intrinsic relations to other patterns, giving them the potential to solve larger design problems [3].

The integration of two or more patterns during software architecture design remains a challenging task. More precisely, we identify the following two challenges:

- Most of the pattern languages described in the literature document relationships among patterns at the conceptual level [4]. However, none of these pattern languages deals with the relationships among participants[1] of related patterns. In this sense, current pattern languages only offer guidance for the selection of related architectural patterns, or hints to design a particular kind of system; they do not provide support for integrating architectural patterns within software architecture

---

[1] The term pattern participants, frequently used in this paper, refers to the elements within the solution of patterns e.g. the Pipe and Filter are participants of the Pipes and Filters pattern.

M. Ali Babar and I. Gorton (Eds.): ECSA 2010, LNCS 6285, pp. 401–408, 2010.

design. Extensive design effort is required to precisely identify participants of related patterns that overlap, interact, or override related pattern participants in the resulting software architecture.

– Depending on the context of a system at hand, the combination of architectural patterns may entail variability, which is weakly addressed by existing pattern relationships approaches. For instance, to model interactive applications, the MVC[2] and Layers[2] pattern can be combined in several different forms like 3-tier layered architecture (where the presentation layer may consist of View and Control participants while the application logic layer owns the Model participant), which may vary for 2-tier or 4-tier software architectures.

To address the challenges described above, we propose to model the combination of patterns using a set of relationships between their participants. We have discovered these relationships by reviewing the patterns used in several industrial software architectures. We present a representative set of these relationships and exemplify them with instances from studied architectures.

The remainder of the paper is structured as follows: in Section 2, we describe the notion of pattern-to-pattern relationships and briefly outline the approach presented in this paper. In Section 3, we list the pattern participants relationships discovered during this work. Section 4 discusses the related work and Section 5 describes future work and concludes this study.

## 2   Relationships among Architectural Patterns

Architectural patterns are often combined with related patterns within software architectures. The value that individual patterns have, as solutions to design problems, is of course substantial, but their tremendous value comes when patterns are effectively combined within software architectures [1]: the combination of patterns is more than the sum of its parts. Unfortunately, individual patterns descriptions are not always explicit on 'how' to combine them with related architectural patterns. For instance, when reading the Reactor [4] pattern description, it is not clear how to apply Active Object [4] or Monitor Object [4]. In principle each participant within the solution of architectural patterns can be quite complex by itself, and often implemented using other patterns. It is therefore of paramount importance to express the intricate relationships between patterns, in order to effectively combine them within software architectures.

Pattern languages are thus far the most common and well-known form used by the software patterns community for defining relationships among architectural patterns. Pattern languages are not formal languages, although they document generic relationships among architectural patterns to address particular design problems [4]. For instance, the Model-View-Controller pattern has a 'change propagation' relationship with the Observer pattern as documented in [2]. Several pattern languages have been documented in the literature e.g. pattern languages for distributed computing [1], domain specific pattern languages [2], architectural views specific pattern language [3] etc.

## 2.1 The Proposed Approach

The underlying idea behind our approach is that architectural patterns can be effectively combined using a set of relationships between their participants. The relationships serve as a basis for identifying the participants of the patterns to be combined, that share responsibilities, overlap, or override each other. In order to come up with such relationships between participants, we have analyzed the architectural patterns used within several software architectures, and mined the relationships between their participants. The sources for eliciting pattern participants relationships were architecture design documents, architecture diagrams, design decisions, and case studies etc. The mined relationships must be recurring in several different examples in order to be considered as good design solutions. In the following section, we present a set of these relationships.

# 3 Mining Pattern-Participants Relationships for Modeling Patterns

The relationships presented in this section are based on the study of 32 industrial software architectures [5]. We provide, as an example, the complete documentation of a selected relationship. Due to space restrictions, a number of other relationships are also documented in an abbreviated form. We also provide a table to exemplify the discovered relationships by mapping pairs of patterns to the relationship between their participants.

### 3.1 Example of a Pattern Participant Relationship: absorbparticipant

In this sub-section, we present the detailed documentation of the absorbParticipant relationship while in the next sub-section we list several other relationships discovered during this study.

*Definition:* An *absorbParticipant* relationship defines how the participants of different patterns performing similar responsibilities are integrated in a single element. In an *absorbParticipant* relationship, certain participants of a pattern are absorbed by the participants of another pattern to avoid redundancy.

*An example to describe the issue:* Both the Reactor and Acceptor-Connector patterns introduce their own event handling solutions for using different services. The separate event handling structures in both patterns would be redundant if these patterns are applied in combination, e.g. the handler participant is present in both the Reactor and Acceptor-Connector patterns. In the Reactor's architectural structure, for each service an application offers, a separate event handler is introduced that processes different types of events from certain event sources. However, the Acceptor-Connector pattern can be suggested as an option to implement the Reactor's event handlers. This ensures that the Reactor pattern specifies the 'right' types of event handlers associated with the Acceptor-Connector pattern. In order to integrate the two patterns, the overlapping pattern participants either need to be merged or participants of one pattern be replaced by the other. However, removing a specific participant within a pattern may impact the solution specified by that pattern and may require new associations between the participants of both patterns, which is not a trivial work and require extensive design effort.

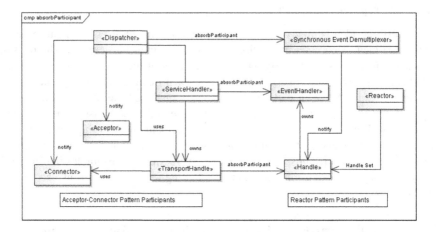

**Fig. 1.** The absorbParticipant relationship between Reactor and Acceptor-Connector

## 3.2   More Pattern Participants Relationships

Due to space restrictions, we will not go into detail for the rest of the pattern participants relationships we have elicited, but we will give a brief overview of these relationships.

*mergeParticipant:* The *mergeParticipant* relationship is used to combine one or more semantically different pattern participants into a single element within the target pattern. Such an integration retains the structural and semantic properties of individual participants into the target element. For instance, integrating the Active-Passive pattern with the Pipes and Filters pattern may result in certain filters passively processing the data. In essence, a passive filter in the Pipes and Filters chain performs the responsibilities of both a filter and a passive element. The *mergeParticipant* relationship is different from the *absorbParticipant* relationship where participants performing similar responsibilities are overridden (i.e. redundant participants are virtually removed in the resulting

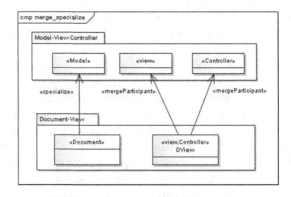

**Fig. 2.** The mergeParticipant relationship

software architecture). Figure 2 shows an example of the occurrence of *mergePartici-pant* relationship among the participants of architectural patterns.

*employ:* In the employ relationship, participants of a pattern make use of another pattern for their complete implementation. Patterns using the 'employ' relationship are often used together within a software architecture where one pattern often 'makes use of' another pattern to fulfill specific design needs. Patterns having an 'employ' relationship can be applied separately to a software architecture as the relationship does not constrain the presence of both patterns within the architecture. For instance, the MVC pattern often employs the Observer pattern for implementing the change propagation mechanism. However, each of these patterns can also be individually applied to a software architecture. Figure 3 shows the employ relationship among the participants of the Iterator and Batch Method patterns.

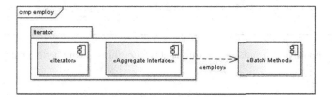

**Fig. 3.** Employ relationship between the Iterator and Batch Method Patterns

*depends:* The depends relationship shows the need of pattern participant(s) to use another pattern for their complete implementation. In comparison to the employ relationship, the depends relationship is a strong dependency of a pattern's participants on another pattern where participants of the source pattern are seldom applied without the use of target pattern participants. The depends relationship is shown in a particular example of Client-Server and Broker pattern in figure 4.

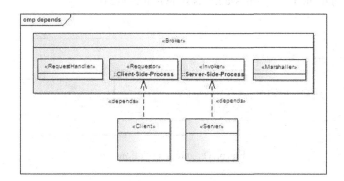

**Fig. 4.** The depends relationship among pattern participants

*importPattern:* In the importPattern relationship, the participants of the target pattern import all participants from the source pattern i.e. all participants of a pattern are modeled within the participant of another pattern. The importPattern relationship is similar to Package import in UML, Family import in ACME, etc. For instance, individual layers in the Layers pattern can import other patterns e.g. the Pipes and Filters pattern is used for implementing data processing layers as illustrated, for example, in figure 5.

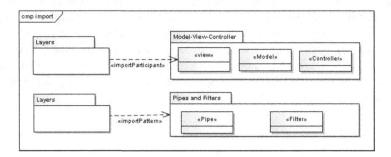

**Fig. 5.** importPattern and importParticipant relationships among pattern participants

*importParticipant:* In the importParticipant relationship, participants of the target pattern import 'specific' participants from the source pattern. For instance, an individual layer in the Layers pattern can import the View and Controller participants of the MVC pattern while the Model participant of the MVC pattern resides in another layer. Figure 5 shows an example of using *importParticipant* relationship.

*interact:* In the interact relationship, certain participants of the source pattern 'interact' with the participants of the target pattern. This relationship represents a loose coupling among the participants of different architectural patterns such as events, procedure calls, etc. For instance, the Request Handler pattern has an interact relationship with the Proxy pattern to send and receive messages as shown in figure 6.

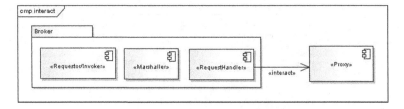

**Fig. 6.** The interact relationship

Table 1 provides a number of examples of pattern participants relationships discovered in pattern combinations in the studied architectures.

**Table 1.** Pattern-Participants Relationships Description

| Pattern A | Pattern B | Relationship | Description |
|---|---|---|---|
| Reactor | Leader/ Follower | absorbParticipant | EventHandler and Handle participants are present in both patterns |
| Reactor | Acceptor-Connector | absorbParticipant | EventHandler and Handle participants are present in both patterns |
| Layers | Pipes and Filters | importPattern | A specific layer can internally implement Pipes and Filters structure |
| Layers | MVC | importParticipant | Individual layers can import specific participants of MVC pattern e.g. Model may reside in one layer while View and Controller reside in another layer |
| Layers | Client-Server | importParticipant | see previous line comments |
| Layers | Broker | importPattern | A specific layer can be implemented as a Broker |
| Layers | Proxy | importPattern | A specific layer can be implemented as a proxy to other layers |
| Layers | Factory Method | importPattern | A layer can be implemented using factory method to handle different requests |
| MVC | Observer | employ | MVC employs observer pattern to implement change notification mechanism |
| MVC | Factory Method | importPattern | The Model participant can be implemented using Factory method |
| Broker | Client-Server | depends | Broker is often modeled in combination with the Client-Server pattern |
| Client-Server | Proxy | interact | The interaction mechanism between Client and Server may use proxy |
| Active Object | Proxy | integrate | A proxy can act as an active object |
| Scheduler | Proxy | interact | A scheduler can monitor the requests to decide when a request needs to be executed |

# 4  Related Work

Several pattern languages have been documented in the literature e.g pattern languages for solving specific design problems [2], domain-specific pattern languages [1], and the pattern languages documented in the Pattern Oriented Software Architecture book series [4]. Buschmann et. al. [1] present a pattern language for distributed computing that includes 114 patterns grouped into 13 problem areas. The problem areas address technical topics related to building distributed applications e.g. Event Demultiplexing, Concurrency, Synchronization etc. Their pattern language serve as an overview about the selection and use of related architectural patterns to solve design problems in specific areas. However, the language in itself presents architectural patterns as components, objects and entities linked through generic textual relationships. For instance Model-View-Controller has a 'request handling' relationship with the Command, Command Processor, Application Controller, and Chain of Responsibility patterns. Our work significantly differs from their work as we document relationships among the 'participants' of architectural patterns that can be used more effectively for combing any two architectural patterns in several different forms.

Some work has been done on proposing patterns languages that address specific architectural concerns such as pattern languages for usability [6], pattern languages for concurrency issues [1], pattern languages for performance-critical systems [2] etc. However, these languages provide relationships that best fit to address the concerns they relate to and do not address the relationships among participants of related architectural patterns. In terms of granularity, pattern languages that deal with specific concerns provide more enriched relationships as compared to general pattern languages but they too do not address the relationships among participants of architectural patterns and overlook possible variation in relationships among the participants of combined architectural patterns.

In our previous work [3], we have documented relationships among architectural patterns in different architectural views that show specific aspects of systems like data flow, interaction decoupling etc. However, though such relationships provide valuable information about pattern-to-pattern relationships (e.g. communication between Layers may use Pipes and Filters), this language too does not focus on relationships among participants of architectural patterns.

## 5   Conclusion and Future Work

The novelty of our work lies in discovering relationships among the 'participants' of architectural patterns which has not been fully addressed before. The use of pattern participants relationships for integrating architectural patterns offers an effective way to integrate architectural patterns within software architecture design. In particular, this approach offers: a) reusability by providing a vocabulary of pattern-to-pattern relationships that help combine the participants of selected architectural patterns; b) model validation support by ensuring that the patterns are correctly combined within a software architecture; and c) explicit representation of 'integrated' architectural patterns participants within software architectures.

As future work, we plan to apply our approach to industrial case studies for designing software architectures and by conducting controlled experiments. We are in the process of developing a pattern modeling tool called Primus [7], which will support integrating architectural patterns and pattern variants, modeling pattern variability, architectural views synchronization, and source code generation. We believe that we can discover more pattern participants relationships in the near future, which will provide a better reusability support to software architects for effectively integrating architectural patterns.

## References

1. Schmidt, D.C., Buschmann, F., Henney, K.: Pattern-Oriented Software Architecture: On Patterns and Pattern Languages. Wiley Series in Software Design Patterns (2007)
2. Buschmann, F., Meunier, R., Rohnert, H., Sommerlad, P., Stal, M.: Pattern-Oriented Software Architecture, vol. 1. Wiley & Sons, Chichester (1996)
3. Avgeriou, P., Zdun, U.: Architectural patterns revisited - a pattern language. Technical Report (2005)
4. Schmidt, D.C., Stal, M., Rohnert, H., Buschmann, F.: Patterns for Concurrent and Distributed Objects. In: Pattern-Oriented Software Architecture, J. Wiley and Sons Ltd., Chichester (2000)
5. Boosch, G.: Handbook of software architecture: Gallery (2010),
   http://www.booch.com/architecture/architecture.jsp?
   part=Gallery
6. Patterns and pattern languages of program (2010), http://hillside.net
7. Kirtley, N., Kamal, A.W., Avgeriou, P.: Developing a modeling tool using eclipse. In: International Workshop on Advanced Software Development Tools and Techniques, Co-located with ECOOP 2008 (2008)

# Software Architecture Recovery Process Based on Object-Oriented Source Code and Documentation

Sylvain Chardigny[1] and Abdelhak Seriai[2]

[1] MGPS
Port-Saint-Louis, France
s.chardigny@mgps.info
[2] LIRMM, university of Montpellier II/CNRS
Montpellier, France
seriai@lirmm.fr

**Abstract.** Architecture recovery aims at providing a high level abstraction of a system using the architectural elements to represent functionalities and interactions. This architecture makes easier the program comprehension and then provides many advantages during all the phases of software life cycle. Nevertheless, most architecture recovery approaches fail to combine the human expertise on the system with a high automation level. In order to solve this issue, we propose to use the intentional architecture of a system, which represent the system as imagined by its designers, to improve the adequation between the resulting software architecture and the architect's expectations without requiring more human expertise. Thus, we present in this paper a semi-automatic process to recover intentional architecture from the available documentation and the expert recommendations. This process is an extension of ROMANTIC, an approach aiming at recovering a component-based architecture of an existing object-oriented system.

## 1 Introduction

Given the explosive growth of the computer systems size and complexity, software architectures are emerging as a valuable ally for both the design and maintenance of these systems. This abstract view of systems has become, during the last decade, a central field of software engineering [1]. Its main advantages is to make easier the program comprehension by allowing us to focus on architectural elements (components, connectors and configuration) rather than implementation details [2]. In addition to program comprehension, this distinction between functionalities (components) and interactions (connectors) is crucial to safely maintain the system [3]. However most existing systems do not have a reliable architecture representation. Indeed these systems could have been designed without an architecture design phase, as it is the case for most legacy systems. In other systems, the available representation can diverge from the system implementation due to the lack of synchronization between software documentation and implementation.

M. Ali Babar and I. Gorton (Eds.): ECSA 2010, LNCS 6285, pp. 409–416, 2010.

Taking into account the previous considerations, we have proposed an approach called ROMANTIC[1] which focuses on recovering a component-based architecture from object-oriented systems [4]. Starting from the source code, our process aims at selecting among all the architectures which can be abstracted from a system, the best one according to our quality model. Then we formulate this model as measurable constraints and modelize the recovery process as a search-based problem aiming at balancing these competing constraints. This choice is motivated by the recent works on the search-based engineering showing that these techniques are very effective to solve this kind of problems [5].

The main advantage of our approach is its automation level which decreases the need of human expertise which is expensive and not always available. However, the code source is insufficient to recover an architecture which fulfills all the expert expectations and allows a complete comprehension of the system. Consequently, we propose to integrate in our process information about the intentional architecture, *i.e.* architecture as imagined by the designers, in order to identify an architecture reflecting all the design decisions.

The remainder of this paper is structured as follows. Section 2 presents an overview of ROMANTIC whereas Section 3 studies the place of the intentional architecture in the related work. In section 4 we describe the impact of the intentional architecture on the search-based process and the intentional architecture recovery process. Conclusion and future works are presented in Section 5.

## 2   Principles of ROMANTIC

ROMANTIC aims at recovering a component-based software architecture from an object-oriented system using a search-based approach [6]: an exploration process of the search space, *i.e.* a representation of all possible architectures, in order to identify the best solution according to a given fitness function.

*Definition of the search-space.* ROMANTIC operates on a search-space consisting of all the instances of a mapping model between object concepts (*i.e.* classes, interfaces, packages, etc.) and architectural ones (*i.e.* components, connectors, interfaces, etc.). According to this model, an architecture is a partition of the system classes. Each element of this partition, named "shape", is mapped to a component and contains classes which can belong to different object-oriented packages. All existing links between shapes are mapped to connectors. Finally, the architecture configuration is mapped to the set of shapes constituting a partition of the system classes.

*Definition of the fitness function.* Our fitness function is based on a quality model for software architecture [7,4]. This model is based on the ISO-9126 norm [8] and refines successively architecture quality characteristics to sub-characteristics, properties on components and then on the shapes, like coupling or cohesion. The

---

[1] ROMANTIC: Re-engineering of Object-oriented systeMs by Architecture extractioN and migraTIon to Component based ones.

first quality characteristic, the semantic correctness, measures the relevance of an entity according to the concept of architecture. Its refinement is based on the most commonly admitted properties of the architectural concepts. The second quality characteristic, the architectural quality, describes the quality characteristics of the architectural elements. We refine it in two sub-characteristics: the maintainability and the reliability.

*Meta-heuristic of the search-based process.* ROMANTIC uses a simulated annealing algorithm in order to explore the solution space and resolve the recovery problem. This algorithm explores one solution by iteration and chooses the following one in its neighborhood [9]. The neighborhood depends on the algorithm operators defined according to the problem, but the choice is also dependent from the evaluation of the solutions according to our fitness function. The algorithm can sometimes accept a worse solution in order to avoid local extrema.

## 3    Place of Intentional Architecture in Existing Recovery Approaches

Various works are proposed in literature in order to recover architecture from an existing system. According to their consideration for the intentional architecture, these approaches can be split in two groups. The first one contains approaches which deal with intentional architecture recovery from available documentation like UML diagrams [10], source code commentaries [11] or physical organization [12]. None of these approaches merge the information recovered from different sources or use the expert recommendations. Moreover, all these approaches trust all the documents whereas the documentation of the system is often outdated.

On the contrary, other approaches use the code source and human expertise to recover the software architecture and ignore available documentation. They use the dependencies presented in the code source and the expert recommendations to regroup the source code entities in order to identify the architecture elements. These approaches can be classified according to their automation level: quasi manual [13], semi-automatic [14] or quasi-automatic [15]. Finally, manual approaches take advantages from the intentional architecture thought the human expertise but are costly whereas automatic approaches are less expensive but refuse to use the information not contained in the code source.

Thereby, the architecture recovery approaches fail to reconcile all the available information sources. They are focused either on the human expertise or the code source, and cannot benefit from their combination.

## 4    Place of Intentional Architecture in the ROMANTIC Process

In order to improve ROMANTIC, we use the intentional architecture to reduce the search-space. This is done in two different ways. Firstly, we define a starting point which is conformed to the intentional architecture. Secondly the process ignores solutions which are obviously in conflict with the intentional architecture. To achieve this reduction, we proceed in four steps. Firstly, we recover one view of the intentional architecture from each type of available documents. Then we collect the expert recommendations. After these steps, we merge all the recovered intentional architectures and the expert recommendations in order to define a hierarchical constraint network, *i.e.* a set of constraints classified per level, from required constraints to optional ones. Finally, we use the constraint network to reduce the search-space according to two ways. Firstly, we use the constraint network solution as starting point for the simulated annealing. Secondly, we modify the acceptance probability in order to depend on the variation of the number of broken constraints in the same way that the fitness function variation. In particular, if a required constraint is broken, the solution cannot be accepted.

### 4.1   Useful Information Sources for the Intentional Architecture Recovery

Intentional architecture is the architecture as imagined, understood and manipulated by its architects and designers. It is not necessary the one that is implemented. Thus the information source about intentional architecture cannot be only the source code. Among available sources, we outline the three followings :

- source code: the entity names and the commentaries contained in the code source are often carefully chosen to make the code more explicit. They contain intentional information which reflect the programmer goals. Consequently we can use them to identify the dependences between two classes according to the semantic similarity between their commentaries and their entity names [16]. For example, consider two JAVA classes which sort a list of object according to different comparators. We will probably find similar names of variables or methods as well ass similar commentaries. Consequently, these classes are semantically closed according to these commentaries and their entity's names, and should be in the same component;
- UML diagrams: UML diagrams are used since the first steps of the software life cycle in order to modelize links between classes and functionalities. We can use these information to identify the intentional architecture components [10]. For example, consider a class diagram where the classes $A$ and $B$ are connected through an aggregation link whereas the class $C$ is disconnected. This implies that intentional architecture should include two components: $\{A, B\}$ and $\{C\}$;
- log of versionning tools: this log contains informations on the time of the file modification and the commits. These information are useful to identify some intentional dependency between the maintained classes[17]. For example, consider two logged commits, the first one describes the modification of two classes $a$ and $b$ whereas the second one describes the modification of the class $c$. It appear that $c$ seems to be independent and this implies that intentional architecture should include two components: $\{a, b\}$ and $\{c\}$.

## 4.2    ROMANTIC Intentional Architecture Recovery Process

In order to use information identified in the previous section, we propose a recovery process from the documentation and architect recommendations. This process is composed of four steps with different automation levels: the class partition step, the recommendation collect step, the constraint network generation step and the last step which solves the constraint network in order to obtain a system class partition. Each element of this partition is matched to an architectural component and so the partition is a view of the intentional architecture.

**Class partition step.** In order to recover a class partition from the three selected type of documents, we use a process based five phases ( *cf.* Fig.1). These phases are of two kinds: computation phases (in blue on the figure 1) which are automatics and validation phases (in green on the figure 1) which allow the architect's interventions.

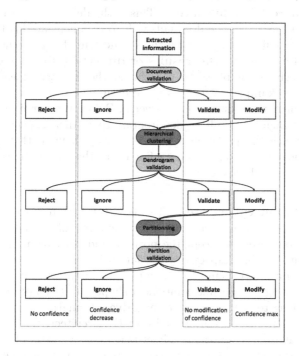

**Fig. 1.** Class partition step and the resulting trust level

*Computation phases.* Computation phases aims to compute the class partition. The first one aims to merge system classes according to a different similarity measure for each document type. To achieve this, we use the hierarchical clustering algorithm, defined by S.C.Johnson [18]. At the beginning, this algorithm assigns each initial element to a cluster. Then, in each step, the two more similar clusters are merged into a single cluster. The process stops when all items are merged into a single cluster. We obtain from this single cluster a dendrogram which represents the class cluster hierarchy.

The second phase aims to compute a class partition from the dendrogram. To obtain this partition, we cut the dendrogram according to its depth. Clusters positioned to the half of the dendrogram depth are part of the system class partition. This default process can be modified by the architect.

*Validation phases.* The architect's interventions may occur at different times during the calculation of the partition of classes: before the first computation phase, between the two computation phases and after the last computation phase. Each of these interventions has a direct impact on confidence in the recovery result (*cf.* Figure 1):

- he can **reject the information** considering they are not sufficiently reliable to be used. This action result in the first trust level : the lack of confidence;
- he can **ignore the information**. This is the default case if no architect is available. In this case, he does not wish to comment at this level and take no decision. This action result in the second trust level, the default ;
- he may also **validate the results** or **directly influence the process**. Before the clustering phase, he can change the similarity measures between classes. For example, he can assess the similarity between two classes is higher than that measured or vice versa. Before the partitioning phase, he can also change the resulting dendrogram to fit their expectations. Finally, he can change the partition results to adjust them to their expectations. These actions give a maximum confidence to the automatic computing and result in the third trust level.

**Recommendation collect step.** To allow the architect to provide all the knew information, our approach takes into account all partial information he has. Thereby, our process accept the positive and negative properties, i.e. the properties that describe respectively a relationship between two entities or the absence of such a relationship. For example, the architect may tell us that two classes must belong to the same component shape (positive information) or they should not belong to the same shape (negative information).

However, depending on the expertise of the architect, we can obtain more accurate information. Thus, the architect may know a cluster of classes which is a component. He can even specify a system architecture which seems correct. In this case, the objective of our process is to refine his proposal.

**Constraint network generation step.** The construction of the constraint network is done in two steps: the constraint creation and their assembly into a hierarchical network.

*Constraint creation.* There is two kinds of constraints: the constraints which have been collected though the expert recommendations and constraints define by the intentional architectures. The first ones are defined directly by the expert and they have a maximum confidence level. For example, it can be a constraint which requires several specific classes to be in the same component shape. The second kind of constraints needs to be extracted from each recovered intentional architecture. For each pair of classes which are in the same shape, we create a constraint requiring to not separate the pair. Then for each pair of classes which are in different shape, we create a constraint requiring to separate the classes in different shapes. Finally all these constraints have a confidence level which is the confidence in their intentional architecture.

*Constraint network assembly.* The constraints recovered from the expert's recommendations and documentation are assembled to form the hierarchical network of constraints, where the hierarchy in the network is determined by the level of confidence of each constraint. However, given the diversity of constraint sources, some conflicts may exist between the constraints, making the network inconsistent. To ensure this consistency, we proceed by hierarchical level. Firstly, we check the consistency of each level. If two constraints are conflicting, the architect can choose the one to keep. If the architect is not available, we delete one of them randomly. Secondly, we check the consistency between levels. If two different level constraints are in conflict, we remove the constraint of the lowest level since it is the constraint that has the least confidence.

# 5   Conclusion

We proposed, in this paper, an approach to recover a component-based architecture from an object-oriented system using a combination of documentation, human expertise and source code. This approach extends a previous one based on the use of the component semantic and quality characteristics which are used to define a fitness function. We presented an algorithm to recover the intentional architectures from documentation and expert recommendations and we described a method to extend ROMANTIC, using the intentional architectures. The new process can identify more accurately the system functionalities and so the recovered architecture is more accurate and useful for the program comprehension.

The intervention of the architect can be see as a major drawback of our process. Nevertheless all interventions are optional and each one is associated to a default action. These default actions allow the architect to focus on his phases of interest according to his knowledge and his availability. Another point of discussion is the similarity measures for each document type. Due to space limitation we only gave examples of these measures, but we need to improve the confidence in these measures and to test their scalability through a case study.

Our current work is realize this case study. We use Jigsaw, a JAVA WEB server to test our approach and compare the results to the classic ROMANTIC process (*cf.* Sect.2) and the known architecture of the system.

Finally we have to document the functionalities of identified components. Indeed, our process groups the classes which participate to a same functionality but it does not explain this functionality. Consequently, the functionality identification is another future work.

# References

1. Garlan, D.: Software architecture: a roadmap. In: ICSE 2000, pp. 91–101. ACM, New York (2000)
2. Garlan, D., Perry, D.: Introduction to the special issue on software architecture. IEEE Transactions on Software Engineering 21(4), 269–274 (1995)
3. Koschke, R.: Atomic Architectural Component Recovery for Program Understanding and Evolution. PhD thesis, University of Stuttgart (2000)
4. Chardigny, S., Seriai, A., Oussalah, M., Tamzalit, D.: Extraction of component-based architecture from object-oriented systems. In: WICSA, pp. 285–288. IEEE ComputerSociety, Los Alamitos (2008)
5. Harman, M.: The current state and future of search based software engineering. IEEE Future of Software Engineering, 342–357 (2007)
6. Chardigny, S., Seriai, A., Oussalah, M., Tamzalit, D.: Search-based extraction of component-based architecture from object-oriented systems. In: Morrison, R., Balasubramaniam, D., Falkner, K. (eds.) ECSA 2008. LNCS, vol. 5292, pp. 322–325. Springer, Heidelberg (2008)
7. Chardigny, S., Seriai, A., Tamzalit, D., Oussalah, M.: Quality-driven extraction of a component-based architecture from an object-oriented system. In: CSMR, IEEE, pp. 269–273 (2008)
8. ISO: ISO 9126-1 Software Engineering - Product Quality - Part 1: Quality Model. International Organization for Standardization (2001)
9. Laarhoven, P.J.M., Aarts, E.H.L. (eds.): Simulated annealing: theory and applications. Kluwer Academic Publishers, Norwell (1987)
10. Riva, C., Selonen, P., Systa, T., Xu, J.: Uml-based reverse engineering and model analysis approaches for software architecture maintenance. In: ICSM 2004, pp. 50–59. IEEE Computer Society, Washington (2004)
11. de Boer, R.C., van Vliet, H.: Architectural knowledge discovery with latent semantic analysis: Constructing a reading guide for software product audits. J. Syst. Softw. 81(9), 1456–1469 (2008)
12. Harris, D.R., Reubenstein, H.B., Yeh, A.S.: Reverse engineering to the architectural level. In: Proc. of ICSE, pp. 186–195. ACM, New York (1995)
13. Medvidovic, N., Jakobac, V.: Using software evolution to focus architectural recovery. Automated Software Engg. 13(2), 225–256 (2006)
14. Kazman, R., Klein, M., Barbacci, M., Longstaff, T., Lipson, H., Carriere, J.: The architecture tradeoff analysis method. In: Engineering of Complex Computer Systems ICECCS 1998, pp. 68–78 (1998)
15. Mancoridis, S., Mitchell, B.S., Chen, Y.F., Gansner, E.R.: Bunch: A clustering tool for the recovery and maintenance of software system structures. In: ICSM, p. 50 (1999)
16. van der Spek, P., Klusener, S., van de Laar, P.: Towards recovering architectural concepts using latent semantic indexing. In: CSMR 2008, pp. 253–257. IEEE Computer Society, Los Alamitos (2008)
17. Beyer, D.: Clustering software artifacts based on frequent common changes. In: IWPC, IEEE, pp. 259–268 (2005)
18. Johnson, S.: Hierarchical clustering schemes. Psychometrika 32, 241–245 (1967)

# Ontological Analysis for Generating Baseline Architectural Descriptions

Arvind W. Kiwelekar and Rushikesh K. Joshi

Department of Computer Science and Engineering
Indian Institute of Technology Bombay
Powai, Mumbai-400076, India
{awk,rkj}@cse.iitb.ac.in

**Abstract.** Mapping elements from an application domain to architectural abstractions is a significant architecture description activity from the point of view of seamlessness in descriptions. For establishing such a mapping of domain elements to architectural abstractions, an approach based on *ontological analysis* is presented. The central idea of the approach is to establish the mapping through a uniform framework of understanding that is applicable over the problem domain as well as the solution domain. The reference ontology used is an adaptation of Bunge-Wand-Weber (BWW) ontology. Typically, an element from an application domain is mapped with an architectural abstraction when both represent the same phenomena from BWW ontology. The approach is realized as a model-driven transformation process.

## 1 Introduction

Domain understanding is one of the concerns that needs to be addressed while deriving architectural descriptions from requirements [1]. Some of the challenges faced while understanding application domains are- (i) Different models are used to represent outcomes of the activities of requirement analysis and architecture design. (ii) Domain requirements are elaborated through domain terminology. (iii) Correspondence among requirements and architectural viewpoints is undefined.

In this paper, an *ontological analysis technique* to guide the transition from requirements to architecture is presented. The technique aims to understand application domains and architectural abstractions through a universal language formalism. The BWW ontology [2,3] is used to interpret domain elements and architectural abstractions. The reason for selecting this ontology was that it has been applied to evaluate the expressive power of various modeling languages such as UML [4], and ebXML [5], and it is a generic ontology capturing diverse phenomena. The outcomes of the application of the analysis technique include identification of architecturally significant domain elements specific to Component-Connector (C&C) viewpoints, and an initial architectural configuration aligned with interactions among domain elements. The technique assumes the availability of domain descriptions in natural language text or scenario descriptions.

M. Ali Babar and I. Gorton (Eds.): ECSA 2010, LNCS 6285, pp. 417–424, 2010.
© Springer-Verlag Berlin Heidelberg 2010

Earlier approaches that derive architectural descriptions from requirements vary in terms of analysis models used. Analysis models such as goal oriented analysis [6,7], global analysis [8,9], and quality attribute based analysis [7] are some of the techniques used earlier. In this paper, it is proposed to perform ontological analysis of application domains for describing domains in terms of ontological categories. Some of the earlier approaches such as the collaborative approach called CBSP [10] target the component-connector (C&C) view. The CBSP approach analyzes requirements in terms of components, buses, systems and properties. A limitation of this approach is that a given requirement may be mapped to a component or a connector by different analysts. The conflicts on the choice of abstraction is resolved through a voting process that lacks analytical reasoning. The approach presented in this paper also targets C&C views. An element from an application domain is mapped with an architectural abstraction only when both represent the same phenomena from BWW ontology. The approach presented in this paper also attempt to address the problem of vagueness [11] in semantics of components and connectors. The problem is handled by performing ontological analysis of components and connectors. The distinctness of these abstractions is brought out by showing that components are the representations of *Things* and connectors represent *Coupled Events*. *Things* and *Coupled Events* are two different phenomena from the reality.

The next section describes the reference model based on BWW ontology. Section 3 presents an overview of the process with various artifacts involved. Ontological interpretations of architectural abstractions and also of domain elements are presented in Section 4. Section 5 discusses transformation rules that transform the output ontological analysis to components and connector specifications.

## 2    BWW Reference Model

Bunge's original ontology [2] is considered as a general system theory. Later, Wand and Weber [12] subsequently adapted it to model information systems. The adapted version is referred to BWW ontology. An *ontological category* capturing a real world phenomenon is a high-level generic notion defined in an ontology. Ontological categories are valuable conceptual abstractions to analyze a particular domain because they can be used to identify the roles played by domain abstractions and relationships among them. BWW ontology includes a comprehensive set of ontological categories that model static and dynamic features of reality. Earlier we developed a classification scheme for ontological categories and a meta-model for BWW ontology that have been reported in [13]. The ontological categories and the relationships among them are represented through a UML meta-model is summarized in Figure 1. The meta-model has been formalized through type-theoretic notations. By specifying the meta-model through type theoretic notations, we learnt that the ontological categories are generic types and they can play the roles of *types* to describe elements from application domains.

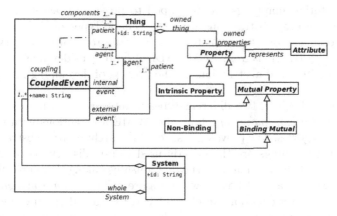

**Fig. 1.** An Object Oriented meta-model for BWW Ontology

# 3   The Process and Its Artifacts

Two different types of modeling artifacts are needed. Firstly, a *domain ontology model* describes an application domain through BWW ontological categories. This model is manually developed after performing ontological analysis of requirements. The second model is automatically generated and it is referred to as a *baseline architectural description*. It consists of a set of architecturally significant elements from application domain. Baseline architectural abstractions i.e., abstractions present in baseline architectural descriptions can be further refined into full-fledged architectural abstractions by adding features found in software modeling languages. For example, in *Meeting Scheduler* domain [14], *getting a preferred date for meeting* is an element of the domain that can be considered as a baseline connector. This baseline connector can be further refined to a full-fledged software connector by adding non-functional features such as distribution, concurrency and security around the baseline connector. Earlier, we have used the concept of the *baseline connector* to extract C&C views from the UML models of existing systems [15]. A baseline connector becomes a *full-fledged* connector by adding non-functional properties to it.

# 4   Interpreting Architectural Abstractions and Domain Elements through BWW Ontology

The existing practices and taxonomies [11,16] provide guidelines to represent solution-domain specific entities through architectural abstractions. For example, computational processes or database entities can be represented through components. The interaction entities such as pipes, semaphores and communication protocols can be represented through connectors. These guidelines are convenient to describe architectures of many software systems. But they offer little assistance to derive architectural abstractions from domain descriptions.

The interpretation mappings are developed to provide an assistance by relating the architectural abstractions with the generic types of domain elements. In this context, the ontological categories play the roles of generic types. The architectural abstractions from ACME ADL [17] are considered as the reference model for architectural abstractions in the process of developing interpretation mappings.

As shown in Table 1, two different types of interpretation mappings are defined. The *abstraction mapping* relates the ACME abstractions with the BWW ontological categories. The prevalent usages of the architectural abstractions and their intended meanings are the criteria used to establish the correspondence. The architectural abstractions and the relationships among them are represented through a UML meta-model as shown in Figure 2. The *domain mapping* assigns exactly one category to a domain element because each domain element represents a single phenomenon from the reality. A noun, or a noun phrase, a verb or a verb phrase or a single sentence describing domain requirements is considered as a domain element. The domain mapping is also referred to as *domain*

**Table 1.** Interpretation Mappings

**(a) Interpretation Mapping for Architectural Abstractions**

| Architectural Abstractions | BWW Category | Architectural Abstractions | BWW Category |
|---|---|---|---|
| Component | Thing | Port | Attributes representing Binding Mutual property |
| Connector | Coupled Process | Roles | Mutual Binding Property |
| System | System | Representation | System Composition |
| Property | BWW Property | Attachments | Representation relation between mutual property and attributes |

**(b) Interpretation Mapping for Example Domain Elements from Meeting Scheduler Problem**

| Sr. No. | Domain Element | BWW Category | Sr. No. | Domain Element | BWW Category |
|---|---|---|---|---|---|
| 1. | Meeting Initiator | Thing | 2. | Meeting Attendee | Thing |
| 3. | To Ask all for exclusion set | Coupled-event | 4 | To ask all for preference set | Coupled-event |
| 5. | Exclusion Set | Property | 6. | Preference set | Property |
| 7. | Meeting Date | Property | 8. | To ask for special Equipment | Coupled Event |
| 9. | To ask for preferred location | Coupled Event | 10. | The proposed meeting date should belong to the stated date range and to none of the exclusion sets | Law |

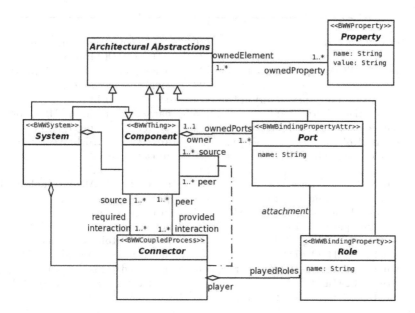

**Fig. 2.** Meta-model for Architectural Abstractions

*ontology model* and it is described as an XMI document. The BWW ontological categories are the tags in XMI document. The XMI document describing application domain follows the schema presented in the meta-model of the reference BWW ontology shown in Figure 1. The mapping from domain elements to BWW ontology is depended on an application domain and it is defined every time for each domain. The mapping from architectural abstractions to BWW ontology is independent of application domains and it is defined only once as a reusable process. The metamodel represented in Figure 2 is used as schema for the output description.

# 5   Transformation Rules

Transformation rules are defined to create architectural abstractions from a domain ontology model. A C&C view described in ACME is the output model that the transformation rules generate. Transformation rules are invoked based on the ontological types of domain elements. Things, Properties, Coupled Events and BWW System are some types of domain elements. They are transformed to ACME Components Properties, Connectors and System respectively. The type of ACME abstraction to be created is guided by the interpretation mapping defined in Table 1(a). Transformation rules are realized in ATLAS Transformation Language (ATL). One example of a transformation rule for transforming coupled event to connector is included below.

An instance of a connector is created when the ontological type of a domain element is *Coupled Event*. Steps involved in creating new instance of connectors

```
1 rule ce2con{                          20        --   Constructing   Ports
2   from                                21 port1 :  C2ADL! Port (
3     ce : BWWOntology! CoupledEvent     22     name<-ce . name  +  'RepPort',
4   to                                   23     owner<-  ce . agent ) ,
5 --Constructing  new  connector.        24 port2 :  C2ADL! Port (
6   con : C2ADL! Connector (             25     name<-ce . name  +  'ReqPort',
7     name<-  ce . name ,                26     owner<-  ce . patient ) ,
8     ownedRoles<-  Sequence { }) ,      27 binding1  :  C2ADL! Attachment (
9   --  Constructing  Properties         28     port <-  port2 ,
10  p :  C2ADL! Property (               29     role <-  role2 ) ,
11    name  <-  'Parameters',            30 binding2  :  C2ADL! Attachment (
12    value <-  ce . parameter ,         31     port <-  port1 ,
13    ownedElement <-  Sequence { }      32     role <-  role1 )
14    ->append ( ce )) ,                 33 do{
15  --  Constructing  Roles              34 con . ownedRoles <-  con .
16  role1 :  C2ADL! Role (               35 ownedRoles ->append ( role1 );
17    name<-ce . name+'Requester'),      36 con . ownedRoles <-  con .
18  role2 :  C2ADL! Role (               37 ownedRoles ->append ( role2 );
19    name<-ce . name  +  'Replier'),    38 }}
```

are (i) defining properties of connectors, (ii) constructing roles of connectors, (iii) creating ports in the components playing the roles of connectors, and (iv) binding ports to roles through attachments. Connectors, Ports, Roles and Attachments are created as a result of processing of instances of *Coupled Events*. In some cases, though the number of connectors, ports, roles and attachments can be minimized by merging all coupled events that share their participant things, this may be undesirable from the point of view of losing flexibility. For example, in Figure 3, the instances of coupled events *askAllPrefSet* and *askAllExSet* are not merged to form a single connector instance. It can be noted that non-functional properties of interactions may depend on the semantics of interactions among things and not on the participant types. In interaction such as *withdraw meeting*, an acknowledgment or reply may not be expected, while in the interaction *askAllPrefSet* an acknowledgment and reply are expected. Coupled events that need an acknowledgment may use a *reliable* communication protocol. In this context, reliability is a non-functional property.

The transformation rules generate a XMI document that conforms to the XMI schema representing meta-model of architectural abstractions. The baseline architectural configuration for *Meeting Scheduler Problem* as generated by the approach is shown in Figure 3. An earlier C&C-based architectural model of *Meeting Scheduler problem* can be found in [18]. The appropriateness of the generated architectural description is checked by comparing it with the existing architectural description.

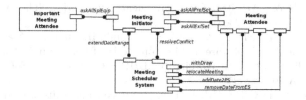

**Fig. 3.** Generated Architectural Configuration for Meeting Scheduler Problem

# 6   Conclusion

A process of mapping domain elements to produce $C\&C$ based architectural descriptions was discussed in this paper. The outcomes of the process include identification of architecturally significant domain elements and an architectural configuration aligned to interactions among things present in the domain. Usefulness of the approach comes from the definition of transformation rules to create an architectural configuration. The transformation rules maintain traceability links between domain requirements and architectural abstractions. By introducing the concept of *baseline architectural descriptions* the approach achieves a separation of application domain specific concerns from software specific concerns. Currently, the task of interpreting domain elements in terms of BWW ontological categories is manually performed by mapping the decisions depend on the judgment of a domain expert. The approach can be explored further-(i) by considering non-functional properties, (ii) validating the approach through non-trivial software systems and (iii) evaluating the approach from scalability point of view and by (iv) developing knowledge-based automated techniques to assist the process.

# References

1. Ferrari, R.N., Madhavji, N.H.: Architecting-problems rooted in requirements. Inf. Softw. Technol. 50(1-2), 53–66 (2008)
2. Bunge, M.: Treatise on Basic Philosophy, 1st edn. Ontology I: The Furniture of the World, vol. 3. D. Reidel Publishing Compant (1977)
3. Yair, W., Weber, R.: An ontological model of an information system. IEEE Transactions on Software Engineering 16(11), 1282–1292 (1990)
4. Opdahl, A., Henderson-Sellers, B.: Ontological evaluation of the uml using the bunge-wand-weber model. Software and Systems Modeling J. 1(1), 43–67 (2002)
5. Green, P.F., Rosemann, M., Indulska, M.: Ontological evaluation of enterprise systems interoperability using ebxml. IEEE Transactions on Knowledge and data Engineering 17(5), 713–724 (2005)
6. Liu, W., Easterbrook, S.: From requirements to architectural designs using goals and scenarios. In: STRAW 2001 located at ICSE 2001 (2003)
7. Kim, J., Park, S., Sugumaran, V.: Drama: A framework for domain requirements analysis and modeling architectures in software product lines. J. Syst. Softw. 81(1), 37–55 (2008)

8. Schwanke, R.W.: Architectural requirements engineering: Theory vs. practice. In: STRAW, pp. 1–8 (2003)

9. Hofmeister, C., Kruchten, P., Nord, R., Obbink, H., Ran, A., America, P.: Generalizing a model of software architecture design from five industrial approaches. In: Proceedings of the 5th Working IEEE/IFIP Conference on Software Architecture, WICSA 2005 (2005)

10. Grunbacher, P., Egyed, A., Medvidovic, N.: Reconciling software requirements and architectures with intermediate models. Journal on Software and System Modeling (December 2003)

11. Mehta, N.R.: Towards a taxonomy of software connectors. In: 22nd International Conference on Software Engineering (June 2000)

12. Yair, W., Weber, R.: On the ontological expressiveness of information system analysis and design grammars. Journal of Information Systems (3), 217–237 (1993)

13. Kiwelekar, A.W., Joshi, R.K.: An object oriented metamodel for bunge-wand-weber ontology. In: Proc. of SWeCKa 2007, Workshop on Semantic Web for Collaborative Knowledge Acquisition at IJCAI 2007 (January 2007)

14. Shaw, M., Garlan, D., Allen, R., Klein, D., Ockerbloom, J., Scott, C., Schumacher, M.: Candidate model problems in software architecture (January 1995)

15. Kiwelekar, A.W., Joshi, R.K.: Extracting high-level component-connector view from detailed uml models: A case study. COMPSAC (2), 527–534 (2007)

16. Liu, W., Easterbrook, S.: Eliciting architectural decisions from requirements using a rule based framework. In: STRAW 2003 located at ICSE (2003)

17. Garlan, D.: Acme: An architecture description interchange language. In: Proceedings of CASCON 1997 (November 1997)

18. Medvidovic, N.: Modeling software architectures in unified modeling language. ACM Transactions on Software Engineering and Methodology 11(1), 2–57 (2002)

# Experiences in Making Architectural Decisions during the Development of a New Base Station Platform

Juha Savolainen[1], Juha Kuusela[2], Tomi Männistö[3], and Aki Nyyssönen[4]

[1] Nokia Research Center, Itämerenkatu 11-13, 00180 Helsinki, Finland
juha.e.savolainen@nokia.com
[2] Nokia Devices, Keilalahdentie 4, 02150 Espoo, Finland
juha.kuusela@nokia.com
[3] Aalto University, Tekniikantie 14, 02150 Espoo, Finland
tomi.mannisto@tkk.fi
[4] Nokia Siemens Networks, Kaapelitie 4, 90650 Oulu, Finland
aki.nyyssonen@nsn.com

**Abstract.** Creating architecture for a complex telecommunication system is a difficult task and requires expertise of many different stakeholders. The software architecture design process relies on understanding the architecturally significant requirements (ASRs) for the system under design. This paper describes experiences in creating a new base station product line. A goal was to create a process to facilitate fulfillment of ASRs during the development of the product line. The approach proved to be feasible for developing large-scale systems in the telecommunications infrastructure domain. This paper describes the approach taken, experiences gathered during the development process and promotes the idea of defining concrete ASRs for each project and refining them through architecture for all relevant subsystems.

**Keywords:** Software architecture, design decisions, architecturally significant requirements process, refinement.

## 1 Introduction

Software architecture has been identified as one of the main development tools that helps system to achieve it's quality requirements [1]. Correct architectural decisions allow the system to meet its quality requirements such as modifiability, performance, reliability and security. In the highest level, architectural styles has been proposed as the way to match architecturally significant requirements to architectural decisions [2]. However, architectural styles cover only the highest levels of software architecture design. In fact, it seems that complex systems tend to be based on many different architectural styles.

The overall system architecture determines the main subsystems. Separation to the subsystems can happen for many reasons, but for large-scale systems the most important is that the subsystems support division of work. That is, each subsystem can be reasonably independently designed and implemented. This is measured by cohesion

M. Ali Babar and I. Gorton (Eds.): ECSA 2010, LNCS 6285, pp. 425–432, 2010.
© Springer-Verlag Berlin Heidelberg 2010

and coupling. By increasing the cohesion within the subsystem and minimizing coupling between the subsystems can make the subsystems more independent.

In this paper, we share experiences from a project in the telecommunication domain. The intention of the project was to build a new base station platform that would allow creating base stations for various telecommunication standards. The base station project was substantial in size. More than one hundred engineers and multiple sites around the globe participated contributed to the project. Because of the geographical division, a way to communicate the decisions and to effectively divide work to the different sites was very important.

In the context of our work, the system had chief architects that were responsible for the whole system and subsystem architects for the system components, the first level of the decomposition. Together these architects intended to create an architecture that would supports ASRs for the whole system. Initial list of ASRs was created by the chief architects together with architecture experts from corporate research. The highest-level software architecture document was created to describe how the ASRs were addressed by the overall architecture.

For each of the system components the system-wide ASRs must be converted to the ones that are relevant to that particular subsystem. As the design progresses each system component will determine its own architecture within the constraints of the higher-level architecture and will again will define new subsystems. We consider architecture design to continue until no new subsystems are needed. At this point the design will continue with classes or code modules, depending on the implementation technology.

The structure of the development project was aligned with the software architecture of the system. This provided easy communication of architectural decisions through software architecture documentation.

The remainder of this paper is organized as follow. Section 2, discusses three main ways in which we made architectural decisions during the base station project. After this, we discuss our findings and conclude in Section 3.

## 2    Observations on Architectural Decisions during the Development of the Base Station Platform

Designing good architectures require making correct design decisions in many different levels of abstraction. On the higher levels many questions relating to overall structure of the architecture must be answered, general approach for division of work established and main responsibilities of software elements decided. On the lower levels APIs must be designed, process structures decided and detailed compile time dependencies managed.

A number of researchers have argued that architectural decisions should be, if possible, delayed. Delaying decisions achieves flexibility and allows improved knowledge taken into account when making the decisions. Lower level decisions are equally difficult to be taken upfront, since not enough is known on the implementation details to make correct decision on e.g. detailed process or threading design issues. We agree with Ruth Malan and Dana Bredemeyer [3] who argue that an architect should make as few decisions as possible, deferring the rest until later in the lifecycle. Delaying decision means that decisions must be made during different time in the system development lifecycle and in a different level of abstraction.

In the base station project, we had three main ways to target architectural concerns. Sometimes an architectural solution was created and described in form of components, their dependencies and interactions, allocation of functionality or interfaces. Often, chief architects could decide to solve the issue later. This was communicated to subsystem architects using system component specific ASRs. In few cases, an additional process step was sometimes added to alleviate the risk of not satisfying the concern at some later point of time.

We believe that understanding the different intent of these different approaches to architectural decisions will help architects to better express their decisions in their own architectures.

## 2.1 Architectural Decision Are Made in Form of the Structure

The most common type of architectural decision is a decision taken to modify the current structure of the software architecture. These decisions affect the architecture on level of abstraction currently under work and typically address the ASRs defined for this level of abstraction. In general, the structure is a good way to communicate decisions. When a decision is expressed as e.g. a defined interface or as a responsibility division between subsystems it makes the decision very explicit and the probability of misunderstandings is low. The decision can be implemented by updating the structure.

For our project, the intent was to use the overall list of ASRs as the way to organize architectural decisions. The main ASRs were included into all versions of the architectural documentation to keep track on the process of facilitating them.

Not all decisions affecting the structure give ready-made solutions to ASRs. Some architectural decisions are made as explicit constraints on future decisions. These are often explicitly documented as constraints or rules [4], but can be sometimes disguised as just another architectural decision on the structure of the architecture.

An architectural constraint restricts the future architectural decisions. Even though it can be argued that all decisions will reduce the available design space [5], for architectural constraints this becomes the essence of the decision. One possible way to express a constraint is to use layer diagrams as shown in Figure 1.

The idea of layer diagram in Figure 1 was to communicate to subsystem architects and other stakeholders the main mechanism to achieve reuse in software product line architecture. Layers were used to achieve reuse across different radio access technologies, that is, to allow derivation of products that differ on the supported radio technology. Hence, two layers were constructed, one specific to radio technology and one generic.

Most subsystems could be mapped to either layer, but some had functionality that belonged to both layers. For these subsystems, the subsystem architects must guarantee that on the component level, the subsystem can be organized to a layered structure that separates components that are specific to a particular radio technology and to those that contain generic functionality.

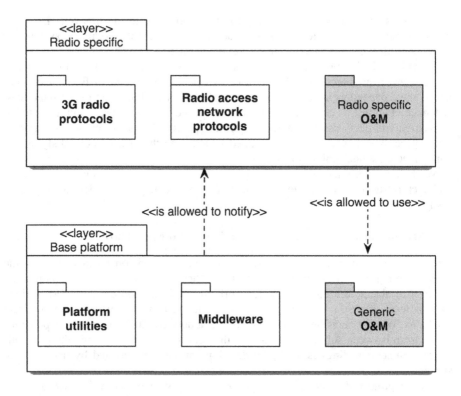

**Fig. 1.** Architectural constraints shown in the context of the structure

## 2.2   Architectural Decisions Are Done in Form of Requirements to the Structure

Making architectural decisions in the form of the structure requires that we can describe the decision in terms of architectural structures. Sometimes, the architects either lack the information, necessary specialized expertise, or some preliminary decisions have not been done so that it is not possible to express the decision in terms of structure.

Decision has to be expressed in form of architectural requirements. Here the intention is not to make the actual decision, but the explain the requirements for the decision to be made later. A requirement places a constraint that is described in a textual form and targets some subsystems (or system components). This way of communicating decisions is typically less precise than making the decision in form of the structure, but is necessary when the architects cannot make the actual decisions right now and must delay them.

However, the decisions on the structure are not independent from decisions in form of requirements. In particular, an architectural decision on the level of the entire system can greatly affect the ASRs for the subsystems. For example, a decision to distribute responsibilities between subsystems defines what ASRs will be relevant for each subsystem. That is, making decisions on the structure of the architecture and making the ASRs are results of an iterative process of architecting and both communicate architectural constraints.

As long as architecture design continues, we believe that it is essential to refine the ASRs, so that for each step of software architecture design, the relevant ASRs are available. To do this, two things must happen. First, for each level of decomposition a subsystem architect must be able to identify the relevant higher level ASRs for it and second, the architect must be able to derive the relevant ASRs into subsystem specific ASR(s). This process is described in Figure 2.

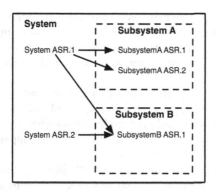

**Fig. 2.** Refining ASRs in general (adapted from [6])

Figure 2 describes how ASR refinement works in general. Two system-wide ASRs refined to the subsystem ASRs. There is a complex mapping between the system ASRs and the subsystem ASRs. Often a system level ASR is refined into many subsystem level ASRs similarly what ASR.1 is refined into subsystem A ASRs SsA_ASR.1 and SsA_ASR.2. This represents how higher-level ASRs become more detailed when transitioning to subsystems. Also many system level ASRs affect a number of subsystems. In Figure 2, the system level ASR.1 if refined to ASRs of both subsystems A and B.

However, not every ASR needs to be relevant to all subsystems. For example, performance may be crucial for data transmission part of the system, but a maintenance system can ignore strict real-time requirements. In Figure 2 this is shown in case of ASR.2 that is only refined into respective ASRs for subsystem B.

For the base station platform we had an extensive excel document describing how the system level ASRs were reflected in the subsystems. The idea was not to repeat the ASRs in the subsystem documentation in the same way as they were described in the overall architecture document, but rather describe the ASR as requirements for the subsystem. We felt that is was crucial to express the subsystem ASRs in those terms that are relevant for the subsystem. The resulted subsystem ASRs were then recorded and represented in the subsystem architecture document.

For example, a system level ASR "The system shall be able to report any fault in the system within 5 seconds of its detection" could be refined to BTS O&M system component ASR as "BTS O&M shall report a detected fault in any of the HW cards within 2 seconds". This means that we intended to make the ASRs always very relevant for the particular subsystem and also communicate e.g. performance budgets.

After defining some of the subsystem level ASRs will start another iteration where decisions on the (subsystem) structure will be made and new detailed ASRs for the components within the subsystems are born.

### 2.3 Architectural Decision as a Process Step

In two previous sections we have discussed two ways to address software architecture development directly by either making architectural decisions in form of the structure or as architectural requirements. However, during the software architecture design, not all decisions address the architecture directly, but affect the process of designing the architecture.

For a large system, the chief architect is typically responsible for the overall system architecture and each subsystem has an own responsible architect. A set of rules cover the whole architecting process and give guidelines on what documentation is required for each subsystem. These rules are often derived from company or domain specific standards on architectural documentation.

Based on the decisions on how to achieve ASRs in the system level, the subsystem ASRs are affected. Besides this, also the ways the architectural decisions are documented or intended to be pursued, could be tailored for some subsystems. This is the essence of architectural decisions as a process step. For example, some subsystems may be required to document how certain aspects of the system are achieved or defined analysis may be required.

In the base station, two large decisions on the process of architecting were done. First, for selected subsystems architectural evaluation was decided to be done in a later stage to verify the fulfilment of a number of key ASRs. Second, a detailed analysis of performance characteristics was selected for a small subset of the architecture. This part of the architecture was agreed to be critical for the overall performance of the messaging functionality of the base station. We decided to perform rate monotonic analysis (see e.g. [7]) for this part of the system after we have better understanding on the actual process structure. This process decision was combined with architectural requirements, because we also decided to estimate worst-case execution times for each system component that limited the design freedom of the system component teams.

## 3  Discussion and Conclusions

Software architecture can be been seen as a series of architecturally significant design decisions. These decisions aim to define the architecture that is then used as the basis for system implementation.

The decisions can manifest themselves as being about requirements, architecture or changes to design process, among others. The kinds of decisions include, for example, requirements, constraints, rules and different decisions about the actual systems, such as structure, interfaces, styles, patterns and detailed design decisions. These all can be seen as restrictions on the allowed design space in the later phases of the design process.

In a broader view, we try to shed light in this paper on the issue that when someone is making architectural decisions, what kind of decisions should she make. There are two main aspects in that. First, the decisions should be made to the appropriate level of detail not to restrict the later design decisions unnecessarily. Second, the decision-making should bear adequate responsibility not to postpone the making of decisions on issues that could and should be resolved here and now. Within these boundaries, the decision-maker should be aware of her capabilities in making the decision, so that she would have the a justified understanding on how concrete decisions to make or what issues to still leave to be determined later, typically by others.

We used a concrete example of the phenomenon in which the ASRs of the whole system were propagated to the subsystems. The propagation was not straightforward and thus illustrated how ASRs for the whole system become refined and take a different form when interpreted within the context of a subsystem and how in this decision-making the structural decision regarding the system decomposition have a major impact on the ASRs of the subsystems.

The used case example is a real example from a complex architecture design problem. However, the example is simple in the broader view of the idea we aim to illustrate, as it only covers a slice of the entire problem area in making different kinds of architectural decisions. There is clearly a room for deeper understanding on the kinds of architectural design decisions and their role in restricting the available design space. With such understanding, a framework and guidelines could be defined to help practitioners to explicate their own boundaries and responsibilities and to assess what kinds of architectural decisions should be applied in a particular situation.

For practitioners it is important to make explicit decisions on how to represent architectural decisions. If the architect's have enough knowledge to make the decision by affecting the structure of the architecture and this simplifies the further development by supporting independent work, then the decision should be made. Otherwise creating new subsystem specific ASRs or adding a process step to e.g. evaluate subsystem architectures may be more appropriate. Despite that we described three ways to make architectural decisions separately; these three options are rarely independent. When making a decision on structure, it tends to change subsystem-level ASRs. In addition, the more decisions are made; typically less process is needed later.

The ability to make correct architectural decisions and how to represent them is ultimately dependent on the competence of the architect. This paper presented three different ways to represent architectural decisions to assist architects to consider all options during the architecting process. In the future, we intend to research more on factors affecting the choice of representing architectural decisions in order to further assist practitioners.

# References

[1] Bass, L., Clements, P., Kazman, R.: Software architecture in practice. Addison-Wesley, Reading (2003)
[2] Shaw, M., Garlan, D.: Software architecture: Perspectives on an emerging discipline. Prentice Hall, Englewood Cliffs (1996)
[3] Malan, R., Bredemeyer, D.: Less is more with minimalist architecture. IEEE IT Professional 4(5), 46–48 (2002)
[4] Bosch, J.: Design and Use of Software Architectures: Adopting and Evolving a Product-Line Approach. Addison-Wesley, Harlow (2000)
[5] Davis, A.: Great Software Depates. Wiley, Hoboken (2004)
[6] Savolainen, J., Kuusela, J.: Transition to Agile Development - Rediscovery of Important Requirements Engineering Practices. In: 18th IEEE International Requirements Engineering Conference. IEEE, Sydney (to appear, 2010)
[7] Nord, R.L., Cheng, B.C.: Using RMA for evaluating design decisions. In: Proceedings of the IEEE Workshop on Real-Time Applications, pp. 76–80 (1994)

# On the Role of Architectural Styles in Improving the Adaptation Support of Middleware Platforms

Naeem Esfahani and Sam Malek

Department of Computer Science
George Mason University
{nesfaha2,smalek}@gmu.edu

**Abstract.** Modern middleware platforms provide the applications deployed on top of them with facilities for their adaptation. However, the level of adaptation support provided by the state-of-the-art middleware solutions is often limited to dynamically loading and off-loading of software components. Therefore, it is left to the application developers to handle the details of change such that the system's consistency is not jeopardized. In this paper, we present an approach that addresses the current shortcomings by utilizing the information encoded in a software system's architectural style. This information drives the development of adaptation patterns, which could be employed to enhance the adaptation support in middleware platforms. The patterns specify both the exact sequence of changes and the time at which those changes need to occur.

**Keywords:** Middleware, Adaptation Patterns, Architectural Styles.

## 1 Introduction

The unrelenting pattern of growth in size and complexity of software systems that we have witnessed over the past few decades is likely to continue well into the foreseeable future. As software engineers have developed new techniques to address the complexity associated with the construction of modern-day software systems, an equally pressing need has risen for mechanisms that automate and simplify the management and modification of software systems after they are deployed, i.e., during run-time. This has called for the development of self-* (self-configuring, self-healing, self-optimizing, etc.) systems. However, the construction of such systems has been shown to be significantly more challenging than traditional, relatively more static and predictable, software systems.

Previous studies have shown that a promising approach to resolve the challenges of constructing complex software systems is to employ the principles of *software architecture* [7], [8]. Software architectures provide abstractions for representing the structure, behavior, and key properties of a software system. They are described in terms of *software components* (computational elements), *connectors* (interaction elements), and their *configurations*. A given software *architectural style* (e.g., *publish-subscribe, peer-to-peer, pipe-and-filter, client-server*) further refines a vocabulary of component and connector types and a set of constraints on how instances of those types may be combined in a system [1].

M. Ali Babar and I. Gorton (Eds.): ECSA 2010, LNCS 6285, pp. 433–440, 2010.

Software architecture has also been shown to provide an appropriate level of abstraction and generality to deal with the complexity of dynamic adaptation of software systems [3]. This observation has led to research on *architecture-based adaptation*, which is the process of reasoning about and adapting a system's software at the architectural level [3], [6].

Architecture-based adaptation is often realized via the run-time facilities provided by an implementation platform, i.e., *middleware*. Unfortunately, the level of adaptation support provided by most state-of-the-art middleware solutions is limited to dynamically loading and offloading of software components. They do not consider the state or dependency among the system's software components. This is driven by the fact that, in the general case, component dependency relationships are application specific, and cannot be predicted a priori by the middleware designers.

The lack of advanced adaptation management and coordination facilities in the existing platforms forces the application developers to implement them on their own. Unfortunately, the status quo places significant burden on the application developers. The developers have to spend a significant amount of time understanding the underlying details of a middleware platform, before they can develop the required adaptation facilities. As a result, the theoretical advances [4], [10] for consistent and sound adaptation of a software system remain untapped, and the application developers rely on the rudimentary adaptation capabilities that the existing middlewares provide by default.

In this paper, we present an approach that attempts to alleviate these shortcomings. The approach relies on the information encoded in a software system's architectural style. More specifically, an underlying insight guiding our research is that a software system's architectural style reveals a lot about the dependency relationships among the system's software components. This information is utilized to identify *adaptation patterns*, which determine the recurring sequence of changes that need to occur for adapting a software system built according to a given style. An adaptation pattern ensures that the system is not left in an inconsistent state and the application's functionality is not jeopardized. We have realized the adaptation patterns on top of an existing middleware platform, called Prism-MW [5].

The paper is organized as follows. Section 2 provides the required background, while Section 3 motivates the work by summarizing the problems with existing approaches. Section 4 describes our overall approach. Section 5 describes the extraction of an adaptation pattern from a given architectural style. Section 6 provides an overview of the application of patterns in improving the capabilities of an existing middleware. Finally, the paper concludes.

## 2  Background and Related Work

For exposition purposes, we are going to use a simple application intended for routing incoming cargo to a set of warehouses. This application was first presented in the seminal work on architecture-based adaptation [6]. We have reproduced its architecture in Fig. 1a. The architectural style of this application is C2 [9]. A software system built in the C2 style consists of layers, where *request* events travel upward, while *notification* events travel downward. *E*vents that are received are evaluated to determine if the component needs to process them.

In Fig. 2, the *Ports, Vehicles,* and *Warehouses* components are abstract data types (ADTs) that keep track of the state of shipping ports, transportation vehicles, and goods warehouses, respectively. The *Telemetry* component determines when cargo arrives at a port, and tracks the cargo from the time it is routed until it is delivered to the warehouse. The *Port Artist, Vehicle Artist,* and *Warehouse Artist* components are responsible for graphically depicting the state of their respective ADTs to the end-user. The *Router* component provides the end-user's last selected port, vehicle, and warehouse. The *Graphics* component renders the drawing requests sent from the artists using the Java AWT graphics package.

## 2.1 Challenges of Architecture-Based Adaptation

Typically, middleware support for architecture-based adaptation is realized in the form of adding, removing, and replacing software components. However, such changes could jeopardize the functionality of a software system, as they could leave the system in an inconsistent state. For instance, consider a scenario where we would like to replace the *Warehouses* component. Such capability may be realized by removing the old *Warehouses* and adding a new instance of it [6]. This solution, however, ignores the other components, such as *Telemetry*, which depend on the *Warehouses* for delivering their services.

Let us assume the end-user makes a "Route Warehouse" request using the *Graphics* component. Fig. 1b shows the interactions (events/messages) that would result in response to this request. If such a request is made while *Warehouses* component is being updated, and thus temporarily unavailable, it is processed by the *Router* and *Warehouse Artist*, but not the new *Warehouses* component. The effect of this may manifest itself in the form of functional failure: the new *Warehouses* component may not receive event 3, resulting in the system to never respond to the user (i.e., events 4-7 do not occur).

At first blush it may seem that buffering events intended for *Warehouses* component would solve the problem. However, buffering by itself cannot address consistency issues that may arise. Consider the situation in which *Warehouses* component is

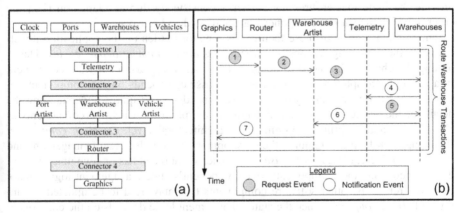

**Fig. 1.** Cargo-routing application: a) its C2 architecture; and b) a transaction for the cargo-routing application and the corresponding component dependencies

replaced after it has replied with event 4, but before receiving event 5. In this case, it is possible for the old component to process request 3, and the new component to process request 5, assuming it is buffered for later processing. However, this may violate the component's interaction protocol (i.e., event 5 can be processed only after event 3 has, which would not be the case with the newly installed component). Since the new component may not have the correct state, the system may become inconsistent.

## 2.2  Change Management Model

A generally applicable solution to this problem was proposed by Kramer and Magee's seminal model of dynamic change management [3], which provides a separation of structural concerns from application concerns. Their work also identifies two possible states for a software component during the adaptation process. Each state defines how a component behaves during the corresponding phase of adaptation:

- *Active*: A component can start, receive, and process transactions.
- *Passive*: A component in this state will continue to receive and process transactions, but will not initiate any new transactions.

*Quiescence* is defined as the required property to adapt a component [4]. Quiescence implies that a component (1) is not currently involved in a transaction, (2) will not start any new transactions, and (3) no transactions have been or will be initiated by other components that require service from this node.

Based on this change management model, Gomaa and Hussein [2] suggest the development of reconfiguration patterns for software product lines. However, their approach does not consider transitive dependencies and their implications.

## 3  Research Problem

It is typically left to the application developers to implement the required change management and coordination facilities mentioned above. These facilities would provide the logic that ensures the system's consistency during adaptation (i.e., the order in which the various components are activated and passivated).

The implementation of these facilities is a major burden on the application developers for the following reasons: (1) *Identifying the component dependencies:* Determining the changes that need to occur in the system to place a software component in a particular adaptation state (i.e., active, passive) depends on the component dependencies. However, identifying transitive dependencies requires understanding the details of the application logic, which defeats the purpose of treating components as black boxes and adapting a system at the architectural level. (2) *High complexity:* Realizing such facilities requires the development of complex state management and coordination logic. (3) *Lack of reuse:* Since each component has its own unique set of dependencies on other components, one component's state management logic cannot be easily reused by other software components that may need to be updated at runtime. (4) *High coupling:* Since the state management logic depends on the component dependency relationships, the resulting software is very fragile. That is as soon as the software evolves (e.g., components change the way they interact and use one another), the state management logic needs to be modified.

Traditionally, one method of reducing complexity and increasing the developer's productivity is to employ middlewares. The middleware engineers develop the frequently needed intra-component facilities (e.g., data marshalling, remote method invocation, service discovery), and provide them as reusable modules to any applications developed on top of the middleware. Unfortunately, employing the same approach in the context of adaptation is not feasible, since it needs inter-component analysis and the middleware designers cannot predict a priori which software components will be deployed on top of a middleware, how they will be configured, and what will be their dependencies. Therefore, modern middleware platforms do not provide change management facilities beyond simple dynamic addition and removal of components. This is precisely the research problem that we have aimed to solve in this paper through the use of knowledge embedded in architectural styles and the capabilities of a unique style aware middleware.

# 4 Approach

In light of the challenges mentioned above, currently three methods of adapting a software system are employed: (1) Query the component itself to provide information about its dependency relationships. This relates to the 1st problem in Section 3, i.e., violates the black-box treatment of components. Moreover, it hinders reusability of components developed in this manner. (2) Yank the old component and replace it with a new one. As exemplified using the Cargo Routing application in Section 2.1, this approach could leave the sytem in an inconsistent state. (3) Bring down (Passivate) the entire system before adapting it, and restart it afterwards. This approach clearly results in severe disruption in system's execution.

We propose a new approach that builds on the existing models of dynamic change management (recall Section 2). The key underlying insight guiding our research is that a software system's architectural style could reveal the dependency relationships among the components of a given system, even if the components are indirectly connected to one another. The dependency relationships are critical when adapting a software system, as they determine the impact of change on the system [4], [10].

We use the rules and constraints of an architectural style to infer the component dependencies for any software system built according to that style. An example of this can be seen in Fig. 1a. In a C2 software system it is generally true that components in lower layer depend on components in higher layer. As a concrete example, take *Warehouse Artist* that depends on *Warehouses*.

The component dependencies are in turn used to determine a reusable sequence of changes that need to occur for placing a component in the appropriate adaptation state. Such a recurring sequence of changes, which are coordinated among the system's architectural constructs (e.g., components, connectors) is called an *adaptation pattern*. An adaptation pattern provides a template for making changes to a software system built according to a given style without jeopardizing its consistency.

An adaptation pattern for a given style is guaranteed to be generally applicable for systems built according to that style, since (1) quiescence is guaranteed to be reachable [4], and (2) applications built according to the style exhibit similar dependency relationships among their components.

## 5  Style-Driven Adaptation Patterns

In this section we describe the process of extracting adaptation patterns from an architectural style. For this purpose we have chosen the C2 style [9]. Note that while the overall approach is generally applicable to any style, the details of the patterns, their accuracy, and level of disruption due to adaptation directly depend on the characteristics of the style. The styles with rich properties and rules inevitably result in more interesting and effective patterns.

During normal operation a C2Component is *Waiting* to receive asynchronous request event from an associated C2Connector. If the event is not intended for the component, it returns to the *Waiting* state. Otherwise, it starts *Processing* the request and additional request and notification events are generated as needed. After the *Processing* has completed and the appropriate events are sent, the component returns to the *Waiting* state.

Adaptation of a software system requires its constituents (e.g., components, connectors) to coordinate the changes that need to occur. It is the responsibility of the adaptation module to track the adaptation state (e.g., active, passive) of the component and neighboring architectural constructs. This recurring coordination constitutes the adaptation pattern for an architectural construct in a given style.

An adaptation pattern may be expressed using statechart models (Fig. 2). Each pattern contains one or more statecharts that define the sequence of steps a component goes through during the adaptation process. In essence, each statechart describes the run-time behavior of a component type (e.g., Client in Client-Server, Publisher in Publish-Subscribe) provisioned by a style during the adaptation process.

The adaptation process requires a component that is to be updated to satisfy the quiescence property. The statechart in Fig. 2 presents the transitions that take an *Active* C2Component that is being adapted to satisfy the quiescence property. When in the *Active* state, the component processes any received events. The first step toward quiescing the component can take one of three paths. Let us first consider the scenario

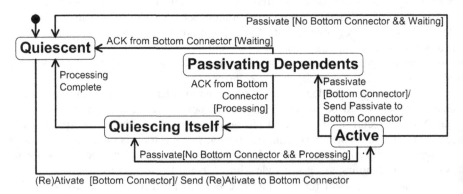

**Fig. 2.** Partial state chart of C2 adaptation pattern: A C2Component that is being adapted

where the component has no bottom connector (i.e., no other component depend on it). In this case, either the component is currently processing or waiting (idle). If the component is waiting, then it simply transitions to *Quiescent*. If the component is processing, it starts *Quiescing Itself*, and waits. When the processing has completed, it transitions to *Quiescent*.

If the component has a bottom connector (i.e., other components depend on it), then the component sends a *Passivate* request to the bottom connector to passivate the dependent components. Once an ACK reply is received from the bottom connector, the component gets *Quiescent* if it is waiting, and starts *Quiescing Itself* if it is processing. In the latter case, the component eventually transitions to the *Quiescent* when the component has completed the work.

The pattern described above, while simple, codify the structural rules and constraints of C2 style into reusable logic that allows for consistent adaptation of any C2 software system. Due to space constraints we have just shown the adaptation patterns for the component being adapted.

# 6 Style-Aware Adaptation

We have leveraged the style-driven adaptation patterns described above to provide advanced run-time adaptation facilities in Prism-MW [5]. Prism-MW is an *architectural middleware*, which supports architectural abstractions by providing implementation-level modules (e.g., classes) for representing each architectural element, with operations for creating, manipulating, and destroying the element. These abstractions enable direct mapping between a system's software architectural model and its implementation. Prism-MW's core functionality provides the necessary support for developing arbitrarily complex applications, as long as one relies on the provided default facilities (e.g., event scheduling, dispatching, and routing). The developer can extend the core functionality as needed. Prism-MW provides three key capabilities that we have relied on to realize the proposed approach. It provides support for (1) basic architecture-level dynamism, (2) multiple architectural styles, and (3) architectural reflection. By codifying the adaptation patterns in Prism-MW, we have been able to provide significantly more advanced adaptation capabilities than that is currently offered by other middleware platforms.

# 7 Conclusion

Most state-of-the-art middleware solutions provide rudimentary support for dynamic adaptation of software systems. They lack the ability to handle the implications of replacing a software component. Therefore, the application developers are burdened with the responsibility of managing the adaptation process at the application-level. We have developed a new approach that addresses the current shortcomings. It leverages the rules and characteristics of an architectural style to determine adaptation patterns for software systems built according to that style. These patterns specify the required sequence of actions to put a software component in a state that can be adapted without jeopardizing the software system's consistency, and hence its functionality. In our future work, we plan to develop a catalog of adaptation patterns for commonly employed architectural styles. Such a catalog would be of great interest to both the software engineering and middleware community. We also plan to include the new patterns in the adaptation support of Prism-MW.

**Acknowledgments.** This work is partially supported by grant CCF-0820060 from the National Science Foundation.

# References

1. Fielding, R.: Architectural Styles and the Design of Network-based Software Architectures. Doctoral Thesis #AAI9980887, Univ. of California Irvine (2000)
2. Gomaa, H., Hussein, M.: Software reconfiguration patterns for dynamic evolution of software architectures. In: Working IEEE/IFIP Conference on Software Architecture, pp. 79–88 (2004)
3. Kramer, J., Magee, J.: Self-Managed Systems: an Architectural Challenge. In: Int'l. Conf. on Software Engineering, Minneapolis, MN, pp. 259–268 (2007)
4. Kramer, J., Magee, J.: The Evolving Philosophers Problem: Dynamic Change Management. IEEE Trans. Softw. Eng. 16(11), 1293–1306 (1990)
5. Malek, S., Mikic-Rakic, M., Medvidovic, N.: A Style-Aware Architectural Middleware for Resource-Constrained, Distributed Systems. IEEE Trans. Softw. Eng. 31(3), 256–272 (2005)
6. Oreizy, P., Medvidovic, N., Taylor, R.N.: Architecture-based runtime software evolution. In: Int'l. Conf. on Software Engineering, Kyoto, Japan, pp. 177–186 (1998)
7. Perry, D.E., Wolf, A.L.: Foundations for the study of software architecture. Softw. Eng. Notes. 17(4), 40–52 (1992)
8. Shaw, M., Garlan, D.: Software architecture: perspectives on an emerging discipline. Prentice-Hall, Inc., Englewood Cliffs (1996)
9. Taylor, R.N., Medvidovic, N., et al.: A component- and message-based architectural style for GUI software. In: Int'l. Conf. on Software Engineering, Seattle, Washington, pp. 295–304 (1995)
10. Vandewoude, Y., Ebraert, P., Berbers, Y., D'Hondt, T.: Tranquility: A Low Disruptive Alternative to Quiescence for Ensuring Safe Dynamic Updates. IEEE Trans. Softw. Eng. 33(12), 856–868 (2007)

# Context-Aware Quality Model Driven Approach: A New Approach for Quality Control in Pervasive Computing Environments

Adel Alti[1], Abdellah Boukerram[1], and Philippe Roose[2]

[1] Computer Science Departement, Engineering Faculty,
Ferhat Abbas University of Setif, 19000 Setif, Algeria
`altiadel2002@yahoo.fr`
[2] LIUPPA / IUT Bayonne, 2 Allée du Parc Montaury, 64600 Anglet, France
`Philippe.Roose@iutbayonne.univ-pau.fr`

**Abstract.** This paper presents extension of MDA called Context-aware Quality Model Driven Architecture (CQ-MDA) which can be used for quality control in pervasive computing environments. The proposed CQ-MDA approach based on ContextualArchRQMM (Contextual ARCHitecture Quality Requirement MetaModel), being an extension to the MDA, allows for considering quality and resources-awareness while conducting the design process. The main idea of presented extension consists in three abstractions levels: PIM (Platform Independent Model), CPIM (Contextual Platform Independent Model) and CPSM (Contextual Platform Specific Model). At the PIM level, a model decomposed into a two interrelated models: software architecture artifacts, which reflect functional requirements and quality model. At the CPIM level a simultaneous transformation of these two models with contextual information details is elaborated and then refined to a specific platform at the CPSM level. Such a procedure ensures that the transformation decisions should be based on the quality assessment of the created models.

**Keywords:** MDA, Context, Quality Model, ADL.

## 1 Introduction

Model Driven Approach (MDA) [5] has been proposed by the OMG (Object management Group). The basic models of MDA are entities able to unify and support the development of computer systems by providing interoperability and portability. MDA approach does not address how to consider non-functional demands, i.e. how to represent and transform them.

In this paper, we present an extended Model Driven Architecture which includes support for software architecture quality control and resources requirements changes, in the framework of CQ-MDA (Context-aware Quality Model Driven Architecture). Some other works concentrate only on quality system architecture or context-aware system architecture [9, 10]. Our approach focuses on separation of two concerns: the architecture and the implementation contexts. This enables us to support them with

M. Ali Babar and I. Gorton (Eds.): ECSA 2010, LNCS 6285, pp. 441–448, 2010.
© Springer-Verlag Berlin Heidelberg 2010

the elaboration of quality model explicitly and to facilitate the system architecture quality control with the continuous evolution of its context.

We have previously introduced the *ArchRQMM* (ARCHitecture Requirement Quality MetaModel) [3] to address a serious gap in architectural styles quality control. *ArchRQMM* extend the common concepts of Architecture Description Languages (ADLs) with the concepts of quality requirements and quality standards [7]. The *ArchRQMM* targets the quality evaluation and selection of application styles at a high level of abstraction. However, our metamodel does not support the definition of a context-awareness and a resource-awareness metamodel.

The paper is organized as follows. Section 2 proposes the main element of CQ-MDA approach, i.e. *ContextualArchRQMM* metamodel which it is an *ArchRQMM* extension used as support for context model description and quality model definition. Section 3 describes the CQ-MDA itself. Section 4 shows an example of applying CQ-MDA for VideoConferencing system development. Section 4 summarizes related works. Section 5 concludes this article and presents some future works.

## 2    ContextualArchRQMM

The main idea of this proposal is to take into consideration the nonfunctional concerns (*adaptation service, communication protocol, security, QoS, etc.*) of the components by connectors at the software architecture level. Our motivation is to extend *ArchRQMM* with contextual connectors in order to support improved composability of heterogeneous components and to integrate a software architecture quality control in the framework CQ-MDA which unifies all modelling[2] approaches.

### 2.1  Context-Awareness MetaModel

We extend our software architecture metamodel, with a context metamodel (Fig. 1). The goal is to represent context information of system architecture at model level. Context is any information that can be collected from artifact needs, resources capacities and user preferences. *ContextualArchRQMM* uses these informations to perform a software architecture quality evaluation and selection in software development process. In our metamodel we have identified two types of context, i.e., required context (user preferences, artifacts needs) and provided context that encompasses the properties of the execution environment of an application. Context elements are realized through *Context* class, are expressed as QoS properties of the contextual architectural artifacts (*Non-Functional-Prop* class).

### 2.2  Resource-Awareness MetaModel

Fig. 2 depicts a resource-awareness metamodel. The hardware components are mobile devices (Class *Device*) like PDAs, PC Portables or smart phone, are constrained in their resources (memory size, CPU power, bandwith, battery, etc) and act as execution environment for architectural artifact (Class *Artifact*).

Network connections (Class *Node*) connect hardware components having a limited bandwith. A resource-awareness about current usage of processing power, memory,

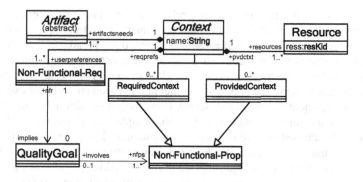

Fig. 1. The context metamodel of ContextualArchRQMM

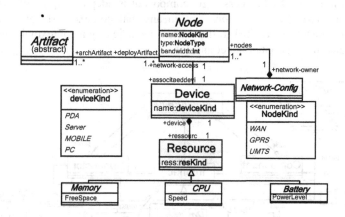

Fig. 2. The resource metamodel of ContextualArchRQMM

network bandwith, etc. is a prerequisite to guarantee a minimum quality of service. Due to heterogeneous architectural components as well as its various communications paradigms (GSM 3G, Bluetooth, ZigBee, etc.) can be specified more easily using a contextual architectural artifact to better support resource-awareness.

## 2.3 Contextual Architectural Artifacts

For an efficient and clear specification of connection points, we have introduced more precise port according to their global roles in a component: the *DataPort*, the *ContextPort*, the *ServiceControlPort*, the *QoSNotificationPort*. The *DataPort* is used to transfer data of any type. The *ContextPort* is responsible for the sending and receiving of the context information available at run-time when the service is active. The *ServiceControlPort* is a standard dedicated port for controlling a service. It allows the service to be (re)started, updated, relocated, stopped and uninstalled. The *QoSNotificationPort* is responsible for sending QoS information to execution platform in order to decide if a service reconfiguration is needed.

As software architecture descriptions rely on a *connector* to express interactions between components, an equivalent abstraction must be used to express a contextual and a heterogeneous interaction (i.e. various interactions paradigms). We extend an architectural connector with a contextual concern in a heterogeneous interaction (see Fig. 3). The traditional connector is not enough to design a contextual and a heterogeneous interaction because the way that a contextual component composes with a business logic component is slightly different from the composition between business logic components only. A contextual (i.e. the adaptation) connector is the central place where the auto-adaptative mechanisms are managed in a connector. Three auto-adaptative mechanisms are distinguished: **communication** (i.e. clarify the connection between various components regarding the communications paradigms), **service adaptation** (i.e. adding, suppression and substitution of adaptation services), and **QoS adaptation** (selecting parameters of service to provide adequate quality to component needs at runtime). The business logic component is adapted explicitly and automatically by a *contextual connector*. This means that context ports of *business logic* components instances, related to the context managed by a contextual connector, are all connected to that contextual connector.

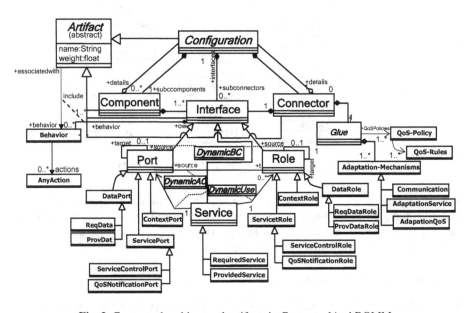

**Fig. 3.** Contextual architectural artifacts in ContextualArchRQMM

# 3   Context-Aware Quality Model Driven Architecture (CQ-MDA)

The general structure of Context-aware Quality – Model Driven Architecture (CQ-MDA) is presented in Fig. 4. The proposed structure consists in five levels representing CIM, PIM, Contextual Platform Independent Model (CPIM), Contextual Platform Specific Model (CPSM), and code. Each level decomposed into three parts: the left part represents architectural artifacts and context concepts; the right part represents quality model and measurements done for these artifacts while the center part represents requirements. Architecture quality should be controlled at each steps of the design. *External requirements* of the system are transformed into *internal ones* for the architecture and its components. *Internal requirements* are needed for assessing designed architecture models. So, particular internal models, being instances of *ContextualArchRQMM* metamodel, are used to assess particular models of CQ-MDA, for example, the requirement reflects both functional and non-functional architects' needs are elaborated on the base of a particular set of criteria's and associated metrics. The software architecture quality model is produced by measurement done for each architectural artifact for a given factor in the context of associated requirement, for a given criteria with associated metric. The quality model is evaluated by the semantic constraints defined by the metamodel.

Two ways of using the *ContextualArchRQMM* metamodel are possible:

-   The first one assumes that the software architecture quality metamodel is used for evaluating an architecture model. The architecture model is tested and validated with the semantic constraints defined by the metamodel. If the verified architecture model gets bad marks then the design process can be stopped or it can go back to the previous stage either to change requirements or to elaborate a different (better) architectural model.
-   The second one, using software architecture quality metamodel considers the case when the metamodel is used for selecting the best architectural model from different choices. In this case the values of a metric are used to classify the models. A metric formula gives a note for the architecture model. The values of the metric function are used to classify the models and to choose the suitable one and we select a first model if we have the same value. After that, the selected architectural model is evaluated by the OCL constraints to remove any quality semantic violation.

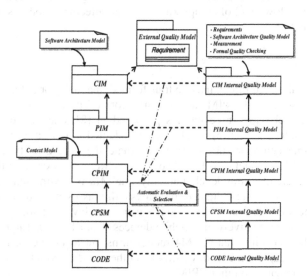

**Fig. 4.** Context-aware Quality Driven Model Architecture

# 4  Case Study: VideoConferencing System

A case study given below is intended to show applicability of CQ-MDA both for evaluation and for selection of the best architectural model from some alternatives. A case study deals with *VideoConferencing* System [13]. The following architect needs and preferences are considered:

- Recording, reviewing user' video and creating respective reports.
- Video should be delivered in quality and in period no longer than one minute from their request.

These demands are processed as external quality requirements. The first one is functional demand while second one is non-functional one. Only non-functional requirements will be considered further.

## 4.1  PIM Level

Several architectural models can be used to design a given system. For the *VideoConferencing* system, the model is designed with *PipesAndFilters* style. The architecture model should be evaluated, tested and validated with the semantic constraints defined by the metamodel.

According to *ContextualArchRQMM*, all these requirements should be associated with a respective architecture quality model with selected quality factors. It is proposed to use the efficiency factor with time-behavior sub-factor and the maintainability factor with modularity, analyzability sub-factors [4].

We have evaluated the PIM model with similar measurements of the whole architecture of the basic metrics (i.e. coupling, cohesion and complexity) [4]. The architectural model provides an acceptable maintainability (a high level of cohesion, a low level of coupling, a low level of complexity). This architectural model is accepted for further transformation.

## 4.2  CPIM Level

PIM software architecture model may be transformed, manually or automatically, into different CPIM models. The PIM model is transformed into four exemplary CPIM models. For time-behavior, three metrics proposed in [8], one of them, *TBM* (the estimated Time Behavior Metric) is selected and adapted in our case. Apart from the evaluation of time behavior sub-factor we evaluate the analyzability sub-factor to select the best CPIM model. In [17] two metrics were proposed for the dynamic adaptivity at the architectural level, but only one, *MaAC* (Minimum architectural Adaptive Cost) was used and validated for analysability assessment in our example.

We have simulated the four CPIMs models using our Java VM simulator and have varied the user (and respectively, the mobile devices) from 1 to 30. Table 1 shows the evaluation results, meaning that CPIM4 model turns out to be the best. Differences can be seen in the adaptation cost of CPIM4 and other CPIMs, which is due to the low adaptation cost compared to other CPIMs.

**Table 1.** CPIM models evaluation results

| CPIM | TBM$^{Benefit}$(ms) | MaAC$^{Cost}$ (artifacts number) |
|------|---------------------|----------------------------------|
| CPIM 1 | 200 ~ 400 | 0 ~ 16 |
| CPIM 2 | 350 ~ 500 | 0 ~ 8 |
| CPIM 3 | 470 ~ 800 | 0 ~ 8 |
| CPIM 4 | 200 ~ 930 | 0 |

# 5 Related Works

The first related area of research are ADLs that have been proposed for representing dynamic architectures including: ACME [12], π-ADL [6], C3 [2] and AADL [1]. However, except for ACME, most ADLs do not support the concept of evaluation function. In addition, most of them are not contextual defined. AADL [1] allows definition of non-functional requirements and their validation at model level. MARTE [15] not treat the problem of heterogeneity by a meta-model which verifies the adequacy of service regarding its context. π-ADL [6] supports dynamic software architecture and evolving software systems. However, contrary to our work, π-ADL does not support contextual connectors and not integrate quality metrics. Recently, Garlan and al. [12] extended ACME ADL in order to support evaluation function in evolution styles and their multiple decision forms. However, this work does not consider exploiting contextual connectors in heterogeneous environment where entities of different nature collaborate: software and hardware components.

The second related area of research are some works involving quality in MDA approach, like QADA (Quality-driven Architecture Design and Quality Analysis) [9] – a methodology targeted at the development of service architectures. Other works involving Context in MDA approach, e.g. Context-aware Model Driven Architecture Model Transformation [11] – a methodology targeted at the development of context-aware applications and other networked systems. These works concentrate only on quality system architecture or context-aware system architecture, while CQ-MDA insisted on the separation of the two concerns: software architecture model and context model. These models based on the quality assessment that enables us to reuse them independently and to achieve a comfortable architectural quality analysis framework.

# 6 Conclusion and Future Work

In this paper we presented *ContextualArchRQMM* metamodel centered on the concept of contextual connector to provide a lightweight support for the definition of some composition facilities such as contextual interfaces at the connector level. In this way, *ContextualArchRQMM* encompasses a reduced set of minor changes. Our goal is a complete ArchRQMM software architecture metamodel that supports structural and contextual description of software systems. Representing components, connectors as first class entities allows us to define the context concerns of each of concept independently and explicitly and to improve composability of heterogeneous components and lowering adaptation cost through self-adaptation policies under resources constraints. We have used our metamodel to extend the MDA's CIM-PIM-PSM with a parallel CPIM-CPSM chain of refinement, to explicitly consider quality and re-sources-awareness while conducting the design and implementation process. We presented an illustrative example to show the applicability of the proposed CQ-MDA approach. The results of the experiments (based on the example of *VideoConferenc-ing system* with four CPIMs) are encouraging. The experiment shows that our ap-proach outperforms two abstractions level in terms of some quality metrics such as adaptation ratio and time response. As future work, we will consider moving our approach to a real execution platform to validate its feasibility.

# References

1. Berthomieu1, B., Bodeveix, J.P., Chaudet, C., Vernadat, F.: Formal Verification of AADL Specifications in the Topcased Environment. In: 14th Ada-Europe International Confer-ence on Reliable Software Technologies, Brest, France, pp. 207–221 (2009)
2. Amirat, A., Oussalah, M.: First-Class Connectors to Support Systematic Construction of Hierarchical Software Architecture. JOT 8(7), 107–130 (2009)
3. Alti, A., Boukerram, A., Smeda, A.: Architectural Styles Quality Evaluation and Selection. In: 9th Conference International NOTERE 2009, Montréal, Canada (2009)
4. Alti, A., Boukerram, A.: QualiStyle: A Tool for Automatic Quality Evaluation and Selec-tion of Architectural Styles. In: 10th Annual Conference on New Technologies of Distrib-uted Systems, pp. 243–248. IEEE Press, Tunisia (2010)
5. Miller, J., Mujerki, J.: MDA Guide, Version 1.0. OMG Technical Report (2003), http://www.omg.org/docs/ptc/03-05-01.pdf
6. Oquendo, F.: $\pi$-ADL: an architecture description language based en the higher order typed $\pi$-calculus for specifying dynamic and mobile software architecture. ACM Software Engi-neering 29(4), 1–13 (2004)
7. Losavio, F., Chirinos, L., Lévy, N., RamdaneCherif, A.: Quality characteristics for soft-ware architecture. JOT 2(2), 133–150 (2003)
8. ISO/IEC 9126-3, Software Engineering Product quality Part 3: Internal metrics (2003)
9. Quality-driven Architecture Design and Quality Analysis, http://virtual.vtt.fi/qada
10. Tarvainen, P.: Adaptability Evaluation at Software Architecture Level. The Open Software Engineering Journal 2, 1–30 (2008)
11. Vale, S., Hammoudi, S.: Context-aware Model Driven Development by Parameterized Transformation. In: 3rd Workshop of MDISIS 2008, pp. 167–180 (2008)
12. Garlan, D., Barnes, J.M., Schmerl, B., Celiku, O.: Evolution Styles: Foundations and Tool Support for Software Architecture Evolution. In: WICSA 2009, pp. 16–25 (2009)
13. Laplace, S., Dalmau, M., Roose, P.: Prise en compte de la qualité de service dans la con-ception et l'exploitation d'applications réparties. In: Workshop GEDSIP@Inforsid (2009)
14. Raibulet, C., Masciadri, L.: Evaluation of Dynamic Adaptivity through Metrics: an Achievable Target? In: WICSA 2009, pp. 65–71 (2009)
15. Gérard, S., Petriu, D., Medina, J.: MARTE: A New Standard for Modeling and Analysis of Real-Time and Embedded Systems. In: 19th Euromicro Conference on Real-Time Sys-tems, Pisa, Italy (2007)

# Many to Many Service Discovery: A First Approach

Anthony Hock-koon and Mourad Oussalah

University of Nantes, LINA Laboratory
2 rue de la Houssiniere, 44322 NANTES, France
{anthony.hock-koon,mourad.oussalah}@univ-nantes.fr
http://www.lina.univ-nantes.fr/

**Abstract.** Dynamic service discovery is one of the main concepts which define the Service Oriented Architectures (SOA). This mechanism ensures loosely coupled services. It supports the reusability of services and the flexibility of applications. This paper provides a new service discovery approach which enhances the number of services potentially discovered and thus, it multiplies the number of candidate services. This multiplication ensures a better selection of the most suitable services and more alternatives is case of failures.

**Keywords:** SOA, Service Composition, Service Discovery.

## 1 Introduction

Service Oriented Architecture (SOA) [8] relies on the service composition which can be divided in three phases: service discovery, service selection and service composition. According to the user's needs the composition system has to discover the set of candidate services which can realize his task; then it selects the most suitable ones following the context (user or system); finally it defines the collaboration between them in order to realize the targeted application. Thereby, the service discovery step is a central mechanism in the SOA paradigm. It is the base towards the dynamic definition of a new composition and it is directly involved in its quality.

The existing service discovery algorithms can be grouped in two approaches [4], *one to one matching* (1-1) [2,11] and *one to many matching* (1-N) [4,1]. The 1-1 approach identifies one abstract service to exactly one concrete service. The 1-N approach identifies one abstract service to one concrete service or to many concrete services which coordinate their actions to realize the targeted service. In this paper, we intend to provide a first step towards the definition of a *many to many matching* (M-N). Our approach relies on a semantic organization between some sets of available services.

The remainder of this paper continues as follows. Section 2 deals with the existing types of service discovery. We present the motivations of our M-N approach and its contributions to the SOA paradigm. In section 3, we define this M-N approach and its related mechanisms. Section 4 concludes and discusses future work.

M. Ali Babar and I. Gorton (Eds.): ECSA 2010, LNCS 6285, pp. 449–456, 2010.

# 2    Service Discovery Overview

Service discovery is a main step of the matching between abstract services and concrete services. Abstract services represent the descriptions of the sought services. These descriptions are extracted from the expression of the user's task which is combined with the user's preferences. Concrete services represent the existing services which are available for possible invocations of their capabilities.

## 2.1    Related Works

There are numerous works on service discovery which focus on different problems such as trust orientation [6], context awareness [9] or user's preferences [5]. However all of them can be grouped in two types of approaches [4], *one to one matching* (1-1) and *one to many matching* (1-N).

The 1-1 approach identifies one abstract service to exactly one concrete service. We distinguish between *strong matching* and *loose matching*. The strong matching represents the exact correspondence between the needs and the available services (Figure 1:L-a). The loose matching represents the ability to discover non exact solutions which can be interesting for the user. These solutions represent 1) the services which can provide more capabilities than the required ones (Figure 1:L-b) or 2) the lower quality services which are identified according to a fixed coefficient of acceptance (Figure 1:L-c).

The 1-N approach is the enhancement of the previous one. Most of them only focus on the entries defined by the abstract service [4,1]. They intend to establish a composition of available services which can fulfill the abstract service's requirements. The different approaches can be classified following their handled types of compositions. We identify three types of potentially identified compositions: *sequential, parallel* and *complex*. A sequential composition (Figure 1:R-a) is a chain of services which are sequentially executed to realize the abstract service. A parallel composition (Figure 1:R-b) is a set of independent services where each of them realizes a specific part of the capabilities required by the abstract service. A complex composition (Figure 1:R-c) represents a combination of sequential and parallel identifications. Moreover, each of them can be combined with *strong matching* or *loose matching*.

## 2.2    Towards M-N Matching

The M-N matching appears as the logical enhancement of the service discovery. This approach allows for discovering new compositions of concrete services which

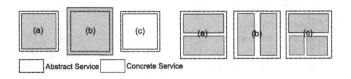

**Fig. 1.** Left: 1-1 matching; Right: 1-N matching

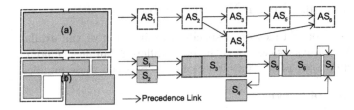

**Fig. 2.** Left:M-N matching; Right: Redefinition of the user's task

are not detectable by the previous matchings. The multiplication of candidate compositions has some potential benefits on the quality of service discovery and selection. According to our knowledge, none of existing works in the SOA paradigm provides its specification. Therefore, we intend to define the theoretical concepts involved in the M-N approach and we clarify its contributions.

We introduce the notion of *cross boundaries* concrete service. This type of concrete service realizes a set of functionalities which are distributed among different abstract services. It is the main concept which defines the M-N matching. In Figure 2:L-a, we show a 2-1 matching where two abstract services are realized by one concrete service. This new concept of services can be easily combined with *strong matching* and *loose matching*, and with the different types of compositions (sequential, parallel, complex). In Figure 2:L-b, two abstract services are realized by a complex composition of five services which includes one cross boundaries service (concrete service 1). Three services were identified with strong matchings (1, 2, 3), and two with loose matchings (4, 5) where (4) is a lower quality and (5) provides more functions than required.

The first goals of the M-N approach is the identification of additional concrete solutions which can fulfill the abstract services. More solutions there are, better the service selection is. The probability of finding adequate concrete services is higher.

In addition to these quantitative benefits related to the number of solutions, the M-N approach could have a significant impact on the quality of a composite. On the contrary to the 1-1 and 1-N approaches which focus on each abstract services one by one, the M-N approach takes account of the overall composition sought by the architect. The quality of the concrete realization is not limited to the individual quality of each abstract service instantiations but it can include a global evaluation of the composition. Some evaluation metrics of compositions [7,10] can be reused to drive the M-N matching and they help the selection of the best identified composition. Figure 2:R shows a user's task defined by a composition of abstract services and its concrete realization identified by a M-N approach. These compositions are represented by a simplified *collaboration schema* [3] which only focuses on the invocation order of the services: AS2 is invoked just after AS1. A complete collaboration schema handles workflow and dataflow between services. The collaboration schema of the abstract services is different from the one between the concrete services, this illustrates a redefinition of user's task.

# 3    Specifying the M-N Approach

Our M-N approach relies on a specific classification of the available concrete services. All these services are gathered in different families (*family of services*), and we define a set of semantic relationships between these families.

## 3.1    Family of Services

A family of services represents a set of services which are semantically close. They have the same kind of capabilities and thus, they share the same ontology of domain [11] related to some specific activities. An ontology of domain is used as description of a family. For example a family Data_conversion can gather different services which ensures money conversions, metrics conversions and so forth. The use of family ensures a faster location of equivalent services.

Moreover, we define three binary semantic relationships between families: the *inheritance link*, the *equivalence link* and the *union link*.

*Inheritance link*: derives from object orientation. A family $A$ inherits from a family $B$ implies that the $A$'s ontology of domain is a specialization of $B$'s ones. For exemple, an ontology luxury_car_rental is a specialization of the ontology car_rental. The services included in the set of the first domain realize at least all the expected capabilities of the second domain. This can be understood as a familial lineage.

*Equivalence link*: represents a functional equivalence between two families. A family $A$ is equivalent to a family $B$ implies that $A$'s services and $B$'s services realize the same functionalities. It represents an equivalence of ontological domains. For example, two ontologies car_rental (english) and location_voiture (french) represent the same domain. However their syntactic description are different, their semantics are identical and their services realize the same functionalities. This can be understood as a brotherly relationship.

The *equivalence link* is transitive, i.e. $A$ is equivalent to $B$ and $B$ is equivalent to $C$ imply that $A$ is equivalent to $C$.

*Union link*: represents some possible compositions between the services of two different families. It expresses the semantical matching between their inputs and outputs. Two families linked by an *union link* can be viewed as a new family. This can be understood as a marital link which defines a new family in the point of view of this "couple" i.e. the composition of services.

The *union link* is transitive, for example two *union links* which associate $A$ and $B$, and $B$ and $C$ can defined a greater family which gathers all of three.

The choice of the term family and the related concepts of lineage (*inheritance link*), brotherhood (*equivalence link*) and marriage (*union link*) ensure a better natural understanding of our approach. Following these semantic relationships between families we are able to define some graphs of families.

## 3.2    Graph of Families

The three semantic links previously defined are used to organize the different families. They allow for building some graphs of families. A graph of families is used to provide a classification of the available services.

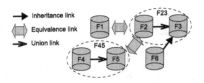

**Fig. 3.** Example: Graph of families

Figure 3 shows an example of graph. This graph is composed by six families which gather all the services. Two *union links* associate $F2$ and $F3$, and $F4$ and $F5$ which define respectively the families $F23$ and $F45$. $F1$ is equivalent to $F23$ and $F45$ is equivalent to $F2$. $F6$ inherits from $F3$. This particular organization and the transitivity of the links ensure other equivalences. For example, $F2$ can potentially be replaced by the union of $F4$ and $F5$ ($F45$) which can defined a new family from $F45$ and $F3$ following the union link between $F2$ and $F3$. This new family is equivalent to $F1$. These complex identifications of equivalences between families are the base of our M-N discovery approach.

A graph of families mixes two levels of relationships. The first level is defined by the semantical equivalence between the ontologies of domains (*inheritance link* and *equivalence link*). We are at the family level. The second level is defined by the ability of composition between available services. This allows for identifying concrete compositions of services. We are at the service level.

These two levels of relationships imply a two levels management: adding or removing services, and adding or removing families.

*Adding services*: a new service has to be registered in the graph of families in order to be discovered and used. Its classification relies on its description of service and this process can be divided in two steps. First, the system has to identify the ontology of domain at which the service can be associated and it is registered in the corresponding family. Then, some *union links* have to be defined between this family and the other ones according to the added service's entries.

A service which becomes unavailable or which is no more supported by its provider has to be removed from the graph. Therefore, the system removes this service from its family and all the related *union links* are deleted.

*Adding families*: the adding of a new family corresponds to the definition of *inheritance* and *equivalence* links between this family and the existing ones. These new links rely on the use of semantic and ontologies which define the domains of applications. Their definitions can partially be automated nevertheless, most of them have to be handled by a human's expertise which decides how to connect the new family.

In general, it is not very useful to remove a family from the graph even if it is empty. Indeed, a family expresses a semantic concept which is automated with difficulty. Moreover, the semantic links associated with this family can be useful to define multiple complex equivalences. The human's expertise has to be stored in order to be reused.

This concept of graph is the cornerstone of our M-N approach.

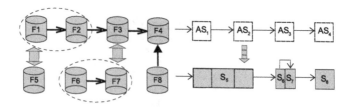

**Fig. 4.** Example: Left available graph of families; Right user's task redefinition

## 3.3   Identifying Concrete Compositions

The notion of family and the associated semantic links are used to organize the services which are available in the system. In order to illustrate our identification process, we use an example. The graph of families presented in the figure 4:L is the representation of the system's available services. Figure 4:R(up) shows the representation of a sought task expressed by the user's needs. This task is described by a composition of abstract services. So as to facilitate the understanding of our method we assume that there is a direct matching between the semantic descriptions of the abstract services and the ontologies of domains associated with the existing families. Therefore, the abstract service $AS1$ can be realized by one concrete service of the family $F1$ (and respectively between $ASi$ and $Fi$).

The discovery algorithm is based on the descriptions of services which are associated with the composition of abstract services extracted from the user's task.

First, it intends to make a direct matching (1-1) between the functional ontologies provided by the descriptions of services and the available ontologies of domains associated with the families. In our example, there are some direct matchings between the couples $(AS1, F1)$, $(AS2, F2)$, $(AS3, F3)$, $(AS4, F4)$. After the identification of the appropriate families, the system tries to define a composition between their registered concrete services. This composition is defined following the *union links*. Finally, the system selects the most suitable composition according to the user's preferences.

However, we can imagine that the available concrete services which are registered by the identified families are no more available or their quality of services is not enough according to the selection criteria. Therefore, the system has to identify some alternative solutions. Now, the system will focus on the family level and the semantic relationships defined by the *inheritance link* and the *equivalence link*.

We rule that the families $F1$ and $F2$ do not have the suitable concrete services. However, the union link between them (which is parallel to the sought composition $AS1$ to $AS2$) defines a new family in the graph. This new family is equivalent to the family $F5$. Then, the system selects in $F5$ the most suitable service according to the preferences. This service has to be able to be composed with the concrete realization of $AS3$. The system identifies a 2-1 matching.

Moreover, the same problem can occur with the family $F3$. Following the equivalence link, some alternatives can be provided by a composition of two concrete services which belong to the families $F6$ and $F7$. The system identifies a 1-2 matching.

A last equivalence can be identified by the inheritance link between $F4$ and $F8$. $F8$'s services realize at least the same functionalities as the $F4$'s ones. They are specialized versions or they have more capabilities. All these alternatives are proposed to the user which has the final decision of the services uses.

Thereby, the composition of abstract services is redefined following the graph of families. Figure 4:R (down) shows the redefinition of the task. However the global matching is 4-4, the structure of the composition is totally different where $S5$ is a concrete service from the family $F5$ and respectively $S6$, $S7$ and $S8$ from $F6$, $F7$ and $F8$.

### 3.4   Toward the Automated Definition of New Families

Our M-N discovery approach relies on a graph of families which has to exist in the system. The specification of all the families and their semantic relationships depend on a human expertise. Indeed, our concept of families is limited by the locks which are encountered by the research area of the ontologies. Therefore, the instantiation of the graph is automated with difficulty. However, we draft a method which allows for dynamic enlargement of a graph of families by reusing the user's tasks. In fact, a user's task defines a complex composition of functionalities in order to realize some high level goals. These goals can defined as new ontology of domains which are associated with a family. Some equivalence links can be specified between this family and the existing ones which were selected for implementing the concrete composite. The composite service's description is registered in this new family. Note that the user's level of comprehension has to be trusted.

In our example (Figure 4), the user's task defines a new family. According to the semantic matching (between $AS1$ and $F1$ and respectively $AS2$, $AS3$, $AS4$ and $F2$, $F3$, $F4$) this new family is equivalent to families $F1$, $F2$, $F3$, $F4$ which are linked by different *union links*.

## 4   Conclusion

In this paper, we present a many-to-many (M-N) service discovery approach. We introduce the notion of family of services which ensures an organized repartition of the available services. The M-N algorithm enhances the potential of alternatives and thus, it reinforces the composite's quality and robustness. Moreover it can be used as development guidelines by proposing some redefinitions of the collaboration schema initially targeted by the architect following the graph of families. Our M-N approach can be combined with works on the composition's quality to provide a dynamic selection of the most suitable task's redefinition following some criteria such as coupling or cohesion [7,10].

In future work, we will focus on the evaluation of our approach's cost. This method is a first step toward a real many-to-many matchings which gives some immediate benefits on numerous aspects (service's quality, robustness, coupling and so forth) nevertheless a prototype still needs to be provided.

# References

1. Beauche, S., Poizat, P.: Automated service composition with adaptive planning. In: Bouguettaya, A., Krueger, I., Margaria, T. (eds.) ICSOC 2008. LNCS, vol. 5364, pp. 530–537. Springer, Heidelberg (2008)
2. Gu, X., Nahrstedt, K., Yu, B.: Spidernet: An integrated peer-to-peer service composition framework. In: HPDC, pp. 110–119 (2004)
3. Hock-koon, A., Oussalah, M.: Expliciting a composite service by a metamodeling approach. In: RCIS (2010)
4. Kalasapur, S., Kumar, M., Shirazi, B.A.: Dynamic service composition in pervasive computing. TPDS 18 (2007)
5. Kwak, D., Lee, J., Kim, D., Lee, Y.: User care preference-based semantic service discovery in a ubiquitous environment. In: Nielsen, M., Kucera, A., Miltersen, P.B., Palamidessi, C., Tuma, P., Valencia, F.D. (eds.) SOFSEM 2009. LNCS, vol. 5404, pp. 365–375. Springer, Heidelberg (2009)
6. Li, L., Wang, Y., Lim, E.P.: Trust-oriented composite service selection and discovery. In: Baresi, L., Chi, C.-H., Suzuki, J. (eds.) ICSOC-ServiceWave 2009. LNCS, vol. 5900, pp. 50–67. Springer, Heidelberg (2009)
7. Ma, Q., Zhou, N., Zhu, Y., Wang, H.: Evaluating service identification with design metrics on business process decomposition. In: IEEE SCC, pp. 160–167 (2009)
8. OASIS: Reference architecture for service oriented architecture 1.0 (April 2008), http://docs.oasis-open.org/soa-rm/soa-ra/v1.0/soa-ra-pr-01.pdf
9. Patel, P., Chaudhary, S.: Context aware semantic service discovery. In: SERVICES II, pp. 1–8 (2009)
10. Perepletchikov, M., Ryan, C., Frampton, K., Tari, Z.: Coupling metrics for predicting maintainability in service-oriented designs. In: Australian Software Engineering Conference, pp. 329–340 (2007)
11. Verma, K., Gomadam, K., Sheth, A.P., Miller, J.A., Wu, Z.: The meteor-s approache for configuring and executing dynamic web processes. LSDIS Lab, University of Georgia Technical Rport (2005), http://lsdis.cs.uga.edu/projects/meteor-s/

# Communicating Architectural Knowledge: Requirements for Software Architecture Knowledge Management Tools

Widura Schwittek and Stefan Eicker

paluno – The Ruhr Institute for Software Technology
University of Duisburg-Essen
Universitätsstr. 9, 45141 Essen, Germany
{widura.schwittek,stefan.eicker}@paluno.de

**Abstract.** Architecting is a communication intensive task in which architectural knowledge is shared between the architect and the stakeholders. The software architect's communicative action is often conducted face-to-face, e.g. in presentations and workshops. A software architecture documentation as a carrier of explicit architectural knowledge can also be seen as an architect's communicative action. This perspective opens the door for treating a software architecture documentation as an expression of an asynchronous knowledge communication process enabling the application of principles from communication theory. In this paper this perspective is taken and specific requirements are derived for software architecture knowledge management tools with respect to the context-oriented communication model.

**Keywords:** software architecture, architectural knowledge, knowledge communication.

## 1 Introduction

Architecting is a communication intensive task in which the architecture serves as a vehicle for communication among stakeholders [1]. Developers must understand their work assignments it requires of them, testers must understand the task structure it imposes on them, management must understand scheduling implications it suggests, and so forth [2].

The shift to viewing a software architecture as a set of architectural design decisions [3, 4] brought the notion of architectural knowledge to the software architecture research community, in which it is defined as "architectural design decisions + design" [5]. This shift underlines that communicating a software architecture is a knowledge intensive process, which occurs often during the development of a software architecture and therefore should be considered adequately.

Communicating knowledge takes a lot of effort because not only facts are communicated, but also their emphasis, underlying assumptions and problem perspectives. Unlike the sole transfer of information, this kind of communication is called "knowledge communication" [6], which aims at creating a common ground between two communication partners. Communicating architectural knowledge is even more tedious because a software architecture is intangible and at first resides only in the

M. Ali Babar and I. Gorton (Eds.): ECSA 2010, LNCS 6285, pp. 457–463, 2010.
© Springer-Verlag Berlin Heidelberg 2010

architect's head. It needs advanced communication skills to achieve a common understanding of the architecture between all stakeholders. Stakeholders from different functional domains with different backgrounds and mindsets speak different languages, which make successful communication even more difficult.

Much research work has been spent on tool support for the architecting process and especially on the subject of sharing architectural knowledge [7, 8, 9, 10]. But to the knowledge of the author there has been no work on the success factors of computer-mediated communication processes underlying many architectural knowledge sharing processes. The research work behind this paper tries to fill this gap recognizing the importance of successful communication for creating a common ground between the architect and the stakeholders, and which otherwise would have a negative impact on software architecting and maintenance processes. The focus of this work lies on software architecture documentations viewed as the expression of a central architectural knowledge communication process. The results are high-level requirements for software architecture knowledge management tools to better support successful communication of architectural knowledge during all software lifecycle phases and to relieve the architect in his role as a "communicator".

This paper is structured as follows: In chapter two, the context-oriented communication model is explained and the rationale behind its selection. An understanding of how computer-mediated communication works is created and the significance of the different communication contexts is highlighted. In chapter three, derived high-level requirements from these insights are presented. In chapter four, a conclusion is made and an outlook is given to further research following this paper.

# 2  Computer-Mediated Knowledge Communication

The field of knowledge communication originating from communication theory tries to find answers to the question how knowledge should be communicated, in order to create a common understanding between two communication partners. In this process the sender has to create a plan, how to construct an expression regarding his target audience choosing the right form and language. While knowledge becomes information in the moment it is expressed, the recipient has to reconstruct the knowledge by integrating the information into his existing knowledge. This constructivist understanding of knowledge is central within the context-oriented communication model [11]. Originally created to explain misunderstandings in computer-mediated communication situations, it was later used to derive requirements for CSCW (Computer Supported Collaborative Work) systems [12]. This model is based on the work of Ungeheuer [13] and the neurobiological insights of Maturana and Varela [14]. While Ungeheuer dealt with the significance of the context in communication processes, Maturana and Varela came to the conclusion, that living systems always perceive their environment through filters and always constructing their own reality.

As its name already says, the importance of the context for creating a common understanding through communication is taken into account and should be explained in detail in the following.

Figure 1 depicts the elements and their interplay of the context-oriented communication model. To create a common understanding between two communication

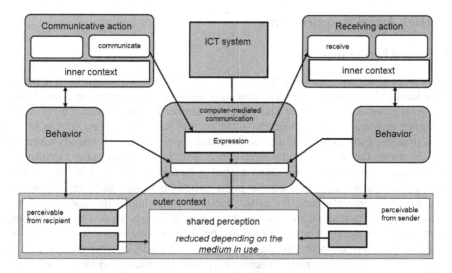

**Fig. 1.** Context-oriented communication model translated from [12]

partners not only the proper expression of an idea is important, but also what additional context information should be given, in order to allow the recipient to interpret the expression correctly. The context-oriented communication model differentiates two kinds of contexts.

The inner context represents the personal existing knowledge, which is not directly accessible by other individuals. The expression of an idea is biased by the inner context of the sender, meaning by his personal background, his attitude, prejudices, values, educational history etc. In order to support the recipient's understanding of the expression, the sender has to check his personal impression of the recipient against congruencies between the inner context of him and the recipient's inner context. Any expected differences between those two inner contexts must be compensated by expressing or referencing those parts and making them explicit.

The outer context consists of everything that is not part of the current communication expression, such as the facial expression, gesture and behavior, but also information and knowledge, which has been shared before. It is divided into things, which are or have been potentially perceivable by the communication partners and into things, which actually are perceived by both communication partners (shared perception). In computer-mediated communication processes the outer context is reduced depending on which medium is used. E.g. using a chat system the outer context is reduced to characters leaving no room to validate the interpretation of the expression against elements from the outer context. While this synchronous type of communication allows immediate check-backs and feedbacks to secure communication, this is not possible in asynchronous communication situations.

Communicating architectural knowledge through a software architecture documentation represents such an asynchronous communication situation. This short introduction into computer-mediated communication should sensitize the reader to consider both inner and outer context, if knowledge communication should be supported adequately.

# 3  High-Level Requirements

## 3.1  Avoid Loss of Inner Context

Knowledge is always bound to a person. If knowledge is separated from a person, more knowledge – part of the inner context – needs to be explicated to raise chances of a good reconstruction of that knowledge by another person. Research work around capturing architectural design decisions to prevent knowledge vaporization [3, 15] show, that the inner context of a communication process is in part already taken into account within the architecture research community: It is not only about capturing the design decisions itself, but also about capturing its rationale, considered alternatives, organizational constraints at a certain point in time and other situative information, that span the context around the actual decision. Referring to the discussion about context-oriented communication in chapter two, it is already known how to communicate decisions the right way. But architectural knowledge does not only comprise decisions and there are probably more measures to be made, in order to overcome the other problems resulting from asynchronicity and computer-mediation. These other aspects are discussed in the following with respect to the context-oriented communication model.

## 3.2  Avoid Loss of Outer Context

As described in chapter two, the conception of an expression is biased by the impression the sender has got of the recipient. He therefore has to estimate the foreknowledge of the recipient. The same applies for interpreting the expression on the recipient's side. During this process the recipient is biased by the impression he has about the sender. Thus having a good impression of your communication partner helps to communicate effectively and reduce misunderstandings. Its creation should therefore be supported on both sides, especially when it comes to computer-mediated communication in which the outer context is reduced depending on the type of media used.

Looking at the research field of CSCW a lot of research work has been spent on this topic labeled "awareness research". In this field awareness is described as "an understanding of the activities of others, which provides a context for your own activity" [16]. Awareness modules in modern CSCW systems offer information about the presence, availability, working activities (e.g. last opened document) etc. of other users. Another source for information, which might enrich the creation of a partner's impression is social software. Social software makes the weak and strong ties of social relationships visible, offering profile information about skills and working experience. Hence, social software supports building up a proper impression of a person and making communication more effective on both sides. Furthermore social software encourages spontaneous and informal synchronous communication, but this is not subject of this paper.

Software architecture research already gave birth to a knowledge sharing community software [17]. But while recognizing the importance of communication, interaction and the outer context for knowledge sharing processes, it focuses on networking and making use of the network. It fulfills not all requirements described in this paper and therefore does not explicitly support knowledge communication processes the way we presented it in this paper.

## 3.3  Support Asynchronous Communication

Asynchronous communication comes with two problems: On the sender's side it is not possible to check, if the conceptualization of an expression was good enough. On the recipient's side it is not possible to validate the interpretation of an expression. The best way to communicate knowledge is face-to-face, being able to establish a common understanding through high interaction. Asynchronous communication has to compensate this.

Asynchronous communication requires even more to focus on the target audience, because there is no possibility to adapt the expression instantaneously. Through the concept of architectural views [18] this requirement is already being applied in software architecture documentations. The concept allows creating viewpoints and instantiating views for different groups of stakeholders to satisfy their demand for information. Views only display specific aspects of an architecture which leads to reduced complexity and a language and notation the target audience understands. The context-oriented communication model speaks of "hide the known and irrelevant" referring to the fact, that having more information at hand does not automatically mean being more informed [13].

Due to the fact that questions on the recipient's side cannot be asked instantaneously, context-oriented communication suggests multiple expressions of the same idea helping to reduce room for interpretation. Mass media like newspapers and magazines fulfill this requirement by not only providing textual representations but also additional images. In software architecture documentations UML diagrams support textual representations and vice versa.

Other visual representations beside the well-known UML diagrams exist and should be considered when offering multiple expressions. E.g. in [19] a proposal is made for different visualizations of architectural design decisions.

## 3.4  The Dynamic Architecture Documentation

On the basis of the insights offered by the context-oriented communication model we propose the concept of a dynamic architecture documentation. By this we mean to simulate synchronicity and the ability to interact instantaneously between two communication partners. This is achieved by certain mechanisms on the sender's and recipient's side.

First, the recipient should be able to bring expressions into a form he chooses and understands best. While an architectural view offers a starting point for a stakeholder of the target group, a dynamic architecture documentation makes it possible to fine tune his "personal" view. This is realized through filters allowing hiding and showing different aspects of an architecture and through transformers to switch to different visual representation forms or to merge them. Second, the sender should be supported in segmenting and semantically enriching an architecture documentation, enabling the functionality on the recipient's side. One way of realization is through the concept of tags. In [9] a word plug-in is presented that allows tagging parts of the document. One use case of this approach is to list all design decisions. All parts of the document, which have been tagged as a design decisions are collected and shown in an aggregated form.

A general requirement for the concept of a dynamic architecture documentation is the provisioning of a repository storing all explicit architectural knowledge, which can be queried the way described above.

One tool originating from architecture research is already close to the realization of the concept of a dynamic architecture documentation: The Knowledge Architect [20] is database-driven and offers a repository, which is queried by a Knowledge Translator component which transforms generic architectural knowledge into a more domain specific form the stakeholder understands. The stakeholder however is not able to configure the Knowledge Translator to fine tune his view, but has to stick to the predefined views the component offers.

# 4  Conclusions and Future Work

In this paper a communication theory perspective is taken, in order to consider a software architecture documentation as an expression of an asynchronous communication process, through which architectural knowledge is shared. With this perspective high-level requirements have been derived for architecture knowledge management tools. The context-oriented communication model has been used to explain how knowledge is communicated and the importance of the inner and outer context has been highlighted. It provided the necessary conceptual framework to look at concepts from other research fields like CSCW, social media and visualization and to make them usable in software architecture research. The result consists of high-level requirements, measures and hints to concepts and tools, already fulfilling parts of these high-level requirements.

The research work presented in this paper is not finished and open research questions remain. These will be addressed in the next step of our research work. One of these questions is, to look more into detail, how existing software architecture knowledge management tools cope with knowledge communication, and how the high-level requirements proposed in this paper can be refined and put into practice. Another open question is, whether these high-level requirements really have an impact on the success of knowledge communication processes and whether they really lead to a better common understanding between the architect and other stakeholders. Therefore an empirical evaluation is planned for which a software prototype will be used. It is based on the Generic Views Concept [21] and fulfills all requirements of a dynamic architecture documentation. The prototype concentrates on delivering user defined and concern related on-demand-views, while still missing other features like avoiding the loss of the outer context, which has been demanded in this paper. Thus, further development of the prototype is planned, while it is not yet clear if it will result in a standalone application or in an enhancement of existing architecture knowledge management tools.

# References

1. Dingsøyr, T., van Vliet, H.: Introduction to Software Architecture and Knowledge Management. In: Ali Babar, M., Dingsøyr, T., Lago, P., van Vliet, H. (eds.) Software Architecture Knowledge Management. Theory and Practice, pp. 1–17. Springer, Heidelberg (2009)
2. Bass, L., Clements, P., Kazman, R.: Software architecture in practice. Addison-Wesley, Boston (2003)

3. Bosch, J.: Software Architecture: The next step. In: Oquendo, F., Warboys, B.C., Morrison, R. (eds.) EWSA 2004. LNCS, vol. 3047, pp. 194–199. Springer, Heidelberg (2004)

4. Jansen, A., Bosch, J.: Software architecture as a set of architectural design decisions. In: Proceedings of the 5th IEEE/IFIP Working Conference on Software Architecture (WICSA), pp. 109–119. IEEE Computer Society, Los Alamitos (2005)

5. Kruchten, P., Lago, P., van Vliet, H.: Building up and Reasoning about Architectural Knowledge. In: Hofmeister, C., Crnković, I., Reussner, R. (eds.) QoSA 2006. LNCS, vol. 4214, pp. 43–58. Springer, Heidelberg (2006)

6. Reinhardt, R., Eppler, M.J.: Wissenskommunikation in Organisationen. Methoden, Instrumente, Theorien. Springer, Heidelberg (2004)

7. Ali-Babar, M., Gorton, I., Jeffery, R.: A tool for managing software architecture knowledge. In: 2nd Workshop on Sharing and Reusing architectural Knowledge – Architecture, Rationale, and Design Intent (SHARK/ADI). ACM, Minneapolis (2007)

8. Farenhorst, R., Lago, P., van Vliet, H.: EAGLE: Effective tool support for sharing architectural knowledge. Int. J. Cooper. Inform. Syst. 16(3/4), 413–437 (2007)

9. Jansen, A., Avgeriou, P., van der Ven, J.S.: Enriching software architecture documentation. J. Syst. Software 82(8), 1232–1248 (2009)

10. Tang, A., Avgeriou, P., Jansen, A., Capilla, R., Ali-Babar, M.: A comparative study of architecture knowledge management tools. J. Syst. Software 83(3), 352–370 (2010)

11. Herrmann, T., Misch, A.: Anforderungen an lehrunterstützende Kooperationssysteme aus kommunikationstheoretischer Sicht. In: Schwill, A. (ed.) Informatik und Schule, pp. 58–71. Informatik aktuell. Springer, Heidelberg (1999)

12. Kienle, A.: Integration von Wissensmanagement und kollaborativem Lernen durch technisch unterstützte Kommunikationsprozesse. Dissertation. Lohmar, Eul (2003)

13. Ungeheuer, G.: Vor-Urteile über Sprechen, Mitteilen, Verstehen. In: Ungeheuer, G. (ed.) Kommunikationstheoretische Schriften, vol. 1, pp. 229–338, Rader, Aachen, (1982)

14. Maturana, H.R., Varela, F.J.: Tree of Knowledge: Biological Roots of Human Understanding. Shambhala Publications, Boston (1987)

15. Tyree, J., Akerman, A.: Architecture Decisions: Demystifying Architecture. IEEE Software 22(2), 19–27 (2005)

16. Dourish, P., Bellotti, V.: Awareness and Coordination in Shared Workspaces. In: Turner, J., Kraut, R. (eds.) CSCW 1992 - Sharing perspectives. Proceedings of the Conference on Computer-Supported Cooperative Work, pp. 107–114. ACM, New York (1992)

17. Lago, P.: Establishing and Managing Knowledge Sharing Networks. In: Ali Babar, M., Dingsøyr, T., Lago, P., van Vliet, H. (eds.) Software Architecture Knowledge Management. Theory and Practice, pp. 113–131. Springer, Heidelberg (2009)

18. Kruchten, P.: The 4+1 View Model of Architecture. IEEE Software 12(6), 42–50 (1995)

19. Lee, L., Kruchten, P.: Visualizing software architectural design decisions. In: Morrison, R., Balasubramaniam, D., Falkner, K. (eds.) ECSA 2008. LNCS, vol. 5292, pp. 359–362. Springer, Heidelberg (2008)

20. Liang, P., Jansen, A., Avgeriou, P.: Collaborative Software Architecting through Knowledge Sharing. In: Finkelstein, A., van der Hoek, A., Grundy, J., Mistrìk, I., Whitehead, J. (eds.) Collaborative Software Engineering, pp. 343–367. Springer, Heidelberg (2010)

21. Eicker, S., Jung, R., Schwittek, W., Spies, T.: SOA Generic Views - In the Eye of the Beholder. In: Congress on Services - Part I, SERVICES 2008, pp. 479–486. IEEE Computer Society, Piscataway (2008)

# Specifying Loose Coupling from Existing Service Composition Approaches

Anthony Hock-koon and Mourad Oussalah

University of Nantes, LINA Laboratory
2 rue de la Houssiniere, 44322 NANTES, France
{anthony.hock-koon,mourad.oussalah}@univ-nantes.fr
http://www.lina.univ-nantes.fr/

**Abstract.** The loose coupling notion associated with the service composition is a key concept which defines the Service Oriented Architectures (SOA) paradigm. Given that this notion is intuitively understood, its definition lacks formalism. Moreover, the existing evaluation metrics are limited and cannot take into account all the specificities of the SOA's composition mechanism. In this paper, we present a set of metrics based on a clear definition of the loose coupling. We combine these metrics in a formula which calculates a weight. This weight allows for clear measurements of a composite's coupling.

**Keywords:** SOA, Composite Service, Loose Coupling, Metrics.

## 1 Introduction

Service Oriented Architecture (SOA) [15] is a software development paradigm which provides a set of mechanisms to ensure *an homogeneous exposition and use of heterogeneous resources*. One of these mechanisms is the service composition. It allows combinations of available resources exposed as services. Many models were developed in order to automatically produce new compositions of services in a secure manner. In this context, the underlying issue of *what makes good compositions of services* is critical for evaluating the existing composition approaches.

The SOA paradigm intends to generalize a loose coupling relationship between reused services in a composition. In fact, their independences ensure immediate improvements on the composition's flexibility (localized failures, easier replacement of services, etc.). However, the lack of formalism in the definition of loose coupling in SOA and the limitations of existing metrics do not allow its clear evaluation. Therefore, we propose a definition of this notion which allows for the specification of evaluation metrics. These metrics are combined into a global formula which evaluates the coupling of a composition of services.

Section 2 deals with the motivations and contributions of a new coupling definition. Section 3 presents this definition and its related metrics. Section 4 presents a formula which reuses the previous metrics. Section 5 concludes and discusses future work.

M. Ali Babar and I. Gorton (Eds.): ECSA 2010, LNCS 6285, pp. 464–471, 2010.

## 2   Related Work

Formal specifications of the SOA paradigm in existence (listed in [6]) present the loose coupling notion as essential in a composition of services. The reduction of the dependencies between constituent services gives immediate benefits to the composition's flexibility. This intuitive understanding of the loose coupling principles is the only definition provided by these specifications. Moreover, existing works in SOA which provide evaluation metrics for loose coupling are not able to evaluate all the mechanisms introduced by the diversity of composition approaches. They cannot give a clear comparison between them.

In [18,9], the authors reuse established metrics which come from the object-oriented (OO) design [5,3]. These metrics have been proved effective for evaluating the OO design structure. However, they focus on the implementation-level concepts of classes and thus they are unsuitable for SOA [17]. The methods proposed by [7,13] rely on message exchanges (number of messages, complexity of the exchanged data, etc.). They only focus on physical aspect of an instantiated composition. Thus, they do not take account of all the high level mechanisms which can be supported by this instantiated composition. Other works exist in CBSE such as [21,10]. However, they cannot be applied directly since there are some theoretical differences between component and service orientation (dynamicity, mechanisms, granularity, black box, etc.).

We believe that these metrics are not enough to take account of all the specificities of the SOA's composition theory. They have to be extended in order to capture all its aspects. Indeed, there are numerous service composition approaches which aim at reducing the coupling inside a composition of services by proposing new mechanisms. Each of them focus on a particular aspects of the service composition. Some approaches [19,1] focus on the heterogeneous nature of the services which are not directly reachable and invokable. In [2,4], the authors focus on adaptation mechanisms which can modify the composition's architecture. Each of these works are linked to the fundamental concepts which characterize the service composition, such as service discovery, service selection, service mediation, adaptation and so forth. All of them have some intuitively tangible benefits on the composition's coupling and, as for the intuitive understanding of the loose coupling, this lack of formalism leads to the impossibility of having some real measurements of their contributions. An architect cannot compare these approaches and thus, he cannot select the suitable one according to his needs.

We aim at proposing an evaluation method of the coupling which takes account of all the aspects underlined by the existing works on the service composition. We aim at providing a quantitative evaluation which provides an objective point of view about a composite's coupling. Since the choice of a composition model heavily depends on the expertise and experience of individual architects, our coupling evaluation wants to be a formal guideline for helping them to make a decision.

# 3    The Loose Coupling Notion

We use a short running example to illustrate our work. We give a simple representation of a car constructor's development process. In the first step, the constructor models its new car by defining its elements and the way they work together to ensure the required functionalities. We use a set of five classic car's functionalities.

The moving capability is composed of three elements: Cooling system, Motor and Wheels. The Cooling system provides a coolant to the Motor which is able to run and thus triggers the Wheels movements. The stopping capability is composed of two elements: Brake and Wheels. The Brake transfers frictions to the Wheels which stop their movement. The direction capability is composed of two elements: Steering_Wheel and Wheels. The Steering_Wheel gives directions to the Wheels. The GPS capability is composed by one element: GPS. The air-conditioning capability is composed by one element: Cooling system. The constructor wants to subcontract the production of all these elements and searches which enterprises are able to produce them.

This scenario is a classic problem which can be supported by a service-based modeling. The specification of the car prototype by the constructor expresses its needs. These needs can be modeled by a set of abstract services organized by a collaboration schema [11] which defines workflow and dataflow. For example, the description of the Motor element defines an abstract service and its sought functionalities and properties. The constructor looks for some enterprises (providers of services) which are able to realize this abstract Motor and provide this concrete service. The realization of the car by composing all the different concrete services represents the composite service.

Our coupling definition deals with all these different notions of abstract and concrete services. Then, it is divided into three couplings:

**The semantic coupling** between abstract services: intends to make explicit the architect's expertise about the application domain of his composite. It is independent of the implementation and represents the dependencies which involve an abstract service and the composite capabilities that this service participates in. Thereby, the semantic coupling measurement of the abstract services depends on the collaboration schema and on the level of importance given by the architect to the composite capabilities.

We define three levels of semantic coupling:

*Strong coupling:* an abstract service and a composite are strongly coupled if this service participates in an essential capability of the composite. A capability is identified subjectively as essential by the architect: without this capability the composite becomes unusable. In our example, the constructor can define the moving capability as essential. Without this capability the composite can no longer be called a car. The abstract services (Cooling system, Motor and Wheels) which the related collaboration schema supports the moving capability, are *strongly coupled* with the composite. They represent some critical points according to the constructor.

*Loose coupling:* an abstract service and a composite are loosely coupled if this service participates in a non essential capability of the composite. However, these capabilities have a direct impact on the composite efficiency. We cannot guarantee the composite quality if one or more of these capabilities are removed. If all of them are removed, we rule that the composite becomes unusable. In our example, the constructor can define the abstract services involved in the stopping capability and the direction capability as loosely coupled with the composite. In fact, the car is totally out of control if it loses these two capabilities.

*Non predominant coupling:* an abstract service and a composite have a non predominant coupling if this service participates in a non-essential capability. Moreover, all non-predominant services can be removed without consequences on the composite availability or on the efficiency of its essential capabilities. These specific capabilities express some optional features. In our example, the constructor can define the abstract services involved in the GPS capability and the air-conditioning capability as non predominant for the composite. These capabilities are optional and their dysfunction does not modify the semantic of the car.

**The syntactic coupling:** an important property of the SOA paradigm relies on the dynamic discovery of available services. Thereby, the syntactic coupling focuses on the dependencies between abstract services and concrete services. We define two levels of syntactic coupling:

*Strong coupling:* an abstract service is strongly coupled with a concrete service if this concrete service is the only available one which can realize the abstract service. Alternative solutions are not available.

*Loose coupling:* an abstract service is loosely coupled with a concrete service if there are alternative solutions. The more suitable concrete services there are, the weaker the coupling is.

In our example, the Motor has a strong syntactic coupling if there is only one enterprise which is able to produce it. On the contrary, it can have a loose syntactic coupling if numerous enterprises are known by the constructor.

Thereby, this notion of syntactic coupling directly depends on two elements:

*The used discovery algorithm:* the existing algorithm can be grouped in two approaches [12], *one to one matching* (1-1) [8,20] and *one to many matching* (1-N) [12,1]. The 1-1 approach identifies one abstract service to exactly one concrete service. The 1-N approach identifies one abstract service to one concrete service or many concrete services in collaboration. Thereby, the 1-N approach has a larger potential of solutions than the 1-1. The syntactic coupling is weaker. In our example, the constructor which wants to identify the future production site of its car will prefer a region which can be easily supplied by a greater potential of industrial subcontractors.

*The selection criteria:* they define the constraints on the identification of concrete services. These constraints are provided to a discovery algorithm. Thereby, the weaker the constraints are, the larger the potential of solutions is. The management of the heterogeneities [11,19,1,16] directly impacts on the syntactic coupling. A composite which does not have implementation considerations can use a larger range of concrete services. In our example, if the constructor can adapt any type of wheels in its car, it will be able to choose between classic producers of car wheels, but also truck or air plane wheels. More enterprises will match its call for tender.

The syntactic coupling expresses the alternatives of realization and completes the semantic coupling. In fact, the semantic coupling allows for identifying the critical aspect of the composite in a functional point view. An architect will uppermost try to reduce the syntactic coupling of services which are related to this critical aspect. For example, the Motor is defined as essential in the car by the constructor. However, the Motor is not critical in a realization point of view since there are numerous enterprises which can produce it. In case of any problems related to the Motor (defects, time of production, etc.) the constructor can call for others enterprises.

The syntactic coupling represents the dynamic possibilities of service selection for the specification of the composite and also its ability to dynamically identifies alternatives solutions in case of failures.

**The physical coupling** between concrete services: it reuses existing researches and it is based on empirical measurements [18,9,7,13] such as method calls, message exchanges, and so forth. These metrics identify the physical dependencies. They are fully linked to the collaboration methods (orchestration, choreography) and to the communication methods (messages, notification of events, and so forth). A purely SOA approach gives priority to the minimization of the transversal communications between services in the same level of composition. There is a preference for a vertical communication (composite and constituent) rather than horizontal communication (constituent and constituent). Following this preference, we rule that a service is strongly coupled if it is linked with numerous services. A service is loosely coupled if it is linked with only one other service (theoretically its composite service).

These three couplings focus on different aspects of the service composition and act in a complementary way. The semantic coupling expresses the architect's expertise and allows for identifying the critical functional aspects of his composite. This semantic coupling acts as guidelines for the syntactic coupling. In fact, the architect intends to reduce the syntactic coupling of the abstract services which are strongly coupled at the semantic level and thus, he makes these critical aspects safer. The physical coupling expresses the dependencies between concrete services and can be used to select the better concrete composition.

## 4   Global Evaluation

Our evaluation takes inspiration from an existing formula of the Preliminary risk analysis [14] and it is commonly used in the automotive industry. This simplified formula is used to measure the risk of failure of car's components: $Risk = A * B * C$. $A$ is the *Criticality* of the component, $B$ is its *Probability* *of Failure Occurrence* and $C$ is the *Probability of non-detected Failure* of this component. We provide our own specification of these three elements so as to calculate the coupling of a service in a specific composition.

**Criticality:** expresses the degree of element's dangerousness. In the automotive industry, it is evaluated by an empirical scale based on the car constructor's experiences. There is a direct match with our notion of *semantic coupling* which represents the architect's expertise. A coefficient is associated with strong coupling $(S)$, loose coupling $(L)$ and non-predominant coupling $(np)$. An abstract service can have multiple semantic couplings insofar as it can participate in multiple composite's capabilities. Therefore, we define that the criticality of a service equals: $A = \{S, L, np\}^{NbCapabilities}$

**Probability of failure occurrence:** can be refined in two others probabilities, $(a)$ the probability of failure on the services which realize the task, and $(b)$ the probability of failure on the management services which define the system responsible of the coordination between the others services.

The $(a)$ **probability** is evaluated by using the informations of the *syntactic coupling* and the *physical coupling*. In fact, the *syntactic coupling* calculates the potential of alternative solutions for instantiating an abstract service. The functionalities required by the abstract service will no longer be supported if all the alternative solutions become unavailable. Therefore, an abstract service fails if all concrete solutions fail. Moreover, this weight has to be level-headed by the *physical coupling* which provides data about the use ratio or the possible propagations of a service's fail and so forth. Therefore, we define that the $(a)$ probability equals:$(a) = P_{allfail} * C_{phys}$

Our $P_{allfail}$ is the probability that all concrete solutions fail. This probability is linked to the number of these solutions. This potential of alternatives heavily depends on the discovery engine (1-1 matching [8,20] or 1-N matching [12,1]) and on the management of the heterogeneities by the composition system.

We define $P_s$ the probability that a service fails. The calculation of $P_s$ has to be done by a precise analyze of the service's implementation. Typically, this analyze is under the responsibility of the service's owner. We define a general formula $P_{allfail}$ which handles M-N matching. However, we do not find significative service discovery engines which realize M-N matching, our approach is able to evaluate them. In fact, M-N approaches represent a natural goal for the thematic of service discovery. The number of possible combinations relies on the numbers $M$ and $N$, and also on the number $X$ of abstract services which are required by the architect in his composite. First, we determine $\lambda$ the number of possible combinations of $M$ in $X$ abstract services. Then, we use this $\lambda$ to calculate the number of compositions which realize these abstract services. $\alpha$ represents the number of concrete alternatives.

$$P_{allfail} = \prod_{k=1}^{\lambda} \prod_{i=1}^{N} \sum_{j=1}^{i} ((P_s)_{kij})^{\alpha_{kij}} \tag{1}$$

$$M < X: \quad \lambda = \sum_{i=X-M}^{X-1} C_{X-1}^i \big|\big| M \geq X: \quad \lambda = 1 + \sum_{i=1}^{X-1} C_{X-1}^i$$

The (b) **probability** focuses on the failure of the coordination system. Its evaluation heavily depends on the implementation techniques and thus it requires a deep analyze of the prototype of the composition approaches. We only define a coefficient called $P_{sys}$ which addresses this probability.

This probability calculation assumes that the composite service is able to dynamically modify its architecture, i.e. it is able to make good use of the alternative solutions. Otherwise, the formula only focuses on selected services which instantiate the composite. We do not take account of the alternatives.

**Probability of non-detected failure:** is determined by the mechanism used by the composite or by the composition system in order to observe the environmental context. Therefore, the evaluation of this criteria requires a deep study of the targeted model. However, a first distinction can be done between centralized and distributed observation systems. Centralized approaches advocate that one entity is responsible for observing the used services. If this entity fails, whatever the failed service, it won't be able to detect it. On the contrary, distributed approaches advocate that each observed services is associated with a dedicated observer. The probability of non-detected failure results in the combination of failures: both service's failure and observer's failure. We define $P_{ndetect}$, the probability of non-detected failure which is higher for centralized approaches than distributed ones. If the composite service is unable to detect failures, the probability of non detected failure equals 1.

## 5 Conclusion

In this paper, we point out the lack of theorization of the loose coupling definition. We demonstrate the limitations of existing coupling measurement techniques which do not take account of all the high level concepts involved in the service composition.

We present our coupling evaluation method which intends to handle all the features which leverage the coupling relationship between the composite's services. Therefore, we combine statical and dynamical aspects of a composite and its modeling approach. We group these aspects in three different couplings: semantic, syntactic and physical. While the physical coupling reuses existing works based on OO metrics, the semantic and syntactic couplings capture the high level concepts of SOA such as service discovery, service mediation and so forth. We combine these three couplings by reusing a formula inspired by the context of preliminary risk analysis. This formula defines our quantitative evaluation of the composite's global coupling. Moreover, it is the base toward a classification of existing service composition approaches and a classification of existing tools. Due to page limitation, we do not focus on our comparison framework of existing service composition approaches which reuses our coupling metrics. This framework will be the topic of another paper.

# References

1. Beauche, S., Poizat, P.: Automated service composition with adaptive planning. In: ICSOC, pp. 530–537 (2008)
2. Bottaro, A., Gérodolle, A., Lalanda, P.: Pervasive service composition in the home network. In: AINA, pp. 596–603 (2007)
3. Briand, L.C., Wüst, J., Daly, J.W., Porter, D.V.: A comprehensive empirical validation of design measures for object-oriented systems. In: IEEE METRICS, pp. 246–257 (1998)
4. Chibani, A., Djouani, K., Amirat, Y.: Semantic middleware for context services composition in ubiquitous computing. In: MOBILWARE, p. 9 (2008)
5. Chidamber, S.R., Kemerer, C.F.: A metrics suite for object oriented design. IEEE Trans. Software Eng. 20(6), 476–493 (1994)
6. Erickson, J., Siau, K.: Web services, service-oriented computing, and service-oriented architecture: Separating hype from reality. J. Database Manag. 19(3), 42–54 (2008)
7. Erradi, A., Kulkarni, N.N., Maheshwari, P.: Service design process for reusable services: Financial services case study. In: Krämer, B.J., Lin, K.-J., Narasimhan, P. (eds.) ICSOC 2007. LNCS, vol. 4749, pp. 606–617. Springer, Heidelberg (2007)
8. Gu, X., Nahrstedt, K., Yu, B.: Spidernet: An integrated peer-to-peer service composition framework. In: HPDC, pp. 110–119 (2004)
9. Gui, G., Scott, P.D.: New coupling and cohesion metrics for evaluation of software component reusability. In: ICYCS, p. 1181 (2008)
10. Gui, G., Scott, P.D.: Ranking reusability of software components using coupling metrics. Journal of Systems and Software 80(9), 1450–1459 (2007)
11. Hock-koon, A., Oussalah, M.: Expliciting a composite service by a metamodeling approach. In: RCIS (2010)
12. Kalasapur, S., Kumar, M., Shirazi, B.A.: Dynamic service composition in pervasive computing. TPDS 18 (2007)
13. Ma, Q., Zhou, N., Zhu, Y., Wang, H.: Evaluating service identification with design metrics on business process decomposition. In: IEEE SCC, pp. 160–167 (2009)
14. Mortureux, Y.: Preliminary risk analysis. Techniques de l'ingenieur. Securite et gestion des risques SE2(SE4010), SE4010.1–SE4010.10 (2002)
15. OASIS: Reference architecture for service oriented architecture 1.0 (April 2008), http://docs.oasis-open.org/soa-rm/soa-ra/v1.0/soa-ra-pr-01.pdf
16. OASIS: Service component architecture assembly model specification version 1.1 (2009), http://www.oasis-opencsa.org/
17. Perepletchikov, M., Ryan, C., Frampton, K.: Comparing the impact of service-oriented and object-oriented paradigms on the structural properties of software. In: OTM Workshops, pp. 431–441 (2005)
18. Perepletchikov, M., Ryan, C., Frampton, K., Tari, Z.: Coupling metrics for predicting maintainability in service-oriented designs. In: Australian Software Engineering Conference, pp. 329–340 (2007)
19. Roman, D., de Bruijn, J., Mocan, A., Lausen, H., Domingue, J., Bussler, C., Fensel, D.: Www: Wsmo, wsml, and wsmx in a nutshell. In: Mizoguchi, R., Shi, Z.-Z., Giunchiglia, F. (eds.) ASWC 2006. LNCS, vol. 4185, pp. 516–522. Springer, Heidelberg (2006)
20. Verma, K., Gomadam, K., Sheth, A.P., Miller, J.A., Wu, Z.: The meteor-s approache for configuring and executing dynamic web processes. LSDIS Lab, University of Georgia Technical Report (2005), http://lsdis.cs.uga.edu/projects/meteor-s/
21. Yu, L., Ramaswamy, S.: Multiple-parameter coupling metrics for layered component-based software. Software Quality Journal 17(1), 5–24 (2009)

# Dynamic Adaptive Service Architecture – Towards Coordinated Service Composition

Claus Pahl

School of Computing
Dublin City University
Dublin, Ireland
cpahl@computing.dcu.ie

**Abstract.** With software services becoming a strategic capability for the software sector, software architecture needs to address integration problems to help services to collaborate and coordinate their activities. The increasing need to address dynamic and automated changes can be answered by a service coordination architecture with event-based collaboration that enables dynamic and adaptive architectures. Intelligent service and process identification and adaptation techniques are suitable solutions for event-driven and on-demand service architectures. We define an architectural solution space and identify research challenges.

## 1 Introduction

Service-oriented architecture (SOA) is a methodological framework for software architectures, supported by Web services as the platform technology. Particularly scalability and suitability for open, collaborative applications are limited due to the restrictive nature of current service composition, collaboration and interaction techniques such as orchestration and choreography languages as the core principles of SOA.

Interoperation and coordination of services is a major challenge service-oriented architecture in the context of on-demand scenarios - as the emergence of cloud computing as a form of service architecture virtualisation demonstrates [4]. Today, hand-crafted service architectures are in place and provide support for software systems in classical sectors such as finance or banking. However, their inherent structural inflexibility makes changes and evolution difficult, resulting in major costs.

## 2 A Changing Architectural Landscape – SOA Challenges

The vision behind recent initiatives such as cloud and on-demand computing is to enable collaboration of service communities [4]. These exhibit a more dynamic nature of interaction, which requires novel software architecture techniques for the identification of needs and behaviours and the adaptation and customisation of provided services to requested needs. The coordination of activities between

M. Ali Babar and I. Gorton (Eds.): ECSA 2010, LNCS 6285, pp. 472–475, 2010.

communities of users and providers needs to be supported [5]. Architecture-based solutions for these evolving and software-intensive systems are sought.

Currently, orchestration and choreography approaches describe business interaction protocols that coordinate and control collaborating services [8]. Challenges for architectural configuration to support future needs are [7]:

- Dynamic and adaptive processes. Services and processes need to provide adaptive capabilities in order to respond to evolving demands and changes without compromising operational and financial efficiencies. A challenge is to provide self-management support for dynamic service compositions.
- QoS-aware service compositions. Service compositions must be QoS-aware - including business regulations, performance levels, reliability requirements or service-level agreements (SLA).

## 3  Architecture Implications – Coordination

The changing architectural landscape requires flexible composition techniques such as event-driven and decentralised coordination instead of tightly coupled synchronous and centralised compositions [9] – resulting in three objectives:

- *Objective 1: provide a technology framework (platform + methodology) that allows flexible composition of services for dynamic service architectures.* The core solution can be built around a notion of a coordination space. This coordination space acts as a passive infrastructure to allow communities of users and providers to collaborate through the coordination of requests and provided services. The coordination space can be governed by event-driven principles: tasks to perform some activity on an object occur are requested, services collaborative and coordinate their activities to execute these tasks.
- *Objective 2: provide flexible infrastructure mechanisms to support dynamic, changing service architectures.* Dynamic selection and adaptive, process-centric composition of services to meet user needs requires a considerable degree of flexibility: user requests might be incomplete or incorrect and need to be corrected, individual requests can be part of an ongoing process that can be derived from the context and the execution history, and provided service might need to be adapted and customised to meet user needs.
- *Objective 3: provide a solution to support future Internet objects and applications.* Users are concerned with the processing of objects. In classical enterprise scenarios these objects are electronic documents passing through business processes, but within the Future Internet, the notion of objects will broaden, capturing any dynamic, evolving entity.

The central concepts are objects and processes. Evolving objects are dynamic entities that represent an end-to-end view. The process notion refers to business processes on these objects. States of the process are points of variation for objects: data evolves as it passes through a process. Process-centricity is the first aspect that characterise this new architecture [3]; the second is a paradigm shift from a pull- to a push-model of communication. Instead of requesting services directly (pull), requests are published (push) and responded to independently.

# 4   A Challenges Framework and Architectural Solutions

Fig. 1 represents an architectural solution framework that we use here to locate and describe specific research challenges. The conceptual framework is goal-driven, event-based collaboration of services. We can identify two *core* facets: the data representing processable objects and the processes themselves and the operation of coordination based on event handling and self-management.

Based on a core architecture, we look into challenges for the information architecture, the operational aspects of dynamic and adaptive service architecture and quality considerations – forming the advanced layer in our framework.

*Information Architecture.* The architecture needs to process object and process information in many ways:

– static and incremental process identification aiming to determine individual tasks, i.e. steps of a larger process, to achieve goals based on an abstract, user-centric and object-based goal specification. Static determination can identify processes based on static knowledge, e.g. in the form of common structural patterns. Incremental determination based on mining approaches can incrementally identify behaviour patterns based on historical data.
– adaptation of provided services to meet the needs of identified process and requestor via mediation between client and provider. Based on identified processes that should enable an object goal to be achieved, adaptations of existing services or subprocesses might be necessary to bridge the gap between requirements and actual services: service-level adaptation as data-centric mediation based on identified process patterns and process-centric adaptation to adapt processes locally to include user profile and context aspects.

*Operation through Coordination*

– Event handling is the challenge. A variety of coordination models has been proposed [1],[6],[2], e.g. based on tuple spaces. Domain- and application context-specific solutions and approaches based on semantic extensions need to be further investigated and applied to service composition and mediation.
– Self-management is a requirement in dynamic systems. A critical aspect is fault-tolerance [10]. The classical security aspects prevention, detection and recovery can be applied to define challenges. Correction of incorrect or

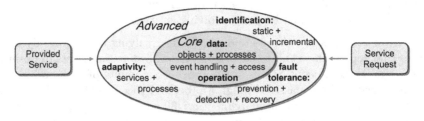

**Fig. 1.** An Architectural Challenges Framework

incomplete input is a fault prevention technique; constraint monitoring is detection or remedial strategies can be defined for recovery purposes.

- Governance is a management-related aspect that also bridges into quality. Compliance with not only technical constraints is needed for self-management, but also wider regulatory and business constraints are of importance for virtualisation environments such as the cloud that bridge organisational boundaries and therefore need to reconcile different regulatory needs.

The coordination models selected to support a solution determines notational aspects we would expect an architectural description language to deal with.

*Quality Reflections.* We have discussed different technology challenges for dynamic, adaptable service coordination architectures. As quality is a central concern of software architecture, the respective techniques need to be considered from a quality perspective:

- The infrastructure techniques suggested here require specifically qualities related to the dynamic context in which they need to be provided, i.e. performance and reliability are central challenges.
- The services (i.e. applications themselves) are subject to varying qualities as required by the context, but need to be dealt with dynamically, i.e. efficiency and reliability are again critical requirements.

Accountability through governance is another quality aspect of importance.

# References

1. Balzarotti, D., Costa, P., Picco, G.P.: The LighTS tuple space framework and its customization for context-aware applications. Web Intelligence and Agent Systems 5(2), 215–231 (2007)
2. Doberkat, E.-E., Franke, W., Gutenbeil, U., Hasselbring, W., Lammers, U., Pahl, C.: PROSET - Prototyping with Sets, Language Definition. Software-Engineering Memo 15, Universitt GH Essen (1992)
3. Gacitua-Decar, V., Pahl, C.: Automatic Business Process Pattern Matching for Enterprise Services Design. In: 4th International Workshop on Service- and Process-Oriented Software Engineering (SOPOSE 2009). IEEE Press, Los Alamitos (2009)
4. Hayes, B.: Cloud computing. Communications of the ACM 51(7), 9–11 (2008)
5. Johanson, B., Fox, A.: Extending Tuplespaces for Coordination in Interactive Workspaces. Journal of Systems and Software 69(3), 243–266 (2004)
6. Nixon, L., Antonechko, O., Tolksdorf, R.: Towards semantic tuplespace computing: the semantic web spaces system. In: Symp. on Appl. Computing, SAC 2007 (2007)
7. Papazoglou, M.P., Traverso, P., Dustdar, S., Leymann, F.: Service-Oriented Computing: State of the Art and Research Challenges. Computer, 38–45 (November 2007)
8. Rao, J., Su, X.: A Survey of Automated Web Service Composition Methods. In: Cardoso, J., Sheth, A.P. (eds.) SWSWPC 2004. LNCS, vol. 3387, pp. 43–54. Springer, Heidelberg (2005)
9. Utschig-Utschig, C.: Architecting Event-Driven SOA: A Primer. Oracle (2008), http://www.oracle.com/technology/pub/articles/oraclesoa_eventarch.html
10. Wang, M., Yapa Bandara, K., Pahl, C.: Integrated Constraint Violation Handling for Dynamic Service Composition. In: IEEE International Conference on Services Computing, SCC 2009. IEEE, Los Alamitos (2009)

# Identity Management Mismatch Challenges in the Danish Municipality Administration System

Mads Schaarup Andersen and Henrik Bærbak Christensen

Department of Computer Science, Aarhus University, Aarhus, Denmark
{masa,hbc}@cs.au.dk

**Abstract.** Integrating a COTS product in a company's product portfolio is appealing from a business perspective but highly challenging from the perspective of the software architecture. In this paper we outline research challenges regarding authorization in the identity management part of the Danish municipality administration system, called Opus BRS, a system that integrates SAP, legacy mainframe systems, and other systems present in the individual municipalities. Each of these systems defines their own access control model and architecture, which leads to architectural mismatch that impacts security, usability, as well as maintainability. We outline a three-year research project and discuss our research method that will include elements of action research as well as experiments using architectural prototyping. The project is carried out in cooperation with KMD, one of the largest Danish IT companies, who is the producer of the Opus system.

**Keywords:** Architectural Mismatch, Identity Management, Architectural Prototyping, Action Research, COTS.

## 1 Motivation

Commercial Off-The-Shelf (COTS) products offer business value as they encapsulate complex domain functionality in thoroughly tested components. However, COTS products often also pose serious challenges for the software architects because of *Architectural Mismatch*. Architectural mismatch was first identified and described by Garlan et al. [4] during their development of the AESOP system, and Garlan et al. recently stated that the problem of architectural mismatch persists today [5].

In this paper, we outline our research project that investigates the research challenges of architectural mismatch for *identity management*, with a focus on authorizations. The project is a three year project co-funded by the major Danish supplier, KMD, of administration systems for the Danish municipalities. KMD provides administration services in more than 90% of the Danish municipalities. The Danish municipalities handles vast and complex data concerning each individual citizen in Denmark. The complexity stems from both the Danish social welfare system that entitles a citizen to a large palette of benefits in case of unemployment, retirement, or social or medical problems on one hand, and the

M. Ali Babar and I. Gorton (Eds.): ECSA 2010, LNCS 6285, pp. 476–479, 2010.

Danish legislation that defines very strong limitations of the type of data an individual social worker at the municipality may access.

To illustrate the complexity, a social worker that is responsible for payment of disability pensions in the municipality must have access to the citizens' classification of disability. However, the social worker is not entitled to access a person's full medical record, criminal record, etc. The social worker in the next office, however, aids citizens in getting a job and need access to for instance certain aspects of the criminal record to judge if a person is suitable for a vacant job. Thus, a very fine grained role- and identity management system is required. The architectural challenges are complicated as KMD has a complex and heterogeneous portfolio of applications and systems, including a legacy mainframe system, individual systems, as well as SAP [11]. To further complicate things KMD handles the administration systems for a large set of Danish municipalities on a single centralized solution in which each municipality act as a client. This is done for cost-efficiency but as each municipality has their own peculiar work flows and requirements, this poses even further challenges for the architecture.

## 2    Research Challenge

We will investigate the problems faced by the KMD security division in realizing the first version of the SAP based system called *Opus BRS*. A major problem faced here is in relation to the access control model in SAP. SAP is mainly based on RBAC [3,10] with the addition of structural authorizations [8], which is a way of restricting access based on a company's organizational structure. Currently, the structural authorization model only exists in SAP Human Capital Management (HCM), and hence is not supported by SAP Identity Management (IDM). This presents a mismatch when user access rights need to be provisioned between the different components in the heterogeneous setup of KMD. One of the goals of Opus BRS is to provide a single interface for user administration in the form of a web based portal interface. The portal is based on SAP IDM and hence is not able to handle structural authorizations. This entails that the user administrator needs to log in to the SAP HCM system to assign structural authorizations, thus compromising the idea of the portal as a single interface for managing users. The initial research challenge is to examine and quantify this architectural mismatch and propose an architecture in which structural authorizations can be handled using the portal, enabling the idea of a single interface. The initial idea is to examine whether and how the existing components in SAP IDM can be used to accommodate structural authorizations.

Further research challenges include examining and quantifying whether the SAP access control model is capable of handling all the requirements in the heterogeneous setup in which Opus BRS is deployed.

There have been other efforts to solve the limited expressiveness of the RBAC model [3] which we will use in our analysis. TRBAC (Temporal RBAC) [2] and GTRBAC (Generalized TRBAC) [6] introduces the temporal aspect to RBAC, the latter being more expressive than the first. GRBAC (Generalized RBAC) [9] extends RBAC by introducing object and environment state.

# 3   Research Method

The project is carried out in close cooperation with KMD, and because of this we have the architects and developers involved in the implementation of the Opus BRS system at our disposal. As the project is designed to have an industrial and applicable outcome as well as a research outcome, we have focused on empirical software engineering methods.

Sjøberg et al. distinguishes between four kinds of empirical methods in software engineering research: *Experimentation, Surveys, Case Studies*, and *Action Research* [12]. We have decided on a research agenda based on a *Action Research* which is defined as *"Action research focuses particularly on combining theory and practice. It attempts to provide practical value to the client organization while simultaneously contributing to the acquisition of new theoretical knowledge."* Using the definition proposed by Sjøberg et al. we elaborate the research to be reflective action research, where an already existing system is examined.

The reason for choosing action research is that it fits our needs of investigating a specific problem in practice and identifying a problem. Next our ambition is to combine the obtained knowledge of the system with our knowledge of identity management and software architecture in a number of architectural prototypes [1], which we will then evaluate in cooperation with KMD. Architectural prototypes seek to experiment and evaluate architectural solutions in a "sandbox," a realistic but scaled down version of the real target system.

# 4   The Case

The Danish company KMD is one of the largest IT companies in Denmark with more than 3000 employees [7]. In 2005 they started working with SAP, and recently they started deploying a new system, *Opus*, based on SAP. Opus is KMD's suite of administration systems for Danish municipalities, and *Opus BRS* is the identity management part of this.

We will specifically be collaborating with the *Security Division* of KMD. Our research will be divided into two phases. In *phase 1* we will do a retrospective analysis and documentation of how authorization and identity management is currently implemented in KMD's Opus BRS solution. This will be done as a bottom-up analysis where authorization in identity management and software architecture issues will be examined by interviewing the people involved in the process of implementing and deploying the solution, this being both developers and architects. The retrospective analysis will be based on architecture and document reviews, as well as code tracing. We expect to identify a number of issues in relation to identity management, and the impact on the Opus system software architecture. In *phase 2* we will use the knowledge obtained in phase 1 to create a number of architectural prototypes in which the problems identified will be addressed. These will then be used to propose and experiment with one or several new architectural solutions in collaboration with KMD architects.

# 5  Expected Outcome

The project is expected to have both research as well as industrial outcomes. Regarding research we expect develop detailed models for authorizations in identity management and specifically in relation to COTS product integration and the mismatch that this might introduce. This should in turn lead to a proposal for an architecture incorporating an access control model which solves the authorization problems of identity management identified in phase 1. Regarding industrial outcomes we expect to produce a number of architectural prototypes demonstrating different solutions to the problems which currently exists in the Opus BRS system. These will in turn be evaluated in cooperation with the KMD architects, and hence we will use the method of evolutionary prototypes.

# References

1. Bardram, J., Christensen, H., Hansen, K.: Architectural Prototyping: An Approach for Grounding Architectural Design and Learning. In: Proceedings of Fourth Working IEEE/IFIP Conference on Software Architecture. WICSA 2004, June 2004, pp. 15–24 (2004)
2. Bertino, E., Bonatti, P.A., Ferrari, E.: TRBAC: A temporal role-based access control model. ACM Trans. Inf. Syst. Secur. 4(3), 191–233 (2001)
3. Ferraiolo, D.F., Sandhu, R., Gavrila, S., Kuhn, D.R., Chandramouli, R.: Proposed NIST standard for role-based access control. ACM Trans. Inf. Syst. Secur. 4(3), 224–274 (2001)
4. Garlan, D., Allen, R., Ockerbloom, J.: Architectural Mismatch: Why Reuse is so Hard. IEEE Software 12(6), 17–26 (1995)
5. Garlan, D., Allen, R., Ockerbloom, J.: Architectural Mismatch: Why Reuse Is Still So Hard. IEEE Software 26(4), 66–69 (2009)
6. Joshi, J.B., Bertino, E., Latif, U., Ghafoor, A.: A Generalized Temporal Role-Based Access Control Model. IEEE Transactions on Knowledge and Data Engineering 17, 4–23 (2005)
7. KMD, http://www.kmd.dk/
8. Linkies, M., Off, F.: SAP Security and Authorizations. SAP Press (2006)
9. Moyer, M.J., Ahamad, M.: Generalized Role-Based Access Control. In: International Conference on Distributed Computing Systems, p. 391 (2001)
10. Sandhu, R., Coyne, E., Feinstein, H., Youman, C.: Role-based access control models. Computer 29(2), 38–47 (1996)
11. SAP, http://www.sap.com/
12. Sjøberg, D., Dyba, T., Jørgensen, M.: The Future of Empirical Methods in Software Engineering Research. In: Future of Software Engineering, FOSE 2007, May 2007, pp. 358–378 (2007)

# From Web Components to Web Services: Opening Development for Third Parties

Chouki Tibermacine[1] and Mohamed Lamine Kerdoudi[2]

[1] LIRMM, CNRS and Montpellier University, France
[2] Computer Science Department, University of Biskra, Algeria
Chouki.Tibermacine@lirmm.fr, l.kerdoudi@univ-biskra.dz

**Abstract.** One of the main advantages of the Web component-based development paradigm is the ability to build customizable and composable web application modules as independent units of development, and to share them with other developers by publishing them in libraries as COTS (Commercial Off The Shelf) or free components. Besides this, since many years, Web services confirmed their status of the most pertinent solution for a given service provider, like Google, Amazon or FedEx, to open its solutions for third party development. In this paper, we present an approach to build web services starting from existing web component-based applications and deploy them on a web service provider. This transformation helps server-side web application developers in transforming their "user interface"-based web components into a set of web services intended for remote code extensions. We implemented our solution on a collection of Java EE technologies.

## 1 Introduction: Context and Motivation

Web component-based development aims at decoupling Web application code modules, and making them reusable and customizable software entities. Indeed, in this paradigm a step has been taken forward in modularizing Web applications and thus separating business logic code, from view, model and controller one. One of the technologies leading this field is Java EE[1] and its numerous frameworks like Struts or JSF. Web components in such technologies are entities that can be used and reused in different applications and customized according to the application requirements.

In our opinion, these technologies are currently the ideal solutions for developing large and complex applications with highly critical requirements on maintainability. However, after deploying a Web component-based application within an application server, there is no means to directly publish some services of the application for third party development. In this paper, we present an approach (see Section 2) to build web service-oriented architectures starting from existing web component-based applications and deploy them on a web service provider. In this way, developers of web components offer the opportunity to other developers to build extensions of the services provided by their artifacts.

---

[1] Java Enterprise Edition from Sun Microsystems: http://java.sun.com/javaee/

M. Ali Babar and I. Gorton (Eds.): ECSA 2010, LNCS 6285, pp. 480–484, 2010.
© Springer-Verlag Berlin Heidelberg 2010

This transformation goes through a process composed of several steps, which has been implemented on a collection of Java-related technologies. Java EE components are the input artifacts of the proposed implementation, and a set of Java web services and compositions of these services are provided at output. The paper ends by discussing some related work and presenting our future work.

## 2   Proposed Approach

The transformation process is composed of five steps:

**1. Operation Extraction:** First, a recursive parsing of the different web component elements is performed to extract the potential set of Web services. All operations in classes and other structured code elements are saved. In addition, the code present in server-side programs (JSP pages, for example) is grouped within a single operation and formatted to be executed as stand-alone code. Similar extracted operations are spread out in different Web services using a simple similarity measure (based on operations' names, parameters, ...).

**2. Input and Output Message Identification:** The input and output messages related to each operation in the Web services are extracted starting from the parsed elements in the Web component. For classes and other structured code elements, the parameters and the returned value are formatted as SOAP messages. The code present in other programs (like JSP pages) is parsed to extract the input values received in the HTTP requests. Their types are inferred from the parsed code by analyzing type casts and other conversions. The contents produced by theses programs, which are viewed at the client side (like JSP expressions), are considered as returned values.

**3. Operation Filtering:** After that, the non-pertinent operations of the Web services are eliminated from the starting set, according to a collection of filtering heuristics. These heuristics are boolean expressions which are represented by OCL expressions that can be added/modified/removed by developers. An example of a filtering heuristic is: "Operations that use the session standard script variable are not taken into account". This is formalized in OCL as follows:
not (self.body.usedType->includes(t|t.name='HTTPSession'))
At the end of this step, the developer is asked to choose the less pertinent operations to remove from the Web services that will be published.

**4. Composite Web Service Creation:** In this step, the potential dependencies between the different selected operations in the Web services are identified. There are two kinds of dependencies between operations: operation-call dependencies (which give rise to Web service choreographies) and Web navigation relationships (which allow to generate Web service orchestrations).

**4.1. Web Service Choreography Creation:** All calls to operations in the code are captured. If the called operations are published in the same web service of the caller operation, the calls are left as method invocations. If they are published on a remote host, these operation dependencies are replaced by Web service requests. In this way, we build composite Web services as code-level choreographies. In the near future, we plan to generate high-level choreographies in "WS-CDL"-compliant languages [7].

**4.2. Web Service Orchestration Creation:** Navigation documents such as JSF `faces-config` files are parsed. This allows the identification of the different relationships between Web pages, and potential collaborations of the different Web services extracted from these pages. This task is implemented according to a simple algorithm in which we first create a process, and for each navigation rule in the Web navigation document, we identify the source and destination operations. Before each operation invocation, we prepare the list of parameters.

**5. Web Service Deployment and Indexing:** The validated set of Web services (composite and primitive ones) are deployed on an application server chosen by the developer/administrator of the Web component-based application. If the developer deploys the Web services in different servers, the dependencies between collaborative operations in composite services are resolved. Then, on the Seekda Web server, we create an account and register the services. Once the services indexed, we propose to the developer a smart mechanism of keyword extraction, based on our previous work [2]. This mechanism identifies potential tags for the services starting from their WSDL description. The keyword list (based on identifiers in the service operation names, parameters' names, ...) is proposed to the developer in order to select tags for the deployed services.

# 3    Related Work

In [5], Roger Lee et al. proposed an approach which allows a client to specify a request for searching a given functionality in components deployed in a Web server. As an answer, a Web service or a composition of Web services is generated automatically. Our approach is proactive; it does not react to a client request, but it allows a web application engineer to anticipate the export of some functionalities to third party developers as Web services. In addition, in our work we deal with Web interface conversion into stateless Web services. In Wike [3], developers can define patterns for extracting partial information from Web pages. These patterns are encapsulated in functions that can be exported as Web services. In our work, content-based Web pages are not the main concern. Wike is however a complementary solution to our work. Web services that are generated using our approach starting from Web components, which produce to users during execution a large quantity of content, can be enhanced with new operations that return only partial information (texts, images, ...) using Wike.

Many works in the literature proposed model-driven techniques to generate Web service-oriented applications. Bauer and Müller [1] developed an approach to map elements from UML2 sequence diagrams (considered as PlMs – Platform Independent Models) to a representation of compositions of Web services using BPEL (considered as PSMs – Platform Specific Models). In [8], the authors propose transformation rules for converting orchestration models specified in CCA (Component Collaboration Architecture), which is part of the UML profile for Enterprise Distributed Object Computing (EDOC [6]), into BPEL specifications. Another model-driven approach for creating service-oriented solutions has been proposed in [4]. In this work, a UML profile has been defined for the expression of service-oriented applications. In our work the transformations are made from PSM to PSM. Web components, which are models specific to a given platform (in the current implementation, Java EE), are converted into Web services, which are considered as another platform-specific model (WSDL, Java and BPEL). The UML profile presented in [4] can be used to define high-level models of the generated Web services. The other approaches can be used to make a reverse engineering of the generated Web services or orchestrations and obtain more understandable models (compared to the code).

# 4 Conclusion: Contribution and Future Work

We implemented the proposed solution as a prototype tool called WSGen: Web Service Generator. The components parsed by WSGen are Java Enterprise archives. JSPs, Servlets, JavaBeans, Enterprise JavaBeans and traditional Java classes in these archives are extracted. To deploy services, this tool uses a Tomcat/Axis server.

In our work, we consider the generated and deployed Web services as remote APIs that offer the opportunity for developers to extend the functionalities provided by these services and exploit the resources used by them. Many enhancements still have to be performed in the transformation process implemented in WSGen. We are now working on the implementation of more interesting techniques for grouping complementary operations in Web services, based on "text-mining" of the Web components' documentation. At the conceptual level, we plan to study the formalization of the process as a set of high level declarative (or a combination of declarative and imperative) transformation rules, and thus integrate our solution in the Model-Driven Engineering world. At the tool level, we plan, as introduced previously, to work on the generation of high-level specifications of choreographies in "WS-CDL"-compliant languages [7] starting from collaborations of the generated Web services' operations.

# References

1. Bauer, B., Müller, J.P.: Mda applied: From sequence diagrams to web service choreography. In: Koch, N., Fraternali, P., Wirsing, M. (eds.) ICWE 2004. LNCS, vol. 3140, pp. 132–136. Springer, Heidelberg (2004)
2. Falleri, J.-R., Azmeh, Z., Huchard, M., Tibermacine, C.: Automatic tag identification in web service descriptions. In: Proc. of WEBIST 2010 (April 2010)
3. Han, H., Tokuda, T.: Wike: A web information/knowledge extraction system for web service generation. In: Proc. of ICWE 2008, pp. 354–357. IEEE CS, Los Alamitos (2008)

# Learning from the Cell Life-Cycle: A Self-adaptive Paradigm

Antinisca Di Marco[1], Francesco Gallo[1], Paola Inverardi[1], and Rodolfo Ippoliti[2]

[1] Dipartimento di Informatica - University of L'Aquila
[2] Dipartimento di Biologia di Base ed Applicata - University of L'Aquila
{antinisca.dimarco,francesco.gallo,
paola.inverardi,rodolfo.ippoliti}@univaq.it

**Abstract.** In the software domain, self-adaptive systems are able to modify their behavior at run-time to respond to changes in the environment they run, to changes of the users' requirements or to changes occurring in the system it-self. In life science, biological cells are power entities able to adapt to the (unpredictable) situations they incur in, in a complete decentralized fashion. Learning adaptation mechanism from the cell life-cycle, we propose in this paper a new architectural paradigm for self-adaptive software systems.

## 1 Motivations and Background

Biological systems inspire systems design in many directions [4,6,5]. Among the biological systems, cells represent a model for their ability to undergo adaptation changes as a response to environmental stimuli. Each cell is able to check its status, to duplicate (mitosis) and to kill itself (apoptosis) in case of need[1].

Stem cells are primitive cells with the singular ability to generate all other types of cells and to give rise to progenitor cells in adult tissues able to substitute ageing cells [1]. They, regardless of their origin, have three general properties: *(i)* they are able to divide and renew themselves even after a long period of inactivity, *(ii)* they are not specialized cells, that is they do not make work of a specific organ or tissue and *(iii)* they give rise to several specialized cell types. Once a stem cell is activated, depending on the type of internal or external received signal, it may choose to mutually execute:

- **Symmetric Stem Cell Division (SSCD)** process, in which the stem cell clones itself producing a new stem cell identical to it.
- **Asymmetric Stem Cell Division (ASCD)** process, a first step of specialization, that originates as outcome of the stem cell and a new cell called Transit Amplifying Cell (TAC) or progenitor cell. TAC is the real origin of the (tissue) cell proliferation and it represents an intermediate cell that has lost the status of stem and that can evolve into a tissue cell.
- **Apoptosis (A)** process, it happens when the stem cell is induced to differentiate into cells unable to enter in the cellular process and it is then sent to death.

M. Ali Babar and I. Gorton (Eds.): ECSA 2010, LNCS 6285, pp. 485–488, 2010.

TAC, in turn, can mutually start the **Terminal Differentiation (TD)** process (that represents the final specification step), in which the cell passes to a specific status (Differentiated Cell (DC)), depending on the type of tissue or organ in which it is located; or the **Apoptosis (A)** process. TAC undergoes the apoptosis if it occurs in an errors, or the generation from the stem cell fails in meeting the required behavior specification. Finally the DC may face either to mitosis or apoptosis. **Mitosis (M)** is a process that substitutes the DC with two new daughter cells of the same type (DC').

The basic properties of the cell life-cycle that have inspired our paradigm are *(i)* the reflective properties of stem cells, i.e. the ability to self-preservation in spite of changes induced by the environment and *(ii)* the ability to capture stimuli from the environment and generate the associated behaviors. This two properties can be can be summarized as: *a universal machine that can interpret the signals from the environment and generate the code that implements the desired functionality.* The paradigm also embeds the cell apoptosis process [3] to improve the efficiency of the whole system by means of the programmed death of all cells that are no more useful as they are, and that cannot evolve any more.

## 2    Bio-inspired Paradigm for Self-adaptive Systems

The definition of the paradigm we propose is given by means of a mapping between the paradigm entities and the cellular process concepts inspiring them. Figure 1 shows such a mapping reporting at the left-side the cellular process concepts whereas at the right-side the corresponding paradigm entities.

The key concept of the paradigm is the stem module that is inspired to the stem cell. In our paradigm, we refer to multipotent stem cell as stem cell that is able to generate different types of differentiated cells as required by the organ making up its environment. The organ establishes the boundary of the stem cell specialization capabilities, limiting its generation power to the differentiated cells of the tissues composing it. The organ concept is mapped to the functionalities provided by the system. The system can evolve by adaptation in different ways always guaranteeing the core services (organ functionalities) as required by the users. In other words, the organ functionalities and the user requirements represent the invariant for the biologic and software systems, respectively. In general, the *invariant* (Inv) represents a collection of properties that meets system and which must also be satisfied after successive and repeated adjustments induced in the system. The stem cell represents a huge container of information, which is capable if properly stimulated, to interpret signals from the environment and generate the appropriate behaviour. In particular, the stem cell itself contains all the means to understand the problem shaped as changes, and generate the "solution". It implements the basic functionalities that allow the cell to survive and evolve over time, preserving them in a sort of kernel. In our metaphor, the stem cell can be compared to the universal machine able to execute all possible behaviors throughout interpretation of the corresponding code. To improve the efficiency of the paradigm, the stem module is devised as an engine able

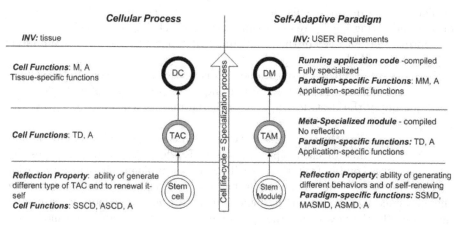

**Fig. 1.** Mapping from the Cell Life-cycle to the Self-adaptive Paradigm

to treat behaviors as data, interprets them to generate compiled code (i.e., the Differentiated Module) implementing the new behavior.

Both the stem cell and the stem module are characterized by the *reflection property*, i.e. the ability to self-renew, to capture changes in the system and in its environment, and to generate code to implement different, possible new, behaviors in case of need.

Generate code suitable for the implementation of specific functionality is equivalent to passing from a condition of generalization to one of specialization. This transition occurs through a series of steps or specialized functions that we describe below. The first step is one of the following *division*:

- **ASMD** (Asymmetric Stem Module Division), this process results in a first step of specialization: our universal machine in response to a given external event, generates a specialized meta module software, called TAM (Transit Amplifying Module), which represents a software module compiled with the ability to further specialize into the final code implementation of the functionalities associated to the event or to self eliminate, mimicking the cellular concept of **Apoptosis (A)**. Moreover, by exploiting the reflection ability of the universal machine, it duplicates by creating an identical copy of itself.
- **MASMD** (Meta Asymmetric Stem Module Division), this process is very similar to the one seen above, but there is no duplication of the universal machine. This is because in most cases this is unnecessary and expensive computationally. This process is not present in the cellular life-cycle. We introduce it to improve the efficiency of the paradigm.
- **SSMD** (Symmetric Stem Module Division), this process results in a duplication of the universal machine only. This process is very rare also in biology, as computationally expensive.

The next step of the specialization process, Terminal Differentiation (TD), is the final generation of specialized code, which in our paradigm is denoted by **DM**

(Differentiated Module). This module represents the compiled code that will run on the underlying hardware and exhibits the highest degree of efficiency. Again, to improve the efficiency of the paradigm, TD step generates a DM maintaining a copy of the TAM.

The concept of mitosis in our framework is very close to the one in the cellular process. The difference is that in our paradigm, the production of multiple copies does not imply the destruction of the original one. It will be denoted by MM (Meta Mitosis).

In our paradigm, the running software system is composed by a stem module, a set of TAM (one for each type) and a set of differentiated modules (possible more instances coming from the same TAM type) implementing the application specific functions. The stem module has the ability to face the unforeseeable changes since it contains all the logic to generate new behaviors in case some unforeseeable changes occur the system must adapt. Whereas the more specialized modules (i.e., the set of DM) provide the services required by users and implement the adaptation logic to foreseen and foreseeable changes. In our mind, the canonical feedback control loop (such as, the MAPE-K loop) [2] is implemented in the DMs either in a centralized or in distributed way. Finally, TAMs implement an intermediate step of specialization between stem module and DM, introduced to reduce the complexity of the specialization step, as it happens in the cellular process. To improve the paradigm efficiency, we maintain a copy of each type of generated TAM from which restarts the TD step in case of necessity without to involve the stem module again.

**Acknowledgement.** This work is partially supported by the EU-funded CON-NECT project (FP7–231167) and by the Italian PRIN d-ASAP project.

# References

1. Alberts, Johnson, Lewis, Raff, Roberts, Walter (eds.): Molecular Biology of the Cell, 4th edn. Garland Publishing, Inc., New York (2004)
2. Brun, Y., Serugendo, G.D.M., Gacek, C., Giese, H., Kienle, H.M., Litoiu, M., Müller, H.A., Pezzè, M., Shaw, M.: Engineering self-adaptive systems through feedback loops. In: Software Engineering for Self-Adaptive Systems, pp. 48–70 (2009)
3. Degterev, Y.J.A.: Expansion and evolution of cell death programmes. Nat. Rev. Mol. Cell Biol. 9(5), 378–390 (2008)
4. Horn, P.: Autonomic computing: Ibm perspective on the state of information technology. In: Presented at AGENDA 2001, Scottsdale, AR, IBM T.J. Watson Labs, NY (2001)
5. Shen, C.-C., Li, K., Jaikaeo, C., Sridhara, V.: Ant-based distributed constrained steiner tree algorithm for jointly conserving energy and bounding delay in ad hoc multicast routing. ACM Trans. Auton. Adapt. Syst. 3(1), 1–27 (2008)
6. Snyder, P.L., Greenstadt, R., Valetto, G.: Myconet: A fungi-inspired model for superpeer-based peer-to-peer overlay topologies. In: SASO, pp. 40–50 (2009)

# Toward an Aspect Oriented ADL
# for Embedded Systems

Sihem Loukil, Slim Kallel, Bechir Zalila, and Mohamed Jmaiel

ReDCAD Laboratory, University of Sfax
B.P. 1173, 3038 Sfax, Tunisia
sihem.loukil@redcad.org, slim.kallel@fsegs.rnu.tn,
{bechir.zalila,mohamed.jmaiel}@enis.rnu.tn

**Abstract.** Managing embedded systems complexity and scalability is
one of the most important problems in software development. To better address this problem, it is very recommended to have an abstraction
level high enough to model complex systems. Architectural description
languages (ADLs) intend to model these systems and manage their structure at a high abstraction level. Traditional ADLs do not provide appropriate formalisms to separate any kind of crosscutting concerns. This
frequently results in poor descriptions of the software architectures and
a tedious adaptation to constantly changing user requirements and specifications. AOSD (Aspect Oriented Software Development) deals with
these problems by considering crosscutting concerns in software development. The effectiveness of AOSD appears when aspect concepts are
considered throughout the software's life-cycle.

In this paper, we propose a new aspect language called AO4AADL
that adequately manipulates aspect oriented concepts at the software
architecture level to master complexity and ensure scalability.

## 1 Introduction

Implementing and managing software embedded systems are tedious tasks, due
to the complexity and strict requirements of such systems. A possible solution
to manage this complexity is to model these systems at architecture level. Architecture description languages [1,2] are an important tool for early analysis
and feasibility testing. They can also support code generation and allow easier
management of the configuration and the deployment of systems.

Traditional ADLs provide formalisms to describe functional concerns (what
the system does) and non-functional concerns (the quality of service and the
conditions under which the system correctly operates). They lack of appropriate formalisms representing crosscutting concerns (behavior that cuts across the
typical divisions of responsibility). This lack frequently results in poor descriptions of the architectures and a tedious adaptation to the constantly changing
user requirements and execution context. The specification of non-functional
concerns is not well-modularized, as it is *tangled* with the specification of each
component's core functionality or *scattered* across the specification of different

M. Ali Babar and I. Gorton (Eds.): ECSA 2010, LNCS 6285, pp. 489–492, 2010.
© Springer-Verlag Berlin Heidelberg 2010

components. This results in an increase of the model complexity. Furthermore, when the designer modifies one of the concerns, he should manipulate all parts of the model related to that concern which is challenging as these parts are mixed with elements of other concerns. AOSD deals with these problems by considering crosscutting concerns in software development.

In this paper we propose AO4AADL, an aspect oriented language for AADL [2], a well known ADL. This language considers aspects as an extension of AADL using "annexes", an intrinsic mechanism to extend the AADL language. We consider that aspects can be specified in a language other than AADL, and then integrated in AADL models as annexes. The remainder of this paper is organized as follows. Section 2 overviews the syntax and the semantics of a new aspect oriented language for AADL in terms of pointcut and advice. Section 3 gives the related works and Section 4 concludes the paper and presents ongoing work.

## 2  The AO4AADL Language

Considering aspect concepts at the beginning of software life cycle is considerably valuable: it improves comprehensibility, evolution and reuse in the development of complex software systems. For this purpose, we extended AADL. Many reasons led us to this choice. AADL is a concrete ADL in which all elements correspond to concrete entities that allows describing both hardware and software parts of the system. It introduces two extension mechanisms: properties and annexes. These mechanisms make the language much easier to enrich. Moreover, they offer a good foundation for additional capabilities in analysis, automated system integration, distribution, and dynamism. Based on the annex extension mechanism, we propose to enrich AADL specifications with aspect concepts.

An AO4AADL aspect consists of two parts: (1) *pointcut_specification* determines the conditions under which the aspect is invoked by the corresponding functional components and (2) *advice_specification* encapsulates the behaviour of the aspect depending on its location. If the aspect influences only one component, it should be declared as an annex inside this component. If the aspect influences the behaviour of more than one component, it should be declared as an annex library in an AADL package outside the components.

### 2.1  Pointcut Specification

A pointcut is defined as a set of joinpoints which are used to accomplish the composition between the aspect description and the base description of the software system. Pointcut definitions consist of a left-hand side containing the specification of the pointcut name and parameters (the data available when the events happen) and a right-hand side consisting of the pointcut itself.

A joinpoint specifies a well-defined point of the aspect behaviour execution. AO4AADL explicitly defines the architectural joinpoints as places where the effect of aspect annex can occurs. They include: (1) the subprograms already declared in the AADL specifications (2) the outgoing data flow emerging from an AADL component and (3) the incoming data into an AADL component with either a call or an execution primitive. Moreover, a joinpoint can expose instance of checks and control to specify when the arguments are instances of specific types or the types of the specified identifiers.

In real architectural configuration, aspect behaviour may be executed by several architectural joinpoints. Hence, an architectural pointcut should be defined as an expression that specifies the set of joinpoints to which the behaviour of an aspect is applicable. In order to express the architectural quantification mechanism, we introduce the operators "and" ("&&") and "or" ("||") as well as wildcards such as "*" to describe sets of joinpoints invoking the same advice.

Listing 1 shows an example of an aspect code, CheckCode, described in AO4AADL. It belongs to the software part of an automated teller machine (ATM). It specifies that the client has exactly three authentication attempts. Each time it gets an incorrect code, the system prompts for the code again. If it reaches the third time, the card will be rejected and an explanatory message is displayed to the customer. The example shows also the interaction between the AO4AADL code and the corresponding AADL entities (here, the out port RestoreCode_out specified in the AADL thread containing the annex).

**Listing 1.** Example of AO4AADL aspect

```
1    aspect CheckCode{
2    pointcut Verification (): call outport RestoreCode_out (..);
3    advice around (): Verification () {
4      variables{counter : Integer_Type; message : String_Type;}
5      initially{counter:=1; message:="Card Rejected !";}
6      if (counter = 3){
7        RejectedCard_out! (message);
8        counter := 1;}
9      else{
10       proceed();
11       counter := counter + 1;}}}
```

## 2.2  Advice Specification

The advice defines the crosscutting relationships among the aspect behaviour and the place where to inject this behaviour (joinpoint). AO4AADL provides three kinds of crosscutting interactions listed by the keywords: **before** (the advice action runs before the joinpoint), **after** (the action runs after each joinpoint) and **around** (the action runs before and after of each joinpoint. The joinpoint itself can be executed by calling **proceed**). To each pointcut, we can associate one or more crosscutting behaviour which is expressed in an advice section allowing one or more advice sections can be associated to the same pointcut.

The syntax used to specify the action performed by the advice action on the functional component is inspired from the AADL Annex Behavior [2] with some modifications to express other requirements[1].

In our aspect CheckCode (Listing 1), the advice is presented in lines (3 – 12). We use an **around** advice to execute the joinpoint only if the user has remaining attempts. In the other case, the card will be rejected.

[1] The full AO4AADL grammar can be found on www.redcad.org/projects/AO4AADL

# 3   Related Work

There are several points of view on how to represent aspects at architectural level but most of existing Aspect-Oriented architectural approaches agree on that the semantics of the composition should be somehow extended in order to ensure the connection between the aspects and the basic components.

As stated by [3], extending a component based formalism to AOSD is performed either symmetrically or asymmetrically. Some existing implementation of AOSD in an ADL used the asymmetric approach [4,5]. They use two different formalism to describe the model and the aspect. Some other implementations use the symmetric approaches [6]. They use components to model both functional components and aspects. In our case, we integrated the aspect code in the model (in the same document) while keeping out model compatible with tools that do not support AO4AADL. Therefore we used the AADL annex extension mechanism. This allows us to have a whole new formalism to describe the aspects (benefit of the asymmetric approach) while keeping a single model which can be reusable among different tools (benefit of the symmetric approach).

# 4   Conclusion and Future Work

In this paper, we presented AO4AADL, an aspect-oriented ADL, which extends the AADL language using the annex extension mechanism to capture crosscutting concerns at architectural level. We defined a rigorous grammar that supports most of aspect concepts. We are currently working on the implementation of the code generator from AO4AADL aspect to AspectJ aspect. Future work include using AO4AADL for defining an approach for managing "at runtime" configurable (adaptive) embedded systems.

# References

1. Medvidovic, N., Taylor, R.N.: A classification and comparison framework for software architecture description languages. IEEE Trans. Softw. Eng. 26, 70–93 (2000)
2. SAE: Architecture Analysis & Design Language (2004), http://www.sae.org
3. Harrison, W.H., Ossher, H.L., Tarr, P.L., Harrison, W.: Asymmetrically vs. symmetrically organized paradigms for software composition. Technical report, Research Report RC22685, IBM Thomas J. Watson Research (2002)
4. Navasa, A., Pérez-Toledano, M.A., Murillo, J.M.: An ADL dealing with aspects at software architecture stage. Inf. Softw. Technol. 51, 306–324 (2009)
5. Jing, W., Shi, Y., LinLin, Z., YouCong, N.: AC2-ADL: Architectural description of aspect-oriented systems. In: Proc. of the ASEA, pp. 147–152. IEEE, Los Alamitos (2008)
6. Pinto, M., Fuentes, L.: AO-ADL: An ADL for describing aspect-oriented architectures. In: Early Aspects: current challenges and future directions, pp. 94–114 (2007)

# On the Need of Safe Software Product Line Architectures

Roberto E. Lopez-Herrejon and Alexander Egyed

Institute for Systems Engineering and Automation
Johannes Kepler University Linz, Austria
{roberto.lopez,alexander.egyed}@jku.at

**Abstract.** A Software Product Line (SPL) is a family of related software systems distinguished by the different sets of features each system provides. Over the last decade, the substantial benefits of SPL practices have been extensively documented and corroborated both in academia and industry. Several architecture methods have been proposed that employ different artifacts for expressing the components of a SPL, their properties and relationships. Of crucial importance for any SPL architecture method is to guarantee that the variability, for instance as expressed in feature models, is not only preserved but also kept consistent across all artifacts used. In this research challenge paper we argue that Safe Composition – the guarantee that all programs of a product line are type safe – can be leveraged to address this guarantee for structural properties of SPL architectures and the challenges that that entails.

## 1 Motivation

A *Software Product Line (SPL)* is a family of related software systems distinguished by the different sets of features each system provides [1,2,3]. Extensive research and industrial experience have widely proven the significant benefits of SPL practices, some of them are: reduced time to market, increase in asset reuse and increase in software quality [4,2]. *Variability* is the capacity of software artifacts to vary [5], and its effective management is a core tenet of the research in SPL.

An adequate underlying software architecture support is a crucial factor for the success of any software system [6]. Such support is even more critical in the case of a SPL because its architecture must cope with variability [3]. This means that from the SPL architecture it should be possible to instantiate *all* individual product architectures [7]. This instantiation requires preserving the variability expressed in feature models [8](i.e. considering all feature combinations of the SPL), and assuring consistency amongst the software artifacts used to express each individual product architecture (e.g. in UML or an *Architecture Description Language (ADL)* [6]). The research question addressed by our paper is precisely this: How can the correct instantiation of *all* product architectures of a SPL be guaranteed?

We argue that *Safe Composition* [9], the guarantee that *all* program members of a SPL are type safe (i.e. absent of references to undefined elements), can be leveraged to address this guarantee for structural properties of SPL architectures. Thus in a *Safe SPL Architecture* all the product architectures that can be instantiated are devoid of

M. Ali Babar and I. Gorton (Eds.): ECSA 2010, LNCS 6285, pp. 493–496, 2010.
© Springer-Verlag Berlin Heidelberg 2010

references to undefined elements. First we describe some key emerging trends in SPL development that bear relation to Safe Composition.

## 2    The Road to Composition

SPL development approaches can be broadly divided in two main categories depending on how they manage variability in software artifacts [10]. In *integrative* approaches, artifacts contain both the common and variable parts. Building a system member of the product family means preserving the common parts and removing the unneeded parts of the unselected features of the system being built [11,12]. In contrast, in the *compositional* approaches the variable parts are encapsulated in modular units. These variable units are put together (composed) in accordance to the feature set of the system to be built [13,1,14,10,15][1].

It has been shown that both categories can complement each other (and in some cases can be regarded as expressive) [16], none-the-less compositional approaches have modularity as a key advantage. Though most of the early research on this area has focused on source code artifacts, there is a growing awareness and research in other types of artifacts such as models [15,17]. Furthermore, work such as Bosch et. al. strongly advocates the use of a compositional perspective throughout the overall development of a SPL not only on its implementation at programming level [18,19].

There has been research on extending ADLs such as xADL to represent variability [20], and proposals that exploit Aspect-Orientation concepts for modularizing ADLs for SPL architectures [21,22,23]. However, to the best our knowledge, checking that structural properties of SPL architectures hold for all the products of a SPL is a topic that remains largely unexplored.

## 3    Principles of Safe Composition

Safe composition uses propositional logic to express and relate two terms [9]: *i)* domain constraints denoted as $PL_f$ which are derived from a mapping of feature models to propositional logic (see details in [24]), and *ii)* implementation constraints denoted as $IMP_f$ which correspond to the concrete instances of structural properties to validate. Because we are interested in verifying that *all* members of the product line satisfy a given structural property, the following formula should not be satisfiable: $\neg(PL_f \Rightarrow IMP_f)$. In case it is satisfiable, it would mean that there is a member of the product line that does not meet constraint instance $IMP_f$. By using a *satisfiability (SAT)* solver, the violating feature combination(s) can be identified. This process is performed for each instance of each structural property we want to verify.

For example, consider an architecture with feature $F$ that contains a component with a required interface $I$ which is provided by components in either feature $G$ or $H$. This particular implementation constraint instance is denoted as $IMP_f \equiv F \Rightarrow (G \vee H)$. When plugged in the previous expression and expanded, the resulting proposition which is passed to the SAT solver is: $PL_f \wedge F \wedge \neg G \wedge \neg H$. Intuitively, this expression

---

[1] This classification appears with different names in the literature, for example *negative* or *positive* variability respectively [10].

checks that it is not the case that a product with feature F does not have neither feature G nor H as well. Again, this process is performed for each instance of each structural property we want to verify. For details on Safe Composition please consult [9].

## 4 Open Challenges

This section summarizes the challenges and research venues identified by our work:

- Scalability. Safe Composition relies on SAT solvers which inherently present scalability issues as the size and complexity of a feature models increase. Other less exhaustive alternatives that exploit knowledge of the artifact structure could be employed to address this limitation [25].
- Generic Safe Composition. Our recent work applied Safe Composition in basic UML artifacts [26]; however, for other artifact types an adequate underlying theory and tool support is required. Model-Driven Engineering technologies could be used to meet this requirement.
- SPL quality attributes. There exist extensive research results on formal analysis of feature models which can be potentially used for assessing quality attributes such as performance in SPL architectures [24,27].
- Non-structural architectural properties. This paper focused on structural properties of SPL architectures; however, non-structural properties such as behavioral conformance are equally important. Recent work such as Brito et al. on fault tolerance goes in that direction [28]. Drawing a relation with Safe Composition may lead to benefits on both kinds of approaches.

**Acknowledgments.** This work was partially funded by the Austrian FWF under agreement P21321-N15 and Marie Curie Actions - Intra-European Fellowship (IEF) project number 254965.

## References

1. Batory, D.S., Sarvela, J.N., Rauschmayer, A.: Scaling step-wise refinement. IEEE Trans. Software Eng. 30(6), 355–371 (2004)
2. Pohl, K., Bockle, G., van der Linden, F.J.: Software Product Line Engineering: Foundations, Principles and Techniques. Springer, Heidelberg (2005)
3. Bosch, J.: Design and Use of Software Architectures. In: Adopting and evolving a product-line approach, Addison-Wesley, Reading (2000)
4. van der Linden, F.J., Schimd, K., Rommes, E.: Software Product Lines in Action: The Best Industrial Practice in Product Line Engineering. Springer, Heidelberg (2007)
5. Svahnberg, M., van Gurp, J., Bosch, J.: A taxonomy of variability realization techniques. Softw., Pract. Exper. 35(8), 705–754 (2005)
6. Taylor, R.N., Medvidovic, N., Dashofy, E.: Software Architecture: Foundations, Theory, and Practice. John Wiley & Sons, Chichester (2009)
7. Perry, D.E.: Generic architecture descriptions for product lines. In: van der Linden, F.J. (ed.) ESPRIT ARES. LNCS, vol. 1429, pp. 51–56. Springer, Heidelberg (1998)
8. Czarnecki, K., Eisenecker, U.: Generative Programming: Methods, Tools, and Applications. Addison-Wesley, Reading (2000)

9. Thaker, S., Batory, D.S., Kitchin, D., Cook, W.R.: Safe composition of product lines. In: Consel, C., Lawall, J.L. (eds.) GPCE, pp. 95–104. ACM, New York (2007)
10. Groher, I., Völter, M.: Aspect-oriented model-driven software product line engineering. T. Aspect-Oriented Software Development VI 6, 111–152 (2009)
11. Gomaa, H.: Designing Software Product Lines with UML. In: From Use Cases to Pattern-Based Software Architectures, Addison-Wesley, Reading (2004)
12. Zhang, H., Jarzabek, S.: Xvcl: a mechanism for handling variants in software product lines. Sci. Comput. Program 53(3), 381–407
13. Batory, D.: AHEAD Tool Suite (2008),
    http://www.cs.utexas.edu/users/schwartz/ATS.html
14. Mezini, M., Ostermann, K.: Variability management with feature-oriented programming and aspects. In: Taylor, R.N., Dwyer, M.B. (eds.) SIGSOFT FSE, pp. 127–136. ACM, New York (2004)
15. Jayaraman, P., Whittle, J., Elkhodary, A., Gomaa, H.: Model Composition in Product Lines and Feature Interaction Detection Using Critical Pair Analysis. In: Engels, G., Opdyke, B., Schmidt, D.C., Weil, F. (eds.) MODELS 2007. LNCS, vol. 4735, pp. 151–165. Springer, Heidelberg (2007)
16. Kästner, C., Apel, S., Kuhlemann, M.: A model of refactoring physically and virtually separated features. In: Siek, J.G. (ed.) GPCE, pp. 157–166. ACM, New York (2009)
17. Lopez-Herrejon, R.E., Rivera, J.E.: Realizing feature oriented software development with equational logic: An exploratory study. In: Vallecillo, A., Sagardui, G. (eds.) JISBD, pp. 269–274 (2009)
18. Bosch, J.: Software product families: Towards compositionality. In: Dwyer, M.B., Lopes, A. (eds.) FASE 2007. LNCS, vol. 4422, pp. 1–10. Springer, Heidelberg (2007)
19. Bosch, J., Bosch-Sijtsema, P.: From integration to composition: On the impact of software product lines, global development and ecosystems. Journal of Systems and Software 83(1), 67–76 (2010)
20. Dashofy, E.M., van der Hoek, A., Taylor, R.N.: A comprehensive approach for the development of modular software architecture description languages. ACM Trans. Softw. Eng. Methodol. 14(2), 199–245 (2005)
21. Pinto, M., Fuentes, L., Valenzuela, J.A., Pires, P.F., Delicato, F.C., Marinho, E.: On the need of architectural patterns in aosd for software evolution. In: [29], pp. 245–248
22. Loughran, N., Sánchez, P., Garcia, A., Fuentes, L.: Language support for managing variability in architectural models. In: Pautasso, C., Tanter, É. (eds.) SC 2008. LNCS, vol. 4954, pp. 36–51. Springer, Heidelberg (2008)
23. Adachi, E., Batista, T., Kulesza, U., Medeiros, A.L., Chavez, C., Garcia, A.: Variability management in aspect-oriented architecture description languages: An integrated approach, pp. 1–11 (2009)
24. Benavides, D., Segura, S., Ruiz-Cortés, A.: Automated analysis of feature models 20 years later: A literature review. Information System (in Press, 2010) (Corrected Proof)
25. Egyed, A., Wile, D.S.: Support for managing design-time decisions. IEEE Trans. Software Eng. 32(5), 299–314 (2006)
26. Lopez-Herrejon, R.E., Egyed, A.: Detecting inconsistencies in multi-view models with variability. In: ECMFA (to appear, 2010)
27. Etxeberria, L., Mendieta, G.S.: Variability driven quality evaluation in software product lines. In: SPLC, pp. 243–252. IEEE Computer Society, Los Alamitos (2008)
28. Brito, P.H.S., Rubira, C.M.F., de Lemos, R.: Verifying architectural variabilities in software fault tolerance techniques. In: [29], pp. 231–240
29. Joint Working IEEE/IFIP Conference on Software Architecture 2009 and European Conference on Software Architecture 2009, WICSA/ECSA 2009, Cambridge, UK, September 14-17. IEEE, Los Alamitos (2009)

# Expert Activities Automation through Enhanced Business Services Orchestration

Asta Krupaviciute and Jocelyne Fayn

MTIC-EA4171, INSA de Lyon, Université de Lyon 1, F69677, Bron, France
asta.krupaviciute@insa-lyon.fr, jocelyne.fayn@insa-lyon.fr

**Abstract.** Automating sophisticated, personalized expert activities, which are based on the application of professional knowledge to process an individual case, remains a great challenge. It is all the more relevant in some complex domains such as preventive medicine or e-learning where reliable and self-adaptive solutions are expected by users. In this paper we analyze differences between typical procedure-based business processes automation and expert activities automation. We propose to integrate context related knowledge into the business process modeling via the development of an intelligent process management agent. The latter is designed to dynamically orchestrate the set of services that will build up the process reproducing an expert activity, adapted to the concrete client's context.

**Keywords:** Expert activity, Dynamic business process, Ontology-based approach, Web services orchestration, Data and Model driven SOA.

## 1 Introduction

Business activities are increasingly being automated in order to expand their accessibility by overcoming time and distance limitations and reducing their costs. Usually, this automation is performed for activities based on a well known, defined procedure and are implemented as reusable atomic or composite business services accessible via the Internet. Examples of such procedure-based activities include well known services as booking an hotel room and flight tickets or creating a bank account. However, if a user demand is more complex, specific or intrinsic to the user, the implemented service cannot fulfill the request and so the task is forwarded to a human domain's expert. In particular, this situation occurs when the user request cannot be guided by a set of questions with multiple modalities. Then, in his turn, the expert analyzes the user situation and proposes the most adequate personalized solution.

This paper addresses the challenge of automating such complex, nonstandard and expert-requiring business activities, which we call expert activities in order to distinguish them from typical, procedural business activities. The target of such expert activities is to assist the user in an application of a specific domain knowledge, which depends on the circumstances of use and which is capable to respond to a concrete demand of the user. This activity, typically, covers a human intellectual process, such as teaching, diagnosing or deciding. Sasa et al. [1] called it a *mental process task*, where the final result can vary and *depends on an individual* expert.

M. Ali Babar and I. Gorton (Eds.): ECSA 2010, LNCS 6285, pp. 497–500, 2010.
© Springer-Verlag Berlin Heidelberg 2010

In the following, we further discuss the issue of expert activity automation by comparing it with the automation of a procedure-based business activity. Then, we propose a dynamic business process approach for modeling expert activities and a way to implement these processes by means of ontology driven services orchestration.

## 2 Expert Activities Automation

Procedure-based activities are being successfully automated in various domains, while the expert activity automation is often presented as a *long-term future vision* [1], although both activity types have at a first glance many similarities. They both tend to replace a human, to give a personal assistance, and they both require specific domain knowledge. Thereinafter, we overview the issues which make an automation of expert activities a complex and great challenge.

First of all, let us give two simplified examples of each activity type. We name PA a procedure-based activity helping a system user to book plane tickets and EA an automated expert activity, which is capable to locate the correct electrodes position on a human torso enabling the user to record the best quality electrocardiogram (ECG) by himself. Here, EA aims to replace a skillful nurse in a specialized hospital unit, who is recording an ECG that provides a patient specific body signal for a further medical diagnosis. Our goal is then to analyze the modeling of these two examples according to their input data, working practice and output, seeking to highlight challenges EA type activities are raising.

Typically, five broad stages underlie both activities: there is *a situation* (a), from which *a need* (b) is rising, then *a formal request* (c) is formed and *a process* (d) is launched in order to obtain *an answer* (e) to the user needs. Obviously, input data shall be described before the process is launched, so stages (a), (b) and (c) include the design of input parameters. In the PA case, the system user is an active client, capable to manage the online booking service on his own. He analyzes by himself his situation, he clearly understands his need and is able to formulate his demand in a formal request form. For example, a travel type – one way, a destination – Berlin, an outbound date – 2010.07.01. In the EA case, a service user is on the contrary a passive client, who has no specific medical or anatomy knowledge to evaluate his own situation and is not sure how to express his needs. So he is not really able to formulate his demand. Here, a service performing an optimal electrode-system selection should guide the user in order to obtain the possible user related contextual information that would help this service to determine the user situation and his needs as a formal request. Hence, the request form, in the EA case, can differ and basically depends on contextual information and on available methods used to acquire this information.

Then, when the user specific formal request (c) is set, the input data treatment (d) seeking to obtain a final result (e) is launched. For the procedure based activities, a chain of tasks is usually designed, where each task might demand additional information (or decision) from a client and a final task in the chain provides an answer (e) to the user primal request. Intuitively, we even can define a chain of tasks for the PA case: a flights search, a flight selection, a client identification, payment and confirmation. The latter answers to the initial user demand with a confirmation of booked tickets and details upon flights. Actually, we could use another online service to book the flight to Berlin and we would obtain the same final result (a confirmation and the same flight details), what shows that procedure based activities tend to produce repetitious results and are easy to test.

Meanwhile, the expert activity is often seen as a black box, which produces hardly tailored results. Here, we suggest perceiving a mental process not as a black box and not as a complex chain of tasks, but rather as a labyrinth, which can have several entries and several exits, and for which some passing rules (obtained from a previous experience or from the current steps evaluation) can be set in advance and/or at runtime. Indeed, an expert activity design strongly depends on a specific request, that is an entry point to the labyrinth, and on the expert knowledge base (practice / experience / habits), which holds also labyrinth passing rules. So the model of an expert activity (the labyrinth) instantiated for different clients may contain different passing routes or workflows of tasks to be performed, as a human expert would have proposed to each client a personal and individualized service. In our simplified EA example, if a client is a man and the signal quality is not sufficient (or qualified not to be sufficient), he might be asked to shave his chest in order to reduce skin conductivity. Also, several iterations of signal recording or an identification of various possible postures, electrode places or other changes might be done in order to improve the signal quality depending on the client context, available data processing methods and on intermediate results. Then, the labyrinth can be roughly seen as a state machine, where a pointer changes its state by choosing one out of four possible directions: the next state is the exit (x), the next state is a new task (+), the next state is an error, the pointer comes back to one of the previous states and sets a rule based on the error analysis (-), or finally the next state is the repetition of the current task using another method in order to gather additional information, which shall improve the confidence about the next direction to take (°). This state machine presents well the dynamism of the expert activity, herewith challenging to create advanced, adaptive business processes, which could provide intelligent assistance.

# 3   Dynamic Business Process

As it's briefly presented in the previous section, a business process, which is capable to adapt to a context, could be used to simulate expert type activities. We call such a business process a dynamic business process. A dynamic business process is composed of two main elements: a set of tasks and an intelligent management agent, which is responsible for the design of a business process that is specific to each client. Here, a set of tasks corresponds to various business process functionalities, which are typically implemented through atomic or composite services. However, the realization of the management agent, capable to orchestrate business functionality services according to each client's specificities, requires further research.

We are currently investigating knowledge management and business process management integration. Instead of modeling separately the domain knowledge and its context, we propose to model process knowledge on the basis of the context-aware domain knowledge. In this approach, the process knowledge is formally expressed via an ontology and a rules engine that provides a solid base to implement process related services and to compose them into a business process which is dynamically orchestrated according to the client specificities.

This approach is being tested on a decision support system called a Personal Cardiac Assistant [2] helping a non-professional user to select a personal sensor-system for biosignals recording on his own.

# 4 Conclusion

Expert activities automation is awaited in several domains such as preventive medicine, where early diagnosis is expected to be performed automatically at anytime and anyplace [3]. Also a thorough automatic follow up of the knowledge assimilation processes [4] could ameliorate and boom e-learning. Alike, the sales and consulting sectors may benefit from services proposing the user an automatic help that is most adequate to his needs. All these processes are domain specific and require professional knowledge that normally a typical user does not have.

Our ontology driven approach for enhancing services orchestration is especially promising for context-aware modeling. We thus firmly believe that intelligent assistance shall be grounded by a knowledge model upon each specific expert activity, and not only upon a specific business domain. Reusable expert activities automation could thus be performed thanks to domain independent core-ontologies that are related to the generic scope of the services, such as decision making. A research challenge is now to expand the Services Oriented Architecture (SOA) approach towards a data and model driven SOA approach.

**Acknowledgement.** This research work has been supported by a Marie Curie Early Stage Research Training Fellowship of the European Community Sixth Framework Programme under the contract number MEST-CT-2005-021024 within the project Wide Area Research Training in Health Engineering (WARTHE).

# References

1. Sasa, A., Juric, M., Krisper, M.: Service-Oriented Framework for Human Task Support and Automation. IEEE Transactions on Industrial Informatics 4, 292–302 (2008)
2. Krupaviciute, A., Fayn, J., Verdier, C., McAdams, E., Nugent, C., Rubel, P.: Information system architecture for wearable cardiac sensors personalization. In: 14th IEEE International Conference on Engineering of Complex Computer Systems, pp. 265–272. IEEE Computer Society, Washington (2009)
3. Fayn, J., Rubel, P.: Towards a Personal Health Society in Cardiology. IEEE Transactions on Information technology in Biomedicine 14(2), 401–409 (2010)
4. Macris, A., Papakonstantinou, D., Malamateniou, F., Vassilacopoulos, G.: Using ontology-based knowledge networks for user training in managing healthcare processes. International Journal of Technology Management 47, 5–21 (2009)

# Architecture Decision-Making in Support of Complexity Control

Andrzej Zalewski and Szymon Kijas

Warsaw University of Technology,
Institute of Automatic Control and Computational Engineering
a.zalewski@ia.pw.edu.pl, s.kijas@elka.pw.edu.pl

**Abstract.** The main challenge of software engineering has always been to bring software complexity under control. Different kinds of abstractions have been devised and applied for that purpose at different levels of software design. Some of them have proven successful, such as function hierarchies, layers, API's, abstract classes, encapsulation, interfaces etc. and are widely used in practice. Concepts from the genre of software architecture should also help to manage software complexity. We argue that, before architecture decisions and architecture decision-making become a common industrial practice, they have to support software complexity management much more efficiently than at present. Despite the substantial progress already made, it is still a major challenge both in theory (architecture decisions representation and architecture decision-making methods) and practice (tool support).

**Keywords:** architecture decisions, architecture decision-making, architectural styles, software complexity.

## 1 Introduction

Complexity has always been a primary concern of software engineering. Its ultimate objective was to overcome software complexity with software design methods, models, approaches and programming paradigms. Brooks, in his famous paper [1], has called them "silver bullets" and argued pessimistically that there are no such bullets in sight. The discussion over bullets killing software complexity seems to have faded out now. We have made tremendous progress in software development methods and tools over the last fifteen years: software we could not even imagine in 1996 can be created nowadays in just a couple of hours.

This does not mean that "silver bullets" have been found. We have rather managed to transform a complexity werewolf into a genie, and to devise means of keeping him in a tightly sealed bottle of abstractions such as API's, interfaces, layers or styles/patterns [9]. Hence, we have devised numerous successful abstractions that allow us to successfully manage software complexity. This is why these most popular abstractions are widely applied in practice.

The concept of architecture decisions (AD) [2], [3] and architecture decision-making have not achieved a maturity level similar to the abstractions mentioned above, and are still far from being everyday industrial practice. The main

M. Ali Babar and I. Gorton (Eds.): ECSA 2010, LNCS 6285, pp. 501–504, 2010.

challenge to be met in order to achieve industrial maturity of architectural decision-making, is to transform it into an efficient means of managing software complexity. In the conclusion of the paper we try to envisage future developments in the area of AD making aimed at meeting this general challenge.

# 2    Does AD Making Help to Control Software Complexity?

Architecture decisions (AD) have been conceived as a model of software architecture alternative to the views [4]. Software modelling has always been about abstracting from details that are unimportant at a given level of abstraction. Software architecture plays the same role.

ADs successfully capture knowledge that usually evaporates during system design and evolution. However, the question of whether architectural decision-making helps to overcome software complexity has not even been raised yet. We think that in current state-of-the-art, architectural decision-making contributes very little to overcoming design complexity, while it introduces an additional complexity of its own. These limitations of architectural decision-making arise mainly from: the textual form of ADs documentation; the diversity of abstraction levels of ADs, accompanied by insufficient and often ambiguous classifications; extremely complex structures of relations between ADs and a lack of guidelines on how to properly shape these relations in the decision-making process.

## 2.1    Representation of Architectural Decisions

Architecture decisions are still represented as text records [3], [5], [6], certain prototype tools link ADs with some illustrating diagrams, see [7] for example. The weaknesses of textual documentation have long been identified and are a kind of mantra of software engineering: incompleteness, inconsistency, ambiguity, inefficiency in representing and sharing engineering concepts. ADs have inherited these weaknesses in full.

Diagrammatic representations of ADs could help resolve this problem, as they did in the case of structured and object-oriented analysis and design methods. However, it is very difficult to express the heart of ADs graphically, as only existence decisions [6] can easily be linked to a specific element of software design, while most ADs describe certain properties, design assumptions or constraints.

## 2.2    Abstraction Level and Classifications of Architectural Decisions

ADs comprising certain software architecture usually concern different levels of abstraction, different levels of architectural scope or detail. Most influential classifications by Kruchten [6] (existence, non-existence, property and management ADs) and Zimmermann [8] (executive, conceptual, technology, vendor asset ADs) substantially help to navigate through a set of ADs. However, these categories are not always precise, and in many cases can confuse engineers (consider, for example, the decision of implementing access to data via web services - engineers can treat it either as a management (technology decision) or as an existence decision). The same category can contain decisions concerning different levels of abstraction, impacting different sets of design elements or engineering artefacts. The means of creating hierarchies of ADs (to hide unimportant details) or of aggregating ADs defining the same design element have not been devised yet.

### 2.3 Relations between Architecture Decisions and the Architecture Decision-Making Process

Relations between architecture decisions are used both to represent the architectural decision-making process and to supplement software architecture modelled as a set of ADs. Kruchten in [6] indicates ten kinds of relations between ADs, a number exceeding the famous $7 \pm 2$ rule. Thus, it could take some time to learn how to recognise each of these kinds.

ADs often represent a cross-cutting concern and can potentially be related to many other ADs (e.g. certain ADs can constrain many other ADs). This usually leads to the extremely complex structures of such relations - compare, for example, figures in [6] - pages 51-54. At the same time, there are scarcely any clues on how to shape the relations between ADs, which relations and under what conditions should or should not be modelled.

Sets of ADs do not comprise a uniform set of states similar to those known from the decision-making theory. This makes tree or graph representation of the architectural decision-making process difficult to achieve, as trees and graphs are most suitable for representing transitions between states of the same structure. This explains why design decision-making models, although developed for at least the past fifteen years [8], [10], [11], have not yet become popular in software industry. At the same time, existing tree or graph representations of architectural decision-making lack the ability to represent ADs hierarchically.

## 3  Challenges for Architecture Decision-Making

Architectural decision-making does not sufficiently address the concerns of software complexity control. This makes its "value proposition" disputable and will limit the transfer of the approach to the industry. We do think that the success of architectural decision-making depends mainly on its transformation into an efficient means of coping with software complexity, as in case of API's, layers, interfaces, architectural styles or design patterns.

To meet the above challenge, the following advances are needed:

- modelling ADs: developing models of ADs representing them in terms of engineering artefacts easily comprehensible for software engineers,
- organisation of ADs:
  - extending techniques of classification and clustering of ADs to improve complexity management. This should aim at the identification of ADs at a given level of abstraction, concerning certain design elements as well as clustering ADs with the structures recognised as contributing to complexity control, e.g. hierarchies or layers;

- developing means of aggregating ADs comprising a certain design element;
- developing means of defining and managing links between ADs and software engineering artefacts.
- structuring architectural decision-making process and providing more efficient ways of managing relations between ADs:
  - minimising the number of relations between ADs captured during the architectural decision-making process to a reasonable minimum defined by architectural decision-making methods,
  - extending existing architectural decision-making approaches to minimise dependencies between ADs by defining more precise paths of architectural decision-making while preserving the necessary level of design freedom,
  - developing predefined structures of relations between ADs, probably for chosen application domains.

# References

1. Brooks, F.P.: The Mythical Man-Month: Essays on Software Engineering, 2nd Anniversary edn. Addison-Wesley Professional, Reading (1995)
2. Bosch, J., Jansen, A.: Software Architecture as a Set of Architectural Design Decisions. In: WICSA 2005, pp. 109–120. IEEE Computer Society, Los Alamitos (2005)
3. Tyree, J., Akerman, A.: Architecture Decisions: Demystifying Architecture. IEEE Software (2005)
4. Kruchten, P.: The 4+1 View Model of Architecture. IEEE Software 12, 45–50 (1995)
5. Harrison, N.B., Avgeriou, P., Zdun, U.: Using Patterns to Capture Architectural Decisions. IEEE Software 24(4), 38–45 (2007)
6. Ali Babar, M., et al.: Architecture knowledge management. Theory and Practice. Springer, Heidelberg (2009)
7. Capilla, R., et al.: A Web-Based Tool for Managing Architectural Design Decisions. In: Proc. SHARK 2006, Software Eng. Notes. ACM SIGSOFT, vol. 31(5) (2006)
8. Zimmermann, O., et al.: Managing architectural decision models with dependency relations, integrity constraints, and production rules. Journal of Systems and Software 82(8), 1249–1267 (2009)
9. Avgeriou, P., Zdun, U.: Architectural patterns revisited - a pattern language. In: 10th European Conference on Pattern Languages of Programs (EuroPlop 2005), Irsee, Germany (2005)
10. Ran, A., Kuusela, J.: Design decision trees. In: Eighth International Workshop on Software Specification and Design, pp. 172–175 (1996)
11. Workshop summary: Patterns for decision-making in architectural design, Conference on Object Oriented Programming Systems Languages and Applications, pp. 132-137 (1995)

# Software Architecture Constraints as Customizable, Reusable and Composable Entities

Chouki Tibermacine[1], Christophe Dony[1], Salah Sadou[2], and Luc Fabresse[3,4]

[1] LIRMM, CNRS and Montpellier University, France
[2] VALORIA, Université Bretagne-Sud, Vannes, France
[3] Université Lille Nord de France, France
[4] École des Mines de Douai, France
{tibermacin,dony}@lirmm.fr, sadou@univ-ubs.fr, luc.fabresse@mines-douai.fr

**Abstract.** One of the major advantages of component-based software engineering is the ability for developers to reuse and assemble software entities to build complex software. Whereas decomposition of software into components has been and is largely addressed for what concerns the business (functional) part of applications, this is not yet the case for what concerns their documentation (non-functional) part. In this paper, we propose a new and original solution to express component-based software non-functional documentation, and we will focus more especially on architecture constraints, which formalize parts of architecture decisions, as executable, customizable, reusable and composable building blocks represented by components. Component-based applications using business and constraint components can be modeled with CLACS, a dedicated ADL which is also introduced in the paper. Architecture constraints can be executed at design-time within CLACS. CLACS is implemented as a plugin in the Eclipse IDE.

## 1 Introduction: Context and Motivation

Architecture constraints play an important role in design decision documentation and architecture validation. These constraints are often specified either textually or formally, but no means are proposed to customize them for their reuse in different contexts or to compose them in order to define complex constraints. The goal of the work presented in this paper is to propose a way to build architecture constraints as checkable entities embedded in a special kind of software components that can be reused, assembled, composed into higher-level ones and customized using standard component-based techniques. The purpose is as well to put reusable constraint-component on shelves (design for reuse) and to produce new constraints by composition of existing ones (design by reuse) and then to simplify the expression and definition of constraints (ascending design). An additional fundamental goal is to define a uniform paradigm to develop business and non-functional (constraint-) components. We aim thus at proposing an operational component-based design environment providing new capabilities to

M. Ali Babar and I. Gorton (Eds.): ECSA 2010, LNCS 6285, pp. 505–509, 2010.

506 C. Tibermacine et al.

express architecture constraints that can be executed at design-time to check the conformity of architecture designs and in which business components can be compiled into instructions of a component-based programming language.

The remaining of the paper is organized as follows. In the following section, we first introduce CLACS, the ADL we built for the SCL [4] component programming language which has been developed in our team. We then explain how using this ADL we can describe constraints as components and how these components can be connected to other constraint components or business ones. Before concluding and presenting the future work at the end of this paper, we make an overview of the related works.

## 2 Architecture Constraint-Components

Our solution is embedded into an operational software suite (CLACS-SCL) made of an architecture description language (ADL) called CLACS (*Constraint Language for Architectures of Component-based SCL-like software*), and of a component-oriented programming language named SCL (*Simple component language* [4]). CLACS is a modeling alternative for SCL.

### 2.1 Constraint-Components vs. Business Components

In order to not add (yet-)other constructs for constraint-component modeling, we chose to use the same constructs as for business component modeling. SCL business components and CLACS constraint components share most of their characteristics. The difference between them is expressed in the implementation of services. In business components, services represent traditional operations with a body containing the SCL code implementing the business logic. In constraint-components, the body contains the code of the constraint to be checked (specified in ACL [7] which is an adaptation of OCL).

### 2.2 Constraint-Component Specification in CLACS

Suppose we define a constraint-component which checks the Façade pattern. The descriptor of this component can be specified in CLACS and instantiated in a given architecture description. Each *Façade checker*, instance of this descriptor, owns one provided port named `Checking` that exports a constraint checking service having this signature : `boolean isFacade(aPort:Port,aSubComp:Component)`. Each *Façade checker* can then be connected, through that checking port, to any business component requiring this service i.e. having a corresponding required interface.

### 2.3 Connecting Constraints to Architectures

When designing a software architecture, the developer can connect constraint-components to business ones. The binding used to connect these two model elements makes it possible to validate the architecture design according to the constraints embedded in the constraint-component. When invoked within our modeling environment, a constraint-component provided service returns true if the architecture of the business component to which it is connected fulfills the constraint. When such a connection is established and a constraint evaluated, the constraint expressions interpretor automatically binds the context identifier, used in constraints expressions, to the business-component to which the constraint will be applied. When composite constraint-components are built in which a constraint-component is connected to another one, a transitive closure is computed on that link until a business-component is found.

## 2.4 Constraint-Component Composition

A constraint-component can be assembled together with other constraint-components to build more complex ones. We have defined one kind of binding for each logical operator (and, or, xor and implies). Delegation bindings linking constraint-components can be of kind "affirmative" or "negative". In the first case, if the constraint-component is bound to a business-component, this means that the architecture of the latter component should respect the constraint embedded in the former component. However, in the second case (negative delegation binding), the architecture of the business component should not respect the architecture choice formalized within the constraint-component.

## 2.5 Constraint Checking

Architectural constraint checking is performed at design time. Thus, constraint-components are interpreted at this stage contrarily to business-components which are executed after their deployment. The constraint checking is implemented by a simple function. Depending on the kind of constraint-components (composite or primitive), the local evaluation corresponds to a delegation to another sub-component or to an ACL interpreter. The propagation of the context within the different constraint-components is done during constraint checking. This allows the evaluation of the constraints on the appropriate business component.

# 3  Related Work

Different existing ADLs embed constraint languages. Acme [5] and Wright [2] are two representative examples of them. Constraints in Acme and Wright do not represent first-class entities for composition. In addition, constraints in these languages are fixed expressions, which cannot be parameterized to reference a part of the architecture description (with identified components). As presented in the previous sections, CLACS implements a customizability feature at the architecture constraint description level, which allows designers to define reusable constraints. Being embedded in components, these constraints can be easily assembled to extend existing architecture constraint specifications.

Design pattern schemas [6] and component specification patterns [1] are descriptions which allow the definition of templates of OCL constraints with some parameters which are fixed during the instantiation of the templates. As in our work, constraints are parameterized with model elements and are used as library modules. However, model elements (parameters) in our case are architectural elements and constraints target structural descriptions, whereas, in [6], model elements are UML class entities and in [1] constraints target the functional (behavioral) aspect of components.

## 4   Conclusion and Future Work

Sometimes, defined manually (from scratch) architectural decisions' documentation is complex, error-prone and time-consuming. Having a means to define such documentations by hierarchical composition of constraints is beneficial for two accounts: First, by decomposing the models of architecture constraints in several small interfaced documentation parts, a common repository of reusable (parametrized) assets is provided for software architects; and second, this is a logical way of doing in the continuum of artifact development in component-based software engineering[1].

We implemented CLACS as a prototype in the Eclipse IDE by using some existing plugins [3]: the EMF (Eclipse Modeling Framework) module which allowed us to define an Ecore metamodel of CLACS to generate an editor, and the GMF (Graphical Modeling Framework) plugin to give a graphical dimension to the editor. SCL code generation feature in this editor allows to generate SCL code starting from EMF models. This has been done using the JET (Java Emitter Templates) Eclipse plugin [3]. At the conceptual level, we plan to enrich constraint-components with the other parts of architecture decision documentation. This will help to incrementally build complex non-functional documentations by composition and thus get the advantages of component-based software engineering. In addition, we are investigating the proposition of a model of reflective components. At the tool level, we plan in the near future to work on constraint-component code generation. This will help to check architecture constraints at the evolution stage on implementation artifacts (SCL code). Our aim in the future is also to build a repository of classified architecture constraints.

## References

1. Ackermann, J., Turowski, K.: A library of ocl specification patterns for behavioral specification of software components. In: Dubois, E., Pohl, K. (eds.) CAiSE 2006. LNCS, vol. 4001, pp. 255–269. Springer, Heidelberg (2006)
2. Allen, R.: A Formal Approach to Software Architecture. PhD thesis, Carnegie Mellon University, Pittsburgh, PA, USA (May 1997)

---

[1] In the same spirit, the Eiffel language has been proposed for, at the same time, programming applications' business-logic and formalizing functional constraints (contract programming with assertions).

3. Eclipse. Eclipse Modeling Project. Eclipse Board Web Site: http://www.eclipse.org/modeling/
4. Fabresse, L., Dony, C., Huchard, M.: Foundations of a Simple and Unified Component-Oriented Language. Journal of Computer Languages, Systems & Structures 34(2-3), 130–149 (2008)
5. Garlan, D., Monroe, R.T., Wile, D.: Acme: Architectural description of component-based systems. In: Leavens, G.T., Sitaraman, M. (eds.) Foundations of Component-Based Systems, pp. 47–68. Cambridge Univ. Press, Cambridge (2000)
6. Giese, M., Larsson, D.: Simplifying transformations of OCL constraints. In: Briand, L.C., Williams, C. (eds.) MoDELS 2005. LNCS, vol. 3713, pp. 309–323. Springer, Heidelberg (2005)
7. Tibermacine, C., Fleurquin, R., Sadou, S.: A family of languages for architecture constraint specification. Journal of Systems and Software, JSS (2010)

# A Framework for Dynamic Self-optimization
# of Power and Dependability Requirements
# in Green Cloud Architectures

Rami Bahsoon

School of Computer Science
The University of Birmingham
Edgbaston, B15 2TT, Birmingham, UK
r.bahsoon@cs.bham.ac.uk

**Abstract.** I report on the activities and research challenges, their rationales, and
the work in progress related to the ongoing EPSRC/UoB Bridging the Gap Fellowship project on Green Cloud Architectures. The initiative is aimed at a
framework for dynamic self-optimization of cloud architectures taking into
account the tradeoffs involved in maintaining acceptable dependability requirements/Quality of Service (QoS) with minimal power at runtime. I argue
that linkage between dependability requirements and power should be explicit. I
motivate the need for new meters for Power-per-QoS value (and sacrifices) for
cloud architectures. I motivate the need for an economics-inspired approach for
dynamic self-optimization of cloud architectures. I discuss the role of Data
Driven Simulation Systems in implementing such framework.

## 1 Introduction

*Cloud computing* is claimed for enabling convenient, on-demand network access to a
shared pool of configurable computing resources (e.g., networks, servers, storage,
applications, and services) that can be rapidly provisioned and released with minimal
management effort[1,3]. The popularity of the cloud is rapidly increasing: many computing services have now moved to the cloud and many new applications are emerging either as standalone or in orchestration with existing services. As a result, the
cloud architecture is *dynamically* scaling up to accommodate such growth in services,
data, and users. From the architecture point of view, scaling up such ultra-large scale
architectures does continuously introduce additional *computational power*, as meeting
*dependability requirements* such as *scalability, availability, reliability, real time performance, fault-tolerance, openness and security* essentially imply the need for additional computational resources: this may, for example, entail hardware and software
redundancy to be deployed in realization to some architectural mechanisms and tactics, like load balancing, replication, migration transparency, and so forth. It would
be expected that more servers/nodes to be deployed to realize dependability requirements and consequently more operating and cooling power will be required. The
situation will lead to an uncontrolled growth of computational power consumption.
Such growth, if left unmanaged, is expected to contribute to the degradation of our

M. Ali Babar and I. Gorton (Eds.): ECSA 2010, LNCS 6285, pp. 510–514, 2010.

ecosystem and more $CO_2$ emissions, as we move and heavily depend on the cloud. Meanwhile, meeting dependability and Quality of Service (QoS) requirements are critical and can't be neglected in favor of power savings.

I report on the activities and research challenges, their rationales, and the work in progress related to the ongoing *EPSRC Bridging the Gap Fellowship project* on Green Cloud Architectures. The initiative is aimed at a framework for *dynamic self-optimization* of cloud architectures taking into account the tradeoffs involved in maintaining acceptable dependability requirements with minimal power at runtime. The research initiative is multidisciplinary, involving Software Architectures and Dynamic Data Driven Simulation Systems (DDDAS), Economics, Dynamic Power Management and Energy Policy, Modeling and Optimization research.

# 2 Self-managed Green Cloud Architectures: Research Challenges and Work in Progress

Below, I report on the software architecture related challenges, their rationales, and work in progress in realizing the framework for *dynamic self-optimization* of cloud architectures taking into account the tradeoffs of dependability on power.

## 2.1 Linking Dependability Requirements to Power and New Meters for QoS per Cloud Power Value

Green-aware constraints such as power bring new challenges to the way we systematically develop, evolve and scale ultra large-scale software architectures, as it is the case for the cloud. We argue that the software architecture should be green aware, where the architecture design decisions should not only be judged by their technical merits, but also by their contributions to energy savings. The software system architecture is the appropriate level of abstraction to address green-aware concerns, as the architectural design decisions in addressing dependability requirements and managing their evolution trends and tradeoffs are crucial determinant for power consumptions and savings. Current practice to architecting software systems does not make the linkage between power and design decisions explicit (or even implicit). The need for such linkage becomes more important especially in the case of evolving large-scale architectures, such as cloud architectures. In practice, dynamic changes and evolution of dependability requirements like scalability, availability, security, and performance requirements may suggest additional hardware/software resources, which need to be deployed at runtime. This may effectively translate to additional computing power. As result, power could be best modeled in relation to dependability and QoS demands and provision of a runtime instance. There are several research challenges to address, however. One of the challenges is to relate power to dependability requirements in cloud architectures. Another challenge is to arrive on mechanisms for measuring, logging, controlling, actuating and calibrating power as the cloud architecture dynamically evolves in response to dependability and QoS demands and provision. One intuition is to leverage on the state-of-art and state-of-practice in Dynamic Power Management to benefit the case of the cloud. The challenge, however, is to express and formulate models for expressing dependability and QoS demands and provision-values per power usage or savings. Inversely, new meters for QoS-per-power value will be needed. Such meters will show the value of QoS on the expense of power sacrificed (and vice versa). We envision further refinement of these meters to include individual QoS quality-per-power value (e.g. performance-per-power value, availability-per-power value etc.) and how they can be expressed in isolation or when combined. Such meters will be useful for performing what-if analyses, when matching resources provision to power demands, for facilitating sensitivity and tradeoffs analyses-either statically or dynamically (at runtime). The fundamental premise is that the cloud architecture (and its components) experiences no uniform workloads exhibiting variation in QoS requirements during its operation. Such an assumption is valid for most systems, both when considered in isolation and when internetworked as for the case of the cloud. A second assumption is that it is possible to monitor, with a certain degree of confidence, the fluctuations of QoS and their power. Such observation and prediction should not consume significant energy, however.

## 2.2  Economics-Inspired Approach for Self-optimizing the Cloud Architecture

We argue that dynamic change and evolution of the cloud architectures is a value-seeking and value-maximizing process, where the architecture is undergoing a dynamic change (at runtime) and seeking value. We treat dependability provision and their power consumption as scare resources, which need to be dynamically optimized. Performing a runtime search for best architectural instances, which addresses the dependability requirements with minimal power is a problem, which is appealing to "dynamic" or "on line" Search-based Software Engineering (SBSE), where the optimization problem is rapidly changing and the current best solution must be continually adapted. The challenge is to maximize the value added and select the optimal execution plans.

The highly dynamic nature of the cloud architecture requires a simple, scalable, and inexpensive runtime optimization technique. This is necessary as the search for the optimal runtime instance addressing the tradeoffs between power and dependability requirements/QoS is continuously active and may be initiated at various time intervals of the execution. This is not only for seeking to find an optimal solution to the said problem, but rather, for seeking to improve upon the current runtime situation. Classical and static optimization techniques may be ineffective and expensive to use in this dynamic setting for the representation of the problem and the definition of the fitness function are mere active at runtime and very volatile with respect to time. Furthermore, the problem entails judging the tradeoffs not only from a technical perspective but also from an economics driven one. We are investigating how economics-inspired approaches, based on market-control theory and/or game theory, can address the problem of dynamic runtime optimization and self-adaptation of the cloud architecture in addressing such tradeoffs. Together with Economists, we will formulate models and scenarios, utilizing the meters developed in 2.1. We are investigating how classical market based theory and it various simple concepts and scenarios like supply, demand, inflation, recession, and equilibrium could be mapped to the case of matching supply and demand of power vs. that of dependability requirements (individual or combined) in the cloud. We have reported on some preliminary results on the analogy for the case of standalone software architectures [2]. The relevance to the cloud architecture is promising.

## 2.3 Implementation Framework Using Dynamic Data Driven Simulation Systems (DDDAS)

We are investigating how Dynamic Data Driven Simulation Systems (DDDAS) paradigm, which the University of Birmingham is a key contributor to the field, can benefit the cloud architecture. In particular, we are investigating how elements of DDDAS – *including measurement, simulation, control, and feedback* can extend various cloud architectural styles to assist in the problem of dynamic runtime self-optimization of the cloud in relation to power and QoS. This layer is expected to utilize the meters of 2.1 and the economics-inspired models developed in 2.2. One important aspect of DDDAS in this setting is the ability to use *runtime simulation* (through the use of high performance computing) in order to improve the prediction and the self-management process of the runtime configuration through symbiotic control and feedback loops. To achieve this objective, the simulation will require mining data stored from previous runtime instances to inform and tune the prediction and execution plans to self-adaptation. In particular, the simulation (i) will identify scenarios and possible moves leading to robust and stable runtime configurations in the cloud topology showing efficiency of power use and acceptable QoS. Simulation can also predict situations leading to QoS sacrifices in relation to power savings; (ii) can assist in predict the rippling impact of such sacrifices on the robustness of individual nodes/services and the cloud as whole; (iii) shall provide the basis for dynamic analysis for QoS value sacrifices with respect to power savings. Simulation can also determine the long-term implications of favoring QoS requirements and policies over power savings for some instances, where QoS can't be compromised. These implications can be in relation to cost and stability of the cloud architecture; (iv) can also have static use: For example, the simulation can inform the cloud management decisions and long-term policies related to cloud service provision, management, deployment, and capacity restriction or leasing in relation to various cloud services – ranging from software-, platform-; infrastructure-, data- services. The DDDAS layer is expected to form a standalone and independent layer, which can be integrated in the cloud to make it green-aware and energy efficient.

## 3 Conclusions and Expected Impact

Green-aware constraints such as power bring new challenges to the way we systematically develop, evolve and scale ultra large-scale software architectures, as it is the case for the cloud. We have argued that the software architecture should be green aware, where the architecture design decisions and their evolution trends should not only be judged by their technical merits, but also by their contributions to energy savings. We have reported on the activities and research challenges of the ongoing EPSRC Bridging the Gap Fellowship project on Green Cloud Architectures. The initiative is aimed at a framework for *dynamic self-optimization* of cloud architectures taking into account the tradeoffs involved in maintaining acceptable dependability requirements with minimal power at runtime. We have argued that linkage between dependability requirements and power should be explicit. We have motivated the need for new meters for Power-Per-QoS value and sacrifices. We have discussed the role of DDDAS in such framework. The research will raise the understanding of evolution trends in ultra large sale dynamic cloud architectures and improve their quality and robustness through dependability and power measurement and control. More widely, we hope the research results will feed into long-term vision of helping in reducing power consumption and $CO_2$ emissions in ICT infrastructures.

# References

1. Nallur, V., Bahsoon, R., Yao, X.: Self-Optimizing Architecture for Ensuring Quality Attributes in the Cloud. In: Proceedings of the Joint Working IEEE/IFIP Conference on Software Architecture 2009 & European Conference on Software Architecture 2009, Cambridge, UK (2009)
2. Rangaraj, G., Bahsoon, R.: A Market-based Approach for Self-Managing Power in Software Architectures – in submission. Technical Report, School of Computer Science, University of Birmingham, CSR-10-01 (2010)
3. Nallur, V., Bahsoon, R.: Design of a Market-Based Mechanism for Quality Attributes Tradeoffs of Services in the Cloud. To appear in the Proceedings of the 25th ACM Symposium of Applied Computing, ACM SAC 2010 (2010)
4. EDSER 1-8: Proceedings of the Workshops on Economics-Driven Software Engineering Research. In conj. with the 21st through 28th International Conference on Software Engineering (1999-2006)

# Identifying Architectural Connectors through Formal Concept Analysis of Communication Primitives

Arvind W. Kiwelekar and Rushikesh K. Joshi

Department of Computer Science and Engineering
Indian Institute of Technology Bombay, Mumbai-400076, India
awk@cse.iitb.ac.in, rkj@cse.iitb.ac.in

**Abstract.** A set of interaction primitives and properties are systematically analyzed through Formal Concept Analysis (FCA) leading to identification of connector types and relationships among them. The approach is illustrated through a set of communication primitives from the web services modeling languages. The identified concepts are elaborated in terms of UML/OCL descriptions. The FCA based analysis and OCL descriptions can be used to automatically build an ontology of architectural connectors.

## 1 Introduction

Architectural connectors encapsulate protocols of interactions among components of software systems [1]. They differ in terms of properties they possess. For example, implementations of Remote Procedure Call may vary on type of binding between clients and servers, exceptions, argument copying, and security [2]. Architectural connectors can be conceptualized in terms of such properties. Earlier researchers have formalized the semantics of connectors through various techniques such as process calculus [1], taxonomies and description logics. In this paper, we attempt a systematic identification of connectors through *Formal-Concept Analysis* [3]. The approach also brings out differences and commonalities between connectors.

## 2 Interaction Primitives and Properties

Eight interaction primitives from WSDL and BPEL interaction patterns [4] are considered to demonstrate the use of FCA in identifying connectors. They are characterized by the properties that they possess. From WSDL, the data transfer primitives that are considered are simple output data transfer, robust output data transfer, and simple and robust input of data. From BPEL, the activity primitives considered are an activity to reply to a request, an invocation of an activity, an activity to receive data and an event handler activity. The WSDL primitives are data transfer primitives, while the BPEL primitives are control

M. Ali Babar and I. Gorton (Eds.): ECSA 2010, LNCS 6285, pp. 515–518, 2010.
© Springer-Verlag Berlin Heidelberg 2010

transfer primitives that start activities. The former primitives are of descriptive nature, while the latter are executional primitives.

The following properties can be associated with a characterization of these interaction primitives: (i) *Bilateral.* Only two participants are involved in the interaction. (ii) *Anonymity.* The identity of the peer participant is not known in advance. (iii) *Round trip Interaction.* The sender of a message is also the recipient of the reply. (iv) *Synchronized.* A recipient is ready to receive messages when messages arrive. (v) *Single Message Transfer.* Only a reply or a request is sent, but not both. (vi) *Reliable Delivery.* The messages are guaranteed to be delivered despite the failure of a communication medium. (vii) *Blocked Sender.* The initiator of an interaction gets blocked until a message is successfully delivered or delivery failure is reported. (viii) *Correlating Interactions.* Messages that have been sent and their replies are correlated. (ix) *Fault Generation.* A fault message is generated if the interaction is not successful. (x) *Racing of Messages.* If many messages are received at the same time, a race condition may occur. (xi) *Thread-based handling.* A new thread is created to process an incoming message. (xii) *Exception-based fault handling.* Faults are handled separately by exceptions. An association of various primitives and these properties is captured in Table 1. It can however be noted that the table represents one view in a possible application context, and other variations may be possible due to application specific architectural considerations.

**Table 1.** Building Formal Context

| | BILAT | ANON | ROUND | SYNCH | ONETX | RELI | BLOCK | COREL | FAULT | RACE | THREAD | EXCEP |
|---|---|---|---|---|---|---|---|---|---|---|---|---|
| wsdlOut | × | | | × | | | | | | | | |
| wsdlRobustOut | × | × | | × | | | × | | | | | × |
| wsdlIn | × | | | × | × | | | | | | | |
| wsdlRobustIn | × | × | | × | × | | | × | | | | × |
| bpelRepAct | × | × | × | × | × | × | × | × | × | | | × |
| bpelRecvAct | × | | × | × | × | × | × | × | × | | × | × |
| bpelInvokeAct | × | × | | × | × | × | × | | × | | | × |
| bpelOnEvent | × | | × | × | × | | | | | × | × | |

BILAT    *Bilateral*
ANON    *Anonymous*
ROUND    *Round Trip*
SYNCH    *Synchronized*
ONETX    *Single Transfer*
RELI    *Reliable Delivery*
BLOCK    *Blocked Sender*
COREL    *Message Correlation*
FAULT    *Fault Message*
RACE    *Race Avoider*
THREAD *Threaded Handling*
EXCEP    *Exception Handling*

# 3   Conceptualization of Connector Types

To identify concepts a *formal context* as shown in Table 1 can be used. A formal context is a 3-tuple $(O, A, R)$, where $O$, $A$ and $R$ are sets of objects, attributes, and relations between objects and attributes respectively. The interaction primitives are mapped to objects and properties to attributes. Objects and attributes are related if a communication primitive possesses a given property. A *concept* $C$ is a pair $(X, Y)$ where $X \subseteq O$, $Y \subseteq A$, X'=Y and Y'=X, where X'={a ∈ A |

(a) Connectors as Formal Concepts

| Concepts Definitions | Identified Connectors |
|---|---|
| Descriptive Connector Types | |
| $c1$ = {(wsdlIn, wsdlRobustIn, wsdlOut, wsdlRobustOut), (BILAT, ONETX)} | Simple Transfer |
| $c2$ = {(wsdlIn, wsdlRobustIn), (BILAT, ONETX, RELI)} | Reliable Transfer |
| $c4$ = {(wsdlRobustOut, wsdlRobustIn), (BILAT, ONETX, FAULT, EXCEP, ROUND)} | Robust Transfer |
| Executable Connector Types | |
| $c6$ = {(bpelRecvAct), (BILAT, ONETX, SYNCH, BLOCK, EXCEP, FAULT, RELI, ROUND, COREL, THREAD)} | Threaded Receiver |
| $c8$ = {(bpelInvokeAct, bpelRepAct), (BILAT, ONETX, SYNCH, BLOCK, EXCEP, FAULT, RELI, ANON)} | Anonymous Invocation |
| $c9$ = {(bpelRepAct), (BILAT, ONETX, SYNCH, BLOCK, EXCEP, FAULT, RELI, ANON, ROUND, COREL)} | Round Reliable Callback |
| $c11$ = {(bpelOnEvent), (BILAT, ONETX, SYNCH, ROUND, THREAD)} | Event Listener |

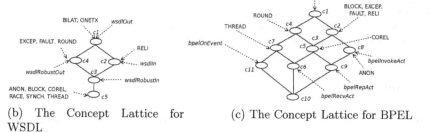

(b) The Concept Lattice for WSDL

(c) The Concept Lattice for BPEL

**Fig. 1.** Conceptualization of Connector Types

(o,a) ∈ R for all o ∈ X }, and Y'={o ∈ O | (o,a) ∈ R for all a ∈ Y }. The set $X$ is known as an *extent* of the concept and $Y$ is the *intent*. The concept lattices for the interaction primitives and properties considered are shown in Figure 1. A *concept lattice* relates two concepts through a *sub-concept* relationship. Two concepts may be related through *sub-concept* relationships For example, in the wsdl lattice, reliable connector is a sub-connector of simple connector. Reliable connector adds more attributes to simple connector. Similarly, reliable connector and robust connector are siblings, both being subconnectors of the simple connector. Robust and reliable connector is a specialization derived from these two specializations. The lattice brings out these relationships.

# 4   OCL Descriptions

Towards building connector ontologies, the connector types are further specified with OCL invariants against UML based reference communication model shown

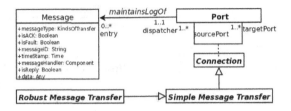

Fig. 2. UML based Communication Model

in Figure 2. For example, a simple message transfer connector has two properties. Firstly, a simple message transfer is a bilateral interaction, i.e. only one source is involved for a message received. Secondly only one message is transferred between source and target participant for a given message Id.

```
context SimpleMessageTransfer inv smt:
self.sourcePort ->allInstances()->size() = 1 and
self.targetPort ->allInstances()->size() = 1 and
self.sourcePort.entry->collect(sm: Message|
self.targetPort.entry->select(tm : Message|
tm.messageID = sm.messageID and
sm.messageType = KindsOfTransfer::OUT and
tm.messageType = KindsOfTransfer::IN))-> size() =1
```

## 5   Conclusion

The FCA approach demonstrates a method of systematic analysis of interaction properties to bring out connectors and relationships between them. Connectors derived through the analysis are specified through OCL specifications with reference to a metamodel towards building connector ontologies. However, the challenges faced in this work include handling properties in different domains, subtle variations in interpretations of properties and scale of contexts.

## References

1. Allen, R., Garlan, D.: A formal basis for architectural connection. ACM Trans. Softw. Eng. Methodol. 6(3), 213–249 (1997)
2. Birrell, A.D., Nelson, B.J.: Implementing remote procedure calls. ACM Trans. Comput. Syst. 2(1), 39–59 (1984)
3. Ganter, B., Stumme, G., Wille, R. (eds.): Formal Concept Analysis. LNCS (LNAI), vol. 3626. Springer, Heidelberg (2005)
4. Alistair, B., Dumas, M., ter Hofstede, A.H.: Service interaction patterns: Towards a reference framework for service-based business process interconnection. In: van der Aalst, W.M.P., Benatallah, B., Casati, F., Curbera, F. (eds.) BPM 2005. LNCS, vol. 3649, pp. 302–318. Springer, Heidelberg (2005)

# MDA Tool for Telecom Service Functional Design

Ankit Ahuja[1,2], Jacques Simonin[2], and Rémi Nedelec[1]

[1] Orange Labs, 2 avenue P. Marzin,
22300 Lannion, France
{Ankit.Ahuja,Remi.Nedelec}@orange-ftgroup.com
[2] Institut Télécom, Télécom Bretagne, Lab-STICC UMR CNRS 3192, UEB,
Technopole Brest-Iroise, 29238 Brest, France
{Ankit.Ahuja,Jacques.Simonin}@telecom-bretagne.eu

**Abstract.** Telecom service development process followed at Orange consists of a sequence of interrelated tasks. We present an MDA tool which describes this process using SPEM 2.0 compatible graphical editor, and then associates a model to each defined task for its execution. These models are validated for conformance to functional rules embedded inside the tool. Task automation is achieved using MDA model transformations, which use Orange knowledge model as the basis to extract the existing reusable functional components and their interdependencies. Graphical editor and model transformations have been integrated together in an ECLIPSE environment. Finally, the validated functional design model is transformed towards a UML2 profile, so as the telecom architect can manipulate it in an environment he is familiar with.

**Keywords:** model-driven architecture, SPEM 2.0, model transformation, component reuse.

## 1 Introduction

A telecom service is a service provided to an end-user by a telecommunication operator. For telecom service development, an enterprise architecture assisted method called Enterprise Architecture for Unified Processes (EA4UP) [1] is used at Orange. This method aims at improving the process continuity and reuse of existing components. We have developed a Model-Driven Architecture (MDA) tool around EA4UP method which firstly describes this development process graphically using a SPEM 2.0 (Software Process Engineering Meta-model) compatible editor, and secondly associates an input/output model to each task defined. The target audiences for this tool are on one hand the telecom architects at Orange, and on the other, the quality engineers who could thus check telecom service development traceability. The input and output models conform to EA4UP meta-model and are generated automatically using model transformations. For these transformations, MDA approach is used which consists of transforming a Platform Independent Model (PIM) into a Platform Specific Model (PSM) using a Platform Dependent Model (PDM). In our approach, PIM is a model extracted from the graphically defined components and PSM is the functional design model obtained using PDM which is the Orange knowledge model

M. Ali Babar and I. Gorton (Eds.): ECSA 2010, LNCS 6285, pp. 519–522, 2010.

consisting of existing reusable functional components. PSM model is validated for correctness based on functional rules of enterprise architecture defined in the transformation, and the telecom architect is warned of anomalies, if any. Finally, the validated EA4UP model is transformed towards a UML2 profile, so that it can be analyzed in a modeling tool like Rational Software Modeler (RSM).

This tool presents a new paradigm for creating functional architecture of a telecom service, as the architect describes graphically the required functional components without intervening directly into the complex EA4UP model. Of these components, ones already available in the knowledge model are extracted along with their interdependencies. The functional design model is then transformed towards a UML2 profile which can be imported in RSM, with which the telecom architect is familiar. Hence, an automatically generated visual model of functional design is obtained.

## 2  Tool Architecture

Tool architecture consists of three different layers as shown in Figure 1: Process description layer, Input/output model layer and UML2 profile layer. *Firstly*, in Process description layer, the EA4UP development process is described in terms of activities and tasks using a SPEM 2.0 compatible editor Top-Process Modeler (TPM) [2]. TPM meta-model has been evolved to integrate with it the EA4UP and Orange knowledge models as input/output for a task. Additional classes and attributes are added in TPM meta-model in order to make links of tasks with EA4UP models. A new graphical editor is generated using TOPCASED [3] approach for the evolved TPM meta-model. *Secondly*, in Input/output model layer, each of the tasks defined in TPM is executed by linking it with an input or output model. These models conform to the EA4UP or the Orange knowledge meta-model, and are generated using MDA model transformations. Model transformations are realized using the open-source ECLIPSE plug-in SmartQVT [4], developed at Orange Labs. Hence, the tasks defined in the Process

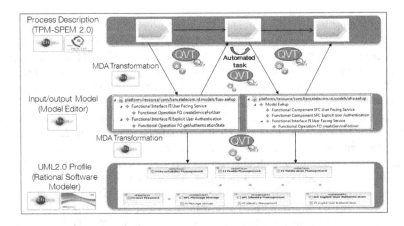

**Fig. 1.** MDA tool 3-layer architecture

description layer are executed with the help of models generated by MDA transformations in Input/Output model layer. These models are validated for conformance to functional rules defined by a telecom architect which are coded in model transformation. *Thirdly*, in UML2 profile layer, the hence obtained validated EA4UP model is transformed to a UML2 profile, so as it can be viewed and edited in software modeling tool like RSM. This is also achieved using a SmartQVT transformation.

# 3  Task Execution Using MDA Tool

The tool has been implemented for the functional view defined in EA4UP process. This view further consists of a sequence of tasks shown in Figure 2. In task 1, the telecom architect graphically creates various Functional Operations (FO) required for a particular telecom service. In task 2, these FOs are extracted into an EA4UP model and a look-up is performed in the Orange knowledge model for their pre-existence. This task generates a warning to the telecom architect as shown in Figure 3, in case the created FO does not exist in the knowledge model. In task 3, the corresponding functional interfaces (FI) are extracted from Orange knowledge model for each FO. Also, for newly created FOs in task 2, new FIs are created. In task 4, the functional components (FC) related to each FI are extracted from knowledge model. Here, it is to be noted that a FC has a list of *provided* FIs and *used* FIs which, in turn, gives a chain of interdependent FIs and FCs. Hence, all the required FCs are extracted from the knowledge model. In task 5, the telecom architect creates new FCs corresponding to new FIs not existing in knowledge model. Here, he has to comply with the functional rule that the FI-FC interdependency should never create a loop, as it would lead to unnecessary redundant data flow. Finally in task 6, functional architecture is validated for conformance to this functional rule and error message is generated in case of non-compliance.

The EA4UP functional design model hence obtained is then transformed towards a UML2 profile, which is shown in layer 3 in the tool architecture. UML2 stereotypes

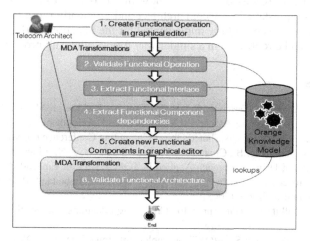

**Fig. 2.** Execution of functional design tasks using MDA tool

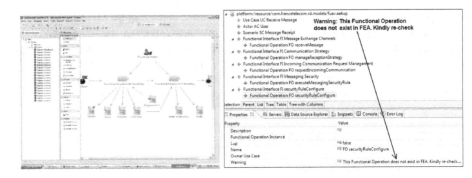

**Fig. 3.** MDA tool screenshots showing EA4UP graphical model and a warning message generated during model transformation

are created for each FI, FO and FC defined in the EA4UP functional design. The UML model hence obtained is imported in a software modeling tool like Rational Software Modeler to visualize the functional design. It is during this stage of telecom service development that the functional component interaction is visualized. This interaction thus allows the realization of scenarios for the telecom service. Tasks defined inside MDA transformation box in Figure 2 are automated. Figure 3 shows screenshots of MDA tool functionalities.

## 4 Conclusion

The main expectation of telecom architect from this tool is to obtain a validated UML functional design of a telecom service containing the existing reusable components and their interdependencies. Hence, the output of this MDA tool is an automatically generated UML model which can be manipulated and analyzed by the architect according to his functional knowledge.

Experimentation results of this tool show that it is able to automate majority of functional design tasks of a telecom architect and efficiently reuse the existing components. This tool has been fully implemented for the Functional MDE sub-process of EA4UP, and can be replicated in a similar way for the other sub-processes.

## References

1. Simonin, J., Alizon, F., Deschrevel, J.-P., Le Tron, Y., Jézéquel, J.-M., Nicolas, B.: EA4UP: an Enterprise Architecture-Assisted Telecom Service Development Method. In: 12th International IEEE Enterprise Distributed Object Computing Conference (2008)
2. Garcia, A., Combemale, B., Cregut, X., Vandeur, J., Guyot, J.-N., Libert, B.: topPROCESS: a Process Model Driven Approach Applied in TOPCASED for Embedded Real-Time Software. In: Proceedings of the 4th European Congress Embedded Real Time Software (ERTS), Toulouse, France (2008)
3. Topcased: Toolkit in Open-source for Critical Applications and SystEms Development, http://www.topcased.org
4. Belaunde, M., Dupe, G.: SmartQVT, an implementation of the MOF QVT Opertational language in top of EMF. In: eclipseCON 2007 (2007)

# A NUI Based Multiple Perspective Variability Modeling CASE Tool

Rabih Bashroush

School of Computing, IT and Engineering,
University of East London,
London, United Kingdom
rabih@uel.ac.uk

**Abstract.** With current trends towards moving variability from hardware to software, and given the increasing desire to postpone design decisions as much as is economically feasible, managing the variability from requirements elicitation to implementation is becoming a primary business requirement in the product line engineering process. One of the main challenges in variability management is the visualization and management of industry size variability models. In this demonstration, we introduce our CASE tool, MUSA. MUSA is designed around our work on multiple perspective variability modeling and is implemented using the state-of-the-art in NUI, multi-touch interfaces, giving it the power and flexibility to create and manage large-scale variability models with relative ease.

**Keywords:** Software Product Lines, Variability Management, Feature Modeling.

## 1 Introduction

Software Product-line Engineering (SPLE) has emerged as a major strategy for maximizing reuse when a family of related software systems is developed. In this approach, commonality-variability analysis [1] (Variability Management - VM) of the member products is a major phase of the process and plays an important role in its success.

One of the main challenges within VM is the handling and visualizing "industry-size" models which usually comprise a large number of variability points along with the dependency relationships that exist among them. The challenge comes from the large amount of information captured within a model (business related, dependency and relationships, etc.) as well as the current techniques and I/O devices used to visualize the model which do not inherently scale.

The MUSA CASE tool was designed to overcome these challenges. MUSA is based on our successful work on multiple-perspective based variability management which provides a rich modeling framework while using the concept of separation-of-concerns to alleviate the problem of information overloading. MUSA implements this theory using a mind-mapping modeling approach over the state-of-the-art in HCI, the multi-touch Microsoft Surface [2]. This provides a scalable solution that taps on the

M. Ali Babar and I. Gorton (Eds.): ECSA 2010, LNCS 6285, pp. 523–526, 2010.

latest in Natural User Interface (NUI) [3] design providing an intuitive and large display for VM. In addition, the MUSA solution provides interfaces over other multitouch platforms including Windows 7 (using its native multi-touch support). The theory behind MUSA is highlighted in section 2. An overview of the MUSA CASE tool is then presented in section 3. Finally, section 4 ends with related work and conclusion.

## 2 Theoretical Background

The Four Views Model (4VM) forms the theoretical foundation upon which MUSA is designed as a Proof-of-Concept. The original version of the 4VM can be found here [4] and to appear here [5].

It is generally agreed that different stakeholders have interest in considering different views of the product line variability model [4],[6]. So, it is important for a VM mechanism to be able to extract and present relevant information about the family model in dedicated views for different groups of stakeholders (users, system analysts, developers, etc.). This could considerably contribute to alleviating the graphical overload when showing all the information in one view (as compared to using multiple views). This is one of the core concepts behind 4VM.

The 4VM proposes a four view presentation of the feature model. The views are:

- *Business View*: where the information related to the project management, cost/benefit analysis, closed/open sets of features, etc. is presented.
- *Hierarchical & Behavioral View*: where the way the different features are organized (usually presented in a tree structure) along with the behavior attached to each feature is presented.
- *Dependency & Interaction View*: where the dependency and interaction among features is presented.
- *Intermediate View*: where some design decisions are injected into the feature model to take it one step further towards the architecture domain in an attempt to bridge the gap between the feature model and the system architecture.

For further information about 4VM, please refer to [4],[5].

## 3 Technical Foundation

MUSA was funded as a Proof-of-Concept project to demonstrate the theoretical foundation provided in 4VM. The MUSA system provides an end-to-end variability management solution as shown in Figure 1 below. MUSA provides a rich and collaborative interface to elicit and manage requirements and variability from stakeholders while allowing for appropriate access to the variability model to different teams including: implementation, testing and deployment teams. In addition, MUSA automates model verification (with the use of SAT solvers) and maintains consistency among the different views with the help of a centralized Database (as shown in Fig. 1).

This is the first official demonstration of the toolset and will focus on the interface that is used for variability management and requirements elicitation by Software Architects/Requirements engineers. The main features of this interface are:

- Based on the Microsoft Surface platform [2], it provides a large gesture based interface for managing the variability model.
- The interface design principles followed (360-D UI and NUI [3]) support a seamless multi-user simultaneous interaction and collaborative environment.
- The variability model itself is implemented using a mind-mapping approach based on hyperbolic trees providing an unprecedented potential for scalability

MUSA is considered among the very first CASE tools to move into the NUI space in order to overcome scalability issues.

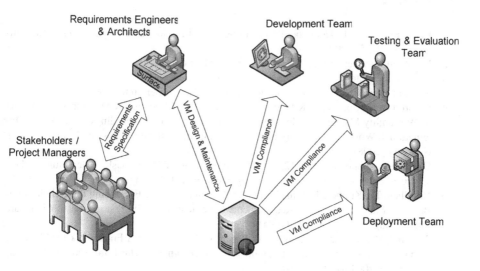

**Fig. 1.** The end-to-end MUSA System overview

# 4 Conclusion and Related Work

Over the past few years, a number of VM approaches have been developed ranging from research techniques [7],[8],[9] to commercial products [10],[11],[12].

The major challenge for most research techniques is scalability. The scalability issue arises from the graphical modeling techniques traditionally adopted (e.g. trees) and the I/O devices used (standard keyboard, mouse, and monitors). Although virtual reality technologies have been recently reported as being explored as a potential approach for VM, it is hard to see how such techniques could make their way to commercial environments due to the difficulty involved in integrating such approaches within existing industrial development settings.

Commercial products on the other hand have managed scalability by largely moving away from graphical representation of models. File system tree like structures and even text listings (e.g. using MS Excel sheets) have been seen in use. Although such approaches scale and are in industrial use, adopting NUI interfaces such as the one we implemented in MUSA will increase productivity, time-to-market and allow for the creation and management of larger and more complex product families.

**Acknowledgments.** The work on the MUSA project has been funded by the European RD Fund through INI under the Proof of Concept funding scheme [2008-2010]. It has just received further funding under the Challenge Fund scheme at the University of East London [2010-2011]. We thank all the postgraduate students at the CITE school at UEL who contributed to some of the testing and development of the MUSA toolset as part of their thesis work.

# References

1. Kang, K.C., Lee, J., Donohoe, P.: Feature-Oriented Product Line Engineering. IEEE Software 19, 58–65 (2002)
2. Microsoft Surface, http://www.microsoft.com/surface/
3. Natural User Interfaces,
   http://en.wikipedia.org/wiki/Natural_user_interface
4. Bashroush, R., Spence, I., Kilpatrick, P., Brown, T.J., Gillan, C.: A Multiple Views Model for Variability Management in Software Product Lines. In: Proceedings of the Second International Workshop on Variability Modelling of Software-intensive Systems, Essen, Germany (2008)
5. US Patent Application No. 12/349,797, Inventor: Rabih Bashroush, Title: Multiple Perspective Feature-based Variability Management (Patent Pending)
6. Nuseibeh, B., Kramer, J., Finkelstein, A.: A Framework for Expressing the Relationships Between Multiple Views in Requirements Specification. IEEE Transactions on Software Engineering 20(10), 760–773 (1994)
7. Sinnema, M., Deelstra, S., Nijhuis, J., Bosch, J.: COVAMOF: A Framework for Modeling Variability in Software Product Families. In: Proceedings of Third Software Product Line Conference 2004, Boston (2004)
8. Antkiewicz, M., Czarnecki, K.: FeaturePlugin: feature modeling plug-in for Eclipse. In: Proceedings of the 2004 OOPSLA workshop on eclipse technology eXchange (2004)
9. Asikainen, T., Männistö, T., Soininen, T.: Kumbang: A domain ontology for modelling variability in software product families. Advanced Engineering Informatics 21, 23–40 (2007)
10. Beuche, D.: Variant Management with pure: Variants, Pure-Systems GmbH (2003)
11. Pure-Systems Pure:Variants,
    http://www.pure-systems.com/Variant_Management.49.0.html
12. BigLever Software Gears,
    http://www.biglever.com/solution/product.html

# ByADL: An MDE Framework for Building Extensible Architecture Description Languages*

Davide Di Ruscio, Ivano Malavolta, Henry Muccini,
Patrizio Pelliccione, and Alfonso Pierantonio

University of L'Aquila, Dipartimento di Informatica
{davide.diruscio,ivano.malavolta,henry.muccini,
patrizio.pelliccione,alfonso.pierantonio}@univaq.it

**Abstract.** In order to deal with evolving needs and stakeholder concerns, next generation ADLs should support incremental extension and customization. In this direction we proposed BYADL (Build Your ADL), a framework which allows software architects to (i) extend existent ADLs with domain specificities, new architectural views, or analysis aspects, (ii) integrate an ADL with development processes and methodologies, and (iii) customize an ADL. This paper presents the BYADL tool and its features.

## 1 Introduction

A broader view of Software Architecture (SA), which is being accepted today, is far beyond the traditional perception of an SA as a set of constituting elements (such as components, connectors and interfaces) and looks at the multiple stakeholder's concerns and their design decisions [1,2,3]. Many Architecture Description Languages (ADLs) have been proposed in the last years. Software engineers found existent ADLs inadequate for modelling concerns judged unavoidable by system's stakeholders. Furthermore, stakeholders's concerns vary from system to system and from domain to domain; this demonstrates that it is not possible to define a general, optimal ADL once and forever. Therefore, ADLs should be extensible in order to be able to adapt to different stakeholder's concerns and to different domain specificities. However, first attempts of extensible ADLs do not deal with semantic aspects of extensions in a satisfactory way.

BYADL (Build Your ADL) [4] is a framework that supports a software architect in defining its own ADL, which is optimal according to specific stakeholder's concerns, starting from an existent ADL. BYADL provides extensibility mechanisms for: (i) adding domain specificities, new architectural views, or analysis aspects, (ii) integrate ADLs with development processes and methodologies, (iii) customize ADLs by fine tuning them. These mechanisms are implemented in the BYADL tool that is the main objective of this paper. The tool supports different features such as model editing, visualization with different views, extensibility, interoperability, and analysis. The tool has been applied on a real system called Integrated Environment for Communication on Ship (IECS); the case study comes from a project developed within Selex Communications, a company mainly operating in the naval communication domain.

---

* This work is partly supported by the Italian PRIN d-ASAP project.

M. Ali Babar and I. Gorton (Eds.): ECSA 2010, LNCS 6285, pp. 527–531, 2010.

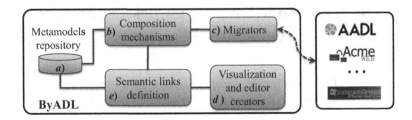

**Fig. 1.** The high-level design of the BYADL framework

The paper is organized as follows: Section 2 presents the main aspects of the BYADL framework, Section 3 presents the tool, and finally Section 4 concludes the paper.

## 2  The ByADL Framework

Figure 1 shows the high-level design of the BYADL framework. The main input of BYADL is the metamodel of the ADL to be extended. For this reason BYADL contains a repository of metamodels as shown in Figure 1.a. The metamodel is extended by means of composition mechanisms (see Figure 1.b) that rely on specific composition operators for metamodels.

It is important to note that, even though this could be technically possible, we do not allow to compose two different ADLs since this could lead to the creation of a "chaotic" and "vague" language. In such cases we believe that it is better to keep the two ADLs separated, and to use interoperability techniques to translate from one ADL to a different one [5]. The composition operators are: *Match*, *Inherit*, *Reference*, and *Expand*, whose semantics is detailed in [4]. The composition engine performs also semantic checks to avoid incidental errors. The *Migrators* (see Figure 1.c) component is used to automatically generate model transformations able to reflect the architectural models defined within the newly created ADL, back to the original tools. In the BYADL framework, migrators are automatically generated by means of higher-order model transformations. The ADL obtained at the end of the process is a modeling language consisting of (i) an *abstract syntax*, i.e. the metamodel obtained by means of the composition mechanisms, (ii) a set of *concrete syntaxes*, i.e., textual and graphical notations to visualize and edit models conforming to the composed metamodel (see Figure 1.d), and (iii) *semantics* describing the meaning of the language constructs [6] (see Figure 1.e). The semantics of the extended language is given by means of semantic relationships between the language's elements and elements of a target semantic domain called $A_0$ [5].

## 3  The ByADL Tool

The BYADL tool[1] is implemented as a plugin of the Eclipse[2] platform. More specifically, it extends the ATLAS Model Management Architecture (AMMA)[3]. Metamodel

---

[1] BYADL Web site: http://byadl.di.univaq.it/

[2] Eclipse Project Home Page: http://www.eclipse.org

[3] AMMA: http://wiki.eclipse.org/AMMA

**Fig. 2.** Metamodels composition user interface

compositions are specified as weaving models defined by using the ATLAS Model Weaver (AMW). All the involved model transformations are based on the ATLAS Transformation Language (ATL), a hybrid model transformation language with declarative and imperative constructs. Models and metamodels are managed by means of EMF[4], a modeling framework for Eclipse. In the following we present how the features of the BYADL framework described in Section 2 are realized in its supporting tool.

**Metamodels import.** Importing a metamodel into the *Metamodels repository* is a three-steps process:

1. *Obtaining a metamodel.* The BYADL tool works on EMF metamodels. If the metamodel of an architectural notation is not available, many techniques exist to obtain such a metamodel, like using TCS[5] in case of textual notations, or using the DUALLy importing engine in case of UML-based notations.

2. *Tagging a metamodel.* Tagging metamodels guides ADLs extensions and keeps the involved metamodels organized. The tags available in BYADL reflect the different kinds of metamodel involved in the composition scenarios, namely: ADL, Domain, Analysis, Viewpoint, Process, Methodology, Customization. The importing wizard allows the user to associate one or more tags to the metamodel being imported.

3. *Providing semantics to a metamodel.* As stated in Section 2, in BYADL a kind of translational semantics is provided to a metamodel by linking it to the $A_0$ semantic domain. We extended the AMW interface so that the semantic links to the $A_0$ metamodel guide the application of the composition operators. More precisely, once applying an operator, the BYADL tool highlights as target the metaclasses that are semantically compatible with the source metaclass.

**Metamodels composition.** Software engineers create a new ADL by composing two metamodels already imported into the *Metamodel Repository*. Metamodels are composed by specifying weaving models which represent the application of the composition operators. Figure 2 shows the AMW graphical interface we extended for metamodel composition. The woven metamodels are rendered into two lateral panels (points *a* and

---

[4] Eclipse Modeling Framework (EMF) project Web site: http://www.eclipse.org/emf
[5] TCS: http://wiki.eclipse.org/TCS

*c* in the figure) using the standard EMF tree-based interface. The central panel (point *b* in the figure) represents the composition weaving model. Our extension consists of a specific weaving metamodel defining the four kinds of composition operators and a dedicated weaving toolbar (see Figure 2.*d*). The composed metamodel is generated by clicking on a button of the BYADL weaving toolbar; the result is a metamodel which is automatically loaded into the *Metamodels repository* and tagged as *ADL*.

**Model migrators generation.** A model migrator is a specific ATL transformation; its inner logic is represented by the operators applied in the weaving model during the composition phase. The BYADL weaving toolbar contains functionalities (see Figure 2.*d*) to automatically generate the migrators starting from the current composition weaving model. Model migrators may be used also outside the BYADL tool.

**Editors generation.** In BYADL there are three possibilities to produce an editor for the ADL being developed: *tree-based*, *textual*, and *graphical*. Each editor has different levels of usability and requires different efforts for the customization (if needed). The tree-based editor, with its collapsible and hierarchical structure, is automatically provided by EMF. The textual editor is automatically generated and conforms to the Human-Usable Textual Notation (HUTN) specification[6]. The produced textual editor supports syntax highlighting and automatic conformance check with respect to the metamodel of the new ADL. The graphical editor is based on the EuGENia[7] tool: exploiting specific annotations of the metamodels involved in the composition (included $A_0$), a graphical editor is automatically generated. Obviously the generation of the editor is limited to elements for which EuGENia annotations are provided. Special policies regulate the choice of the graphical element to be used when more than one metamodel provide EuGENia annotations for a specific concept.

# 4    Conclusions

In this paper we presented the BYADL tool. Starting from an existing ADL, BYADL allows software architects to incrementally extend and customize an ADL according to stakeholder's concerns. BYADL ensures the compatibility with existing tools by means of automatically generated migrators. Our tool also supports the generation of textual and graphical editors for the newly created ADL. The generation of graphical editors is in its prototypal version, this aspect is one of the main future work directions.

# References

1. ISO: Fourth working draft of Systems and Software Engineering – Architectural Description (ISO/IECWD4 42010). Working doc.: ISO/IEC JTC 1/SC 7 N 000. IEEE, Los Alamitos (2009)
2. Kruchten, P., Lago, P., van Vliet, H.: Building up and reasoning about architectural knowledge. Quality of Software Architectures (2006)

---

[6] HUTN specification: http://www.omg.org/spec/HUTN/

[7] EuGENia: http://www.eclipse.org/gmt/epsilon/doc/eugenia/

3. Taylor, R.N., Medvidovic, N., Dashofy, E.M.: Software Architecture: Foundations, Theory, and Practice. John Wiley & Sons, Chichester (2009)
4. Di Ruscio, D., Malavolta, I., Muccini, H., Pelliccione, P., Pierantonio, A.: Developing next generation adls through mde techniques. In: ICSE 2010. IEEE Computer Society, Los Alamitos (2010)
5. Malavolta, I., Muccini, H., Pelliccione, P., Tamburri, D.: Providing architectural languages and tools interoperability through model transformation technologies. IEEE TSE 36(1) (2010)
6. Cuadrado, J.S., Molina, J.G.: A model-based approach to families of embedded domain specific languages. IEEE TSE 99(RapidPosts), 825–840 (2009)

# Author Index